# VIRGINIA DOMESTIC RELATIONS HANDBOOK

## 2020 Edition

**JOHN E. BYRNES**, Contributing Author from 2015
*Kelly Byrnes & Danker, PLLC*

**MARGARET F. BRINIG**, Original Author, 1984 to 2004
*Professor of Law*
*George Mason University*
*School of Law*

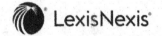 LexisNexis

## QUESTIONS ABOUT THIS PUBLICATION?

For questions about the **Editorial Content** appearing in these volumes or reprint permission, please call:

Cathy Seidenberg at ............................................................................. (908) 673-3379
Email: ...................................................................... Cathy.J.Seidenberg@lexisnexis.com
Outside the United States and Canada, please call . . . . . . . . . . . . . . . . (973) 820-2000

For assistance with replacement pages, shipments, billing or other customer service matters, please call:

Customer Services Department at . . . . . . . . . . . . . . . . . . . . . . . . . . (800) 833-9844
Outside the United States and Canada, please call . . . . . . . . . . . . . . . . (518) 487-3385
Fax Number . . . . . . . . . . . . . . . . . . . . . . . . . . . . . . . . . . . (800) 828-8341
Customer Service Website . . . . . . . . . . . . . . . . http://www.lexisnexis.com/custserv/

For information on other Matthew Bender publications, please call

Your account manager or . . . . . . . . . . . . . . . . . . . . . . . . . . . . . (800) 223-1940
Outside the United States and Canada, please call . . . . . . . . . . . . . . . (937) 247-0293

Virginia Domestic Relations Handbook (Print) ISSN: 2474-4905

96-77726

ISBN: 978-1-6633-0262-5 (print)

Cite this publication as:

Virginia Domestic Relations Handbook, 2018 Edition, Ch. no., § [sec. no.] (Matthew Bender)

Example:
Virginia Domestic Relations Handbook, 2018 Edition, Ch. 1, § 1.01 (Matthew Bender)

Because the section you are citing may be revised in a later release, you may wish to photocopy or print out the section for convenient future reference.

Editorial Office
230 Park Ave., 7th Floor, New York, NY 10169 (800) 543-6862
www.lexisnexis.com

# Introduction to First Edition

This book was written to aid Virginia practitioners who occasionally or often handle cases dealing with family relationships.

Despite the fears of some family lawyers in the nineteen eighties, domestic relations practice has changed dramatically. It has become at once more complicated and more lucrative. The low status family lawyers bore because of the problems with fault divorce is a thing of the past. The work family practitioners do now resembles corporate practice: much more is accomplished through contracts and negotiation. Since emotions are almost always involved, however, and children take center stage in most families, dissolution of families, whether through termination of parental rights or divorce, isn't exactly like winding up a business partnership.

Though most family law, in this state and others, begins with statutes, courts still exercise their equitable powers. Judges continue to wrestle with the discretion they are given to determine which custodial arrangement will be in a child's best interest and how much property should equitably be awarded to each spouse. Increasingly, their task involves expert testimony, whether about valuing pensions, closely held corporations, or deciding whether a parent or the state has proven child abuse.

As I prepare this edition, many of the assumptions of the past twenty years are being rethought. Virginia, with other states, is reconsidering no-fault divorce, custody arrangements, parental rights, and the basis for alimony. The changes contemplated are not minor tinkering; they will have real consequences for the citizens of the state. In contrast to earlier editions of this book, this volume has citations to authorities that may be helpful in making these important public policy choices.

Additionally, there are increasing opportunities for attorneys dealing with cases involving status. For example, Virginia has abolished interspousal immunity, and has engrafted many exceptions onto the rule prohibiting suits between parent and child. Although there are no longer actions in the common law field of "heartbalm actions," a cause of action is available for parents who have emotional distress as the result of being deprived of the custody or visitation with their children. Increasingly, individuals in status relationships such as parent and child or husband and wife are being granted court recognition of their individual rights.

# Introduction to 2020 Edition

The 2020 Virginia legislature implemented monumental legislation by repealing Va. Code §§ 20-45.2 and .3, which banned same-sex marriage and civil unions. These legislative acts helped conform Virginia law with the ruling of the United States Supreme Court in *Obergefell v. Hodges*, 135 S. Ct. 2584 (2015) which recognized the rights of same sex people to marry. In addition, the legislature amended the Virginia Code to include gender neutral terms in recognition that marital and custodial rights apply to same sex couples. However, Article I, Section 15-A of the Constitution of Virginia, which restricts marriage to the union of one man and one woman, has not been repealed and this article of the Virginia Constitution will certainly be addressed in the courts and the general assembly. The transformation of the Virginia Code has been expected by many practitioners, but the dispute between Article I, Section 15-A of the Constitution of Virginia and same-sex marriages will continue to linger and be the source of contentious debate and litigation.

The Virginia legislature also repealed the criminal fornication statute, Va. Code § 18.2-344, in 2020, while the Virginia Supreme Court had declared the statute unconstitutional back in 2005. *Martin v. Ziherl*, 269 Va. 35, 42, 607 S.E.2d 367, 371 (2005). The private sexual behavior of people nonetheless continues to be of significant importance in Virginia divorce law. Adultery continues to be a criminal act pursuant to Virginia Code § 18.2-365, adultery remains a viable ground for divorce (Va. Code § 20-91(A)(1), a spouse can be denied permanent spousal support if the spouse has committed adultery (Va. Code § 20-107.1(B), and adultery is to be considered by the court when determining whether or not to award spousal support (Va. Code § 20-107.1(E), and in determining the amount and duration of spousal support (Va. Code § 20-107.1(E)(13). Despite the emphasis that adulterous behavior has on divorce, and the devastating impact that adultery poses to a spouse's potential claim for spousal support, the legislature curiously decreased the protections afforded by asserting the Fifth Amendment when it modified Va. Code § 8.01-223.1 to state that "in any civil proceeding for spousal support, custody, or visitation under Title 16.1 or any civil action for divorce or separate maintenance under Title 20 filed on or after July 1, 2020, if a party or witness refuses to answer a question about conduct described in subdivision A (1) of § 20-91 or in § 18.2-365 on the ground that the testimony might be self-incriminating, the trier of fact may draw an adverse inference from such refusal." Whether or not this statutory amendment is constitutional is questionable and hopefully the issue will be addressed. More important is the potential unintended consequence resulting from minimizing the Fifth Amendment protections, as this change will negatively impact the more economically deprived spouse who is a stay-at-home parent and less able to financially provide for himself or herself. This change in our law magnifies the great imbalance of power that often exists in marriage, and distorts the emphasis on adulterous behavior to the prejudice of the person who is frequently the more impoverished and less sophisticated spouse.

Finally, as mentioned in prior introductions, citing to unpublished appellate decisions has become common and many of those decisions will be referenced in this treatise. Rule 5A:1(f) of the Rules of the Supreme Court of Virginia permits the citation to unpublished decisions as being informative rather than establishing binding authority.

# About the Author

John E. Byrnes has been practicing exclusively in the area of family law since 1996. He practices in all of the northern Virginia circuit courts and juvenile and domestic relations district courts as well as the Virginia Court of Appeals. While most matters are amicably resolved through negotiation or mediation, John has extensive litigation experience. During his career, John's practice has covered virtually every aspect of family law, from: complex equitable distribution matters involving business valuations and detailed tracing issues; forensic accounting considerations for determining a party's income; intricate custody concerns dealing with non-parental rights, international legal considerations, and abuse claims; as well as unique family law issues such as litigating the validity of divorces obtained in foreign countries. Over his career, John has identified an array of talented expert witnesses to assist his clients on various issues. John also prepares marital settlement agreements and pre-marital agreements tailored to meet the client's goals. John provides his clients with candid advice—be it favorable or unfavorable—and he explains the benefits and negatives that are associated with litigation, mediation, and other alternative dispute resolution alternatives.

John graduated from the George Mason University School of Law, where he was selected to be in the Dean's Scholar Program and was also chosen to be the Lead Articles Editor for the George Mason University Independent Law Review. Since his completion of a one-year clerkship for the Honorable J. Howe Brown of the Fairfax County Circuit Court in August of 1996, John's law practice has concentrated solely on the area of family law and divorce.

John is the former Chairperson of the 5th District Disciplinary Committee of the Virginia State Bar, and previously served on the Virginia State Bar Judicial Candidate Evaluation Committee, and the Virginia State Bar Mid-Year Seminar Committee. He has also lectured for the Virginia CLE, attended the Bar Leadership Institute, was previously recognized by Legal Services of Northern Virginia for providing pro bono legal services, and is a past Chair of the Fairfax Bar Association's Membership Committee. Lastly, John is a member of the Virginia State Bar, the Fairfax Bar Association, and the Loudoun Bar Association.

# Volume 1 Table of Contents

A COMPLETE SYNOPSIS FOR EACH CHAPTER APPEARS AT
THE BEGINNING OF THE CHAPTER

# Volume 1 Table of Contents

# Volume 1 Table of Contents

# Volume 1 Table of Contents

## Volume 1 Table of Contents

# Volume 1 Table of Contents

# Volume 1 Table of Contents

## Chapter 18      Divorce from Bed and Board

# Volume 1 Table of Contents

## Chapter 19      Absolute Divorce

| **Chapter 20** | **Spousal Support and Maintenance** |
|---|---|

# Volume 1 Table of Contents

# Volume 1 Table of Contents

# Volume 1 Table of Contents

# Volume 1 Table of Contents

# CHAPTER 1

# Contracts Between Unmarried Cohabitants

## SYNOPSIS

## § 1.01  Introduction

Before the Married Women's Property Acts, Va. Code §§ 55-35 to 55-47.1, contracts made by a married woman were ineffective, since by marrying, a wife went under her husband's protection or coverture. See, e.g., *Virginia R. & P. Co. v. Gorsuch*, 120 Va. 655, 662, 91 S.E. 632, 634 (1917); *Wynn v. Southan's Adm'r & Heirs*, 86 Va. 946, 11 S.E. 878 (1890). The parties owned everything together, and the husband was the only one who could act to bind the parties. The woman lacked capacity to contract. *Wynn*, 86 Va. at 949, 11 S.E. at 879.

Contracts between a man and a woman living together who were not married were also invalid. If they thought that they were married, but the marriage was void, the parties' agreement did not amount to a contract because it was presumed to have been undertaken out of love and affection rather than hope of a pecuniary gain. *Alexander v. Kuykendall*, 192 Va. 8, 10, 11, 63 S.E.2d 746, 747 (1951). Many of the services that might be performed by a married couple would obviously not be the subject of a separate contract because of the promises the spouses made to each other through their wedding vows. They were in any event not dealing with each other at arm's length. If they knew that they were not married, the contract was not valid either because the relationship's illegality tainted it, or because there was no legal consideration, since payment in sexual services outside

1-1

marriage was invalid. See, e.g., *Grant v. Butt*, 198 S.C. 298, 17 S.E.2d 689 (1941); *Restatement, Contracts* § 589; 6A *Corbin on Contracts* § 1476 (1962).

Today these positions have changed. Married women can contract with the same efficacy as all other persons. Va. Code § 55-36. Husbands and wives generally contract between themselves; this will be discussed further in Chapter 8. Va. Code § 55-36; *Moreland v. Moreland*, 108 Va. 93, 60 S.E. 730 (1908) (contract after separation); *Capps v. Capps*, 216 Va. 378, 219 S.E.2d 901 (1975) (contract after marriage).

If one (or both) of the parties to a void marriage thinks in good faith that the marriage is valid, there are several ways in which relief may be sought.

## § 1.02     Seeking Relief Under Contract Law

**[1]     *Tort Action in Fraud and Deceit.*** In *Alexander v. Kuykendall*, 192 Va. 8, 63 S.E.2d 746 (1951), a woman gave up her employment and moved in order to marry a man who was, unknown to her, already married. When she discovered the truth, she sued in contract to recover the value of the services she performed while the two lived together, and in tort for damages for fraud and deceit. The Virginia Supreme Court denied her contractual relief since she thought she was married, and therefore did not bargain for financial remuneration at arm's length. However, she recovered in tort, for she had suffered damage as the result of his intentional misrepresentation.[1]

Similarly, in *Allen v. Jackson*, 9 Va. Cir. 60 (Nottoway Co. 1987), Mrs. Jackson placed George Jackson's name on a deed as co-owner of her separate property, thinking they had been validly married when in fact he was still married to another woman. George died intestate, leaving his daughter, the plaintiff, as his survivor. Both Mr. and Mrs. Jackson contributed to the construction of the house. The trial court found that Mrs. Jackson would not have purchased or put property in his name if she had known that he was not divorced from his prior wife, and proceeded to invalidate the deed on grounds of fraud.

**[2]     *Common Law Marriage.*** Virginia does not recognize common

---

[1] This action would lie despite the statutory invalidation of actions involving breach of promise to marry and seduction, since both of these actions involve a sexual performance that is knowingly unlawful. Va. Code § 8.01-220. In *Kuykendall*, the action involved a totally innocent party, so that the action existed because "a woman so induced has changed her status from that of a virtuous single woman and has been forced to live meretriciously with defendant, to her humiliation, disgrace and mental anguish." 192 Va. at 12, 63 S.E.2d at 748.

law marriages contracted within the state. Va. Code § 20-13; *Offield v. Davis,* 100 Va. 250, 263, 40 S.E. 910, 914 (1902). However, if parties entered into a common law marriage valid in another state, it will be recognized even though an attempted ceremonial marriage occurred in Virginia. For example, in *Metropolitan Life Ins. Co. v. Holding,* 293 F. Supp. 854 (E.D. Va. 1968), a serviceman, relying upon his wife's attorney's erroneous statement that their divorce was final, married another woman in France. The couple lived in various places abroad during the man's career in the Armed Forces and foreign service, but travelled through the common law marriage jurisdictions of Florida and Ohio when they were on leave in the United States. When the husband died in Virginia, the French woman was able to recover insurance money as a surviving spouse since she had never known of the invalidity of the ceremonial marriage and the couple had agreed to and ratified a common law marriage recognizable in Virginia.

[3] *Estoppel.* Although there are no Virginia cases on point, cases from other jurisdictions frequently allow a dependent would-be spouse relief on grounds of estoppel, if there was a change in position based upon a bona fide reliance upon the validity of a marriage (or a prior divorce).[2] *Alexander v. Kuykendall,* supra, may be read in part as a protection of the putative wife's change in position. Virginia recognizes the efficacy of the doctrine of estoppel generally.[3] Until it was overturned, the decision by the Virginia Court of Appeals in *MacDougall v. Levick,* 66 Va. App. 50, 76–77, 782 S.E.2d 182 (2016) confirmed that the application of equitable doctrine of estoppel is generally rejected in modern divorces which are governed by statutes. Nonetheless, the Virginia courts recognize generally that equitable principles are inapplicable to divorce cases since divorce is now a matter of statute. *Bajgain v. Bajgain,* 64 Va. App. 439, 457–58, 769 S.E.2d 267, 276 (2015).

[4] *Putative Spouse.* Several important states,[4] following a civil law formulation, allow recovery for persons who mistakenly believe that they

---

[2] See, e.g., Spellens v. Spellens, 49 Cal. 2d 210, 317 P.2d 613 (1957); Poor v. Poor, 381 Mass. 392, 409 N.E.2d 758 (1980); Rosen v. Sitner, 274 Pa. Super. 445, 418 A.2d 490 (1980). See generally Restatement, Conflict of Laws (Second) § 74; 24 Am. Jur. 2d *Divorce and Separation* §§ 971, 972; 27B C.J.S. *Divorce* §§ 364–366.

[3] See 7 Michie's Jurisprudence *Estoppel* § 14.

[4] These states include Illinois, Ill. Rev. Stat. ch. 40, § 305; and Texas, Hupp v. Hupp, 235 S.W.2d 753 (Tex. Civ. App. 1950). Both the Illinois formulation, enacted in 1977, and that occurring in Michigan, Mich. Stat. Ann. § 26-190.1, enacted in 1978, have occurred through legislative action.

are validly married. They are permitted the share of property to which they would have been entitled had the marriage been valid. This doctrine is not available to plaintiffs in Virginia, and would not be absent a legislative change.

**[5]   *Support Following Annulment.*** If the parties went through a marriage ceremony and the dependent spouse can show need and lack of fault, there may be recovery under the general spousal support and maintenance statute unless the marriage was void ab initio. *Bray v. Landergren,* 161 Va. 699, 706, 172 S.E. 252, 254 (1933) (dictum). In *Fulton v. Fulton,* Chancery No. 87732 (1985), the supposed husband was wed to another before he took part in a marriage ceremony with the plaintiff. When plaintiff amended her annulment action to include a count for equitable distribution under Va. Code § 20-107.3, the Circuit Court sustained defendant's demurrer on the grounds that a marriage, at least a voidable marriage, must have existed in order for distribution to take place. See also *Mato v. Mato,* 12 Va. Cir. 153 (Spotsylvania Co. 1988) (substantially the same facts as in *Fulton*). The case for disallowing support was even stronger in *Kleinfield v. Veruki,* 7 Va. App. 183, 372 S.E.2d 407 (1988), where the alleged wife had a preexisting marriage. She had married a would-be immigrant in order to keep him from being deported, and had the marriage annulled only after her marriage to defendant, making this second marriage bigamous and void.

**[6]   *No Recovery Absent a Contract.*** In the case of *Cooper v. Spencer,* 218 Va. 541, 238 S.E.2d 805 (1977), a man and a woman mistakenly believed that their prior marriages had ended in divorce. They went through a marriage ceremony and lived together for many years, supporting the family in large part through an egg and poultry business called Jo-Bets farm (an acronym made of portions of each party's first name). When the relationship ended, and the parties discovered that they were not married, the woman attempted to sue the man for some of the farm's assets. The Supreme Court disallowed relief, because the woman did not sufficiently prove a partnership. If there were no partnership, an implied contract would not lie since the woman believed herself married and therefore acted out of love and affection rather than the hope of pecuniary gain. Although the court did not take note of the landmark California decision in *Marvin v. Marvin,* 18 Cal. 3d 660, 134 Cal. Rptr. 815, 557 P.2d 106 (1976), even if an action were allowed for express contract, the result would be the same. There was no proof that a business relationship between the man and woman had been established, and therefore all that remained was the presumed affectionate relationship between them. *Cooper v. Spencer,* 218 Va. at 543–44, 238 S.E.2d at 806–07.

A wife was permitted to receive *pendente lite* spousal support pursuant to the terms of a marital settlement agreement even though the parties were ultimately found never to have been married. *MacDougall v. Levick,* 66 Va. App. 50, 782 S.E.2d 182 (2016). Although their marital settlement agreement was set aside, the purported wife was not required to reimburse the purported husband for the *pendente lite* spousal support, or the substantial attorney fee award. *MacDougall,* 66 Va. App. at 87–92.

A reported circuit court case used an implied contract to allow a putative wife to recover reasonable compensation for her services. In *Paxton v. Paxton,* 29 Va. Cir. 496 (Craig Co. 1977), the woman believed in good faith that she was married to decedent, performing various services for him and receiving support and maintenance from him. The court did not mention *Cooper v. Spencer,* but permitted the woman to recover the difference between the value of services rendered and the support and maintenance paid by the supposed husband before he died.

If the parties know that they are not married, but nevertheless live together, a growing number of jurisdictions allow relief on the basis of an express contract.[5] Although there will be no recovery based upon the illicit exchange of sexual favors, the decisions state that there is no reason that the other forms of consideration, such as performance of household tasks, work in the other's business, or entertainment of business friends, cannot be a valid exchange for a promise of support. In other words, the fact that the parties to a contract are living together in an unmarried relationship will not invalidate an otherwise valid contract. However, it may be difficult to prove that other forms of consideration are involved. In a West Virginia case, *Thomas v. LaRosa,* 184 W. Va. 374, 400 S.E.2d 809 (W. Va. 1990), a woman who lived for some years with a man she knew to be already married was not permitted to recover under an alleged oral contract under which he agreed to provide her with financial security for her lifetime and to educate her children. The contract was found to be unenforceable because it was explicitly and inseparably founded on illegal sexual services. In that state, cohabitation outside marriage is illegal.

---

[5] See, e.g., Mason v. Rostad, 476 A.2d 662 (D.C. App. 1984) (quasi-contract); Morone v. Morone, 50 N.Y.2d 481, 429 N.Y.S.2d 592, 413 N.E.2d 1154 (1980) (express contract); Crowe v. De Gioia, 90 N.J. 126, 447 A.2d 173 (N.J. 1982); see generally Hunter, *An Essay on Contract and Status: Race, Marriage and the Meretricious Spouse,* 64 VA. L. REV. 1039 (1978); Comment, 30 STAN. L. REV. 359 (1978).

The states not following the majority position, which finds express agreements enforceable, reason that heterosexual non-marital living arrangements are illegal. See, e.g., *Hewitt v. Hewitt,* 77 Ill. 2d 49, 31 Ill. Dec. 827, 394 N.E.2d 1204 (1979); *Merrill v. Davis,* 100 N.M. 552, 673 P.2d 1285 (1983); *Roach v. Buttons,* 6 Fam. L. Rep. (BNA) 2355 (Tenn. Ch. App. 1980). Additionally, to recognize financial repercussions from such relationships would be, in effect, to create a type of common law marriage, abolished as difficult to prove and tending towards collusion many years ago. See, e.g., *Hewitt v. Hewitt,* 77 Ill. 2d 49, 63, 31 Ill. Dec. 827, 394 N.E.2d 1204, 1209–10 (1979); *Merrill v. Davis,* 100 N.M. 552, 554, 673 P.2d 1285, 1287 (1983); cf. *Morone v. Morone,* 50 N.Y.2d 481, 488, 596, 429 N.Y.S.2d 592, 413 N.E.2d 1154, 1156 (1980) (relief allowed for express contracts only). Further, the extramarital relationship, because it allows participants to escape many of the duties and responsibilities of marriage, might become so popular as to threaten the institution of marriage, at the heart of the fabric of society. *Hewitt v. Hewitt,* 77 Ill. 2d 49, 58, 31 Ill. Dec. 827, 394 N.E.2d 1204, 1207 (1979); *Merrill v. Davis,* 100 N.M. 552, 554, 673 P.2d 1285, 1287 (1983).

### § 1.03    The Virginia Position

Although the Virginia Supreme Court declared Virginia's fornication statute unconstitutional, *Martin v. Ziherl,* 269 Va. 35, 42, 607 S.E.2d 367, 371 (2005), the Virginia legislature did not repeal the criminal fornication statute, Va. Code § 18.2-344, until 2020. Nonetheless, adultery remains a Class 4 misdemeanor under Va. Code § 18.2-365. There is therefore a basis for arguing the minority position. However, unlike Illinois at the time of *Hewitt v. Hewitt,* 77 Ill. 2d 49, 31 Ill. Dec. 827, 394 N.E.2d 1204 (1979), Virginia recognizes no-fault divorce and does not provide the alternative relief of the putative spouse doctrine. Although it appears from an analysis of *Cooper v. Spencer,* 218 Va. 541, 238 S.E.2d 805 (1977), that an express contract will be necessary, the older *Alexander v. Kuykendall,* 192 Va. 8, 63 S.E.2d 746 (1951), would cast doubt upon the availability of recovery in any case. The question really becomes whether the parties lacked the arm's length necessary for a valid transaction. It could certainly be argued that the difference between *Cooper* and *Alexander* and the modern cohabitation case is the express intent not to be married in the latter. The counterargument would be that the feelings of affection noted in *Cooper* and *Alexander* are just as likely to be present where a couple contemplates a meretricious relationship. The desire not to be entangled with the complex of rights and duties that arises from the marital status should arguably be sufficient to keep the same sort of financial responsibilities from being incurred.

However, there is lower court support for the contrary view, allowing recovery without an express contract in a situation where the supposed husband had died. In *Paxton v. Paxton,* 29 Va. Cir. 496 (Craig Co. 1977), the court cited a North Carolina case and permitted the woman to recover the difference between the reasonable value of the services she had performed before the man's death and the support and maintenance she had received from him.

If the Virginia Supreme Court were to recognize such a contract, the attorney would have to prove: (1) the parties were not married; (2) they knew they were not married; (3) they contracted at arm's length and expressly for the service arrangement; and (4) sexual favors were not the major part of the consideration. Recovery would be possible if factors (1) and (2) could not be proven. It would not be possible if (3) or (4) were not susceptible of proof.

In the first Virginia Supreme Court case to consider the question of the division of property of cohabitants, *Tiller v. Owen,* 243 Va. 176, 413 S.E.2d 51 (1992), Tiller purchased property in her own name while the couple lived together. She used $23,000 obtained from Owen for the down payment, but was the sole purchaser named in the real estate contract and the only party obligated on the note that secured the deed of trust on the property. Owen was married to another woman during this whole time, but furnished Tiller with sufficient money to make each mortgage payment from October 1987 until June 1989, when their relationship ended. At that point Tiller moved out of the home since Owen refused to leave. He continued making mortgage payments directly, and asked the trial court to declare a resulting trust on the property in his favor since he had delivered to Tiller both the money for the down payment and the monthly mortgage payments. The Supreme Court reversed the trial court's imposition of a resulting trust, finding that Owen had not obligated himself to purchase all or part of the property in question. When he delivered the checks to Tiller, therefore, he was not acting in satisfaction of any obligation he had regarding purchase of the property, so a resulting trust could not arise.

Cohabitation may have another effect that would seem to justify the different treatment of voidable from void marriages apparent in *McConkey v. McConkey,* 216 Va. 106, 215 S.E.2d 640 (1975). Amended Va. Code § 20-109(A) provides that if the dependent spouse has been cohabiting with another person in a relationship analogous to marriage for a year or more, the court will decrease or terminate spousal support or maintenance unless termination would be unconscionable. The court will not terminate spousal support if the divorcing parties' agreement otherwise provides, or if the dependent spouse proves by a preponderance of the evidence that termination of support would constitute a manifest injustice. The cohabitation must be proved by clear and convincing evidence, and termination of support must follow a court order.

# CHAPTER 2

## Antenuptial Contracts

### SYNOPSIS

### § 2.01   Historical Perspective

For many years, Virginia, like most common law jurisdictions, did not recognize antenuptial contracts. This was because such agreements might promote or facilitate divorce, and they might attempt to affect the incidents of marriage. 2 A. Lindey, *Separation Agreements and Ante-Nuptial Contracts* § 90, at 90–93 (1979). Additionally, persons contemplating marriage have always been held to be in a confidential relationship. *Batleman v. Rubin*, 199 Va. 156, 160, 98 S.E.2d 519, 522 (1957). Since in many cases the husband to be was the dominant partner in this relationship, he might too easily take advantage of his fiancée who would then be left without viable means of support. *Volid v. Volid*, 6 Ill. App. 3d 386, 286 N.E.2d 42, 46 (1972).

Virginia abandoned any reluctance to accept antenuptial agreements before most other states, *Cumming v. Cumming*, 127 Va. 16, 102 S.E. 572 (1920), and now recognizes that antenuptial contracts tend to promote rather than discourage marital stability. *Estate of Gillilan v. Estate of Gillilan*, 406 N.E.2d 981 (Ind. App. 1980); 12B Michie's Jurisprudence *Marriage Contracts and Settlements* § 2; cf. *Capps v. Capps*, 216 Va. 378, 219 S.E.2d 901 (1975) (agreement between spouses after their marriage). "Marital property settlements entered into by competent parties upon valid consideration for lawful purposes are favored in the law and such will be enforced unless their illegality is clear and certain." *Cooley v. Cooley*, 220 Va. 749,

752, 263 S.E.2d 49, 52 (1980); *Doherty v. Doherty*, 9 Va. App. 97, 99, 383 S.E.2d 759, 760 (1989); *Drewry v. Drewry*, 8 Va. App. 460, 466, 383 S.E.2d 12, 14 (1989).

In 1985, Virginia became the first state to adopt the Uniform Premarital Agreement Act, codified after ratification by the 1986 General Assembly in Va. Code § 20-147 et seq. The Act applies to any premarital agreement executed on or after July 1, 1986, and codifies the case law as developed in this chapter. "Marital agreements between competent parties are favored in the law and will be enforced unless its illegality is clear and certain." *Doherty v. Doherty*, 9 Va. App. 97, 99, 383 S.E.2d 759, 760 (1989); *Drewry v. Drewry*, 8 Va. App. 460, 466, 383 S.E.2d 12, 14 (1989).

### § 2.02    Reasons for Antenuptial Contracts

Although, as previously mentioned, Virginia has recognized antenuptial agreements for many years, they have become increasingly popular recently for several reasons.

The first is the relatively high divorce rate. Since many divorced persons marry again, there may be families from a first marriage to support, or a reluctance to risk further dividing scarce resources should the second marriage fail. See, e.g., *Posner v. Posner*, 233 So. 2d 381, 384 (Fla. 1970).

The second reason is the social trend toward marrying later in life, when substantial assets have already been accumulated. Since women are very frequently employed outside the home, there is an increased probability that the wife as well as the husband will have substantial personal assets, or will at least have the capacity to be self-supporting by the time the marriage takes place. This reason relates to the general tendency toward private ordering of married life that began in the nineteen seventies. Private ordering allows spouses to tailor marriage, at least in part, to their own specifications.

A final reason that the antenuptial agreement should be considered is the equitable distribution statute, which, absent a contract entered into prior to or during the marriage, will require all marital property to be divided in cases of divorce. As we will see in Chapter 21, the law presumes that any property acquired during marriage is marital. After a lengthy marriage, even separately acquired property may take on the character of marital assets.

The careful attorney might advise a contract before marriage if: (1) the client has been previously married, particularly if there is another family to support; or (2) if the client is older and has already accumulated a substantial estate. See the facts in *Batleman v. Rubin*, 199 Va. 156, 98 S.E.2d 519 (1957), where the husband was a 54-year-old widower with two children and successfully engaged in real estate ventures and a storage business.

## § 2.03  Subjects of a Valid Agreement

Parties to antenuptial contracts may contract to a wide variety of obligations. Va. Code § 20-150 specifies that in a premarital agreement, parties can contract to:

1. The rights and obligations of each of the parties in any of the property of either or both of them whenever and wherever acquired or located;

2. The right to buy, sell, use, transfer, exchange, abandon, lease, consume, expend, assign, create a security interest in, mortgage, encumber, dispose of, or otherwise manage and control property;

3. The disposition of property upon separation, marital dissolution, death, or the occurrence or nonoccurrence of any other event;

4. Spousal support;

5. The making of a will, trust, or other arrangement to carry out the provisions of the agreement;

6. The ownership rights in and disposition of the death benefit from a life insurance policy;

7. The choice of law governing the construction of the agreement; and

8. Any other matter, including their personal rights and obligations, not in violation of public policy or a statute imposing a criminal penalty.

Case law prior to Virginia's enactment of the Premarital Agreement Act may provide insight as to obligations under an antenuptial contract that may be unenforceable due to violating public policy or criminal statutes. See e.g., *Burke v. Shaver*, 92 Va. 345, 23 S.E. 749 (1895) (a contract is void where the consideration is for illicit sexual relations).

There is also a clear prohibition against encouraging divorce. Agreements are illegal and unenforceable where "the specific object and the actual result of the antenuptial contract" encourages or facilitates a separation after the marriage. *Cumming v. Cumming*, 127 Va. 16, 25, 102 S.E. 572, 574 (1920).

> The public policy rendering such agreements void is the policy to foster and protect marriage, to encourage the parties to live together, and to prevent separation, marriage being the foundation of the family and of society, without which there would be neither civilization nor progress.

*Shelton v. Stewart*, 193 Va. 162, 166, 67 S.E.2d 841, 843 (1951) (separation agreement). "Consequently, agreements between spouses dealing with a division of property, even though in contemplation of divorce, are valid unless part of a scheme to effect a separation or to obtain a divorce by collusion." *Cooley v. Cooley,* 220 Va. 749, 752, 263 S.E.2d 49, 52 (1980).

In *Cumming,* the husband and wife married to legitimize the child of the parties who had been born before the marriage. The only condition under which the husband would marry was the execution of an agreement, which provided that each party was to retain separate property and the husband was to pay the wife a trivial sum for her and the child's support. The husband never intended to live with the wife and in fact never did so. The wife later sued for divorce based upon his desertion and sought alimony pendente lite and child support. The antenuptial agreement was found void since it was made to encourage or facilitate a separation after the marriage. 127 Va. at 25, 102 S.E. at 574 (citing 1 Bishop on *Marriage, Divorce and Separation* § 1277 (1891)). The contract was distinguished from bona fide antenuptial agreements not made with the specific object of providing a contractual limitation of the support obligation. *Id.* at 30, 102 S.E. at 576. See also *Schmidt v. Schmidt,* 9 Va. Cir. 273 (City of Richmond, 1988).

The prohibition against contracts facilitating divorce and separation would also exclude agreements whose language limited the duration of the marriage or specified grounds for divorce. For example, where before their separation at the instigation of the husband, a contract was drawn between husband and wife giving her $6,000 and some personal property and relieving the husband of any further duties of support, the agreement was void as contrary to public policy because "any contract between the parties having for its object the dissolution of the marriage or facilitating that result is void as contra bonos mores." *Arrington v. Arrington,* 196 Va. 86, 94, 82 S.E.2d 548 (1954) (postnuptial agreement) (citing 1 Bishop on *Marriage, Divorce and Separation* § 1261 (1891)); cf. *In re Marriage of Dawley,* 17 Cal. 3d 342, 131 Cal. Rptr. 3, 551 P.2d 323 (1976).

However, the parties may validly contract regarding support should the marriage fail. Va. Code § 20-150(4). The parties in *Schmidt v. Schmidt,* 12 Va. Cir. 313 (City of Richmond, 1988), had a prenuptial agreement limiting the wife's right to support following divorce. When the matter was litigated in their divorce proceedings, res judicata barred the wife's later claim that during the marriage the husband had promised to always take care of her. A waiver of property rights in an antenuptial agreement does not waive a spouse's claim to support and maintenance. In *Davis v. Davis,* 239 Va. 657, 391 S.E.2d 255 (1990), a valid antenuptial agreement provided that each spouse would keep property separate and waive any property interests that might accrue in the future by operation of law. After the husband shot and paralyzed the wife, she filed for divorce and obtained support pendente lite.

On the day before the divorce hearing, the husband conveyed his real property to a friend. The circuit court awarded the wife a divorce, and found that the husband was in arrears by $9,000. The Supreme Court agreed with the wife that the agreement did not preclude her obtaining spousal support, so that the judgment against him was valid. The deed was set aside as fraudulent, and was subject to her lien. Any waiver of spousal support must be expressly stated in the agreement reached by the parties. *Davis v. Davis*, 239 Va. 657, 661, 391 S.E.2d 255, 257 (1990).

An obvious candidate for inclusion in an agreement continues to be parties' property.

An antenuptial agreement stating that each party's property will remain separate after marriage and that each party waives any right to the other party's property will not satisfy the requirements for waiver of surviving spouse rights in a pension plan that is qualified under the Employee Retirement Income Security Act of 1974, as amended by the Retirement Equity Act of 1984 (ERISA—29 U.S.C. § 1055(a)). In order to waive spousal rights under ERISA, a spouse must execute a writing, witnessed by a plan representative or a notary public, in which the spouse designates a beneficiary other than himself or herself and acknowledges that he or she is giving up the rights conferred by ERISA. However, a party to an antenuptial agreement does not possess the spousal rights conferred by ERISA, because, before marriage, he or she is not a spouse; therefore, the party cannot waive those rights. *Hagwood v. Newton*, 282 F.3d 285 (4th Cir. 2002).

If an antenuptial agreement expressly states that the parties' incomes will remain separate property during marriage, then a joint income tax refund that is specifically attributable to that separate property will be part of each party's separate estate in a property distribution at divorce. Tracing is used to determine the correct distribution of the income tax refund. To the extent that a party can show that any portion of a joint refund is directly traceable to that party's separate income and losses, then the funds will be that party's separate property, but any portion of the refund in excess of what the party can trace to separate property will be marital property. *King v. King*, 40 Va. App. 200, 578 S.E.2d 806 (2003) (*King I*). In *King v. King*, 46 Va. App. 677, 621 S.E.2d 159 (2005) (*King II*), the court of appeals applied the "*King I* mandate" to the particular facts of the case. A husband and wife, although separated, had filed joint tax returns that claimed a loss to the husband's separately owned beach property. By filing jointly, they generated federal and state tax refunds of $25,447 and $8,526, respectively. If they had filed separately, the husband would have received federal and state tax refunds of $14,987 and $6,006, and the wife would have received a federal refund of

$679 and have owed state taxes of $175. The amounts that the husband and wife would have received if they had filed separately constituted their separate property, and the remainder constituted their marital property, which was to be divided equally according to their premarital agreement. The federal and state refunds of $14,987 and $6,006 derived from, and were traceable to, the husband's separate property (the loss to his beach property), but the remaining $12,301 in federal and state refunds derived from the parties' marital state and their marital act in filing jointly.

In *Smith v. Smith,* 43 Va. App. 279, 597 S.E.2d 250 (2004), the court of appeals enforced a provision in a divorcing couple's antenuptial agreement that stated: "all property—real, personal and mixed—which each party may hereafter acquire in his or her own name or possession shall remain the separate property of that person . . . ."

## § 2.04 Formalities

Although no specific form must be used, the antenuptial agreement must be in writing and signed by both parties. Va. Code § 20-149. This eliminates many problems of proof, see, e.g., *Hannon v. Hounihan,* 85 Va. 429, 434–35, 12 S.E. 157, 158–59 (1888), and satisfies the statute of frauds. Va. Code §§ 11-1 and 11-2. The subsequent marriage would not otherwise take the contract out of the statute. 85 Va. at 435, 12 S.E. at 158. While prospective spouses are required to have their agreement be in writing and signed by both parties, married people can enter into agreements that are not necessarily in writing or signed by them. *See* Va. Code § 20-155.

However, in one famous case, *T . . . v. T . . .* 216 Va. 867, 224 S.E.2d 148 (1976), the parties agreed orally that if the woman, who was pregnant by another, did not go to New York and put the child up for adoption, the man would marry her and support the child as if it were his. The woman in fact gave up prospects of a job in New York, married the man, and gave birth. The man was named as the child's father on the birth certificate, and claimed the child as his on income tax returns until the couple divorced. The contract was upheld although not in writing because not only had the marriage taken place, but also because the wife had terminated her employment plans and reconsidered her decision to place the baby for adoption. These changes in the lives of both mother and child constituted part performance, as did the husband's marriage and acceptance of her services as a housewife. The partial performance took the case out of the statute of frauds, and the husband's promises to the wife, in reliance upon which she changed her position, acted to her detriment, so that when she substantially performed her obligations, he was estopped from pleading the statute of frauds.

Antenuptial agreements are contracts subject to the rules of construction applicable to contracts generally, including the application of the plain meaning of unambiguous contractual terms. *Pysell v. Keck*, 263 Va. 457, 559 S.E.2d 677 (2002). Thus, in *Pysell*, the court of appeals held that the plain language of an antenuptial agreement referred only to the separate property owned by the parties during their lifetimes, and not to the property in a deceased party's estate, so that a widow's rights as a surviving spouse in her deceased husband's estate were not waived by the antenuptial agreement. See *Dowling v. Rowan*, 270 Va. 510, 621 S.E.2d 397 (2005) (premarital agreement containing express waiver of rights to specific, listed property upon spouse's death operated as waiver of surviving spouse's rights in listed property).

Virginia courts resolve contractual vagaries in one of three ways: (1) if no patent or latent ambiguities exist, a court should enforce the plain meaning of the contractual language; (2) if an ambiguity exists, a court should still enforce the contract if the real meaning of the ambiguous provision can be discerned from extrinsic evidence; and (3) if an ambiguity renders the alleged contract too indefinite for a determination of the parties' intent, even after the consideration of extrinsic evidence, a court should not enforce the contract. See *Vilseck v. Vilseck*, 45 Va. App. 581, 612 S.E.2d 746 (2005) (ambiguity in antenuptial agreement necessitated court's consideration of extrinsic evidence); *Smith v. Smith*, 43 Va. App. 279, 597 S.E.2d 250 (2004) (court's findings that prenuptial agreement was "less than clear" and used "imprecise and conflicting language" were insufficient to invalidate agreement).

Under Virginia choice-of-law rules, unless the parties clearly intend for a prenuptial agreement to be governed by the laws of a specific jurisdiction, the validity of the agreement is governed by the jurisdiction where the agreement was executed, unless the substantive law of that jurisdiction is contrary to the established public policy of Virginia. *Black v. Powers*, 48 Va. App. 113, 628 S.E.2d 546 (2006). In *Black*, a prenuptial agreement signed by two Virginia residents on the day before their wedding in St. Croix, Virgin Islands, was governed by the law of the Virgin Islands rather than by the law of Virginia.

In *Marks v. Marks*, 36 Va. App. 216, 548 S.E.2d 919 (2001), the parties agreed that their antenuptial agreement would be governed by Virginia law, and that any unresolved disputes related to the agreement would be remedied through arbitration. Consequently, the husband's exclusive means for challenging the arbitration award incorporated in his divorce decree was The Uniform Arbitration Act, as adopted in Va. Code § 8.01-581.01 et seq.

## § 2.05    Mutuality of Agreement

Va. Code § 20-147 provides that antenuptial agreements are "valid without consideration and . . . become effective upon marriage." However, from a historical perspective, prior to the enactment of Virginia's Premarital Agreement Act, where the consideration for the promise of one party is a promise, there must be absolute mutuality of agreement, so that each has the right to hold the other to a positive agreement. *Capps v. Capps,* 216 Va. 378, 219 S.E.2d 901 (1975) (agreement made between married couple in which the wife agreed that she would relinquish her interest in property held in joint names should she file any matrimonial action in return for a release on the mortgage note). See also *Osborne v. Osborne,* 384 Mass. 591, 428 N.E.2d 810 (1981).

The consideration for an antenuptial agreement is the marriage itself. When the husband called off the wedding after execution of a premarital agreement, although the parties eventually married nearly a year later, the agreement did not govern the terms of their divorce. The court of appeals agreed with the trial court that the contract had been repudiated and no subsequent mutual consent of the parties had been given to revitalize it. *Hurt v. Hurt,* 16 Va. App. 792, 433 S.E.2d 493 (1993). "[F]or a repudiation of a contract to constitute a breach, the repudiation must be clear, absolute, unequivocal, and must cover the entire performance of the contract." *Hurt v. Hurt,* 16 Va. App. 792, 798, 433 S.E.2d 493, 497 (1993) (citing *Vahabzadeh v. Mooney,* 241 Va. 47, 51, 399 S.E.2d 803, 805 (1991)).

An Iranian marriage contract obligated the husband to give the wife "one holy Qur'an, a piece of flower, and 20 million Rials" in Iranian currency. This contract became due and payable upon consummation of the parties' marriage, and was therefore the wife's exclusive property upon their divorce six years later. This contract did not fall within Virginia's prohibition against immoral contracts because sexual intercourse in marriage is neither illicit nor morally reprehensible, but on the contrary, is automatically part of the promise to marry. *Derakhshan v. Derakhshan,* 42 Va. Cir. 411 (Fairfax Co. 1997).

If the agreement was formulated according to foreign laws, it will be enforceable in Virginia if it satisfies existing Virginia law pertaining to prenuptial agreements. *Carpenter v. Carpenter,* 19 Va. App. 147, 449 S.E.2d 502 (1994). Each spouse must be reasonably and fairly provided for, or, in the alternative, there must be full and fair disclosure to the wife of the husband's worth before she signs. A contract called a *nikah nama* prepared before the parties' 1982 Pakistan marriage was not enforceable according to

*Chaudhary v. Ali*, 1994 Va. App. LEXIS 759 (Dec. 27, 1994) (not designated for publication).

In *Black v. Powers*, 48 Va. App. 113, 628 S.E.2d 546 (2006), the parties decided to marry and chose the island of St. Croix in the U.S. Virgin Islands as the location of their wedding. Several months before the wedding, the husband gave the wife a proposed prenuptial agreement. The wife never sought legal advice about the terms and conditions of the agreement. While in St. Croix, the day before the wedding, the husband gave the wife another copy of the agreement, which she signed. There was no exchange of financial documents prior to execution of the agreement. Upon their divorce, the wife sought equitable distribution of the marital property, and the husband sought dismissal of the action based on the terms of the premarital agreement, which defined each party's property rights. The trial court applied Virginia law to uphold the agreement and also noted that the agreement would also be valid under Virgin Island law. The wife's request for equitable distribution was denied. On appeal, the court of appeals affirmed the trial court's decision, but held that Virgin Islands law applied insofar as a prenuptial agreement is governed by the law of the jurisdiction where the agreement was executed, unless the substantive law of that jurisdiction is contrary to the established public policy of the Commonwealth of Virginia. The court further found that the wife was given the opportunity to obtain independent legal advice concerning the terms and conditions of the agreement, but failed to do so, even though the husband encouraged her to obtain such advice. Thus, the court held that the prenuptial agreement was valid and enforceable.

## § 2.06 Capacity to Contract

The usual rules relating to capacity to contract will apply to antenuptial agreements. Each party must voluntarily sign the agreement. Va. Code § 20-151(A)(1).

Every adult party who executes an agreement is presumed to be mentally competent to enter into a contract. In order to be competent to enter into a legally binding obligation, a party is not required to exercise good judgment or to make wise decisions so long as he or she understands the nature and character of the agreement and consequences of entering into it. *Drewry v. Drewry*, 8 Va. App. 460, 467, 383 S.E.2d 12, 15 (1989). "The law does not require that one have the ability to make a reasoned judgment concerning an agreement but only that he or she understand the nature and consequences of his acts." *Drewry v. Drewry*, 8 Va. App. 460, 468, 383 S.E.2d 12, 16 (1989). "A contracting party is competent if, at the time he executes the agreement, he had sufficient mental capacity to understand the nature of the transaction and agree to its provisions." *Bailey v. Bailey*, 54 Va. App. 209, 215, 677 S.E.2d 56, 60 (2009) (citation omitted).

Duress is not generally accepted as an excuse. The party claiming duress must prove its existence by clear and convincing evidence, and the threatened act must be wrongful. *Pelfrey v. Pelfrey*, 25 Va. App. 239, 246, 487 S.E.2d 281, 284 (1997).

Va. Code § 20-151 establishes the grounds upon which antenuptial agreements will not be enforced. Agreements will not be enforced where either (1) a party did not voluntarily execute the agreement, or (2) the agreement was unconscionable when executed and the party was not provided a fair and reasonable disclosure of the property and financial obligations of the other party, or the party did not voluntarily waive any right to a disclosure of the property and financial obligations of the other party.

The disclosure of property and financial obligations is critical when drafting antenuptial agreements. A fair and reasonable disclosure of property and financial obligations means that something less than a full disclosure is permitted. *Chapin v. Chapin*, 2017 Va. App. LEXIS 225 (Aug. 29, 2017) (unpublished opinion). However, determining reasonableness and fairness "is a fact-intensive inquiry that will turn on multiple factors, including, but not limited to, the information actually disclosed, the information not disclosed, whether any information regarding obligations is provided, the totality of the party's financial situation, and the relative size of the non-disclosed information to the totality of the party's financial situation." *Id.* In the *Chapin* case, the antenuptial agreement was not enforceable because the husband who disclosed approximately $1,800,000 in assets, failed to disclose liabilities exceeding $500,000. Since the undisclosed liabilities reduced the husband's assets by almost one-third of its total value, the trial court did not err by finding that the disclosure provided to the wife was neither fair nor reasonable, and accordingly, the antenuptial agreement was not enforced. *Id.*

Lastly, where "a marriage is determined to be void, an agreement that would otherwise have been a premarital agreement shall be enforceable only to the extent necessary to avoid an inequitable result." Va. Code § 20-151(C).

### § 2.07    Equality of Bargaining Position

Court may invalidate antenuptial agreements if there exists unequal bargaining positions and there was no waiver to a disclosure of assets and liabilities. *Batleman*, discussed *infra*, established the legal standard prior to the enactment of the Premarital Agreement Act. Va. Code § 20-151(a)(2) provides that an unconscionable antenuptial agreement will not be enforced where the party was neither provided a fair and reasonable disclosure of the property or financial obligations of the other party nor voluntarily and expressly waived such disclosure. Each party should have knowledge about what might normally accrue upon death or divorce. *Batleman v. Rubin*, 199 Va. 156, 160, 98 S.E.2d 519, 522 (1957). In *Batleman*, husband and wife agreed before their marriage that in lieu of all marital rights, husband would leave wife $25,000 in his will. At the time of the antenuptial contract, husband was worth $250,000. The agreement was void because the husband did not make any disclosure to his intended wife of the value of the property, nor did she know it. The wife agreed to less than one-third of the value of her rights, if married, in the property. The evidence raised a presumption, since the amount received was disproportionate, that there had not been full disclosure. The husband was unable to rebut the presumption. *Id.* at 161, 98 S.E.2d at 523–24.

*Chaplain v. Chaplain*, 54 Va. App. 762, 682 S.E.2d 108 (2009), is a modern equivalent of *Batleman*. In *Chaplain*, a husband failed to disclose his net worth of approximately $20 million dollars to his fiancée prior to her execution of an antenuptial agreement. The agreement provided that, in the event of a divorce, each party waived their interest in the other party's property, their right to inherit from the other, their right to equitable distribution, spousal support, retirement and life insurance benefits, and attorney's fees and costs. The only asset the wife was entitled to under the agreement was the sum of $100,000, on the condition that she and the husband were married and living together at the time of his death. At divorce, the husband argued that his wealth was his separate property and not subject to equitable distribution, because most of it was accumulated prior to the marriage. However, the wife was able to establish *prima facie* that the antenuptial agreement was unenforceable. Under the Premarital Agreement Act, an antenuptial agreement is not enforceable if, in addition to being found unconscionable when it was executed, the individual challenging its enforceability establishes either (1) that he or she did not execute the agreement voluntarily, or (2) that he or she was not provided "a fair and reasonable disclosure of the property or financial obligations of the other party; and did not voluntarily and expressly waive, in writing, any right to disclosure of the property." See Va. Code § 20-151(A). Not only did the husband fail to disclose his assets and liabilities to the wife prior to her signing the agreement, but the wife also did not waive further disclosure in writing before the execution of the agreement, as required by the statute.

In *Makoui v. Makoui*, 2011 Va. App. LEXIS 360 (Nov. 22, 2011), the wife appealed the property distribution and spousal support awards entered in her divorce, arguing that the trial court erred in finding that the parties' premarital agreement was enforceable. The wife claimed that the husband did not make a fair and reasonable disclosure of his finances prior to execution of the agreement, and that the agreement was unconscionable pursuant to Virginia's Premarital Agreement Act. Va. Code Ann. § 20-151. The Act provides that a premarital agreement is not enforceable if the person against whom enforcement is sought proves that:

> The agreement was unconscionable when it was executed and, before execution of the agreement, that person (i) was not provided a fair and reasonable disclosure of the property or financial obligations of the other party; and (ii) did not voluntarily and expressly waive, in writing, any right to disclosure of the property or financial obligations of the other party beyond the disclosure provided.

The wife claimed that the husband undervalued his net worth by disclosing only about $68,000 worth of stock in the financial statements attached to the premarital agreement executed in 1993, but that in 2009 he testified that he owned $250,000 to $300,000 of stock at the time he signed the 1993 agreement. The financial statements disclosed by the husband in 1993 set forth the market value of the majority of shares of stock listed but also included thousands of shares of named stocks for which no value was listed. The trial court held that, without evidence of their value, nothing in the record compelled a finding that the husband failed in 1993 to disclose the $250,000 to $300,000 worth of stock he later testified he had owned at that time

The appellate court affirmed the trial court ruling and held that the evidence supported the trial court's finding that the husband's disclosure was fair and reasonable under the standard set forth in the Premarital Agreement Act. The court also stated that the recitation in the prenuptial agreement that each party had given fair and reasonable disclosure of his or her property and financial obligations created a prima facie presumption that it was factually correct. Va. Code Ann. § 20-147 et seq.

However, where the husband underestimated his financial condition but had no intent to conceal property from his wife, the misstatement did not invalidate an otherwise valid antenuptial agreement. Nor could the contract be voided because, in hindsight, there existed a better opportunity for the wife. *Schmidt v. Schmidt*, 9 Va. Cir. 273 (City of Richmond, 1988).

See generally 12B Michie's Jurisprudence *Marriage Contracts and Settlements* § 3.

## § 2.08   General Sources

For further reading, see Lenore Weitzman, *The Marriage Contract* (1981); Howard Hunter, *An Essay on Contract and Statutes: Race, Marriage, and the Meretricious Spouse,* 64 Va. L. Rev. 1039 (1978); Marjorie Macguire Schultz, *Contractual Ordering of Marriage: A New Model for State Policy,* 70 Calif. L. Rev. 707 (1982); Elizabeth Scott, *Rational Decisionmaking About Marriage and Divorce,* 76 Va. L. Rev. 9 (1990); Peter Swisher, *Divorce Planning in Antenuptial Agreements: Towards a New Objectivity,* 13 U. Rich. L. Rev. 175 (1979); Homer Clark, *The New Marriage,* 12 Willamette L.J. 441 (1976); Comment, *Marital Contracts for Support and Services: Constitutionality Begins at Home,* 49 N.Y.U. L. Rev. 1161 (1974); 12B Michie's Jurisprudence *Marriage Contracts and Settlements;* 26 Am. Jur. *Husband and Wife* § 277; West Digest, *Husband and Wife* Key No. 29(9).

# CHAPTER 3

# Unmarried Parents and Their Children

## SYNOPSIS

## § 3.01 Introduction

At common law, the illegitimate child was *nullius filius*, no one's son. *Brown v. Commonwealth,* 218 Va. 40, 45, 235 S.E.2d 325, 329 (1977). This meant that he could not inherit, *Bond v. Bond,* 16 Va. L. Reg. 411 (1910), nor generally advance in society, since tainted by his parents' meretricious relationship. See *Goodman v. Goodman,* 150 Va. 42, 45, 142 S.E. 412, 413 (1928). See generally Lasoh, *Virginia Bastardy Laws: A Burdensome Heritage,* 9 Wm. & Mary L. Rev. 402 (1967).

Because the fate of the illegitimate was so harsh, the law has provided several avenues of relief. These include: (1) the presumption of legitimacy; (2) statutory legitimation following void marriage, Va. Code § 20-31; see *Henderson v. Henderson,* 187 Va. 121, 46 S.E.2d 10 (1948); (3) legitimacy if parents are later wedded, Va. Code § 20-31.1, and the father acknowledges the child, *Hoover v. Hoover,* 131 Va. 522, 105 S.E. 91 (1921); and (4) the paternity proceeding allowing support from the unwed father. Va. Code § 20-61.3.

The child of unmarried parents lived with his mother since birth. The father failed to acknowledge the child at birth, so the mother selected a last name for the child other than the father's. After a court found paternity, the father regularly paid $500 per month child support and had temporary-custody visitation. The father's petition to change the child's surname to his own was granted by the circuit court and this decision was affirmed on appeal. *Long-Molnar v. Dean*, 1996 Va. App. LEXIS 681 (Nov. 5, 1996). However, when the mother conceived a son during her separation, but the child was born after his mother and her husband had reconciled, the birth father could not have the boy's surname changed to match his own.

In *Rowland v. Shurbutt*, 259 Va. 305, 525 S.E.2d 917 (2000), the father did not file the name change petition until the child was nearly seven, although the parents litigated custody, visitation and support issues "most of the child's life." Although the mother and father had joint legal custody of the child, the child resided with the mother and her husband since birth. Citing *Flowers v. Cain*, the court reasoned that the burden of proving that a name change "is in the best interests" of a minor rests upon the petitioning parent. The father's evidence in *Rowland* rested upon the deposition of a psychiatrist who had never met the child's mother or her husband, and who concluded that "a child should be able to carry the name of both his parents" and that the father "has been extensively involved with the child." The court noted that the psychiatrist's opinions focused mainly on the father's "rights" and "only tangentially" addressed the child's best interests. The court concluded that the child's best interest would be served without the name change, since with his present name he is "healthy, happy, developing normally in school and socially, and is the best balanced of all the parties."

When a child lives with her mother and her mother's male companion, she does not become his "relative" or a "foster child" so that his uninsured motorist insurance will cover her injuries. Living together outside marriage and adoption does not create a legal family even though the companion acted like the child's father and "look[ed] upon her as though she were his own daughter" while in return she looked to him exclusively for "paternal love, affection, care, comfort, education, emotion[al] support, and guidance." *Virginia Farm Bureau Mut. Ins. Co. v. Gile*, 259 Va. 164, 524 S.E.2d 642 (2000).

In more recent times, much of the stigma has passed from the illegitimate child and his parents. Fit fathers of illegitimate children must be given the right to refuse consent to their child's adoption, *Stanley v. Illinois*, 405 U.S. 645, 92 S. Ct. 1208, 31 L. Ed. 2d 551 (1972); support is due since provided for by statute for legitimate children, *Gomez v. Perez*, 409 U.S. 535, 93 S. Ct. 872, 35 L. Ed. 2d 56 (1973); *Brown v. Commonwealth*, 218 Va. 40, 235 S.E.2d 325 (1977), and custody may be granted to the father if in the child's best interests. Compare *Caban v. Mohammed*, 441 U.S. 380, 99 S. Ct. 1760, 60 L. Ed. 2d 297 (1979), with *Commonwealth v. Hayes*, 215 Va. 49, 205 S.E.2d 644 (1974). A variety of United States Supreme Court decisions have allowed illegitimate children to recover under workman's compensation laws, *Weber v. Aetna Cas. & Sur. Co.*, 406 U.S. 164, 92 S. Ct. 1400, 31 L. Ed. 2d 768 (1972), and wrongful death statutes, see *Levy v. Louisiana*, 391 U.S. 68, 88 S. Ct. 1509, 20 L. Ed. 2d 436 (1968); *Carroll v. Sneed*, 211 Va. 640, 179 S.E.2d 620 (1971) (where child can prove damages), and have clarified inheritance under the intestacy laws, *Labine v. Vincent*, 401 U.S. 532, 91 S. Ct. 1017, 28 L. Ed. 2d 288 (1971) (distinguishing between classes of illegitimate children constitutional) all on constitutional grounds. However, it is constitutional to grant preferential immigration status to children of unwed parents whose mothers are citizens, while withholding it from those whose fathers alone are citizens. *Miller v. Albright*, 523 U.S. 420, 118 S. Ct. 1428, 140 L. Ed. 2d 575 (1998). See generally Krause, *Equal Protection for the Illegitimate*, 65 Mich. L. Rev. 402 (1967); Lasoh, *Virginia Bastardy Laws: A Burdensome Heritage*, 9 Wm. & Mary L. Rev. 402 (1967).

## § 3.02   Presumption of Legitimacy

Because of the ancient problems of proof and the societal preference for the marital status, it was conclusively presumed that a child born during the mother's marriage was that of her husband. In fact, the spouse was frequently unable to testify at all due to the evidentiary maxim called Lord Mansfield's Rule. *Stegall v. Stegall*, 22 F. Cas. 1226, F. Cas. No. 13351 (C.C. Va. 1825). See *Bowles v. Bingham*, 16 Va. (2 Munf.) 442, 17 Va. 599 (1811) (quoting 2 Blackstone's *Commentaries* 466). See generally McCormick *Evidence* § 343, 9 Wigmore, *Evidence* § 21537. This continues to remain the rule in some states, and was upheld against due process challenges by the Supreme Court. *Michael H. v. Gerald D.*, 491 U.S. 110, 109 S. Ct. 2333, 105 L. Ed. 2d 91 (1989).

Gradually it became possible in paternity proceedings, where the parties had never entered into a marriage, to show non-access by the husband during the period of likely conception. See, e.g., *Smith v. Perry*, 80 Va. 563, 569 (1885) (if beyond the seas, etc.); *Scott v. Hillenberg*, 85 Va. 245, 7 S.E. 377 (1888) (not overcome where husband was a soldier in the Confederate Army who frequently deserted and returned home).

In *Gibson v. Gibson*, 207 Va. 821, 153 S.E.2d 189 (1967), the wife gave birth to a son 314 days after the husband and she had last cohabited together, according to evidence adduced at their divorce hearing. The wife alleged that they had resumed cohabitation only after the child was born, and in fact denied that she was pregnant less than three months before his birth. The Virginia Supreme Court allowed the husband's appeal from a support order, stating that "[i]mprobability of known access by the husband merely of itself is not sufficient to repel the presumption; but when the evidence forces the conclusion of non-access beyond all reasonable doubt, it is sufficient to repel the presumption." *Id.* at 825, 153 S.E.2d at 192 (citing 3 Michie's Jurisprudence *Bastardy* § 7, at 132, 10 C.J.S. *Bastards* § 3, at 25 et seq., § 5(a) at 30–31; 10 Am. Jur. 2d *Bastards* § 15, at 855). The burden, therefore, is upon the person claiming illegitimacy. *Scott v. Hillenberg,* 85 Va. 245, 7 S.E. 377 (1888). See generally Friend, *The Law of Evidence in Virginia* § 129 (2d ed. 1983). When the juvenile and domestic relations district court ruled that blood test results had not been timely filed, the Division of Child Support Enforcement was a proper party to appeal. *Jones v. Division of Child Support Enforcement,* 19 Va. App. 184, 450 S.E.2d 172 (1994). However, the notice of appeal must be filed by the Division's attorney. Because the rules for appeal were not followed, the circuit court never acquired jurisdiction over the appeal.

Va. Code § 20-49.1 et seq. set forth the procedure to establish the parent-child relationship, which includes completing court ordered genetic testing. A father was able to establish paternity beyond 99.9999% probability pursuant to this code section where the mother used a turkey baster to inseminate herself. *Bruce v. Boardwine,* 64 Va. App. 623, 631, 770 S.E.2d 774, 777–78 (2015). A party may also under limited circumstances use the results of genetic testing to set aside a final judgment, court order, administrative order, or other obligation to pay child support or any legal determination of paternity. See Va. Code § 20-49.10.

In *Slagle v. Slagle,* 11 Va. App. 341, 398 S.E.2d 346 (1990), the wife told the husband prior to their marriage that she was pregnant with his child. After the child was born, the parties married and lived together for more than a year. They separated, and the wife was awarded $600 per month in pendente lite support. A final divorce was granted several years later, and the wife was given child custody, while the husband was ordered to pay $250 in child support and $350 in spousal support. After the decree was entered, the husband obtained blood tests conclusively establishing that he could not be the father of the child. The juvenile court, which had ordered the blood tests performed at the husband's request, abated his child support payments, but continued his spousal support obligation and ordered payment of support arrearages. Both parties appealed. The circuit court found that the final decree of divorce constituted a final adjudication of the husband's paternity and thus was not subject to collateral attack. The court of appeals agreed that the husband was collaterally estopped from challenging the support obligation established by the final divorce decree, which stated that the child was born of the marriage. See also *Comer v. Comer,* 1996 Va. App. LEXIS 277 (April 23, 1996).

A child born more than 10 months after a parent's death shall not be recognized as the parent's child for intestacy purposes. Va. Code § 2-164 (1994). Although a child is presumed to be the child of his or her married mother's husband, the presumption may be rebutted by a preponderance of the evidence of the paternity of another man or the impossibility or improbability of conception by the husband. Va. Code § 63.1-220.3(D). The presumptive father must give consent to adoption under Va. Code § 63.1-220.3(C).

## § 3.03    Support of Children Born Out of Wedlock

Beginning in 1576, the English Poor Laws provided that the parish should be responsible for the maintenance of children born out of wedlock, with the power to punish both parents and to make orders for the upkeep of the illegitimate by charging the mother or the father with payment. 18 Eliz. 1, c. 3; Comment, *Support of Children Born Out of Wedlock: Virginia at the Crossroads,* 18 Wash. & Lee L. Rev. 343 (1961). The Virginia equivalent was found in L. 1769, 8 Hening 374. The brunt of illicit sexual relations was to be borne by the mother and the child through indenture into service or the workhouse. However, in *McClaugherty v. McClaugherty,* 180 Va. 51, 21 S.E.2d 761 (1942), the Virginia Supreme Court stated that support was due even in the absence of statute where a child sued the father to collect support. The parents had gone through a secret ceremonial marriage and then lived together for twenty years, after which they separated and the father eventually married another, *id.* at 65, 21 S.E.2d at 767 (citing 1 Minor's *Institutes* 405). *McClaugherty* did not signal a trend, however. A later case with less compelling facts stated that the father was under no legal obligation to support or to contribute to the support to his illegitimate offspring. *Brown v. Brown,* 183 Va. 353, 32 S.E.2d 79 (1944). This lack of a legal obligation continued until Virginia adopted its paternity statute, which was originally Va. Code § 20-61.1 et seq. (and is now at Va. Code § 20-49.1 et seq.) See generally Comment, *Support of Children Born Out of Wedlock: Virginia at the Crossroads,* 18 Wm. & Mary L. Rev. 343 (1961). More recently, the Supreme Court has compelled such a result since legitimate children are provided for by statute. *Gomez v. Perez,* 409 U.S. 535, 93 S. Ct. 872, 35 L. Ed. 2d 56 (1973); Va. Code § 20-61.1; *Brown v. Commonwealth,* 218 Va. 40, 235 S.E.2d 325 (1977).

In *T . . . v. T . . .,* 216 Va. 867, 224 S.E.2d 148 (1976), an unwed pregnant woman gave up employment prospects in New York and plans to put the child up for adoption upon a man's oral agreement that he would marry her and support the child as if it were his own. The husband's name was placed as father on the birth certificate, and the husband claimed the child on income tax returns until the couple divorced. Although the agreement was oral, it was upheld despite the statute of frauds on grounds of estoppel and partial performance. See also *Dunnaville v. Department of Social Servs.,* 1995 Va. App. LEXIS 222 (March 7, 1995) (husband required to pay unless he could demonstrate fraud). Similarly, where the husband refused to make court-ordered child support payments in contempt of the divorce order, he was later refused equitable relief to recover whatever payments he did make or any withheld tax funds, despite the fact that H.L.A. testing revealed that he could not be the child's father. *Stover v. Stover,* 31 Va. Cir. 484 (City of Roanoke 1990).

When the parties agreed during their deposition that the husband would acknowledge paternity of a child born during the marriage and would support that child, and the divorce decree recited that there were five children of the marriage, "including one infant child born during the marriage," the decree was a valid, conclusive judgment. *Rose v. Rose,* 1993 Va. App. LEXIS 375 (Aug. 24, 1993,). The husband was therefore obligated to pay support. However, a separation agreement that acknowledged that the husband was not the father of his wife's child, born during the marriage, waived her right to enforce express promises made prior to and after the birth to support the child as if it were his own. The agreement allowed the wife to remain in the marital residence for a year and have $6,500 to cover the birth expenses and care of the infant. *Mills v. Mills,* 36 Va. Cir. 351 (Fairfax Co. 1995).

Likewise, the unwed father in *Lawson v. Murphy,* 36 Va. Cir. 465 (Wise Co. 1995), was unable to enforce a contract according to which he agreed to pay the child's mother $7,500 to replace all child support. The mother received AFDC payments and the father had to reimburse the state. When parties stipulate to a child support "credit" for $157 paid in child support for another child outside the marriage as a deduction from the presumptive child support amount, a trial court will not err in accepting the stipulated amount to compute the child support obligation. *Sproles v. Lowry,* 1999 Va. App. LEXIS 24 (Jan. 12, 1999). Although the circuit court would normally consider the full amount of support paid for another child in determining how much to deviate, the trial court did not err in accepting the lower amount.

A sworn declaration of paternity is not res judicata of paternity and does not collaterally estop the putative father from adjudicating the issue of paternity, when he never had a hearing to litigate the issue. The putative father in *Dunbar v. Hogan,* 16 Va. App. 653, 432 S.E.2d 16 (1993), was therefore able to introduce H.L.A. tests excluding the possibility that he was the child's biological father in support proceedings brought by the child's mother. However, a putative father who signed a sworn declaration of paternity, and later proved through blood testing that he was not the child's biological father, was nevertheless held liable for child support arrearages that accrued prior to his obtaining a judgment of nonpaternity. *Commonwealth ex rel. Breakiron v. Farmer*, 32 Va. App. 430, 528 S.E.2d 183 (2000). Amendments to Va. Code § 20-49.1 substitute "genetic" for "blood tests" throughout the language about establishing paternity.

A father was responsible for paying child support although he maintained that the mother had seduced him, refused to obtain an abortion, and refused to place the child for adoption. *Hur v. Commonwealth Dep't of Social Services Div. of Child Support Enforcement ex rel Klopp*, 13 Va. App. 54, 409 S.E.2d 454 (1991). The court of appeals quoted from a New York case, *L. Pamela P. v. Frank S.*, 59 N.Y.2d 1, 6–7, 462 N.Y.S.2d 819, 821–22, 449 N.E.2d 713, 715–16 (1983):

> [The father] seeks to have his choice regarding procreation fully respected by other individuals and effectuated to the extent that he should be relieved of his obligation to support a child that he did not voluntarily choose to have. But [the father's] constitutional entitlement to avoid procreation does not encompass a right to avoid a child support obligation simply because another private person has not fully respected his desires in this regard. However unfairly [the father] may have been treated by [the mother's] failure to allow him an equal voice in the decision to conceive a child, such a wrong does not rise to the level of a constitutional violation.

The court expressly rejected the father's argument that the mother's intentional conduct deprived him of a right to decide whether to father a child. The trial court had correctly found that Hur had not shown any seduction on the part of the child's mother and that he was voluntarily underemployed, so that imputation of an income was appropriate. However, the court of appeals reversed the ruling that Hur was not entitled to visitation.

In 2020, Va. Code § 20-108.(D)(1) was enacted to require that, as part of any initial child support hearing brought within six months of the birth of a child, the parents are to pay "any reasonable and necessary unpaid expenses of the mother's pregnancy and the delivery of such child" pursuant to their respective proportionate income shares.

## § 3.04  Custody of Children of Unwed Parents

At common law, custody of illegitimate children rested with their mothers. See, e.g., *State ex rel. Bennett v. Anderson*, 129 W. Va. 671, 41

S.E.2d 241 (1946). This was in contrast to legitimate children, who were under their father's governance. In part this was because of problems of proof of paternity.

Even today, upon the birth of an illegitimate child, the right of the natural mother to immediate custody is superior. *Commonwealth v. Hayes*, 215 Va. 49, 52, 205 S.E.2d 644, 647 (1974). Thus, a biological father who was absent at a child's birth, had not contributed to the child's support, and had not visited the child had no "legal justification" under Va. Code § 18.2-47 for forcibly taking the child from its mother's custody. The father committed the crime of abduction of his illegitimate son. *Taylor v. Commonwealth*, 260 Va. 683, 537 S.E.2d 592 (2000).

Since the Supreme Court case of *Stanley v. Illinois*, 405 U.S. 645, 92 S. Ct. 1208, 31 L. Ed. 2d 551 (1972), unwed fathers must be given an opportunity to demonstrate their fitness before an adoption of their child will be granted. This does not, however, mean that a putative unwed father must give his consent to adoption. In *Commonwealth v. Hayes,* 215 Va. 49, 205 S.E.2d 644 (1974), the trial court found that the father had been "guilty of anti-social, immoral and illegal conduct," *Id.* at 53, 205 S.E.2d at 648, and allowed an adoption despite the "refreshing" desire of the father to have custody. He had never offered any financial assistance to the mother, seen the child, or even inquired about her. His plans were so speculative and unsatisfactory that the court wrote they deserved no comment. *Id.* at 52, 205 S.E.2d at 647. *Hayes* further noted that under Va. Code § 64.1-6, the father's consent was unnecessary since the mother had relinquished the child, in contrast to the involuntary event of the mother's death that produced the custody dispute in Stanley. *Id.* at 52–53, 205 S.E.2d at 647.

If the children have been legitimated because their parents' marriage was void and the husband acknowledged the children, their custody will be decided on the same basis as children born during wedlock. *Henderson v. Henderson,* 187 Va. 121, 46 S.E.2d 10 (1948). Recognition of the child by the natural father will suffice to revoke a prior interlocutory order for adoption. *Harmon v. D'Adamo,* 195 Va. 125, 77 S.E.2d 318 (1953).

A child's parents were never married, and the child lived with the mother after the couple separated, while the father never provided any financial assistance or attention and eventually relocated to Florida. Shortly before the child's second birthday, the mother was killed in an automobile accident. Both the father and the maternal grandmother sought custody. The trial court awarded custody to the father, finding that he had obtained employment in Florida while pursuing education as a "pharmacist assistant," and that he provided an adequate home and attendant support for his son. Although the grandmother initially assumed custody, the father was awarded custody by the trial court. The grandmother complained unsuccessfully that the father had once "picked the child up from the floor" and "slammed him up against the corner of a door and a wall" and that he was living in a "meretricious relationship" with his fiancée. This was not sufficient to clearly and convincingly rebut the presumption that the father's custody best served the child's interests. *Bonds v. Anderson*, 1996 Va. App. LEXIS 504 (July 16, 1996).

There is a great deal of tension between the legal concept of being a parent versus the practical every-day roles taken on by adults who parent a child in a same sex relationship. The distinction between being a legal parent as opposed to parenting a non-biological child is substantial and has significant and prejudicial consequences. *Hawkins v. Grese*, 68 Va. App. 462, 809 S.E.2d 441 (2018), defines who qualifies as a parent. The case involves same-sex partners who had a committed ten-year relationship. Hawkins and Grese discussed having children, Grese became pregnant through artificial insemination, and she gave birth to a son in 2007. The child was raised by both parties and considered them to be his parents. However, Hawkins never adopted the child, and the parties neither married nor formed a civil union. A few years after their relationship ended, Hawkins sued for custody and visitation. *Hawkins v. Grese*, 68 Va. App. at 467, 809 S.E.2d at 443. In recognizing that the Code of Virginia lacks any definition for "parent", the Court determined that "by looking to other areas within the Code of Virginia where parent is used, it is clear that the term "parent" contemplates a relationship to a child based upon either the contribution of genetic material through biological insemination or by means of legal adoption." *Hawkins v. Grese*, 68 Va. App. at 472, 809 S.E.2d at 446. In recognizing that Va. Code § 20-124.1 defines "a person with a legitimate interest" as a class of people other than a parent who may be able to sue for custody and visitation, the Court held that "[i]t seems clear, and we hold that where custody disputes are concerned, the term 'parent' is a relationship to a child only through either biological procreation or legal adoption." *Hawkins v. Grese*, 68 Va. App. at 473, 809 S.E.2d at 446. The case resulted in a devastating impact for Hawkins, and likely the child, as Hawkins' claim for custody was denied since she was unable to rebut the fundamental rights of the biological parent and presumptions respecting the rights of the biological parent against claims made by a third party. *Hawkins v. Grese*, 68 Va. App. at 486, 809 S.E.2d at 452.

## § 3.05    Children of Void Marriages

One of the earliest American statutes lessening the harsh treatment of the illegitimate child, enacted as c. 60 in 1785, Va. Code § 64.1-7 makes children of marriages deemed null at law or dissolved by courts legitimate and therefore capable of inheriting under the intestate statute. This help was extended to children of common law marriages in *McClaugherty v. McClaugherty*, 180 Va. 51, 21 S.E.2d 761 (1942). See also *Murphy v. Holland*, 237 Va. 212, 377 S.E.2d 363 (1989) (attempted common law marriage legitimated children for inheritance purposes). Even a bigamous second marriage will legitimize a child under the statute. *Stones v. Keeling*, 9 Va. (5 Call.) 143 (1804):

> But if it were otherwise, if the legislature should even be supposed to consider every second marriage, living a first husband or wife [sic], as criminal, wherefore should they visit the sins of the parents upon the innocent and unoffending offspring?

See also *Brown v. Commonwealth*, 218 Va. 40, 235 S.E.2d 325 (1977); *Kasey v. Richardson*, 331 F. Supp. 580 (W.D. Va. 1971).

For example, in *Brown v. Commonwealth*, 218 Va. 40, 235 S.E.2d 325 (1977), a child was conceived after the parties to a bigamous marriage ceased cohabiting together as man and wife, but following a period when they were seeing each other for extended periods nearly every day. The mother was not required to prove paternity under the strict standards of Va. Code § 20-61.1 as she would need to in cases involving a meretricious relationship where the parties had never entered into marriage, but rather could claim support under Va. Code § 64.1-7. *Id.* at 43–44, 235 S.E.2d at 327–28. The child should not be deprived of her rights because of statutes affecting the marital status of her parents. *Id.* at 44, 235 S.E.2d at 328.

## § 3.06    Inheritance

Illegitimate children, by statute, Va. Code § 64.2-102, inherit from their mothers and may transmit inheritance on her part as if born in lawful wedlock. For inheritance from fathers, Va. Code § 64.2-102(3) governs how an illegitimate child can qualify to inherit through the father. Decisions under prior law should be examined carefully.

The child has the burden of proving recognition. *Hoover v. Hoover,* 131 Va. 522, 526, 105 S.E. 91, 92 (1921), *reh'g granted,* 131 Va. 522, 109 S.E. 424 (1921). Although in *Hoover* the putative father married the mother after the child's birth since he had been unable to satisfy a seduction prosecution against him, he never had intercourse with her after the marriage and consistently denied that the child was his. *Id.* at 534, 105 S.E. at 94. The child was not legitimated by the mere fact of the marriage, for his acknowledgment must be plain and unequivocal. *Id.* at 540, 105 S.E. at 96. However, upon rehearing the court found that because of the presumption in favor of legitimacy, Hoover's silence when he should have spoken to deny his paternity, and some of his conduct and words, Hoover recognized the child. *Id.* at 545, 109 S.E. at 425.

A child born out of wedlock may establish paternity for inheritance purposes by clear and convincing evidence, which may include cohabitation with the mother during the ten months immediately prior to birth of the child, consent to entry of his name as the father on the birth records of the child, allowance of his surname by a general course of conduct, claiming of the child as his on any government document signed by him, admission before any court having jurisdiction over such matters that he is the child, voluntary admission of paternity in writing and under oath, a judgment for support entered against the man as if the child were born during marriage, the results of medically reliable genetic blood grouping tests, or medical or anthropological evidence relating to the alleged parentage performed by experts. See Va. Code § 64.2-103. See *Hart v. Posey,* 31 Va. Cir. 284 (Stafford Co. Cir. Ct. 1993) (clear and convincing evidence shown when alleged father placed his name on the child's birth certificate and later appeared before a notary to have the spelling of his name changed).

In *Jones v. Eley,* 256 Va. 198, 501 S.E.2d 405 (1998), two children filed a paternity action after the death of their putative father. The trial court found by clear and convincing evidence that the decedent was the biological father of the petitioners. The co-administrators contended that the evidence was insufficient to prove paternity because the eight items set forth in Va. Code § 64.1-5.2 were not proved, and the mother of the children had failed in court to be awarded child support from Jones. The Supreme Court, however, stated that the code expressly provides that the evidence relating to paternity shall not be limited to the eight items mentioned in the statute. The court looked to other evidence, such as the mother and Jones' seven-year relationship, Jones' acknowledgment of his paternity of the Eleys to his physician and others, and his actions with the Eleys that "were indicative of a father and children relationship." Most significantly, Jones named the Eleys as his son and daughter on the insurance beneficiary designation form.

When a child born out of wedlock is attempting to establish paternity for inheritance purposes under Va. Code §§ 64.2-5.1 and 64.2-103, a trial court may order the exhumation of a dead person's body for the conduct of scientifically reliable genetic tests, including DNA tests, to prove a biological relationship. Va. Code § 32.1-286(C). See *Martin v. Howard*, 643 S.E.2d 229 (2007).

A child born out of wedlock may not share in a putative parent's estate unless an affidavit alleging the parent-child relationship and an action seeking adjudication of the alleged relationship are filed within one year of the parent's death. Va. Code § 64.2-102(4). See *Belton v. Crudup*, 641 S.E.2d 74 (2007) (limitations period not tolled by administrator's filing of list of heirs). In 2008, the requirement for filing within one year was held to be inapplicable to determination of title to real property passing by intestate succession because the statute then applied only "in the settlement of" a decedent's estate. *Jenkins v. Johnson*, 276 Va. 30, 661 S.E.2d 484 (2008). The reference to settlement of an estate was removed from Va. Code § 64.1-5.1(4) effective July 1, 2009, to make it clear that the statutory limitation does apply to intestate succession of real property and not just personal property. See 2009 Va. Acts 449.

### § 3.07 Children Conceived Through Artificial Means

According to statute, Va. Code § 64.2-102, children conceived by a wife after written permission of her husband through artificial insemination by a third party donor are legitimate, and able to inherit from and through the married couple. Va. Code § 32.1-257. There are also out-of-state cases holding that even absent such a statute, the husband owes the duty of support under a theory of estoppel. See, e.g., *Gursky v. Gursky,* 39 Misc. 2d 1083, 242 N.Y.S.2d 406 (1963); *People v. Sorensen,* 68 Cal. 2d 280, 66 Cal. Rptr. 7, 437 P.2d 495 (1968).

Children conceived through the in vitro method of fertilization would be legitimate so long as both the sperm and ovum were obtained from the married couple, and the wife was implanted with the resulting embryo. Presumably, if a third party's sperm were utilized instead of the husband's Va. Code § 64.2-102 would apply.

The case of *In re Baby M,* 109 N.J. 396, 537 A.2d 1227 (1988), demonstrates many of the problems posed by agreements attempting to regularize surrogate parenthood. The lower court specifically enforced a contract, awarding the biological mother, who had agreed to give up her child, the $10,000 promised in the contract, terminating her parental rights, and allowing the wife of the natural father to adopt the child. The New Jersey Supreme Court found that the surrogate contract conflicted with state laws prohibiting use of money in connection with adoptions, requiring proof of parental unfitness or abandonment before termination of parental rights, and making surrender of custody and consent to adoption revocable in private placement adoptions. Although the contract was void, custody of the infant was awarded to the natural father and his wife on the usual standards of best interest of the child, with the natural mother awarded visitation.

In 1991, the legislature enacted Va. Code §§ 20-156 through 20-165, providing that contracts for surrogate motherhood, whether the pregnancy is naturally or artificially created, are enforceable so long as there is compliance with a detailed set of requirements including a home study, and there is no payment of fees to the mother beyond reimbursement for medical care.

In *Baby Doe v. Doe*, 15 Va. App. 242, 421 S.E.2d 913 (1992), the court of appeals reversed the district court's denial of a continuance sought by the guardian ad litem of an infant born to a surrogate mother in a declaratory judgment action brought by her genetic parents. The genetic parents sought to have an original birth certificate listing themselves as the infant's parents issued to replace one listing the surrogate mother. The trial court had terminated the infant's relationship with her birth mother and had directed that an original birth certificate issue with the genetic parents listed as the infant's parents. The guardian ad litem argued successfully that the trial court abused its discretion in denying her motion for a continuance because the summary proceedings prejudiced and impaired Baby Doe's due process rights.

When a child is born after artificial conception, the birth certificate shall name the mother's husband as the father and the gestational mother as the mother of the child. Donors of sperm or ova do not have any parental rights or duties for such child. Va. Code § 32.1-257(D) [amended 1994].

See generally Richard Epstein, *Surrogacy: The Case for Full Contractual Enforcement*, 81 Va. L. Rev. 2305 (1995); Margaret Friedlander Brinig, *A Maternalistic Approach to Surrogacy: Comment on Richard Epstein's Surrogacy: The Case for Full Contractual Enforcement*, 81 Va. L. Rev. 2377 (1995).

In *L.F. v. Breit*, 285 Va. 163, 736 S.E.2d 711 (2013), the Virginia Supreme Court affirmed a court of appeals decision that upheld the rights of a father who was cohabiting with the mother when in vitro fertilization resulted in the birth of his biological daughter. The unmarried couple wanted to have a child, but were unable to conceive naturally. The father donated his sperm and the mother underwent a successful in vitro fertilization procedure. The father was present during the procedure, and the parents entered into a written custody and visitation agreement during the pregnancy, which provided the father with "reasonable visitation." The father's name was placed on the baby's birth certificate and health insurance, and the parents sent out birth announcements. The parents continued to cohabit after the baby was born, and a relationship was formed between the father and daughter and the father's extended family. The following year, shortly after the child turned one year old, the mother ended all contact between the father and daughter. The father subsequently filed a custody petition, citing Va. Code § 20-49.1(B)(2), which provides that a parent-child relationship can be established by a voluntary written statement, under oath, by the father and mother acknowledging paternity. Nevertheless, the mother successfully argued that, pursuant to Va. Code § 20-158(A)(3), a sperm donor does not have any parental rights unless the donor is married to the mother. The trial court agreed and dismissed the father's custody petition. The father appealed to the circuit court and argued that the paternity acknowledgment executed the day after the child was born created a final binding parent-child relationship. The circuit court dismissed the father's petition, finding that construing the statute in favor of the father would make the sperm donor statute meaningless. The father appealed to the court of appeals, which found that using the sperm donor statute against a natural father after the mother acknowledged him as the child's father was absurd. The court of appeals found that the purpose of the sperm donor statute was to make sure an infertile married couple would not be threatened with a paternity claim from an anonymous donor, and was not intended to deny parentage to a natural father simply because he was not married to the mother at the time of conception. The Virginia Supreme Court affirmed.

As our societal relationships evolve, it is apparent that the laws do not necessarily treat people fairly or equally. See the discussion above in § 3.06 of *Hawkins v. Grese*, 68 Va. App. 462, 809 S.E.2d 441 (2018), which details the legal consequences, advantages and disadvantages for custodial and visitation claims by same sex partners who decided that one of them would have a child through artificial insemination. The legal construct of being the biological parent gives that parent far superior rights to the child, and the non-biological parent's rights will be severely undermined if that person does not adopt the child.

## § 3.08   Paternity Proceedings

Parentage proceedings may be instituted by a child, a parent, a person claiming parentage, a person standing in loco parentis to the child or having legal custody of the child, or a representative of the Department of Social Services or the Department of Juvenile Justice. Va. Code § 20-49.2. A parentage proceeding is a civil action. Va. Code § 20-49.7. All relevant evidence on the issue of paternity is admissible, and the standard of proof is clear and convincing evidence. Va. Code § 20-49.4. The circuit court has concurrent original jurisdiction with the juvenile and domestic relations district court when the parentage of a child is at issue in a matter otherwise before the circuit court. Va. Code § 20-49.2. Judgments may include support or custody provisions, or provisions on other matters in the best interest of the child. Va. Code § 20-49.8. Former Va. Code §§ 20-61.1, 20-61.2 concerning evidence of paternity were repealed at the time of the original enactment Va. Code § 20-49.1 et seq., which now governs determination of parentage in any proceeding. See Va. Code § 20-49.2. According to Va. Code § 20-49.2, a child may bring an action to declare that a man is the natural father. Paternity proceedings in some ways resemble criminal actions, since the person convicted of nonsupport may be sentenced to jail or workhouse. Va. Code §§ 20-62 and 20-64. Under new Va. Code § 8.01-328.1(8)(iii), personal jurisdiction may be asserted over a person alleged by affidavit to have conceived or fathered a child in this Commonwealth, but only upon proof of personal service on a nonresident pursuant to Va. Code § 8.01-320.

Many recipients of Aid for Dependent Children or public housing have been required to sign statements naming the fathers of their children so that the agencies may be reimbursed. This is apparently constitutional as a condition of receiving government largesse. *Edelman v. Jordan,* 415 U.S. 651, 94 S. Ct. 1347, 39 L. Ed. 2d 662 (1974); *King v. Smith,* 392 U.S. 309, 88 S. Ct. 2128, 20 L. Ed. 2d 1118 (1968). See generally 3A Michie's Jurisprudence *Bastardy* §§ 11–20.

The party seeking to prove paternity must do so by clear and convincing evidence if there has been no admission by the alleged father. Va. Code § 20-49.1 et seq. See, e.g., *Wellington v. Broadwater,* 1994 Va. App. LEXIS 736 (Dec. 20, 1994) (H.L.A. testing showed probability of over 99% that Wellington was the father, and he had access to the mother during the period of time when the child was conceived). See also *Department of Social Servs., Div. of Child Support Enforcement ex rel. Comptroller v. Flaneary,* 22 Va. App. 293, 469 S.E.2d 79 (1996). The putative father may have the right to a free blood test if he is indigent and has the right to cross-examine witnesses called to testify for the plaintiff. Va. Code § 20-48. The clear and convincing standard of proof required under § 20-49.1, which became effective in 1988, is appropriate even though the child in question was born (and juvenile court proceedings begun) when repealed Code § 20-61.1, requiring proof beyond a reasonable doubt, was still in effect. *Wyatt v. Virginia Dep't of Social Services,* 11 Va. App. 225, 397 S.E.2d 412 (1990).

Results of scientifically reliable genetic tests, including blood tests, are admissible to prove paternity. Amendments to Va. Code § 20-49.1 substitute "genetic" for "blood tests" throughout the language about establishing paternity. Bills for expenses incurred for pregnancy, childbirth, and genetic testing shall be admissible as prima facie evidence of the facts stated, without requiring third-party foundation testimony, if the party offering such evidence is testifying under oath. Va. Code § 20-49.7. Va. Code §§ 20-49.1 and 20-49.4. The genetic blood grouping tests were made mandatory by 1989 amendments to Va. Code § 20-49.3, which provides that upon its own motion or upon motion of either party, where child support is in issue, the court *shall* direct the parties to submit to such tests. The uncorroborated testimony of the mother will not be sufficient to establish paternity. Blood tests may be ordered upon motion of either party, and the court, in its discretion, may require the person requesting such blood grouping tests to pay the cost. In order to be admissible, the results must be filed with the clerk of the court at least fifteen days prior to the hearing. An expert personally appearing to make his or her analysis may, upon motion of either party, be required to appear as a witness and be subject to cross-examination provided that such motion is made within not less than seven days prior to the trial. Va. Code § 20-71.2, as amended in 1988. Code § 20-49.1 et seq. provides for procedures in proceedings to determine paternity, including admission of blood grouping tests, clear and convincing evidence as the standard of proof, and proceedings to establish paternity or enforce support of minor parents aged fourteen to eighteen. If a putative father fails to appear after having been personally served with notice, the court may proceed in hearing the evidence in the case, according to Code § 20-61.3. Putative fathers between the ages of fourteen and eighteen who are represented by a guardian ad litem may testify pursuant to Code § 20-61.1. However, a guardian ad litem need not be appointed for the child in paternity proceedings. *Rowland v. Shurbutt,* 1993 Va. App. LEXIS 353 (Aug. 17, 1993).

Amendments to Va. Code § 20-49.1 allow establishment of paternity by a written sworn statement of the father and mother acknowledging paternity or by blood testing that affirms at least a ninety-eight percent probability of paternity. The voluntary written statement may be rescinded by either party within 60 days of its signing, or, within this period, at an administrative or judicial proceeding relating to the child, such as one to establish child support. Va. Code § 20-49.1(B)(2) (amended 1998). Without either the acknowledgement or the strong indication of paternity through blood testing, paternity may be established as described above. Va. Code § 20-49.1B. However, the sworn statement of paternity will not provide the same res judicata effect as the hearings. Thus a putative father may introduce evidence in a support proceeding that shows he could not be the child's father even though he previously executed a sworn declaration of paternity. *Dunbar v. Hogan,* 16 Va. App. 653, 432 S.E.2d 16 (1993). Also, a sworn statement of paternity by one putative father will not have res judicata effect that bars blood testing of a second putative father. See *Whitaker v. Day*, 32 Va. App. 737, 530 S.E.2d 924 (2000); *Bedell v. Price*, 70 Va. App. 497, 828 S.E.2d 263 (2019) (the party's sworn statement of paternity was deemed a "material mistake of fact" pursuant to Va. Code § 20-49.1(B)(2) where genetic testing proved another man was the biological father); *Matzuk v. Price and Bedell*, 70 Va. App. 474, 828 S.E.2d 252 (2019) (petition to disestablish paternity granted where genetic test proved the biological father was not the person who executed an acknowledgment of paternity). Because the true identity of the father became a substantial issue in *Myers v. Brolin*, 1995 Va. App. LEXIS 560 (July 5, 1995), the trial court should have required him to verify two relevant and material facts: his identity and his employment.

Section 20-49.8 now allows equitable apportionment of the expenses incurred for the child in establishing paternity. These may be recovered by the natural parent or by any other person or agency incurring the expenses.

Va. Code § 20-49.10, enacted in 2001, provides for relief from a legal determination of paternity. If a scientifically reliable genetic test for paternity excludes a legal father as a possible father, a court may set aside a final judgment, court order, administrative order, child support obligation, or legal determination of paternity pertaining to the named father. However, the court cannot grant relief from a legal determination of paternity if the individual named as the father (1) acknowledged paternity knowing he was not the father, (2) adopted the child, or (3) knew that the child was conceived through artificial insemination. Va. Code § 20-49.10 further states that no existing child support order may be retroactively modified, although a child support order may be modified with respect to the period after service when the petition for relief from legal determination of paternity is pending.

Res judicata will not bar a finding of nonpaternity as far as a child is concerned, although his mother may be barred by the findings in the prior proceeding, since the child and mother's interests are not the same. *Commonwealth ex rel. Gray v. Johnson,* 7 Va. App. 614, 376 S.E.2d 787 (1989). On the other hand, a prior finding that a man was the father of a child in a divorce proceeding acts to collaterally estop him from establishing through conclusive blood testing that he was not the biological parent. *Slagle v. Slagle,* 11 Va. App. 341, 398 S.E.2d 346 (1990).

The child of unmarried parents lived with his mother since birth. The father failed to acknowledge the child at birth, so the mother selected a last name for the child other than the father's. After a court found paternity, the father regularly paid $500 per month child support and had temporary-custody visitation. The father's petition to change the child's surname to his own was granted by the circuit court and this decision was affirmed on appeal. *Long-Molnar v. Dean*, 1996 Va. App. LEXIS 681 (Nov. 5, 1996).

A finding of paternity in the mother's divorce suit was not binding against the children, third parties to the divorce action. *Maher v. Alcon*, 40 Va. Cir. 238 (City of Virginia Beach 1996).

Finally, laches can bar paternity suits. A father's inexcusable delays in asserting paternity for more than ten years kept him from claiming any rights he might have as a parent. *Payne v. Lynchburg Div. of Soc. Servs.*, 1997 Va. App. LEXIS 366 (June 10, 1997). The children were 11 and 12 at the time he brought the paternity action.

### § 3.09    Assisted Conception and Unmarried Biological Father

A 2013 Virginia Supreme Court case examined a case involving the rights of an unmarried biological father whose child was conceived through in vitro fertilization. In *L.F. v. Breit*,[1] an unmarried couple enjoyed a long-term relationship and lived together for several years. They wanted to have a child together but were unable to conceive. They engaged the services of a fertility doctor and eventually conceived a child through in vitro fertilization using the mother's eggs and father's sperm. Prior to the birth of the child, the parties entered into a custody and visitation agreement providing the father with reasonable visitation rights and stating that such visitation would be in the child's best interests. The father was present at the birth of the child and was listed as the father on the child's birth certificate. The child's last name is a hyphenated combination of both parents' surnames. The day after the child was born, the parties executed an "Acknowledgment of Paternity" agreement stating that the father was the child's legal and biological father. The couple held out to friends and relatives that the child was the father's child.

Four months after the child was born, the parents separated. The father continued to support the child and actively established an ongoing parent-child relationship for a year until the mother unilaterally terminated all contact between father and child. The father filed a petition for custody and visitation in the Juvenile and Domestic Relations District Court of the City of Virginia Beach. The mother filed a motion to dismiss the father's action which was granted without prejudice. The father subsequently filed a petition to determine parentage and establish custody and visitation in the Circuit Court of the City of Virginia Beach pursuant to Va. Code Ann.

---

[1] L.F. v. Breit, 285 Va. 163, 736 S.E.2d 711 (2013).

§ 20-49.2.[2] He filed a motion for summary judgment pursuant to Va. Code Ann. § 20-49.1(B)(2),[3] arguing that the Acknowledgement of Paternity voluntarily signed by both parents created a final and binding parent-child legal status. The mother filed pleas in bar pursuant to Va. Code Ann. §§ 20-158(A)(3)[4] and 32.1-257(D),[5] arguing the father was barred from being the child's legal parent because she was never married to him. The circuit court sustained the mother's pleas in bar and denied the father's summary judgment motion, dismissing his petition for custody and visitation.

The father appealed the circuit court's judgment to the Court of Appeals which reversed the circuit court ruling and held that the father, who acted in the capacity of sperm donor at the request of the mother for the purpose of conceiving their child, and who thereafter executed an Acknowledgement of Paternity, was not barred from filing a parentage action to establish paternity of the child. The Court of Appeals cited the legislature's intent that all children born in the Commonwealth have a known legal mother and legal father. The court further held that it was an "absurdity" to interpret the statutes to foreclose any legal means for an intended, unmarried biological father to establish legal parentage of a child born as a result of assisted conception merely by virtue of his status as a "donor."

The mother appealed to the Virginia Supreme Court. The Supreme Court examined the applicable sections of law to reconcile the apparent inconsistencies that formed the basis of the dispute. The court stated that Va. Code Ann. § 20-49.1 et seq. set forth the statutory scheme designed to establish the legal parentage of a child born to unmarried parents. Pursuant to this section, paternity may be established by a voluntary written acknowledgement of paternity made under oath by the parents. The court found this section to be controlling in all cases concerning children of unwed biological parents who enter into such an agreement.

---

[2] Va. Code Ann. § 20-49.2 allows a child or parent to bring an action to determine parentage of a child.

[3] Va. Code Ann. § 20-49.1(b)(2) states that a parent-child relationship between a parent and a man may be established by (1) genetic testing; and (2) a voluntary written statement of the mother and father under oath acknowledging paternity.

[4] Va. Code Ann. § 20-158(A)(3) states, in part, that a donor is not the parent of a child conceived through assisted conception unless the donor is the husband of the gestational mother.

[5] Va. Code Ann. 32.1-257(D) states, in part, that in the case of a child resulting from assisted conception, donors of sperm or ova shall not have any parental rights or duties for the child.

The court further held that the assisted conception statute, Va. Code Ann. § 20-156 et seq., was enacted to establish legal parentage of children born through assisted conception and protect the interest of married parents against any claims of parentage asserted by a non-biological third party donor. The court discussed the history of the assisted conception statute, which was enacted in response to *Welborn v. Doe*,[6] a case involving a married couple who conceived a child using a third-party sperm donor. In Welborn, the Supreme Court stated that the only way to terminate the rights of the sperm donor and establish a parent-child relationship with the husband of the gestational mother would be through adoption. The assisted conception statute was subsequently enacted to affirmatively establish that (1) the husband of the gestational mother is the child's father; and (2) a donor is not the parent of a child conceived through assisted conception.

Thus, the Supreme Court affirmed the Court of Appeals judgment and held that:

(1) the assisted conception statute does not contemplate situations where unmarried donors have long-term relationships, as well as biological ties, that have been voluntarily acknowledged in writing and have voluntarily assumed responsibilities to their children;

(2) although the assisted conception statute made distinctions based on marital status, the statute did not violate equal protection;

(3) the due process clause protected the biological father's fundamental right to make decisions concerning the child's care, despite his status as unmarried sperm donor; and

(4) prohibiting the sperm "donor" from ever establishing parental rights was contrary to the assisted conception statute's stated purpose and contrary to the due process clause.

In response to the *Breit* case, the legislature codified[7] the parent's "fundamental right to make decisions concerning the upbringing, education, and care of the parent's child."[8] Va. Code § 1-240.1.

---

[6] Welborn v. Commonwealth, 10 Va. App. 631, 394 S.E.2d 732 (1990).

[7] HB 1642: Parental rights; fundamental right to make decisions concerning upbringing, etc., of their child (2013 session).

[8] Va. Code Ann. § 1-240.1.

# CHAPTER 4

# Marriages

## SYNOPSIS

## § 4.01    Introduction

Marriage in theory is a status created by the interaction of three parties—husband, wife and the state. *Maynard v. Hill,* 125 U.S. 190, 205, 8 S. Ct. 723, 31 L. Ed. 654 (1888). In 2020, Virginia HB 623 abolished the ban against same sex marriages by repealing Va. Code §§ 20-45.2 and 45.3, and amended substantial portions of the Code of Virginia by replacing references to Husband and Wife with gender neutral terms like "spouses," "married couple," "they," and "persons married to each other." The fact that the relationship is created by contract requires such factors as agreement between the parties, legality of the union as within public policy, and capacity to contract, all of which will be considered in the next chapter. See generally 12B Michie's Jurisprudence *Marriage* § 2. The fact that status is involved and that therefore the state is interested means that in addition various statutory formalities must be observed or the marriage will not be valid. See *Boddie v. Connecticut,* 401 U.S. 371, 376, 91 S. Ct. 780, 28 L. Ed. 2d 113 (1971):

> It is not surprising, then, that the States have seen fit to oversee many aspects of that institution. Without a prior judicial imprimatur, individuals may fully enter into and rescind commercial contracts, for example, but we are unaware of any jurisdiction where private citizens may covenant for or dissolve marriages without state approval.

See also *Cramer v. Commonwealth*, 214 Va. 561, 565, 202 S.E.2d 911, 915 (1974).

Va. Code § 20-38.1 prohibits marriages entered into prior to the dissolution of an earlier marriage of one of the parties, and between certain familial relationships. Bigamous marriages are void and obtaining a court order is unnecessary. Va. Code § 20-43. For other types of marriages that are void, refer to Va. Code § 20-45.1. The legal age at which a person can be married is 18. Va. Code § 20-48. However, a minor child who is at least age 16 can petition for emancipation if he or she desires to enter into a valid marriage. Va. Code § 16.1-331.

When a question arises about the validity of a marriage, the following questions should be asked: (1) Was a valid license obtained? (2) Was a ceremony performed by one authorized to do so by statute? (3) Was the marriage performed in a jurisdiction where neither party was domiciled, to which the parties travelled to evade Virginia public policy? and (4) Did a common law marriage arise in some state other than Virginia?

If the answers to the foregoing questions do not prove helpful, the annulment chapter, following, should also be consulted.

## § 4.02    Common Law Marriages

At common law, marriages could begin by an agreement between a man and woman to be husband and wife that was made in words of the present tense. *Offield v. Davis*, 100 Va. 250, 40 S.E. 910 (1902); see 12B Michie's Jurisprudence *Marriage* § 8. In order to demonstrate objectively that this agreement had taken place and to show that in fact a marriage contract had been made, it was also necessary for the couple to live together as man and wife and to have the reputation of being man and wife in the community. See *Pickens v. O'Hara*, 120 W. Va. 751, 200 S.E. 746 (1938) (common law marriage not shown where man later ceremonially married another, although relationship with woman continued for forty-one years). Since a contract was involved, the parties needed the capacity to become married at the time of the agreement. See generally Note, *Common Law Marriage and Annulment*, 15 Vill. L. Rev. 134 (1969).

Virginia has not recognized common law marriages created within the state for many years. *Offield v. Davis*, 100 Va. 250, 253, 40 S.E. 910, 914 (1902) (no dower rights created by nonceremonial "marriage"). However, because of the mobility of the population, it may be necessary to consider such marriages even if both husband and wife currently live in Virginia. This is because once a marriage has validly been created, it will be valid everywhere unless grossly against public policy. *Greenhow v. James'*

*Executor,* 80 Va. 636, 640 (1885) (marriage void and children not legitimate when white man married black woman in District of Columbia and returned to Virginia). Where a husband and wife married according to the common law in a foreign country, or even in such neighboring jurisdictions as the District of Columbia or Pennsylvania, they will retain their status in Virginia. *Kelderhaus v. Kelderhaus,* 21 Va. App. 721, 467 S.E.2d 303 (1996); *Farah v. Farah,* 16 Va. App. 329, 429 S.E.2d 626 (1993). 12B Michie's Jurisprudence *Marriage* § 8.

Once a common law marriage has been created, the relationship will be the exact equivalent of a ceremonial marriage. In order to remarry, the parties must divorce. Dower and curtesy exist if they would for any other married couple, husband and wife inherit exactly the same way other married persons do, their children are legitimate, and the same privileges and duties flow between them as for other married couples.

Most of the recent Virginia cases involving common law marriages are concerned not with their consequences, since that is settled law, but rather with whether or not the marital status was in fact created. One recurring problem is whether a common law marriage arises after the impediment to a valid ceremonial marriage is removed. *Travers v. Reinhardt,* 205 U.S. 423, 27 S. Ct. 563, 51 L. Ed. 865 (1907).

For example, in *Metropolitan Life Insurance Co. v. Holding,* 293 F. Supp. 854 (E.D. Va. 1968), the man had been married to another woman for many years when he met a French woman while serving in the Armed Forces. He was informed by his first wife's attorney that a divorce of his first marriage was final, and married in a ceremony. In fact the divorce did not become final until after the ceremony. When his tour of duty ended, he became employed as a foreign service officer, so that for most of their relationship the couple lived abroad, in places not recognizing common law marriages. From time to time, while on leave, the couple visited friends and relatives in the United States, spending as much as a month in the states of Florida and Ohio, both of which recognize common law marriage. Finally the man died in Virginia, to which the couple had moved when he retired. The second wife was allowed to recover insurance proceeds as a surviving spouse, although the ceremonial marriage had not resulted in a valid union, because of the time the couple had spent living together as man and wife and holding themselves out as such in Florida and Ohio. Compare *Goldin v. Goldin,* 48 Md. App. 154, 426 A.2d 410 (1981), where a couple cohabited in Virginia but never married because the man, who had been previously married and divorced, and the woman, who had her first marriage annulled, would not go through a ceremony for religious reasons. Although the couple lived together for many years, had two children, and were regarded by many as husband and wife, a common law marriage was not created when they frequently vacationed in Pennsylvania, since they never really had the intent to be married.

Courts will be apt to recognize a common law marriage where the parties, or at least one of them, has acted in good faith, compare *McPherson v. Steamship South African Pioneer,* 321 F. Supp. 42 (E.D. Va. 1971) (no common law marriage where both parties knew that wife's divorce was not final) and there are no innocent third parties, such as surviving first spouses or children of a prior marriage, who will be hurt. This policy is particularly true when all possible objections to the validity of the union have ceased: in *Holding,* for example, by the death of the husband.

However, a party claiming a common law marriage must prove its existence by a preponderance of the evidence, and the claims of a common law marriage should be closely scrutinized since ceremonial marriage is available and conclusively proves the marriage. *Porter v. Porter,* 69 Va. App 167, 172, 817 S.E.2d 339 (2019). In the *Porter* case, the parties intended to be married, and they scheduled a wedding ceremony in Washington, DC, where one of the parties lived, for February 25, 2006, to which they had invited multiple friends. For some reason though, the parties obtained a marriage license from Virginia on February 24, 2006, and stated on the license that the marriage ceremony occurred in Arlington, Virginia. No marriage ceremony occurred in Virginia, but rather, the marriage ceremony and reception occurred in Washington, D.C. After the reception, the parties spent that evening in a hotel in Washington, D.C. and the next day each party returned to their separate residences—one in Virginia and the other in Washington D.C. In May of 2006, the parties started living together in Virginia, and they considered themselves married until their September 2015 separation. Despite the parties actions in believing they were married, filing joint taxes returns, owning real property as tenants by the entirety, and holding themselves out as being married, the Wife filed a motion for declaration of marriage status in response to a complaint for divorce. The common law marriage elements for the District of Columbia are cohabitation as husband and wife following an express mutual agreement. Although the parties clearly had an express mutual agreement to be married, the Husband was unable to prove that the parties cohabited in Washington, D.C., as their one evening stay at the hotel in Washington, D.C. following their wedding ceremony and reception failed to establish that the parties cohabited in Washington, D.C. *Id.* at 173–76.

See generally Stein, *Common-Law Marriage: Its History and Certain Contemporary Problems,* 9 J. Fam. L. 271 (1970).

## § 4.03 Persons Who May Perform Marriages

> The interest of the state is not only in marriage as an institution, but in the contract between the parties who marry, and in the proper memorializing of the entry into, and execution of, such a contract. In the proper exercise of its legislative power it can require that the person who performs a marriage ceremony be certified or licensed.

*Cramer v. Commonwealth,* 214 Va. 561, 567, 202 S.E.2d 911, 914 (1974).

A member of the clergy may be authorized to perform marriages upon producing proof of his ordination and of his being in regular communion with the religious society of which he is a reputed member, or proof that he is commissioned to pastoral ministry or holds a local minister's license and is serving as a regularly appointed pastor in his denomination. Va. Code § 20-23. Upon petition filed with the clerk and payment of applicable clerk's fees, any circuit court judge may issue an order authorizing one or more persons residing in the circuit in which the judge sits, to celebrate the rites of marriage in the Commonwealth. Any person so authorized shall, before acting, enter into bond in the penalty of $500, with or without surety, as the court may direct. Any judge or justice of a court of record, any judge of a district court or any retired judge or justice of the Commonwealth or any active, senior, or retired federal judge or justice who is a resident of the Commonwealth may celebrate the rites of marriage anywhere in the Commonwealth without the necessity of bond or order of authorization. Va. Code § 20-25. Members of a religious society which has no ordained ministers may be married in accordance with the practice of that religious society provided that one person of the religious society completes the certification of marriage in the same manner as either an ordained minister or any other person authorized to perform marriages. Va. Code § 20-26. In 2016, Va. Code §§ 20-23, 25, and 26 were amended to specify that a marriage celebrant (1) was not required to take an oath, and (2) was not considered to be an officer of the Commonwealth of Virginia.

This statutory scheme has been tested in a few cases, most recently in *In re Kooiman,* 45 Va. Cir. 503 (Fairfax Co. 1998). Va. Code § 20-23 requires that a "minister" of a religious organization may perform marriages. The term "minister" does not include a self-proclaimed high priestess and founding elder of a Nomadic Chantry of the Gramarye, without any evidence of a connection with an established church, nor any proof of ordination. "The Commonwealth of Virginia has historically considered marriage among its most valued and sacred institutions. As such, the Virginia legislature has systematically surrounded the celebration of marriage (as well as its dissolution) with statutory mandates."

In contrast, *Cramer v. Commonwealth,* 214 Va. 561, 202 S.E.2d 911 (1974), involved an action rescinding the authority to perform marriages for six ministers of the Universal Life Church, ordained without instruction for a "free will offering," and holding no particular dogma. Everyone belonging to the church was encouraged to become a minister. The court found that the organization in fact had no "minister" within the contemplation of Va. Code § 20-23, which referred to the head of a religious congregation, society, or order. At that time there was still the paramount and compelling duty of returning the completed certificate within five days after the ceremony. The rescission was therefore consistent with the Code section.

The question remains whether marriages will be valid despite the fact that the person performing the ceremony did not fall into the categories named in the statutes. Generally speaking, if the parties to the marriage acted in good faith, not realizing that the persons marrying them had no authority to do so, the marriage will nevertheless be valid. Va. Code § 20-31; *Stanley v. Rasnick,* 137 Va. 415, 119 S.E. 76 (1923). In such cases, the person performing the ceremony may be subject to punishment. Va. Code § 20-28. The reason for the directory nature of the statute is that the clergyman or official performing the ceremony is really acting in the nature of a witness: the vows or contractual agreements are exchanged by the parties. *Cramer v. Commonwealth,* 214 Va. 561, 567, 202 S.E.2d 911, 914 (1974).

Virginia courts will not recognize a proxy marriage performed in England, which itself does not recognize proxy marriages. In *Farah v. Farah,* 16 Va. App. 329, 429 S.E.2d 626 (1993), both parties resided in the United States, and their marriage had been solemnized by proxy in London. The parties then traveled to the bride's native Pakistan where her father held a reception to symbolize the sending away of the bride with her husband. The parties then returned to Virginia, purchased a house jointly titled in both names, and lived together for about one year. The parties then separated, and the man sought to have the marriage declared void. The woman filed for divorce and equitable distribution. The court of appeals held that the trial judge erred in granting a divorce and by equitably distributing the parties' property because the marriage was not valid in England where celebrated. The court reasoned that because Virginia does not recognize common law marriages where the relationship is created in the state, the parties never entered into a valid marriage. There could therefore be no divorce and no distribution of the parties' property.

## § 4.04 Requirement of a License

Va. Code § 20-13 provides that in order for a marriage to be valid, a license must be obtained. Va. Code § 20-16 governs the issuance of marriage licenses and marriage certificates, and was amended in 2015 to permit the parties to designate themselves on the marriage license as "spouse, bride, or groom." Va. Code § 20-31 is a curative statute that will recognize a marriage's validity where the person performing the marriage lacked proper authority or the certificate was defective, provided that the marriage was otherwise lawful and the parties consummated the marriage believing they were married. In 1988, Va. Code § 20-16.1 was added, allowing the clerk to amend marriage records on his own authority, upon application under oath and submission of evidence deemed by the clerk to be adequate and sufficient, and directing him to forward a certified copy of the corrected marriage record to the State Registrar. The person performing the ceremony may be subject to punishment. Va. Code § 20-28. This is because the license requirements are largely to avoid later problems of proof or possible collusion, and do not really affect the contract.

*Levick v. MacDougall*, 294 Va. 283, 805 S.E.2d 775 (2017) held that Va. Code § 20-13 does not establish any order in which the license and solemnization requirements are to be performed. In addition, the Court found that the solemnization of a marriage need not occur at the ceremony. *Levick v. MacDougall*, 294 Va. at 292, 805 S.E.2d at 779. Guiding the Court's decision is Virginia's long standing public policy "to uphold the validity of the marriage status as for the best interest of society" and that "the presumption of the validity of a marriage ranks as "one of the strongest presumptions known to the law." *Levick v. MacDougall*, 294 Va. at 290, 805 S.E.2d at 778 (citing *Needam v. Needam*, 183 Va. 681, 686, 33 S.E.2d 288, 290 (1945), and *Eldred v. Eldred*, 97 Va. 606, 625, 34 S.E. 477, 484 (1899)). During the parties' divorce proceeding in *Levick*, and after the parties had reached a settlement agreement, the husband challenged the validity of their marriage and sought to invalidate the agreement. The husband argued that the marriage was void ab initio because they had not obtained a marriage license as of the day that the rabbi conducted the wedding ceremony at their home in the presence of their invited guests. In discussing their options with the rabbi, McDougall, Levick and the rabbi all agreed to proceed with the marriage ceremony that day, and the parties would thereafter obtain a marriage license and submit the marriage license and certificate to the rabbi as soon as possible. The parties proceeded with this understanding and sent the rabbi the marriage certificate 16 days after the ceremony. Upon receiving the documents, the rabbi executed the marriage certificate and verified that the parties were married as of the day that the rabbi executed the document rather than the day of the ceremony. In analyzing the statutes, the Court noted that albeit unusual, solemnization of the marriage need not occur at the ceremony. *Levick v. MacDougall*, 294 Va. at 292, 805 S.E.2d at 779.

In *Stanley v. Rasnick,* 137 Va. 415, 119 S.E. 76 (1923), a father sued for loss of the services of his daughter, who obtained a license and married without his permission. She was 16 at the time and therefore above the age of consent (12 years). The marriage was valid despite the defect in the license and the incidental loss of services to the father brought about by the change in the daughter's status.

Despite this trend upholding the validity of the marriage despite defects in licensing, in *Davis v. Davis,* 29 Va. Cir. 110 (Accomac Co. 1992), the court held that a religious ceremony performed in Virginia using a Maryland license was not effective. The license was returned to Maryland and stated that the marriage ceremony took place in that state. The parties lived together in Virginia as husband and wife for seven years after the ceremony. The court found that the Virginia marriage statutes were mandatory rather than directory, citing a West Virginia case decided under a similar statute. Compare *Carabetta v. Carabetta,* 182 Conn. 344, 438 A.2d 109 (1980) (marriage without license following religious ceremony).

In the case of *Makheja v. Kundra*, 39 Va. Cir. 136 (Fairfax Co. 1996), the marriage was arranged by the families of husband and wife, as is customary in Indian culture. They obtained a valid marriage license in Fairfax County, and a Hindu priest authorized to perform religious marriages in Virginia but not in D.C. conducted an elaborate Hindu marriage ceremony in Washington, D.C. Following the ceremony, husband and wife consummated the marriage. The priest signed the marriage certificate in Virginia, although no valid Hindu religious ceremony was conducted at that time. Before departing on their honeymoon, the husband gave the marriage certificate to his father and instructed him to mail it to the Fairfax County Courthouse, which he did. Husband and wife then left on their honeymoon and began their life together, all the time believing they were married. According to the circuit court, the signing of the marriage certificate by one authorized to perform marriages, together with the intent of the couple to become man and wife, constituted a lawful marriage.

## § 4.05 Blood Tests

At the present time Virginia has repealed the statutory requirement for obtaining a blood test for syphilis (Va. Code § 20-1 was repealed in 1984) as well as for receiving information on acquired immunodeficiency syndrome, genetic disorders, and contraceptive measures (for Va. Code § 20-14.2 was repealed in 2012).

## § 4.06 Necessity for Domicile

As will be seen in the chapter on annulments, it is not necessary for persons to be domiciled in a state to be married there. The problems occur when couples leave Virginia to be married in another state in order to evade particular Virginia laws, such as those involving marriage between persons under age, *Needham v. Needham,* 183 Va. 681, 688, 33 S.E.2d 288 (1945) (provision for parental consent at that time was directory and preventive rather than prohibitive of the consummation of the marriage contract), or, in earlier days, those prohibiting interracial marriages, *Naim v. Naim,* 197 Va. 80, 87 S.E.2d 749 (1955); *Greenhow v. James' Executor,* 80 Va. 636 (1885); *Kinney v. Commonwealth,* 71 Va. (30 Gratt.) 858 (1871). If such a marriage would be against Virginia public policy, and is mentioned in Va. Code § 20-38.1 (bigamy and incest), it will be void under the Virginia anti-evasion statute, Va. Code § 20-40, and the parties will be subject to punishment.

## § 4.07 Proof of Ceremonial Marriage

Marriage may be proved by evidence of reputation, *McClaugherty v. McClaugherty,* 180 Va. 51, 60, 21 S.E.2d 761, 764 (1942); *Eldred v. Eldred,* 97 Va. 606, 34 S.E. 477 (1899); civil records, Va. Code § 32-1.272B (prima facie evidence), or the testimony of witnesses to the marriage ceremony. There is a strong presumption in cases of ceremonial marriage that the parties living as husband and wife are in the legitimate state of matrimony. *Newsom v. Fleming,* 165 Va. 89, 181 S.E. 393 (1935); *Reynolds v. Adams,* 125 Va. 295, 99 S.E. 695 (1919); *Eldred v. Eldred,* 97 Va. 606, 625, 34 S.E. 477 (1899) (marriage not proved). However, the presumption of validity was overcome where the woman, a patient with Alzheimer's Disease, shook her head from left to right when asked if she wanted to marry the man and otherwise remained mute throughout the ceremony. The ceremony was witnessed only by the minister, a longtime friend of the man, who was told to keep the marriage a secret. The man also forged her signature to a spurious common law marriage "contract" after the ceremony. *Nicely v. Gardner,* 12 Va. Cir. 216 (City of Roanoke 1988).

There is also a strong presumption, in cases where there have been two marriages by one of the parties, that the first marriage ended in divorce so that the second one is valid. *Parker v. American Lumber Corp.,* 190 Va. 181, 185, 56 S.E.2d 214, 217 (1949).

After 1997, marriage certificates shall include the parties' social security numbers. Va. Code § 32.1-267(B).

## § 4.08   Marriages and Civil Unions Between Persons of Same Sex

2020 was a historic year in Virginia for the recognition of same sex marriages and civil unions. Until July 1, 2020, marriage between persons of the same sex in Virginia was prohibited, any marriage entered into by persons of the same sex in another state or jurisdiction was deemed void in all respects, and any contractual rights created by such marriage were void and unenforceable in Virginia. Va. Code § 20-45.2. Similarly, a civil union, partnership contract, or other arrangement between persons of the same sex, whether established in Virginia or another state, purporting to bestow the privileges or obligations of marriage were prohibited and unlawful. Va. Code § 20-45.3.

On November 7, 2006, a majority of Virginia voters ratified a constitutional amendment (the "Marshall/Newman Amendment"). The Marshall/Newman Amendment provides:

> That only a union between one man and one woman may be a marriage valid in or recognized by this Commonwealth and its political subdivisions. This Commonwealth and its political subdivisions shall not create or recognize a legal status for relationships. of unmarried individuals that intends to approximate the design, qualities, significance, or effects of marriage. Nor shall this Commonwealth or its political subdivisions create or recognize another union, partnership, or other legal status to which is assigned the rights, benefits, obligations, qualities, or effects of marriage.

Va. Const. Art. 1, § 15-A. This Virginia constitutional provision may prove to be a hindrance in Virginia's attempt to recognize and expand the rights of marriage to same sex couples.

Va. Code § 20-16, the statute governing the issuance of marriage licenses and marriage certificates, was amended in 2015. The amendment allows parties to now designate themselves on the marriage license as "spouse, bride, or groom." This amendment can be seen to authorize and permit marriage licenses for same-sex couples. This amendment was viewed by many as an initial step toward recognizing same sex marriages in Virginia.

Despite Va. Const. Art. 1, § 15-A, the 2020 Virginia legislature enacted broad substantive and significant changes to Virginia law by legalizing same sex marriages. Specifically, Va. Code §§ 20-45.2 and 45.3, which banned same sex marriages and civil unions, were repealed. An extensive effort was made to amend multiple provisions of the Virginia Code in a gender neutral manner, and HB 623 replaced gender specific terms like "Husband" and

Wife" with gender neutral terms like "spouses," "married couple," "they," and "persons married to each other." The legislative enactments which took effect on July 1, 2020, erased the discrepancy between Virginia's ban on same sex marriages and civil unions with the ruling of the United States Supreme Court in *Obergefell v. Hodges*, 135 S. Ct. 2584 (2015) which recognized the rights of same sex people to marry.

The repeal of Va. Code §§ 20-45.2 and 45.3 facially conflicts with Va. Const. Art. 1, § 15-A. The Virginia Constitution defines marriage in the Commonwealth of Virginia as being "only a union between one man and one woman" and prohibits the extension of marriage rights to any other status of individuals. It is certainly foreseeable that challenges to marriage status and Virginia's Constitution will arise and be the subject of intense debate and disagreement. Political and social policy changes do not occur quickly, as evidenced by the fact five years transpired from the United States Supreme Court's ruling in *Obergefell* until the Virginia legislature was able to repeal the statutory ban on same sex marriages and civil unions.

Because of Va. Const. Art. 1, § 15-A, there remains a potential dispute as to whether or not same sex marriages and civil unions are legally recognizable in Virginia. The United States Supreme Court and other federal courts have certainly upheld the rights of same sex couples to marry. Nonetheless, and despite the efforts of the 2020 Virginia legislature to conform marriage rights in Virginia to the ruling in *Obergefell*, it is evident that legal challenges to the marriage status will continue.

The debate of how marriage is to be construed, and the tension between the Commonwealth's rights to define and govern the status of a marriage and the impact of federal law, is depicted by the following analysis. In *Bostic v. Schaefer*, 760 F.3d 352 (4th Cir. 2014), the Fourth Circuit recognized that "the right to marry is an expansive liberty interest that may stretch to accommodate changing societal norms," 760 F.3d at 376, and held that the "Virginia Marriage Laws violate the Due Process and Equal Protection Clauses of the Fourteenth Amendment to the extent that they prevent same-sex couples from marrying and prohibit Virginia from recognizing same-sex couples' lawful out-of-state marriages." 760 F.3d at 384. The legality of Va. Const. Art. 1, § 15-A and Va. Code § 20-45.3 (which code section was repealed on July 1, 2020) were greatly impacted by the decision of the United States Supreme Court in *Obergefell v. Hodges*, 135 S. Ct. 2584 (2015). In *Obergefell*, the United States Supreme Court directly addressed the issue of same-sex marriage and reached a landmark 5-4 decision written by Justice Kennedy. The Supreme Court held that the Fourteenth Amendment requires a State to license a marriage between two people of the same sex and to recognize same-sex marriages that were lawfully performed in a foreign state.

*Obergefell*, 135 S. Ct. 2584 (2015) did dramatically impact Virginia's marriage laws in 2020 when the Virginia legislature repealed the ban on same sex marriages (Va. Code § 20-45.2) and civil unions (Va. Code § 20-45.3). However, the Virginia Supreme Court and the Fourth Circuit reached conflicting decisions regarding the constitutionality of Va. Code § 18.2-361 ("Crimes against nature; penalty"). While the Fourth Circuit held the statute to be facially unconstitutional, *MacDonald v. Moose*, 710 F.3d 154, 156, 166 (4th Cir. 2013), the Virginia Supreme Court in *McDonald v. Commonwealth*, 274 Va. 249, 645 S.E.2d 918 (2007) declared the statute to be constitutional. This conflict can exist between the federal and state courts since a decision of the federal appeals court whose circuit includes Virginia is not binding precedent when interpreting a Virginia state statute. *Saunders v. Commonwealth*, 62 Va. App. 793, 804, 753 S.E.2d 602, 607 (2014). Instead, "[o]nly decisions of the United States Supreme Court can supersede binding precedent from the Virginia Supreme Court." *Saunders v. Commonwealth*, 62 Va. App. 793, 804, 753 S.E.2d 602, 607 (2014).

# CHAPTER 5

# Annulments

## SYNOPSIS

## § 5.01    Introduction

For religious reasons it was not possible for Christians to divorce until the time of Henry VIII. In order to escape from unhappy relationships and to be free to marry again, it was sometimes permissible for the ecclesiastical court to declare that the marriage had never taken place. This nullification procedure developed into a most complex set of grounds. It was the sole form of relief for many years, and even after the advent of divorce in the nineteenth century, in many cases (since adultery and desertion for five years were the only causes of action for divorce), the only practical means of severing the relationship. *Bailey v. Bailey,* 62 Va. (21 Gratt.) 43 (1871) (divorce from bed and board only). As the phenomenon of separation, annulment, and remarriage became increasingly popular, more and more grounds for annulment were added, and those existing were more leniently applied. This trend continued until absolute divorce rules were relaxed in Virginia in the 1940s.

As opposed to the problems concerning requisites for marital status discussed in the prior chapter, annulments historically involve problems in the contract between man and woman (but will in the future likely involve same sex couples) that normally would result in a marriage. Unlike divorce, solely a creature of statute, annulment rests within the inherent power of equity inherited from the English ecclesiastical courts. *Pretlow v. Pretlow,* 177 Va. 524, 548–49, 14 S.E.2d 381, 383–84 (1941).

### § 5.02    Reasons for Modern Annulments

Although annulments are not as common as divorces, depending on the circumstances an annulment may be the preferred legal remedy for a spouse if the grounds exist. In addition, a client may want to pursue an annulment if his or her religion prohibits remarriage following divorce. In particular, the fact that a civil annulment was obtained may be an aid to the client who also wishes a canon law annulment.

A second reason to obtain an annulment is that, at least in the case of void marriages, there is apparently no duty to support the person who shared an annulled marriage, *Bray v. Landergren,* 161 Va. 699, 172 S.E. 252 (1933); Va. Code § 20-107.1; see also *Mato v. Mato,* 12 Va. Cir. 153 (Spotsylvania Co. 1988). Although it was subsequently overturned, the case of *MacDougall v. Levick,* 66 Va. App. 50, 76, 782 S.E.2d 182 (2016) provides an insightful analysis explaining that there can be no equitable distribution of marital property under § 20-107.3, when a marriage is voidable since no marriage ever existed.

A corollary is that, at least in cases of void marriages, there may be a resumption of prior benefits that were lost upon marriage, such as insurance or alimony from a first spouse. *McConkey v. McConkey,* 216 Va. 106, 215 S.E.2d 640 (1975).

Finally, there may be some psychological reason for legally declaring that a marriage never existed. The parties, especially when the mistake was youthful and the relationship of short duration, can declare themselves "single" with a clear conscience. See *Crouch v. Wartenberg,* 91 W. Va. 91, 112 S.E. 234 (1922).

### § 5.03    Jurisdiction in Annulment Cases

Va. Code § 20-96 authorizes the circuit courts in Virginia with jurisdiction to hear annulment cases. The grounds for an annulment in Virginia are set forth at Va. Code § 20-13 (License and solemnization required), Va. Code § 38.1 (Certain marriages prohibited), Va. Code § 45.1 (Void and voidable marriages) and Va. Code § 89.1 (additional grounds).

There is case law from other jurisdictions that would support the theory that personal jurisdiction must be obtained in annulment cases. *Sacks v. Sacks*, 47 Misc. 2d 1050, 263 N.Y.S.2d 891 (1965); *Flaxman v. Flaxman*, 57 N.J. 458, 273 A.2d 567 (1971); cf. *Whealton v. Whealton*, 67 Cal. 2d 656, 63 Cal. Rptr. 291, 432 P.2d 979 (1967) (although no domicile of either party, in personam jurisdiction over both is sufficient to confer jurisdiction for annulment). Virginia follows the minority position in requiring only that one party be domiciled in the state, with constructive or substituted service if the other cannot be personally served. Va. Code § 20-104. This is the same requirement as in divorce cases, which are in essence status adjudications. *Williams v. North Carolina*, 317 U.S. 287, 63 S. Ct. 207, 87 L. Ed. 279 (1942). Va. Code § 20-97 provides jurisdiction for annulment to persons in the United States armed forces or their spouses who have been stationed in and resided in the Commonwealth for a period of six months or more preceding separation, and for service persons or foreign service officers domiciled in Virginia for the six months prior to being stationed in a foreign country or territory. Unlike a suit for divorce or legal separation, the person in the armed forces or the spouse apparently need not continue to reside in Virginia until the complaint is filed.

If more than the annulling of the relationship is involved, personal service will clearly be required. This may be by service upon the party within Virginia or by use of the long-arm statute, Va. Code § 8.01-328.1(9), where appropriate in child support or child custody matters. The contacts of the absent party with Virginia and the due process aspects of notice must both be satisfied in such cases. Va. Code § 20-99.2 authorizes service of process in annulment cases is to be made in accordance with Va. Code § 8.01-296 or § 8.01-320.

Statutes enacted in 1989 regarding the experimental family courts were repealed in 1999, including Va. Code §§ 16.1-296.1, 20-96.1, and 20-96.2. There are no longer any such courts, and all appeals from such courts have been completed.

Counsel may be appointed to represent the child in cases involving annulment or affirmation of marriage as provided in § 8.01-9 (Va. Code § 16.1-266(F)). In proceedings to determine parentage, Va. Code § 20-49.2 requires that a guardian ad litem be appointed to represent a child and the guardian may not be either parent. In cases involving the status of marriage, confidentiality of the cases is governed by § 20-124.

For any issue arising in a suit for annulment or affirmation of marriage, the judge shall consider whether to refer the parties to mediation, and, on its own motion or one of the parties, may refer the issue to mediation. Upon referral, the parties must attend one session in which the parties and the mediator assess the case and decide whether to continue the mediation or to proceed to adjudication. Further participation in the mediation shall be by consent of all parties, and attorneys for any party may attend mediation sessions. Va. Code §§ 20-124.2 and 20-124.4. When the court refers parties to mediation, it shall set a return date. The parties shall notify the court in writing if the dispute is resolved prior to this return date. In its discretion, the court may incorporate any mediated agreement into the terms of a final decree. Only if the order is entered incorporating the mediated agreement will the terms of the voluntary settlement agreement affect any outstanding court order.

In *Lewis v. Lewis*, 271 Va. 520, 628 S.E.2d 314 (2006), the court of appeals held that it lacked subject matter jurisdiction to entertain an appeal from an interlocutory decree that dismissed a husband's cross-bill for annulment of his marriage. In the cross-bill, the husband claimed that he was entitled to an annulment because his wife was not validly divorced when they married. However, a circuit court decided that the husband lacked standing to attack the validity of his wife's divorce, and dismissed the cross-bill for that reason. As a result, the circuit court's interlocutory decree did not (1) respond to the chief object of the domestic relations dispute, or (2) determine the principles necessary to adjudicate the cause—because the decree did not determine the status or validity of the parties' marriage, award spousal support, or make an equitable distribution of marital assets. Therefore, the interlocutory decree was not appealable to the court of appeals.

## § 5.04 The Complaint

As in cases of divorce, the complaint for annulment is brought in the circuit court. Va. Code § 20-96. The complaint should allege jurisdiction through domicile of the complainant, the fact that a ceremony occurred on some date and in a particular place, the grounds for relief, and the fact that no ratification occurred after the defect was discovered in cases of voidable marriage.

If the prayers for relief involve more than annulment, personal jurisdiction must also be alleged. Of course, the relief sought should be listed. In a void or voidable marriage, the court can make pendente lite awards of spousal support and child support (Va. Code § 20-103; *MacDougall v. Levick*, 66 Va. App. 50, 86–87, 782 S.E.2d 182 (2016) ("Annulment and *pendente lite* support are longstanding features of Virginia law"); *Kleinfield v. Veruki*, 7 Va. App. 183, 190, 372 S.E.2d 407, 411 (1988)), and also make final determinations of custody, visitation, and child support. There is no equitable distribution in the event of annulment. Va. Code §§ 20-107.1 (spousal support) and 20-107.3 (equitable distribution) provide relief only upon decreeing a dissolution of the marriage. *Shoustari v. Zamani*, 39 Va. App. 517, 520, 574 S.E.2d 314, 315 (2002) (citing the *Kleinfield* decision). If the incidents of the relationship can be resolved in writing between the parties beforehand, their agreement can be made a part of the complaint by incorporation. Courts may make child support or custody orders and decrees in suits for annulment or separate maintenance. Va. Code § 20-107.2.

## § 5.05 Parties to Annulment Actions

Historically the parties to an action declaring a marriage void ab initio are the man and woman involved. However, the code provisions prohibiting same sex marriages (Va. Code § 20-45.2) and civil unions (Va. Code § 45.3) were repealed, and annulments may now likely involve same sex marriages. Either party may initiate suits under Va. Code § 20-89.1(a) for void marriages and voidable marriages except those for impotency, felony conviction, pregnancy by another, or fathering a child by another. The latter actions may only be brought by the innocent party.

In cases of bigamous or incestuous marriages, any third party can bring an action. In cases of marriages annulled for nonage, the parents of the child involved may bring an action on his or her behalf. This was not the case before the statute made such marriage void. *Kirby v. Gilliam*, 182 Va. 111, 28 S.E.2d 40 (1943). In cases of insanity or mental retardation, the guardian or committee of the incompetent may bring an action.

## § 5.06 Void and Voidable Marriages

Two types of marriages may be annulled. The most obvious group consists of void marriages, which require no legal action to declare that the marriage never existed. Grounds are listed in Va. Code § 20-38.1. Void marriages have always included bigamous, *Toler v. Oakwood Smokeless Coal Corp.*, 173 Va. 425, 4 S.E.2d 364 (1939), and incestuous relationships. However, where a spouse is absent for seven years, and thus deemed dead pursuant to Va. Code § 63.2-2300, the remaining spouse is able to remarry and the remarriage will not be bigamous. *Simpson v. Simpson*, 162 Va. 621, 169 S.E. 556 (1934). Until the Supreme Court case of *Loving v. Virginia*, 388 U.S. 1, 87 S. Ct. 1817, 18 L. Ed. 2d 1010 (1967), interracial marriages also fell within the relationships that were prohibited because they were considered grossly against public policy. Va. Code § 20-50 et seq. (now repealed); see *Naim v. Naim,* 197 Va. 80, 87 S.E.2d 749 (1955).

Although Virginia's prohibition against same-sex marriage, Va. Code § 20-45.2, and civil unions, Va. Code § 20-45.3, were repealed on July 1, 2020, Va. Const. Art. 1, § 15-A mandates that marriage in the Commonwealth of Virginia as being "only a union between one man and one woman" and prohibits the extension of marriage rights to any other status of individuals. This article of the Virginia Constitution is most certainly unconstitutional under the United States Supreme Court decision in *Obergefell v. Hodges*, 135 S. Ct. 2584 (2015). In *Obergefell*, the United States Supreme Court held that the Fourteenth Amendment requires a State to license a marriage between two people of the same sex and to recognize same-sex marriages that were lawfully performed in a foreign state. However, Va. Const. Art. 1, § 15-A may pose a problem for a same sex couple who is seeking to annul a voidable marriage.

All marriages occurring on or after July 1, 2016 in Virginia in which one or both of the parties was under the age of 18 and did not obtain legal emancipation if over the age of 16 are voidable. Va. Code § 20-45.1(C). However, if such marriage occurred outside of Virginia and was lawful in that state, Virginia will recognize the marriage if the parties are subsequently domiciled within the Commonwealth.

The other type of annullable marriages is those with contractual defects other than illegality and offense to public policy. These are listed in Va. Code § 20-89.1. Voidable marriages require court action to dissolve, and therefore possess the indicia of status until that time. See, e.g., *Cornwall v. Cornwall,* 160 Va. 183, 190–91, 168 S.E. 439, 442 (1933). In Virginia, such marriages include those where there has been lack of capacity through insanity or mental defect; marriages procured through fraud, coercion or duress; marriages where there is no intent to assume the consequences of marital status, including sham and joke marriages; and those where the spouse has concealed pregnancy, prior prostitution, conviction of a felony or infection with venereal disease.

> A void marriage confers no legal rights, and, when it is determined that the marriage is void, it is as if no marriage had ever been performed . . . . A voidable marriage differs from a void marriage in that it may be afterwards ratified by the parties and become valid and usually is treated as a valid marriage until it is decreed void. [Toler v. Oakwood Smokeless Coal Corp., 173 Va. 425, 4 S.E.2d 364 (1939)]. A void marriage is a mere nullity and its validity may be impeached in any court, whether the question arises directly or indirectly, and whether the parties be living or dead. *Alexander*

*v. Kuykendall,* 192 Va. 8, 10, 63 S.E.2d 746, 748 (1951).

## § 5.07 Homosexual Marriages

On July 1, 2020, Virginia repealed its statutes prohibiting same sex marriages (Va. Code § 20-45.2) and civil unions (Va. Code § 20-45.3), and amended a substantial portion of the Code of Virginia to refer to gender neutral terms, such as "spouse" instead of Husband and Wife. These now repealed statutes were generally seen as unconstitutional based on the United States Supreme Court decision in *Obergefell v. Hodges,* 135 S. Ct. 2584 (2015). In *Obergefell,* the United States Supreme Court held that the Fourteenth Amendment requires a State to license a marriage between two people of the same sex and to recognize same-sex marriages that were lawfully performed in a foreign state. However, despite the repeal of the statutes banning same sex marriages and civil unions, Virginia's constitutional amendment, Va. Const. Art. 1 § 15-A continues the debate as to the legality of same sex marriages. This article defines marriage as being "only a union between one man and one woman" and prohibits the extension of marriage rights to any other status of individuals. Accordingly, until this article is either repealed or declared unconstitutional, the legal status of a same sex marriage in Virginia can be challenged.

The historical analysis supporting the prohibition on same sex marriages follows and is being left in this treatise for the time being as a point of reference and should not be used for any precedential value. Marriages in Virginia must be between persons of the opposite sex. Va. Const. Art. 1 § 15-A, Va. Code § 20-45.2. This is required as well by the state public policy that continues to declare homosexual intercourse a criminal offense. *Doe v. Commonwealth's Attorney for Richmond,* 403 F. Supp. 1199 (E.D. Va. 1975), *aff'd mem.,* 425 U.S. 901, 96 S. Ct. 1489, 47 L. Ed. 2d 751 (1976). See also *Baker v. Nelson,* 291 Minn. 310, 191 N.W.2d 185 (1971), and *Dean v. District of Columbia,* 653 A.2d 307 (D.C. App. 1995), which held that the legislature never intended to sanction same-sex marriages, nor did it intend the Human Rights Act to change the fundamental definition of marriage. The court wrote:

> There is no constitutional basis under the due process clause to find that the fundamental right of heterosexual couples to marry is extended to same-sex partners: Even without reference to *Hardwick*'s constitutional approval of statutes criminalizing consensual sodomy, we cannot say that same-sex marriage is deeply rooted in this Nation's history and tradition. Indeed, the District of Columbia marriage statute reflects an altogether different tradition.

An attempted marriage between two persons of the same sex would be absolutely void even though not mentioned in the statutes listing grounds for annulment. See *Anonymous v. Anonymous,* 67 Misc. 2d 982, 325 N.Y.S.2d 499 (1971) (Plaintiff married defendant mistakenly believing that he was a woman. The parties separated and never resumed cohabitation after the wedding night. The plaintiff did not have to pay support nor medical expenses even before the marriage was annulled).

Although there exists no statutory impediment to same sex marriages in Virginia as of July 1, 2020 since Va. Code §§ 20-45.2 and 45.2 were repealed, Va. Const. Art. 1 § 15-A still provides a basis for refusing to recognize the validity of same sex marriages. However, in *Miller-Jenkins v. Miller-Jenkins,* 49 Va. App. 88, 637 S.E.2d 330 (2006), the Court of Appeals held that the federal Parental Kidnapping Prevention Act (PKPA), 28 U.S.C. § 1738A, requires Virginia courts to grant full faith and credit to other states' custody and visitation orders that arise from litigation involving civil unions, as long as the other states are exercising jurisdiction consistent with the provisions of the PKPA. In *Miller-Jenkins,* a Virginia woman: (1) entered into a civil union in Vermont; (2) gave birth in Virginia to a child conceived by artificial insemination; (3) asked a Vermont court to dissolve the civil union and determine child custody and visitation issues; and (4) asked a Virginia court, following enactment of Va. Code § 20-45.3 (which was repealed following this case on July 1, 2020), to rule that any parental rights claimed by her former civil union partner were "nugatory, void, illegal, and/or unenforceable." Because the woman had invoked the jurisdiction of the Vermont courts and subjected herself and her child to that jurisdiction, the PKPA required the Virginia courts to give full faith and credit to the Vermont custody and visitation orders. See also *Miller v. Jenkins,* 54 Va. App. 282, 678 S.E.2d 268 (2009) (dismissal of collateral attack on Vermont custody and visitation orders brought under Declaratory Judgment Act, Va. Code § 8.01-184 et seq.).

In *Prashad v. Copeland,* 55 Va. App. 247, 685 S.E.2d 199 (2009), a surrogate mother and a same-sex couple agreed to have a child, through artificial insemination with the couple's sperm, that would be raised by the couple. After the child's birth, a custody dispute arose, and a North Carolina court, exercising jurisdiction consistent with the Parental Kidnapping Prevention Act, 28 U.S.C. § 1738A, and the Uniform Child Custody Jurisdiction and Enforcement Act, Va. Code § 20-146.1 et seq., awarded primary custody to the child's father and his same-sex partner, and secondary custody to the mother. Despite the mother's objections, a Virginia court properly registered the North Carolina custody orders for enforcement in Virginia. Registration of the orders did not violate the Marriage Amendment, Va. Const. Art. 1 § 15-A, or the Marriage Affirmation Act, Va. Code

§ 20-45.3, because the North Carolina court awarded custody to the father's same-sex partner on the basis of the partner's relationship with the child that he had cared for, for two years, rather than on the basis of the relationship between the partner and the child's father.

In *Damon v. York*, 54 Va. App. 544, 680 S.E.2d 354 (2009), a mother and her girlfriend married under a Canadian law authorizing same-sex marriage. For about two years, the mother, her daughter, and the girlfriend lived together in a shared household. After the adults' relationship ended, the girlfriend sought court-ordered visitation with the daughter, arguing that she was the child's "quasi-stepparent" or the "functional equivalent of the child's stepparent or former stepparent." The court of appeals held that the girlfriend lacked standing to litigate the question of visitation, because she was not a "person with a legitimate interest" who fit within any of the Va. Code § 20-124.1 categories or their functional equivalents. The Canadian marriage, which was void in all respects under Virginia law, created neither a familial relationship nor a stepparent relationship. See Marriage Amendment, Va. Const. Art. 1 § 15-A; Marriage Affirmation Act, Va. Code § 20-45.3. Furthermore, the girlfriend in *Damon* was a mere "adult presence" in the child's life, and never established any kind of close stepmother-stepdaughter relationship with the child.

For additional discussions of marriage by same-sex couples, see Andrew Sullivan, *Virtually Normal: An Argument about Homosexuality* (Alfred A. Knopf, 1995); William Eskridge, *A History of Same-Sex Marriage*, 79 Va. L. Rev. 1419 (1993); and Judith McDaniel, *Lesbian Couples' Guide* (Harper, 1995).

## § 5.08 Bigamous Marriages

Marriages contracted by parties when one has a living spouse are void. Va. Code §§ 20-38.1(a)(1) and 20-43. Some are also punishable criminally. The marriage will be found void despite the fact that one party was unaware of the impediment to a valid marriage because of concealment by the other or honest mistake regarding the validity of a prior divorce or death of a former spouse.

There is a strong presumption that a later marriage is valid, even though one party asserts that a prior marriage has rendered the later marriage void as bigamous. Rebuttal of this presumption requires proof by clear and convincing evidence that there was a prior marriage, and that the earlier marriage did not end before the later one began. *Rahnema v. Rahnema*, 47 Va. App. 645, 626 S.E.2d 448 (2006) (*Rahnema II*) (unpersuasive evidence of bigamy).

In *Naseer v. Moghal*, 2012 Va. App. LEXIS 259 (Aug. 14, 2012), the wife remarried without obtaining a formal certificate of divorce under Pakistani law. The wife did not tell her second husband that she had been previously married, stating on the marriage certificate that this was her first marriage. The husband subsequently found the wife's marriage certificate from her first marriage and discovered that she never obtained a legal divorce. Pakistani authorities arrested the wife and charged her with bigamy. The husband filed a complaint for annulment, alleging that the wife committed bigamy. The annulment was granted. The wife appealed on grounds that there was insufficient evidence to prove bigamy. The court of appeals found that the husband had carried his burden of "clear and convincing evidence" to prove that the wife committed bigamy and affirmed the trial court's ruling.

The fact that a person believes he is validly divorced from a first spouse does not preclude a subsequent criminal conviction for bigamy as opposed to a mere finding that he had violated § 20-38.1 by entering into a prohibited marriage. *Stuart v. Commonwealth,* 11 Va. App. 216, 397 S.E.2d 533 (1990).

In *Cole v. Commonwealth*, 58 Va. App. 642, 712 S.E.2d 759 (2011), the defendant appealed a judgment by the circuit court that convicted him of bigamy pursuant to Va. Code Ann. § 18.2-362, arguing that if his bigamous marriage was void, it was legally impossible for him to be convicted of a crime. The appellate court upheld the conviction finding that the fact that Virginia does not recognize bigamous marriages does not justify the non-sequitur that such marriages cannot be criminalized. Although the separate statutes may overlap in their proscription of specific conduct, this does not detract from their independent enforcement except when double jeopardy concerns are implicated.

The customary relief for innocent bigamous spouses is the so-called Enoch Arden rule. After a spouse has been missing and presumed dead for seven years, Va. Code § 64.2-2300 (formerly Va. Code § 64.1-105), the other spouse may remarry without fear of a criminal bigamy prosecution. *Simpson v. Simpson,* 162 Va. 621, 175 S.E. 320 (1934); see also *Toler v. Oakwood Smokeless Coal Corp.,* 173 Va. 425, 435, 4 S.E.2d 364, 368 (1939). Should the missing spouse reappear, however, the second marriage would still be absolutely void. *Toler v. Oakwood Smokeless Coal Corp.,* 173 Va. 425, 435, 4 S.E.2d 364, 368 (1939); Va. Code § 18.2-364. See generally Fenton & Kaufman, *Enoch Arden Revisited,* 13 J. Fam. L. 245 (1973). The prudent attorney in such cases would secure a no-fault divorce before a remarriage took place. See *Simpson v. Simpson,* 162 Va. 621, 175 S.E. 320 (1934). The problem is then one of proving that the absent spouse at some time was aware of his spouse's desire, or had himself formed the intent to separate. *Hooker v. Hooker,* 215 Va. 415, 211 S.E.2d 34 (1975).

The section on defenses should be consulted, however, regarding the applicability of estoppel and res judicata.

## § 5.09 Incestuous Marriages

Marriage between close relatives is prohibited by Va. Code § 20-38.1, which lists nephews and nieces, uncles and aunts, grandparents and, of course, parents and siblings or half-siblings. There are two reasons that incestuous marriages are void and subject to criminal penalty. Va. Code § 18.2-366. One is that there may be genetic problems in the offspring of incestuous couples. The second is that if such marriages were permitted, great strains would be placed upon families, particularly in those where stepfathers and young daughters were concerned. The first reason indicates that even if the man and woman have not been raised in the same household, and even if one has been adopted, the marriage cannot take place. See *State v. H.,* 429 A.2d 1321 (Del. Super. 1981); *In re Marriage of Flores,* 96 Ill. App. 3d 279, 51 Ill. Dec. 885, 421 N.E.2d 393 (1981). The second is the rationale for including stepparents and adopted children in the statute, although obviously they are not related by blood. *Simpson v. Simpson,* 162 Va. 621, 175 S.E. 320 (1934).

## § 5.10 Marriages of Persons Under the Statutory Age

Marriages below the age of consent have always been void and against public policy. *Needham v. Needham,* 183 Va. 681, 33 S.E.2d 288 (1945); *Kirby v. Gilliam,* 182 Va. 111, 28 S.E.2d 40 (1943); see *Stanley v. Rasnick,* 137 Va. 415, 119 S.E. 76 (1923). In the years of adolescence, however, parental consent has been required since 1975. Va. Code § 20-89.1. Before that time, if the man and woman chose to live together after reaching majority, the marriage was still valid. If the minor has been emancipated, no parental consent shall be required. Va. Code § 20-49 (new in 1993).

The minimum legal age in Virginia for a person to get married is 18. Va. Code § 20-48. However, a minor child of at least 16 years of age can petition the juvenile court for emancipation if intending to get married. *Id.*

In *Needham v. Needham,* 183 Va. 681, 33 S.E.2d 288 (1945), two young people, without their parents' knowledge or consent, left Virginia and proceeded to Maryland, where they were married. They immediately returned to Virginia, where they lived together for some time. The marriage was valid although they could not have married in Virginia without parental approval since they were above the age of consent (twelve) and the marriage would have therefore merely been voidable. *Id.* at 688, 33 S.E.2d at 291.

Parental consent was required not only to aid the couple in making a rational decision but also to protect the father's right to his children's services.

In *Pifer v. Pifer,* 12 Va. Cir. 448 (Frederick Co. 1975), the circuit court upheld the validity of an underage marriage similar to that of *Needam.* Complainant, who was 17, married a 19-year-old high school graduate in Hagerstown, Maryland after the man applied for a Maryland license, falsely stating that she was 18 and failing to obtain the parental approval required for underage marriages in both Virginia and Maryland. The two wished to marry because the complainant suspected she was pregnant. After the wedding, they continued to live at their respective parents' homes. When the complainant's parents learned of the marriage, they took her to an obstetrician who confirmed the pregnancy. It was the doctor's opinion that she would shortly have a miscarriage. The miscarriage in fact occurred two days later, and shortly thereafter the complainant's mother filed for annulment. Because the complainant had participated in the false application, she could not claim the benefits of her minority. Nor could she complain of mistake, for the marriage would have been upheld on grounds of public policy even if she had not been pregnant in the first place. Finally, there was no duress because, all things considered, she preferred the course that she took.

### § 5.11    Insanity and Mental Defect

Where one of the parties was unable to give a valid consent to marriage because he was incurably insane or mentally defective at the time of the ceremony, see *Counts v. Counts,* 161 Va. 768, 771–72, 172 S.E. 248, 249 (1933). An annulment may be obtained by the sane partner or by the committee or guardian of the incompetent. Va. Code §§ 20-45.1 and 20-89.1. Insanity may also, if acquired after the marriage, be the basis for separate grounds for divorce under Va. Code § 20-45.1. Spousal support may not be awarded to the defendant incompetent when the marriage is found void on these grounds. *Somers-Shiflet v. Shiflet,* 29 Va. Cir. 206 (Fairfax Co. 1992), even though the defendant's guardian sought to have the support awarded before entry of the final decree of nullity.

A woman with Alzheimer's Disease did not give her consent when she moved her head from right to left in response to the question whether she wished to marry Gardner during a ceremony performed by a minister in a car, with no other witnesses present. The only thing she did during the ceremony, according to the minister, was to try to get out of the car, whereupon the groom locked the door. *Nicely v. Gardner,* 12 Va. Cir. 216 (City of Roanoke 1988).

Although there are no Virginia cases on point, case law from other jurisdictions indicates that where one party was involuntarily intoxicated by the other so that during the marriage ceremony there was no capacity for knowing consent, and there was no cohabitation following the ceremony, the marriage was voidable. *Thomas v. Thomas,* 111 Ill. App. 3d 1032, 67 Ill. Dec. 590, 444 N.E.2d 826 (1983).

## § 5.12 Fraud

If one spouse procures the other's consent only through fraud going to some matter essential to the marriage relationship, see *Jacobs v. Jacobs,* 184 Va. 281, 296, 35 S.E.2d 119, 125 (1945) ("There must be some evidence that the appellant did not intend before the marriage or at the time of the marriage to become in truth and fact the wife of the appellee"), the resulting marriage is voidable and may be annulled by the innocent spouse if there is no cohabitation after the defect is discovered. Va. Code § 20-89.1(c).

Falsehoods relating to wealth or social status will not render a marriage voidable, since the spouse received the person bargained for, *Francis v. Francis* (V.I. Territorial Ct. 1985); *McKee v. McKee,* 262 So. 2d 111 (La. App. 1972); *Emmons v. Emmons,* 34 A.D.2d 725, 312 N.Y.S.2d 117 (1970). However, marriages are voidable where there was a misstatement of a desire to have children, *Heup v. Heup,* 45 Wis. 2d 71, 172 N.W.2d 334 (1969) (no fraud found on facts); *Ciarochi v. Ciarochi,* 194 Va. 313, 73 S.E.2d 402 (1952) (question not decided although alleged by wife's testimony), or to ever engage in sexual intercourse. *Pretlow v. Pretlow,* 177 Va. 524, 14 S.E.2d 381 (1941). See Note, 28 Va. L. Rev. 305 (1941). There was no fraud when the woman herself acquiesced in the application process, falsely stating that she was over eighteen. *Pifer v. Pifer,* 12 Va. Cir. 448 (Frederick Co. 1975).

Another type of fraud that has been recognized in recent cases is misleading as to the existence of a prior spouse, or that spouse's continued life, to a person who for religious reasons cannot marry one who is divorced while the former spouse still lives. See, e.g., *Wolfe v. Wolfe,* 62 Ill. App. 3d 498, 19 Ill. Dec. 306, 378 N.E.2d 1181 (1978), and cases cited therein. Compare *State Compensation Fund v. Foughty,* 13 Ariz. App. 381, 476 P.2d 902 (1970), *overruled,* Jackson v. Industrial Comm'n, 121 Ariz. 602, 592 P.2d 1258 (1979) (false assurance that had deep religious convictions made voidable a marriage to a devout Protestant). Fraud regarding pregnancy will not render marriage voidable in Virginia, although concealment of pregnancy by another will be grounds of annulment. Va. Code § 20-89.1. Misrepresentation as to prior marital status will not invalidate a marriage. *Sanderson v. Sanderson,* 212 Va. 537, 186 S.E.2d 84 (1972) (wife alleged one prior marriage and divorce, but had been married and divorced five times).

However, duress is not involved when a pregnant young woman, who under other circumstances might have greatly preferred to delay marriage by some months, considering all things, preferred marrying. *Pifer v. Pifer,* 12 Va. Cir. 448 (Frederick Co. 1975).

There must be a clear setting forth of the facts upon which the alleged fraud is based in the complaint, and the alleged fraud must be clearly proved. *Ciarochi v. Ciarochi,* 194 Va. 313, 73 S.E.2d 402 (1952).

See generally Margaret F. Brinig & Michael V. Alexeev, *Fraud in Courtship: Divorce and Annulment,* 2 Eur. J. Law & Econ. 45 (1995).

### § 5.13  Duress and Coercion

Some older cases involve parents of young women who literally hold a gun to the young man's head in order to get him to marry. Such "shotgun" marriages are voidable. See *Copeland v. Copeland,* 21 S.E. 241, 2 Va. Dec. 81 (1895) (marriage not shown in this case to be product of duress, but rather the result of a prosecution for seduction).

See generally Kingsley, *Duress as a Ground for Annulment of Marriage,* 33 S. Cal. L. Rev. 1 (1959).

### § 5.14  Sham or Joke Marriages

A marriage may be valid regardless of the purpose for which the parties contracted it, so long as they intended to assume a marital status. *Mpiliris v. Hellenic Lines, Ltd.,* 323 F. Supp. 865 (S.D. Tex. 1969). If, however, the parties did not intend to acquire the rights and obligations of married persons, the marriage is voidable as a sham. *Faustin v. Lewis,* 85 N.J. 507, 427 A.2d 1105 (1981), cf. *Boyter v. Commissioner,* 668 F.2d 1382 (4th Cir. 1981).

In *Aboulhosen v. Elawar,* 12 Va. Cir. 157 (Henrico Co. 1988), plaintiff sought to annul a marriage on the grounds that it had been entered into without any intent to live together. The court found that the plaintiff did not carry her burden of proof that the man had always intended it to be a lark.

Sham marriages occur most frequently in cases involving spouses who marry in part to gain lawful United States residence. In *Marblex Design Int'l, Inc. v. Stevens,* 54 Va. App. 299, 678 S.E.2d 276 (2009), a company claimed, after an employee died from injuries sustained in an industrial accident and his widow was awarded dependent worker's compensation benefits, that the employee and his wife had entered into a "sham green-card marriage." However, the couple had a legal marriage, because they obtained a marriage license, went through a ceremony performed by a marriage commissioner, and recorded the marriage at a circuit court clerk's office.

There was no evidence that the couple had conspired to violate federal immigration laws, but even if they had conspired, the validity of their marriage would not have been affected. Also, under Virginia law, a "green-card marriage" is voidable, not void *ab initio*, and thus the marriage was valid because it had never been voided. Furthermore, a putative "green-card marriage" is *not* violative of the public policy of Virginia.

If the marriage is entered into in a spirit of joke or jest, it is likewise annullable. See *Crouch v. Wartenberg,* 91 W. Va. 91, 112 S.E. 234 (1922), where the parties went through a marriage ceremony only in order to alleviate their embarrassment but never lived together, and *Meredith v. Shakespeare,* 96 W. Va. 229, 122 S.E. 520 (1924), where the parties married as a joke in a spirit of great exuberance and fun, but never lived together nor intended to be married. In neither of these cases was there a meeting of the minds in good faith nor any intent to assume the duties and obligations of the marital relationship. See generally 1 J. Bishop, *Marriage and Divorce* §§ 296, 298, 339, 366 et seq.

## § 5.15   Miscellaneous Grounds

Some grounds for annulment are also grounds for divorce. These include impotency, conviction for an infamous offense, prostitution, pregnancy by another, or fathering another's child. Va. Code § 20-89.1. Virginia courts will not recognize a proxy marriage performed in England, which itself does not recognize proxy marriages. In *Farah v. Farah,* 16 Va. App. 329, 429 S.E.2d 626 (1993), both parties resided in the United States, and their marriage had been solemnized by proxy in London. The parties then traveled to the bride's native Pakistan, where her father held a reception to symbolize the sending away of the bride with her husband. The parties then returned to Virginia, purchased a house jointly titled in both names, and lived together for about one year. The parties then separated, and the man sought to have the marriage declared void. The woman filed for divorce and equitable distribution. The court of appeals held that the trial judge erred in granting a divorce and by equitably distributing the parties' property because the marriage was not valid in England where celebrated. The court reasoned that because Virginia does not recognize common law marriages where the relationship is created in the state, the parties never entered into a valid marriage. There could therefore be no divorce and no distribution of the parties' property.

## § 5.16   Defenses

The usual defenses to annulment action include: (1) lack of jurisdiction; (2) lack of proof that the alleged grounds occurred; (3) estoppel; (4) ratification of a voidable marriage by continued or renewed cohabitation after the defect was discovered, Va. Code § 20-89.1(c); (5) res judicata; (6) expiration of more than two years after the ceremony, Va. Code § 20-89.1(c) (voidable marriages only); and (7) laches.

Proving the grounds for annulment is essential. In the case of *Arebalo v. Melendez*, 2020 Va. App. LEXIS 162 (June 2, 2020), the annulment complaint was dismissed because the Plaintiff failed to provide any corroborating evidence to support the annulment. Va. Code § 20-99(1) requires that no "annulment . . . shall be granted on the uncorroborated testimony of the parties or either of them." The foreign records from Bolivia were not admitted into evidence due to procedural and authentication defects, and the annulment could not be granted solely on the Plaintiff's testimony. "The general rule is that where a particular fact or circumstance is vital to complainant's case, some evidence of the same, in addition to the complainant's own testimony, is essential." *Arebalo v. Melendez*, 2020 Va. App. LEXIS at *8 (citing *Graves v. Graves*, 193 Va. 659, 662, 70 S.E.2d 339 (1952) (other citations omitted).

The estoppel cases do not make the marriage valid, but merely state that the innocent party who did not know of the defect and relied upon it to his or her detriment should be able to receive financial remunerations as though the marriage were valid and the parties were now divorcing. See, e.g., *Poor v. Poor,* 381 Mass. 392, 409 N.E.2d 758 (1980); *Rosen v. Sitner,* 274 Pa. Super. 445, 418 A.2d 490 (1980); 24 Am. Jur. 2d *Divorce and Separation* §§ 971, 972; 27B C.J.S. *Divorce* §§ 364–366; Restatement, Conflict of Laws § 112; Clark, *Estoppel Against Jurisdictional Attack on Decrees of Divorce,* 70 Yale L.J. 45 (1960). Compare *George v. King,* 208 Va. 136, 156 S.E.2d 615 (1967), where the husband was not allowed to annul his marriage when he sought to collaterally attack the wife's divorce from a prior marriage, since he had no interest adversely affected at the time of the prior divorce.

Apparently in Virginia the defense of "unclean hands" will be unavailable in cases of void marriages. See *Heflinger v. Heflinger,* 136 Va. 289, 118 S.E. 316 (1923) (husband who remarried before first divorce was effective could bring an action to have second marriage annulled as bigamous).

Res judicata becomes a defense if a prior Virginia proceeding found that a marriage existed. This may be a prior spousal support and maintenance proceeding, see, e.g., *Hosier v. Hosier,* 221 Va. 827, 273 S.E.2d 564 (1981); *Psaroudis v. Psaroudis,* 27 N.Y.2d 527, 312 N.Y.S.2d 998, 261 N.E.2d 108 (1970), or a prior finding that a first divorce was valid. See, e.g., *Kessler v. Fauquier Nat'l Bank,* 195 Va. 1095, 81 S.E.2d 440 (1954) (right to share as surviving spouse in distribution of former wife's estate).

If the impediment to a void or voidable marriage is removed, a valid common law marriage, which requires a divorce to dissolve, may result. See, e.g., *Metropolitan Life Ins. Co. v. Holding,* 293 F. Supp. 854 (E.D. Va. 1968).

Laches was claimed as a defense in *Pretlow v. Pretlow,* 177 Va. 524, 14 S.E.2d 381 (1941), and *Counts v. Counts,* 161 Va. 768, 172 S.E. 248 (1933), but was not substantiated in either case. Laches was found in *Robinson v. Robinson,* 33 Va. Cir. 351 (Fairfax Co. Cir. Ct. 1994) (delay of nearly three years after wife knew of West Virginia divorce proceedings).

## § 5.17  Effects of Annulment

Before an annulment is granted, especially in cases of voidable marriages, the usual incidents of marital status exist. This would include the marital privilege for confidential communications or exemption from testifying, compare *People v. Godines,* 17 Cal. App. 2d 721, 727, 62 P.2d 787, 790 (1936) (voidable marriage; communication protected), with *People v. Mabry,* 71 Cal. 2d 430, 78 Cal. Rptr. 655, 455 P.2d 759 (1969) (no privilege where marriage void); interspousal immunity from suit, *Gordon v. Pollard,* 207 Tenn. 45, 336 S.W.2d 25 (1960) (the immunity is now abolished in Virginia by Va. Code § 8-220.1) and legitimacy of children, *Cornwall v. Cornwall,* 160 Va. 183, 191, 168 S.E. 439, 442 (1933). See also *Henderson v. Henderson,* 187 Va. 121, 46 S.E.2d 10 (1948); Va. Code § 64-7. Dower would also exist where otherwise applicable unless the marriage were annulled.

In many ways, annulments resemble divorces. Child custody, see, e.g., *Brown v. Kittle,* 225 Va. 451, 303 S.E.2d 864 (1983), and support, *Henderson v. Henderson,* 187 Va. 121, 46 S.E.2d 10 (1948), must still be dealt with if children were born of the relationship. These principles were incorporated into Virginia statutes in 1996, when Va. Code Ann. § 20-107.2 added annulment to the list of times child custody and support matters could be determined.

Spousal support is more questionable. Pendente lite awards may be given under Va. Code § 20-103. *MacDougall v. Levick,* 66 Va. App. 50, 86–87 (2016) ("Annulment and *pendente lite* support are longstanding features of Virginia law"). One older Virginia case, *Bray v. Landergren,* 161 Va. 699, 172 S.E. 252 (1933), indicates in dicta that if the marriage is absolutely void, there is no status upon which to base the duty of support. More recently, in *Shoustari v. Zamani,* 39 Va. App. 517, 574 S.E.2d 314 (2002), the court of appeals held unequivocally that a trial court cannot award spousal support or make an equitable distribution in the case of a marriage that is void ab initio (e.g., a bigamous marriage), because a void marriage confers no legal rights to the parties.

In *Farah v. Farah,* 16 Va. App. 329, 429 S.E.2d 626 (1993), the court of appeals held that the trial judge erred by granting the parties a divorce and by equitably distributing their property since their proxy marriage was not valid in England where celebrated. Because Virginia does not recognize common law marriages where the relationship is created in the state, the parties never entered into a valid marriage. There could therefore be no divorce and no distribution of the parties' property.

Following an annulment for a void marriage, it may be possible to recover some monetary benefit that ceased upon the marriage ceremony. One case indicates that this consequence does not adhere to marriages that are voidable only, *McConkey v. McConkey,* 216 Va. 106, 215 S.E.2d 640 (1975), since the former spouse has a right to change his position upon the remarriage of a dependent spouse. *Id.* at 108, 215 S.E.2d at 641. Compare *Stegall v. Stegall,* 22 F. Cas. 1226, 2 Brock. 256, F. Cas. No. 13351, F. Cas. No. 13351, F. Cas. No. 1335 (C.C. Va. 1825), where the wife's gross misconduct in leaving her husband and living with another disqualified her from claiming a dower interest in the husband's estate. There may still be recovery from a fund, such as Social Security, however. See *Johnson County Nat'l Bank & Trust Co. v. Bach,* 189 Kan. 291, 369 P.2d 231 (1962); cf. *Flaxman v. Flaxman,* 57 N.J. 458, 273 A.2d 567 (1971), where a revival of alimony was not allowed after a voidable marriage was annulled but Social Security would have been. There may also be recovery in tort for fraud and deceit. *Alexander v. Kuykendall,* 192 Va. 8, 63 S.E.2d 746 (1951). See generally Comment, *The Aftereffects of Annulment: Alimony, Property Division, Provision for Children,* 1968 Wash. U.L.Q. 148.

# CHAPTER 6

# Adoption

## SYNOPSIS

## § 6.01    Historical Perspective and Introduction

Adoption was unknown at common law, *Fletcher v. Flanary*, 185 Va. 409, 411, 38 S.E.2d 433, 434 (1946), although in Roman times it was customary for childless men to choose adult heirs by adopting them.

Adoption is therefore a creature of statute, *Clarkson v. Bliley*, 185 Va. 82, 92, 38 S.E.2d 22, 26 (1946), and the Virginia procedures and statutes may be quite different from those followed in other states.

In 2000, Virginia reorganized its adoption statutes as ch. 10.2 of Title 63.1 of the Virginia Code. Acts 2000, ch. 830. Then in 2002, Title 63.1 was recodified, and ch. 10.2 was reissued with very minor changes as ch. 12 of Title 63.2 of the Virginia Code. The reorganization in 2000 was a formal change intended to clarify which rules apply to which types of adoption, and no policy changes were intended. Chapter 12 was initially divided into six articles. General provisions applicable to all adoptions are in Article 1, beginning at Va. Code § 63.2-1200. Separate articles govern agency adoptions (Article 2, beginning at Va. Code § 63.2-1221), parental placement adoptions (Article 3, beginning at Va. Code § 63.2-1230), stepparent adoptions (Article 4, beginning at Va. Code § 63.2-1241), and adult adoptions (Article 5, beginning at Va. Code § 63.2-1243). Records are covered in Article 6, beginning at Va. Code § 63.2-1245. Close relative adoption was added to the specially defined types of adoption in 2006 (Article 4.1, beginning at Va. Code § 63.2-1242.1), and provisions effective in 2007 established a Putative Fathers Registry (Article 7, beginning at Va. Code § 63.2-1249).

What occurs in adoption is the creation of status: a new parent-child relationship. Because of its importance and the complex of privileges and duties flowing from it, the state has an interest in adoption. In addition, the state is concerned because in most cases a minor child, over which the state exercises *parens patriae* authority, is the adoptee. See generally Rendleman, *Parens Patriae: From Chancery to the Juvenile Court*, 23 S.C.L.Q. 205 (1971); Zainaldin, *The Emergence of a Modern American Family Law 1796–1851*, 72 Nw. U.L. Rev. 1083 (1979).

## § 6.02 Termination of Natural Parents' Rights and Creation of New Ones

An adoption case has two parts. In the first, the natural parents' rights are severed. In most cases, this is done with the consent of the parents. If a voluntary termination, as this is called, takes place, the concerns are largely contractual: was the consent freely, knowingly and voluntarily given? See Va. Code § 63.2-1202; Va. Code § 63.2-1232(A)(1) (parental placements). On other occasions, the parents' rights are involuntarily terminated because of parental unfitness that cannot be remedied.

Petitions involving custody, visitation, support, or control of a child may be filed in juvenile and domestic relations court by persons with legitimate interests. This standing requirement is to be liberally construed, and includes, but is not limited to, grandparents, stepparents, former stepparents, blood relatives and family members. It does not include any person whose parental rights have been terminated by court order (voluntarily or involuntarily). It also does not include any person whose interest in the child derives from or through a parent whose rights have been terminated, such as relatives of a child who has been legally adopted (unless the adoption was a stepparent adoption). Va. Code § 16.1-241(A). Except in cases of stepparent adoptions, after adoption of a child, the birth parents or previous adoptive parent, including but not limited to grandparents, stepparents, former stepparents, blood relatives and family members lose their visitation and other familial rights. Va. Code § 63.2-1215.

The fundamental nature of the parent's right to raise the child requires that due process be afforded the parent before rights are terminated involuntarily. This may involve appointing counsel for the indigent parent or the child, and certainly involves notice and a hearing in most cases. *Armstrong v. Manzo,*

380 U.S. 545, 85 S. Ct. 1187, 14 L. Ed. 2d 62 (1965). In *M.L.B. v. S.L.J.*, 519 U.S. 102, 117 S. Ct. 555, 136 L. Ed. 2d 473 (1996), the Supreme Court held that an indigent mother had a right to a transcript necessary for her appeal from an adverse termination decision. On July 1, 2020, subsection (L) of Va. Code § 62.2-1202 was enacted and it requires that a child's legal custodian as well as "any other named parties in pending cases in which the custody or visitation of such child is at issue . . . shall be given proper notice of any adoption proceeding and an opportunity to be heard." Va. Code § 63.2-1202(L).

The second step in the adoption proceeding involves a state inquiry into whether adoption by the prospective parents will be in the child's best interests. See Va. Code §§ 63.2-1205, 63.2-1208, 63.2-1209, 63.2-1225 (agency adoption: determination of appropriate home), and 63.2-1231 (parental placement adoption: home study). There are few strict rules about who is eligible to be an adoptive parent, but Virginia law prohibits adoptions by persons who have been convicted of a sexually violent offense or an offense requiring registration in the Sex Offender and Crimes Against Minors Registry. Va. Code § 63.2-1205.1; see Va. Code § 9.1-902 (registration). Before the 2006 enactment of Va. Code § 63.2-1205.1, an adoptive parent's prior conviction for aggravated sexual battery of a minor and his failure to timely register as a sex offender did not render him ineligible, as a matter of law, to adopt a child. *Gray v. Bourne*, 46 Va. App. 11, 614 S.E.2d 661 (2005).

Any child adopted shall "be, to all intents and purposes, the child of the person so adopting him [or her], and . . . shall be entitled to all the rights and privileges, . . . of a child of such a person born in lawful wedlock." Va. Code § 63.2-1215. Accordingly, an adoptive parent obtains all the legal rights and obligations of a natural parent. See *Frye v. Spotte*, 4 Va. App. 530, 533, 359 S.E.2d 315, 317 (1987). Once the child's adoption is final, there is no legal distinction between the biological parent and the adoptive parent, and they become parents of the child with equal rank and responsibility. *Carter v. Carter*, 35 Va. App. 466, 546 S.E.2d 220 (2001). Thus, in *Carter*, when a husband adopted his wife's child and the parents later divorced, the adoptive father and biological mother were equally entitled to be considered as custodial parent of their son; and the court properly awarded custody to the father, in the best interest of the child.

## § 6.03   Voluntary Placement

In parental placements, the hearing at which consent is given cannot be held until the child is in the third calendar day of life. Va. Code § 63.2-1233. Consent may be revoked for seven days after it is given, but once the child is 10 days old, a parent may waive his or her revocation period in writing if the parent acknowledges receiving independent legal counsel. Va. Code § 63.2-1234. A Virginia birth parent may execute consent under the laws of the prospective adoptive parents' state if the birth parent waives Virginia consent in accordance with the requirements of Va. Code § 63.2-1232(C). In agency adoptions where the child is entrusted to an agency, the entrustment can be revoked until the child is ten days old. Va. Code § 63.2-1223. A proper entrustment agreement must be executed in writing and notarized, and it should divest the birth parents of all legal rights and obligations with respect to the child. Va. Code § 63.2-1221.

Va. Code § 63.2-1202(B) and Va. Code § 63.2-903 provide, among other things, that the consent of a parent less than 18 years of age shall be deemed fully competent. The father of a child born out of wedlock need not sign an entrustment agreement if his identity is not known or reasonably ascertainable, if he has not registered with the Putative Father Registry, or if he has been given notice by mail at his last known address and fails to object within 15 days. Va. Code § 63.2-1222. In *Chollette v. Keeling*, 2015 Va. App. LEXIS 279 (Oct. 6, 2015), a father was denied the ability to intervene and object to his child's adoption because he was timely mailed sufficient notice (although the father never received this notice), and he failed to timely register in the putative father registry. An affidavit of the mother that the identity of the father is not reasonably ascertainable can be sufficient evidence of this fact if there is no contradictory evidence before the court. Va. Code § 63.2-1203. The entrustment agreement is revocable until the child has reached the age of 10 days and seven days have elapsed from the date of execution of the agreement, or until the child has been placed in an adoptive home. Va. Code § 63.2-1223. Parental consent to an adoption, or to an entrustment agreement that has not been finalized by the court, is also revocable prior to the final order of adoption upon proof of fraud or duress; after placement of the child in an adoptive home, revocation of parental consent requires written, mutual consent of the prospective adoptive parents or the child-placing agency. Va. Code § 63.2-1204. See *T.S.G. v. B.A.S.*, 52 Va. App. 583, 665 S.E.2d 854 (2008) (absent fraud or mutual consent to revocation, mother's properly executed consent remained in effect). When considering a parental placement adoption, it is imperative that at least one parent consents to the placement. Va. Code 63.2-1233(3). Where neither parent consented to the child's placement with prospective adoptive parents, but rather the child had been placed with them as a result of a removal following an abuse and neglect proceeding against the parents, neither the juvenile court nor the circuit court on an appeal had the statutory jurisdiction to conduct a parental placement adoption. *Knight v. Ottrix*, 69 Va. App. 519, 525–26, 820 S.E.2d 411, 414–15 (2018).

Direct placement of children by the birth or adoptive parent or legal guardian is authorized by Va. Code §§ 63.2-1200 and 63.2-1230. Parental placements may be with adoptive parents of choice but a valid consent must promptly be executed before a juvenile and domestic relations district court. Va. Code §§ 63.2-1230 and 63.2-1233. For the consent to be valid, the court must determine that the birth parents are aware of alternatives to adoption, that their consent is informed and uncoerced, that a licensed or duly authorized child-placing agency has counseled the prospective parents with regard to adoption procedures, that the birth parents and adoptive parents have exchanged identifying information and relevant medical and other records, that any financial agreement or exchange of property or fees for placement have been disclosed, that the parties are aware that no binding contract regarding placement or adoption exists, and that a home study has been conducted by a licensed or duly authorized child-placing agency that has been provided to the court. Va. Code § 63.2-1232.

The birth parents may elect for the parental placement provisions to apply when a licensed child-placing agency or a local board accepts custody of a child for placement with adoptive parents recommended by the birth parents or any person other than an agency or board. Va. Code § 63.2-1226. The agency or board *must* consider the recommendation of a birth parent, physician, attorney, or clergyman who is familiar with the situation of the prospective adoptive parents, Va. Code § 63.2-1225(A); and it *may* give consideration to placement with the recommended adoptive parents if it finds that such placement is in the best interest of the child. Va. Code § 63.2-1225(B). If birth parents make a recommendation, the agency or board must provide information about the two adoption methods, and it must allow the birth parents the opportunity to be represented by independent legal counsel. Va. Code § 63.2-1226.

Previously, the rule was that if the agency or board accepted custody for the purpose of placing the child with designated adoptive parents, then the parental placement provisions applied. See former Va. Code § 63.2-1226. However, in 2003, Va. Code § 63.2-1225 was amended to provide that when an agency or board accepts custody of a child for the purpose of placing the child for adoption with adoptive parents designated by the birth parents, the agency or board "may" consider placement with the designated parents if it "finds such placement to be in the best interests of the child." Earlier stages of the bill that added that language would have repealed, Va. Code § 63.2-1226, but the bill as enacted did not. See 2003 Va. Acts 779; 2002 Va.

HB 1514. In 2006, both Va. Code § 63.2-1225 and Va. Code § 63.2-1226 were reenacted with extensive changes. 2006 Va. Acts 654.

Donors of sperm or ova to assist reproduction have no parental rights or duties when the child is born of a married woman and was conceived with the written consent of her husband. Such a child is deemed to be the natural child of the woman and her husband. Va. Code § 20-158. Consent from surrogate mothers is discussed in § 6.06.

In some cases, the parents will already have placed the child with an adoption agency, or will have died. Consent must then be obtained from the agency. See Va. Code § 63.2-1202(C)(2).

A capital punishment case, *Thomas v. Garraghty*, 258 Va. 530, 522 S.E.2d 865 (1999), involved a question of voluntary consent to adoption. Thomas, the criminal defendant, was 17 at the time of the murder proceedings in 1990. He claimed that his biological father had not been provided notice of the transfer from juvenile court to circuit court for trial as an adult. The problem was that his biological parents separated in 1973, several years before Thomas' birth, divorcing in 1974. Thomas was adopted by his maternal grandparents in 1982. Both parents attempted to qualify their consent for adoption by providing that when the grandparents died, the child would be returned to the mother. In addition, the father's handwritten form provided that if the mother died or became seriously ill (after the death of the grandparents), he would like to obtain custody.

In fact, after both adoptive parents (the grandparents) died, Thomas did live with his biological mother for three years. In 1988, however, when he was about 15, Thomas began living with his aunt and uncle under an informal arrangement. The aunt and uncle never became his legal guardians or custodians. The Court held that the final adoption order (despite the attempted reservations of parental rights) unconditionally divested them of all legal rights with respect to Thomas. Since the order was not appealed within six months, Thomas' biological father was not his "father" for purposes of the transfer notification requirement.

## § 6.04   Fraud, Duress, and Coercion

Consent to an adoption, or to an entrustment agreement that has not been finalized by the court, may be revoked prior to the final order of adoption if there was fraud or duress in procuring the consent. Va. Code § 63.2-1204. In parental placements, the juvenile and domestic relations district court must determine that the birth parents' consent is informed and uncoerced. Va. Code § 63.2-1232. Six months after entry of an unappealed final order of adoption, the order becomes immune from attack on any grounds, including fraud or duress. Va. Code § 63.2-1216. See *McCallum v. Salazar*, 49 Va. App. 51, 636 S.E.2d 486 (2006) (six-month statute of limitations begins to run from date of entry of the final adoption order, not from date on which fraud was or should have been discovered).

Fraud might involve collusion by one parent with the person arranging for the adoption that was unknown by the other parent, as in the case of *Huebert v. Marshall*, 132 Ill. App. 2d 793, 270 N.E.2d 464 (1971).

There may also be fraud on the part of the prospective adoptive parent, such as in *In re Adoption of Robin*, 1977 Ok 219, 571 P.2d 850, where the adoptive mother, the child's step-grandmother, had children taken from her in the past, had assaulted several men including her present husband, and had failed to disclose the known whereabouts of the child's father, who had married the natural mother.

Coercion, although it usually must be more than embarrassment or financial pressure, see, e.g., *In re K.*, 31 Ohio Misc. 218, 282 N.E.2d 370 (1969); *Regenold v. Baby Fold, Inc.*, 68 Ill. 2d 419, 369 N.E.2d 858 (1977); *Bidwell v. McSorley*, 194 Va. 135, 72 S.E.2d 245 (1952), might involve such facts as a group of hostile relatives accusing a young, unwed mother of causing her mother's illness and death, as in *In re Adoption of Susko*, 363 Pa. 78, 69 A.2d 132 (1949).

Va. Code § 63.2-1223 provides that valid entrustment agreements terminating all parental rights and responsibilities to the child shall be revocable by either of the birth parents until the child has reached the age of ten days and seven days have elapsed from the date of execution of the agreement. This implies that the entrustment agreement is not valid unless executed after the child's birth. A three-day age requirement is imposed by § 63.2-1233, which governs direct placement of children by birth parents.

Even though parental rights and responsibilities have been terminated by an entrustment agreement, these rights may be restored to the birth parents and the child by court order prior to entry of a final order of adoption upon proof of fraud or duress, according to Va. Code § 63.2-1221. For revocation requirements applicable to parental placements, see Va. Code § 63.2-1234.

"For good cause shown," however, "means more than the simple changing of the mind by the parent who has given consent for adoption." *Bidwell v. McSorley*, 194 Va. 135, 140, 72 S.E.2d 245, 249 (1952).

### § 6.05     Time for Consent

By statute, Virginia has provided that consent may be revoked for a specified period following the child's birth. Va. Code § 63.2-1223 (entrustment to agency revocable for 10 days after child's birth); Va. Code §§ 63.2-1233 and 1234 (parental placement consent revocable ten days after given in hearing that cannot occur until the child is in its third day, but after child is 10 days old, no executed consent can be withdrawn). This delay is primarily required to prevent placement with prospective parents followed by a change of heart by a natural mother, who did not foresee her attachment to the child:

> [S]uch consents fail to allow for one of nature's strongest instincts. Who knows what the reaction will be of a mother once she sees *her* baby? . . . To deny the mother's natural desire to keep her baby is in derogation of the purpose of our statute to preserve the natural family relationship to the fullest extent possible. *Johnson v. Cupp*, 149 Ind. App. 611, 274 N.E.2d 411 (1971) (Buchanan, J., dissenting).

The rule also ensures that a hasty decision will not be made during the immediate postpartum period, when the natural mother may be taking medication or otherwise may be prevented from thinking through the entire situation. See, e.g., *Bidwell v. McSorley*, 194 Va. 135, 72 S.E.2d 245 (1952) (consent form effective when signed on day of child's birth, but no duress shown; statute then did not require waiting period, but was amended two years later in Act of 1954, ch. 489).

Consent to adoption must be given in writing, under oath. Va. Code § 63.2-1202. In a parental placement, consent must normally be given in a hearing before the juvenile and domestic relations court. Va. Code §§ 63.2-1233 and 63.2-1202. Va. Code § 63.2-1233 provides, however, that the execution of consent before the juvenile and domestic relations court shall not be required of a birth father if he consents under oath and in writing to the adoption. In such cases the father must provide the identifying information required in Va. Code § 63.2-1232(A)(3) to the court, unless the court dispenses with this requirement for good cause, and the birth mother must give her consent in court in accordance with Va. Code § 63.2-1233. Consent is not required from a putative father named by the mother if either (1) the putative father has failed to register with the Putative Father Registry, or (2) the putative father denies paternity under oath and in writing. Va. Code § 63.2-1233(1)(b). Virginia consent is not required if a Virginia birth parent has executed consent under the laws of the prospective adoptive parents' state and the birth parent has waived Virginia consent in accordance with the requirements of Va. Code § 63.2-1232(C).

Blanket consent forms, although administratively convenient, may not suffice to educate the parents of the irrevocability of the adoption decision.

See generally *In re Holder*, 218 N.C. 136, 141, 10 S.E.2d 620, 622 (1940); 2 Am. Jur. 2d *Adoption* § 45.

Va. Code § 6 63.2-1203 requires the court to provide written notice to the birth parent withholding consent of the parent's right to counsel prior to any hearing or decision on a petition for adoption. In addition, the law requires that an indigent parent who does not consent to the adoption of the parent's child, but whose consent to the adoption is required, shall be appointed counsel if requested.

### § 6.06    Contracts to Adopt and Surrogacy

A. *Contracts to adopt.* Contracts to adopt are illegal in Virginia if money is to be paid to a natural mother beyond reasonable expenses. Va. Code § 63.2-1218. Va. Code § 63.2-1208 requires notification by the investigating agency to the court of any fees paid to persons assisting in obtaining the child. A contract for adoption was performed substantially by both parties and therefore was not considered on the merits in *Harry v. Fisher*, 216 Va. 530, 221 S.E.2d 118 (1976) (natural mother attempted to revoke consent executed 11 days after birth of child, pursuant to contract). The state has a strong policy against "baby selling" as well as a strong presumption that it is in most children's interests to be in the custody of their natural parents. See, e.g., *People v. Free Synagogue Child Adoption Committee*, 194 Misc. 332, 337, 85 N.Y.S.2d 541, 546 (Sup. Ct. 1949).

However, an attorney may ethically represent the prospective adoptive parents in drafting a contract providing for payment of the biological mother's medical and legal fees in consideration for her consent to adoption. Representation is permissible if the lawyer determines that such a contract is neither illegal nor against public policy. In such cases the attorney may handle the payment of the pregnant woman's medical and legal bills as the prospective adoptive parents' agent. Va. State Bar Ethics Opinion No. 1227, May 8, 1989.

The exchange of fees or other consideration for the placement or referral of adoption does not necessarily invalidate the adoption, Va. Code §§ 63.2-1218 and 63.2-1232, but under Va. Code § 63.2-1218 results in commission of a Class 6 felony. Payment to a licensed or duly authorized child-placing agency for reasonable and customary services, reimbursement for the mother's medical expenses directly related to the pregnancy, payment for necessary transportation, and usual and customary fees for legal services in adoption are not prohibited under this section.

B. *Surrogacy in general.* Virginia has enacted legislation discussed below governing assisted conception and surrogacy contracts. In the absence of such legislation, contracts with surrogate mothers would presumably be treated as contracts to adopt, although if the genetic father were to agree to raise the child, he might not be seen as "adopting" his own child. See *Surrogate Parenting Associates, Inc. v. Commonwealth*, 704 S.W.2d 209 (Ky. 1986). Without judicial approval, surrogacy contracts would not be enforceable through specific performance because consent for adoption may not be given until after the child's birth. Va. Code § 63.2-1233. The trial court in the much publicized case of *In re Baby "M,"* 217 N.J. Super. 313, 525 A.2d 1128 (1987), *aff'd in part and rev'd in part*, 109 N.J. 396, 537 A.2d 1227 (1988), awarded the child in question to the father and his wife, specifically enforcing the contractual arrangement between them and the surrogate. Although the Supreme Court found that the agreement was void because it went against public policy, the award of custody was upheld on the usual "best interests" test.

Because the surrogate mother bears the child, she would presumably have a right to custody equal to that of any other natural mother, at least where the parties did not have judicial approval. Custody would be decided, in cases of a dispute, on the basis of the best interests of the child rather than any contract the natural parents might have made. Other problems involving surrogates include the restriction of the surrogate mother's sexual behavior during the period of conception, submission to tests such as amniocentesis, with a view towards abortion of a fetus with genetic problems, limitations on the ingestion of alcohol and various drugs during gestation, and decisions regarding custody of a physically or mentally handicapped child.

In the first reported Virginia case involving surrogate contracts, *Baby Doe v. Doe*, 15 Va. App. 242, 421 S.E.2d 913 (1992), the court of appeals remanded a declaratory judgment action. The case was originally filed by the genetic parents of the child called Baby Doe, who was born to a surrogate mother. The trial court had terminated the infant's relationship with her birth mother and had directed the Virginia Registrar of Vital Records to issue an original birth certificate with the genetic parents listed as the infant's parents. The guardian ad litem for the child successfully appealed from this ruling, arguing that the trial court abused its discretion in denying her motion for a continuance because the summary proceedings prejudiced and impaired Baby Doe's due process rights.

C. *Surrogacy legislation.* Virginia enacted legislation, effective July 1, 1993, allowing surrogacy contracts when at least one of the intended parents will be a genetic parent. Va. Code § 20-156 et seq. However, the intended parents only become parents of the child at its birth if the surrogacy contract has been judicially approved. Va. Code § 20-158(D). Consent after birth by the gestational mother does not appear to be required, as it usually would be under Va. Code § 63.2-1233, although many of the usual biological reasons for requiring a waiting period would seem to be present. Judicial approval is available only when there was no payment of fees to the mother beyond reimbursement for medical care and when a home study has been made and the intended mother cannot bear a child without unreasonable risk. Va. Code § 20-160. The surrogate may revoke during the first six months of pregnancy, with a penalty as set forth in the agreement between the parties. Va. Code § 20-161. There may be few such agreements when there is no payment for the surrogate's services, and attempts to avoid this requirement are all but inevitable. The legislation specifically provides for penalties for receiving compensation for providing brokerage services. Va. Code § 20-165.

The intended parents under a nonapproved surrogacy contract can become parents if the surrogate relinquishes her parental rights to them after a specified time has passed after the birth. Va. Code § 20-162. A sperm donor who has an unapproved surrogacy contract with a married gestational mother and her husband cannot assert fatherhood if the gestational mother elects to keep the child because in those circumstances, "the surrogate and her husband are the parents." Va. Code § 20-158(E)(2). The required genetic relationship between the child and at least one intended parent must be established by a signed and acknowledged statement from the physician who performed the assisted conception, but DNA testing can be substituted if a physician's statement is not available. Va. Code § 20-162(A)(3).

Those matters involving "clinical management of the pregnancy" are left to the surrogate mother under the statute. Va. Code § 20-163(A). A child born under an approved contract, since no longer deemed the child of the surrogate mother, is the responsibility of the natural father even if handicapped. Va. Code § 20-163(C).

If neither of the intended parents is a genetic parent of the child, then they can become the child's parents only by going through the process of adoption. Va. Code § 20-158(D), (E).

See generally Margaret F. Brinig, *A Maternalistic Approach to Surrogacy*, 81 Va. L. Rev. 2377 (1995); Comment, *Surrogate Mother Agreements: Contemporary Legal Aspects of a Biblical Notion*, 16 U. Rich. L. Rev. 467 (1982).

## § 6.07    Placement by Third Parties

In Virginia, as in most states, it is illegal to act as a child welfare agency without obtaining a license. Va. Code § 63.2-1701, 1712; see also Va. Code

§ 63.2-1225 (birth parent, physician, attorney or clergyman recommending a placement to a board or agency may not charge a fee and may not advertise availability to make such recommendations). Only a licensed child-placing agency, a local board of social services, an agency duly authorized outside Virginia, and a child's parent or legal guardian are authorized to place a child for adoption. Va. Code § 63.2-1200. Taking a fee to place a child with a set of prospective adoptive parents or any activity that provides assistance to a parent or guardian in locating an adoptive home or moving a child to an adoptive home may raise questions of violation of these statutes. Attorneys in particular should be cautioned to avoid even the appearance of acting as "baby brokers." However, it is permissible for an attorney to charge for legal fees and services rendered in connection with the placement he recommended. Va. Code § 63.2-1225.

## § 6.08  Interstate Compact on the Placement of Children

Virginia participates in the Interstate Compact on Child Placement, which appears at Va. Code § 63.2-1000, with implementing rules at Va. Code § 63.2-1100 and following at Va. Code §§ 63.2-1233(10) and 63.2-1240. The policy of the Compact is similar to the adoption policies of the state in general: assuring insofar as possible that a child coming to or from Virginia will be placed in an atmosphere with desirable care. In order to achieve this goal, the Compact requires state agencies in both the receiving and sending states to make appropriate investigations regarding the child and his future placement. (Article III). Jurisdiction over the child's welfare is retained until the child is adopted, reaches majority, or is emancipated. (Article V). The Compact does not apply to placement by close relations. (Article VIII).

## § 6.09  Foreign and Out-Of-State Adoptions

By statute enacted in 2011, adoption of a foreign child has the same effect as a Virginia adoption if the adoption was finalized pursuant to the laws of the country from which the child was adopted, and the child was admitted to the United States with an appropriate visa. Va. Code § 63.2-1200.1(A). The adoptive parents may obtain a new birth certificate by filing a specified report. Va. Code § 63.2-1200.1(B). Under prior case law, foreign adoptions would be recognized in Virginia so long as the court rendering the adoption had jurisdiction to render the decree, and so long as the foreign country's laws of adoption did not violate the public policy of *Virginia. Doulgeris v. Bambacus,* 203 Va. 670, 127 S.E.2d 145 (1962) (Greek adoption not recognized for purposes of determining descent and distribution since Greek view of adoption was contrary to Virginia public policy).

Virginia residents who have adopted a child in a foreign country and are seeking a Virginia birth certificate may petition the circuit court for a report of adoption if the country of adoption has post-adoption reporting requirements and has diplomatic relations with the United States. Va. Code § 63.2-1220(B).

Adoptive parents, including same-sex couples, who have adopted a Virginia-born child in another state may obtain a new birth certificate under Va. Code § 32.1-261. *Davenport v. Little-Bowser*, 269 Va. 546, 611 S.E.2d 366 (2005).

When a Virginia birth parent places a child for adoption with adoptive parents in another state, and the laws of that state govern the adoption proceeding, the birth parent may execute consent to the adoption pursuant to the laws of the adoptive parents' state, but the birth parent must waive the consent required under Virginia law in a manner complying with Va. Code § 63.2-1232(C).

### § 6.10    Revocation of Consent

An entrustment agreement under Va. Code § 63.2-1221 is revocable under Va. Code § 63.2-1223 until (1) the child has reached the age of ten days, and (2) seven days have elapsed from the date of execution of the agreement; or until the child has been placed in an adoptive home. Although the entrustment agreement must divest the birth parents of all legal rights and obligations with respect to the child, it must provide that the rights and obligations may be restored to the birth parents and the child by circuit court order prior to the entry of a final order of adoption upon proof of fraud or duress, and must be revocable prior to entry of an order finalizing the agreement (1) upon proof of fraud or duress, or (2) after placement of the child in an adoptive home upon written mutual consent of the birth parents and prospective adoptive parents. Va. Code § 63.2-1221.

Although the parent may revoke his or her consent, the entrustment agreement may still be used as evidence in the case. "The Code does not indicate that stipulations made in connection with an entrustment agreement are revoked in the event that the entrustment agreement is revoked. Rather, the Supreme Court has held that 'if the stipulation was agreed to, there can be no objection to it.' " (citing *Burke v. Gale*, 193 Va. 130, 137, 67 S.E.2d 917, 920 (1951)). *Boatright v. Wise County Dep't of Soc. Servs.*, 64 Va. App. 71, 85, 764 S.E.2d 724, 731–32 (2014).

The revocation rules for parental placement adoptions appear in Va. Code § 63.2-1234. Revocation of consent must be in writing, and may be made for any reason for up to seven days from the execution of consent, except that once the child is 10 days old, a party may waive his or her revocation period in writing if he or she acknowledges receiving independent legal counsel. The prior prohibition against withdrawal of an executed consent after the child is 10 days old has been repealed. 2008 Va. Acts 662. Even after the expiration of the seven-day revocation period, consent may be revoked prior to the final order of adoption where fraud or duress is shown. After placement of the child in an adoptive home, revocation occurs only upon written mutual consent of both the birth parents and the prospective adoptive parents.

After the applicable revocation period has passed, if a birth parent attempts to gain custody of or exercise parental rights to a child who has been placed for adoption, there is no parental presumption in favor of any party. Va. Code § 63.2-1206.

Once there has been a voluntary relinquishment, which must be shown by clear and convincing evidence, the natural parents must bear the burden of showing that the change of custody to them is in the child's best interests. *Shortridge v. Deel*, 224 Va. 589, 299 S.E.2d 500 (1983). In *Shortridge*, the natural mother asked another woman to take her baby at some point during her pregnancy. Once the child was born, the natural mother did not remove her from the foster mother's home for 17 months. The foster mother had taken custody only upon the assurance of the natural mother that she would not want the baby back, and had nourished him to good health. Although the natural parents had married and stabilized their lives by the time of trial, custody was not transferred since the child was thriving with the foster parents. *See also Harry v. Fisher*, 216 Va. 530, 221 S.E.2d 118 (1976); *Szemler v. Clements*, 214 Va. 639, 202 S.E.2d 880 (1974).

Revocation of consent after the petition for adoption has been filed does not divest the court of its jurisdiction. *Szemler v. Clements*, 214 Va. 639, 643, 202 S.E.2d 880, 884 (1974). Thus, the trial court was free to find that custody should be continued in the prospective adoptive parents since a change to the natural parents would be detrimental to the child, and an interlocutory order of adoption was correctly entered.

See generally Margaret F. Brinig, *The Effect of Transaction Costs on the Market for Babies*, 18 Seton Hall Legis. J. 553 (1994) (discussing the relationship between the length of the consent revocation period and the number of completed adoptions).

## § 6.11    Consent of Minor Parent

Even though a natural parent is less than age 18, a valid consent may be given relinquishing a child for adoption and terminating all parental duties and rights. Va. Code §§ 63.2-1202(B) and 63.2-1222.

## § 6.12    Procedural Requirements for Termination of Parental Rights

In 1998, through the "Adoption and Safe Families Act of 1997," Congress amended 42 U.S.C. § 671(a)(15)(D), the Social Security Act, and mandated that the health and safety of the child be the paramount concern in child protective actions including foster care and termination proceedings. Va. Code §§ 16.1-281(B) and 16.1-283(E) reflect the Congressional language. The foster care plan required under Va. Code § 16.1-281 must, "if consistent with the child's health and safety," be designed to support reasonable efforts that lead to the return of the child. See *Strong v. Hampton Dep't of Soc. Servs.*, 45 Va. App. 317, 610 S.E.2d 873 (2005) (parental rights termination reversed because foster care plan did not satisfy Va. Code § 16.1-283 requirements). However, efforts to reunite the child with a parent are not required if the residual parental rights of the parent regarding a sibling of the child have previously been involuntarily terminated or the parent has been convicted of certain felonies against the parent's children or members of the parent's household. See *Brown v. Spotsylvania Dep't of Soc. Servs.*, 43 Va. App. 205, 597 S.E.2d 214 (2004); Va. Code § 16.1-281(B). Even without a prior judicial determination such as a criminal conviction, efforts to reunite will not be required if there is clear and convincing evidence that the parent has subjected any child to aggravated circumstances, or has abandoned a child under circumstances that would justify termination of residual parental rights. "Aggravated circumstances" is defined as including torture, chronic or severe abuse, or chronic or severe sexual abuse against the parent's child or a child living with the parent. It includes failure to protect from abuse as well as active conduct. However, the conduct or failure to protect must either show "wanton or depraved indifference to human life," or have resulted in death or serious bodily injury. Such offenses and conduct can also be grounds for termination of residual parental rights under Va. Code § 16.1-283.

Va. Code § 16.1-281(B) does *not* require that rehabilitative services be provided in all cases as a prerequisite to termination of residual parental rights. Following a finding of neglect or abuse, a circuit court is merely required to *consider* efforts made to rehabilitate a parent and to make a judgment call regarding the parent's ability to substantially remedy the underlying problems. *Toms v. Hanover Dep't of Soc. Servs.*, 46 Va. App. 257, 616 S.E.2d 765 (2005) (no duty to provide rehabilitative services to schizophrenic parent prior to parental rights termination under either state law or principles of constitutional due process).

Because the right of a child to its parent's custody is so strong and the privilege of being a parent so fundamental, involuntary termination of parental rights involves substantial substantive and procedural safeguards. *Weaver v. Roanoke Dep't of Human Res.*, 220 Va. 921, 926, 265 S.E.2d 692, 695 (1980); Va. Code § 16.1-283. A parent is entitled to attend or otherwise participate in a hearing to terminate his or her parental rights. See *Haugen v. Shenandoah Valley Dep't of Soc. Servs.*, 274 Va. 27, 645 S.E.2d 261 (2007) (incarcerated parent); *Mabe v. Wythe County Dep't of Soc. Servs.*, 53 Va. App. 325, 671 S.E.2d 425 (2009) (incarcerated parent); *Alvis v. Thornton*, 2018 Va. App. LEXIS 91 (April 10, 2018) (unpublished opinion) (adoption overturned where the father, an incarcerated felon, was denied his request for transportation to the hearing and thereby was precluded from participating at the adoption hearing). A parent must be informed of his or her right to counsel before an adjudicatory hearing on a petition in which a child is alleged to be abused or neglected or at risk of abuse or neglect or a hearing at which the parent could be subjected to the loss of residual parental rights. Va. Code § 16.1-266.

Involuntary termination requires clear and convincing proof that natural parents' rights should be terminated due to unfitness. See *Santosky v. Kramer*, 455 U.S. 745, 102 S. Ct. 1388, 71 L. Ed. 2d 599 (1982); *Rocka v. Roanoke County Dep't of Pub. Welfare*, 215 Va. 515, 211 S.E.2d 76 (1975). A specific finding of unfitness is not required, however, if one of the statutory factors is present. *Knox v. Lynchburg Div. of Soc. Servs.*, 223 Va. 213, 288 S.E.2d 399 (1982). See also *Edwards v. County of Arlington*, 5 Va. App. 294, 361 S.E.2d 644 (1987), where the county's termination of an immigrant mother's parental rights was held not supported by clear and convincing evidence. The termination had been based upon a finding of mental illness on the mother's part. Language difficulties and problems with cultural acclimation significantly affected her ability to function properly. There was therefore no clear and convincing showing that her problems in parenting sprang from a "mental or emotional illness or mental deficiency of such severity that there is no reasonable expectation" that she would be able to care responsibly for the child.

Thus, unfitness must be proven by clear and convincing evidence according to *Bailes v. Sours*, 231 Va. 96, 100, 340 S.E.2d 824, 827 (1986), and according to the United States Supreme Court case of *Santosky v. Kramer*, 455 U.S. 745, 102 S. Ct. 1388, 71 L. Ed. 2d 599 (1982). For example, in *Brittingham v. Commonwealth*, 10 Va. App. 530, 394 S.E.2d 336

(1990), a father's parental rights were permanently terminated when it was not reasonably likely that the conditions resulting in the neglect of the child could be substantially corrected or eliminated so as to allow the child's return within a reasonable amount of time. Kaywood had been sentenced to a 20 year penitentiary term for malicious wounding of his then 10-month-old son. There was no regular visitation between the father and son, and on those occasions when there were visits, the child became visibly upset and clung to the social worker as soon as he entered the room. The child was apparently prospering in foster care, and the father "has not demonstrated any increased ability, or desire" to fulfill his child's needs in the years since their separation. Likewise, in *Helen W. v. Fairfax County Dep't of Human Dev.*, 12 Va. App. 877, 407 S.E.2d 25 (1991), the parents' residual rights to their daughter were terminated after supervised visitation was fraught with conflict between the mother and the child's social workers while the father either would not participate or, when he did, was unable to alleviate the conflict. When allowed unsupervised visitation, the parents repeatedly violated the conditions placed on the visitation and removed the child to unknown locations. During one of these visits, the child, who was multiply-handicapped, inflicted serious injuries to herself. In addition, the parents refused to participate in recommended mental health treatment, in spite of requirements in the foster care service plan and court orders that they do so. Termination was found to be in her best interest. See also *Logan v. Fairfax County Dep't of Human Dev.*, 13 Va. App. 123, 409 S.E.2d 460 (1991) (failure to have child attend therapy and medical appointments, attend school conferences, or visit child in foster care except when threatened with termination of parental rights); *Edwards v. Fairfax County Dep't of Human Dev.*, 1993 Va. App. LEXIS 332 (Aug. 10, 1993) (girls unable to form attachments because they felt abandoned; mother not amenable to accepting services offered her); *Morris v. Fairfax County Dep't of Human Dev.*, 1993 Va. App. LEXIS 422 (Sept. 14, 1993) (mother failed to keep scheduled visits and only occasionally contacted children by phone, failed to plan for return of children after incarceration, and failed to request services available to her after her release); *Gray v. Commonwealth, Alexandria Dep't of Soc. Servs.*, 1993 Va. App. LEXIS 496 (Oct. 19, 1993) (mother abusive; plaintiff father incarcerated and failed to comply with rehabilitative plan); *Gault v. Commonwealth*, 1994 Va. App. LEXIS 49 (Feb. 8, 1994) (failure to follow substance abuse program); *O'Dell v. Department of Soc. Servs.*, 1993 Va. App. LEXIS 380 (Aug. 24, 1993) (mother not able to provide adequate parenting for child, but could only enjoy supervised visitation; child had suffered neglect and abuse from mother and was afraid he would be taken away from foster home); *Hughes v. Department of Soc. Servs. Arlington*

*County*, 1996 Va. App. LEXIS 77 (Feb. 6, 1996) (termination appropriate when mother participated in Satanic cult that still existed at the time of hearings; child doing well in foster care and no longer showing signs of attachment disorder); *Jackson v. Alexandria Div. of Soc. Servs.*, 1995 Va. App. LEXIS 888 (Dec. 12, 1995) (Parental rights should not have been terminated where mother had mastered substance abuse problem while maintaining an unbroken stream of visits with her daughter). Even though the custodial mother acted to alienate the children from their father, he may not act to terminate his own parental rights. *Willis v. Gamez*, 20 Va. App. 75, 455 S.E.2d 274 (1995). A termination proceeding should be brought in juvenile and domestic relations district court, and only after filing of a foster care plan. *Tallent v. Rosenbloom*, 32 Va. Cir. 61 (1993).

An agreed consent order does not qualify as prima facie evidence of the Department's requirement of establishing by clear and convincing evidence that the children suffered abuse, and whether such abuse is reasonably related to the programs offered to the family. *Department of Family Servs. v. Desouza*, 46 Va. Cir. 48 (1998). In the absence of findings of the nature and extent of the abuse, the court could not evaluate whether programs offered to the parents constituted the reasonable or appropriate efforts to rehabilitate them required by Va. Code § 16.1-283. But see *Jenkins v. Winchester Dep't of Soc. Servs.*, 12 Va. App. 1178, 409 S.E.2d 16 (1991), where after 11 years of involvement with the Department, the mother had not progressed to a point where she was capable of functioning as an independent parent. It was appropriate for the county to remove the youngest child from her custody at age three months because "the child would be subjected to an imminent threat to life or health to the extent that severe or irreversible injury would be likely to result if the child were . . . left in the custody of his parent."

Long-term incarceration does not by itself constitute clear and convincing evidence that parental rights termination is in a child's best interest. In *Ferguson v. Stafford County Dep't of Soc. Servs.*, 14 Va. App. 333, 417 S.E.2d 1 (1992), a father's parental rights were terminated after he was imprisoned for two years and then sentenced to life imprisonment on another charge. The court held that "while long-term incarceration does not, per se, authorize termination of parental rights or negate the Department's obligation to provide services, it is a valid and proper circumstance which, when combined with other evidence concerning the parent/child relationship, can support a court's finding by clear and convincing evidence that the best interests of the child will be served by termination." See also *Harrison v.*

*Tazewell County Dep't of Soc. Servs.*, 42 Va. App. 149, 590 S.E.2d 575 (2004) (termination of parental rights of incarcerated father of special needs child).

The "clear and convincing" standard necessary for termination of parental rights is not required by a change of foster care plans from "return to parent" to "goal for adoption." *Padilla v. Norfolk Div. of Soc. Servs.*, 22 Va. App. 643, 472 S.E.2d 648 (1996).

The Virginia Department of Social Services has adopted a Protective Services Manual for use by its local departments. It contains guidelines interpreting the definition of an abused or neglected child. For the statutory definition, see Va. Code § 63.2-100; former Va. Code § 63.1-248(A). In *Jackson v. W.*, 14 Va. App. 391, 419 S.E.2d 385 (1992), these guidelines were upheld over a father's constitutional challenge. The terms "rejecting, intimidating, humiliating, ridiculing, chaotic, bizarre, violent, hostile, or excessively guilt-producing" were not too ambiguous when interpreting types of behavior constituting mental abuse. Nor was a finding that the child abuse charges were "founded" a disposition that required full due process hearings or the criminal standard of proof "beyond a reasonable doubt."

Unfitness may involve abandonment, Va. Code § 16.1-283. Abandonment must be shown by clear, cogent and convincing evidence. Because termination of parental rights is so final and serious, even if abandonment is found, termination may still not be appropriate. *Robinette v. Keene*, 2 Va. App. 578, 347 S.E.2d 156 (1986). In *In re Slayton*, 13 Va. Cir. 511 (1982), a father placed his children in the custody of his uncle when the paternal grandparents, who had been caring for the children, became ill. The father consented to adoption. The mother, who was then incarcerated, objected, but the court allowed adoption by the uncle, noting that she had not sent any letters or cards nor provided or offered financial support during the eight years in question. The court found that broadening the mother-child relationship might well be disruptive to the child.

The burden of proof for a *temporary* showing of unfitness, sufficient to remove the child from the parental home and for placement in foster care, is a preponderance of the evidence. This is because the placement is only temporary and the risk of an improper placement can be corrected by later action. *Wright v. Arlington County Dep't of Soc. Servs.*, 9 Va. App. 411, 388 S.E.2d 477 (1990). For example, in *Accomack County Dep't of Soc. Servs. v. Muslimani*, 12 Va. App. 220, 403 S.E.2d 1 (1991), the trial court erred in not reopening a custody proceeding based upon contradictory evidence casting doubt upon the father's testimony. Finality is important, held the court, but the child's best interests are paramount. In *Muslimani*, the father had admitted to having sexual relations with his 11-year-old stepdaughter, whom he had eventually married.

In cases of temporary placement in foster care, written consent by the foster parents must usually be obtained in advance. However, in cases of emergency placement in a residential institution or shelter, verbal consent must be obtained within eight hours of the child's arrival, and written consent must be obtained within 24 hours. Va. Code § 63.2-900.

Under amended Va. Code § 16.1-253, the court may enter a preliminary protective order removing the child if the allegations of abuse or neglect have been proven by a preponderance of the evidence. If a parent, the child's guardian ad litem, or the social services department objects to the temporary removal, an adjudicative hearing will be held within 30 days, during which protective orders or removal shall be in full force and effect. If abuse or neglect is found in the preliminary removal proceeding, the court may prohibit or limit contact between the child and his parent or other adult occupant of the same dwelling whose presence tends to endanger the child's life, health or normal development. *Altice v. Roanoke County Dep't of Soc. Servs.*, 45 Va. App. 400, 611 S.E.2d 628 (2005) (construing Va. Code § 16.1-278.2(A)(3)). After a finding of abuse or neglect, a dispositional hearing under § 16.1-278.2 shall be scheduled within 75 days of the preliminary removal order hearing. If the child has been placed in foster care, the foster care plan will be reviewed at the dispositional hearing. Any preliminary protective orders entered on behalf of the child shall also be reviewed at the dispositional hearing, and may be incorporated, if appropriate, in the dispositional order. The dispositional order is final, so that an appeal may be taken from it. Permanency planning hearings are to be held within six months thereafter. If an appeal is taken, a stipulation by the child's parents to the apparent correctness of the juvenile and domestic relations court's findings of abuse and neglect is not binding to the extent that the parents' stipulation conflicts with the circuit court's duty to determine what disposition will serve the best interests of the child. *Anonymous B v. Anonymous C*, 51 Va. App. 657, 660 S.E.2d 307 (2008).

If a child is 16 or over, the foster care plan may allow independent living, with assistance, if other permanent alternatives such as return to the birth parents or adoption are not available. Va. Code § 16.1-281. In *Richmond Dep't of Soc. Servs. v. Carter*, 28 Va. App. 494, 507 S.E.2d 87 (1998), the circuit court rejected the Department's proposal to change the foster care plan's goal from reuniting the child and his mother to allowing the child to be adopted. This rejection incorrectly used the "clear and convincing" standard of proof rather than the lower "preponderance of evidence" standard.

The Virginia Code now allows placement with relatives or other individuals if they are willing and qualified to receive and care for the child, are willing to have a positive and continuous relationship with the child in a permanent and suitable home and have the willingness and ability to protect the child from abuse and neglect. Va. Code § 16.281(C1); see also Va. Code § 16.1-252; 16.1-281 et seq.; 2000 Va. Acts Ch. 385. Under Va. Code § 16.1-283(A), DSS has a duty to consider placing a child with relatives before terminating residual parental rights. *Hawthorne v. Smyth County Dep't of Soc. Servs.*, 33 Va. App. 130, 531 S.E.2d 639 (2000). See also *Sauer v. Franklin County Dep't of Soc. Servs.*, 18 Va. App. 769, 446 S.E.2d 640 (1994) (agency seeking termination of parental rights has affirmative duty to investigate all reasonable options for placement with immediate relatives); *Logan v. Fairfax County Dep't of Human Dev.*, 13 Va. App. 123, 409 S.E.2d 460 (1991) (DSS has duty to produce evidence sufficient to enable court to determine whether there are relatives willing and suitable to take custody of child).

If he or she is of the age of discretion, the minor child must also be consulted before parental rights are terminated. *Deahl v. Winchester Dep't of Soc. Servs.*, 224 Va. 664, 299 S.E.2d 863 (1983). A juvenile court investigating alleged child abuse has the authority to appoint a guardian ad litem for the infant in question, according to one circuit court. *In re J.B.*, 19 Va. Cir. 158 (Fairfax Co. 1990). A validly appointed guardian may file a petition for termination of parental rights. *Stanley v. Fairfax County Dep't of Soc. Servs.*, 10 Va. App. 596, 395 S.E.2d 199 (1990), *aff'd*, 242 Va. 60, 405 S.E.2d 621 (1991). In *Stanley*, the Court of Appeals found insufficient evidence for terminating a mother's parental rights for one of her three children because the most recent foster care plan did not recommend termination. Termination was clearly and convincingly shown to be in the best interests of the other two children. However, a "legal custodian," e.g., a relative providing temporary foster care, is not a "guardian," and cannot enter into a custody entrustment agreement with the DSS. Without a valid entrustment agreement, a juvenile and domestic relations court has no jurisdiction to consider a DSS petition for termination of parental rights. *Fredericksburg Dep't of Soc. Servs. v. Brown*, 33 Va. App. 313, 533 S.E.2d 12 (2000). See Va. Code § 16.1-241(A)(4) and Va. Code § 63.2-900.

Abandonment must be intentional. See *In re Adoption of J.J.P.*, 175 N.J. Super. 420, 419 A.2d 1135 (1980). However, a presumption that when a child has been in continuous foster care for two years, it is in the child's best interest to be placed for adoption is constitutional even as to an incarcerated parent. *Keeney v. Prince George's County Dep't of Soc. Servs.*, 43 Md. App. 688, 406 A.2d 955 (1979). Virginia creates such a presumption after six months of foster care, if the parent has not maintained contact with the child; and after 12 months of foster care, if the parent has failed, without good cause, to substantially remedy the conditions that led to the foster care placement. Va. Code § 16.1-283(C). However, termination of parental rights is not automatic or mandatory when a parent goes beyond 12 months without substantially remedying the conditions that led to the foster care placement, because Va. Code § 16.1-283(C) also requires the trial court to find that termination of parental rights is in the best interests of the child. *Roanoke City Dep't of Soc. Servs. v. Heide*, 35 Va. App. 328, 544 S.E.2d 890 (2001) (father only became serious about substance abuse treatment after children's foster care plan goal was changed to adoption; but DSS failed to present evidence sufficient to overcome presumption that children's best interests would be served by not separating them permanently from their natural parents).

The facts will be construed against abandonment, which must be the intention of giving up the child, never to resume or claim the right of interest in it, *Meyers v. State*, 124 Ga. App. 146, 183 S.E.2d 42 (1971) (mother did not abandon child when she placed the newborn in phone booth with money and a bottle and called the suicide "hotline"; and several days later, accompanied by her mother, came to get the baby back). Other forms of unfitness include nonsupport, neglect, or abuse. See Va. Code § 63.2-100.

Statutes enacted in 1989 regarding the experimental family courts were repealed in 1999, including Va. Code §§ 16.1-296.1, 20-96.1, and 20-96.2. There are no longer any such courts, and all appeals from such courts have been completed.

Neither Va. Code § 16.1-277.02(C) nor Va. Code § 16.1-278.3(D) permits a noncustodial parent to petition for *voluntary* relinquishment and termination of parental rights. Both statutes provide a parent with relief from the "care and custody" of a child, but a noncustodial parent is not invested with actual "care and custody" from which he or she can be relieved. *Cartwright v. Cartwright*, 49 Va. App. 25, 635 S.E.2d 691 (2006).

A divorce court lacks jurisdiction to terminate parental rights. *Church v. Church*, 24 Va. App. 502, 483 S.E.2d 498 (1997). Therefore, the divorce court's finding that the parties' child "ha[d] been abandoned by his father; and that it [wa]s in the best interest of the child to terminate [father's] residual parental rights" was void for want of jurisdiction. The court of appeals affirmed even though the parents had apparently agreed that termination was in the best interests of the child.

Competent evidence by a physician constitutes a prima facie showing of abuse or neglect to justify temporary removal of a child from the parents' home. Va. Code § 63.2-1525. Abuse and neglect are cause for termination of parental rights. Abuse and neglect characterized by a willful act or omission or by a refusal to provide any necessary care for a child's health that causes or permits serious injury to the child's life or health is punishable as a Class 4 felony. Va. Code § 18.2-371.1(A). Abuse and neglect characterized as a willful act or omission in the care of a child that is so gross, wanton, and culpable as to show a reckless disregard for human life is punishable as a Class 6 felony. Va. Code § 18.2-371.1(B). See, e.g., *Shanklin v. Commonwealth*, 53 Va. App. 683, 674 S.E.2d 577 (2009) (parent's failure to seek medical attention for child's burns did not show reckless disregard for human life). Va. Code § 63.2-1516 provides that tape recordings may be made of conversations between people who are the subjects of child abuse investigations and child protective services if all parties are aware that the conversation is to be recorded.

A court may terminate the residual parental rights of a parent whose child has been placed in foster care as a result of a court commitment, entrustment agreement, or other voluntary relinquishment by the parent. Va. Code §§ 16.1-283(B), (C). See *Butler v. Culpeper County Dep't of Soc. Servs.*, 48 Va. App. 537, 633 S.E.2d 196 (2006) (court properly relied on entrustment agreement in terminating parental rights, when parent failed to provide written revocation pursuant to Va. Code § 63.2-1223).

Parental rights termination under Va. Code § 16.1-283(B), after a child is found to be neglected or abused and placed in foster care, requires three findings by clear and convincing evidence: (1) parental rights termination is in the child's best interests; (2) neglect or abuse presents a serious and substantial threat to the child's life, health, or development; and (3) it is not reasonably likely that the conditions that resulted in neglect or abuse can be substantially corrected or eliminated so as to allow the child's safe return to a parent or parents within a reasonable period of time. *Kaywood v. Halifax County Dep't of Soc. Servs.*, 10 Va. App. 535, 538, 394 S.E.2d 492, 494 (1990). See *Butler v. Culpeper County Dep't of Soc. Servs.*, 48 Va. App. 537, 633 S.E.2d 196 (2006) (parental rights termination based on parent's continued drug use). See also *City of Newport News Dep't of Soc. Servs. v. Winslow*, 40 Va. App. 556, 580 S.E.2d 463 (2003) (termination of parental rights under Va. Code §§ 16.1-283(B) and (C) distinguished).

Parental rights termination under Va. Code § 16.1-283(C) for failure to remedy the conditions leading to a child's foster care placement may require the state social services agency to put forth evidence that it made appropriate efforts to assist the parent in remedying those conditions. *Weaver v. Roanoke Dep't of Human Res.*, 220 Va. 921, 265 S.E.2d 692 (1980) (record contained no evidence of measures taken by DSS to assist parent in remedying his financial inability to support child). See also *Richmond Dep't of Soc. Servs. v. Crawley*, 47 Va. App. 572, 625 S.E.2d 670 (2006) (insufficient evidence that parental rights termination would serve children's best interests, when foster care placement was precipitated by loving mother's poverty, hospitalization, and marital circumstances); *Akers v. Fauquier County Dep't of Soc. Servs.*, 44 Va. App. 247, 604 S.E.2d 737 (2004) (agency not required to provide services following approval of plan for permanent foster care); *C. S. v. Virginia Beach Dep't of Soc. Servs.*, 41 Va. App. 557, 586 S.E.2d 884 (2003) (insufficient evidence for termination of parental rights when parent remedied conditions); *L.G. v. Amherst County Dep't of Soc. Servs.*, 41 Va. App. 51, 581 S.E.2d 886 (2003) (Va. Code § 16.1-283(C) does not restrict court's consideration to events that occurred only during 12-month period after child was placed in foster care); *City of Newport News Dep't of Soc. Servs. v. Winslow*, 40 Va. App. 556, 580 S.E.2d 463 (2003) (termination of parental rights under Va. Code § 16.1-283(B) and (C) distinguished); *Babb v. Scott County Dep't of Soc. Servs.*, 1996 Va. App. LEXIS 41 (Jan. 23, 1996) (unpublished opinion); *Rivenbark v. Fairfax County Dep't of Human Dev.*, 1995 Va. App. LEXIS 459 (May 23, 1995) (unpublished opinion). The very length of time children remain in foster care may indicate that parental rights termination would be in their best interests. For an example, see *Price v. Arlington Dep't of Human Servs.*, 1995 Va. App. LEXIS 902 (Dec. 19, 1995) (unpublished opinion) (six years of foster care). *But see Norfolk Div. of Soc. Servs. v. Hardy*, 42 Va. App. 546, 593 S.E.2d 528 (2004) (parental rights termination was not in children's best interests after children developed strong emotional bond to foster parent). Parental disabilities or conditions that prevent discharge of parental responsibilities and that cannot be remedied within a reasonable time do not constitute a valid legal excuse ("good cause") under Va. Code § 16.1-283(C)(2) for failure to remedy conditions leading to a child's foster care placement, and do not forestall termination of parental rights. See *Richmond Dep't of Soc. Servs. v. L.P.*, 35 Va. App. 573, 546 S.E.2d 749 (2001) (parent's mental retardation); *Lecky v. Reed*, 20 Va. App. 306, 456 S.E.2d 538, 540 (1995) (parent's young age).

Due process does not require in every case that a parent whose rights in a child may be terminated have an appointed attorney if indigent. *Lassiter v.*

*Department of Soc. Servs.*, 452 U.S. 18, 101 S. Ct. 2153, 68 L. Ed. 2d 640 (1981). However, the Virginia Code requires that a parent must be informed of the right to counsel before an adjudicatory hearing on a petition in which a child is alleged to be abused, or neglected, or at risk of abuse or neglect, or a hearing at which the parent could be subjected to the loss of residual parental rights. Va. Code § 16.1-266. Some cases hold that a minor should also have independent counsel. See *New Jersey Div. of Youth & Family Servs. v. Wandell*, 155 N.J. Super. 302, 382 A.2d 711 (1978); Va. Code § 16.1-266. In Virginia, the child must at least be asked his opinion at the hearing. *Deahl v. Winchester Dep't of Soc. Servs.*, 224 Va. 664, 299 S.E.2d 863 (1983) (13-year-old was "of sufficient discretion"). These proceedings are held in an informal setting and are usually uncomplicated. *Lassiter v. Department of Soc. Servs.*, 452 U.S. at 29, 32–33 (1981). The parent and the parent's attorney must be given a copy of the social services' investigation report, Va. Code § 16.1-274. In a trial de novo in circuit court after appeal of a termination proceeding in juvenile and domestic relations court, it was error to place the burden of proving or disproving parental unfitness on the natural parents rather than on the county. *Walker v. Department of Pub. Welfare*, 223 Va. 557, 290 S.E.2d 887 (1982). It was an abuse of discretion for a circuit court to summarily dispose of a mother's parental rights termination appeals from the juvenile court without a hearing on the merits, after the mother failed to fully comply with the circuit court's pretrial orders. *Ange v. York/Poquoson Dep't of Soc. Servs.*, 37 Va. App. 615, 560 S.E.2d 474 (2002).

The trial court is not required to bifurcate termination and custody proceedings, because "the issues of custody and termination of parental rights are so interrelated that to bifurcate the issues may well obfuscate both proceedings." *Etzold v. Loudoun County Dep't of Soc. Servs.*, 1993 Va. App. LEXIS 458, at *7 (Sept. 28, 1993) (custody granted to county with goal of adoption although grandparents petitioned for custody). However, there must be a hearing on termination of parental rights in addition to an abuse and neglect proceeding. *Cogan v. Fairfax County Dep't of Human Dev.*, 1994 Va. App. LEXIS 87 (Feb. 22, 1994) (harmless error in this case).

In *M.L.B. v. S.L.J.*, 519 U.S. 102, 117 S. Ct. 555, 136 L. Ed. 2d 473 (1996), the Supreme Court held that an indigent mother had a right to a transcript necessary for her appeal from an adverse termination decision.

Termination of "all parental rights" includes termination of "residual parental rights and responsibilities," which is defined in Va. Code § 16.1-228 as "all rights and responsibilities remaining with the parent after the transfer of legal custody or guardianship of the person, including but not limited to the right of visitation, consent to adoption, the right to determine religious affiliation and the responsibility for support." *Cage v. Harrisonburg Dep't of Soc. Servs.*, 13 Va. App. 246, 410 S.E.2d 405 (1991). Thus, in *Cage*, once a mother's parental rights were terminated, she could not have contact with her children following adoption. See also *Wright v. Alexandria Div. of Soc. Servs.*, 16 Va. App. 821, 433 S.E.2d 500 (1993) (child had standing, through her guardian, to raise issues on mother's behalf in termination proceeding, but was not entitled as a constitutional matter to maintain some parent-child relationship after termination). Once a termination order has been entered, the natural parents no longer must give consent for adoption. *Shank v. Department of Soc. Servs.*, 217 Va. 506, 230 S.E.2d 454 (1976). Prior to termination of their parental rights, parents must support children who are in the custody of social services or in foster care, but the parents' duty of support ends once a termination order is entered. *Commonwealth Dep't of Soc. Servs. Div. of Child Support Enforcement ex rel. Spotsylvania v. Fletcher*, 266 Va. 1, 581 S.E.2d 213 (2003). Entry of a final, unappealed termination order moots any appeal from an order approving a foster care plan that recommends parental rights termination, because there are no parental rights left to protect once a parent's residual parental rights have been terminated. *Najera v. Chesapeake Div. of Soc. Servs.*, 48 Va. App. 237, 629 S.E.2d 721 (2006).

A parent's rights may be terminated even though the parent objects that placement with the child's paternal grandmother might be possible. *Sauer v. Franklin County Dep't of Soc. Servs.*, 18 Va. App. 769, 446 S.E.2d 640 (1994).

In both the juvenile and domestic relations courts, persons with legitimate interests, as defined in Va. Code § 16.1-241(A), may file petitions involving custody, visitation, support, or control of a child. This standing requirement is to be liberally construed, but shall not include either any person whose parental rights have been terminated by a court order (voluntarily or involuntarily), or any person whose interest in the child derives from or through such person. This includes grandparents, stepparents, former step-parents, blood relatives, or family members. The exception to this limitation is for relatives of children legally adopted by a stepparent. Va. Code § 16.1-241. In other adoption cases, birth parents, parents by the child derives from or through them, lose their visitation and other familial rights. Va. Code § 63.2-1215. See *Crockett v. McCray*, 38 Va. App. 1, 560 S.E.2d 920 (2002) (denial of natural parent's request for post-adoption visitation was proper under Va. Code §§ 20-124.1 and 63.2-1215).

Former Va. Code § 63.1-233, the predecessor of this section, was amended in response to *Thrift v. Baldwin*, 23 Va. App. 18, 473 S.E.2d 715 (1996). In *Thrift*, the Court of Appeals decided that the "legitimate interest" terminology of Va. Code § 16.1-241(A) expressly conferred standing to seek visitation, and remanded to the trial court for consideration on the merits of the paternal grandparents' and older sister's petition.

In cases involving the custody, visitation, or support of a child pursuant to Va. Code § 16.1-241(A)(3), the Juvenile and Domestic Relations district court (J&DR court) may make any order of disposition to protect the welfare of the child and family as may be made by the circuit court. Va. Code § 16.1-278.15(A). The J&DR court's authority to consider a petition involving the custody of a child is not proscribed or limited by the fact that the child has previously been awarded to the custody of a local board of social services. Va. Code §§ 16.1-241(A) and 16.1-278.15(B). However, when the J&DR court adjudicates a custody case involving a child subject to a foster care plan, the J&DR court must make the required foster care statutory findings and state those findings in its order. See *Lynchburg Div. of Soc. Servs. v. Cook*, 276 Va. 465, 666 S.E.2d 361 (2008) (J&DR court lacked authority to award custody of child who was subject to foster care plan to child's grandparents under custody-related statutes that authorized award of custody to any petitioning party with legitimate interest).

If a *de novo* appeal is taken from a J&DR court's order granting a petition for involuntary termination of parental rights, and the circuit court grants a request for nonsuit of the termination petition, then any new termination petition must be filed in the J&DR court because the circuit court lacks original jurisdiction over involuntary termination of parental rights. *Lewis v. Culpeper County Dep't of Soc. Servs.*, 50 Va. App. 160, 647 S.E.2d 511 (2007), *overruled in part by Davis v. County of Fairfax*, 282 Va. 23, 710 S.E.2d 466 (2011). See Va. Code §§ 8.01-380, 16.1-241, and 16.1-244.

See generally Levy, *Using "Scientific" Testimony to Prove Child Sexual Abuse*, 23 Fam. L.Q. 383 (1989); Sobelson, *Termination of Indigents' Parental Rights After Lassiter: Ignoring Complexity and Protecting the Best Interests of Psychological Parents*, 16 U. Rich. L. Rev. 731 (1982); Comment, *Termination of Parental Rights in Adoption Cases: Focusing on the Child*, 14 J. Fam. L. 547 (1975–1976); Comment, *Termination of Parental Rights—An Analysis of Virginia's Statute*, 15 U. Rich. L. Rev. 213 (1981).

## § 6.13    Substantive Standards for Termination of Parental Rights

Although the types of physical abuse we will see in Section 15.06 typify grounds for termination, this definition is at once over-and under-inclusive.

Even if the court finds serious abuse has taken place, for termination to occur, the condition must be permanent as well as grave. The parent must not be able to remedy the situation, even with the help of social services. Parental rights are not terminated solely because of abuse. The state may act to permanently sever the parent-child bond when the child is abandoned or neglected as well.

For example, in *Edwards v. County of Arlington*, 5 Va. App. 294, 361 S.E.2d 644 (1987), the termination was based upon a finding of mental illness on the mother's part. Language difficulties and problems with cultural acclimation significantly affected her ability to function properly. There was therefore no clear and convincing showing that her problems in parenting sprang from a "mental or emotional illness or mental deficiency of such severity that there is no reasonable expectation" that she would be able to care responsibly for the child. But see *Jenkins v. Winchester Dep't of Soc. Servs.*, 12 Va. App. 1178, 409 S.E.2d 16 (1991), where after 11 years of involvement with the Department, the mother had not progressed to a point where she was capable of functioning as an independent parent. It was appropriate for the county to remove the youngest child from her custody at age three months because "the child would be subjected to an imminent threat to life or health to the extent that severe or irreversible injury would be likely to result if the child were . . . left in the custody of his parent." See also *Fields v. Dinwiddie County Dep't of Soc. Servs.*, 46 Va. App. 1, 614 S.E.2d 656 (2005) (termination upheld when schizophrenic mother remedied living conditions but remained unwilling to accept mental illness and obtain necessary treatment); *Lecky v. Reed*, 20 Va. App. 306, 456 S.E.2d 538 (1995) (termination upheld when 14-year-old mother was given reasonable time to correct unfitness); *Midgette v. City of Va. Beach*, 1995 Va. App. LEXIS 216 (Mar. 7, 1995) (termination upheld even though children entered foster care only upon mother's voluntary hospitalization); *Frye v. Winchester Dep't of Soc. Servs.*, 1993 Va. App. LEXIS 235 (June 29, 1993) (termination upheld even though parents not at fault since mentally retarded).

A birth father's consent to an adoption is not necessary when the birth father committed rape, statutory rape, or incest; the child was conceived as a result of the crime; and the father was convicted of the crime. Va. Code § 63.2-1202(F). Furthermore, the convicted birth father is not within the definition of a "person with a legitimate interest" who may assert custody or visitation claims concerning the child. Va. Code §§ 16.1-241, 18.2-61, 18.2-63, and subsection B of § 18.2-366. These statutes, which previously had addressed only the father's conviction under Virginia law, were amended in 2005 to include a father's conviction for an equivalent offense of another state, the United States, or any foreign jurisdiction.

The Virginia Department of Social Services has adopted a Protective Services Manual for use by its local departments. It contains guidelines interpreting the definition of an abused or neglected child. For the statutory definition, see Va. Code § 63.2-100; former Va. Code § 63.1-248(A). In *Jackson v. W.*, 14 Va. App. 391, 419 S.E.2d 385 (1992), these guidelines were upheld over a father's constitutional challenge. The terms "rejecting, intimidating, humiliating, ridiculing, chaotic, bizarre, violent, hostile, or excessively guilt-producing" were not too ambiguous when interpreting types of behavior constituting mental abuse. Under § 16.1-253, the court may enter a preliminary protective order removing the child if the allegations of abuse or neglect have been proven by a preponderance of the evidence. If a parent, the child's guardian ad litem, or the social services department objects to the temporary removal, an adjudicative hearing will be held within 30 days, during which protective orders or removal shall be in full force and effect.

Unfitness may involve abandonment, Va. Code § 16.1-283. Abandonment must be shown by clear, cogent and convincing evidence. And, because termination of parental rights is so final and serious, even if abandonment is found, termination may still not be appropriate. *Robinette v. Keene*, 2 Va. App. 578, 347 S.E.2d 156 (1986). However, in *In re Slayton*, 13 Va. Cir. 511 (Henrico Co. 1982), a father placed his children in the custody of his uncle when the paternal grandparents, who had been caring for the children, became ill. The father consented to adoption. The mother, who was then incarcerated, objected, but the court allowed adoption by the uncle, noting that she had not sent any letters or cards nor provided or offered financial support during the eight years in question. The court found that broadening the mother-child relationship might well be disruptive to the child. Abandonment justifying termination may also occur if the parent of a child in foster care fails to maintain continuing contact with the child for six months. Va. Code § 16.1-283. If a parent safely delivers a child within 14 days of birth to a hospital that provides 24-hour emergency services or to an attended rescue squad that employs emergency medical technicians, the parent has a defense against prosecution or civil action based on abuse or neglect, but for purposes of terminating parental rights and placement for adoption, a court may find the child a neglected child upon the ground of abandonment. Va. Code §§ 16.1-228, 18.2-371.

## § 6.14 Due Process and the Termination of Parental Rights

In *Farrell v. Warren County Dep't of Soc. Servs.*, 59 Va. App. 375, 719 S.E.2d 329 (2012), the father appealed the termination of his parental rights arguing that the trial court erred in upholding the constitutionality of Va. Code Ann. § 16.1-283(B) insofar as the law allows termination of parental rights based on a trial court's finding of abuse or neglect by the preponderance of the evidence. An appellate court is not permitted to conduct a trial *de novo* on appeal to second guess a trial court's credibility determination. However, because the argument required the appellate court to interpret a statute's compliance with the Due Process Clause, the court had to apply a *de novo* standard based on the law. Due Process Clause, U.S. Const. amend. XIV.

When a state infringes upon a parent's constitutional right to the companionship of his or her child in order to protect the child from abuse and neglect, it must satisfy the mandates of procedural due process, which requires that a department of social services prove each of the necessary allegations of parental unfitness by *clear and convincing* evidence. Due Process Clause, U.S. Const. amend. XIV.

Upon reading the statute, the appellate court held the statute complied with the Due Process Clause. Va. Code Ann. § 16.1-283(B) requires a social services department to prove, based upon *clear and convincing* evidence, that termination is in the best interests of the child and that: (1) the neglect or abuse suffered by such child presented a serious and substantial threat to his life, health or development; and (2) it is not reasonably likely that the conditions which resulted in such neglect or abuse can be substantially corrected or eliminated so as to allow the child's safe return to his parent or parents within a reasonable period of time. The court further held that the father ignored the plain language of the statute that required the trial court to find that the abuse or neglect rose to a level that presented a substantial threat to the child's life, health, or development, and further required that the finding be made upon a showing of *clear and convincing* evidence. Va. Code Ann. § 16.1-283(B).

See also *Copeland v. Todd*, 282 Va. 183, 715 S.E.2d 11 (2011) (in determining custody, court shall give primary consideration to best interests of the child, however, meaning of best interests of child is different in context of adoptions and must be read in light of biological parent's due process rights in relationship to the child); *Fauquier County Dep't of Soc. Servs. v. Ridgeway*, 59 Va. App. 185, 717 S.E.2d 811 (2011) (when considering termination of parental rights, paramount consideration of trial court is child's best interests); *Switzer v. Fridley*, 2011 Va. App. LEXIS 286

(Sept. 27, 2011) (although presumption favoring parent over non-parent is strong, it is rebutted when certain factors, such as parental unfitness, are established by clear and convincing evidence).

## § 6.15    Restoration of Parental Rights

In 2013, the Legislature created a procedure for restoring parental rights to a parent whose rights were previously terminated under certain limited circumstances. Under Va. Code § 16.1-283.2(A), if a child is in the custody of the local department of social services and a pre-adoptive parent or parents have not been identified and approved for the child, the child's guardian ad litem or the local board of social services may file a petition to restore the previously terminated parental rights of the child's parent under the following circumstances:

1.  The child is at least 14 years of age;

2.  The child was previously adjudicated to be an abused or neglected child, child in need of services, child in need of supervision, or delinquent child;

3.  The parent's rights were terminated under a final order pursuant to subsection B, C, or D of Va. Code § 16.1-283 at least two years prior to the filing of the petition to restore parental rights;

4.  The child has not achieved his permanency goal or the permanency goal was achieved but not sustained; and

5.  The child, if he is 14 years of age or older, and the parent whose rights are to be reinstated consent to the restoration of the parental rights.

The court may accept a petition involving a child younger than 14 years of age if the child is the sibling of a child for whom a petition for restoration of parental rights has been filed and meets all other criteria for restoration of parental rights set forth above, or the child's guardian ad litem and the local department of social services jointly file the petition for restoration. Va. Code § 16.1-283(B).

## § 6.16    Unwed Fathers

Consent of a father whose child was born out of wedlock must be sought if the parents acknowledged paternity under Va. Code § 20-49.1, if paternity has been adjudicated, or if the father has registered as a putative father. Va. Code § 63.2-1202(C); see Va. Code § 63.2-1249 et seq. (Putative Father Registry). An agency entrustment agreement is valid without the father's signature if the father's identity is not ascertainable or the father failed to register with the Putative Father Registry, but if the father's identity is reasonably ascertainable, he must be given notice to enable him to register. Va. Code § 63.2-1222(B). For example, in *Unknown Father of Baby Girl Janet v. Division of Soc. Servs,* 15 Va. App. 110, 422 S.E.2d 407 (1992), the mother said that she did not know which of several men was the father of her child. After publication of the date of the child's birth together with the woman's name, the unknown father's rights were terminated because the court found that his identity was not "reasonably ascertainable." The court contrasted this case with *Augusta County Dep't of Soc. Servs. v. Unnamed Mother,* 3 Va. App. 40, 348 S.E.2d 26 (1986), where the unwed mother knew but refused to reveal the identity of the father, and notice of termination proceedings by order of publication was required. The court noted that "protection of the privacy rights of the mother and the child under specific circumstances argue well for not requiring publication to notify a mere biological father so that his rights, if any, may be protected." See also Va. Code § 63.2-1203(A)(4) (mother's affidavit sufficient to establish that identity of father not ascertainable unless there is refuting evidence). The consent of the father will not be required if the father is unfit, as where he had shown no interest in the child, not given any support, and failed to have a concrete plan for the child's care. *Commonwealth v. Hayes,* 215 Va. 49, 205 S.E.2d 644 (1974). See also *Quilloin v. Walcott,* 434 U.S. 246, 98 S. Ct. 549, 54 L. Ed. 2d 511 (1978); *Lyle v. Eskridge,* 14 Va. App. 874, 419 S.E.2d 863 (1992) (15-year-old father; adoption not allowed). There can be no irrebuttable presumption that a natural father of an illegitimate child is unfit to have custody. *Stanley v. Illinois,* 405 U.S. 645 (1972). When a child's mother is married to a man who is not the child's father, there is a presumption that the child is the legitimate child of the mother's husband, but if the presumption is rebutted, then consent of the husband need not be obtained. Va. Code § 63.2-1202(D). Beginning July 1, 2007, this rebuttable presumption also applies if the parents contracted an invalid marriage that was in apparent compliance with the law, or if the child was born within 300 days after termination of the marriage or after the date of separation evidenced by a written agreement or decree of separation. Va. Code § 63.2-1202(D)(2) and (3).

A father is not required to appear before the juvenile and domestic relations district court to give his consent to adoption. Va. Code § 63.2-1233(1) (amended in 2007 to remove limitation to child born to unmarried woman). The father must consent under oath and in writing, with advice of his opportunity for legal representation, and he must provide the identifying information required in Va. Code § 63.2-1232(3) unless the court dispenses with the information requirement for good cause. In addition, the mother must give her consent in court if the father does not.

A father may consent to the termination of all of his parental rights prior to the birth of the child. Va. Code § 63.2-1202(I) (amended in 2007 to remove limitation to unwed fathers). No consent is required from a birth parent who has neither visited nor contacted the child for six months before the adoption petition was filed, even if the parent was paying child support, unless there was just cause for the parent's behavior. Va. Code § 63.2-1202(H). See *Todd v. Copeland*, 55 Va. App. 773, 689 S.E.2d 784 (2010) (plain language of Va. Code § 63.2-1202(H) refers to six months that *immediately precede* filing of adoption petition), *aff'd in part, rev'd in part*, 282 Va. 183, 715 S.E.2d 11 (2011).

The parental rights of an unwed father to his daughter who was conceived through *in vitro* fertilization was an issue in *Breit v. Mason*, 59 Va. App. 322, 718 S.E.2d 482 (2011). The unmarried couple were in a long-term relationship and lived together as an unmarried couple. The mother wanted a baby but they were unsuccessful in trying to conceive naturally so they tried assisted conception. The father was the sperm donor and the procedure was successful. Prior to the birth, the parties entered into a custody and visitation agreement. The mother gave birth to a daughter and the father executed an acknowledgement of paternity pursuant to Va. Code Ann. § 20-49.1(B)(2). Both parties signed the application for the baby's birth certificate and the child was given a hyphenated surname combining the mother's and father's surnames. The couple continued to live together for months after the birth during which time the father and his extended family bonded with the child.

When the child was a little over one year old, the mother unilaterally terminated all contact between the child and father. The father filed a custody and visitation petition. The mother filed a motion to dismiss claiming that the father was not the child's legal father. The motion relied on Va. Code Ann. § 32.1-257(D), which provides that donors of sperm or ova shall not have any parental rights or duties for any child conceived as a result of assisted conception, and Va. Code Ann. § 20-158(A)(3), which provides that a donor is not the parent of a child conceived through assisted conception, unless the donor is the husband of the gestational mother.

The JDR district court dismissed the father's custody and visitation petition. The father appealed the dismissal to the trial court and filed a Petition to Determine Parentage and Establish Custody and Visitation. The circuit court, strictly reading the statutes cited by the mother, upheld the lower court's judgment, and the father appealed. Because the case involved a question of law involving the interpretation and application of the statutes, the court applied a *de novo* review of the circuit court's judgment.

The appellate court cited two statutes in support of the father's case. Va. Code Ann. § 20-49.2 provides, in part, that "a parent . . . may commence an action . . . to determine parentage of the child." Va. Code § 20-49.1(B)(2) provides that the parent and child relationship between a child and a man may be established by ". . . [a] voluntary written statement of the father and mother made under oath acknowledging paternity . . . and that the acknowledgement may be rescinded by either party within sixty days from the date on which it was signed . . . ." The statute also provides that "[a] written statement shall have the same legal effect as a judgment . . . and shall be binding and conclusive unless, in a subsequent judicial proceeding, the person challenging the statement establishes that the statement resulted from fraud, or a material mistake of fact." In this case, neither the mother nor the father rescinded the acknowledgment, and neither party claimed that the acknowledgment resulted from fraud or a material mistake of fact.

The appellate court concluded the legislature did not intend to permanently bar a parentage action by a sperm donor under the factual circumstances presented in the record on appeal, including the voluntary acknowledgment of parenthood under oath by the undisputed biological mother and biological father, solely because the mother and sperm donor were unmarried at the time of conception. The court rejected the mother's reliance on Va. Code Ann. § 20-158(A)(3) and held that to impose a permanent bar to a known biological father's petition to determine parentage, where the biological father's sperm was donated for *in vitro* fertilization at the request and with the consent of the birth mother, who voluntarily signed a birth certificate application under oath acknowledging the biological father to be the legal father of the child, results in a manifest absurdity because the intended, biological father of the child could never establish parentage of the child, and such a holding ignores the intent of the legislature to ensure that all children born in the Commonwealth have a known legal mother and legal father. The court reversed the holding of the trial court and remanded the case for further proceedings.

See generally David D. Meyer, *Family Ties: Solving the Constitutional Dilemma of the Faultless Father*, 41 Ariz. L. Rev. 753 (1999); Weinhaus, *Substantive Rights of the Unwed Father: The Boundaries Are Defined*, 19 J. Fam. L. 445 (1981).

## § 6.17  Dispensing with Consent

Consent is not required from any person whose parental rights have been terminated by a court of competent jurisdiction, including a foreign court, and no notice need be given to such persons. Va. Code § 63.2-1202(G). For example, in *Shank v. Department of Soc. Servs.*, 217 Va. 506, 230 S.E.2d 454 (1976) (mother had abused children before parental rights were terminated, and the children were placed in a foster home; only defense to adoption was a showing that prospective adoptive parents were unfit. A dissenting opinion suggested that the natural mother should have the chance to demonstrate that she had been rehabilitated since the original order).

Consent is also not required of a birth parent who, without just cause, has neither visited nor contacted the child for a period of six months immediately prior to the filing of the petition for adoption or the filing of a petition to accept consent to an adoption. Va. Code § 63.2-1202(H). The prospective adoptive parent(s) establish by clear and convincing evidence that the birth parent(s), without just cause, has neither visited nor contacted the child for a period of six months immediately prior to the filing of the petition for adoption or the filing of a petition to accept consent to an adoption. *Id.*

In other cases, the unwed father's identity or whereabouts are unknown, and consent cannot be obtained. Only reasonable efforts need be made to ascertain the father's identity, considering the relative interests of child, mother, and father. Va. Code § 63.2-1203(A)(4). If the identity of the birth father is reasonably ascertainable, but his whereabouts are not reasonably ascertainable, verification of compliance with the Putative Father Registry must be provided. Va. Code § 63.2-1233. If personal service is unobtainable, the circuit court may grant an adoption petition without consent 10 days after completion of the execution of an order of publication. Va. Code § 63.2-1203(A)(2). Requirements for an order of publication under Va. Code § 8.01-317 include mailing a copy of the order of publication to the last known address of the party on whom service is sought in addition to posting the order on the courthouse door and publishing it in a newspaper. Noncompliance will apparently be sufficient to vacate a final adoption order. *Carlton v. Paxton*, 14 Va. App. 105, 415 S.E.2d 600, *reh'g granted, en banc, and remanded*, 15 Va. App. 265, 422 S.E.2d 423 (1992). Not only must the adoption be in the child's best interests, but a continuation of the relationship between the nonconsenting parent and the child must be detrimental to the child's welfare. *Knight v. Laney*, 1996 Va. App. LEXIS 4 (Jan. 11, 1996).

Obviously if both parents are deceased and the child has not yet been placed with an agency, consent is not required. Va. Code § 63.2-1203(B). The circuit court may grant a petition without the consent of a deceased parent when the death certificate is filed with the court. Va. Code § 63.2-1203(A)(3).

## § 6.18     Adoption over Objection of Natural Parent

Va. Code § 63.2-1203 and its predecessors (see former Va. Code § 63.1-225) have long provided that if the parent's consent is unreasonably withheld contrary to the best interests of the child, the judge may nevertheless order the adoption. In 1995, the predecessor of Va. Code § 63.2-1205 (see former Va. Code § 63.1-225.1) was enacted to provide standards for determination of the child's best interests in this context. As enacted, former Va. Code § 63.1-225.1 required the judge to consider whether denying the petition would be detrimental to the child, and specified factors for the judge to consider. The new statute reflected case law standards developed under the prior law when there was no explicit statutory standard. See *Hickman v. Futty*, 25 Va. App. 420, 489 S.E.2d 232 (1997). In 2006, Va. Code § 63.2-1205 was amended to remove the detriment test, and to require the court instead to consider whether granting the petition would be in the child's best interest. The factors for the court to consider were retained, and one more was added, requiring the court to address whether the birth parents were currently willing and able to assume full custody. Under the current version of Va. Code § 63.2-1205, the court is not required to make a specific finding that continuing a parent's relationship with his or her child would be detrimental to the child. *Gooch v. Harris*, 52 Va. App. 157, 662 S.E.2d 95 (2008), *superseded by statute as stated in Crabb v. Jara*, 2009 Va. App. LEXIS 42 (Feb. 3, 2009). However, the Fourteenth Amendment to the United States Constitution requires prospective adoptive parents to prove, by clear and convincing evidence, *both* that the entry of an adoption order over the objection of a nonconsenting parent is in the best interest of the child, *and* that a continuing relationship with the birth parent would be detrimental to the child's welfare. *Todd v. Copeland*, 55 Va. App. 773, 689 S.E.2d 784 (2010), *aff'd in part, rev'd in part*, 282 Va. 183, 715 S.E.2d 11 (2011). Thus, the court of appeals concluded in *Todd* that the trial court must make a detriment to the child determination, regardless of the language of the relevant Virginia statute, before it enters an adoption order, in order to protect the Fourteenth Amendment rights of the nonconsenting birth parent.

Despite father's parental rights not being terminated, the adoption by the paternal grandmother was granted over the father's objection. *Hardy v. Poston*, 2014 Va. App. LEXIS 368 (Nov. 4, 2014).

A similar standard from the District of Columbia, D.C. Code § 16-304, was challenged in *In re Petition of J. O. L.*, 409 A.2d 1073 (D.C. 1979), but, since the stepfather withdrew his petition to adopt, was never resolved by the Supreme Court, 449 U.S. 989 (1981). Virginia not only has required unreasonableness, as the District does, but also that the withholding of adoption serves to harm the child. *Ward v. Faw*, 219 Va. 1120, 253 S.E.2d 658, 662 (1979); *Malpass v. Morgan*, 213 Va. 393, 399, 192 S.E.2d 794, 799 (1972). Cf. *In re Morton*, 25 Va. Cir. 531 (Spotsylvania Co. 1991) (grandparents had custody for eight years; mother successfully objected to adoption). Under Va. Code § 63.2-1241(B) a parent who does not consent to adoption cannot waive reference of the petition to the local director of social services. *In re Reynaud*, 21 Va. Cir. 293 (Stafford Co. 1990) (interpreting former Va. Code § 63.1-231). Due process does not require that a court-appointed social services investigator conduct a formal interview with the parent whose rights are subject to divestment, although it must make a "thorough investigation." *Key v. Beckstoffer*, 1994 Va. App. LEXIS 102 (Mar. 1, 1994) (parent incarcerated).

A schizophrenic mother unreasonably withheld consent for adoption by her parents in *Starrs v. Starrs*, 1997 Va. App. LEXIS 212 (Apr. 8, 1997). A licensed clinical social worker testified that he had seen no cure for the mother's condition and that prognosis for her recovery was "very poor" since she did not consistently adhere to treatment or consume her medications as prescribed. The child had lived with the grandparents since shortly after his birth and had known no other home, while the mother's parental rights to her first-born child were terminated by court order.

In cases where the parents of a child are not married, the consent of the father must be sought if the parents acknowledged paternity under Va. Code § 20-49.1, if paternity has been adjudicated, or if the father has registered as a putative father. Va. Code § 63.2-1202(C); see Va. Code § 63.2-1249 et seq. (Putative Father Registry). An agency entrustment agreement is valid without the father's signature if the father's identity is not ascertainable or if the father did not register with the Putative Father Registry, but if the father's identity is reasonably ascertainable, he must be given notice to enable him to register. Va. Code § 63.2-1222(B). The consent of the father is not required if his identity is known and he is given notice by registered or certified mail to last known address, and fails to object to the proceeding. Va. Code §§ 63.2-1222 (entrustment agreement) and 63.2-1233 (parental placement). The father need not be notified if convicted of rape or statutory rape that resulted in the child's conception. Va. Code § 63.2-1202(F).

In *Ward v. Faw*, a mother had custody of the child after separation, and the father made regular support payments and sent cards and gifts. He had not seen the son, however, for three and one-half years. The child's stepfather was not allowed to adopt although he was unquestionably fit and loving. There was no finding that the natural father was unfit, nor that he had by legal action or conduct lost his rights to the child. See also *Doe v. Doe*, 222

Va. 736, 284 S.E.2d 799 (1981); *Cunningham v. Gray*, 221 Va. 792, 273 S.E.2d 562 (1981) (no evidence presented by natural mother or her new husband that continuation of the limited relationship, with only one face-to-face encounter in eight years, would be disruptive of her well-being); *Jolliff v. Crabtree*, 224 Va. 654, 299 S.E.2d 358 (1983) (father was unable to exercise visitation rights since he did not know mother's location, and had provided no support). But compare *Frye v. Spotte*, 4 Va. App. 530, 359 S.E.2d 315 (1987), where the father deserted his wife and daughters for another woman, taking all the food from the family home and disconnecting the electricity and water, intentionally leaving the family in such necessitous circumstances that his wife was forced to apply for public assistance. In addition, he failed to support the children regularly, and demonstrated recurring incidents of spousal and child abuse, including sexual abuse. The custodial mother whose husband sought to adopt the children therefore demonstrated that a continuing or expanded relationship with the children might well present a threat to their emotional, physical, and sexual well-being. *Id.* at 537–538. See also *In re Buchanan*, 13 Va. Cir. 53 (Washington Co. 1987) (no affirmative steps toward pursuing a father-son relationship; no relationship to continue); *In re Tabb*, 18 Va. Cir. 355 (Chesterfield Co. 1989). In *Linkous v. Kingery*, 10 Va. App. 45, 390 S.E.2d 188 (1990), the court allowed a stepparent adoption over the objection of a natural father who had been incarcerated for armed robbery and who had committed a further crime while incarcerated. The court noted that not only must the proposed adoption be in the best interests of the child but also that the fit non-consenting parent must be shown to be "obstinately self-willed in refusing to consent" and "acting prejudicially to the child's interest." See also *Winfield v. Urquhart*, 25 Va. App. 688, 492 S.E.2d 464 (1997) (father's consent to adoption was not necessary when he had murdered the children's biological mother and adoption was by the maternal aunt and her husband). The same result would be reached under Va. Code § 16.1-283(E).

In *Gray v. Bourne*, 46 Va. App. 11, 614 S.E.2d 661 (2005), the court allowed a registered sex offender to adopt, despite the objections of the child's incarcerated birth parent. The court concluded that the adoptive parent's prior conviction for aggravated sexual battery of a minor and his failure to timely register as a sex offender did *not* render him ineligible, as a matter of law, to adopt a child. Therefore, pursuant to Va. Code § 63.2-1203, the birth parent's withholding of his consent to adoption was contrary to the child's best interests, given that the trial court had carefully considered all relevant factors under Va. Code § 63.2-1205 before approving the adoption. Subsequent legislation prohibits adoption by any person who has been convicted of a sexually violent offense or an offense requiring registration in the Sex Offender and Crimes Against Minors Registry. Va. Code § 63.2-1205.1, added in 2006; see Va. Code § 9.1-902 (registration).

A very helpful discussion of the general rule concerning dispensing with parental consent can be found in *Hickman v. Futty*, 25 Va. App. 420, 489 S.E.2d 232 (1997). The adopting parents, the Futtys, were the child's paternal grandmother and her husband, and the child had lived with them since she was three weeks old. In *Gooch v. Harris*, 52 Va. App. 157, 662 S.E.2d 95 (2008), *superseded by statute as stated in Crabb v. Jara*, 2009 Va. App. LEXIS 42 (Feb. 3, 2009), the trial court had approved an adoption over a mother's objection on the basis of its determination that clear and convincing evidence demonstrated that the mother was either unwilling or unable to care for the child. The mother appealed on the sole ground that the trial court erred by granting the adoption without a finding that a continuance of the legal parent-child relationship would be detrimental to the child. The court of appeals held that Va. Code § 63.2-1205 no longer requires any specific finding that the failure to grant the adoption petition would be detrimental to the child. The court specifically noted that the mother did not argue any constitutional issues. The *Gooch* court observed that cases rejecting the best interests test as a basis for overriding parents' objections to nonparent visitation were concerned with *fit* parents. See *Troxel v. Granville*, 530 U.S. 57, 65–68, 120 S. Ct. 2054, 147 L. Ed. 2d 49 (2000); *Griffin v. Griffin*, 41 Va. App. 77, 581 S.E.2d 899 (2003). Thus, in *Gooch*, the court of appeals expressly declined to address the constitutionality of the amended Va. Code § 63.2-1205, because the issue was not raised by the parties. Subsequently, the court of appeals decided that the Fourteenth Amendment to the United States Constitution requires prospective adoptive parents to prove, by clear and convincing evidence, that (1) the entry of an adoption order over the objection of a nonconsenting parent is in the best interest of the child, *and that* (2) a continuing relationship with the birth parent would be detrimental to the child's welfare. *Todd v. Copeland*, 55 Va. App. 773, 689 S.E.2d 784 (2010), *aff'd in part, rev'd in part*, 282 Va. 183, 715 S.E.2d 11 (2011). Therefore, in *Todd*, the court of appeals decided that a trial court must make a detriment to the child determination before it enters an adoption order, regardless of the language of the relevant Virginia statute, in order to protect the federal constitutional rights of the nonconsenting birth parent.

Standard adoption procedures must be adhered to even after the court finds that the natural parent has unreasonably withheld consent to adoption. *Crockett v. McCray*, 38 Va. App. 1, 560 S.E.2d 920 (2002). In *Crockett*, an incarcerated mother who unreasonably opposed adoption by foster parents who had cared for her child for four years was able to successfully argue on appeal that the social services' report contained insufficient information for the court to determine that the best interests of the child would be served by entry of the final order of adoption—because the social services' report did not show that three home visits mandated by Va. Code § 63.2-1212 had been performed after entry of the interlocutory order of adoption.

In some cases, a natural parent who is homosexual wishes to prevent the adoption of a child. In *Doe v. Doe*, 222 Va. 736, 284 S.E.2d 799 (1981), the Virginia Supreme Court indicated that a natural mother's objection to adoption by the child's stepmother could prevent his adoption. This was in a case where the natural mother was not only fit but also according to all accounts was an extremely creative and loving parent who maintained an excellent relationship with her son. The court indicated that if custody as opposed to visitation were in question, or at some later point if the child's well-being were threatened by continued contact through visitation, the mother might have to cease living with her lover. Homosexuality per se does not make a parent unfit. *Doe v. Doe*, 222 Va. 736, 284 S.E.2d 799 (1981). Compare the decision in *Roe v. Roe*, 228 Va. 722, 324 S.E.2d 691 (1985), changing custody from a father who lived with his male lover because of the necessarily adverse impact upon the child.

Since Virginia's focus is upon the *child's* rights as opposed to the parent's, the Virginia statute would better withstand constitutional challenge than that of the District of Columbia. The "rights of parents may not be lightly severed but are to be respected if at all consonant with the best interests of the child." *Malpass v. Morgan*, 213 Va. 393, 400, 192 S.E.2d 794, 799 (1972). See generally Wadlington, *The Divorced Parent and Consent for Adoption*, 36 U. Cin. L. Rev. 196 (1967).

### § 6.19 Consent by State Licensed Agency

When the natural parents have relinquished their child to a state licensed agency for adoptive placement, or when the parents' rights have been terminated because of their unfitness, the agency having custody of the child must give consent to adoption. Va. Code § 63.2-1202(C)(2).

### § 6.20 Equitable Adoption

Although some states recognize the concept of equitable adoption, see, e.g., *In re Estate of McConnell*, 268 F. Supp. 346 (D.D.C. 1967), and cases cited therein, Virginia does not. *Clarkson v. Bliley*, 185 Va. 82, 38 S.E.2d 22 (1946). Under the doctrine, when an adult agrees to take a child into the adult's home and adopt, but fails to acquire a judicial decree of adoption, the child may nevertheless recover as would an adopted child from the adult's estate. The action belongs to the child, and those inheriting through the child, not to the adult or those inheriting through the adult.

However, a man who believed he had fathered a child and supported the infant after her birth, even after testing showed that he was not the biological father, had a legitimate interest in the child pursuant to Va. Code § 16.1-278.15, and was granted custody when the child's mother was found unfit. *In re* Davis, Shenandoah Cir. Ct., No. CH 94-275 (1995).

When children were entrusted to a couple who planned to adopt them but the adoption was never completed before the adoptive parents divorced, the husband had no legal obligation to continue supporting the child. *Schalton v. Schalton*, 31 Va. Cir. 47 (1993) (distinguishing *T. v. T.*, found *below*).

Equitable adoption has not been accepted in Virginia because, as in the case of common law marriages, allowing such a remedy would be to invite fraud and collusion. *Clarkson v. Bliley*, 185 Va. 82, at 93–94, 38 S.E.2d 22, 27 (1946).

### § 6.21 Procedure for Adoption

Proceedings for adoption begin with a petition to the circuit court, which may be filed by (1) any person who resides in Virginia, (2) a person who has custody of a child placed by a Virginia child-placing agency, (3) an adopting parent of a child who was subject to a consent proceeding in juvenile and domestic relations district court, or (4) intended parents who are parties to a surrogacy contract. Va. Code § 63.2-1201. In the case of married persons, or formerly married persons who are permitted to adopt, the spouses or former spouses must petition jointly, but if one petitioner is already the legal parent of the child, that petitioner joins in the petition only to indicate consent. Va. Code § 63.2-1201; see Va. Code § 63.2-1201.1 (previously married persons who stood in loco parentis during marriage may adopt in the same manner as married persons). The requirement that both spouses in a marriage must join the petition cannot be waived. *Sozio v. Thorpe*, 22 Va. App. 271, 469 S.E.2d 68 (1996). However, Va. Code § 63.2-1201 has been amended to provide that when an adoption procedure applies to only one of the adoptive parents, it may be waived for the spouse of the adoptive parent to whom it applies.

The petition must contain a full disclosure of the circumstances under which the child came to live, and is living, in the petitioner's home. Va. Code § 63.2-1201. The required consent to the adoption in writing by the natural parents or state-licensed child placement agency must be attached. Va. Code § 63.2-1202. A petition for adoption of a child placed by an agency is filed in the name by which the child will be known after adoption followed by the registration number of the child's original birth certificate. Va. Code § 63.2-1227. A petition for a parental placement adoption must state with documentation that the findings required for such adoptions have been made. Va. Code § 63.2-1237; see Va. Code § 63.2-1232. Documentation that must accompany the petition includes copies of documents executing consent and transferring custody of the child to the prospective adoptive parents, and a copy of the required home study report. See Va. Code § 63.2-1231.

If a child has been properly entrusted to an agency under a notarized written agreement that divests the birth parents of all legal rights and obligations with respect to the child, the agency is then empowered to give the required consent. Va. Code §§ 63.2-1202 and 63.2-1221. Establishing the required consent in a parental placement usually requires that a separate hearing was held in the juvenile and domestic relations district court. Consent proceedings are to be advanced on the court's docket so as to be heard within ten days of the filing of the petition, or as soon thereafter as practicable. Va. Code § 63.2-1230. The court cannot accept consent without making specified findings, including a finding that an agency has conducted and reported to the court a home study of the prospective adoptive home that includes the agency's recommendation regarding the suitability of the placement. If the court cannot make these required findings, it will refer the birth parent to an agency for investigation and recommendation. Va. Code § 63.2-1232. If the juvenile and domestic relations court is satisfied that all requirements have been met with respect to at least one birth parent and the child is at least in its third calendar day of life, the court will accept the consent and transfer custody of the child to the adoptive parents, pending notification to any nonconsenting birth parent. Va. Code § 63.2-1233.

After the petition is filed in an agency adoption, it is referred to the placing agency to conduct further investigation and make a report to the court within 90 days. If the placement was from outside Virginia and no Virginia agency was involved, the petition is forwarded to the director of social services. Va. Code § 63.2-1228. The petition will be forwarded to the agency that conducted the home study in a parental placement, and the court may order an investigation and report, but further investigation at this point is not mandatory if consent was properly executed. Va. Code § 63.2-1238.

The circuit court will issue an interlocutory order of adoption in parental placement adoptions generally and in agency adoptions as necessary. To issue an interlocutory order, the court must be satisfied, after considering the home study or any required report, that all the applicable requirements have been met, that the petitioner is financially able to maintain the child and is morally suitable and a proper person to care for and train the child, that the child is suitable for adoption by the petitioner, and that the best interests of the child will be promoted by the adoption. Va. Code § 63.2-1209. Following the interlocutory order, there is a probationary period of six months during which supervisory visits are conducted by the agency that placed the child or conducted the original home study. Va. Code § 63.2-1212.

After the agency has reported on the supervisory visits made during the probationary period, the court will issue a final order of adoption if it is satisfied that the best interests of the child will be served. Va. Code § 63.2-1213. See *Crockett v. McCray*, 38 Va. App. 1, 560 S.E.2d 920 (2002) (report on supervisory visits is required before entry of final order of adoption). Until there is a final order, the interlocutory order may be revoked for good cause shown at the motion of the petitioner, the birth parents, the child himself or herself by his or her next friend, the placement agency, the Commissioner of Social Services, or the court on its own motion. Va. Code § 63.2-1211. If a name change was requested and the court finds it in the child's best interest, the change will be given effect upon entry of the final order. Va. Code § 63.2-1209. Upon entry of a final order or other final disposition, all records regarding the investigation and the natural parents will be sealed. Va. Code § 63.2-1246. The court may issue a final order directly without an interlocutory order and probationary period in specified circumstances, notably a stepparent adoption, an agency placement when the agency has already performed visits with the child in the custody of the adoptive parents, or an adoption of a child who has been in the physical custody of the adoptive parent for a specified time. Va. Code § 63.2-1210.

If a petition for adoption is filed before a child's 18th birthday, an order of adoption may be issued after the 18th birthday, but then the consent of the adoptee must be obtained. Va. Code § 63.2-1201.

As discussed elsewhere in this chapter, the procedures for stepparent adoptions, close relative adoptions, adult adoptions, and foster parent adoptions are modified to suit the circumstances of these kinds of adoptions. Va. Code §§ 63.2-1241, 63.2-1242.1, 63.2-1243, and 63.2-1229. Separate procedures enable the parties to an approved surrogacy contract to determine the parentage of children conceived under the contract. Va. Code § 20-156 et seq.

## § 6.22    Inspection by State Agency

In an agency adoption, the circuit court will forward a copy of the petition and all its exhibits both to the Commissioner of Social Services and to the agency that placed the child. If the child was placed by an out-of-state agency, the petition will go to the Virginia agency that completed the home study or provided supervision, if there was one, and otherwise to the local director of social services. Va. Code § 63.2-1228. On receiving a petition and order of reference from the circuit court, the applicable agency must investigate and report to the circuit court within 90 days, with a copy served on the Commissioner. The court will then withhold consideration of the petition for 21 days to give the Commission time to review the agency report and notify the court of any disapproval or any recommendations. Va. Code § 63.2-1208(B).

In a parental placement adoption, the initial investigation should be a home study conducted by a licensed or duly authorized child-placing agency prior to the consent hearing in juvenile and domestic relations court. Va. Code § 63.2-1231. In parental placement adoptions when consent has been properly executed, no further investigation and report is mandated at the time the petition for adoption is filed in circuit court. If the court orders investigation at this point, the rules of Va. Code § 63.2-1208 apply. Va. Code § 63.2-1238.

An investigation requested by the circuit court under Va. Code § 63.2-1208 must cover: (1) whether the petitioner seeking adoption is financially able, morally suitable, in satisfactory physical and mental health and a proper person to care for and to train the child; (2) what the physical and mental condition of the child is; (3) why the parents desire to be relieved of the responsibility for the child, and what their attitude is toward the proposed adoption; (4) whether the parents have abandoned the child or are morally unfit to have custody over the child; (5) the circumstances under which the child came to live, and is living, in the physical custody of the petitioner; (6) whether the child is a suitable child for adoption by the petitioner; and (7) what fees have been paid by the petitioners or on their behalf for assistance in obtaining the child. Any report made to the circuit court must include a recommendation for the action to be taken on the petition. The report must also include the relevant physical and mental history of the birth parents, if known, and a statement that all reasonably ascertainable background, medical, and psychological records of the child have been provided to the prospective adoptive parents. The records of the child that have been provided must be listed.

Some of the requirements of Va. Code § 63.2-1231 are similar. A home study must cover: (1) whether the prospective adoptive parents are financially able, morally suitable, and in satisfactory physical and mental health to enable them to care for the child; (2) the physical and mental condition of the child, if known; (3) the circumstances under which the child came to live, or will be living, in the home of the prospective adoptive family; and

(4) what fees have been paid by the prospective adoptive family or in their behalf in the placement and adoption of the child. In addition, the home study must cover whether the requirements of Va. Code § 63.2-1232 for counseling and exchange of information have been met, and the investigating agency's social worker must meet at least once in the course of the home study with the two sets of parents either simultaneously or separately. Under Va. Code § 63.2-1231(B), the home study is valid for 36 months, but a regulation may require an additional state criminal background check if more than 18 months have passed from the completion of the home study.

The circuit court may add additional inquiries under both Va. Code § 63.2-1208 and Va. Code § 63.2-1231. Ordinarily, no investigation is required for either a stepparent adoption or an adult adoption, but the circuit court has discretion to order a Va. Code § 63.2-1208 investigation and report, and in one variety of adult adoption, is required to do so. Va. Code §§ 63.2-1242, 63.2-1244.

After an interlocutory decree of divorce is entered, there is a probationary period during which the adoptive home is reinspected, so that the child can be observed as part of the new family unit. The investigating agency must visit the child at least three times in a six-month period, normally the six months immediately after the placement of the child in the physical care of the adoptive parents or immediately after the interlocutory decree, with the first and last visits at least 90 days apart. All three visits must be in the presence of the child, and at least one must be conducted in the home of the adoptive parents with both parents present, unless a single parent is seeking adoption or one of the adoptive parents has left the home. After these visits, a final report is submitted to the circuit court. Va. Code § 63.2-1212.

See generally Cynthia E. Cordle, *Open Adoption: The Need for Legislative Action*, 2 Va. J. Soc. Pol'y & L. 275 (1995).

### § 6.23   Adoption by Foster Parents

By statute, Virginia has created a network of foster families. Va. Code §§ 16.1-281 and 16.1-282. In exchange for a monthly remission from the Department of Social Services, these families contract to accept children whose parents are unable to care for them on a temporary basis. This may be because the parents have voluntarily placed the custody of the children with a state agency, or because the children have been adjudicated dependent because of the parents' neglect or abuse.

Although the foster parents may have some liberty interest in the custody of the child, *Kyees v. County Dep't of Pub. Welfare*, 600 F.2d 693 (7th Cir. 1979), the overall objective of the program is to return the children as quickly as possible to their natural parents. In addition, the foster parents have contracted for the temporary nature of their custody, and are compensated for their care of the child. *Smith v. Organization of Foster Families for Equal. & Reform (OFFER)*, 431 U.S. 816, 97 S. Ct. 2094, 53 L. Ed. 2d 14 (1977).

Except in cases where a relative acts as a foster parent, see, e.g., *Rivera v. Marcus*, 696 F.2d 1016 (2d Cir. 1982), the state agency retains the right, after hearing, to remove a child for placement with another foster family or for return to the natural parent. This removal may only take place upon court order. Va. Code § 63.2-902.

Of course, children as well as foster parents may develop psychological bonds, particularly after long residence together, that make it in the child's best interests to remain with the foster family. Some foster parents do end up adopting the children whose custody they have been given. See Va. Code § 63.2-1229, for the requirements in addition to the best interests of the child requirement: (1) residence for 18 months in foster home; (2) termination of natural parents' rights; and (3) investigation and report by agency not having custody of the child. See also *Yokshas v. Bristol Dep't. of Soc. Servs.*, 2017 Va. App. LEXIS 286 (Nov. 14, 2017) (unpublished opinion) (finding that foster parents who cared for the child for nine months constituted persons with a legitimate interest despite the child being placed back with the custodial parent and the foster care contract being terminated, and therefore had standing to petition for custody and for adoption).

See generally Karoline S. Homer, *Program Abuse in Foster Care: A Search for Solutions*, 1 Va. J. Soc. Pol'y & L. 177 (1993); Musewicz, *The Failure of Foster Care: Federal Statutory Reform and the Child's Right to Permanence*, 54 S. Cal. L. Rev. 633 (1981); and Michael P. Kennedy, Comment *In the Best Interest of the Child: Religious and Racial Matching in Foster Care*, 3 Geo. Mason U. Civ. Rts. L.J. 299 (1993).

## § 6.24 Care of Children During Trial Period

Before a decree of adoption becomes final, the inquiry becomes whether adoption by this particular family is in the child's best interests. The child at this juncture is in the physical custody of prospective adoptive parents, while legal custody remains with the state agency in most cases. The prospective adoptive parents are responsible for the child's support, education, and care during this interim period, when strong psychological bonds may also form.

Once the child has been placed in the adoptive home, removal from the home is governed by Va. Code § 63.2-1207, and may occur only upon consent of the adoptive parents, upon order of the Juvenile and Domestic

Relations District Court or Circuit Court, pursuant to Va. Code § 63.2-904, or upon order of the court which accepted consent when such consent has been revoked. In *Carter v. Dinwiddie County Dep't of Soc. Servs.*, 1993 Va. App. LEXIS 149 (May 25, 1993), the child's natural mother placed him with the Carters shortly after his birth in December of 1988. The Department officially recognized them as foster parents in February of 1989. When the natural mother terminated her parental rights in 1990, the goal of the Carters' foster care plan was changed to adoption. The parties signed an Adoptive Homes Agreement approved by the Board of Public Welfare. Some time later, the child, who had "special needs," became difficult for the Carters to manage. After "several equivocal requests" for help with the child, the parties agreed to place him in a therapeutic foster home. During this placement the child did well. The Department, after discussion with the Carters, decided not to return the child to them, and instead withdrew consent for adoption. Because the Carters did not appeal, the decision became final. The Carters subsequently filed a petition for custody pursuant to Va. Code § 16.1-241(A)(3), which allows petitions from "parties with a legitimate interest" in the custody of a child. The Carters alleged that as former potential adoptive parents they had standing to sue. On appeal, the Court of Appeals agreed, but found that they had not met their burden of showing that the best interests of the child would be served by changing his custody to them. Ample credible evidence showed that he had caused stress in their household while he had flourished in his new foster placement.

## § 6.25 Social Considerations

A prospective adoptive family's wealth or social position has no bearing upon whether a child may be adopted by them. *Rocka v. Roanoke County Dep't of Pub. Welfare*, 215 Va. 515, 211 S.E.2d 76 (1975). The proper inquiry is whether it is in the child's best interests. The attachments that develop between child and parent remain of paramount importance.

## § 6.26 Permanent Placement Alternatives to Adoption

For quite some time, many states (and the federal government) have struggled to maintain some balance between the child's needs for permanent placement and for connection to racial and cultural heritage. On the federal level, legislation prohibits states from delaying or denying the placement of a child for adoption or into foster care on the basis of the race, color, or national origin of the adoptive or foster parent, or the child, involved. 42 U.S.C. § 671. The Virginia General Assembly enacted legislation that allows permanent placement with relatives or other individuals if they are "willing and qualified to receive and care for the child," are "willing to have a positive and continuous relationship with the child in a permanent and suitable home" and "have the willingness and ability to protect the child from abuse and neglect." Va. Code § 16.1-281 et seq. (added in 2000). For termination of residual parental rights, the child must also consent if he or she is age 14 or older "or otherwise of an age of discretion." Va. Code § 16.1-283(G). The same session of the legislature, in Senate Joint Resolution No. 208, provided for study of kinship care by the Virginia Commission on Youth.

A 2006 enactment requires that when placing a child in foster care, a local board must determine whether the child has a relative who is eligible to become a kinship foster parent. Va. Code § 63.2-900.1(A); see Va. Code § 63.2-900(A). Kinship foster care placements are subject to all requirements of foster care placement, and are eligible for all services related to foster care placement. Va. Code § 63.2-900.1(B). A kinship foster parent can receive payment at the full foster care rate. Va. Code § 63.2-900.1(C).

For academic discussions of the debate on kinship care, see generally Rebecca Hager & Maria Scannapieco, *From Family Duty to Family Policy: The Evolution of Kinship Care*, 74 Child Welfare 200 (1995). At least a few African-American scholars favor kinship care and remain highly critical of trans-racial adoption, particularly because there has been no reciprocal movement to allow black parents to adopt white children. See, e.g., Dorothy E. Roberts, *Killing the Black Body: Race, Reproduction and the Meaning of Liberty*, 136–243 (1997); R. Richard Banks, *The Color of Desire: Fulfilling Adoptive Parents: Racial Preferences Through Discriminatory State Action*, 107 Yale L.J. 875 (1998); Twila L. Perry, *Race Matters: Change, Choice, and Family Law at the Millennium*, 33 Fam. L.Q. 461 (1999).

## § 6.27 Definition of "Relative"

In termination cases, when entering a custody order, a court must give consideration to granting custody to relatives of the child, including grandparents. Va. Code Ann. § 16.1-283(A). The law requires a department of social services to consider all reasonable options for placement with immediate relatives as a prerequisite to a parental termination decision. However, a department of social services does not have a duty in every case to investigate the home of every relative of the child, however remote, as a potential placement.

In *Bagley v. City of Richmond Dep't. of Soc. Servs.*, 59 Va. App. 522, 721 S.E.2d 21 (2012), the mother appealed the circuit court judgment and challenged the validity of the termination of her parental rights because the Richmond Department of Social Services failed to consider granting custody to a couple she described as the child's "relatives" as required by statute. Va.

Code Ann. § 16.1-283(A). The only connection the prospective couple had with the mother's child was that their daughter was dating the mother's brother. The court found this to be a tenuous relationship at best that did not satisfy the statute and affirmed the circuit court's judgment. In a custody context, under the common law, a *relative* means someone related by consanguinity or affinity. Consanguinity is a "relation by blood," *Doyle v. Commonwealth*, 100 Va. 808, 811, 40 S.E. 925, 926 (1902), and between those sharing "a common ancestor," *Surles v. Mayer*, 48 Va. App. 146, 163 n.5, 628 S.E.2d 563, 571 n.5 (2006). Affinity "is the relation of one spouse to the other spouse's kindred." *Brooks v. Commonwealth*, 41 Va. App. 454, 460, 585 S.E.2d 852, 855 (2003).

In *Pilenza v. Nelson Cty. DSS*, 71 Va. App. 650, 839 S.E.2d 116 (2020), Pilenza, the father of a minor child whose parental rights were being terminated, had approved of the custody petition filed by his biological cousin. However, when Pilenza testified that he had been adopted, the Court determined that his biological cousin was not a relative within the meaning of Va. Code § 63.1-1215. *Id.* at 653–54. "Pursuant to Code § 63.1-1215 a person's 'blood connection' and status as a 'relative' ceases to exist once that person is adopted." *Id.* at 655. Therefore, despite having a blood connection, Father's cousin did not qualify as his relative and the cousin could not be considered to take custody of the child when Father's parental rights were terminated.

## § 6.28   Stability of Family

Placement by state agencies or licensed child placement facilities is most often with married couples. This is because it is presumed to be in the child's best interest to have both a father and a mother take part in the child's growth and development. *Adoption of H.*, 69 Misc. 2d 304, 330 N.Y.S.2d 235 (1972). However, Va. Code § 63.2-1225 specifically allows placement with unmarried individuals as well as married couples.

Should a separation occur between the prospective parents, adoption may not be granted since to do so would jeopardize the child's opportunities for being reared in a two-parent home. This negative factor continues despite a declaration by the prospective parents that they are, and intend to remain, friends, since they could stop being friendly, or divorce and remarry, leaving the child with yet another set of parents. *Watson v. Shepard*, 217 Va. 538, 229 S.E.2d 897 (1976). In *Watson*, custody was retained in the foster mother, who was the child's paternal aunt.

## § 6.29    Race

Although one state court held, in *Blackburn v. Blackburn*, 168 Ga. App. 66, 308 S.E.2d 193 (1983), that considering the race of a child or prospective adoptive parent was permissible in granting a change of custody, *Palmore v. Sidoti*, 466 U.S. 429, 104 S. Ct. 1879, 80 L. Ed. 2d 421 (1984), held that it is not. See also *Roe v. Conn*, 417 F. Supp. 769 (M.D. Ala. 1976). Federal legislation also prohibits consideration of race from hindering adoptive placement. 42 U.S.C. § 671(a).

See generally Bonnie Kae Grover, *Aren't These Our Children? Vietnamese Amerasian Resettlement and Restitution*, 2 Va. J. Soc. Pol'y & L. 247 (1995).

## § 6.30    Religious Preference

If the natural parents, in voluntarily giving their child up for adoption, indicate a religious preference, compare *Scott v. Family Ministries*, 65 Cal. App. 3d 492, 135 Cal. Rptr. 430 (1976), or if the child is old enough to have particular religious needs, the prospective adoptive parents may be chosen from the desired religious affiliation, if such are available, *In re C.*, 63 Misc. 2d 1019, 314 N.Y.S.2d 255 (Sup. Ct. 1970). Both of these cases were decided in states, like Virginia, that have religious matching clauses in their statutes.

However, the state agencies or licensed child care facilities may not otherwise discriminate on the basis of prospective parents' religious preference without violating constitutional prohibitions. *Scott v. Family Ministries*, 65 Cal. App. 3d 492, 135 Cal. Rptr. 430 (1976).

See generally *Religious Matching Statutes and Adoption*, 51 N.Y.U. L. Rev. 262 (1976).

## § 6.31    Age of Adoptive Parents

Some cases involve adoption by older parents, whose age more closely resembles that of grandparents. Such adoptions are usually not in the child's best interests since the child has already suffered disruption in life and will need stability through the formative years when the older adoptive parent may die or be in declining health.

In some cases, however, because of an exceptional bond with a particular child, see *In re Haun*, 31 Ohio App. 2d 63, 286 N.E.2d 478 (1972), or if the older parent is related to the child, such adoptions will be in the child's best interests.

## § 6.32    Sexual Preference of Natural Parents

In some cases, a natural parent who is homosexual wishes to prevent the adoption of the child. In *Doe v. Doe*, 222 Va. 736, 284 S.E.2d 799 (1981), the Virginia Supreme Court indicated that the natural mother's objection to adoption by the child's stepmother could prevent his adoption. This was in a case where the natural mother was not only fit but also to all accounts was an extremely creative and loving parent who maintained an excellent relationship with her son. The court indicated that if custody were in question, or at some later point if the child's well-being were threatened by continued contact through visitation, the mother might have to cease living with her lover. Compare the decision in *Roe v. Roe*, 228 Va. 722, 324 S.E.2d 691 (1985), changing custody from a homosexual father who lived with a male lover since there must of necessity be an adverse impact on the child.

## § 6.33    Presence of Siblings

In some cases, there is a question whether one set of prospective adoptive parents is preferable to another where the child's siblings already reside. In such cases, courts will prefer to keep the siblings together, assuming that both sets of prospective parents are fit. See, e.g., *Watson v. Shepard*, 217 Va. 538, 229 S.E.2d 897 (1976) (custody kept in home of aunt where there was also a cousin with whom child had spent most of her life).

## § 6.34    Consent of Child

Va. Code § 63.2-1202(C)(3) provides that consent to adoption is required of a child 14 years of age or over, unless the court finds that the best interests of the child will be served by not requiring such consent. He or she must also be consulted before parental rights may be terminated at the age of sufficient discretion. *Deahl v. Winchester Dep't of Soc. Servs.*, 224 Va. 664, 299 S.E.2d 863 (1983).

## § 6.35    Adoption of Adults

Adoption of an individual who is over 18 years old is permitted in the case of: (1) a stepchild, (2) a niece or nephew whose parents are deceased and who has lived in the home of the adopting parent for three months, (3) any person who had lived with the adopting parent for three months before age 18, or (4) upon showing of good cause, any person who has known the adopting parent for five years (during two of which both parties resided in Virginia) and who is 15 years younger than the adopting parent. Both parties must consent, but no consent from parents is required. Va. Code § 63.2-1243.

The first three types of adult adoption can proceed without the usual investigation and report by social agencies unless the circuit court in its discretion decides to order investigation. For a proposed adoption under (4) above, where the required connection between the parties is merely that they have known each other for five years, the court must order an investigation and report. Va. Code § 63.2-1244.

The entry of a final adoption order which incorporates a name change meets the requirements of Va. Code § 8.01-217, according to Va. Code § 63.2-1243.

If a petition for adoption is filed before a child's 18th birthday, an order of adoption issued after the 18th birthday has the same effect as if the child was still a minor, provided that the circuit court obtains the consent of the adoptee. Va. Code § 63.2-1201.

## § 6.36 Removal from Prospective Adoptive Parents

Should the investigating agency find prospective parents unfit, the child may be removed from their home under Va. Code § 63.2-1207. This should not be accomplished without a prior hearing with opportunities for cross-examination and confrontation except in cases of an immediate threat to the child's health and well-being. In such event, a hearing should be scheduled in the very near future to assure due process. *C.V.C. v. Superior Court*, 29 Cal. App. 3d 909, 106 Cal. Rptr. 123, 130–31 (1973).

## § 6.37 Finality of Adoption

Before 1995, an adoption decree was not subject to attack after six months, except on jurisdictional grounds. *Shank v. Department of Soc. Servs.*, 217 Va. 506, 230 S.E.2d 454 (1976). After 1995, an adoption decree becomes final "for all purposes" after six months, and is no longer subject to direct or collateral attack in any proceedings, for any reason, including but not limited to fraud, duress, failure to give notice, failure of a procedural requirement, or lack of jurisdiction over a person. Va. Code § 63.2-1216. See, e.g., *Thomas v. Garraghty*, 258 Va. 530, 522 S.E.2d 865 (1999) (final adoption decree divested biological parents of all legal rights to child, despite limiting conditions expressed in consent forms, and validity of decree that was not appealed within six months was not subject to attack in any proceedings, pursuant to former Va. Code § 63.1-237, a predecessor statute identical to Va. Code § 63.2-1216). But compare *McCallum v. Salazar*, 49 Va. App. 51, 636 S.E.2d 486 (2006) (father's as-applied constitutional due process challenge to Va. Code § 63.2-1216, based on alleged extrinsic fraud resulting in father's receiving only constructive notice by publication, depended on threshold showing of "actual relationship of parental responsibility" with the child); *F.E. v. G.F.M.*, 35 Va. App. 648, 547 S.E.2d 531 (2001) (with respect to grant of grandmother's demurrer to father's untimely challenge to her adoption of his son, court's application of former Va. Code § 63.1-237, a predecessor statute identical to Va. Code § 63.2-1216, was unconstitutional on due process grounds, and court's adoption decree was void ab initio because of alleged extrinsic fraud and resulting lack of notice to and personal jurisdiction over father. Holding in case was narrowly limited to facts alleged, that: (1) biological father had an established relationship with child, (2) nature of father's relationship with child did not change until after six-month statute of limitation had run, and (3) father had no understanding of content of consent to adoption form that he signed, due to language barrier, and relied on grandmother's representations that consent to adoption form was merely a form for consent to access child's medical records).

Other jurisdictions are finding that adoptive parents may sue agencies that fail to disclose or misrepresent information regarding the adopted children. See, e.g., *Gibbs v. Ernst*, 615 A.2d 851 (1992). Va. Code § 63.2-1216 provides that after six months from the date of the final adoption order, where no appeal has been taken, the order may not be attacked for any reason, including fraud, duress, failure to give required notice to any person, failure of any procedural requirement, or lack of jurisdiction over any person. This rule (adopted in 1995) should prevent cases like the well-publicized *In re Clausen*, 442 Mich. 648, 501 N.W.2d 193 (1993), *aff'd in part, vacated in part & remanded,* 502 N.W.2d 649 (Mich. 1993), in which birth parents were able to regain custody of a child despite the fact that her adoption had been finalized for some time, because the birth father had not given consent.

An adoption could not be revoked by an adoptee who had been adopted at the age of 14 without giving her consent. The adoptive father was a necessary party to the proceeding to set aside the adoption. *In re Dwyer*, 18 Va. App. 437, 445 S.E.2d 157 (1994).

## § 6.38   Special Needs

Since 1974 Virginia has provided for special subsidy payments for children with special needs, such as handicapped or mentally retarded children, to be made to adoptive parents who would otherwise be financially unable to care for such a special child. Va. Code § 63.2-1300 et seq.; see also 42 U.S.C. § 673. Under 2010 legislation, a child who has developed significant emotional ties with foster parents during a year or more of foster care is regarded as a child with special needs for purposes of state-funded maintenance payments. Va. Code § 63.2-1301(B).

## § 6.39 Inheritance Rights of Adopted Child

The adopted child takes as would a natural child through and by the adoptive parent. Va. Code §§ 63.2-1215 and 64.1-5.1; *McFadden v. McNorton*, 193 Va. 455, 69 S.E.2d 445 (1952). The adopted child is thus an heir at law. *Dickenson v. Buck*, 169 Va. 39, 192 S.E. 748 (1938). However, he or she may not be able to take as "issue" of an adopted parent's deceased relatives, *Fletcher v. Flanary*, 185 Va. 409, 38 S.E.2d 433 (1946), or as "heir of the body," see *Newsome v. Scott*, 200 Va. 833, 108 S.E.2d 369 (1959) ("die without heirs" did not include an adopted child), or as a "direct lineal descendant," see *McGehee v. Edwards*, 268 Va. 15, 23, 597 S.E.2d 99 (2004) (Va. Code § 64.1-71.1 does not apply to trusts executed before 1978).

By statute, the adopted child may also inherit from the natural parent, Va. Code §§ 63.2-1215, 64.1-5.1(2), if the adoption is by a stepparent.

Virginia does not, however, permit "equitable adoption." Cf. *In re Estate of Cregar*, 30 Ill. App. 3d 798, 333 N.E.2d 540 (1975), and cases cited therein. Thus, if the adoption is by a relative of the natural parent, the child may inherit only one share rather than both the share received as an adopted child and as a natural relative. See generally Johnson, *Inheritance Rights of Children in Virginia*, 12 U. Rich. L. Rev. 275 (1978).

## § 6.40 Access to Records

Access to records involving the adoption that do not reveal the identity of the natural parents may be obtained by an adopted child after the child turns 18. Agencies providing services to the child or the adoptive parents also may have access to nonidentifying information. Other persons must generally show good cause and obtain a court order to obtain information. Va. Code § 63.2-1246.

However, the agency that made the investigation must attempt to convey medical, psychological, or genetic information, preserving the confidentiality of all parties, to an adult adoptee, adult birth siblings, or either set of parents when a physician or licensed mental health provider indicates that the information is critical. Va. Code § 63.2-1247(C). Moreover, the agency involved in the adoption may exchange nonidentifying information and pictures in accordance with a written agreement by an adoptive parent and a birth parent, unless the agreement has been withdrawn by either party or an adult adoptee. Va. Code § 63.2-1247(D).

When identifying information is requested by an adult adoptee, the Commissioner of Social Services will direct the agency that made the original home study to attempt to locate the biological family and advise family members of the application. The agency will report the results of the attempt to locate and advise the biological family to the Commissioner, including the relative effects that disclosure of the identifying information may have on the adopted person, the adoptive parents, and the biological family. Upon a showing of good cause, the Commissioner must disclose the identifying information. If the Commissioner denies disclosure of identifying information after receiving the report, the adopted person may apply to the circuit court for an order to disclose, which will be entered only upon a showing of good cause. Va. Code § 63.2-1246.

Upon receipt of notice of a decision or order granting an adult adopted person access to identifying information regarding his birth parents from the Commissioner of Social Services or a circuit court, and proof of identification and payment, the State Registrar will mail an adult adopted person a copy of the original certificate of birth. Va. Code § 32.1-261(B). Constitutionality of an Oregon public initiative making original birth certificates available to adult adoptees was upheld in *Doe 1 v. State*, 164 Or. App. 543, 993 P.2d 822 (1999).

For adoptions finalized on or after July 1, 1994, after the adopted child turns 21, the child's birth parents and adult birth siblings may apply to the Commissioner for disclosure of identifying information from the adoption file after an appropriate report and showing of good cause. Va. Code § 63.2-1247(A). While the child is under 18, the adoptive parents or other legal custodian of the child may apply to the Commissioner for disclosure of identifying information about the birth family after a report and showing of good cause. Va. Code § 63.2-1247(B). In parental placement adoptions where consent was executed after July 1, 1994, the entire adoption record is open to adoptive parents, adult adoptees, and the biological parent consenting to the adoption. Va. Code § 63.2-1247(E).

See generally Klibanoff, *Genealogical Information in Adoption: The Adoptee's Quest and the Law*, 11 Fam. L.Q. 185 (1977).

### § 6.41    Visitation by Natural Relatives

In most cases, and unless the child is adopted by a stepparent, visitation with the natural parent will only disturb the new relationships formed by adoption. *Kattermann v. Di Piazza*, 151 N.J. Super. 209, 376 A.2d 955 (1977). Visitation will therefore not be permitted except with the consent of the adoptive parents. Specifically, Va. Code § 63.2-1215 provides that the final order of adoption divests the natural parent of the right to petition any court for visitation. See *Crockett v. McCray*, 38 Va. App. 1, 560 S.E.2d 920 (2002) (court properly refused parent's request for post adoption visitation).

Virginia will apparently follow the tendency of many other states to allow relatives continued contact after a child is adopted by blood relatives. For example, in *In re Adoption of K.B.M.*, 30 Va. Cir. 343 (City of Radford 1993), the circuit court permitted continued visitation by the maternal aunts of an orphan child after he was adopted by his paternal aunt and her husband.

Dale and Nancy Thrift had five children. Her paternal grandparents adopted the eldest. Social Services removed the other four children from their parents' home in early 1990. The Baldwins adopted three of the children. Another family adopted the youngest of these four. The paternal grandparents and eldest child petitioned for visitation with the children who had been adopted by the Baldwins. In *Thrift v. Baldwin*, 23 Va. App. 18, 473 S.E.2d 715 (1996), the Court of Appeals decided that the "legitimate interest" terminology of Va. Code § 16.1-241(A) expressly conferred standing to seek visitation, and remanded to the trial court for consideration on the merits of the Thrifts' petition. Apparently in response to this case, the predecessor of Va. Code § 63.2-1215 was amended in 1997 to provide that except in cases of stepparent adoptions, family members of the birth parents, former stepparents, and stepparents of a child who has been adopted lose all their visitation and other privileges in the adopted child. They cease to be what the statute terms "interested persons."

## § 6.42  Marriage of Adopted Children

Adopted children are subject to the same incest prohibitions as are natural children. Va. Code § 20-38. This is because the incest taboos are partly concerned with the unusual social relationships that might otherwise occur within the family.

On the other hand, adopted children may not marry their natural relatives. Although upon adoption the child becomes the child of the adopting family, the genetic relationship is not changed. Because of the greater tendency for inherited diseases among children of close relatives, marriage between natural relatives, one of whom has been adopted into another family, is prohibited. *State v. H.*, 429 A.2d 1321 (Del. Super. Ct. 1981).

## § 6.43  Close Relative Adoption

A "close relative placement" is an adoption by the child's grandparent or great-grandparent or the child's adult nephew, niece, brother, sister, uncle, aunt, great uncle, or great aunt. In a close relative placement the court may accept the written and signed consent of the birth parents that is signed under oath and acknowledged by an officer authorized by law to take such acknowledgements. Va. Code § 63.2-1242.1. See *T.S.G. v. B.A.S.*, 52 Va.

App. 583, 665 S.E.2d 854 (2008) (revocation of consent to close relative adoption is governed by Va. Code § 63.2-1204).

If the child has continuously resided in the home or has been in the continuous physical custody of the adoptive parent for at least three years, the parental placement provisions do not apply to a close relative placement. The adoption proceeding commences in circuit court, which may waive appointment of a guardian ad litem for the child. No investigation will be made unless the circuit court in its discretion requires it. The circuit court may omit the probationary period and the interlocutory order and enter a final order of adoption. Va. Code § 63.2-1242.3.

If the period of residence or physical custody is less than three years, adoption proceedings begin in juvenile and domestic relations district court and follow a streamlined version of the parental placement provisions. The district court must approve a home study, but it may accept the birth parents' consent without holding a hearing. There is no requirement for a meeting of the adoptive and birth parents with the social worker. Once the district court accepts consent or otherwise deals with birth parents' rights, and appoints the close relative the custodian of the child, proceedings in circuit court are similar to those for a close relative placement with a longer period of residence or custody. Va. Code § 63.2-1242.2.

### § 6.44    Putative Father Registry

A man who registers with the Putative Father Registry before the birth of a child or within ten days after the birth is entitled to notice of proceedings for adoption or termination of parental rights. Va. Code § 63.2-1250(A). Failure to register waives a man's right to withhold consent to an adoption proceeding unless the man was led to believe through the birth mother's fraud that the pregnancy was terminated, the mother miscarried, or the child died. Va. Code § 63.2-1250(C); see also *Chollette v. Keeling*, 2015 Va. App. LEXIS 279 (Oct. 6, 2015) (father was denied the ability to intervene and object to his child's adoption because he was timely mailed sufficient notice (although the father never received this notice), and he failed to timely register in the putative father registry).

Registration is not required if a father-child relationship has been established by acknowledgement, genetic testing, or adjudication, or if the man is a presumed father, or if he commences a proceeding to adjudicate paternity before filing of a petition to accept consent or waive adoption consent, a petition for adoption, or a petition for the termination of his parental rights. Va. § 63.2-1250(B), see Va. Code §§ 20-49.1, 20-49.8, 63.2-1202.

A birth father's lack of knowledge of the pregnancy does not excuse failure to timely register. A father whose identity is reasonably ascertainable is entitled to written notice, either before or after the birth of the child, of the existence of an adoption plan and the availability of registration with the Putative Father Registry. To preserve his rights, the man must register within 10 days from the date of mailing of this notice. Va. Code § 63.2-1250(E).

## § 6.45  Stepparent Adoption

After divorce, adoption of a legitimate child of the marriage by the new spouse of a birth parent requires consent of the other birth parent if living. Va. Code § 63.2-1241(B). Many of the cases discussed in § 6-16 concerning adoption over the objection of a natural parent have involved attempted stepparent adoptions.

A child born to unmarried parents may be adopted by the new spouse of the custodial birth parent without consent of the other birth parent in the circumstances listed in Va. Code § 63.2-1241(C). For example, consent is not required if the child is 14 years of age or older and has lived in the home of the person desiring to adopt the child for at least five years. Va. Code § 63.2-1241(C)(iv). Consent is also not required from a putative father who is neither an acknowledged father nor an adjudicated father nor a presumed father and who failed to register with the Putative Father Registry. Va. Code § 63.2-1241(C)(vi).

In stepparent adoptions, the circuit court may proceed to order the adoption without referring the matter to the local director. Va. Code § 63.2-1241(A), (B), (C), (D). A former stepparent who stood in loco parentis to his or her former spouse's child during marriage, and who could have obtained a stepparent adoption during marriage, may utilize the stepparent adoption procedures after the marriage has been terminated if the parent/former spouse consents. Va. Code § 63.2-1201.1(B).

The court may waive appointment of a guardian ad litem for the child in a stepparent adoption case. Va. Code § 63.2-1241(E).

The adoption by a stepparent has significant legal consequences, and the stepparent cannot simply seek to dissolve the adoption because of custodial difficulties. In an unpublished decision from the Virginia Court of Appeals in *Chand v. Chand*, the circuit court correctly determined that it did not have jurisdiction on the stepmother's petitions to dissolve the stepparent adoptions that had been finalized five years earlier. *Chand v. Chand*, 2016 Va. App. LEXIS 253 (Oct. 4, 2016). Under Virginia law, termination of parental rights is solely covered by Va. Code § 16.1-283, and compliance with the parental termination statutory scheme is jurisdictional. *Id*.

## § 6.46    Post-Adoption Contact and Communication

Contact and communication with the child after the adoption may be arranged by a written agreement between the birth parents and the adoptive parents. Va. Code § 63.2-1220.2(A); see also Va. Code § 16.1-283.1 (post-adoption contact and communications agreement may be considered at permanency planning hearing).

This agreement will be enforceable if it is approved by the circuit court and incorporated into the final order of adoption. Va. Code § 63.2-1220.3(B). However, the finality of the adoption is not affected by any breach of the agreement. Va. Code § 63.2-1220.2(C). A post-adoption contact and communication agreement cannot be required of any parties and cannot be a condition for approving an adoption. Va. Code §§ 63.2-1220.2(D), 63.2-1220.3(C).

The circuit court must determine that approving a post-adoption contact and communication agreement will serve the best interest of the child. Va. Code § 63.2-1220.3(A)(1). An agency that is sponsoring the adoption or has prepared the adoption report must recommend in favor of the agreement, as must the child's guardian ad litem if there is one. Va. Code § 63.2-1220.3(A)(3). The child's consent is required if the child is 14 years of age. Va. Code § 63.2-1220.3(A)(4).

A petition to modify the agreement or to compel compliance with it may be brought by either a birth parent or an adoptive parent, but the court may not award monetary damages for noncompliance. Va. Code § 63.2-1220.4(B). Furthermore, a party's failure to comply cannot affect the consent to the adoption, the relinquishment or termination of parental rights, or the finality of the adoption. Va. Code § 63.2-1220.2(C).

A party requesting modification of a post-adoption contact and communication agreement must establish that (1) there has been a change of circumstances, and (2) the agreement is no longer in the child's best interest. Va. Code § 63.2-1220.4(C).

A post-adoption contact and communication agreement must include acknowledgements (1) by the birth parents that the adoption is irrevocable even if the adoptive parents do not abide by the agreement, and (2) by the adoptive parents that the birth parents have the right to seek enforcement of the agreement. Va. Code § 63.2-1220.2(B). The governing statute does not limit what an agreement may include, but it does specifically authorize provisions related to contact and communication between the child, the birth parents, and the adoptive parents, as well as provisions for sharing information about the child, including photographs and information about the child's education, health, and welfare. Va. Code § 63.2-1220.2(A).

# CHAPTER 7

# Interspousal Torts

## SYNOPSIS

## § 7.01  Interspousal Immunity and Abrogation by Statute

In 1980, the Virginia Supreme Court, in *Counts v. Counts,* 221 Va. 151, 266 S.E.2d 895 (1980), was asked to carve an exception to the doctrine of interspousal immunity. In *Counts,* a wife had hired another man to kill her husband. The attempt failed, although the husband was seriously injured. After the parties were divorced, the husband sued the wife in tort. The supreme court declined to extend the doctrine of *Korman v. Carpenter,* 216 Va. 86, 216 S.E.2d 195 (1975), which had permitted the estate of a wife, who had been murdered by her husband, to sue the committee of the imprisoned spouse. The court reasoned that when there remained a marriage that might be preserved, to allow a tort action might destroy that marriage. 221 Va. at 156, 266 S.E.2d at 898.

In 1981, the Virginia legislature enacted Va. Code § 8.01-220.1, which abolished the doctrine of interspousal immunity for causes of action arising on or after July of 1981. Reasons for abrogating the doctrine are explored at Comment, *The Legislative Abrogation of Interspousal Immunity in Virginia,* 15 U. Rich. L. Rev. 939, 948 (1981). See generally W. Prosser, *Handbook of the Law of Torts* § 122, at 864 (4th ed. 1971).

## § 7.02  What Marriages are Covered by Interspousal Immunity

Interspousal immunity pertains to actions brought after marriage even though the tort occurred before the marriage. *Furey v. Furey,* 193 Va. 727, 71 S.E.2d 191 (1952). The doctrine remains in effect even though the parties are separated and even though they are divorced at the time of suit. *Counts v. Counts,* 221 Va. 151, 266 S.E.2d 895 (1980). See also *Soedler v. Soedler,* 89 Ill. App. 3d 74, 44 Ill. Dec. 425, 411 N.E.2d 547 (1980). See West Digest,

*Husband and Wife* Key No. 205(2). It is also in effect during a voidable marriage, even though the later decree of annulment says the marriage is "void ab initio." *Gordon v. Pollard,* 207 Tenn. 45, 336 S.W.2d 25 (1960). See also *State ex rel. Angvall v. District Court,* 151 Mont. 483, 444 P.2d 370 (1968). See generally Annot., 92 A.L.R.3d 901.

## § 7.03   Exceptions to the Doctrine

The subjects of most tort actions not barred by the statute of limitations in tort would have taken place after the 1981 enactment of Va. Code § 8.01-220.1, abrogating the doctrine. However, for completeness, a few additional words regarding exceptions to the doctrine follow. See, e.g., *Byrd v. Byrd,* 657 F.2d 615 (4th Cir. 1981) (interspousal immunity would not bar federal admiralty negligence action; case brought before the statute).

1.   It has not been a defense to tort suits arising from automobile accidents since *Surratt v. Thompson,* 212 Va. 191, 183 S.E.2d 200 (1971), because of ubiquitous and mandatory automobile insurance.

2.   Even for suits before 1981, if the death of one spouse was caused by the intentional action of the other, and there were no children or grandchildren surviving, the estate of the deceased spouse may bring an action in tort. *Korman v. Carpenter,* 216 Va. 86, 216 S.E.2d 195 (1975), since there was no marriage to be saved, nor union to be preserved, *id.* at 90, 216 S.E.2d at 198.

3.   There may be some other areas where the doctrine does not apply. The first is where the tort did not occur based upon the marriage relationship, but rather upon a coincidental business one, such as that of master and servant, or common carrier and passenger. A Virginia case recognized that when a father owned a bus company, and his child was injured due to the negligence of one of the father's employees, the child could recover in tort. *Worrell v. Worrell,* 174 Va. 11, 26–27, 4 S.E.2d 343, 349–50 (1939). Although many of the ancient bases for the interspousal immunity doctrine[1] are different from the more recent parent/child immunity,[2] the goal of preserving family harmony would not seem to be affected by either suit. See

---

[1] The idea that husband and wife are of one flesh and therefore unable to sue each other, Keister's Adm'r v. Keister's Ex'rs, 123 Va. 157, 177, 96 S.E. 315, 322 (1918) (Burke, J., concurring) (The duties of marriage "forbid the idea that this 'one flesh' may so divide itself that either spouse may sue the other."). See also Korman v. Carpenter, 216 Va. at 90, 216 S.E.2d at 197; Surratt v. Thompson, 212 Va. 191, 194, 183 S.E.2d 200, 202 (1971); 1 W. BLACKSTONE, COMMENTARIES *442 (1809).

[2] See Worrell v. Worrell, supra, 174 Va. at 19, 4 S.E.2d at 346 (idea that the father controlled the family's exchequer).

*Worrell v. Worrell,* 174 Va. 11, 19, 4 S.E.2d 343, 346 (1939); *Counts v. Counts,* 221 Va. at 154, 266 S.E.2d at 896.

4. In places where the doctrine still exists,[3] if an outrageous intentional tort in effect destroyed the family relationship, there would be no immunity defense since the spouse or parent was no longer acting within the marital or familial role. See, e.g., *Lusby v. Lusby,* 283 Md. 334, 352, 390 A.2d 77, 88 (1978) (interspousal immunity; "no domestic tranquility to be preserved"); and *Mahnke v. Moore,* 197 Md. 61, 68, 77 A.2d 923, 926 (1951) (parental immunity; "complete abandonment of the parental relation"); see generally Comment, *Defining the Parent's Duty after Rejection of Parent-Child Immunity: Parental Liability for Emotional Injury to Abandoned Children,* 33 Vand. L. Rev. 775 (1980); Note, *Intrafamilial Tort Immunity in Virginia,* 21 Wm. & Mary L. Rev. 273 (1979). Apparently, according to *Counts,* the Virginia public policy of saving even troubled family relationships if at all possible would preclude such a suit.

## § 7.04 Matters Not Subject to Suit

In *Merenoff v. Merenoff,* 76 N.J. 535, 388 A.2d 951 (1978), the Supreme Court of New Jersey mentioned that despite the court's abolition of the doctrine of interspousal immunity for that state, some subjects would still not be susceptible of suit.

To paraphrase *Merenoff, id.* at 555, 388 A.2d at 961, suits that still could not be brought might:

(1) involve marital intimacy (but cf. *Kathleen K. v. Robert B.,* 150 Cal. App. 3d 992, 198 Cal. Rptr. 273 (1984), where a suit was brought for intentional fraud in failing to warn the prospective sexual partner that defendant was infected with genital herpes; cf. *Stephen K. v. Roni L.,* 105 Cal. App. 3d 640, 164 Cal. Rptr. 618 (1980); *P. v. S.,* 110 Misc. 2d 978, 443 N.Y.S.2d 343 (1981). As noted in *Smith v. Smith,* 205 Ore. 286, 314, 287 P.2d 572, 584 (1955), "[There is an] area in which the intimacy of the family relationship forbids recovery by the spouses."

(2) Related cases might involve such relatively normal marital exchanges as the "uninvited kiss," *Furey v. Furey,* 193 Va. 727, 733 n.5, 71 S.E.2d 191, 194 n.5 (1952) (quoting from *Wait v. Pierce,* 191 Wis. 202, 209 N.W. 475, 482 (1926) (Eschweiler, J., dissenting), or the nonactionable exchange of harsh words in a domestic quarrel not amounting to a cause of action for divorce on grounds of cruelty:

---

[3] Maryland abolished the immunity in Boblitz v. Boblitz, 296 Md. 242, 462 A.2d 506 (1983).

In arriving at this conclusion we are mindful that the rights and privileges of husbands and wives with respect to one another are not unaffected by the marriage they have voluntarily undertaken together. Conduct, tortious between two strangers, may not be tortious between spouses because of the mutual concessions implied in the marital relationship.

*Lewis v. Lewis,* 370 Mass. 619, 351 N.E.2d 526, 532 (Mass. 1976) (abrogating interspousal immunity in automobile accident cases).

(3) Some injuries might be based upon simple domestic carelessness, such as a slip and fall due to a newly mopped floor or an unshoveled driveway. Compare *Wright v. Wright,* 213 Va. 177, 191 S.E.2d 223 (1972), where a child was injured by sharp awnings left in the back yard where she played, with *Merenoff v. Merenoff,* 76 N.J. 535, 388 A.2d 951 (1978), which involved injuries through dangerous instrumentalities such as electric hedge trimmers and highly flammable formica cement.

## § 7.05 Special Considerations

Because the parties are married, there has always been a concern that they might fraudulently or collusively bring an action, especially where insurance was involved. This argument was dismissed in *Smith v. Kauffman,* 212 Va. 181, 182, 183 S.E.2d 190, 192 (1971), since judges and juries are accustomed to making similar judgments regarding credibility in many cases. See generally Note, *Litigation Between Husband and Wife,* 79 Harv. L. Rev. 1650, 1659–63 (1966).

# CHAPTER 8

## Interspousal Contracts

### SYNOPSIS

### § 8.01 Historical Analysis

At common law, husband and wife were one, and that one was the husband. The husband held all his wife's property during the marriage, and in return owed her duties of protection and support. *Vigilant Insurance Co. v. Bennett*, 197 Va. 216, 218, 89 S.E.2d 69, 71 (1955) (interspousal tort case). See generally McDowell, *Contracts in the Family*, 45 B.U.L. Rev. 43, 44–45 (1965). The *feme covert*, or woman under coverture, was legally incapable of contracting with anyone. See *Wynn v. Southan's Adm'r & Heirs*, 86 Va. 946, 948–49, 11 S.E. 878 (1890).

The Married Women's Property Acts, Acts of 1876–1877, ch. 329, ended this general disability by providing:

> A married woman may contract and be contracted with and sue and be sued in the same manner and with the same consequences as if she were unmarried, whether the right or liability asserted by or against her accrued heretofore or hereafter.

(Now codified at Va. Code § 55-36).

However, married women were still incapable of contracting with their spouses. This was because of the inherent unity of the marital relationship, *Atwell v. Gordon*, 135 Va. 264, 273–80, 116 S.E. 386, 388–90 (1923), and also because such contracts might either tamper with the marital relationship or lead to its untimely dissolution.

Today, in a series of cases beginning with *Ficklin v. Rixey*, 89 Va. 832, 17 S.E. 325 (1890) (wife could receive land from her husband in exchange for dower rights); see also *Stonebraker v. Hicks*, 94 Va. 618, 27 S.E. 497 (1897) (wife could purchase land from husband); and *De Baun's Ex'x v. De Baun*,

119 Va. 85, 89 S.E. 239 (1916) (wife could lend money to husband; relationship creditor to debtor), married women are capable of making contracts with their husbands, and vice versa, providing that certain requisites are met. The primary modern concern is the integrity of the marriage relationship.

See generally 9B, Michie's Jurisprudence, *Husband and Wife*, §§ 72–80.

## § 8.02   Validity of Interspousal Contracts

Generally speaking, any agreement which does not promote divorce or separation and does not attempt to regulate the essential incidents of the marriage will be valid so long as the usual requisites of contract are met.

In 1986, Virginia became the first state to adopt the Uniform Premarital Agreement Act, 9A U.L.A. 333 (1986 Cum. Supp.), which is now codified at Va. Code § 20-147 et seq. Va. Code § 20-155 gives married persons rights to make similar agreements during marriage, to be effective immediately upon execution.

Marital agreements must involve rights and obligations that arise from the marital relationship, dealing with rights and obligations between spouses, not third parties; but marital agreements are not limited to agreements made in contemplation of divorce. *Shenk v. Shenk*, 39 Va. App. 161, 571 S.E.2d 896 (2002). In *Shenk*, several businesses that were marital property were converted into the wife's separate property during marriage, after the husband and wife signed a document in which he agreed to assign all of his right, title, and interest in the businesses to her.

## § 8.03   Contracts Promoting Divorce and Separation

A marital agreement will be upheld unless its illegality is clear and certain. Public policy serves "to foster and protect marriage, to encourage the parties to live together and to prevent separation, marriage being the foundation of the family and of society, without which there would be neither civilization nor progress." *Capps v. Capps*, 216 Va. 378, 380, 219 S.E.2d 901, 904 (1975) (*citing Shelton v. Stewart*, 193 Va. 162, 166, 67 S.E.2d 841, 843 (1951). Antenuptial or post-nuptial agreements are therefore void when they tend to encourage or facilitate separation or divorce. *Id.* (*citing Cumming v. Cumming*, 127 Va. 16, 25, 102 S.E. 572, 575 (1920); *Arrington v. Arrington*, 196 Va. 86, 95, 82 S.E.2d 548, 553 (1954)). However, "agreements between husband and wife relating to the adjustment of property rights, even though in contemplation of divorce, are not violative of established public policy unless collusive or made to facilitate a separation or to aid in procuring a divorce." *Capps*, 216 Va. at 380, 219 S.E.2d at 904. In *Capps*, the contract tended to promote a continuation of the marriage rather than a divorce or separation, and was therefore upheld. *Id.* Agreements between husband and wife relating to the adjustment of property rights, even though in contemplation of divorce, are not violative of established public policy unless collusive or made to facilitate a separation or to aid in procuring a divorce. *Id.*

## § 8.04 Contracts Attempting to Regulate Incidents of Marriage

Contracts will not be recognized if they are attempts to change the nature of marriage. Thus, any contract purporting to waive the duty of spousal support during the marriage will be invalid. *In re Marriage of Higgason*, 10 Cal. 3d 476, 110 Cal. Rptr. 897, 516 P.2d 289 (1973), *overruled,* In re Marriage of Dawley, 17 Cal. 3d 342, 131 Cal. Rptr. 3 (1976) (antenuptial agreement). Likewise, there can be no enforceable contract regarding the performance of the usual marital services, such as entertainment, cooking or laundry. *Matthews v. Matthews*, 2 N.C. App. 143, 146, 162 S.E.2d 697, 698–99 (1968); see generally McDowell, *Contracts in the Family*, 45 B.U.L. Rev. 43, 47–54 (1965). These are performed out of duty or for love and affection. See *Cooper v. Spencer*, 218 Va. 541, 238 S.E.2d 805 (1977) (services performed on egg farm when woman thought she was married). However, if an extraordinary duty is to be performed by a spouse, there may be a contract for consideration. *Department of Human Resources v. Williams*, 130 Ga. App. 149, 202 S.E.2d 504 (1973). See generally *Marriage Contracts for Support and Services: Constitutionality Begins at Home*, 49 N.Y.U. L. Rev. 1161 (1974). However, a Virginia wife was not permitted to recover for "healthcare services necessary" during the last year of her terminally ill husband's life. She tried to recover on an implied contract theory, claiming that the services "were not such as would be required . . . as a result of the marital relationship per se" and were "in lieu of provision of same by healthcare professionals." A divided Virginia Supreme Court in *Dade v. Anderson*, 247 Va. 3, 439 S.E.2d 353 (1994), declined to overrule *Alexander v. Kuykendall*, repeating that

> [t]he authorities which allow a recovery on the theory of implied contract seem to us to place the marriage relation on too much of a commercial basis, and to treat the marital relation as any other business association, whereby each expects to obtain material advantage from the marriage. This is not, in our opinion, the true concept of the relation.

*Id.* at 8, 439 S.E.2d at 356. The dissenting opinions noted that the services involved were beyond normal household duties, and that the public policy against commercialization or disruption of marriage was not furthered when the marriage had terminated through death of a spouse.

As noted in the section regarding antenuptial agreements, contracts purporting to limit the duration of marriage are unenforceable.

Likewise, agreements affecting matters of marital intimacy will not be valid subjects of contract. This would include sexual relations, birth control, and the procreation of children. See generally Comment, *Litigation Between Husband and Wife*, 79 Harv. L. Rev. 1045 (1965). Should the parties disagree about such matters, once they have been married, there may be relief through dissolution of the marriage.

Of course, any contract that would be illegal for another reason, such as an attempt to regulate support of the spouses' children, will not be enforceable.

See generally *Marriage Contracts for Support and Services: Constitutionality Begins at Home*, 49 N.Y.U. L. Rev. 1161 (1974).

## § 8.05   Usual Requisites of Contract

Because the parties are husband and wife, they stand in a confidential relationship to one another. McDowell, *Contracts in the Family*, 45 B.U.L. Rev. 43, 59 (1965). Their contracts will be carefully scrutinized to make sure that one party did not have an unfair advantage over the other and that there was mutuality of consideration. *Capps v. Capps*, 216 Va. 378, 381, 219 S.E.2d 901, 903–04 (1975).

Of course there must be agreement between the parties, who must at the time have the mental capacity to contract.

In 1986, Virginia became the first state to adopt the Uniform Premarital Agreement Act, 9A U.L.A. 333 (1986 Cum. Supp.), which is codified at Va. Code § 20-147 et seq. Va. Code § 20-155 gives married persons corresponding rights to execute agreements during marriage, and requires an agreement to be in writing and signed by both parties unless the agreement is incorporated in a court order or is transcribed by a court reporter and affirmed by the parties on the record. In *Flanary v. Milton*, 263 Va. 20, 556 S.E.2d 767 (2002), the Virginia Supreme Court held that property or spousal support agreements made in contemplation of resolving a pending divorce action are subject to Va. Code § 20-155: and that an oral property settlement agreement made between spouses during a deposition in furtherance of a divorce action was not valid, because it was not in writing or signed by the parties.

Marital property settlements entered into by competent parties upon valid consideration for lawful purposes are favored in the law and such will be enforced unless their illegality is clear and certain. *Webb v. Webb*, 16 Va.

App. 486, 491, 431 S.E.2d 55, 59 (1993) (quoting *Cooley v. Cooley*, 220 Va. 749, 752, 263 S.E.2d 49, 52 (1980)). In forming a marital agreement, Va. Code § 20-149 states that the agreement is enforceable without consideration. If an agreement is negotiated after the spouses have separated, they owe no fiduciary obligations to each other. *Barnes v. Barnes*, 231 Va. 39, 41–42, 340 S.E.2d 803, 804 (1986).

See generally Mary Ann Glendon, *The New Family and the New Property* (1981); Lenore Weitzman, *The Marriage Contract* (1981); Marjorie Macguire Schultz, *Contractual Ordering of Marriage: A New Model for State Policy*, 70 Calif. L. Rev. 207 (1982); *Marriage by Contract*, 8 Fam. L.Q. 27 (1974); Judith Younger, *Perspectives on Antenuptial Agreements*, 40 Rutgers L. Rev. 1059 (1988).

# CHAPTER 9

# Property in the Marital Relationship

## § 9.01   Historical Perspective

The marital rights of spouses in Virginia are the legacy of a common law system in which spouses held property "per tout and not per my," *Vasilion v. Vasilion,* 192 Va. 735, 743, 66 S.E.2d 599 (1951): husband and wife were one, and that one was the husband. When a woman married, the use of all her property belonged to her husband, and she had no control over her property whatsoever. *Edmonds v. Edmonds,* 139 Va. 652, 657, 124 S.E. 415 (1924). Upon his death, she regained the property. The only recompense made to her by the law was the dower right: at the husband's death, she held a life estate in the property, or part of it, if there was issue of the marriage.

Since the time of Jefferson, steps have been taken to ameliorate the inequities inherited from the common law system. The Jeffersonian statute permitted the wife to inherit, if there was no will, on the fourth step: after issue, parents, and siblings of the spouse or their descendants. Spies, *Property Rights of the Surviving Spouse,* 46 Va. L. Rev. 157 (1960). The Married Woman's Property Acts had still greater effect, since they allowed spouses to own their own property while under coverture. *Moreland v.*

*Moreland,* 108 Va. 93, 60 S.E. 730 (1908). See also *Moore v. Glotzbach,* 188 F. Supp. 267, 269 (E.D. Va. 1960). In 1956, spouses were made able to inherit immediately after surviving issue. Va. Code § 64-1. In 1982, the rule was amended by Va. Code § 64-1.1 to allow recovery *before* surviving issue, unless there are surviving issue who are not children of the surviving spouse, who then gets one-third.

The 1990 Legislature abolished the rights of dower and curtesy for property vesting after January 1, 1991. Va. Code § 64.1-19.2. Instead, § 64.1-1 was amended to provide that two-thirds of an intestate decedent's estate shall pass to the intestate's children and to their descendants, and the remaining one-third of such estate shall pass to the intestate's surviving spouse. The surviving share may also claim an elective share of one-third of the testate decedent's augmented estate, if there are children, or one-half, if there are no surviving children. Va. Code § 64.1-16. The definition of "augmented estate" appears in § 64.1-16.1. These statutory shares are barred if the surviving spouse willfully deserts or abandons his or her spouse and the desertion or abandonment continues until the death of the spouse. Va. Code § 64.1-16.3. Finally, the surviving spouse may continue to live in the family residence without payment of rent, taxes, or insurance until that spouse's rights in the principal family residence have been determined and satisfied by an agreement between the parties or a final court decree. It is noted that effective October 1, 2012, Va. Code §§ 64.1-01 through 64.1-206.8 were repealed and recodified generally as Title 64.2 § 64.2-100 et seq.

Despite the abolition of dower and curtesy, the Virginia attorney confronts a confusing mosaic of common law and statutory rules, with many exceptions. These are made no less confusing by the equitable distribution law, enacted in 1981, which will be discussed in Chapter 22.

See generally Ann Lacquer Estin, *Love and Obligation: Family Law and the Romance of Economics,* 36 Wm. & Mary L. Rev. 989 (1995); Joan C. Williams, *Married Women and Property,* 1 Va. J. Soc. Pol'y & L. 383 (1994); Glendon, *Marriage and the State: The Withering Away of Marriage,* 62 Va. L. Rev. 663 (1976); Spies, *Property Rights of the Surviving Spouse,* 46 Va. L. Rev. 157 (1960).

## § 9.02   Creation of the Tenancy by the Entirety

When real property is conveyed to husband and wife, a deed must specify that a tenancy by the entirety is intended, or a tenancy in common results. Va. Code §§ 55-20, 55-20.1, and 55-20.2.

For example, a husband and wife owned property as tenants by the entireties. They sold this residence, and the proceeds were used to purchase other real property. When the husband declared bankruptcy, he was unable to claim this second residence exempt as a tenancy by the entirety since the deed did not specify that a tenancy by the entirety was intended, and the proceeds of the sale of the original property lost their character as "proceeds," which could be traced back to the tenancy by the entirety. *In re Manicure,* 29 B.R. 248 (Bankr. 1983).

However, when husband and wife customarily took title as tenants by the entirety, it was reasonable to conclude that the husband acted as the wife's agent when he agreed with a third party that he and the other would jointly bid on property. *Leonard v. Counts,* 221 Va. 582, 272 S.E.2d 190 (1980).

When land was conveyed to two people as tenants by the entirety and they were not married at the time, they held the property as tenants in common even though they were later married. *Vaughn v. McGrew,* 12 Va. Cir. 125 (Chesapeake Co. 1988).

Finally, in *Allen v. Jackson,* 9 Va. Cir. 60 (Nottoway Co. 1987), a woman put a man's name on the deed as co-owner under the false impression that the two had been validly married, and the man died intestate. His personal representative was required to convey back his interest in the property because there was fraud in the procurement of the deed.

Upon a final decree of divorce, property owned as tenants by the entirety becomes property owned by tenants in common by operation of law. Va. Code § 20-111; *Fox v. Fox,* 61 Va. App. 185, 734 S.E.2d 662 (2012).

### § 9.03   Personalty Held by the Entireties

Personalty that is derived from realty held as tenants by the entirety takes on the character of entirety property. For example, a husband and wife owned a home as tenants by the entirety. They sold the home less than twelve months before the husband declared bankruptcy, and the proceeds were held by the wife. The trustee was unable to recover one-half of these proceeds to satisfy the husband's debt since the estate by entireties exists in personalty as well as realty. *Sprouse v. Griffin,* 250 Va. 46, 458 S.E.2d 770 (1995); *Oliver v. Givens, Trustee,* 204 Va. 123, 129 S.E.2d 661 (1963). See also 26 Am. Jur. *Husband and Wife* § 77, pp. 702–03.

Similarly, when a husband owed cabaret taxes, the Internal Revenue Service unsuccessfully sought to collect from rents paid by tenants of husband and wife who held as tenants by the entirety. *Moore v. Glotzbach,* 188 F. Supp. 267 (E.D. Va. 1960).

### § 9.04   Effect on Creditors

When husband and wife own property as tenants by the entirety, the property may not be reached by creditors of either spouse, although it may be available to creditors of both spouses. *Vasilion v. Vasilion,* 192 Va. 735, 742–43, 66 S.E.2d 599 (1951) (citing *Burroughs v. Gorman,* 166 Va. 58, 184 S.E. 174 (1936)). The interest of the wife in entireties property therefore does not pass to the trustee in bankruptcy. *In re Bishop,* 482 F.2d 381, 383 (4th Cir. 1973). When a husband and wife file a joint Chapter 7 bankruptcy petition, and have only individual creditors (apart from their mortgage lender), they may exempt a home they own as tenants by the entirety from their bankruptcy estates, to the extent of their equity in the home. *Bunker v. Peyton (In re Bunker),* 312 F.3d 145 (4th Cir. 2002).

Va. Code § 55-20.2 provides that if a husband and wife convey a family residence held by them as tenants by the entireties to a joint revocable or irrevocable trust, they will have the same immunity from creditors' claims as if the property had remained a tenancy by the entirety, so long as: (1) they remain husband and wife, (2) the property continues to be held in trust, and (3) the property continues to be their principal family residence.

According to the parties' property settlement agreement incorporated into their final divorce decree, Mr. Tribby was to transfer his interest in the jointly owned marital residence to his wife within fifteen days. Although Mrs. Tribby occupied the house following the separation and made payments on the deed of trust, Mr. Tribby never conveyed his interest to her. Instead, he failed to make payments on a loan from the National Bank of Fredericksburg, and the bank obtained a judgment against him. In *Tribby v. Tribby,* 26 Va. Cir. 372 (Spotsylvania Co. 1992), the circuit court found that the property settlement agreement and divorce decree, while binding on the Tribbys, had no effect on third parties. The court reasoned that because the parties held the house as tenants by the entireties, the bank could not reach their home while they were married. After the divorce, however, the bank could extend their judgment lien to Mr. Tribby's interest in the home since the former spouses had become tenants in common. The court noted that Mrs. Tribby could still seek specific performance of the property settlement agreement against Mr. Tribby. She could also obtain damages in an amount equal to the amount of the judgment lien, plus attorney's fees and costs.

## § 9.05    Restriction on Conveyances

When a husband and wife owned property as joint tenants with common law right of survivorship and the husband deserted, the wife conveyed her share to her daughter. The daughter was unable to compel a partition, where the original deed manifestly intended that the portion of the spouse dying should then belong to the cotenant. *Burroughs v. Gorman,* 166 Va. 58, 184 S.E. 174 (1936). This would obviously be true of the spouses as well.

## § 9.06   Division of Marital Property on Divorce

The division of marital property is governed by Va. Code § 20-107.3. Marital property is not limited to property that is jointly titled. See Va. Code §§ 20-107.3(A)(2)(iii) and 20-107.3(B).

When spouses who held property as tenants by the entirety divorce, their property is converted to a tenancy in common. Va. Code § 20-111.

When the wife then continued to live in the home with the children, while the husband paid alimony and child support, and the wife made insurance and mortgage payments, the wife was able to collect for the sums she had expended, since a cotenant discharging an encumbrance is entitled to a ratable contribution. *Jenkins v. Jenkins,* 211 Va. 797, 180 S.E.2d 516 (1971).

## § 9.07   Devolution of Property upon Death

Where husband and wife were joint owners of a home, and the wife died intestate, leaving her father as her only heir, the husband was unable to seek contribution from her share of the realty for expenses of her last illness, since these were necessaries he had a duty to provide. Nor was he able to recover for funeral expenses since these were his own debt. *Hall v. Stewart,* 135 Va. 384, 116 S.E. 469 (1923).

Money spent by the husband for improvement on the jointly held home was presumed to be a gift for the wife's benefit, even though the couple was estranged. *Norris v. Barbour,* 188 Va. 723, 51 S.E.2d 334 (1949). See also *Eaton v. Davis,* 165 Va. 313, 182 S.E. 229 (1935) (husband not entitled to compensation for improvements, nor wife to accounting for husband's use of home after divorce).

In *Connor v. Mooney,* 1998 Va. Cir. LEXIS 559 (Oct. 28, 1998), a husband was in the insurance business with another man. Their partnership agreement was revised to provide that a deceased partner's spouse would not be part of the business unless the surviving partner consented. To provide purchase money for the stock to the provider, each took out life insurance on the other. Mooney did not give his stock to Mrs. Mooney before his death or leave it to her in his will. The court refused to reform the contract made by an experienced businessman in order to benefit his surviving wife.

Va. Code § 55-20.1 provides that when a person causes any real or personal property to be titled, registered, or endorsed in the name of two or more persons "jointly," as "joint tenants," in a "joint tenancy," or other similar language, the persons will own the property in a joint tenancy *without* survivorship; but if the expression "with survivorship," or any equivalent language is employed, it will be presumed that the persons are intended to own the property as joint tenants *with* the right of survivorship as at common law.

## § 9.08 Defeat of Spousal Interests

If a spouse commits a crime in order to inherit the property of the other, he may not profit by the crime, but is rather entitled only to the share held by him otherwise. *Sundin v. Klein,* 221 Va. 232, 269 S.E.2d 787 (1980) (husband not entitled to whole of property held as tenants by the entirety when he murdered wife; rest of property held in constructive trust). Virginia's slayer statute is codified at Va. Code § 64.2-2500 et seq. (formerly Va. Code § 64.1-18). The estate of tenancy by the entireties can be terminated only by the voluntary action of both tenants or the death of one as the result of a cause reasonably contemplated at the time the tenancy is created.

A spouse convicted of illegal criminal activity may be ordered to forfeit to the federal government the proceeds derived from or used in the criminal activity. If these assets have been disposed of or cannot be located, the convicted spouse may be ordered to forfeit substitute property. An innocent spouse may prevent forfeiture of the substitute property if he or she petitions the federal court and establishes that he or she (1) has a legal right, title, or interest in the property that invalidates the forfeiture, or (2) is a bona fide purchaser for value of the property. 21 U.S.C. § 853(a), (p), (n). However, the innocent spouse must show more than bare legal title to property or ownership under state law: he or she must prove some dominion or control or other indicia of true ownership to demonstrate that he or she is not a nominal or straw owner. *United States v. Morgan,* 224 F.3d 339 (4th Cir. 2000). Thus, in *Morgan,* when a husband was convicted of drug activity and money laundering, his wife was unable to halt the forfeiture of substitute assets because she lacked dominion and control over money in a checking account and a certificate of deposit. See also *United States v. Cox,* 575 F.3d 352 (4th Cir. 2009) (former wife who filed successful bona fide purchaser claim to bank account proceeds seized in former husband's criminal forfeiture proceedings was *not* entitled to award of attorney's fees).

In addition to losing property rights by the commission of crime, a spouse may be barred from enjoying statutory inheritance or dower if she wilfully deserts or abandons her husband, and such desertion continues until his death. See *Purce v. Patterson,* 275 Va. 190, 654 S.E.2d 885 (2008) (husband who willfully abandoned estranged wife prior to and during her final illness was not entitled to elective share of her augmented estate); *Brinson v. Metropolitan Life Ins. Co.,* 226 F. Supp. 94 (E.D.N.C. 1963) (not widow for purposes of Federal Employees' Group Life Insurance Act; parties divorced *a mensa et thoro* on grounds of wife's desertion; wife "married" another).

Similarly, when the husband's physical cruelty forced his wife to leave the marital home, he forfeited his statutory curtesy right to share in her estate upon her death, so that he took nothing since she had not provided for him in her will. *Noland's Executors v. Noland,* 13 Va. Cir. 14 (Fauquier Co. 1987).

Although the husband died intestate during the couple's divorce proceedings in *Sprouse v. Griffin,* 250 Va. 46, 458 S.E.2d 770 (1995), the fund made up of the proceeds from the sale of the marital home became a res over which the divorce court had jurisdiction. The wife could therefore seek a rule on the status of the funds the court held in escrow.

## § 9.09  Dower and Curtesy

Va. Code § 64.2-301 abolished the rights of dower and curtesy for property vesting after January 1, 1991. Instead, Va. Code §§ 64.2-302 and 64.2-304 permit a surviving spouse to make elective shares in the decedent's estate. The surviving spouse may also claim an elective share of one-third of the testate decedent's augmented estate, if there are children, or one-half, if there are no surviving children. The definition of "augmented estate" appears in Va. Code § 64.2.-305. See, e.g., *Chappell v. Perkins,* 266 Va. 413, 587 S.E.2d 584 (2003) (determining contents of deceased wife's augmented estate for purposes of establishing husband's elective share). These statutory shares are barred if the surviving spouse willfully deserts or abandons his or her spouse and the desertion or abandonment continues until the death of the spouse. Va. Code § 64.1-16.2-308. See *Purce v. Patterson,* 275 Va. 190, 654 S.E.2d 885 (2008) (explaining that "abandonment," which is defined as termination of normal indicia of marital relationship combined with intent to abandon marital relationship, is analyzed differently in elective share and domestic relations cases). Finally, the surviving spouse may continue to live in the family residence without payment of rent, taxes, or insurance until that spouse's rights in the principal family residence have been determined and satisfied by an agreement between the parties or a final court decree. It is noted that effective October 1, 2012, Va. Code §§ 64.1-01 through 64.1-206.8 were repealed and recodified generally as Title 64.2 § 64.2-100 et seq. Cases before the 2012 amendments will refer to the prior code sections.

Although new dower and curtesy interests are no longer vesting, property conveyed prior to 1991 still retains the incidents of dower and curtesy, so the common law cases are still relevant. This section may be of historical interest, but with the passage of time becomes less relevant to current legal issues. For example, when a woman is married, and the husband held property separately, the wife had a dower interest in that property. This meant that upon his death, the surviving wife would have a fee simple estate in the surplus if there were no issue, their descendants who are not children, or their descendants of the surviving spouse, and one-third of the realty, if there were such issue. Va. Code § 64.1-1. There is a life estate in the entire personal property. Va. Code § 64.1-19. A wife did not obtain a dower interest in the property her husband bought during a bigamous second marriage. Upon his death, his companion acquired his entire estate by right of survivorship, since the couple had purchased the property as "tenants by the entirety." Since the couple was never lawfully married, they took title as joint tenants with right of survivorship. *Funches v. Funches,* 243 Va. 26, 413 S.E.2d 44 (1992).

The husband had similar rights in the wife's separate estate called curtesy, which devolve upon her death. Va. Code § 55-35. Both dower and curtesy were effective only if the spouse has not taken property under a will designed to be in lieu of curtesy (called jointure). Va. Code § 64.1-29.

Where a husband made a postnuptial agreement releasing curtesy and any distributive share in the wife's estate, and the wife released dower, and the wife died intestate with no issue, the husband was not entitled to curtesy since there was no issue but only a foster child, and the postnuptial agreement was valid. *Powell v. Tilson,* 161 Va. 318, 170 S.E. 750 (1933).

Dower rights are cut off by divorce in Virginia. Va. Code §§ 20-107.3 and 20-111 (divorce *a mensa*), even if the divorce is obtained ex parte in another state. *Simons v. Miami Beach First Nat'l Bank,* 381 U.S. 81, 85 S. Ct. 1315, 14 L. Ed. 2d 232 (1965).

## § 9.10    Defeating the Interest of a Spouse

For some time there has been concern that spouses may, by inter vivos gift or establishment of a trust causa mortis, leave no property for a surviving spouse. See Johnson, *Interspousal Property Rights at Death,* 10 Va. B.A.J. 10 (1984); see also Spies, *Property Rights of the Surviving Spouse,* 46 Va. L. Rev. 157, 164 (1960). The commentators suggest that there should be legislation protecting the public policy in favor of the surviving spouse.

## § 9.11    Separately Held Property

Since the Married Woman's Property Acts, both spouses have been able to hold property in their own name.

Women are able to hold property free of curtesy through Va. Code § 55-47, "nothing contained in the previous sections of the chapter shall be construed to prevent the creation of the wife's equitable separate estates."

The husband may also hold property free of dower according to *Jacobs v. Meade,* 227 Va. 284, 315 S.E.2d 383 (1984).

In one case, the husband gave the wife land in Norfolk, upon which an apartment was later built. The couple lived for some years in part of the property, until the wife deserted the husband. She was able to bring a successful ejectment action against the husband, since if the husband has a right to go upon the wife's premises and jointly occupy them with her, it is solely because he has a right of access to *her* because of his marital rights, and not a right of access to her property. *Edmonds v. Edmonds,* 139 Va. 652, 660, 662–63, 124 S.E. 415 (1924). See also *Moreland v. Moreland,* 108 Va. 93, 60 S.E. 730 (1908); *Norris v. Barbour,* 188 Va. 723, 51 S.E.2d 334 (1949). Even though a husband solely owned the marital home, he could not evict his wife when they were in joint possession of the home. In *Singer v. Singer,* 30 Va. Cir. 80 (Fairfax Co. 1993), the court found that "public policy requires a right of access by one spouse to the other during a marriage, and a limited right to go upon, and remain upon the property exists so long as there is a joint occupancy." *Id.* at 82.

## § 9.12   Crimes Against Property of Spouse

Since it is possible for a spouse to hold property separately, it is also possible for one spouse to commit a crime against the property of the other spouse. See, e.g., *Stewart v. Commonwealth,* 219 Va. 887, 252 S.E.2d 329 (1979) (larceny by estranged husband of wife's station wagon); *Knox v. Commonwealth,* 225 Va. 504, 304 S.E.2d 4 (1983) (burglary of estranged wife's apartment).

# CHAPTER 10

## Crimes Involving Spouses and Family Members

### SYNOPSIS

## § 10.01    Historical Perspective

At common law, a man was not subject to prosecution for many actions that would have been crimes if the victim had not been his wife. This was because in law the two spouses were one, and he was the one. The system was not reciprocal. Since the use of all property of the wife belonged to the husband during coverture, it was impossible to steal from her. *Stewart v. Commonwealth,* 219 Va. 887, 889, 252 S.E.2d 329, 331 (1979). One ancient commentator, 1 M. Hale, *The History of the Pleas of the Crown* 629 (1736), fostered the doctrine that since by marrying him the wife had given her consent to sexual intercourse, she could not be a victim of nonconsensual intercourse or rape by her husband. Part of the husband's duties as a spouse were to give his wife moderate chastisement and correction, which could involve beating with a stick so long as the punishment inflicted was reasonable. Pollack & Maitland, *A History of the English Law* 436.

Even a "reasonable" chastisement would be criminal behavior today. A number of developments have changed the common law concepts. Since the wife is now able to hold property in her own name, the husband may commit larceny from her. Certainly since the advent of no-fault divorce, it is possible for a wife to maintain a separate domicile with no access given to the husband. During this period of separation, nonconsensual intercourse will be rape. *Weishaupt v. Commonwealth,* 227 Va. 389, 315 S.E.2d 847 (1984). However, the termination of the marriage must be known by the husband. *Kizer v. Commonwealth,* 228 Va. 256, 321 S.E.2d 291 (1984); Va. Code § 18.2-67.2. Although there are no recent cases, the doctrine of corporal punishment of a wife has probably changed as well with her legal equality of status to her husband, so that there will be more prosecutions for spousal abuse or assault that would have gone unnoticed before. At common law, the woman was to obey the husband in all things, so that if she acted under his direction in committing a crime, she was his agent and he the guilty principal. She will now be guilty in her own right unless coerced by threat of physical violence. Indeed, the defense of coercion may be taking a new form that follows the modifications to the doctrine of self-defense occasioned by emerging concepts of long-term inter-spousal abuse. See *State v. Lambert,* 173 W. Va. 60, 312 S.E.2d 31 (1984).

## § 10.02  Assault and Corporal Punishment of Wives and Family Members

For some time it has been possible for a wife to complain of the assault of the husband. See, e.g., *Counts v. Counts,* 221 Va. 151, 266 S.E.2d 895 (1980).

Although at common law a husband could punish his wife, if the blows inflicted were not reasonable, he was subject to punishment for assault. *Bradley v. State,* 1 Miss. (Walker) 156 (1824); Pollack & Maitland, *A History of the English Law* 436. For the Virginia approach to a similar topic, see *Wimbrow v. Wimbrow,* 208 Va. 141, 156 S.E.2d 598 (1967) (husband divorced for constructive desertion when he severely beat his wife for taking money from his wallet and she left the marital home).

As the Virginia Supreme Court noted in *Weishaupt v. Commonwealth,* 227 Va. 389, 315 S.E.2d 847 (1984):

> The trend in the recent cases which have analyzed problems of spousal rape is in accord with the trend in recent Virginia cases touching upon the property rights of women. Both sets of cases point to an increasingly recognized role of the autonomy and independence of women. Both sets of cases suggest a break with the ancient rules that cast women in a subservient posture.

Virginia has enacted a criminal prohibition against abuse of family and household members that encompasses spousal abuse. Va. Code § 18.2-57.2. The statute penalizes assault and battery of "a family or household member," which includes spouses, former spouses, children, close blood relatives, in-laws who live in the same home as the defendant, persons who are the parent of a child of the defendant, and individuals who have been cohabiting with the defendant during the previous 12 months. Va. Code §§ 16.1-228 and 18.2-57.2. In the domestic abuse context, factors to be considered in determining "cohabitation" include the sharing of familial or financial responsibilities, consortium, and the length and continuity of the relationship. *Rickman v. Commonwealth*, 33 Va. App. 550, 535 S.E.2d 187 (2000). Va. Code § 18.2-57.2. Likewise, a husband or former husband may be convicted of stalking a wife or former wife. *Woolfolk v. Commonwealth*, 18 Va. App. 840, 447 S.E.2d 530 (1994). Va. Code § 18.2-60.3 survived constitutional challenges of vagueness and overbreadth in *Woolfolk*. In affirming the entry of a civil protective order based on stalking, the Virginia Supreme Court confirmed the necessary elements to prove stalking under Va. Code § 18.2-60.3(A), which are: (1) the defendant directed his or her conduct toward the victim on at least two occasions; (2) the defendant intended to cause fear or knew or should have known that his or her conduct would cause fear; and (3) the defendant's conduct caused the victim "to experience reasonable fear of death, criminal sexual assault, or bodily injury." *Stephens v. Rose*, 288 Va. 150, 762 S.E.2d 758, 761 (2014).

The Juvenile and Domestic Relations Court had jurisdiction to hear a number of assault cases where the defendant and the victim had resided together for six months. The defendant kept his clothing at the residence, the couple regularly engaged in sexual relations, resulting in the birth of a child, he shared expenses and child rearing responsibilities for her other four children in the household, and generally established a relationship similar to a marital relationship. The defendant was therefore a "family or household member" of the victim under Va. Code § 16.1-228. *Buck v. Robertson*, 39 Va. Cir. 447 (1996). See also *Rickman v. Commonwealth*, 33 Va. App. 550, 535 S.E.2d 187 (2000) (defendant who contributed to his victim's household expenses, set rules for her child, slept in same bed with her, and resided with her continuously for a three-month period was "cohabiting" under Va. Code § 18.2-57.2, even though he remained married to another woman).

When a law enforcement officer or an allegedly stalked person asserts under oath that the person has been or is being stalked, the judge or magistrate may issue a protective order. The judge or magistrate must first find probable danger of a further such offense, and that a warrant for the arrest of the respondent has been issued. Va. Code § 19.2-152.9.

Although Virginia does not recognize the so-called battered wife syndrome as a defense to a charge of homicide, the husband's past history of criminal assaults upon the wife would be admissible to prove justifiable self-defense. *Commonwealth v. Hackett,* 32 Va. Cir. 338 (1994).

According to Va. Code § 16.1-106 (amended 1997), there is an appeal of right from protective orders issued pursuant to Va. Code § 19.2-152.10 by the juvenile and domestic relations court. However, the order shall remain in effect while the appeal is pending unless ordered suspended by a judge of the Circuit Court or under a writ of supersedeas issued by the Court of Appeals.

An individual cannot be punished for violation of a protective order unless (1) the order has been personally served on the individual, or (2) the individual has received actual notice of the existence of the protective order. See *Hsiu Tsai v. Commonwealth,* 51 Va. App. 649, 659 S.E.2d 594 (2008).

## § 10.03   Criminal Sexual Assault

Although at common law a woman's consent to her husband's sexual advances could not be retracted, 1 M. Hale, *The History of the Pleas of the Crown* 629 (1736), women today, if living separately from their husbands, have a right to be protected from their society or unwanted intercourse. *Weishaupt v. Commonwealth,* 227 Va. 389, 315 S.E.2d 847 (1984). See also *State v. Smith,* 85 N.J. 193, 202, 426 A.2d 38, 42–43 (1981).

However, the termination of the marriage must be known by the husband; the woman's conduct cannot be equivocal. *Kizer v. Commonwealth,* 228 Va. 256, 321 S.E.2d 291 (1984). In *Kizer,* the husband's conviction was reversed even though on the particular occasion involved, the wife's lack of consent was obvious.

The Virginia no-fault divorce statute, Va. Code § 20-91(A)(9), embodies a legislative endorsement of a woman's unilateral right to withdraw an implied consent to marital sex. The very scheme of the statute contemplates a voluntary withdrawal, by either spouse, from the marital relationship—a de facto termination of the marriage contract. *Weishaupt,* 227 Va. at 403, 315 S.E.2d at 854. The *Weishaupt* court declined, *id.* at 404, 315 S.E.2d at 855, to formulate a rule that would also apply when spouses were living together in a less obvious suspension of the marital relationship; any change must come from Virginia legislature.

The legislature responded to *Weishaupt* by enacting statutes providing for penalties for marital sexual assault as well as special procedures for hearings in such cases. Va. Code §§ 18.2-57.2, 18.2-67.2:1, 19.2-11.01. The marital sexual assault statute, former Va. Code § 18.2-67.2:1, was repealed in 2005 when the rape, forcible sodomy, and object sexual penetration statutes were amended to remove the different standards that formerly applied if the victim and perpetrator were married to each other. See Va. Code §§ 18.2-61,

18.2-67.1, 18.2-67.2. The special procedures of Va. Code § 19.2-218.1 and Va. Code § 19.2-218.2 were retained and made applicable in prosecutions for rape, forcible sodomy, or object sexual penetration when the complaining witness is the spouse of the accused. The terms of a previous court order prohibiting a husband from having contact with his wife and evidence of previous bad assaults the husband committed against his wife were appropriately admitted into evidence according to *Melville v. Commonwealth*, 1994 Va. App. LEXIS 705 (Nov. 29, 1994) (not designated for publication).

Multiple statutes also protect the welfare of a child. See Va. Code § 18.2-63 (Carnal knowledge of child between 13 and 15 years of age); Va. Code § 18.2-67.3 (Aggravated sexual battery; penalty); Va. Code § 18.2-67.4:2 (Sexual abuse of a child under 15 years of age; penalty); Va. Code § 18.2-370; Va. Code § 18.2-371; and Va. Code § 18.2-374.3. Under Va. Code § 18.2-63, each proscribed act establishes a separate offense under the statute. *Paduano v. Commonwealth*, 64 Va. App. 173, 181, 766 S.E.2d 745, 749 (2014).

See generally Waterman, *For Better or for Worse: Marital Rape*, 15 Northern Ky. L. Rev. 611 (1988); Comment, *The Marital Relationship Exemption*, 52 N.Y.U. L. Rev. 306 (1977).

## § 10.04 Theft

When a wife is living separate and apart from her husband, the husband has no right of access to her society and conjugal relations that would allow him to break into her home to commit assault and battery. *Knox v. Commonwealth*, 225 Va. 504, 304 S.E.2d 4 (1983). This is because his "right of consortium is subordinate to the wife's right of exclusive possession." *Id.* at 507, 304 S.E.2d at 6. Neither his right to curtesy nor his traditional marital rights give him any more power or authority over his wife's property than a total stranger would possess. *Id.* (quoting from *Edmonds v. Edmonds*, 139 Va. 652, 124 S.E. 415, 417 (1924)). A husband may also be guilty of larceny of his wife's chattels taken without her permission. *Stewart v. Commonwealth*, 219 Va. 887, 252 S.E.2d 329 (1979). A husband may be guilty of burglary of his jointly-owned home, when the home is solely occupied by his estranged wife and he is under order not to contact her. In such circumstances, the husband's proprietary interest is relegated to the wife's superior possessory interest and right to exclusive habitation. *Turner v. Commonwealth*, 33 Va. App. 88, 531 S.E.2d 619 (2000).

## § 10.05 Conspiracy

Because husband and wife were one, it was conceptually and legally impossible at common law for them to join together in a criminal activity requiring two persons, such as conspiracy. See authorities cited in *United States v. Dege*, 364 U.S. 51, 53, 80 S. Ct. 1589, 4 L. Ed. 2d 1563 (1959). Two of the leading cases collected there, *Dawson v. United States*, 10 F.2d 106 (9th Cir. 1926); and *People v. Miller*, 82 Cal. 107, 22 P. 934 (1889), have since been overruled. *United States v. Dege*, 364 U.S. 51, 80 S. Ct. 1589, 4 L. Ed. 2d 1563 (1959), *People v. Pierce*, 61 Cal. 2d 879, 40 Cal. Rptr. 845, 395 P.2d 893 (1964). *Dege* noted that the medieval status of women should not obfuscate the Court's view of the conspiracy statute, *id.* at 52, and that imposing the culpability for a couple's criminal enterprise would not lead to unacceptable risks of disharmony between them. The Court rejected the notion that a wife must be presumed to act under the coercive influence of her husband. *Id.* at 53. See also *Commonwealth v. Lawson*, 454 Pa. 23, 309 A.2d 391 (1973) (husband and wife could be convicted of conspiracy to sell illegal drugs).

However, it may still be possible to prevent conviction of a spouse for both conspiracy to commit and commission of one substantive offense when the activity that is the object of the conspiracy in itself requires agreement between two persons, such as in the case of bigamy or adultery. This doctrine is called "Wharton's Rule," and was followed in Virginia in the case of *Stewart v. Commonwealth*, 225 Va. 473, 303 S.E.2d 877 (1983) (no conspiracy to pander where the only alleged coconspirators were prostitutes, and the statute said that pandering required a prostitute). Although *Dege* and *Stewart* involved statutes, their analytical patterns are clearly applicable to common law versions of conspiracy, such as bigamy. Of course, Wharton's Rule does not apply where the conspiracy to commit bigamy, adultery, etc. is joined by a third person. See, e.g., *Gebardi v. United States*, 287 U.S. 112, 122, 53 S. Ct. 35, 77 L. Ed. 206 (1932); *People v. MacMullen*, 134 Cal. App. 81, 24 P.2d 794 (1933) (conspiracy conviction of husband and wife reversed when alleged coconspirators acquitted).

See generally 16 Am. Jur. 2d *Conspiracy* § 12, 41 Am. Jur. 2d *Husband and Wife* § 2.

## § 10.06    Crimes of Omission

Several cases from other states have considered the question of whether a spouse is criminally responsible for failure to provide aid to a dying husband or wife who does not wish such aid. The modern cases, where the decision not to be helped is made while the spouse is capable of making an intelligent choice, hold that the spouse is not so responsible. See, e.g., *Commonwealth v. Konz*, 498 Pa. 639, 450 A.2d 638 (1982); *People v. Robbins*, 83 A.D.2d 271, 443 N.Y.S.2d 1016 (1981).

## § 10.07   Agency or Coercion

At common law, the wife was under the domination of her husband. If he ordered her to commit a crime other than murder or treason, he would be responsible criminally and she would not be guilty since she was merely his instrumentality to commit the crime. *Brown v. Commonwealth,* 135 Va. 480, 115 S.E. 542 (1923); see generally Perkins on *Criminal Law* 909 (2d ed. 1969); 4 Blackstone *Commentaries* *28.

The case of *Wampler v. Norton,* 134 Va. 606, 113 S.E. 733 (1922), modified the rule, so that the presence of the husband of a married woman during her commission of a criminal act no longer excused the wife from responsibility. The modified rule was that the presence of the husband merely raised a prima facie presumption that his wife was acting under his coercion and control. Within a year, the Virginia Supreme Court, in *Brown v. Commonwealth,* 135 Va. 480, 115 S.E. 542 (1923), criticized even this rule on the basis of the change in status of women toward greater independence and capacity. *Id.* at 484, 115 S.E. at 543.

The modern rule is that a wife, like any other adult, is competent to make decisions and therefore capable both of committing and of refusing to commit a crime. She no longer has the defense of her coverture. The nearest related defense is that of compulsion: reasonably acting out of fear of imminent death or grievous bodily injury. See, e.g., *State v. Lambert,* 173 W. Va. 60, 312 S.E.2d 31 (1984) (wife's conviction for welfare fraud reversed where corroborated evidence showed that she might have acted out of fear of physical abuse by her husband).

See generally Perkins on *Criminal Law* 954 (2d ed. 1969).

## § 10.08   Computer Crimes

Va. Code § 18.2-152.1 et seq. is known as the Computer Crimes Act. This Act contains many provisions that directly apply to divorcing spouses that can result in criminal violations. See Va. Code § 18.2-152.7:1.

Va. Code § 18.2-152.3 makes it a crime for a person to use a computer or computer network, without authority, and: (1) obtain property or services by false pretenses; (2) embezzle or commit larceny; or (3) convert the property of another.

Va. Code § 18.2-152.4 is referred to as the computer trespass statute. This provision makes it a crime for a person, with malicious intent, to: (1) temporarily or permanently remove, halt, or otherwise disable any computer data, computer programs, or computer software from a computer or computer network; (2) cause a computer to malfunction, regardless of how long the malfunction persists; (3) alter, disable, or erase any computer data, computer programs or computer software; (4) effect the creation or alteration of a financial instrument or of an electronic transfer of funds; (5) use a computer or computer network to cause physical injury to the property of another; (6) use a computer or computer network to make or cause to be made an unauthorized copy, in any form, including, but not limited to, any printed or electronic form of computer data, computer programs, or computer software residing in, communicated by, or produced by a computer or computer network; (7) [Repealed]; (8) install or cause to be installed, or collect information through, computer software that records all or a majority of the keystrokes made on the computer of another without the computer owner's authorization; or (9) install or cause to be installed on the computer of another, computer software for the purpose of (i) taking control of that computer so that it can cause damage to another computer or (ii) disabling or disrupting the ability of the computer to share or transmit instructions or data to other computers or to any related computer equipment or devices, including but not limited to printers, scanners, or fax machines. A Fairfax County Circuit Court judge permitted discovery of information that was otherwise protected by Va. Code § 18.2-152.5. *Albertson v. Albertson*, 73 Va. Cir. 94 (2007).

Va. Code § 18.2-152.5:1 makes it a crime for any person who uses a computer through the use of material artifice trickery, or deception, to obtain another person's identifying information.

Va. Code § 18.2-152.5:7, referred to as personal trespass by computer, makes it a crime for any person who uses a computer or computer network to cause physical injury to an individual.

Va. Code § 18.2-157.1, referred to as harassment by computer, makes it a crime for any person who, with the intent to coerce, intimidate, or harass another, uses a "computer or computer network to communicate obscene, vulgar, profane, lewd, lascivious, or indecent language," or makes "any suggestion or proposal of an obscene nature," or threatens "any illegal or immoral act." A husband's conviction for harassment resulting from emails he sent to his wife was ultimately overturned by the Virginia Supreme Court since the emails were found not to be obscene as defined by Va. Code § 18.2-372. *Barson v. Commonwealth*, 284 Va. 67, 726 S.E.2d 292 (2012). To support a conviction under Va. Code § 18.2-152.7:1, the Commonwealth had to prove: 1. the accused used a computer or computer network; 2. to communicate obscene language; 3. with the intent to coerce, intimidate, or harass. *Id.* 284 at 71, 726 S.E.2d at 294 (2012). Husband did not dispute that he intended to harass his wife, but instead he argued that the language he used was not obscene. Despite finding that husband's emails to his wife were "offensive, vulgar, and disgusting," they were not obscene and his conviction was overturned. *Id.* 284 Va. at 75, 726 S.E.2d at 296 (2012).

The Virginia Computer Crimes Act criminalizes a broad range of conduct that divorcing spouses must be aware of and cognizant not to violate. A party injured by a violation of the Computer Crimes Act may also pursue civil relief and recover the costs of the suit. Va. Code § 18.2-152.12.

### § 10.09    Interception of Wire, Electronic, or Oral Communications

Va. Code § 19.2-62 makes it unlawful, when any person who, either lacks advanced consent or is not party to the communication, intercepts, or endeavors to intercept, any wire, electronic, or oral communication. This section also makes it unlawful to use or disclose, and to attempt to use or disclose, the contents of any such unlawfully obtained oral communication. A violation of this section also results in the exclusion of any evidence that is derived from the unlawfully intercepted communication. Where a wire or oral communication has been intercepted, Va. Code § 19.2-65 excludes from evidence any part of the contents of the communication as well as any evidence derived therefrom. This exclusion of evidence applies to "any trial, hearing or other proceeding in or before any court, grand jury, department, officer, commission, regulatory body, legislative committee or other agency of this Commonwealth or a political subdivision thereof."

A party who has had his or her wire, electronic, or oral communication unlawfully intercepted, disclosed, or used, can maintain a civil action against any person "who intercepts, discloses or uses, or procures any other person to intercept, disclose or use such communications" and is entitled to recover damages and reasonable attorney's fees and other litigation costs. Va. Code § 19.2-69.

### § 10.10    Unauthorized Use of Electronic Tracking Device

In 2013, Va. Code § 18.2-60.5 was enacted. This provision makes it illegal, except under enumerated exceptions, for any person to install or place, or cause to be installed or placed "an electronic tracking device through intentionally deceptive means and without consent . . . uses such device to track the location of any person." Exceptions exist for a parent to track a minor, as well as for an owner of the vehicle to hire a registered private investigator. The broadly written statute appears to make it illegal for the actual car owner to install the tracking device though. Although it is a circuit court opinion, a husband was found guilty of violating Va. Code § 18.2-60.5 when he installed a tracking device on a vehicle that was solely owned by his wife. *Commonwealth v. Blacker,* 94 Va. Cir. 50 (2016).

## § 10.11    Kidnapping

Withholding a child in contravention to a custody order can result in significant problems for the offending parent. Va. Code §§ 18.2-47 and 49.1 proscribe criminal penalties for such behavior. Any person, including a parent, who abducts a child and remains in Virginia is subject to a Class 1 misdemeanor, but if the child is removed from Virginia the offense increases to a Class 6 felony. Va. Code § 18.2-47(D). A parent or any person who "knowingly, wrongfully, and intentionally" withholds a child from a parent or legal guardian in a clear and significant violation of a custody order is guilty of a Class 6 felony (Va. Code § 18.2-49.1(A)) if the child is removed from Virginia or a Class 1-3 misdemeanor (Va. Code § 18.2-49.1(B)) if the child remains in Virginia. Va. Code § 18.2-49.1. The level of misdemeanor depends on the number of violations that occur within a specified time period. The first conviction is a Class 3 misdemeanor, and it can increase to a Class 1 misdemeanor if there is a third conviction within 24 months of the first conviction. Va. Code § 18.2-49.1(B).

Federal law also provides criminal penalties for parents and other people who kidnap a child and withhold the child from a custodial parent or legal guardian. The Parental Kidnapping Prevention Act, 28 U.S.C. § 1738A, is only available where the crime is a felony in Virginia and the child is removed from Virginia. The federal Kidnapping crime, 18 U.S.C. § 1201, generally does not apply to parents. However, there is one explicit exception, 18 U.S.C. § 1204, which provides a fine and incarceration up to three years for any parent who takes a child "outside the United States with intent to obstruct the lawful exercise of parental rights."

See §§ 23.21 and 23.22 in the Child Custody chapter for additional details and discussion regarding kidnapping.

# CHAPTER 11

## Testimony by Spouses

### SYNOPSIS

## § 11.01   Introduction

Although the historical immunity from tort and many criminal actions has largely been abolished in Virginia, attorneys may come across other types of immunities when spouses are involved in lawsuits. These are testimonial immunities and marital privileges.

Va. Code §§ 8.01-398 and 19.2-271.2 codify spousal immunity and testimony in civil and criminal prosecutions. Va. S. Ct. R. 2:504 sets forth the evidentiary rule for such testimony at both civil and criminal trials.

At common law, the spouse was unable to testify at all, since in law the spouses were one, and there was an inability to give evidence for or against one's self. *Trammel v. United States*, 445 U.S. 40, 44, 100 S. Ct. 906, 63 L. Ed. 2d 186 (1980); *Hoge & Hutchinson v. Turner*, 96 Va. 624, 629, 32 S.E. 291 (1899).

The more modern position has been that the spouse is competent to testify against a spouse without that spouse's permission. This is not a requirement of federal constitutional law, *Trammel v. United States*, 445 U.S. 40, 100 S. Ct. 906, 63 L. Ed. 2d 186 (1980), but is found at Va. Code § 19.2-271.2, which is more protective of individual rights. Each witness is capable of testifying in favor of a spouse at any time, but spouses may testify without the other's permission in criminal actions only where the witness or the child of either the witness or the spouse was a victim, in actions between the spouses, or when the marriage has been dissolved by divorce before trial. The status of the marriage at the time of trial determines the competency.

*Stewart v. Commonwealth*, 219 Va. 887, 252 S.E.2d 329 (1979). In *United States v. Golding*, 168 F.3d 700 (4th Cir. 1999), a prosecutor threatened to prosecute a man's fiancée, later his wife, if she testified on his behalf in a criminal case. The prosecutor repeatedly pointed out her decision not to testify against her husband at the trial so as to draw an adverse inference. The misconduct of the prosecutor, not corrected by the judge at the trial, constituted reversible error.

In addition to the incompetence to testify, there is also the matter of the marital privilege. If a matter is communicated to the other spouse by virtue of the marital relationship, *Menefee v. Commonwealth*, 189 Va. 900, 912, 55 S.E.2d 9, 15 (1949), it may not be disclosed without permission of the spouse. This is true even though the parties are divorced at time of trial if the privileged communication took place while the spouses were married. Under 2005 amendments of the statutes defining the marital privilege, confidential communications made by one spouse to another during the course of the marriage may not be disclosed without the agreement of both spouses, regardless of marital status at the time disclosure is proposed; but this privilege may not be asserted in any proceeding in which the spouses are adverse parties or a spouse is charged with a crime or tort against the person or property of the other or against the minor child of either spouse. Va. Code §§ 8.01-398, 19.2-271.2. Retroactive application of the marital privilege statutes as amended in 2005 does *not* violate (1) the ex post facto or due process clauses of the federal constitution, (2) the federal constitutional right to be free from unreasonable searches and seizures, or (3) the federal privilege against compelled self-incrimination. See *Carpenter v. Commonwealth*, 51 Va. App. 84, 654 S.E.2d 345 (2007).

The spousal privilege exists because of the public policy encouraging free communication between husband and wife. See, e.g., *Hawkins v. United States*, 358 U.S. 74, 79, 79 S. Ct. 136, 3 L. Ed. 2d 125 (1958); *Wolfle v. United States*, 291 U.S. 7, 14, 54 S. Ct. 279, 78 L. Ed. 617 (1934):

> That would render susceptible of and expose to public observation and knowledge all confidential conduct, transactions and acts not consisting of spoken or written words, which the continued tranquility, integrity and confidence of their intimate relation demands to be shielded and protected by the inviolate veil of the marital sanctuary.

*Menefee v. Commonwealth*, 189 Va. 900, 912, 55 S.E.2d 9, 15 (1949).

See generally Friend, *The Law of Evidence in Virginia* §§ 57, 64 (2d ed. 1983); "Spousal Privileges," in Stone & Liebman, ed., *Testimonial Privileges* (1983).

## § 11.02   Need for Valid Marriage

The 1996 legislature amended Va. Code Ann. § 19.2-271.2 to revoke the spouse's immunity from adverse testimony. The witness spouse still has the privilege to refuse to testify, in accordance with federal law. The witness spouse may be compelled to testify in cases where the state prosecutes one of the spouses for criminal offense against the other or the child of either, where either is charged with forgery of the other's name or with certain sexual offenses such as child abuse, sodomy, and incest. This changed the common law doctrine. For example, under the former rule, if the parties were not married at the time the crime was committed, but they married before trial, one spouse could not be compelled to give testimony against the other. *Stevens v. Commonwealth,* 207 Va. 371, 150 S.E.2d 229 (1966) (assault by man against woman; marriage after indictment).

In any event, when a marriage was void, the privilege against adverse spousal testimony did not apply. *Leigh v. Commonwealth,* 192 Va. 583, 595, 66 S.E.2d 586 (1951) (woman whose marriage to defendant was void apparently because it was contracted too soon after his divorce was allowed to testify against him at trial for killing her father, even though the wife had believed in good faith that marriage was valid). See also *United States v. Neeley,* 475 F.2d 1136 (4th Cir. 1973) (for both immunity and privilege).

Although there are no Virginia cases on the subject, cases from other jurisdictions hold that the immunity does not exist for unmarried cohabitants. See, e.g., *United States v. Neeley,* 475 F.2d 1136 (4th Cir. 1973); *People v. Torres,* 90 Misc. 2d 358, 360, 394 N.Y.S.2d 546, 547 (1977); *People v. Delph,* 94 Cal. App. 3d 411, 156 Cal. Rptr. 422 (1979).

## § 11.03   Action Against Spouse or Child of Spouse

The 1996 legislature amended Va. Code Ann. § 19.2-271.2 to revoke the spouse's immunity from adverse testimony. The witness spouse still has the privilege to refuse to testify, in accordance with federal law. See, e.g., *Turner v. Commonwealth,* 33 Va. App. 88, 531 S.E.2d 619 (2000) (defendant husband's privilege to bar wife's testimony against him, regarding burglary of her home, was revoked by legislature). The witness spouse may be compelled to testify in cases where the state prosecutes one of the spouses for a criminal offense against the other spouse, against child of either, or against the property of either; or where either is charged with forgery of the other's name or with certain sexual offenses. See, e.g., *Carpenter v. Commonwealth,* 51 Va. App. 84, 654 S.E.2d 345 (2007) (tape recording of conversation between wife and husband was admitted at husband's trial for rape of stepdaughter). Even when the privilege was still in effect, there was an exception for alleged crimes against family members. For example, in

*Osborne v. Commonwealth,* 214 Va. 691, 204 S.E.2d 289 (1974), the defendant's wife was permitted to testify against him in his trial for the rape of her daughter. See generally Annot., 93 A.L.R.3d 1018.

The privilege applied, and a husband could prevent his wife from testifying, in a criminal proceeding for assault where the shot fired by the husband was aimed at the wife but hit another. The exception to the statute was limited to the prosecution by one spouse for an offense committed by the other. *Jenkins v. Commonwealth,* 219 Va. 764, 250 S.E.2d 763 (1979). However, it need not be a crime against the person. A spouse could testify adversely when the crime was against the testifying spouse's property. *Brown v. Commonwealth,* 223 Va. 601, 292 S.E.2d 319 (1982). However, a wife could not testify at her estranged husband's arson trial without his consent. *Creech v. Commonwealth,* 242 Va. 385, 410 S.E.2d 650 (1991). Although her furniture was destroyed in the fire at the marital home and she testified that he had threatened to "torch" her property when she told him she was leaving him, he was not charged with nor tried for an offense committed against her. The indictment and trial was for arson of the home, which was owned solely by him.

See generally Comment, *Confidential Communication Privileges under Federal and Virginia Law,* 13 U. Rich. L. Rev. 593 (1979).

## § 11.04  Testimony Following Separation or Divorce

The privilege did not end when the parties separated. *State v. Freeman,* 302 N.C. 591, 276 S.E.2d 450, 455 n.2 (1981), and cases cited therein. However, once the parties divorced, whether *a vinculo, Menefee v. Commonwealth,* 189 Va. 900, 55 S.E.2d 9 (1949) (confidential communications case, but wife allowed to testify), or a mensa, *Stewart v. Commonwealth,* 219 Va. 887, 252 S.E.2d 329, 333 (1979), the privilege was no longer in effect. In Stewart, a wife was allowed to testify against the husband she had divorced *a mensa* in his trial for stealing her automobile. The Virginia Supreme Court reasoned that "[w]hatever vestige of marital harmony might have remained to be protected by Stewart's exercise of his right to eliminate Mrs. Stewart as a witness had been thoroughly disrupted, if not totally destroyed, by the entry of the *a mensa* decree."

In 2005, Va. Code § 8.01-398 was amended to specify that the spousal privilege may not be asserted in any proceeding in which the spouses are adverse parties, or in which either spouse is charged with a crime or tort against the person or property of the other or against the minor child of either spouse. Va. S. Ct. R. 2-504 sets forth the evidentiary rule governing spousal testimony in civil and criminal proceedings.

## § 11.05　What Constitutes a Privileged Communication

In *Menefee v. Commonwealth,* 189 Va. 900, 55 S.E.2d 9 (1949), a wife testified at her husband's murder trial that he had appeared nervous on the night of the crime, and had placed a gun (later found to be the murder weapon) on the mantel, and had "messed around" with the lid of the car trunk. He also asked her to drive him to the vicinity of the crime several times. These actions and gestures were found to be privileged communications. *Id.* at 912, 55 S.E.2d at 15:

> The immunity and ban of the statute applies to and includes all information or knowledge privately imparted and made known by one spouse to the other by virtue of and in consequence of the marital relation through conduct, acts, signs, and spoken or written words.

However, a wife was allowed to testify concerning the beating her husband had given her, for it did not impart knowledge or information. *Osborne v. Commonwealth,* 214 Va. 691, 204 S.E.2d 289, 290 (1974).

In *Nowlin v. Commonwealth of Va.,* 40 Va. App. 327, 579 S.E.2d 367 (2003), police arrested a wife after her husband reported that she had shot at him and tried to kill him. When questioned, the wife confessed, stating that she and her husband kept guns in the marital home. Later, the husband, a convicted felon, was prosecuted for illegal possession of a firearm. At his trial, the wife invoked her spousal privilege and refused to testify against her husband. After she invoked the privilege, she could not be compelled to testify. However, because the wife was then unavailable as a witness, her hearsay statement to police about guns in the marital home was admissible at the husband's trial, under the "statement against declarant's penal interest" exception to the hearsay rule.

*Nowlin* and its approach to the admission of hearsay statements by unavailable witnesses has been overruled by the United States Supreme Court. In *Crawford v. Washington,* 541 U.S. 36, 124 S. Ct. 1354, 158 L. Ed. 2d 177 (2004), the Supreme Court held that when testimonial statements are at issue, the only indicium of reliability sufficient to satisfy constitutional demands is confrontation. Testimonial statements include, at a minimum, prior testimony at preliminary hearings, before grand juries, or at former trials, and statements made during police interrogations. After *Crawford*, the admission of testimonial hearsay evidence requires both unavailability and a prior opportunity for cross-examination.

A "confidential communication" subject to the marital privilege is defined as "a communication made privately by a person to his spouse that is not intended for disclosure to any other person." Va. Code §§ 8.01-398, 19.2-271.2.

## § 11.06    Waiver of the Privilege

The party who could otherwise claim the privilege may waive it by asking the party to testify in favor of him or herself regarding a particular subject matter. *Osborne v. Commonwealth,* 214 Va. 691, 204 S.E.2d 289 (1974) (waiver by defense attorney's questions on cross-examination).

When a defendant at his murder trial adopted the statement made by his wife to a sheriff, he could not claim that her version of the events in question was inadmissible, since his adoption of her words made them his own. His objection to her testimony prevented her from being examined as a witness at trial. *Shiflett v. Virginia,* 447 F.2d 50, 58 (4th Cir. 1971), *cert. denied,* 405 U.S. 994 (1972).

In a divorce case, the trial court properly allowed a marriage counselor to testify regarding his observations of the parties and statements made by the parties during marital counseling sessions that occurred before their separation. *Bullano v. Bullano,* 2007 Va. App. LEXIS 31 (Jan. 30, 2007). The equitable distribution and spousal support factors required the trial court to consider the physical and mental condition of each party, and thus the trial court did not err in admitting the marriage counselor's testimony.

The legislature placed upon the commonwealth the burden of first obtaining the consent of the spouse before it will be allowed to call the adverse spousal witness. *Wilson v. Commonwealth,* 157 Va. 962, 968, 162 S.E. 15 (1932).

## § 11.07    Effect of the Privilege

If a spouse witness elects not to testify, or is prevented from testifying by his or her spouse, no comment may be made by opposing counsel regarding the failure to testify. Va. Code § 19-271.2. If such a comment is made a conviction may be reversed. *Jones v. Commonwealth,* 218 Va. 732, 736–37, 240 S.E.2d 526 (1978).

# CHAPTER 12

## Necessaries

### SYNOPSIS

§ 12.01    Introduction
§ 12.02    What is Necessary
§ 12.03    Reimbursement from Estate
§ 12.04    Necessity for a Valid Marriage

## § 12.01   Introduction

In common law, the husband was responsible for his wife's support. He was entitled to the use of all her property during coverture as well as her services and consortium. If she was injured, he could sue the tortfeasor for actual damages and also for loss of companionship, sexual attention, and other services. A woman was unable to make contracts while married, but she could purchase goods if her husband did not supply her the necessaries of life: food, clothing, shelter, and medical care. *Hall v. Stewart,* 135 Va. 384, 116 S.E. 469 (1923). In such cases, the third party merchant or professional had a cause of action against the husband. *Richmond Ry. & Elec. Co. v. Bowles,* 92 Va. 738, 24 S.E. 388 (1896). This is the doctrine of necessaries.

Even though the right to recover for loss of consortium was abolished by statute in 1919, the husband was still liable for his wife's necessaries. *Floyd v. Miller,* 190 Va. 303, 307, 57 S.E.2d 114 (1950).

The modern developments of the doctrine of necessaries in Virginia involve its abolition in 1983 in the case of *Schilling v. Bedford County Mem. Hosp.,* 225 Va. 539, 303 S.E.2d 905 (1983), on the basis of unconstitutional gender discrimination, and its reinstatement in 1984 in Va. Code § 55-37, which makes *either* spouse liable for the necessary expenses of the other.

## § 12.02   What is Necessary

Generally speaking, food, clothing, shelter, and medical care must be provided to one's spouse. *Richmond Ry. & Elec. Co. v. Bowles,* 92 Va. 738, 24 S.E. 388 (1896). The degree of luxury required varies with the affluence of the couple. Cf. *Burton v. Commonwealth,* 109 Va. 800, 63 S.E. 464, 466 (1909) (criminal nonsupport). For example, a car may well be a necessary item in today's society, with its reliance upon private transportation. See generally Annot., 56 A.L.R.3d 1335 (for child). One famous case holds that a fur coat was necessary for a wealthy wife. *Louis Berman Co. v. Dahlberg,* 336 Ill. App. 233, 83 N.E.2d 380 (1948) (under a statute permitting recovery for "family expenses," which may be broader than necessaries). However, elective surgery, such as a voluntary abortion, would not be the foundation for such recovery. *Akron City Hosiptal v. Anderson,* 68 Ohio Misc. 14, 22 Ohio Op. 3d 238, 428 N.E.2d 472 (1981). A recent case holds that the wife was responsible for her husband's legal expenses at trial, although the criminal incident occurred before their marriage. *United States v. O'Neill,* 478 F. Supp. 852 (E.D. Pa. 1979).

## § 12.03    Reimbursement from Estate

Once a necessary service has been provided a spouse, the responsible party cannot successfully sue for reimbursement from either the spouse, the committee appointed for the spouse, *Floyd v. Miller,* 190 Va. 303, 309, 57 S.E.2d 114 (1950), or the estate of the deceased spouse. *Hall v. Stewart,* 135 Va. 384, 389, 116 S.E. 469 (1923).

In 2012, the legislature passed HB 229, which provides that a lien arising out of a judgment under the doctrine of necessaries shall not attach to the principal residence of a husband and wife that was held by the spouses as tenants by the entireties prior to the death of either spouse where the tenancy terminated as a result of such death.

## § 12.04    Necessity for a Valid Marriage

The doctrine depends upon at least the appearance of a valid marriage. If the parties have gone through a ceremony and are living together apparently as husband and wife, third party creditors can recover payment for necessaries even though the marriage turns out to be void. *Abrams v. Traster,* 244 Ill. App. 533 (1927); *Frank v. Carter,* 219 N.Y. 35, 113 N.E. 549 (1952).

If the parties divorce, the doctrine is no longer in effect. *Hess v. Slutsky,* 224 Ill. App. 419 (1922); *Kleefield v. Funtanellas,* 201 N.Y.S.2d 907 (1960). However, if the parties have separated, there is no longer a family in fact, so a husband will not be liable for his wife's purchases. *Schlesinger v. Keifer,* 30 Ill. App. 253 (1889), *aff'd,* 131 Ill. 104, 22 N.E. 814 (1889). The duty continues where one spouse has abandoned the other without just cause, *Mihalcoe v. Holub,* 130 Va. 425, 429, 107 S.E. 704 (1921), unless the deserting spouse is the one seeking the support.

See generally Annot., 24 A.L.R. 1480; Annot., 11 A.L.R.4th 1160; Annot., 60 A.L.R.2d 7, 41 C.J.S. *Husband and Wife* §§ 307, 309, 355; 41 Am. Jur.

*Husband and Wife* § 348; 9B Michie's Jurisprudence *Husband and Wife* § 21.

# CHAPTER 13

# Use of Maiden Name and Acquisition of Domicile

## SYNOPSIS

## § 13.01    Use of Maiden Name

[1]    *Introduction.* In Virginia, a woman may change her married name to her maiden name while married so long as: (1) no fraud is being perpetrated; (2) her husband consents; and (3) minor children will bear the husband's surname. *In re Strikwerda,* 216 Va. 470, 220 S.E.2d 245 (1975). She might also continue to use her maiden name after she marries. *In re Strikwerda,* 216 Va. 470, 220 S.E.2d at 246 (1975) (citing *Stuart v. Board of Supvrs.,* 266 Md. 440, 295 A.2d 223, 225–27 (Md. 1972)).

Va. Code § 8.01-217 is the current name change statute in Virginia. Upon the submission of the proper application, the circuit court shall consider the application provided that good cause exists under the alleged circumstances, and the court shall order the name change unless finding fraud or the name change would infringe upon the rights of others.

Va. Code § 20-121.4 permits a spouse to file a name change application to restore a former name or maiden name as part of the divorce case. All requirements of Va. Code § 8.01-217 must be met.

[2]    *Limitations on Use of Maiden Name. Flowers v. Cain,* 218 Va. 234, 237 S.E.2d 111 (1977), indicated that where the parties were divorced the custodial parent had no right to change their children's names to match her new husband's surname. This decision was based upon the need for the children to maintain the strongest relationship possible with their divorced father. The need for a lack of a disruptive effect on the family is made clear in *In re Strikwerda,* 216 Va. 470, 473, 220 S.E.2d 245, 247 (1975), where the court specifically notes that the husband has consented in each case to the name change and it has been agreed between the spouses that any children born of the marriage will bear the husband's surname.

See generally Annot., 92 A.L.R.3d 1091.

## § 13.02    Acquisition of Separate Domicile

At common law the domicile of a married woman was necessarily that of her husband, since the parties were "one flesh" and the wife did not have an independent legal capacity. *Commonwealth v. Rutherfoord,* 160 Va. 524, 530–31, 169 S.E. 909, 915 (1933). This disability was removed in *Commonwealth,* where the wife was held not liable for Virginia taxes although her husband was domiciled in the state and the parties maintained an amicable relationship, since she had retained from before the marriage a separate domicile in New York. This is one of the leading cases in the United States on this subject. See Restatement of Laws, Conflict of Laws, Second § 21.

This would of necessity be true where the parties had separated pursuant to obtaining a no-fault divorce. *Williamson v. Osenton,* 232 U.S. 619, 34 S. Ct. 442, 58 L. Ed. 758 (1914); cf. *Knox v. Commonwealth,* 225 Va. 504, 506, 304 S.E.2d 4, 6 (1983).

For purposes of obtaining long-arm jurisdiction, the marital domicile cannot be unilaterally changed by one spouse. *Stellwagen v. Stellwagen,* 48 Va. Cir. 451 (Fairfax Co. 1999), involved a husband and wife who moved from Georgia, where they had been domiciled, to Virginia. They stayed for a year in Virginia, living on the lower floor of the wife's mother's home, intending to remain in the state, and receiving mail at the Virginia residence. Though the husband worked for a year in Virginia, in 1996 he left the state and moved first to New Hampshire and later to Florida. Although he claimed that his domicile had changed, "Husband and wife never were present in any other place with the intent to live there indefinitely"; therefore, the Virginia court continued to have personal jurisdiction over him.

# CHAPTER 14

# Torts Involving Parent and Child

## SYNOPSIS

## § 14.01    Introduction

At common law, the father held all the property for his children. He owed them support, protection, see *Flippo v. Commonwealth*, 122 Va. 854, 861, 94 S.E. 771, 773 (1918), discipline and education, both secular and religious. In return, the child owed his father his earnings, *Fletcher v. Taylor*, 344 F.2d 93, 95 (4th Cir. 1965); 14A Michie's Jurisprudence *Parent and Child* § 15, obedience, *Cribbins v. Markwood*, 54 Va. (13 Gratt.) 495, 506 (1856) (dicta), respect, and, by statute, care in his old age. This family system was based primarily on the incapacity of children to make decisions, and their inability to defend themselves from enemies in armed combat.

The rules regarding relationships between parent and child, and between the child and the outside world, have been slow to change despite the increasing individual rights of minors. One major area of change in tort law stems from to the universal presence of automobile insurance.

See generally Katz & Schroeder, *Disobeying a Father's Voice: A Comment on Commonwealth v. Brasher*, 57 Mass L.Q. 43 (1971); Zainaldin, *The Emergence of a Modern American Family Law*, 73 Nw. U.L. Rev. 1038 (1979).

## § 14.02    Intrafamilial Immunity

Although parents were not immune from their children's suits at common law, in this country the judicially created doctrine arose in the late 19th century. *Hewellette v. George,* 68 Miss. 703, 9 So. 885 (1891). In Virginia it was adopted in the case of *Norfolk Southern Railroad v. Gretakis,* 162 Va. 597, 600, 174 S.E. 841, 842 (1934). Intrafamily immunity does not apply when the death of an unemancipated child results from the intentional act of his parent. *Pavlick v. Pavlick,* 254 Va. 176, 491 S.E.2d 602 (1997). Together with interspousal immunity, the doctrine has been receding in many states. See, e.g., *Goller v. White,* 20 Wis. 2d 402, 122 N.W.2d 193 (1963); *Gibson v. Gibson,* 3 Cal. 3d 914, 92 Cal. Rptr. 288, 479 P.2d 648 (1971) (and cases cited therein); Restatement (Second) of Torts § 895G; see generally *Defining the Parent's Duty After Rejection of Parent-Child Immunity,* 33 Vand. L. Rev. 775 (1980).

In Virginia, the immunity persists except in cases of automobile accidents, *Smith v. Kauffman,* 212 Va. 181, 186, 183 S.E.2d 190, 194 (1971), or where the relationship of parent and child is purely incidental to the injury: for example, in cases of common carrier, *Worrell v. Worrell,* 174 Va. 11, 26–27, 4 S.E.2d 343, 349–50 (1939), and master and servant, *Norfolk Southern Railroad v. Gretakis,* 162 Va. 597, 600, 174 S.E. 841, 842 (1934).

The immunity stems from the reluctance of courts to disturb family tranquility, their hesitation to second-guess parental decision-making and discipline, *Worrell v. Worrell,* 174 Va. 11, 19, 4 S.E.2d 343, 346 (1939), and their concern about collusion. Generally, so long as the parent is acting in the usual parental role with respect to the actions in question, the doctrine obtains. *Wright v. Wright,* 213 Va. 177, 179, 191 S.E.2d 223, 225 (1972); see generally Note, 7 U. Rich. L. Rev. 571 (1973); Note, *Virginia's Intrafamily Immunity Decisions: What Public Policy Giveth, Will the Insurance Policy Taketh Away?,* 22 Cath. U.L. Rev. 167 (1972).

In other jurisdictions, there has been another exception carved for cases in which the action of the parent destroyed the family unit and was so outrageous an intentional tort as to place the parent outside the usual role. See *Mahnke v. Moore,* 197 Md. 61, 77 A.2d 923 (1951); cf. *Korman v. Carpenter,* 216 Va. 86, 216 S.E.2d 195 (1975) (before abolition of interspousal immunity, action maintainable by wife's estate against husband's committee for her murder). This exception is also suggested by the Virginia case of *Brumfield v. Brumfield,* 194 Va. 577, 583, 74 S.E.2d 170, 174 (1953), which mentioned that the result of immunity barring an action despite the parent's grossly negligent driving might be different if an intentional wrong were charged.

There is certainly a reason for a continued refusal to hear tort cases brought by children regarding parent's failure to provide support, see *Yost v. Yost,* 172 Md. 128, 134, 190 A. 753, 756 (1937), or where institutionalized children brought suit for their neglect. Such cases inevitably involve exercises of parental judgment, and if the conduct is extreme, the state provides other relief through nonsupport or neglect and abuse proceedings. *Burnette v. Wahll,* 284 Or. 705, 588 P.2d 1105 (1978); see generally *Defining the Parent's Duty After Rejection of Parent-Child Immunity,* 33 Vand. L. Rev. 775 (1980).

See generally *Intrafamilial Immunity,* 21 Wm. & Mary L. Rev. 273 (1979); and Sandra L. Haley, *The Parental Tort Immunity Doctrine: Is it a Defensible Defense?* 30 U. Rich. L. Rev. 575 (1996).

## § 14.03  Wrongful Life and Birth

Until very recently a suit against a doctor for negligently allowing a child to be born would have been unthinkable, since life was always preferable to nonlife, and the joy of being a parent was held to outweigh any of the inconvenience or expenses of an unwanted birth, or the pain and suffering of parenting a handicapped or terminally ill child. *Gleitman v. Cosgrove,* 49 N.J. 22, 227 A.2d 689 (1967). With the advent of effective means of sterilization and voluntary abortion, there have been numerous suits by parents or children against physicians allegedly negligent in failing to give appropriate advice or cautions, or failing to competently perform surgical or diagnostic care. Virginia follows the majority rule, which allows a medical malpractice action for not preventing pregnancy or for failing to terminate an unwanted pregnancy. Damages will be limited to medical expenses, pain and suffering, and lost wages for a reasonable period. Compensation may be for harm directly resulting from a negligently performed abortion, the continuing pregnancy, and the ensuing childbirth, as well as for causally related emotional distress. *Miller v. Johnson,* 231 Va. 177, 343 S.E.2d 301, 305 (1986). However, recompense does not include the costs of rearing a reasonably healthy child to majority, since damages in such cases are not capable of determination with any reasonable certainty. *Id.* at 307.

Cases brought by children complaining that they should never have been born have been unsuccessful in most jurisdictions, excepting California, *Turpin v. Sortini,* 31 Cal. 3d 220, 182 Cal. Rptr. 337, 643 P.2d 954 (1982), and Washington, *Harbeson v. Parke Davis,* 98 Wash. 2d 460, 656 P.2d 483 (1983). However, parents have been able to recover when their offspring would not have been born handicapped, *Procanik v. Cillo,* 97 N.J. 339, 478 A.2d 755 (1984), or seriously ill, *Schroeder v. Perkel,* 87 N.J. 53, 432 A.2d 834 (1981), absent the physician's negligence. See also *Glascock v. Laserna,* 30 Va. Cir. 366 (Spotsylvania Co. 1993).

One Virginia case on the subject, *Burger v. Naccash,* 223 Va. 406, 290 S.E.2d 825 (1982), involved negligence on the part of the supervising physician whose laboratory technician mixed up two patients' blood samples, with the result that the plaintiffs were assured that their expected child would not suffer from the inevitably fatal genetic Tay Sachs' disease. Since they did not have correct information, the parents did not abort the child, who was ultimately born with Tay Sachs'. The court allowed recovery for medical expenses and the pain and suffering the parents suffered watching their daughter become ill and die at less than three years of age. Funeral expenses and a burial marker were held not to be consequences of the doctor's negligence. Of course, neither was the disease itself, or the consequent death. The statute of limitations for a wrongful birth action, where the physical problems were not caused by the defendants, is the two-year period prescribed by Va. Code § 8.01-243(A) for actions for personal injuries, not those specified by § 8.01-243(B), which allows five years for injuries to property, including actions by a parent for "expenses of curing or attempting to cure such infant from the result of personal injury or loss of services." *Glascock v. Laserna,* 247 Va. 108, 111, 439 S.E.2d 380, 382 (1994). The plaintiffs were attempting to recover for medical expenses incurred after defendants negligently failed to inform them of the fetus' abnormalities. Their action was not an action for injury to property, defendants did not cause "personal injury" to the child, and the plaintiffs did not suffer loss of services because of defendants' acts.

Where a sonogram would have shown that the plaintiff's baby had spina bifida and hydrocephalus, viability of the fetus was not a defense to an action when the physician failed to perform the sonogram or advise plaintiff that she could obtain an abortion. *Sawyer v. Childress,* 12 Va. Cir. 184 (City of Norfolk 1988).

See generally Comment, *A Rational Approach to Negligent Infliction of Mental Distress,* 1981 B.Y.U. L. Rev. 208.

## § 14.04   Vicarious Parental Liability

At common law parents were liable for the intentional torts of their child only if they knew of the propensity of the child to commit such antisocial acts. See, e.g., *Mitchell v. Wiltfong,* 4 Kan. App. 2d 231, 604 P.2d 79 (1979). The common law rule naturally extends to parents of adult children, as long as the child is not an actual agent or employee of the parent. For example, in *Parlett v. Nelson,* 25 Va. Cir. 257 (City of Winchester 1991), the father was held not legally responsible for the sexual assault made by his 23-year-old son, even though the assault occurred on property the father had recently owned and rented to the victim plaintiff.

However, the Virginia Supreme Court has noted that a parent is generally not liable for the torts of a minor child absent some type of special relationship other than paternity:

> A father is not liable for the torts of his minor son simply because of paternity. There must exist an authority from the father to the son to do the tortious act or a subsequent ratification and adoption of it, before responsibility attaches to the parent. * * * The wrongful act must be performed by the son in pursuance of the business, incident, or undertaking authorized by the father before the latter can be held liable. * * * If the act is not done by the son in furtherance of the father's business, but in performance of some independent design of his own, the father is not liable. The controlling rules of law are the same whether the business in question concerns the operation of an automobile or any other matter.

> *Blair v. Broadwater*, 121 Va. 301, 308, 93 S.E. 632 (1917) (*citing Smith v. Jordan*, 211 Mass. 269, 97 N.E. 761 (1912)).

Another exception to the rule was for cases in which the parent entrusted the child with a dangerous instrumentality that caused the injury. *Howell v. Hairston*, 261 S.C. 292, 199 S.E.2d 766 (1973) (air rifle). However, parents are not responsible for accidental gun injuries suffered by one of their child's guests when the gun was stored separately from the ammunition and the parents took other reasonable precautions. Hughes v. Brown, 36 Va. Cir. 444 (Stafford Co. 1995).

By statute, Virginia has made parents liable for limited damages to private and public property. Va. Code §§ 8.01-43 and 8.01-44. In 1996, the legislature amended Va. Code Ann. § 8.01-43 to raise the limit for vicarious liability of a parent to $2,500.

A child care provider or babysitter, who stands in the place of the parent during the time of the hire, owes a duty to the child to exercise reasonable care in controlling the conduct of third parties, where the babysitter knew he or she had the ability to control the third person and that such control was needed. A church babysitter who sent her son to care for minor children, knowing that he had a propensity for sexual perversion, was liable in tort to the parents when the son sexually abused the children. *Doe v. Bruton Parish Church*, 42 Va. Cir. 467 (City of Williamsburg 1997). This provider's duty did not arise out of her status as the assailant's mother, and thus did not fall under the rule of *Bell v. Hudgins*, 232 Va. 491, 352 S.E.2d 332 (1987), which rejected civil liability for parents who fail to control their minor children's criminal behavior.

See generally Shong, *The Legal Responsibility of Parents for Their Children's Delinquency,* 6 Fam. L.Q. 145 (1972); 14A Michie's Jurisprudence *Parent and Child* § 21.

## § 14.05   Kidnapping and False Imprisonment in Religious Deprogramming

A number of unpopular religious groups have attracted converts among high school and college-aged youths. When their parents attempt to "rescue" their children through the practice known as "deprogramming," or through bringing actions in tort for alienation of the children's affections, *Orlando v. Alamo,* 646 F.2d 1288 (8th Cir. 1981) (no cause of action for alienation of child's affections, and no showing that cult was "intolerable in civilized society" as required for intentional infliction of emotional distress in Arkansas), they have met with little legal success.

Many states have found that the children, particularly if adults, *Schuppin v. Unification Church,* 435 F. Supp. 603 (D. Vt. 1977), were free to make their own decisions regarding religious affiliation, so that the parents had no ability to interfere, despite their natural concern. Similarly, the parents have been unsuccessful in having their children declared incompetent so that a guardian might be appointed. See, e.g., *Cooper v. Molko,* 512 F. Supp. 563 (N.D. Cal. 1981); *Katz v. Superior Court of San Francisco,* 73 Cal. App. 3d 952, 141 Cal. Rptr. 234 (1977).

Some courts have been reluctant to hold the parents liable for an unsuccessful "deprogramming" attempt when the parents believed their child had been coercively persuaded to join the religious group. See, e.g., *Peterson v. Sorlien,* 299 N.W.2d 123 (Minn. 1980), *cert. denied,* 450 U.S. 1031, 101 S. Ct. 1742, 68 L. Ed. 2d 227 (1981). However, in *Ward v. Connor,* 657 F.2d 45 (4th Cir.), *cert. denied,* 455 U.S. 907, 102 S. Ct. 1253, 71 L. Ed. 2d 445 (1982), the court of appeals reversed dismissal of a conspiracy charge under the private civil rights action statute, § 1985(c), where an adult's parents allegedly kidnapped him, held him captive, and subjected him to deprogramming while on his way from Virginia to New York. The court of appeals found that while the parents were motivated out of concern for his well-being, they also acted out of animosity towards members of the Unification Church. *Id.* at 49. Similarly, persons assisting parents in kidnapping their own minor children are not liable criminally under the federal kidnapping statute, 18 U.S.C. § 1201(a), according to a recent Fourth Circuit Court of Appeals case. *United States v. Boettcher,* 780 F.2d 435 (4th Cir. 1985).

See generally Anthony, *The Fact Pattern Behind the Deprogramming Controversy: An Analysis and an Alternative,* 9 N.Y.U. Rev. L. & Soc. Change 73 (1980); Le Moult, *Deprogramming Members of Religious Sects,* 46 Ford. L. Rev. 599 (1978).

## § 14.06 Corporal Punishment

The first Virginia case involving the measure of punishment that might be inflicted upon a child was *Carpenter v. Commonwealth,* 186 Va. 851, 44 S.E.2d 419 (1947). In that case, a conviction for assault and battery upon a child was affirmed when the man who stood in loco parentis whipped the child over most of her body for stealing candy from his wife. The court stated the Virginia position: "A parent has the right to administer such reasonable and timely punishment as may be necessary to correct faults in his growing children," *id.* at 860, 44 S.E.2d at 423, but "if he exceeds due moderation, he becomes criminally liable." *Id.* at 861, 44 S.E.2d at 423. See also *Bowers v. State,* 283 Md. 115, 389 A.2d 341 (1971).

Under Virginia law, any person who commits an assault and battery against a family or household member, including one's child, is guilty of a Class 1 misdemeanor. Va. Code § 18.2-57.2. Upon a conviction for assault and battery against a family or household member, where it is alleged that the person has been previously convicted of two offenses against a family or household member of (i) assault and battery against a family or household member in violation of Va. Code § 18.2-57.2, (ii) malicious wounding or unlawful wounding in violation of Va. Code § 18.2-51, (iii) aggravated malicious wounding in violation of Va. Code § 18.2-51.2, (iv) malicious bodily injury by means of a substance in violation of Va. Code § 18.2-52, (v) strangulation in violation of Va. Code § 18.2-51.6, or (vi) an offense under the law of any other jurisdiction which has the same elements of any of the above offenses, in any combination, all of which occurred within a period of 20 years, and each of which occurred on a different date, such person is guilty of a Class 6 felony. In *Farmer v. Commonwealth,* 62 Va. App. 285, 746 S.E.2d 504 (2013), three certified criminal warrants from Juvenile and Domestic Relations District Court (JDR court) were admissible to prove that the defendant was previously "convicted" of at least two predicate offenses in prosecution for felony assault and battery of a family member, third offense.

There are multiple code sections in Virginia mandating a duty to report child abuse. Va. Code § 22.1-291.3 pertains to the duty to report of a teacher or other person employed in a public or private school. Va. Code § 63.2-1509 obligates the following professionals to report child abuse:

(1)  any person licensed to practice medicine or any of the healing arts;

(2)  any hospital resident or intern, and any person employed in the nursing profession;

(3)  any person employed as a social worker or family-services specialist;

(4)  any probation officer;

(5)  any teacher or other person employed in a public or private school, kindergarten or nursery school;

(6)  any person providing full-time or part-time child care for pay on a regularly planned basis;

(7)  any mental health professional;

(8)  any law-enforcement officer or animal control officer;

(9)  any mediator eligible to receive court referrals pursuant to § 8.01-576.8;

(10)  any professional staff person, not previously enumerated, employed by a private or state-operated hospital, institution, or facility to which children have been committed or where children have been placed for care and treatment;

(11)  any person 18 years of age or older associated with or employed by any public or private organization responsible for the care, custody, or control of children;

(12)  any person who is designated a court-appointed special advocate pursuant to Article 5 (§ 9.1-151 *et seq.*) of Chapter 1 of Title 9.1;

(13)  any person 18 years of age or older who has received training approved by the Department of Social Services for the purposes of recognizing and reporting child abuse and neglect;

(14)  any person employed by a local department as defined in § 63.2-100 who determines eligibility for public assistance;

(15)  any emergency medical services provider certified by the Board of Health pursuant to § 32.1-111.5, unless such provider immediately reports the matter directly to the attending physician at the hospital to which the child is transported, who shall make such report forthwith;

(16)  any athletic coach, director, or other person 18 years of age or older employed by or volunteering with a private sports organization or team;

(17)  any administrators or employees 18 years of age or older of

public or private day camps, youth centers, and youth recreation programs; and

(18)    any person employed by a public or private institution of higher education other than an attorney who is employed by a public or private institution of higher education as it relates to information gained in the course of providing legal representation to a client.

Child protective services are required to receive child abuse complaints 24 hours a day, seven days per week, and must "widely publicize a telephone number for receiving complaints and reports." Va. Code § 63.2-1503. Child abuse information involving active duty military personnel or members of their family is required to be transmitted to the appropriate family advocacy representatives of the United States Armed Forces.

See generally Rosenberg, *Ingraham v. Wright: The Supreme Court's Whipping Boy,* 78 Colum. L. Rev. 75 (1978); Prele, *Neither Corporal Punishment Cruel Nor Due Process Due: The Supreme Court's Decision in Ingraham v. Wright,* 7 J.L. & Educ. 1 (1978); 6 Am. Jur. 2d *Assault and Battery* §§ 57, 58; 67A C.J.S. *Parent and Child* § 12.

## § 14.07  Interference with Family Relations

At common law there was no cause of action for alienation of a parent's affection, for the injury depended upon the loss of consortium that applied only to husband and wife. *Hyman v. Moldovan,* 166 Ga. App. 891, 305 S.E.2d 648 (1983) (conspiracy); *Edwards v. Edwards,* 43 N.C. App. 296, 259 S.E.2d 11 (1979); see also Restatement (Second) of Torts § 699. In any event, Virginia has abolished the case of action for alienation of affections. Va. Code § 8.01-220.

However, several cases have allowed recovery in tort for intentional infliction of mental distress, a cause of action recognized in *Womack v. Eldridge,* 215 Va. 338, 210 S.E.2d 145 (1974), for a parent's interference with the other's custodial or even visitation rights. *Raftery v. Scott,* 756 F.2d 335 (4th Cir. 1985); *Lloyd v. Loeffler,* 694 F.2d 489 (7th Cir. 1982); *Wasserman v. Wasserman,* 671 F.2d 832 (4th Cir. 1982) (diversity jurisdiction); *Bennett v. Bennett,* 682 F.2d 1039, 221 U.S. App. D.C. 90 (D.C. Cir. 1982); *Kajtazi v. Kajtazi,* 488 F. Supp. 15 (E.D.N.Y. 1978). These actions are most often used when there is no other remedy possible: where one parent has disappeared completely, as in *Lloyd,* or spirited the children out of the country, as in *Kajtazi.*

A Circuit Court in Virginia has allowed a verdict in a tort case where the custodial parent interfered with the other's visitation rights. *Memmer v.*

*Memmer,* Civ. No. L-45503 (Fairfax Co. Cir. Ct. 1982) (unreported case). Such interference is now specifically mentioned as a reason for changing a custody award. Va. Code § 20-108.

A case for intentional infliction of emotional distress was not made out when a woman misrepresented to the plaintiff that she was pregnant with his child, he developed a bond of love and affection with the child and paid child support, and then plaintiff proved he was not the father and terminated his visitation rights when her husband wished to adopt the child. The reason plaintiff was unable to recover was that there was no proof that the woman's conduct was "intentional or reckless." *Ruth v. Fletcher,* 237 Va. 366, 377 S.E.2d 412 (1989).

Abduction or kidnapping by the parent of a child abducted is also a Class 1 misdemeanor and shall also be punishable as contempt of court. Va. Code § 18.2-47. If the abduction involves a state other than Virginia, the criminal offense is a felony.

A biological father who was absent at his child's birth, had not contributed to the child's support, and had not visited the child, had no "legal justification" under Va. Code § 18.2-47 for forcibly taking the child from the mother's custody. Thus, the father committed the crime of abduction of his illegitimate son. The father's "fiancée," who assisted in the abduction, was liable as an accomplice. *Taylor v. Commonwealth,* 260 Va. 683, 537 S.E.2d 592 (2000).

In 2018, upon hearing a mater certified to the Virginia Supreme Court by the United States District Court for the Eastern District of Virginia, Alexandria Division, the Court held that an action lies in Virginia for the tortious interference with parental rights. *Wyatt v. McDermott,* 283 Va. 685, 692, 725 S.E.2d 555, 558 (2018). The Court determined that tortious interference with parental rights "existed at common law and continues to exist today." *Id.* In recognizing that the parent-child relationship is protected by due process clause of the Fourteenth Amendment to the United States Constitution, and that a parent's right to raise a child is "perhaps the oldest fundamental liberty interest," the Court rationalized that parents must have "a cause of action against third parties who seek to interfere with this right." *Id.* In distinguishing tortious interference of parental rights with alienation of affection, which was abolished by Va. Code § 8.01-220, the Court explained that intentional interference "intimates that the complaining parent has been deprived of his/her parental or custodial rights" whereas alienation of affection implies that the parent is not able to enjoy the company of the child. *Wyatt v. McDermott,* at 698, 561–62. The elements that comprise tortious interference are:

(1) the complaining parent has a right to establish or maintain a parental or custodial relationship with his/her minor child;

(2) a party outside of the relationship between the complaining parent and his/her child intentionally interfered with the complaining parent's parental or custodial relationship with his/her child by removing or detaining the child from returning to the complaining parent, without that parent's consent, or by otherwise preventing the complaining parent from exercising his/her parental or custodial rights;

(3) the outside party's intentional interference caused harm to the complaining parent's parental or custodial relationship with his/her child; and

(4) damages resulted from such interference.

*Wyatt v. McDermott*, at 699, 562 (citation omitted).

The case of *Coward v. Wellmont Health Sys.*, 295 Va. 351, 812 S.E.2d 766 (2018) explained that not any interference with parental rights is actionable under this tort, but rather, the complaining conduct must amount to "tortious interference as that concept is summarized both in the text of and the comments to the Restatement." *Id.* at 360 (additional citation omitted). The interfering person must have knowledge that the parent did not consent and "that the child is away from the home against the will of the parent." *Id.* at 361 (additional citation omitted). The "against-the-will-of-the-parent require-ment serves as an overarching limitation on the tort." *Id.* In *Coward*, the Court of Appeals sustained a demurer filed by health care workers and an attorney since there was no allegation that these people participated in a conspiracy or concert of action with the allegedly offending party.

In *Padula-Wilson v. Landry*, 841 S.E.2d 864 (2020), the Court held that on the facts of this specific case an action for tortious interference could not be maintained against a guardian ad litem and several counselors and therapists who participated in a contested custody litigation. The Court noted that "intentional interference with parental rights applies only to a tortious interference" and must involve knowingly keeping a child from a parent who is "legally entitled" to custody. *Id.* at 870. The Court noted that this matter involved a contested custody and visitation proceedings, and throughout the litigation the mother "was afforded ample due process." *Id.* The allegedly false and misleading statements that mother complained about had been subject to cross-examination, rebuttal evidence and the appropriate weight afforded by the trial judge in the custody litigation. *Id.* at 870–71. As the Court noted, the custody of the minor children "was adjudicated in a series of hearing and orders," "[d]ivorce and custody cases inherently involve enough frustration, heartache, stress, and expense," and it was not appropriate to "expand the scope of the tort of interference with parental rights by opening a new front for disappointed, angry, frustrated, or vindictive parents to renew battle." *Id.* at 871. The Court ultimately concluded that "no cause of action for tortious interference with a parental or custodial relationship may be maintained against a guardian ad litem or an adverse expert witness based upon his/her expert testimony and/or participation in a child custody and visitation proceeding." *Id.* Although the case claims to be limited to its facts, its preclusive effects of barring an action for tortious interference with parental rights against a guardian ad litem or adverse expert witness in a contested custody case seems too broadly apply to any such litigation in Virginia.

## § 14.08    Failure to Provide Support

Most often, when a parent fails to provide support, the child does not have a cause of action in tort, even upon reaching majority. When the parties live together as a family, a nonsupport action in juvenile and domestic relations court is appropriate. This may lead to a finding of criminal nonsupport.

For a child to sue directly might have a damaging effect upon the parent's control over the family budget, and upon the harmony of the family itself. See, e.g., *Wright v. Wright,* 213 Va. 177, 191 S.E.2d 223 (1972).

The other possibility is a creditor's action against the parent for the furnishing of necessaries, which operates in the same fashion as the action for necessaries furnished a spouse, discussed at Chapter 12.

# CHAPTER 15

# Duties of Parent and Child

## SYNOPSIS

## § 15.01    Child Support

[1]    *Introduction.* Children are incapable, at least at an early age, of supporting themselves. From time immemorial, it has been the parents' responsibility, and particularly the father's, to see that the minor child has adequate food, clothing, and shelter. *Buchanan v. Buchanan,* 170 Va. 458, 471, 197 S.E. 426, 432 (1938) (quoting from 1 Minor's *Institutes* 405). In return for support, education and protection, the child's earnings, income from property and services belonged to the parent, together with obedience and respect. Katz, Schroeder & Sidman, *Emancipating Our Children— Coming of Legal Age in America,* 7 Fam. L.Q. 211, 212, 214 (1973).

The questions involving child support are basically three: Who is owed support? What kind of support is due? What kind of proceedings are involved in establishing a duty of support or in collecting support? Although some parts of the problem will be treated elsewhere, the following sections are designed to answer these questions.

See generally Margaret F. Brinig, *Finite Horizons: The American Family*, 2 Intl. J. Children's Rts. 293 (1994); Elizabeth S. Scott & Robert E. Scott, *Parents as Fiduciaries*, 81 Va. L. Rev. 2401 (1995); Barbara Bennett Woodhouse, *"Who Owns the Child?" Meyer and Pierce and the Child as Property*, 33 Wm. & Mary L. Rev. 995 (1992); 14A Michie's Jurisprudence *Parent and Child* § 17.

**[2]   *Married Parents and Natural Children.*** At common law only the father of a legitimate child had the duty of providing support, since the married woman owned no property of her own, and her wages belonged to her husband. The duty is now, by statute, given to both husband and wife. Va. Code §§ 20-61, 20-107.2, 20-108.1, 20-108.2, and 20-124.2. See, e.g., *Featherstone v. Brooks,* 220 Va. 443, 448, 258 S.E.2d 513, 516 (1979) ("Both parents of a child owe that child a duty of support during minority").

This rule holds true even though the marriage between the parents is absolutely void because bigamous. *Brown v. Commonwealth ex rel. Custis,* 218 Va. 40, 48, 235 S.E.2d 325, 330 (1977). See also *Kasey v. Richardson,* 331 F. Supp. 580 (W.D. Va. 1971) (recovery of social security after attempted bigamous common law marriage by parents).

**[3]   *Married Parents: Artificial Insemination.*** By statute, a child of a married woman conceived through artificial insemination with her husband's consent is treated as the natural child of the husband. Both parents, therefore, owe the child the duty of support. Va. Code § 20-158. *L.M.S. v. S.L.S.,* 105 Wis. 2d 118, 122, 312 N.W.2d 853, 855 (1981); *People v. Sorensen,* 68 Cal. 2d 280, 66 Cal. Rptr. 7, 437 P.2d 495 (1968). Another way of reaching the same result is through estoppel or implied contract. See *L.M.S. v. S.L.S.,* 105 Wis. 2d 118, 121–22, 312 N.W.2d 853, 855 (1981); *Anonymous v. Anonymous,* 41 Misc. 2d 886, 246 N.Y.S.2d 835 (1964).

**[4]   *Unwedded Parents, Natural Children.*** The child of unwedded parents was historically the responsibility of the mother, and, secondarily, the state. The father did not become legally responsible until the Supreme Court case of *Gomez v. Perez,* 408 U.S. 920, 92 S. Ct. 2479, 33 L. Ed. 2d 331 (1972), which stated that if the parents of legitimate children owed a duty of support, unwedded parents did likewise. This is now confirmed in Va. Code § 20-61.3, which requires support by the father once paternity has been admitted or proven beyond a reasonable doubt. However, a separation agreement that acknowledged that the husband was not the father of his wife's child, born during the marriage, waived her right to enforce express promises made prior to and after the birth to support the child as if it were his own. The agreement allowed the wife to remain in the marital residence for a year and have $6,500 to cover the birth expenses and care of the infant. *Mills v. Mills*, 36 Va. Cir. 351 (Fairfax Co. 1995).

A dependent illegitimate child is able to receive compensation under the wrongful death statute, Va. Code § 8.01-53. *Carroll v. Sneed*, 211 Va. 640, 642, 179 S.E.2d 620, 622 (1971); *Withrow v. Edwards*, 181 Va. 344, 25 S.E.2d 343 (1943). Having established paternity, the illegitimate child must also prove damages—that by the decedent's death he sustained pecuniary loss, and was damaged by the loss of decedent's care, attention, and society or suffered mental anguish. *Carroll v. Sneed*, 211 Va. at 643, 179 S.E.2d at 622 (1971). This is now confirmed in Va. Code § 20-49.1, which requires support by the father once paternity has been admitted or proven by clear and convincing evidence.

**[5]  *De Facto Parents*.** Frequently, a stepparent will assume the role of supporting his new family. The question is whether this role is legally binding, and the answer is that it is, if the stepparent is in other respects acting as a de facto parent, or if some detrimental reliance has taken place. Obviously if there is a contract between the natural parent and the stepparent, it will be binding between them, but if the child's welfare is in question, the court will not hesitate to require the natural parent to support the child. See, e.g., *Huckaby v. Huckaby*, 75 Ill. App. 3d 195, 30 Ill. Dec. 909, 393 N.E.2d 1256 (1979); *Pappas v. Pappas*, 247 Iowa 638, 75 N.W.2d 264 (1956); cf. *Goodpasture v. Goodpasture*, 7 Va. App. 55, 371 S.E.2d 845 (1988); and *Buchanan v. Buchanan*, 170 Va. 458, 477, 197 S.E. 426, 434 (1938) (contract between natural parents relieving one of support ineffective).

In *T . . . v. T . . .*, 216 Va. 867, 224 S.E.2d 148 (1976), a man married a woman he knew was pregnant by another. After the child's birth, the couple lived together for some time, during which the husband supported the child. When the couple separated, the husband was estopped to deny his responsibility for supporting the child, since the woman had given up employment and her plans for relinquishing the child for adoption in reliance upon his promise to support the child as if he were the natural father. Generally though, a stepparent has no duty to support his or her former spouse's child absent a clear agreement to do so or the formal adoption of the child. See *NPA v. WBA*, 8 Va. App. 246, 249, 380 S.E.2d 178, 180 (1989). It is noted that *T . . . v. T . . .* was decided before the enactment of

Virginia's Pre-Marital Agreement Act (Va. Code § 20-147 et seq.), and that result could be very different today since agreements between married people are generally required to be in writing and signed by them (see Va. Code §§ 20-149 and 20-155).

Where the husband allowed language to be entered in the final degree that acknowledged his responsibility to pay for the infant child born during the parties' marriage, the decree was held res judicata. When the wife sought to collect child support, the husband was barred from introducing genetic evidence showing that he could not have been the child's father. *Rose v. Rose*, 1993 Va. App. LEXIS 375. See also *Stover v. Stover*, 31 Va. Cir. 484 (City of Roanoke 1990).

A grandparent who is a child's "legal custodian" under a parental consent order has the duty to provide the child with food, shelter, education, and ordinary medical care while the child is residing with the grandparent. Va. Code § 16.1-228. However, absent formal adoption or a clear support contract or agreement, the grandparent has no duty to support the child. *Russell v. Russell*, 35 Va. App. 360, 545 S.E.2d 548 (2001) (court erred in ordering grandfather to pay child support to grandmother, when divorced grandparents were "legal custodians" of child who lived with grandmother).

**[6]   *Adopted Children.*** Adopted children, by statute, are to be treated in all respects like legitimate children. Va. Code § 63.2-1215. They are therefore owed the duty of support by both adoptive parents, but not by their natural parents.

**[7]   *Institutionalized Children.*** Institutionalized children are still owed the duty of support, unless a court removes that responsibility from their natural parents. Va. Code § 16.1-290.

Likewise, Va. Code § 63.2-1908 provides that any payment for a child's welfare under public assistance constitutes a debt on the part of the persons responsible for the child. See, e.g., *Hodges v. Dep't of Soc. Servs, Div. of Child Support Enforcement*, 45 Va. App. 118, 609 S.E.2d 61 (2005) (construing meaning of "public assistance moneys" in Va. Code § 63.2-1908). The homestead exemption in bankruptcy does not apply to debts for child support. Va. Code § 34-5.

**[8]   *Children in Foster Placement.*** By statute in Virginia, children in foster care must be supported by their natural parents. Va. Code § 16.1-290. Failure to provide support will be one of the indicia in determining whether parental rights should be terminated, or whether children should be returned to their parents. See Va. Code § 16.1-283B(2). This rule is in effect even if the child has been involuntarily removed from the parents through a dependency proceeding. See also Va. Code § 16.1-252(F)(3) and Va. Code § 63.2-909, which provide for support of a child placed involuntarily in foster care after removal from the parents. Payment is to be made to the local department of social services. The department is to be subrogated to the right of the child to bring a support action for money expended by the department.

If the person responsible for the child fails or refuses to pay for such support on a timely basis, the local board may petition the juvenile court to order payment. Va. Code § 63.2-910.

**[9]    *Emancipation of Minors, in General.*** In general, a child is emancipated when there is no longer any need for parental support and control. In many cases, emancipation occurs when some other person or agency, such as a spouse or the armed forces, takes responsibility for the child. In other cases, the minor takes on the responsibilities by becoming financially or otherwise independent from the parents. Finally, emancipation occurs in the majority of cases when the child comes of age, and is deemed by law to be able to make critical decisions independently. Emancipation, except by age, usually requires consent of the parents. These general rules are now codified in Va. Code §§ 8.01-229, 16.1-241, 16.1-331 through 16.1-334, which provide for a uniform procedure governing emancipation of minors over sixteen, and authorize court emancipation if the minor is (1) validly married, (2) in the armed forces, (3) willingly living apart from his or her parents, or (4) seeks to marry. In one recent case, the father was able to show that his employed daughter was emancipated, although she continued to live with her mother. *Ware v. Ware,* 10 Va. App. 352, 391 S.E.2d 887 (1990).

Va. Code §§ 8.01-229 and 16.1-334 detail the effects of an emancipation order, which are to free the minor to enter into contracts, execute a will, sue or be sued, and to buy and sell real estate. Va. Code § 16.1-334. An emancipated minor may marry without parental consent. Va. Code § 16.1-334(16).

See generally Katz, Schroeder & Sidman, *Emancipating Our Children— Coming of Legal Age in America,* 7 Fam. L.Q. 211, 217 (1973).

**[10]    *Emancipation by Reaching Majority.*** A husband and wife executed a separation agreement that was incorporated into a final decree of divorce and provided that the husband was to pay child support until the child's education was complete. This amount was later modified upwards, and finally reduced. After the youngest child reached eighteen, the statutory age of majority in Virginia since 1975, the mother sought general relief, alleging arrearages. The Virginia Supreme Court held that although the legal obligation of support terminated the husband's obligation to pay the modified amount under Va. Code § 20-61, the contractual obligation to pay the original amount continued. *Cutshaw v. Cutshaw,* 220 Va. 638, 640–41, 261 S.E.2d 52, 53–4 (1979). See also *Eaton v. Eaton,* 215 Va. 824, 213 S.E.2d 789 (1975) (although parties had an agreement providing for support to age 21, the age of majority changed. They were operating under a court decree modifying the original agreement when the child reached eighteen, so that the court's statutory jurisdiction ceased at the child's reaching majority).

Va. Code §§ 20-124.2 and 20-103 require that divorcing parents provide support for any child of the marriage until age 18, and if the child is in high school, is not self-supporting, and remains living in the home of the child support payee, the child support obligation continues until the earlier of the child graduating from high school or turning the age of 19.

**[11]** *Emancipation by Marriage.* Generally speaking, when a child marries, the parents will no longer be responsible for support, since that duty devolves upon the new spouse. See, e.g., *Bennett v. Bennett,* 179 Va. 239, 243, 18 S.E.2d 911, 913 (1942). Va. Code § 16.1-334(12) provides that a minor who petitioned for, and was granted emancipation, can no longer receive support from his or her parents.

**[12]** *Emancipation by Joining Armed Forces.* Traditionally, emancipation through enlistment in the armed services constitutes a shifting of responsibility from the parent to the government. See, e.g., *Iroquois Iron Co. v. Industrial Commission,* 294 Ill. 106, 128 N.E. 289 (1920); Va. Code § 8.01-229.

**[13]** *Emancipation by Independence.* In the case of *Buxton v. Bishop,* 185 Va. 1, 37 S.E.2d 755 (1946), a minor son supported himself, working away from home, drew his own wages and spent them as he alone desired. His father could not have successfully proceeded against his employer for his wages, and accordingly was not responsible for the hospital expenses occasioned by the son's last illness. See also *Ware v. Ware,* 10 Va. App. 352, 391 S.E.2d 887 (1990) (minor living with mother but employed full-time and able to support herself). A parent who is ready and able to pay support need not do so if a child chooses a different lifestyle against the parent's advice and wishes. *Parker v. Stage,* 43 N.Y.2d 128, 400 N.Y.S.2d 794, 371 N.E.2d 513 (1977). Va. Code § 16.1-331 provides authority for a child of at least 16 years of age, or the parent of the child, to file a petition for emancipation.

**[14]** *Support of Disabled Child or Aged Parent.* Va. Code § 20-61 provides for misdemeanor punishment for any person deserting or willfully neglecting or refusing to pay support of an adult child who is handicapped or otherwise incapacitated when the child is in necessitous circumstances. Va. Code § 20-88 imposes a similar requirement for children to support parents who are in necessitous circumstances, and authorizes juvenile and domestic relations courts to order a child to contribute his or her proper share of the support of a necessitous parent.

Necessitous is a relative term. The son or daughter of sufficient means "must do more than relieve the pangs of hunger, provide shelter and furnish only enough clothes to cover the nakedness of the parent." The necessary support should comport with the health, comfort, and welfare of normal individuals according to their standards of living and the means of the child. *Mitchell-Powers Hardware Co. v. Eaton*, 171 Va. 255, 263, 198 S.E. 496, 500 (1938).

The court of appeals has held that the child support guidelines, Va. Code § 20-108.2(B), should be the basis for awards to adult disabled children unless the court gives written reason for deviation from them. *Miller v. Miller*, 1993 Va. App. LEXIS 646 (Dec. 28, 1993) (unpublished). See *Rinaldi v. Dumsick*, 32 Va. App. 330, 528 S.E.2d 134 (2000) (court's decision not to deviate from guideline support amount, when disabled child had independent financial resources consisting of SSI benefits and part-time wages, was within court's discretion). The support required for adult disabled children will thus normally be higher than that given to needy parents under Va. Code § 20-88.

Language requiring support of disabled children past the age of majority is found in Va. Code § 16.1-278.15, which applies to juvenile and domestic relations district courts, and in Va. Code § 20-124.2(C), which applies to courts of record. In 2015, Va. Code §§ 16.1-278.15 and 20-124.2(C) were amended to clarify that an initial child support award could be made for a disabled child over the age of 18 or 19 provided that the child's disability existed either before the child turned 18 or 19 (as long as the child met the requirements of clauses (i), (ii), and (iii) of Section 20-124.2(C)). The test for determining the need for continued support is the same in both statutes. *Germek v. Germek*, 34 Va. App. 1, 537 S.E.2d 596 (2000). Under the statutes, a court may order continued support for a child over the age of 18 who is (1) severely and permanently mentally or physically disabled, (2) unable to live independently and be self-supporting, and (3) residing in the home of a parent seeking child support. Proof of all three elements is required, and an award of continued support requires a finding that the statutory elements are causally linked, that is, that the child's severe and permanent disability renders the child unable to live independently and be self-supporting. *Germek v. Germek*, 34 Va. App. 1, 537 S.E.2d 596 (2000) (evidence was insufficient to establish that disability rendered child unable to live independently and be self-supporting). See *Mullin v. Mullin*, 45 Va. App. 289, 610 S.E.2d 331 (2005) (no requirement for child's "severe and permanent" disability to be established by expert medical testimony); *Rinaldi v. Dumsick*, 32 Va. App. 330, 528 S.E.2d 134 (2000) (continued support was appropriate for child with physical and cognitive impairments, even though child held part-time grocery clerk's job).

In *Jacobs v. Church*, 36 Va. Cir. 277 (Spotsylvania Co. 1995), the reciprocal duty of caring for an aged parent is discussed. Mrs. Church took her mother, an Alzheimer's patient, into her home and cared for her during her last two years of life. Mrs. Church reimbursed herself $96 a day for the services she provided. These had to be paid back to her mother's estate because the daughter proved no express contract, and "services performed by a child to an aging parent are presumably rendered in obedience to natural promptings of love and affection, loyalty, and filial duty, rather than upon an expectation of compensation."

**[15]** *Termination of Parental Rights and Responsibilities.* Termination of parental rights also terminates the parent's responsibility of parental support. The issue of support after termination is not settled by statute, but the concept that a party whose parental rights have been terminated is a "legal stranger" to the child implies that the parent no longer has a duty to support the child. *Commonwealth ex rel. Spotsylvania County Dep't of Soc. Servs. v. Fletcher*, 38 Va. App. 107, 562 S.E.2d 327 (2002), *aff'd*, 266 Va. 1, 581 S.E.2d 213 (2003).

**[16]** *Death of Obligor Parent.* The death of a parent obliged to provide support will terminate the duty to support a child. Thus, there can be no recovery against the estate of a deceased parent, absent a written agreement to the contrary. Va. Code § 20-107.2. This statute supersedes the decision of *Morris v. Henry*, 193 Va. 631, 70 S.E.2d 417 (1952), which found "no express or implied inhibition against the right of a court in a divorce suit to decree that liability for the support of minor children shall survive the death of the parent against whom it is decreed." *Id.* at 639, 70 S.E.2d at 422. There may be a suit against the estate for arrearages, however. On *Morris v. Henry*, see generally Note, 10 Wash. & Lee L. Rev. 226 (1953).

**[17]** *Contract Between Parents Regarding Support.* A contract between parents involving support of a child will not operate to relieve a parent of his duty to support the child. *Goodpasture v. Goodpasture*, 7 Va. App. 55, 371 S.E.2d 845 (1988); *Buchanan v. Buchanan*, 170 Va. 458, 197 S.E. 426

(1938). A contract between parents involving child support that is incorporated into a divorce decree will not affect the trial court's power to modify the decree with respect to the maintenance of minor children. *Edwards v. Lowry*, 232 Va. 110, 112, 348 S.E.2d 259, 261 (1986). *See also Goldin v. Goldin*, 34 Va. App. 95, 538 S.E.2d 326 (2000) (contract for post-minority child support).

An agreement between parents that is incorporated into a divorce decree and provides for "renegotiation" of child support on the happening of certain future events, such as the emancipation of a child, is not void, although the parents' renegotiation of child support must be submitted to the divorce court for approval. *Riggins v. O'Brien*, 263 Va. 444, 559 S.E.2d 673 (2002). In contrast, a "self-executing" agreement incorporated into a divorce decree that provides for child support adjustments without further court action on the happening of certain future events, such as fluctuation in child care costs, may be valid and enforceable if it (1) is consistent with the children's best interests, (2) does not circumvent the divorce court's jurisdiction to enforce or modify support, (3) does not "contract away" the children's right to support from either parent, and (4) has been determined by the divorce court to be consistent with the children's best interest and not void as against public policy. *Shoup v. Shoup*, 37 Va. App. 240, 556 S.E.2d 783 (2001).

Under Va. Code § 20-109.1 as amended in 2003, an agreement between the parties concerning modification of child support that is incorporated in a decree is valid and enforceable without a further court decree, but the court retains the power to revise the decree under Va. Code § 20-108.

Likewise, the unwed father in *Lawson v. Murphy*, 36 Va. Cir. 465 (Wise Co. 1995), was unable to enforce a contract according to which he agreed to pay the child's mother $7,500 to replace all child support. The mother received AFDC payments and the father had to reimburse the state.

Nor could a noncustodial father complain that the child's mother had forgiven the child support obligation years ago because receipt of it caused the mother and her new husband to receive a smaller military dependent's allowance. *Carter v. Hall*, 42 Va. Cir. 437 (City of Roanoke 1997).

[18] *What Type of Support is Due: Standard of Living.* Although alimony will not increase based upon a change in the obligor parent's income following a divorce, child support is not contingent upon either providing the barest necessities for the child or the continued vitality of the parents' marriage. Therefore, a dramatic increase in a parent's ability to provide support will be reflected in a change of circumstances for child support regardless of when the increase occurs. See, e.g., *Conway v.*

*Conway,* 10 Va. App. 653, 395 S.E.2d 464 (1990); *Cole v. Cole,* 44 Md. App. 435, 409 A.2d 734 (1979).

The fact that the father of two illegitimate children also had two legitimate children to support should not have been ignored by the trial court when applying the guidelines of Va. Code § 20-108.2. Treating the father as though he had only two children was not in the best interests of the legitimate children. *Zubricki v. Motter,* 12 Va. App. 999, 406 S.E.2d 672 (1991).

Income under Chapter 63 of the Code includes not just earnings from employment but rather "any periodic form of payment due an individual from any source." This includes commissions, dividends, severance pay, social security benefits, unemployment insurance benefits, capital gains, spousal support, and gifts, prizes, and awards. Va. Code § 63.2-1900.

Orthodontic care, day camp, and music lessons are additional permissible expenses attributable to the increased needs of growing children, and therefore may evidence a need for increased child support payments. *Featherstone v. Brooks,* 220 Va. 443, 447, 258 S.E.2d 513, 515–16 (1979). However, a noncustodial father was not required to pay necessary hospital care for his minor daughter when she gave birth to an illegitimate child when the mother assumed responsibility for the cost of services and signed the hospital admission form. The mother had merely provided the hospital with information concerning hospital insurance carried by the noncustodial father, which did not cover maternity benefits to a child. *Winchester Medical Center v. Giffin,* 9 Va. Cir. 260 (City of Winchester 1987). The court found that any changes in child support provisions would be better served by proceedings for that purpose than by independent actions instituted by ostensible third-party creditors. According to new Va. Code § 20-60.3, all orders directing payment of child support shall state whether there is an order for health care coverage for dependent children. The cost of health care coverage is a guideline factor used in setting support under amended Va. Code § 20-108.1.

**[19]  *College Education.*** Although generally parents have no duty to supply their children with higher education, courts have upheld orders for college tuition costs as part of divorce decrees. The reasoning is that the children of divorced parents may otherwise be less likely to receive the benefits of higher education than those of married parents. See, e.g., *In re Marriage of Vrban,* 293 N.W.2d 198, 202 (Iowa 1980). This result is typically reached in Virginia through an agreement between the parents. See, e.g., *Cutshaw v. Cutshaw,* 220 Va. 638, 261 S.E.2d 52 (1979).

The Circuit Court of Fairfax County determined in *Ackerson v. Ackerson,* 22 Va. Cir. 215 (1990), that a clause in a property settlement agreement providing that "Husband shall pay all reasonable expenditures for a college education for the minor children" should be construed under the circumstances as including the approximately $21,000 annual tuition at Duke University. The father contended that all he was required to pay was the approximately $10,000 for tuition at a state school. The court found that the school was a reasonable place for the daughter to attend college given the father's income and social circumstances. He is a partner at a Washington, D.C. law firm who attended graduate and law school at Harvard University.

Where a father agreed to pay for his child's "college expenses," the trial court correctly interpreted the phrase broadly and included not only the costs for tuition, room, board, and books, but also other ordinary living expenses such as an allowance and a computer. *Douglas v. Hammett,* 28 Va. App. 517, 507 S.E.2d 98 (1998).

See generally Washburn, *Post-Majority Support: Oh Dad, Poor Dad,* 44 Temple L.Q. 319 (1971).

   **[20]   *Domicile or Fault of Parent or Child.*** Where the husband is willing to support his children but the wife, without reasonable excuse, refuses to live with him and keeps the children from him, he is not guilty of "willfully neglecting and refusing to support them" within the criminal nonsupport statute. *Butler v. Commonwealth,* 132 Va. 609, 613, 110 S.E. 868, 869 (1922); see also *Mihalcoe v. Holub,* 130 Va. 425, 107 S.E. 704 (1921). This is because the duty to support children is based largely upon his right to their custody and control. *Butler v. Commonwealth,* 132 Va. at 614, 110 S.E. at 869 (1922). He has a right at common law to maintain them in his own home, and he cannot be compelled against his will to do so elsewhere.

However, when one parent has rendered it impossible for his spouse and children to remain in the marital home, "he cannot by his misconduct escape the performance of the duty which the law imposes upon him." *Owens v. Owens,* 96 Va. 191, 195, 31 S.E. 72, 74 (1898). The wife may clearly obtain child support if she is establishing a domicile for the purpose of getting a divorce, Va. Code § 20-97, or if the husband's actions are placing unconstitutional restraints upon her exercise of religion. See *I. v. I.,* 107 Misc. 2d 663, 435 N.Y.S.2d 928 (1981).

If a child refuses to live with a parent or to obey his reasonable suggestions, abandoning the parent, the parent no longer has a duty to support the child, *Parker v. Stage,* 43 N.Y.2d 128, 400 N.Y.S.2d 794, 371

N.E.2d 513 (1977), even though the child must otherwise be supported by public welfare. However, a family disagreement relative to a child's living in a college dormitory is not sufficient grounds to deny support. *Anthony v. Anthony,* 213 Va. 721, 722, 196 S.E.2d 66, 67 (1973).

[21]  *Necessaries.* If a father abandons a child or drives him from his home, he is liable to any persons furnishing necessary support. The person furnishing support must prove that there was an unjustified abandonment, that the support furnished was necessary, and that the credit of the father was legally the basis of the advances. *Mihalcoe v. Holub,* 130 Va. 425, 430, 107 S.E. 704, 706 (1921). A defense to an action for necessaries will be that the child was emancipated, so that the parent no longer owed the duty of support. *Buxton v. Bishop,* 185 Va. 1, 37 S.E.2d 755 (1946). Similarly, if the medical expenses that the child incurred were voluntary, as in the case of an elective abortion, the parent will have no duty to pay for them unless authorized by him. *Winchester Medical Center v. Giffin,* 9 Va. Cir. 260 (City of Winchester 1987); *Akron City Hospital v. Anderson,* 68 Ohio Misc. 14, 22 Ohio Op. 3d 238, 428 N.E.2d 472 (1981).

[22]  *Standing to Bring Cause of Action for Support.* Actions or suits by a child against a parent will not be encouraged since they tend to disturb familial relationships, and disrupt parental discipline and authority. *Buchanan v. Buchanan,* 170 Va. 458, 472–73, 197 S.E. 426, 432 (1938). Children do not therefore have the power to compel their father to provide them an income out of his estate for their future support and education. Nor do they have a property right in the agreement between their parents regarding their support. *Yarborough v. Yarborough,* 290 U.S. 202, 54 S. Ct. 181, 78 L. Ed. 269 (1933).

However, if a child is in necessitous circumstances, an action in circuit court may be brought by the child through that child's next friend, *McClaugherty v. McClaugherty,* 180 Va. 51, 68–69, 21 S.E.2d 761, 768 (1942), in addition to the usual nonsupport action.

See generally 14A Michie's Jurisprudence *Parent and Child* § 19.

[23]  *Types of Actions Available.* The Uniform Interstate Family Support Act, Va. Code §§ 20-88.32 to 20-88.95, allows a Virginia parent to enforce a foreign support judgment against a nonresident parent under the doctrine of comity. This is true despite the fact that the foreign decree may be retroactively modified, *Scott v. Sylvester,* 220 Va. 182, 184–85, 257 S.E.2d 774, 775 (1979), and despite the fact that all arrearages did not accrue while the custodial parent was in Virginia. The duty of support is that imposed by the law of the state where the obligor was present during the period for

which support is sought. *Id.* at 186, 257 S.E.2d at 776 (citing Childers v. Childers, 19 N.C. App. 220, 224–25, 198 S.E.2d 485, 488 (1973)).

The support decree of a juvenile and domestic relations court under Va. Code § 20-61.2 et seq. will not be terminated by a final divorce when the divorce decree is silent as to support. Va. Code § 20-79; *Werner v. Commonwealth,* 212 Va. 623, 625, 186 S.E.2d 76, 78 (1972). See also *Jones v. Richardson,* 320 F. Supp. 929 (W.D. Va. 1970) (ex parte divorce).

**[24]    *Jurisdiction over Defendant.*** Under the Virginia long-arm statute, Va. Code § 8.01-328.1, an action for child support may be maintained against a nonresident defendant if pursuant to a divorce or separate maintenance action where the matrimonial domicile was in Virginia and the plaintiff spouse resides in Virginia, or when based upon a prior court decree of support pursuant to an absolute or *a mensa* divorce, where in personam jurisdiction was obtained. Virginia's long-arm statute also provides for personal jurisdiction over a non-resident parent who conceived or fathered a child in this Commonwealth.

In other cases, jurisdiction is obtained pursuant to Va. Code § 8.01-460, which provides that a decree of judgment for support or maintenance of a spouse or child that is payable in future installments shall be a lien upon real estate designated by the court.

**[25]    *Procedural Rules Applicable.*** A prior finding that a man was the father of a child in a divorce proceeding acts to collaterally estop him from establishing through conclusive blood testing that he was not the biological parent. *Slagle v. Slagle,* 11 Va. App. 341, 398 S.E.2d 346 (1990).

Where a father signed an acknowledgment of paternity, but there had never been a judicial determination of paternity, the putative father was able to contest paternity in a child support proceeding. *Dunbar v. Hogan,* 16 Va. App. 653, 432 S.E.2d 16 (1993). Although Va. Code § 20-49.1 provided that an acknowledgment of paternity has the same effect as a judgment entered pursuant to Va. Code § 20-49.8, the statute did not preclude a putative father from contesting paternity where there had been no prior adjudication.

Although an adult who was a party to a proceeding and determined to be the natural father may be collaterally estopped from subsequently denying paternity, a child who was not a party to that law suit is not bound by that parental determination. A child, through his next friend, was able to successfully maintain a petition for child support against his natural father despite a judicial determination in a prior divorce suit that another man was his father. *Shelton v. An Infant,* 12 Va. App. 859, 406 S.E.2d 421 (1991).

Under Va. Code § 19.2-305(B), a father who is placed on probation following a conviction may be required to provide for the support of his children or others for whose support he may be legally responsible. *Martin v. Commonwealth*, 274 Va. 733, 652 S.E.2d 109 (2007).

Under amended Va. Code § 20-49.6, fathers between the ages of fourteen and sixteen who are represented by a guardian ad litem may testify and may be required to provide for support and maintenance just as they would be if adult.

When the possible sentence for misdemeanor nonsupport is six months or greater, counsel must be provided indigent parents. *Potts v. Superintendent of Virginia State Penitentiary*, 213 Va. 432, 192 S.E.2d 780 (1972) (rule applied prospectively only).

Forms useful in prosecuting and defending actions for custody and support may be found in L. Bean, *Virginia Law Practice System, Domestic Relations* § 6655 et seq. Forms for *Juvenile and Domestic Relations Actions for Support* appear in § 6905.2 et seq.

## § 15.02 Education

**[1] Introduction.** Until the nineteenth century, most education of minor children took place in the home and was conducted by the parents. See *Wisconsin v. Yoder*, 406 U.S. 205, 226 n.15, 92 S. Ct. 1526, 32 L. Ed. 2d 15 (1972). At that time, Virginia, along with all other jurisdictions, established a system of public education. Va. Const. art. VIII, § 3; *Brown v. Board of Education*, 347 U.S. 483, 489 n.4, 74 S. Ct. 686, 98 L. Ed. 873, 53 Ohio Op. 326 (1954). Education until a certain age became compulsory. Va. Code § 22.1-254.

Even though parents no longer have direct control over their children's formal education in most cases, teachers have only the privileges ceded to them by the parents. Parents may choose between public, parochial, *Pierce v. Society of Sisters*, 268 U.S. 510, 45 S. Ct. 571, 69 L. Ed. 1070 (1925), and private education, and home instruction; for the most part, local school boards control curriculum and library content in the public schools.

**[2] Compulsory Education.** Va. Code § 22.1-254 provides that every parent of a child between the ages of five and seventeen shall send that child to a public, parochial or private school or have the child specially taught by an approved tutor. The right to a free public education is guaranteed by Va. Const. art VIII, § 3.

Va. Code § 22.1-3.1, amended in 1991, provides that the principal or the principal's designee shall record the student's official state birth number from a certified copy of the student's birth record before first admission. If there is no birth certificate, the student shall be admitted to public school upon presentation of information sufficient to estimate the age of the child with reasonable certainty.

In *Rice v. Commonwealth,* 188 Va. 224, 49 S.E.2d 342 (1948), parents sought exemption from compulsory education statutes because their deeply held religious beliefs included the commandment that parents teach and train their children in the ways of life. They were held not to be exempt from the compulsory education statutes. *Id.* at 234, 49 S.E. at 347. The court also upheld the validity of compulsory education, *id.* at 236, 49 S.E.2d at 348, which it found reasonable.

This holding would apparently be valid despite the intervening United States Supreme Court decision in *Wisconsin v. Yoder,* 406 U.S. 205, 92 S. Ct. 1526, 32 L. Ed. 2d 15 (1972), which held that the first amendment, as incorporated through the fourteenth, precluded application of the compulsory education statute for children ages fourteen to sixteen where the children were members of the Amish religion, which had for centuries maintained a position of other-worldliness, at the same time preparing young adults for their role in the Amish religious community by a vocational training. *Grigg v. Commonwealth,* 224 Va. 356, 297 S.E.2d 799 (1982) (home schooling required approval of district superintendent).

Following the lead of Justice Douglas' separate opinion in *Yoder,* when a parent seeks to exempt a 16-year-old child on the grounds of religion, the child must also conscientiously object to school attendance. *Downing v. Fairfax County Sch. Bd.,* 28 Va. Cir. 310 (Fairfax Co. 1992). The school board may consider the views of pupils age fourteen or older after interviewing them, and need not base its decision on the training provided by the parents. To qualify for the exemption, the Virginia Supreme Court has held that the objection must not be on the basis of essentially political, sociological, or philosophical views, or a merely personal moral code, but rather must be the product of bona fide religious beliefs. *Johnson v. Prince William County Sch. Bd.,* 241 Va. 383, 404 S.E.2d 209 (1991). In 1995 and 1996, the legislature added and amended Va. Code Ann. § 22.1-279.3 to require parents to acknowledge receipt of the school board's standards of student conduct. These materials reserve parental rights to disagree with a school's policies or decisions.

**[3]  *Immunization.*** Before admission to any Virginia school, a parent must satisfy the requirement of Va. Code § 22.1-271.2 that the child be immunized, unless the student or parent submits an affidavit to the admitting official of the school stating that the administration of immunizations conflicts with the student's religious tenets or practices, or that immunization would be detrimental to the student's specified medical condition. See, e.g., *Davis v. State*, 294 Md. 370, 451 A.2d 107 (1982).

Pupils' sight and hearing shall be tested in the public schools free of expense under Va. Code § 22.1-273.

**[4]   *Curriculum and Rights of Students.*** Parents acting through local boards of education have a great influence on school curriculum. They may not, however, decide which books are to be placed in the school libraries. *Minarcini v. Strongsville City School Dist.*, 541 F.2d 577 (6th Cir. 1976).

A school may not offer elective classes in transcendental meditation, since this is really a religion and to do so would violate the constitutional prohibition against establishment of religion, *Malnak v. Yogi*, 592 F.2d 197 (3d Cir. 1977), nor require students to participate in coeducational physical education classes when close contact with members of the opposite sex while scantily attired violated the student's deeply held religious beliefs. *Moody v. Cronin*, 484 F. Supp. 270 (C.D. Ill. 1979).

A school may not interfere with a student's first amendment rights so long as the exercise does not interfere with the normal educational process. *Tinker v. Des Moines Independent Community School Board*, 393 U.S. 503, 89 S. Ct. 733, 21 L. Ed. 2d 731, 49 Ohio Op. 2d 222 (1969) (arm bands protesting Vietnam War); *Gambino v. Fairfax County School Board*, 564 F.2d 157 (4th Cir. 1977) (student newspaper censorship of article on birth control).

**[5]   *Home Instruction.*** Education, according to Va. Code § 22.1-254, must be in a public school, a private school, a parochial school or in home instruction given by a qualified tutor or teacher approved by the district superintendent. The question of whether parents without such approval could nevertheless withdraw their children from the public schools and establish their own private school was answered in the negative in *Grigg v. Commonwealth*, 224 Va. 356, 297 S.E.2d 799 (1982). The parents were ordered to provide their children with one of the forms of education listed in the statute.

**[6]   *Controversial Subjects in the Curriculum.*** A variety of cases has addressed the problem of state control over curriculum dealing with controversial topics such as sex education, now required in Virginia public schools by Va. Code § 22.1-207.1 et seq. Most cases have held that, so long as excusal privileges are afforded parents, such classes are appropriate subjects for the curriculum and do not violate the parents' first amendment or fourteenth amendment rights nor amount to an establishment of religion. See, e.g., *Citizens for Parental Rights v. San Mateo County Board of*

*Education,* 51 Cal. App. 3d 1, 124 Cal. Rptr. 68 (1975), *appeal dismissed,* 425 U.S. 908, 96 S. Ct. 1502, 47 L. Ed. 2d 759 (1976); see also *Medeiros v. Kiyosaki,* 52 Hawaii 436, 478 P.2d 314 (1970). Should the state desire to omit such a topic from study completely, as Michigan did with methods of birth control, that would be permissible as well. *Mercer v. Michigan State Board,* 379 F. Supp. 580 (E.D. Mich. 1974), *aff'd mem.,* 419 U.S. 1081, 95 S. Ct. 673, 42 L. Ed. 2d 678 (1974): "The authorities must choose which portions of the world's knowledge will be included in the curriculum's programs and courses, and what portions will be left for grasping from other sources, such as the family, peers or other institutions." *Id.* at 586.

An attempt to make family life education the province of the State Board of Education rather than local school boards was vetoed by the Governor in 1998. H. 478.

See generally Hirschoff, *Parents and the Public School Curriculum, Is There a Right to Have One's Child Excused From Objectionable Instruction?,* 50 S. Cal. L. Rev. 871 (1977).

Likewise, a series of cases beginning with *Epperson v. Arkansas,* 393 U.S. 97, 89 S. Ct. 266, 21 L. Ed. 2d 228 (1968), has allowed public schools to teach the theory of evolution. An attempt to require a concurrent instruction in the theory of scientific creationism failed in *McLean v. Arkansas Board of Education,* 529 F. Supp. 1255 (E.D. Ark. 1982), since no basis other than a religious one had been established for the creationist theory. See also *Daniel v. Waters,* 515 F.2d 485 (6th Cir. 1975) (evolution might be taught only at the same time as Biblical creation).

[7]  *Due Process.* Because education is one of the most important functions of the state, *Brown v. Board of Education,* 347 U.S. 483, 74 S. Ct. 686, 98 L. Ed. 873, 53 Ohio Op. 326 (1954), and one of the most important assets to an individual, children may not be suspended from public schools without a hearing affording them notice, an opportunity to be heard, and the privilege of confronting witnesses against them, as well as a written statement of reasons for the suspension. *Goss v. Lopez,* 419 U.S. 565, 95 S. Ct. 729, 42 L. Ed. 2d 725 (1975).

The Supreme Court, in the case of *New Jersey v. T.L.O.,* 469 U.S. 325, 105 S. Ct. 733, 83 L. Ed. 2d 720 (1985), held that a search of a student's purse by school officials must be based upon reasonable suspicion that criminal activity is taking place. In *T.L.O.,* the search of a student's purse was upheld when she had been accused of smoking in the restroom by a teacher.

[8]  *Discipline.* Public school teachers do have the right, without a prior hearing, to punish students corporally for infraction of rules. *Ingraham*

*v. Wright,* 430 U.S. 651, 97 S. Ct. 1401, 51 L. Ed. 2d 711 (1977). The punishment must be reasonable, or tort liability will result. The ability of teachers to use corporal punishment derives from the state's authority to regulate the educational process through compulsory attendance laws.

In Virginia, teachers, principals, and other employees of a school board or school are prohibited by statute from inflicting corporal punishment on a child. Va. Code § 22.1-279.1. Child Protective Services' finding of Level Three physical abuse by a teacher against a student was upheld by the Virginia Court of Appeals. *Mulvey v. Jones,* 41 Va. App. 600, 587 S.E.2d 728 (2003).

See generally Piele, *Neither Corporal Punishment Cruel Nor Due Process Due: The U.S. Supreme Court's Decision in Ingraham v. Wright,* 7 J.L. & Educ. 1 (1978); Rosenberg, *Ingraham v. Wright: The Supreme Court's Whipping Boy,* 78 Colum. L. Rev. 75 (1978).

## § 15.03    Religious Rights of Minors

[1]    *Introduction.* Until very recently, the religious preference of a minor was unquestionably that of his parent. A parent had the responsibility for the religious upbringing, and any preference the child might have could only be exercised upon his reaching majority.

The opinion of Justice Douglas, concurring and dissenting in part in *Wisconsin v. Yoder,* 406 U.S. 205, 245, 92 S. Ct. 1526, 32 L. Ed. 2d 15 (1972), suggested that the child's wishes regarding exemption from public education should be consulted; that it need not necessarily be the same as the parental desire for separation from non-Amish society.

The other indication that children might now possess rights separate from those of their parents comes from the decisions in the abortion, *Planned Parenthood v. Danforth,* 428 U.S. 52, 96 S. Ct. 2831, 49 L. Ed. 2d 788 (1976), and contraception cases, *Carey v. Population Services Int'l,* 431 U.S. 678, 97 S. Ct. 2010, 52 L. Ed. 2d 675 (1977), which hold that in these areas involving intimate decisions the parents need not give their consent. This suggests an independent right of religious exercise, if the abortion decision is taken as a relinquishment of a matter of choice to the individual because it is essentially a religious determination.

See generally Hafen, *Children's Liberation and the New Egalitarianism: Some Reservations About Abandoning Youth to Their "Rights,"* 1976 B.Y.U. L. Rev. 605; Minow, *Rights of the Next Generation: A Feminist Approach to Children's Rights,* 9 Harv. Women's L.J. 1 (1986); *Adjudicating What Yoder Left Unresolved: Religious Rights for Minor Children After Danforth and Carey,* 126 U. Pa. L. Rev. 1135 (1978).

## § 15.04    Sexual Activities of Minors

[1]    *Introduction.* In perhaps no area of family law has the change toward individual rights been more apparent than in the cases involving the sexual activities of minors. See, e.g., *Planned Parenthood of Central Missouri v. Danforth,* 428 U.S. 52, 74, 96 S. Ct. 2831, 49 L. Ed. 2d 788 (1976). The Supreme Court, in a series of cases that began with the "marital privacy" case of *Griswold v. Connecticut,* 381 U.S. 479, 85 S. Ct. 1678, 14 L. Ed. 2d 510 (1965), has held that the personal right of autonomy in matters involving birth control and abortion extends to unmarried minors as well as married adults. State statutes have extended the privacy protection further to include treatment for venereal diseases without parental notification or consent.

[2]    *Contraception.* In *Griswold v. Connecticut,* 381 U.S. 479, 85 S. Ct. 1678, 14 L. Ed. 2d 510 (1965), the Supreme Court declared that the due process clause prevented a statute from prohibiting the use of contraceptive devices to married adults. This new right of privacy was extended to unmarried adults in *Eisenstadt v. Baird,* 405 U.S. 438, 453, 92 S. Ct. 1029, 31 L. Ed. 2d 349 (1972), and to minors in *Carey v. Population Services Int'l,* 431 U.S. 678, 97 S. Ct. 2010, 52 L. Ed. 2d 675 (1977). The most recent cases have involved parental notification when prescription contraceptives are purchased. Again, the holdings have been that this requirement interferes with the unmarried minor's right to privacy. *Planned Parenthood Federation of America, Inc. v. Schweiker,* 712 F.2d 650, 229 U.S. App. D.C. 336 (D.C. Cir. 1983); *New York v. Heckler,* 719 F.2d 1191 (2d Cir. 1983), 10 Fam. L. Rep. (B.N.A.) 1024.

Information regarding contraceptives may be included within secondary school student newspapers without the administration's consent. *Gambino v. Fairfax County School Board,* 564 F.2d 157 (4th Cir. 1977).

[3]    *Abortion.* A mature, unmarried minor possesses the right, with her doctor, to elect regardless of whether to have an abortion. *Bellotti v. Baird,* 443 U.S. 622, 99 S. Ct. 3035, 61 L. Ed. 2d 797 (1979). A state may require a minor seeking an abortion to obtain the consent of a parent or guardian, provided that there is an adequate judicial bypass procedure. *Planned Parenthood of S. Pa. v. Casey,* 505 U.S. 833, 899, 112 S. CT. 2791, 120 L. Ed. 2d 674 (1992). Information regarding abortions may be published in newspapers circulated throughout the state, and a Virginia statute prohibiting publications advertising abortion was held unconstitutional in *Bigelow v. Virginia,* 421 U.S. 809, 95 S. Ct. 2222, 44 L. Ed. 2d 600 (1975).

Under Virginia law, physicians are prohibited from performing abortions on unemancipated minors without written consent from at least one parent or other authorized person (legal guardian or custodian or person standing in loco parentis) unless the minor obtains a court order. The minor may petition the Juvenile and Domestic Relations Court, and after a confidential hearing, the judge must authorize the abortion if the judge finds either that the minor is mature enough and well enough informed to make her abortion decision, in consultation with her physician, or that the desired abortion would be in her best interest. An ordering authorizing an abortion on the basis of the minor's best interests must require the physician to give at least 24 hours notice to a parent or authorized person unless the judge finds that notice would not be in the minor's best interest. Va. Code § 16.2-241(W).

A physician may perform an abortion without consent or notice or court order in cases of medical emergency or reportable abuse or neglect. A medical emergency is a condition that, in the physician's good faith clinical judgment, necessitates an immediate abortion to avert the pregnant minor's death or that creates a serious risk of substantial and irreversible impairment of a major bodily function. The abuse or neglect exception applies if the pregnant minor declares that she is abused or neglected and the physician has reason to suspect that the minor may be an abused or neglected child and makes a report in accordance with Va. Code § 63.2-1509. Abuse or neglect can also be raised at the bypass hearing, and the judge must find that notice to a parent or other authorized person is not in the minor's best interest if the judge finds that all authorized persons either are abusive or neglectful or have refused to accept their responsibilities. Va. Code § 16.2-241(W).

The provisions for dispensing with parental consent or notice do not authorize physicians to perform abortions on minors when it would be illegal to perform an abortion on an adult. Va. Code § 16.2-241(W). Virginia Code § 18.2-76, defines informed written consent to abortion, and requires that certain basic information to effect consent be given to the pregnant woman at least 24 hours before the abortion. The information must include an explanation of the proposed procedures or protocols, an instruction that she may withdraw her consent at any time prior to the procedure, an offer to speak with the physician who is to perform the abortion, a statement of the probable gestational age of the fetus at the time the procedure is to be performed, and an offer to review printed materials that must be developed by the Department of Health.

A parent may not force her minor child to undergo an abortion for financial reasons against the child's wishes. See, e.g., *In re P.,* 111 Misc. 2d 532, 444 N.Y.S.2d 545 (1981).

A state may regulate abortion, like any medical procedure, to further the health or safety of a woman seeking an abortion, but may not impose an undue burden on the right to abortion with unnecessary health regulations that have the purpose or effect of presenting a substantial obstacle to a woman seeking an abortion. *Planned Parenthood of S. Pa. v. Casey*, 505 U.S. 833, 878, 112 S. Ct. 2791, 120 L. Ed. 2d 674 (1992). Virginia's requirement that a second trimester abortion occur in a hospital has been upheld. *Simopoulos v. Virginia*, 462 U.S. 506, 103 S. Ct. 2532, 76 L. Ed. 2d 755 (1993); see Va. Code § 18.2-73. State statutes regulating methods of abortion cannot subject women's health to significant risks by forcing women to use riskier methods of abortion. *Stenberg v. Carhart*, 530 U.S. 914, 120 S. Ct. 2597, 147 L. Ed. 2d 743 (2000). Thus, former Va. Code § 18.2-74.2, which was virtually identical to the Nebraska statute, struck down by *Stenberg*, that attempted to criminalize "partial birth abortions," was likewise struck down as unconstitutional. *Richmond Med. Ctr. for Women v. Gilmore*, 224 F.3d 337 (4th Cir. 2000). Former Va. Code § 18.2-74.2 was repealed in 2003 and replaced with Va. Code § 18.2-71.1 prohibiting "partial birth infanticide."

[4]    *Sexually Transmitted Diseases.* Under Va. Code § 54.1-2969(E), minors are to be deemed adults in cases of "medical or health services needed to determine the presence of or to treat venereal disease . . . ." This means that parental consent or notification is not necessary.

[5]    *Sterilizations.* According to Va. Code § 54.1-2975, a person aged over 13 and under 18 may be sterilized against his or her will only if a petition requesting the operation is filed in circuit court by the custodial parent or parents or by the child's guardian, spouse, or next friend. The court must make the child a party defendant; serve notice of the proceedings on the child, the child's guardian or spouse, if any, and the custodial parent; and appoint an attorney-at-law for the child. The court must also determine that a full, reasonable, and comprehensible medical explanation with respect to the sterilization operation and regarding alternative methods of contraception has been given to the child and also to any guardian, spouse, or custodial parent, and must take the child's views into account. The court must determine by clear and convincing evidence that the child's mental abilities are so impaired that the child is incapable now and will be incapable in the foreseeable future of making an informed decision on sterilization, and it must also comply with the requirements applicable to involuntary sterilization of adults. If the court issues an order authorizing sterilization, it must require a 30-day waiting period from the date of the order.

The statute in effect until 1974 was upheld in *Buck v. Bell,* 274 U.S. 200, 47 S. Ct. 584, 71 L. Ed. 1000 (1927). A procedural challenge was unsuccessfully made in *Poe v. Lynchburg Training School & Hospital,* 518 F. Supp. 789 (W.D. Va. 1981). Compare *Wentzel v. Montgomery General Hospital,* 293 Md. 685, 447 A.2d 1244 (1982), *cert. denied,* 459 U.S. 1147, 103 S. Ct. 790, 74 L. Ed. 2d 995 (1983).

**[6]    *Indecent Liberties.*** A teenager who knowingly exposes him or herself to a child five or more years younger shall be guilty of a Class 1 misdemeanor under Va. Code § 18.2-370.01. This section supplements the statutory rape law, Va. Code §§ 18.2-61 and 18.2-63, which proscribes sexual intercourse with minors.

## § 15.05    Medical Care for Children

**[1]    *Introduction.*** One of the duties a parent owes a minor child is the provision of adequate medical care. Failure to provide necessary services and drugs may result in a conviction for child abuse, Va. Code § 18.2-314 and Va. Code § 63.2-100, or in a finding that the child is neglected and deprived and therefore dependent, see, e.g., *In re Alyne E.,* 113 Misc. 2d 307, 448 N.Y.S.2d 984 (1982) (mental health neglected), warranting state intervention. Va. Code §§ 54.1-2969 and 63.2-1517. However, a noncustodial parent need not pay for necessary medical care in a suit by a third-party creditor when the custodial parent had assumed responsibility on admission for the cost of obstetrical care and hospitalization of the parties' child. *Winchester Medical Center v. Giffin,* 9 Va. Cir. 260 (City of Winchester 1987).

Although there are few Virginia cases involving medical care for minor children, the law from other states is reasonably settled. Although the state will usually not intervene in a parent's considered decision regarding a method of treatment, the state will exercise its parens patriae power in certain circumstances. The easiest of these times to identify are the occasions when the child's very life, or the general well-being of the community, are threatened by parental failure to select an efficacious and accepted course of treatment. The theory in these cases is that the child must be allowed to reach the age when he or she could make the decision for or against treatment independently. *People ex rel. Wallace v. Labrenz,* 411 Ill. 618, 104 N.E.2d 769 (1952); *Custody of a Minor,* 375 Mass. 733, 379 N.E.2d 1053 (1978); see generally *The Rights of Children: A Trust Model,* 46 Ford. L. Rev. 669 (1978).

On the other extreme are the cases where the corrective treatment is elective, particularly when the treatment itself may carry some measurable risk. In such cases the decision will be made by the parents in consultation with their physician.

In most of the intermediate possibilities, state intervention does not occur, especially when the parents' objections to the usual forms of treatment are based upon their religious beliefs.

Finally, there are cases in which the critical decision is whether treatment should be continued, in the case of critically ill terminal patients, or even offered, in the case of handicapped newborns. Petitions involving medical care for children will be heard in the new family court, once it is funded. Statutes enacted in 1989 regarding the experimental family courts were repealed in 1999, including Va. Code §§ 16.1-296.1, 20-96.1, and 20-96.2. There are no longer any such courts, and all appeals from such courts have been completed.

Both parents, regardless of custody, are entitled to access their child's health records, "unless otherwise ordered by the court for good cause shown." Va. Code § 20-124.6. In *Green v. Richmond Dep't of Soc. Servs.*, 35 Va. App. 682, 547 S.E.2d 548 (2001), an incarcerated father was denied access to his 16-year-old daughter's medical records, when the daughter viewed the access as an invasion of her privacy, her treating professionals maintained that access would interfere with the daughter's treatment, the father had no specialized training or education in child development or counseling, and there was no evidence explaining how the daughter would benefit or progress in resolving her psychological issues if the father were allowed access to her records. Under a 2005 amendment, access to health records may be denied if a minor's treating physician or treating clinical psychologist has put in the minor's record a written statement that, in the exercise of the physician's or psychologist's professional judgment, the furnishing to or review by the requesting parent of such health records would be reasonably likely to cause substantial harm to the minor or another person. Va. Code § 20-124.6(B). Either the minor or the parent has the right to have the denial reviewed by a comparable professional. See Va. Code § 32.1-127.1:03(F).

[2]   *Compulsory Medical Treatment.* In some instances, the state has acted out of its interest in the welfare of the community or its parens patriae interest in each individual, and has compelled forms of medical care.

One familiar example is compulsory vaccination before the child enters school, Va. Code § 22.1-271.1, and eye and hearing tests during elementary school. Va. Code § 22.1-273. Perhaps less obvious are the silver nitrate drops placed in each newborn baby's eyes to treat possible infection, Va. Code

§§ 32.1-61 to 32.1-64, phenylketonuria tests, Va. Code § 32.1-65, and vaccinations and quarantines in times of epidemics. Va. Code § 32.1-48.

Drivers of cars are responsible for ensuring that children up to the age of eight are secured in a proper child restraint device, and that rear-facing child restraint devices are to be in the vehicle's back seat. However, where there is no back seat, the child restraint device may be placed in the front passenger seat only if there is no passenger side airbag or the passenger side airbag has been deactivated. A driver is also responsible to ensure that passengers less than 18 who do not require a child restraint device are properly secured by an appropriate safety belt system. Va. Code § 46.2-1095.

[3]   *Life-Threatening Situations.* Even when the strongest interests of a parent are pitted against the life-saving treatment of his child, these religious freedoms or parental abilities to control family resources will not prevail. Compare *Ginsberg v. New York,* 390 U.S. 629, 639, 88 S. Ct. 1274, 20 L. Ed. 2d 195, 44 Ohio Op. 2d 339 (1968). The state's interest in assuring that the child reaches maturity will justify a course of court-ordered medical treatment.

Thus, if a child has an illness that requires surgery, a parent must consent or the surgery will be ordered despite a religious tenet prohibiting blood transfusions. This same doctrine has been used to justify a court-ordered transfusion for a woman seven months pregnant, *Raleigh Fitkin-Paul Morgan Memorial Hospital v. Anderson,* 42 N.J. 421, 201 A.2d 537 (1964), and a parent with several small children to care for, *Application of President & Directors of Georgetown College, Inc.,* 331 F.2d 1000, 118 U.S. App. D.C. 80 (D.C. Cir. 1964). See generally *Constitutional Limitations on State Intervention in Prenatal Care,* 67 Va. L. Rev. 1051 (1981).

Even if a small child suffers some discomfort, such as stomach cramps, nausea, and pain from injections, a course of treatment for a frequently curable cancer will be followed despite parental objection. *In re Custody of a Minor,* 375 Mass. 733, 379 N.E.2d 1053 (1978).

Regimes of diet and prayer will not suffice if there is an accepted medical treatment that is usually efficacious and a child's life is endangered. *Custody of a Minor,* 375 Mass. 733, 379 N.E.2d 1053 (1978). But so long as a parent follows the advice of a physician who subscribes to a course of treatment accepted by some segment of the medical commentary, even though it is unusual, there will be no state intervention. *In re Hofbauer,* 47 N.Y.2d 648, 419 N.Y.S.2d 936, 393 N.E.2d 1009 (1979).

See generally J. Nelson Thomas, Note, *Prosecuting Religious Parents for Homicide: Compounding a Tragedy,* 1 Va. J. Soc. Pol'y & L. 409 (1994).

If a child's life is threatened, some states have found parental liability for improper prenatal care. See, e.g., *Curlender v. Bio-Science Laboratories,* 106 Cal. App. 3d 811, 829, 165 Cal. Rptr. 477, 488 (1980); N.J. Stat. Ann. § 30:4C-11; see generally Note, *Parental Liability for Prenatal Injury,* 14 Colum. J.L. & Soc. Probs. 47 (1978).

[4]  *Elective Therapy—Religious Objection.* Where the child's life is not at stake and the parent has a religious objection to his undergoing a particular treatment, a court will not adjudicate neglect and order treatment. If the child is of an age and maturity to have a religious preference to make a decision independently, his opinion will be given great weight, see, e.g., *In re Green,* 448 Pa. 338, 292 A.2d 387 (1972), if not always followed.

When a child's decision does not accord with the parent's—as when a child wishes an abortion but the mother objects on a religious basis, *In re Smith,* 16 Md. App. 209, 295 A.2d 238 (1972); *J.B. v. Detroit-Macomb Hospital Ass'n,* 9 Fam. L. Rep. (B.N.A.) 2219 (1983), the child's view will prevail if the child is mature, especially when, as in the case of abortion, there are independent constitutional rights of the child at stake.

[5]  *Elective Therapy.* When a parent opposes a particular type of therapy, but not on a religious basis, the parent's wish will usually prevail unless the condition is life-threatening. *In re Hudson,* 13 Wash. 2d 673, 126 P.2d 765 (1942).

A parent may volunteer a child for drug research, but only if there is no appreciable risk to the child. The doctrine of substituted judgment, discussed below, will prevail, as well as the utilitarian policy that important medical information can often not be gleaned absent testing on human subjects.

See generally Glantz et al., *Scientific Research with Children: Legal Incapacity and Proxy Consent,* 11 Fam. L.Q. 253 (1977).

Minors may be voluntarily committed by their parents after a hearing held in the institution with a third party, such as a psychiatrist, acting as an impartial decisionmaker. *Parham v. R.,* 442 U.S. 584, 99 S. Ct. 2493, 61 L. Ed. 2d 101 (1979).

Va. Code § 16.1-346.1 requires that predischarge plans be formulated and explained to the minor admitted to inpatient treatment. Copies shall be sent to the minor's parents or, if the minor is in the custody of the local department of social services, to the department's director or designee. The plan shall, at a minimum, specify the services required by the patient in the community to meet the minor's needs for treatment, housing, nutrition, physical care, and safety; specify any income subsidies for which the minor is eligible, identify all local and state agencies that will be involved in providing treatment and support to the minor, and specify services that would be appropriate for the minor's treatment and support in the community that are currently unavailable.

See generally Richard E. Redding, *Children's Competence to Provide Informed Consent for Mental Health Treatment*, 50 Wash. & Lee L. Rev. 695 (1993).

**[6] *Life Sustaining Therapy—Risk to Other Child.*** On a few occasions one of two children in a family is ill and in need of an organ that can best be obtained from a healthy sibling. In one well-known case, *Hart v. Brown*, 289 A.2d 386, 29 Conn. Supp. 368 (1972), a kidney removal from a healthy eight-year-old twin was ordered in order to save the life of her ill sister. The court's reasoning was that when the healthy sister reached the age when she could understand a decision of that kind, she would choose to donate her organ—the "doctrine of substituted judgment." See, e.g., *Superintendent of Belchertown State School v. Saikewicz*, 373 Mass. 728, 370 N.E.2d 417 (1977) (discontinuance of treatment for elderly retarded leukemia patient).

In another case, the healthy twin was mentally defective. In *In re Guardianship of Pescinski*, 67 Wis. 2d 4, 226 N.W.2d 180 (1975), the transplant was never ordered because the institutionalized healthy twin could never understand why he would suffer pain in giving up his kidney. But see *Strunk v. Strunk*, 445 S.W.2d 145 (Ky. 1969) (institutionalized brother could be operated on to save healthy sibling dying of kidney disease).

See generally Note, 9 J. Fam. L. 309 (1969–1970).

**[7] *Decisions to Forego Therapy.*** The landmark case of *In re Quinlan*, 70 N.J. 10, 355 A.2d 647 (1976), brought to the public scrutiny the issue of whether a family should ever be permitted to discontinue extraordinary medical treatment from a child who would not recover from an illness that had already irreversibly terminated conscious mental functions.

More recently, Congressional legislation has addressed the question of whether parents, together with doctors, could decide to forego treatment, extraordinary or routine, of handicapped newborns. The legislation makes the life-terminating omission child abuse under state statutes, except in rare cases when the baby would die in any case in a short time.

See generally Robertson, *Involuntary Euthanasia of Defective Newborns: A Legal Analysis*, 27 Stan. L. Rev. 213 (1975); Bennett, *Allocation of Child Medical Care Decision-Making Authority: A Suggested Interest Analysis*, 62 Va. L. Rev. 285 (1976); Goldstein, *Medical Care for the Child at Risk, On State Supervision of Parental Autonomy*, 86 Yale L.J. 645 (1977).

## § 15.06   Child Abuse and Neglect and Family Abuse

In 1998, through the "Adoption and Safe Families Act of 1997," Congress amended 42 U.S.C. § 671(a)(15)(D), the Social Security Act, and mandated that the health and safety of the child be the paramount concern in child protective actions including foster care and termination proceedings. Accordingly, the Virginia legislature amended §§ 16.1-281(D) and 16.1-283(E) to reflect the Congressional language. The sections also substantively change foster care and termination standards. The new language states that social services shall no longer plan to reunify the family if the parent has been convicted of murder, involuntary manslaughter, felony sexual assault or felony assault or bodily wounding resulting in serious injury if the victim was a child of the parent or the parent with whom the child resided. Such offenses can also be sufficient for termination of parental rights. See, e.g., *M.G. v. Albemarle County Dep't of Soc. Servs.*, 41 Va. App. 170, 583 S.E.2d 761 (2003) (parental rights termination based on "felony sexual assault" conviction). The time frame for failing to maintain continued contact with a child in foster care was shortened from 12 to six months. Failing to maintain contact is also a basis for terminating parental rights, as is involuntary termination of parental rights with respect to a sibling.

Following the national trend, Virginia has enacted statutes protecting children and adults from the abuse of other family members. Under Va. Code § 16.1-228, "family abuse" is defined to mean any act "involving violence, force, or threat that results in bodily injury or places one in reasonable apprehension of death, sexual assault or bodily injury and that is committed by a person against such person's family or household member." A "family or household member" is defined to include a person's spouse, former spouse, parents, stepparents, children, stepchildren, brothers, sisters, half-brothers, half-sisters, grandparents, grandchildren, in-laws, any individual "who has a child in common with the person," cohabitants, recent cohabitants, and cohabitants' children. In-laws and cohabitants' children must reside in the same household with the person. Va. Code § 16.1-228 also provides a multi-part definition of an "abused or neglected child."

Under Virginia law, any person who commits an assault and battery against a family or household member, including one's child, is guilty of a Class 1 misdemeanor. Va. Code § 18.2-57.2. Upon a conviction for assault and battery against a family or household member, where it is alleged that the person has been previously convicted of two offenses against a family or household member of (i) assault and battery against a family or household member in violation of Va. Code § 18.2-57.2, (ii) malicious wounding or unlawful wounding in violation of Va. Code § 18.2-51, (iii) aggravated malicious wounding in violation of Va. Code § 18.2-51.2, (iv) malicious bodily injury by means of a substance in violation of Va. Code § 18.2-52, or (v) strangulation in violation of Va. Code § 18.2-51.6, or (vi) an offense under the law of any other jurisdiction which has the same elements of any of the above offenses, in any combination, all of which occurred within a period of 20 years, and each of which occurred on a different date, such person is guilty of a Class 6 felony. In *Farmer v. Commonwealth*, 62 Va. App. 285, 746 S.E.2d 504 (2013), three certified criminal warrants from Juvenile and Domestic Relations District Court (JDR court) were admissible to prove that the defendant was previously "convicted" of at least two predicate offenses in prosecution for felony assault and battery of a family member, third offense.

An abused or neglected child is defined by Va. Code § 63.2-100. Local child protective service departments are authorized to conduct investigations pursuant to Va. Code § 63.2-1505 and assessments pursuant to Va. Code § 63.2-1506. A person who is found to have abused or neglected a child can be placed into a child abuse central registry. Va. Code § 63.2-1515. A person who is found to have abused or neglected a child has various appeal rights pursuant to Va. Code § 63.2-1526.

In *Carrington v. Commonwealth*, 59 Va. App. 614, 721 S.E.2d 815 (2012), the mother was living with her boyfriend and three small children. When the mother's 12-month old son would not stop crying, the boyfriend punched the baby in the thigh three times, fracturing the baby's femur. Upon investigation, the boyfriend was arrested, convicted and sentenced to 10 years' incarceration with four years suspended. He appealed the conviction, arguing that the evidence was insufficient to support a conviction for child neglect where appellant was not a "person responsible for the care of [the] child" pursuant to Va. Code Ann. § 18.2-371.1(A), which reads, in part:

> Any parent, guardian, or other person responsible for the care of a child under the age of 18 who by willful act or omission or refusal to provide any necessary care for the child's health causes or permits serious injury to the life or health of such child shall be guilty of a Class 4 felony.

The appellate court held that the plain language of the statute applies to "*any . . . person responsible for the care of a child,*" which is the only proof required, and at the time of the child's injury, the appellant's conduct demonstrated that he was a person responsible for the child's care. Although appellant was not the child's biological father, he held himself out as the father, and even helped feed, bathe, and put the child to sleep. Thus, the conviction was affirmed.

In *Farrell v. Warren County Dep't of Soc. Servs.*, 59 Va. App. 375, 719 S.E.2d 329 (2012), the court of appeals held that, along with her history of substance abuse, a mother's cover-up of the father's child abuse justified the termination of her parental rights. The Department of Social Services (DSS) filed a petition seeking to terminate the mother and father's parental rights to their three children, "A," "E," and "W." The children had previously been removed twice from their home by DSS and, at subsequent hearings, the court determined that the children were abused or neglected, as defined in Va. Code § 16.1-228(1):

"*Abused or neglected child*" means any child:

1. Whose parents or other person responsible for his care creates or inflicts, threatens to create or inflict, or allows to be created or inflicted upon such child a physical or mental injury by other than accidental means, or creates a substantial risk of death, disfigurement or impairment of bodily or mental functions . . . .

The first removal occurred after the mother gave birth to premature twins who tested positive for cocaine at birth, and the mother also tested positive for drugs. All three children were placed in foster care, and a plan to return the children to their parents was put in place. The children were returned to their parents' legal custody after the parents completed their obligations under the foster care plan. At a subsequent medical appointment, "A" was found to be suffering from malnourishment. A follow-up appointment was scheduled, but the parents missed the appointment. The child did not receive further medical treatment until he was so malnourished that the parents ended up bringing him to the hospital, where the child spent one week. During testing, the child was diagnosed with subdural hematomas of various ages along with bilateral retinal hemorrhaging, which were consistent with non-accidental trauma. It was subsequently determined that the father inflicted the injuries upon "A."

Based upon this report, DSS removed the children from their home a second time. At a subsequent hearing, it was determined again that the children were abused or neglected. The court found that "A" was abused by the father and neglected by the mother and that "E" and "W" were "at risk" of being abused or neglected due to the father's abuse of "A." The mother refused to acknowledge that the father caused physical injury to "A," although she admitted that she had been involved in physical altercations with the father. The trial court found that it was in the best interests of all three children to terminate both parents' rights, noting that DSS had investigated all reasonable options for placement with relatives and no reasonable alternatives existed. Both parents appealed the decision. The court of appeals affirmed the trial court's decision to terminate parental rights.

In order to terminate parental rights, Va. Code § 16.1-283(B) requires "clear and convincing evidence" that termination is in the best interests of the child and that:

1. The neglect or abuse suffered by such child presented a serious and substantial threat to his life, health or development; and

2. It is not reasonably likely that the conditions which resulted in such neglect or abuse can be substantially corrected or eliminated so as to allow the child's safe return to his parent or parents within a reasonable period of time.

On appeal, the mother argued that the trial court erred in terminating her parental rights without giving her the opportunity to remedy the conditions leading to the children's removal, as required by the statute. Even though the mother was not the parent responsible for the physical abuse of "A," the court nevertheless affirmed termination of her parental rights, citing her history of substance abuse and her failure to acknowledge that the father physically abused "A," thus putting all of the children in peril by leaving them unsupervised with the father.

A mere threat of physical injury will suffice to sustain a finding of physical abuse of a child. See *Chabolla v. Va. Dep't of Soc. Servs.*, 55 Va. App. 531, 687 S.E.2d 85 (2010) (father displayed loaded handgun in response to daughter's temper tantrum).

Under Va. Code § 18.2-57.2, a person who is convicted of assault and battery against a family or household member, as defined in Va. Code § 16.1-228, is guilty of a misdemeanor or a felony. When family abuse is involved, protective orders are available under Va. Code §§ 16.1-253, 16.1-253.1, 16.1-253.4, 16.1-278.14, 16.1-279.1, and 20-103(B). See, e.g., *Elliott v. Commonwealth*, 277 Va. 457, 675 S.E.2d 178 (2009) (order prohibiting "contact of any type"). Criminal penalties for violations of protective orders are established in Va. Code § 16.1-253.2.

Jurisdiction for proceedings alleging family abuse or child neglect or abuse lies exclusively in the juvenile and domestic relations (J&DR) district court. Va. Code § 16.1-241.

In *Oxenham v. J.S.M.*, 256 Va. 180, 501 S.E.2d 765 (1998), a 10-year-old boy's mother filed a juvenile petition charging him with assault and battery. The juvenile court had the authority to appoint counsel to represent the child. The child's parents were in the midst of acrimonious divorce proceedings and could not agree on a private attorney to represent him.

Guidelines enacted by the Commissioner of the Virginia Department of Social Services for use by child-protective units in interpreting Virginia's child abuse and neglect statute, including guidelines related to mental abuse, have been upheld as constitutional. *Jackson v. W.*, 14 Va. App. 391, 419 S.E.2d 385 (1992). See also *Doe v. Virginia Department of Social Services*, 33 Va. Cir. 538 (Prince William Co. 1992) (setting aside finding of mental/emotional abuse).

Social workers or other professionals acting in good faith in cases involving abuse enjoy qualified immunity. See, e.g., *Martin v. St. Mary's Dep't of Soc. Servs.*, 346 F.3d 502 (4th Cir. 2003). However, if they violate court orders or act completely outside the proper conduct of family therapy practitioners, they will not be protected from suit. *Tomlin v. McKenzie*, 251 Va. 478, 468 S.E.2d 882 (1996). Social workers who involuntarily remove children from their homes and take the children into state custody owe the children a duty not to make foster care placements that are deliberately indifferent to the children's rights to personal safety and security. *Doe v. S.C. Dep't of Soc. Servs.*, 597 F.3d 163 (4th Cir. 2009).

However, autoeroticism by the parents that may have been witnessed by the child did not constitute abuse warranting a change of custody when the father showed "an involvement more extensive" than the trial judge had seen "in the great bulk of most of the cases that" he had heard. *Davenport v. Davenport*, 1995 Va. App. LEXIS 75 (Jan. 31, 1995). When the parties were accused of abusing their children, the trial court found that there had been no abuse, and when the Department of Human Development unsuccessfully appealed, the wife was appropriately awarded attorney's fees and costs from the department.

In *Eggleston v. Virginia Dep't of Soc. Servs.*, 1999 Va. App. LEXIS 166 (Mar. 16, 1999), substantial evidence to support a finding of sexual molestation is a test that is met when arousal (as required by Va. Dep't of Soc. Servs., Child Protective Servs., Vol. VII, § III, Ch. A. 1.5 (internal guidelines)) can be inferred from "the very nature of the touching under the circumstances" described by the child. Va. Code § 63.2-1514(D) allows a person who is the subject of an unfounded child abuse charge to petition the court to require the Department's release of that file if the person believes that the complaint may be malicious or in bad faith. In *Gloucester County Dep't of Soc. Servs. v. Kennedy*, 256 Va. 400, 507 S.E.2d 81 (1998), the father presented sufficient evidence demonstrating that the complaint was filed by the mother or her live-in boyfriend to prevent the father's visitation with his daughter. The court of appeals viewed the file *in camera*, and the decision to order the department to provide the father with a copy of the records was affirmed.

In *Fairfax County Dep't of Family Servs. v. Nordel*, 29 Va. App. 400, 512 S.E.2d 830 (1999), the circuit erred in prohibiting the Department of Family Services from introducing evidence of physical abuse to determine whether a child was "abused and neglected" when the particular subparagraph of the child abuse statute had not been considered at the juvenile court. The appellate court affirmed that there was no error in finding the evidence insufficient to support a finding of child abuse and neglect. "A court's conclusion that a party has failed to carry its burden of proof is conclusive upon this Court as a finding of fact." Although there was conflicting expert testimony, the trial court, as the finder of fact, "may determine the weight to be given to an expert's opinion," and it did just that, siding with the testimony presented by the expert for the Neidigs.

In *Carter v. Ancel*, 28 Va. App. 76, 502 S.E.2d 149 (1998), the circuit court held that DSS lacked jurisdiction when it issued a "founded" finding of child sexual abuse against the father, who then appealed that ruling to the court. Although DSS had taken 60 days, rather than the 45 days provided in former Va. Code § 63.1-248.6(E)(7), the appellate court held that section was directive rather than jurisdictional and reversed. See current Va. Code § 63.2-1505(B)(5).

If the local department of social services finds that a complaint of abuse is unfounded, records of the complaint shall be kept for one year in order to provide local departments with information regarding prior investigations. The exception to the rule is when the accused, through a civil suit, proves that the report was made in bad faith or with malicious intent. Va. Code § 63.2-1514. The other important consequence of making a false report of child abuse or neglect is that the complainant shall be subject to criminal action. The first such conviction is a Class 4 misdemeanor; a subsequent conviction is a Class 2 misdemeanor. *Id.* § 5:101 [added 1996].

Substance abuse by a mother during her pregnancy that goes untreated shall be reported as child abuse under Va. Code § 63.2-1509, when the newborn is found dependent on a controlled substance or alcohol and an attending physician makes a diagnosis within seven days of a child's birth. This includes the presence of a non-prescription controlled substance in the child's blood or urine and a diagnosis of fetal alcohol syndrome. Such a report triggers a child abuse or neglect investigation and may warrant a protective order under § 16.1-251 et seq. Intra-family immunity does not apply when the death of an unemancipated child results from the intentional act of his parent. *Pavlick v. Pavlick*, 254 Va. 176, 491 S.E.2d 602 (1997).

Pursuant to Virginia's Sex Offender and Crimes Against Minor's Registry Act, Va. Code § 9.1-900 et seq., a person convicted of sexual offenses against a minor must register with local law enforcement either upon conviction, within three days of suspension of a sentence, within three days of release from confinement, within three days of a name change, and within three days of moving into the Commonwealth. Va. Code §§ 9.01-903 and 9.01-905. Va. Code § 9.01-910 govern the length of time that a person must remain registered and when a petition to remove his name from registration can be filed. However, any person who has been convicted of (i) any sexually violent offense, (ii) murder, or (iii) former § 18.2-67.2:1 shall have a continuing duty to reregister for life. Va. Code § 9.1-908. The offenses that require a convicted person to register are listed at Va. Code § 9.01-902.

Petitions involving custody, visitation, support, or control of a child may be filed in Juvenile and Domestic Relations Court by persons with legitimate interests. This standing requirement is to be liberally construed, and includes, but is not limited to, grandparents, stepparents, former stepparents, blood relatives and family members. It does not include any person whose parental rights have been terminated by court order (voluntarily or involuntarily). It also does not include any person whose interest in the child derives from or through a parent whose rights have been terminated, such as relatives of a child who has been legally adopted (unless the adoption was a stepparent adoption). Va. Code § 16.1-241.

If a parent safely delivers a child within 14 days of birth to a hospital that provides 24-hour emergency services or to an attended rescue squad that employs emergency medical technicians, the parent has a defense against prosecution or civil action based on abuse or neglect, but for purposes of terminating parental rights and placement for adoption, a court may find the child a neglected child upon the ground of abandonment. Va. Code §§ 16.1-228, 18.2-371.

# CHAPTER 16

## Separate Maintenance

### SYNOPSIS

### § 16.01  Introduction

Unlike the divorce *a mensa*, the action for separate maintenance is not dependent upon a statutory framework. *White v. White*, 181 Va. 162, 24 S.E.2d 448 (1943). It is a direct descendant of the common law duty of the husband to support his blameless wife, see *Almond v. Almond*, 25 Va. (4 Rand.) 662, 664 (1826), and jurisdiction comes from the inherent equitable power of the chancery court.

Although it is a distinct action from the *a mensa* divorce, and its consequences are different; courts are apt on occasion to confuse separate maintenance with a divorce from bed and board. See, e.g., *Montgomery v. Montgomery*, 183 Va. 96, 101, 31 S.E.2d 284, 286 (1944).

The separate maintenance action is not often used today. Its utility rests with its tax advantage of making payments deductible as alimony by the payor. In addition, the marital relationship continues, with its privileges in case of the obligor spouse's death. *Wilson v. Wilson*, 195 Va. 1060, 81 S.E.2d 605 (1954). There may also be occasions where the cause of action for a fault divorce needed for a divorce *a mensa* could not be made out, but the dependent spouse needs an immediate award of support pending a maturing of a no fault cause of action. See, e.g., *Rowand v. Rowand*, 215 Va. 344, 210 S.E.2d 149 (1974) (husband's ordering "get out" on two occasions was not enough to give wife grounds for divorce *a mensa* on constructive desertion; but since the wife was free from fault, she could be awarded alimony). See also *Alls v. Alls,* 216 Va. 13, 216 S.E.2d 16 (1975). In most of these cases an appropriate separation agreement will not have been agreed to by both parties.

## § 16.02     Jurisdiction

Although jurisdiction does not depend upon statute, as it does in cases of divorce, *White v. White,* 181 Va. 162, 24 S.E.2d 448 (1943), several things must be proven: (1) personal service over the defendant; (2) the existence of a valid marriage, see, e.g., *Purcell v. Purcell,* 14 Va. (4 Hen. & Mun.) 507 (1810); and (3) cause for the living apart. A divorce need not be granted to either party for maintenance to be awarded. See, e.g., *Graham v. Graham,* 210 Va. 608, 172 S.E.2d 724 (1970); *Alls v. Alls,* 216 Va. 13, 216 S.E.2d 16 (1975). When a court obtains jurisdiction over a nonresident under the long-arm statute, such service shall have the same effect as service on the nonresident within Virginia. Va. Code § 8.01-320 (amended 1997). This statute specifically includes divorce and annulment cases.

Statutes enacted in 1989 regarding the experimental family courts were repealed in 1999, including Va. Code §§ 16.1-296.1, 20-96.1, and 20-96.2. There are no longer any such courts, and all appeals from such courts have been completed.

The Virginia Beach Circuit Court determined that it had jurisdiction over a separate maintenance action where neither party resided in the Commonwealth of Virginia. *Hart v. Hart,* 41 Va. Cir. 456 (1997).

Where custody or visitation is disputed, the court can refer the parties to mediation. Va. Code §§ 20-124.2 and 20-124.4. Upon referral, the parties must attend one evaluation session during which the parties and the mediator assess the case and decide whether to continue with mediation or with adjudication. The parties shall notify the court in writing if the dispute is resolved prior to this return date. The court may, in its discretion, incorporate any mediated agreement into the terms of its final decree. Only if the order is entered incorporating the mediated agreement will the terms of the voluntary settlement agreement affect any outstanding court order. Procedure in cases of separate maintenance shall be governed by provisions of Title 20.

Venue does not come under Va. Code § 20-96, but rather under the general venue of suits in equity. *Rochelle v. Rochelle,* 225 Va. 387, 392, 302 S.E.2d 59 (1983). Objections to venue must be made within 21 days after service of process by a plea in abatement. It may shift with the abode of children of separated parents. *White v. White,* 181 Va. 162, 24 S.E.2d 448 (1943). See also *Rochelle v. Rochelle,* 225 Va. 387, 393, 302 S.E.2d 59, 62 (1983).

The marriage required for a separate maintenance decree will not be extinguished by a prior ex parte divorce, *Newport v. Newport*, 219 Va. 48, 54–56, 245 S.E.2d 134, 138–39 (1978), but will be by a proceeding in which the dependent spouse generally appeared. *Osborne v. Osborne*, 215 Va. 205, 207 S.E.2d 875 (1974). Following divorce, payments made will be support rather than separate maintenance. Thus, a wife's right to support established under a separate maintenance decree ended upon entry of a final divorce decree, since the court had personal jurisdiction over her. The court did not have jurisdiction to award her support in a subsequent separate maintenance proceeding. *Scott v. Scott*, 24 Va. App. 364, 482 S.E.2d 110 (1997). The rights under the separate maintenance decree depend on the continuance of the marriage.

## § 16.03  Proof

As in a divorce action, witnesses need to be corroborated to make out the essential elements. See, e.g., *Aichner v. Aichner*, 215 Va. 624, 626, 212 S.E.2d 278, 279 (1975).

## § 16.04  Grounds

Constructive desertion will be grounds for a decree of separate maintenance. For example, permanent alimony was proper where a husband refused to let the wife return to the marital home following her visit to relatives. *Purcell v. Purcell*, 14 Va. (4 Hen. & Mun.) 507 (1810).

However, the presence and undue curiosity of the husband's mother were not excuses for the wife's departure from the marital home and subsequent suit for separate maintenance. *Montgomery v. Montgomery*, 183 Va. 96, 31 S.E.2d 284 (1944). There is no duty for a husband to provide separate maintenance when he has committed no breach of a marital duty, and the wife cannot claim separate maintenance on grounds of her own misconduct. However, had the mother-in-law in *Montgomery* caused the wife to suffer from her cruelty and misconduct, as in the case of a physical beating and an enforced subservience of the wife to the mother-in-law, the husband would have had a duty to protect her and breach of that duty would result in liability for separate maintenance. See *Hutchins v. Hutchins*, 93 Va. 68, 70, 24 S.E. 903, 904 (1896).

Generally, the wife may depart and maintain a separate maintenance action where the husband's mistreatment by ill usage, personal violence, or lack of an adequate and fit home destroy her health or endanger her life by affecting her mind. *Williams v. Williams*, 188 Va. 543, 549–50, 50 S.E.2d 277, 279–80 (1948), citing 42 C.J.S. *Husband and Wife* § 611.

## § 16.05    Defenses

The dependent spouse, or complainant, cannot recover if he or she departed without lawful excuse, *Almond v. Almond,* 25 Va. (4 Rand.) 662 (1826); see also *Anthony v. Anthony,* 213 Va. 721, 196 S.E.2d 66 (1973), although the justification need not rise to the level of proof needed for a divorce. An inexcusable refusal to engage in sexual intercourse on a permanent basis would bar a separate maintenance award. *Aichner v. Aichner,* 215 Va. 624, 626, 212 S.E.2d 278 (1975).

Where the wife continued to live with the husband after securing a court order that he cease his improper relationship with another woman, she forfeited her right to separate maintenance unless there was a repetition of the offense. *Williams v. Williams,* 188 Va. 543, 551, 50 S.E.2d 277 (1948).

A valid divorce decree will extinguish the duty to pay separate maintenance, but only if there was personal jurisdiction over the dependent spouse. Compare *Ceyte v. Ceyte,* 222 Va. 11, 13, 278 S.E.2d 791, 792 (1981), with *Newport v. Newport,* 219 Va. 48, 54–56, 245 S.E.2d 134, 138–39 (1978). Therefore, a wife's right to support established under a separate maintenance decree ended upon entry of a final divorce decree, since the divorce court had personal jurisdiction over her. The court did not have jurisdiction to award her support in a subsequent separate maintenance proceeding. *Scott v. Scott,* 24 Va. App. 364, 482 S.E.2d 110 (1997). The rights under the separate maintenance decree depend on the continuance of the marriage.

## § 16.06    Consequences

Since there has been no divorce, a decree of separation will not sever rights to a share of a deceased spouse's estate, *Wilson v. Wilson,* 195 Va. 1060, 81 S.E.2d 605 (1954) (dower), and so will be greater protection through support for a faultless spouse than alimony, which ceases at the death of the obligor. The court may, however, provide for the custody and support of minor children of the marriage. Va. Code Ann. § 20-107.2 [amended 1996].

However, the separate maintenance decree will not give the court power to award a spouse the use of specific marital property, just as it cannot be awarded in a proceeding for alimony. *Wilson v. Wilson,* 195 Va. 1060, 81 S.E.2d 605 (1954). See also *Almond v. Almond,* 25 Va. (4 Rand.) 662 (1826) (no ability to obtain judgment requiring return of a slave). It should be noted though, that Va. Code § 20-103, authorizing *pendente lite* relief in separate maintenance cases, permits a court to make temporary rulings regarding the use of property during the pendency of a case, including the use of a home and restrictions on spending from bank accounts.

An award of separation will cease upon one party's being awarded an absolute divorce. *Hagen v. Hagen*, 205 Va. 791, 139 S.E.2d 821 (1965) (three years' separation as cause of action; statute allowing no-fault divorce enacted after separate maintenance decree). Of course, unless the dependent spouse was seriously at fault, there may be an award of support following divorce. *Lancaster v. Lancaster*, 212 Va. 127, 183 S.E.2d 158 (1971).

The Internal Revenue Code § 71 requires that, for periodic payments to be deductible to the payor and taxable to the payee, they be made under court decree of separation, a divorce, or a property settlement agreement. If the cause of action for divorce has not yet matured, and the parties cannot agree on a property settlement, support payments may still be deductible under an award of separate maintenance.

Property would not be equitably divided at this time under Va. Code § 20-107.3, which requires a dissolution of marriage or divorce.

Separate maintenance will signify a revocation of the wife's implied consent to marital intercourse. See *Weishaupt v. Commonwealth*, 227 Va. 389, 315 S.E.2d 847, 855 (1984).

The amount of the separation allowance lies within the sound judicial discretion of the chancellor, who must take into account the needs of the dependent spouse and the ability of the obligor to pay by virtue of earning capacity and financial resources. *Hinshaw v. Hinshaw*, 201 Va. 668, 670, 112 S.E.2d 902 (1960); *Oliver v. Oliver*, 202 Va. 268, 271–72, 117 S.E.2d 59 (1960).

## § 16.07   Life Insurance

Va. Code § 20-107.1:1 was enacted in July 2017, and authorizes a trial court to require a spouse who owes spousal support to maintain life insurance for the payee spouse upon the entry of an order for separate maintenance. The following conditions must exist before a court can impose this obligation on the support payor: the life insurance policy must have existed during the marriage, whether it was purchased by either party or provided through the spouse's employment, or be within the effective control of the insured; the payor spouse must have the right to designate a beneficiary; the payee spouse must have been designated as a beneficiary during the marriage; and the payee spouse must have an insurable interest pursuant to Va. Code § 38.2-301(B). Va. Code § 20-107.1:1(A). The cost for the life insurance premiums can be allocated between the parties but all premiums must be billed to the policyholder. *Id.* The obligation to maintain any such life insurance ceases upon the termination of the spousal support. *Id.*

Pursuant to Va. Code § 20-107.1:1(B), in determining to require a payor spouse to maintain life insurance for the payee spouse, the court must consider the following factors:

- The age, health, and insurability of the insured party;
- The age and health of the payee spouse;
- The cost of the life insurance policy;
- The amount and term of the award of spousal support or separate maintenance;
- The prevailing insurance rates at the time of the order;
- The ability of either spouse to pay the premium cost of the life insurance; and
- Such other factors as the court deems necessary or appropriate to consider in order to arrive at a fair order.

# CHAPTER 17

# Property Settlement or Separation Agreements

## SYNOPSIS

## § 17.01    Introduction—Advantages

Although formerly any contract between spouses that contemplated a division of property or financial obligations in the event of a separation or divorce was void as against public policy, courts have long recognized that spouses might contract to settle potential disputes concerning the distribution of property upon the death of either.

In the twentieth century, the contract between spouses after they have separated has been seen as a realistic and efficient method of resolving disputes. See, e.g., *Eschner v. Eschner*, 146 Va. 417, 131 S.E. 800 (1926). Especially since the advent of no-fault divorce, private agreements have streamlined the dissolution process so that in the great majority of cases there is no contest either as to the divorce itself or as to the disposing of the incidents of the marriage. See generally Mnookin & Kornhauser, *Bargaining in the Shadow of the Law: The Case of Divorce*, 88 Yale L.J. 950 (1979).

Although they will be regarded with greater scrutiny than the average contract, many of the concerns for the attorney will be the same. The parties, because they are still in a confidential relationship at the time of making, will need roughly equivalent bargaining power. This is most often assured by keeping each party fully informed of the assets and benefits of the other, and by seeing that each is represented by independent counsel. See, e.g., *Friedlander v. Friedlander*, 80 Wash. 2d 293, 494 P.2d 208 (1972). There will also need to be adequate consideration supporting the promises that are made in the contract. *Capps v. Capps,* 216 Va. 378, 219 S.E.2d 901 (1975).

However, once the parties engage attorneys, are dealing at arm's length, and begin the negotiation process, the confidential relationship is severed, for some purposes at least. *Wells v. Wells,* 12 Va. App. 31, 401 S.E.2d 891; 12 Va. App. 31, 401 S.E.2d 891 (1991). Thus, the failure by the wife to disclose a sexual relationship with another man was not fraud in the inducement justifying cancellation of the agreement executed by the parties. *Barnes v. Barnes,* 231 Va. 39, 41, 340 S.E.2d 803 (1986).

Since this is an agreement dealing with the marriage relationship, there are special concerns. These include the requirement that the agreement not "facilitate or promote a divorce or separation." See *Cooley v. Cooley,* 220 Va. 749, 263 S.E.2d 49 (1980). See also *Bailey v. Bailey,* 12 Va. Cir. 67 (1987) (property settlement is not void as against public policy when it is prepared before grounds for divorce have ripened). Further, the parties may not divest the court of matters under its jurisdiction, such as those dealing with child custody and support. Va. Code § 20-108; *Wickham v. Wickham,* 215 Va. 694, 213 S.E.2d 750 (1975). "Marital property settlements entered into by competent parties upon valid consideration for lawful purposes are favored in the law and such will be enforced unless their illegality is clear and certain." *Cooley v. Cooley,* 220 Va. 749, 752, 263 S.E.2d 49, 52 (1980).

Marital agreements generally are subject to the same requirements as premarital agreements. Va. Code § 20-155. Thus, they must be in writing and signed by both parties. See Va. Code § 20-149. However, an agreement is not required to be in writing and is considered to be executed if its terms are (i) contained in a court order endorsed by counsel or the parties or (ii) recorded and transcribed by a court reporter and affirmed by the parties on the record personally. Va. Code § 20-155. Marital agreements between competent parties are favored in the law and will be enforced unless illegality is clear and certain. *Cooley v. Cooley,* 220 Va. 749, 752, 263 S.E.2d 49, 52 (1980); *Doherty v. Doherty,* 9 Va. App. 97, 99, 383 S.E.2d 759, 760 (1989); *Drewry v. Drewry,* 8 Va. App. 460, 466, 383 S.E.2d 12, 14 (1989).

In *Flanary v. Milton,* 263 Va. 20, 556 S.E.2d 767 (2002), the Virginia Supreme Court held that an oral property settlement agreement made between spouses during a deposition in furtherance of a divorce action was not valid. The Virginia Supreme Court reasoned that a property or spousal support agreement made in contemplation of resolving a pending divorce action was subject to Va. Code § 20-155, which by reference to Va. Code § 20-149 required the agreement to be signed by the parties and in writing. See also *Bryant v. McDougal,* 49 Va. App. 78, 636 S.E.2d 897 (2006) (oral property settlement agreement, read into record by wife's counsel, was invalid for lack of mutual consent, when husband's affirmation "subject to" execution of formal written agreement created condition precedent to existence of valid agreement); *Gaffney v. Gaffney*, 45 Va. App. 655, 613 S.E.2d 471 (2005) (attorneys' stipulations and proffers did not bind parties to terms of oral property settlement agreement); *Shackelford v. Shackelford*, 39 Va. App. 201, 571 S.E.2d 917 (2002) (husband's oral spousal support proposal was not binding on trial court).

Prior to the current statutes, the statute of frauds might require a writing if the contract involved real property or could not be performed within one year. In an earlier case, *Troyer v. Troyer*, 231 Va. 90, 341 S.E.2d 182 (1986), the Virginia Supreme Court upheld an agreement by the husband to convey his interest in the marital home to the wife after their separation when the only "writing" was a deposition in the divorce proceedings. Also earlier, in *Richardson v. Richardson*, 10 Va. App. 391, 392 S.E.2d 688 (1990), the Court of Appeals reasoned that "compromises and settlement agreements to pending litigation which incidentally include issues of property and spousal support" did not have to be in writing because they were not within the purview of Va. Code § 20-155, and upheld an oral property settlement agreement that had been read into the trial court record. However, the Virginia Supreme Court in *Flanary* expressly overruled the rationale and holding of *Richardson*. In yet another earlier case, *Baskerville v. Baskerville*, 18 Va. Cir. 487 (1990), a husband refused to sign a written agreement based on an oral agreement made during depositions. Although Va. Code § 20-109.1 did not require that an agreement be signed or in writing, the trial court disapproved incorporation of the agreement into the final decree to the extent it involved real property or spousal debts. Thus, the agreement remained valid as a contract, but the husband could not be placed in contempt for violating its terms, because there was doubt whether he entered the settlement voluntarily.

An oral marital agreement will be enforceable if one of the Va. Code § 20-155 exceptions to the Va. Code § 20-149 writing requirement applies. Thus, an oral agreement will be valid and binding if its terms are (i) contained in a court order endorsed by counsel or the parties, or (ii) recorded and transcribed by a court reporter and affirmed by the parties on the record personally. Va. Code §§ 20-155(i), (ii). To satisfy the "court reporter" exception, the terms of the parties' agreement must be read or recited into the record in the presence of a court reporter, and the parties must specifically and affirmatively manifest their assent to those terms on the record. The mere introduction into evidence of written exhibits reflecting various terms of the agreement, combined with testimony of the parties that merely reflects the existence of the agreement, will not satisfy Va. Code § 20-155(ii). *Gaffney v. Gaffney*, 45 Va. App. 655, 613 S.E.2d 471 (2005). If one of the parties to an oral property settlement agreement manifests an intent that his or her affirmation of the terms is "subject to" the execution of a formal, written agreement, then execution of a formal, written agreement is a condition precedent to the existence of a valid and binding property settlement agreement. If the condition precedent is not satisfied by the execution of a written property settlement agreement, then the Va. Code § 20-155(ii) exception to the writing requirement of Va. Code § 20-149 is not invoked, and the oral property settlement agreement is ineffectual, as if it never existed. *Bryant v. McDougal*, 49 Va. App. 78, 636 S.E.2d 897 (2006).

Parole evidence is admissible where an ambiguity exists in the agreement. Contractual vagaries are resolved in one of three ways.

> First, if no patent or latent ambiguities exist, a court should enforce the plain meaning of the contractual language without resort to extrinsic evidence. *See Eure v. Norfolk Shipbuilding & Drydock Corp.*, 263 Va. 624, 632, 561 S.E. 2d 663, 667 (2002); King, 40 Va. App. at 206, 578 S.E. 2d at 810. Second, if an ambiguity exists, a court should still enforce the contract if the real meaning of the ambiguous provision can be discerned from extrinsic evidence. *See Cascades N. Venture Ltd. P'ship v. PRC Inc.*, 249 Va. 574, 579, 457 S.E. 2d 370, 373 (1995). Third, if an ambiguity renders the alleged agreement too indefinite, even after the consideration of extrinsic evidence, for the court to determine the parties' intent, the contract cannot be enforced due to the absence of any discernable meeting of the minds. *See, e. g., Allen v. Aetna Casualty & Surety*, 222 Va. 361, 364, 281 S.E. 2d 818, 820 (1981).

*Smith v. Smith*, 43 Va. App. 279, 287, 597 S.E.2d 250, 254 (2004) (citations omitted).

The contractual provisions are usually viewed as a whole, and therefore are not severable. See, e.g., *Buchanan v. Buchanan*, 174 Va. 255, 6 S.E.2d 612 (1939); *Eschner v. Eschner*, 146 Va. 417, 131 S.E. 800 (1926).

The parties may specify which jurisdiction's law is to govern their agreement. Thus, although the agreement was executed in New Jersey, when the intent was that the agreement be governed and construed by the laws of North Carolina, and a paragraph of the agreement reflected this intent, North Carolina law governed. *Knight v. Knight*, 22 Va. Cir. 485 (1981) (citing *Tate v. Hain*, 181 Va. 402, 25 S.E.2d 321 (1943)).

The lawyer will also need to consider whether the agreement should be incorporated into the final decree of divorce, so that the court's contempt power can be used in enforcing support clauses. *Durrett v. Durrett,* 204 Va. 59, 129 S.E.2d 50 (1963). Such incorporation will also make it impossible for the court to modify provisions dealing with spousal support, except as provided in the contract itself for agreements that were entered into prior to July 1, 2018. Va. Code § 20-109. Prior to July 2018, if an Agreement merely recited the amount and duration of spousal support, and it did not reserve a court's authority to modify spousal support, no court could ever modify the spousal support obligation. *Pendleton v. Pendleton,* 22 Va. App. 503, 506–07, 471 S.E.2d 783 (1996). In July 2018, Va. Code § 20-109(C) was amended to require agreements executed on or after July 1, 2018, to expressly state that the spousal support is not modifiable. To ensure that the spousal support non-modifiability is preserved the statute mandates that the agreement must include the following precise language, *"The amount or duration of spousal support contained in this [AGREEMENT] is not modifiable except as specifically set forth in this [AGREEMENT]."* In 2020, the same statute was amended to remove the mandatory language noted in quotations in the preceding sentence. However, the statute still modifies the pre-July 2018 law and requires that post July 2018 Agreement contain an affirmative statement that "the amount or duration of spousal support is non-modifiable" in order for the spousal support to be non-modifiable. It will be interesting to see the impact of this statute on agreements that do not include the precise requisite language or where the parties waived spousal support but did not include the requisite language in the agreement.

The tax advantages of various transactions are also important, and should be considered before a recommendation is made.

See generally 27 C.J.S. *Divorce* § 301(1)–(5); Mnookin & Kornhauser, *Bargaining in the Shadow of the Law: The Case of Divorce,* 88 Yale L.J. 950 (1979).

## § 17.02    Capacity of Parties to Make Agreement

In general, as with any other contract, the parties must be of sufficient age and discretion to make a knowing disposition of their assets and marital rights. See generally 4B Michie's Jurisprudence *Contracts* § 24. Each party must voluntarily sign the agreement. Va. Code § 20-151(A)(1).

The person seeking to invalidate the agreement because of lack of mental competence must prove that he or she did not understand the nature and character of the agreement and the consequences of executing a legal document. Proof of severe mental depression does not of itself render a person legally incompetent. *Drewry v. Drewry,* 8 Va. App. 460, 383 S.E.2d 12 (1989). In *Bailey v. Bailey,* 54 Va. App. 209, 677 S.E.2d 56 (2009), a trial court refused to enforce a marital agreement signed by a schizoaffective psychotic husband while he was on weekend furlough from a hospital's psychiatric ward. The agreement provided (1) that the husband would execute a power of attorney authorizing his wife to solely manage all financial affairs of the marriage, (2) that all debts incurred during the marriage would be solely attributed to the husband, (3) that all real and personal property acquired during the marriage would become the sole property of wife in the event of divorce, and (4) that the husband would pay the wife continuous and adequate support in the event of divorce. Testimony by the husband's treating psychiatrist and by the husband's long-time colleague demonstrated that the husband lacked the requisite mental competence to execute the agreement at the time he signed it.

Every adult party who executes an agreement is presumed to be mentally competent to enter into a contract. In order to be competent to enter into a legally binding obligation, a party is not required to exercise good judgment or to make wise decisions so long as he or she understands the nature and character of the agreement and consequences of entering into it. *Drewry v. Drewry*, 8 Va. App. 460, 467, 383 S.E.2d 12, 15 (1989). "The law does not require that one have the ability to make a reasoned judgment concerning an agreement but only that he or she understand the nature and consequences of his acts." *Drewry v. Drewry*, 8 Va. App. 460, 468, 383 S.E.2d 12, 16 (1989). "A contracting party is competent if, at the time he executes the agreement, he had sufficient mental capacity to understand the nature of the transaction and agree to its provisions." *Bailey v. Bailey*, 54 Va. App. 209, 215, 677 S.E.2d 56, 60 (2009) (citation omitted).

There was no mutual mistake of fact justifying rescission of a property settlement agreement even though the parties referred to Virginia's equitable distribution statute as entitling the wife to 50% of the royalties from the husband's books. *Jennings v. Jennings*, 12 Va. App. 1187, 409 S.E.2d 8 (1991).

## § 17.03 Knowledge of Assets—Disclosure

The attorney must take care that each party fully understands the implications of the agreement. This will include a full disclosure of the assets of the other, and a discussion of how much could be expected if the parties chose litigation rather than a property settlement agreement. *Feinberg v. Feinberg*, 96 Misc. 2d 443, 409 N.Y.S.2d 365 (1978). See also *Vinson v. Vinson*, 41 Va. App. 675, 588 S.E.2d 392 (2003) (attorney's responsibility to contact husband when drafting spouses' settlement agreement at wife's request).

Va. Code § 20-151 provides that a marital agreement is not enforceable where the agreement was unconscionable at the time it was executed and the party either "was not provided a fair and reasonable disclosure of the property or financial obligations of the other party" or did not waive such disclosure. The parties' premarital agreement was found to be unenforceable where the husband failed to disclose his net worth of approximately 20 million dollars. *Chaplain v. Chaplain*, 54 Va. App. 762, 682 S.E.2d 108 (2009).

In *Derby v. Derby,* 8 Va. App. 19, 378 S.E.2d 74 (1989), the court of appeals considered the validity of a settlement agreement executed in a parking lot before the husband's lawyer was available for consultation, in which the parties' real property (the major asset of the marriage) was given completely to the wife. The court found the agreement unconscionable because of the gross disparity of assets each would receive under the agreement, Mr. Derby's emotional weakness, and particularly because the wife had concealed an extramarital relationship and misrepresented her willingness to reconcile.

In *Galloway v. Galloway*, 47 Va. App. 83, 622 S.E.2d 267 (2005), a wife freely and voluntarily signed a property settlement agreement that gave a marital business and residence to her husband, and also waived spousal support. She could have consulted an attorney before signing, but chose not to do so. The spousal support waiver taken together with the gross disparity in value of the property received by the parties constituted inequitable circumstances, but the agreement itself was not unconscionable. Although a "gross disparity" existed because the agreement gave the husband approximately 94% of the marital assets, there was no evidence of overreaching or oppressive behavior by the husband. Therefore, the two-step test for unconscionability set forth in *Derby v. Derby*, 8 Va. App. 19, 378 S.E.2d 74 (1989) was not satisfied.

In a typical case alleging unconscionability of a property settlement agreement, a court must consider (1) whether there was a gross disparity in the division of assets, and (2) whether the evidence demonstrates oppressive or overreaching influences. See *Galloway v. Galloway*, 47 Va. App. 83, 622 S.E.2d 267 (2005). Proof of may be established by either (1) a showing of bad faith, such as concealments, misrepresentations, undue advantage, or oppression by the advantaged spouse, or (2) ignorance, weakness of mind, sickness, old age, incapacity, pecuniary necessities, and the like, on the part of the disadvantaged spouse. See *Derby v. Derby*, 8 Va. App. 19, 378 S.E.2d 74 (1989). Thus, the unconscionability of a property settlement agreement can be established by showing a gross disparity in the division of assets in conjunction with pecuniary necessity on the part of the disadvantaged spouse. *Sims v. Sims*, 55 Va. App. 340, 685 S.E.2d 869 (2009). In *Sims*, a property settlement agreement was unconscionable, even though a husband did not engage in any overt overreaching or oppressive conduct. By entering into a contract in which the wife waived spousal support and relinquished almost 100% of the marital estate, the husband left the wife, who was disabled by numerous health conditions, both penniless and without any practical means of supporting herself.

However, the fact that, at the time the settlement agreement was executed, any or some property was not subject to distribution need not invalidate all or a portion of the agreement. *Eberhardt v. Eberhardt*, 2018 Va. App. LEXIS 343 (Dec. 11, 2018) (the trial court was without authority to distribute in IRA that was not addressed in the parties' oral agreement which was read into the record pursuant to Va. Code § 20-155.) In *Bragan v. Bragan*, 4 Va. App. 516, 358 S.E.2d 757 (1987), the husband and wife executed releases of all existing and future claims as part of a settlement agreement that did not expressly provide for the husband's pension plan. Although the agreement was signed before the equitable distribution statute was enacted, the divorce took place afterward, and the wife sought a monetary award under Va. Code § 20-107.3 based on the value of this plan. The court of appeals held that the release of future claims barred the monetary award. *Id.* at 519. However, there was no unconscionability in *Jennings v. Jennings,* 12 Va. App. 1187, 409 S.E.2d 8 (1991), when the husband, a successful author, suggested an agreement, negotiated its terms, and was not misled by the wife's attorney or the wife. He was afforded and declined an opportunity to obtain his own legal counsel. The agreement was upheld even though it gave the wife a 50% share of the royalties in his books, and even though he "may have possessed some human frailty or compelling personal agenda." 409 S.E.2d at 12. See also *Pillow v. Pillow,* 13 Va. App. 271, 410 S.E.2d 407 (1991), where no unconscionability was found although the husband was not represented by counsel and did not read the agreement thoroughly. The husband retained the car he drove, a boat, personal property, and an interest in the marital home with the right of first refusal should the wife decide to sell the home. In *Thomas v. Thomas*, 36 Va. Cir. 427 (1995), the court found that "all of the benefits available to the Wife" in connection with the Uniformed Services Former Spouses' Protection act means medical and dental care but not the husband's military pension. The wife and her attorney had drafted the property settlement agreement.

## § 17.04 Divorce Mediation

In many civil proceedings, including divorce and separation matters, courts may refer the parties to mediation under Va. Code § 8.01-576.4 et seq. The judge shall consider whether to refer the parties to mediation, and may do so sua sponte or on motion of one of the parties. Upon referral, the parties must attend one evaluation session during which the parties and the mediator assess the case and decide whether to continue with mediation or with adjudication. However, if a party objects to mediation pursuant to Va. Code § 8.01-576.6, the party shall be excused from participating in mediation. Further participation in the mediation shall be by consent of all parties, and attorneys for any party may be present during mediation. Va. Code § 8.01-576.5. Mediation for parties disputing custody is also authorized by Va. Code §§ 20-124.2 and 20-124.4.

When the parties are referred to mediation, the court shall set a return date. The parties shall notify the court in writing if the dispute is resolved prior to the set date. The court may, in its discretion, incorporate any mediated agreement into the terms of its final decree. Only if the order is entered incorporating the mediated agreement will the terms of the voluntary settlement agreement affect any outstanding court order.

The court shall vacate a mediated agreement or an incorporating order if it was procured by fraud or duress or is unconscionable, if disclosure of financial or property information was inadequate, or where evident partiality or misconduct by the mediator prejudiced the rights of a party. Misconduct includes failure of the mediator to inform the parties in writing at the beginning of mediation that:

(1)    the mediator does not provide legal advice;

(2)    an agreement will affect the legal rights of the parties;

(3)    each party may consult with independent legal counsel at any time and is encouraged to do so; and

(4)    each party should have any draft agreement reviewed by independent counsel prior to signing the agreement, or should waive this opportunity. Va. Code § 8.01-576.12.

A motion to vacate an order or agreement must be made within two years after the agreement is reached. However, if the motion is based upon fraud, it shall be made within two years after these grounds are discovered or reasonably should have been discovered. Va. Code § 8.01-576.12.

Alternatives to courtroom battles are generally less expensive than an adjudicated procedure, both in terms of attorneys' fees and the emotional costs on the parties. For example, Joyce Hauser-Dann found in a recent study of divorced couples that those who had participated in the usual adversary process, even though they did not have a court trial, felt that their involvement with the legal process had made the relationship with their spouse even more difficult than before. This was particularly true of the men who responded to her questionnaire. *Divorce Mediation: A Growing Field?*, 43 Arb. J. 15, 17 (June 1988); and Margaret F. Brinig & Michael V. Alexeev, *Trading at Divorce: Preferences, Legal Rules and Transaction Costs*, 8 Ohio St. J. on Disp. Res. 279 (1993) (analyzing data from Fairfax County and a similar county in Wisconsin).

Particularly where there are children, if the parties can resolve their disputes without resorting to judicial decision making, these non-parties will not have to testify and theoretically will not have to experience their parents' being involved in an expensive and acrimonious procedure. See, e.g., Cochran, *"The Search for Guidance": Reconciling the Primary Caretaker and Joint Custody Preferences*, 20 U. Rich. L. Rev. 1 (1985); Elster, *Solomonic Judgments: Against the Best Interests of the Child*, 54 U. Chi. L. Rev. 1 (1987); Murray, *Improving Parent-Child Relationships Within the Divorced Family: A Call for Legal Reform*, 19 U. Mich. J.L. Ref. 563 (1986).

Further, if the parties have agreed on amounts to be paid in child or spousal support, the obligor spouse will be more likely to carry through on his or her obligations. Noncustodial parents refuse to support their offspring in an alarming number of cases. See D. Chambers, *Making Fathers Pay: The Enforcement of Child Support* (1979); Czapanskiy, *Child Support and Visitation: Rethinking the Connections*, 20 Rutgers L.J. 619 (1989). One reason for this may be that noncustodial parents, primarily fathers, may have little control over how the support money is being spent. See Weiss & Willis, *Children as Collective Goods and Divorce Settlements*, 1 J. Lab. Econ. 268 (1985).

Finally, divorce mediation is designed to focus not only on legal issues, but also on the emotional process of unravelling the marriage. See, e.g., Silberman, *Professional Responsibility Problems of Divorce Mediation*, 16 Fam. L.Q. 107 (1982). Although the stated goal of divorce mediation is not to reconcile the spouses, one of the objectives mentioned by mediators is that of increasing the communication skills of the divorcing couple, who will have to continue in their role as parents regardless of their marital status. In this connection, there is some concern that mediators may have to skillfully intervene to protect power imbalances within the family. The court may also require the parties to attend courses in parenting responsibilities, conflict resolution, and financial responsibilities, according to the amendments to Va. Code § 20-103 passed in 1997. See Folger & Bernard, *Divorce Mediation: When Mediators Challenge the Divorcing Parties*, 10 Mediation Q. 5 (1985).

The mediator, attorney or not, must refrain from attempting to legally represent either party or from giving legal counsel to either or both. In Virginia, any memoranda, work products and other materials, or communications made during a mediation are confidential, and thus are not subject to disclosure in any judicial or administrative proceeding except where all parties agree to waive confidentiality, in an action involving damages arising out of the mediation. Va. Code Ann. § 8.01-581.22 (1990); see generally Comment, *Protecting Confidentiality in Mediation,* 98 Harv. L. Rev. 441 (1984).

Counsel must take care, especially in representing the spouse who has been the dominant or most knowledgeable partner in the marriage, to make sure that the other spouse is adequately represented by counsel. In no event should the attorney undertake to advise the non-represented spouse except to urge that he or she obtain counsel. Virginia ethics opinions also forbid the preparation of a waiver of process for the other spouse. Where the wife assured the husband that the attorney she hired would represent both of their interests, and, because of the special relationship of trust between him and his wife, the husband relied on this statement and did not obtain independent legal counsel, the wife's demurrer to his amended complaint attacking the agreement should not have been sustained. *Zdanis v. Deely,* 1995 Va. App. LEXIS 423 (May 9, 1995).

Mr. and Mrs. Bandas executed a separation agreement that provided for binding arbitration of the issues of spousal support and equitable distribution. The final decree of divorce incorporated this agreement, referring specifically to the arbitration provision. The court retained jurisdiction under § 8.01-77 et seq. because of the agreement to arbitrate. After the divorce, the parties chose the arbitrator, who took evidence over seventeen days and heard argument for an additional seven. During the course of the arbitration, the arbitrator issued five awards concerning spousal and child support, visitation, and property distribution. In *Bandas v. Bandas,* 25 Va. Cir. 492 (City of Richmond 1991), the wife sought to have the court confirm the awards, while the husband argued that they were unconscionable, and that they "gave license to Kay to commit adultery." *Id.* at 496. The Virginia Code sections governing arbitration, §§ 8.01-581.01–581.010, require that the party seeking to vacate an arbitrator's award must show arbitrator misconduct by clear proof, and must overcome a presumption that the award is binding. The circuit court found that the record did not reveal anything manifestly unfair or illegal about the arbitrator's determinations. Because there was no plausible view of the law available to defendant that justified him to contest confirmation, causing unnecessary delay and expense to the wife, the court imposed sanctions in the amount of the wife's attorney's fees.

## § 17.05  Consideration

It should be noted that Va. Code § 20-149 provides that premarital agreements are "enforceable without consideration and shall become effective upon marriage." Pursuant to Va. Code § 20-155, lack of consideration also applies to marital agreements.

In 2017, well after the enactment of Virginia's Premarital Agreement Act, the Court of Appeals held that a party's agreement not to divorce for over 20 years constitutes valid consideration for a property settlement agreement. *Allen v. Allen*, 66 Va. App. 586, 594 (2016).

In cases that pre-date the Virginia Premarital Agreement Act, an agreement between the parties affecting property rights had to be supported by mutuality of consideration, binding both parties to perform their promises. This consideration may consist of indemnification on a joint debt. *Capps v. Capps*, 216 Va. 378, 219 S.E.2d 901 (1975). See also *Buchanan v. Buchanan*, 174 Va. 255, 277, 6 S.E.2d 612, 621 (1939). Consideration for a promise may be forbearance by one spouse to bring or prosecute a meritorious suit for divorce against the other. *Upton v. Ames & Webb, Inc.*, 179 Va. 219, 18 S.E.2d 290 (1942). There is also sufficient consideration if one party forgoes a claim for spousal support. *Troyer v. Troyer*, 231 Va. 90, 94, 341 S.E.2d 182 (1986).

## § 17.06  Special Requirements—Fraud and Overreaching

The agreement must satisfy the approving court as reasonable. *Vellines v. Ely*, 185 Va. 889, 896, 41 S.E.2d 21, 24 (1947). There must not be fraud regarding the purpose of the agreement, *Francois v. Francois*, 599 F.2d 1286 (3d Cir. 1979), or the true nature and extent of financial worth. See, e.g., *Feinberg v. Feinberg*, 96 Misc. 2d 443, 409 N.Y.S.2d 365 (1978).

However, there is no fraud justifying rescission if, after the parties have separated and begun negotiations, one fails to disclose a sexual relationship to the other. *Troyer v. Troyer*, 231 Va. 90, 341 S.E.2d 182 (1986), held that the foregoing would be true even if the parties had not retained counsel at the time of the negotiations. Nor was there reason to declare an agreement invalid in a case where the wife had been receiving psychological counseling for depression and had been hospitalized for this condition. The wife was unable to prove by clear and convincing evidence that she lacked mental capacity to contract or that her husband coerced her into executing the agreement. *Drewry v. Drewry*, 8 Va. App. 460, 383 S.E.2d 12 (1989). The trial court also found no unconscionability since there was no "gross disparity in value exchanged" in the agreement.

A husband could not claim that there had been mutual mistake vitiating an agreement where he participated with counsel in the negotiation and execution of the contract, but did not notice that the agreement contained an error that gave the wife 100% of the net equity in the marital residence. The wife alleged that, although she was surprised when she noticed the apparent change in her husband's position, she thought he had agreed to the change because he "was getting rid of" her. *Ward v. Ward,* 239 Va. 1, 387 S.E.2d 460 (1990). Even though the wife mistakenly believed that the parties' camper would be conveyed along with their North Carolina real estate, she violated their separation agreement by refusing to execute a deed to the property. *Clarke v. Clarke,* 1993 Va. App. LEXIS 113 (May 11, 1993). Since she breached, the wife was liable for her husband's resulting expenses and attorney's fees, but she was not in contempt.

A husband "stunned" his wife by asking her for a divorce. Although the parties continued to live together and to engage in sexual relations, they negotiated a property settlement agreement without the assistance of attorneys. During this time, the husband failed to disclose that he had retained legal counsel, that he had collected a library of "how-to" divorce books and that he was engaged in an extra-marital affair. The husband also met several times with the family's accountant of many years, who prepared a financial statement dramatically understating some of the assets the husband was to retain. Although the wife expressed concern about the accuracy of the property values, the husband and accountant assured her that "that's the way you do it." The court of appeals agreed with the trial court that the agreement was procured by fraud and was unconscionable, and upheld the equitable distribution award giving the wife one-half of the parties' property. *Adams v. Adams,* 1994 Va. App. LEXIS 42 (Feb. 1, 1994). See also *Webb v. Webb,* 16 Va. App. 486, 431 S.E.2d 55 (1993), where an agreement was invalidated because of nondisclosure and overreaching by the attorney husband who prepared the agreement and discouraged his wife from seeking separate legal counsel. The parties negotiated much of the agreement while still living together in the same house and sleeping in the same room, and the husband handled all major financial transactions during the marriage. On the other hand, the unhappy wife was not able to prove she relied on the husband's representations to establish fraud in *Miller v. Miller,* 1994 Va. App. LEXIS 116 (Mar. 8, 1994), nor duress in *Duc Van Nguyen v. Lan Phoung Dang,* 1994 Va. App. LEXIS 138 (Mar. 1, 1994).

However, fraud could be shown where the wife discovered after entry of the decree that part of the real property that was to be conveyed to her according to the separation agreement had been conveyed by the husband to one of his attorneys almost eighteen months before the agreement, and that her signature on that deed had been forged. *Holmes v. Holmes*, 8 Va. App. 457, 382 S.E.2d 27 (1989).

A wife filed a petition requesting vacation of the final decree of divorce, alleging that the husband had made material misrepresentations in a deposition taken before execution of the parties' separation agreement. Although the husband argued that the wife should be held to a standard of knowledge akin to that of a fiduciary relationship, the court of appeals found that such a relationship no longer existed during creation of the agreement, so that she was entitled to rely upon the husband's statements made under oath even though she had suspicions concerning their veracity. *Wells v. Wells*, 12 Va. App. 31, 401 S.E.2d 891 (1991). The court of appeals therefore remanded the case to determine the parties' property and spousal support rights resulting from the invalidity of the settlement agreement. The wife accused her husband of a fraudulent conveyance in *Chattin v. Chattin*, 245 Va. 302, 427 S.E.2d 347 (1993). He moved out of the marital home and began residing with one Barbara Soukup, who was married to another man at the time. He then gave $268,000 to a Delaware corporation in which Soukup was the president and sole stockholder, so that she could purchase property in Henrico County. This property was later sold, and Soukup's corporation used the proceeds to purchase, in its name, a condominium in which Chattin and Soukup were residing at the time of suit. The Virginia Supreme Court agreed with Mrs. Chattin that the conveyance was void as to her, since, before the transfer occurred, she was her husband's creditor under the parties' property settlement agreement. In addition, the court agreed that there was no valuable consideration for the conveyance. Soukup was married at the time the money was given to her, and the transfer was made as an inducement to Soukup to terminate her marriage, which was contrary to public policy.

The court found an agreement unconscionable because of the gross disparity in the assets received through the "over-reaching and oppressive conduct" of the husband at a time when the wife was patently suicidal and operating under impaired judgment. *Scroggins v. Scroggins*, 1996 Va. App. LEXIS 207 (Mar. 26, 1996).

In *Plogger v. Plogger*, 1997 Va. App. LEXIS 249 (Apr. 22, 1997) (unpublished decision), a husband successfully overturned a separation agreement on grounds of its unconscionability. The court first found that there was a "gross disparity in the value exchanged" under the agreement, since it imposed a shocking monthly support obligation on the husband that the wife knew was essentially impossible for him to perform. The agreement provided that he was to pay her $1,200 of his $1,386 monthly income, and had been drafted by the wife's attorney. The husband signed without reading the agreement. But see *Pelfrey v. Pelfrey*, 25 Va. App. 239, 487 S.E.2d 281 (1997), where the husband, who did not consult an attorney after he was presented with the wife's property settlement agreement, but did make changes to several drafts, was found not to have been coerced into signing. Before the wife began to prepare the agreement, the husband had given her his attorney's draft agreement, which she refused to sign. A party cannot claim fraud on the part of husband's counsel in a property settlement agreement when the wife reviewed the agreement prior to signing, initialed each page, signed the agreement, had counsel present, received a copy of the agreement immediately and subsequently used the executed agreement in her attempts to enforce its provisions. *Venie v. Venie*, 1998 Va. App. LEXIS 469 (Sept. 1, 1998) (unpublished decision).

In *Ellett v. Ellett*, 35 Va. App. 97, 542 S.E.2d 816 (2001), a husband failed to allege facts sufficient to support his claim of extrinsic fraud in connection with a property settlement agreement incorporated into a divorce decree. His allegations that: (1) his wife misrepresented the status of the family's bills and accounts, (2) she discouraged him from obtaining an attorney, (3) he executed the agreement under duress and undue influence, (4) the agreement's property division, child and spousal support, and child custody provisions were unconscionable, and (5) his wife misrepresented her intent to abide by the terms of the agreement, were all matters that could have been raised during the divorce proceeding. Thus, they did not involve "extrinsic" fraud, or fraud upon the court, that would sustain a challenge to the divorce decree itself as void. See *Wallihan v. Hughes*, 196 Va. 117, 82 S.E.2d 553 (1954) (when parties are before a court and a separation agreement is approved, confirmed, and decreed upon, its validity is *res judicata* between the parties, and a party cannot later "go behind the judgment of the court" and say that the contract was secured through fraud).

Duress is not generally accepted as an excuse. The party claiming duress must prove its existence by clear and convincing evidence, and the threatened act must be wrongful. *Pelfrey v. Pelfrey*, 25 Va. App. 239, 246, 487 S.E.2d 281, 284 (1997).

## § 17.07   Facilitating or Promoting Divorce

Husband and wife executed an agreement upon separation. After some negotiation about an increased amount of support, the increase was agreed to in exchange for a written promise by the wife that she would not contest the husband's divorce. This was valid since at the time the second agreement was executed there was no dispute that the parties had been separated for one year, so that the husband had valid grounds for an absolute divorce; the general purpose of the contract was to adjust property rights, not to facilitate a divorce, and the agreement was valid. *Cooley v. Cooley,* 220 Va. 749, 263 S.E.2d 49 (1980).

However, where a separation agreement was made solely at the urging of the husband, who wanted to pay his wife not to return to him, it was void as contrary to public policy. *Arrington v. Arrington,* 196 Va. 86, 82 S.E.2d 548 (1954). Likewise, a contract by a wife with a third party that depended upon the continued estrangement of husband and wife and the prosecution of a divorce by the wife was against public policy and void from its inception. *Shelton v. Stewart,* 193 Va. 162, 67 S.E.2d 841 (1951). See also *Upton v. Ames & Webb, Inc.,* 179 Va. 219, 18 S.E.2d 290 (1942).

The public policy rendering agreements facilitating or promoting separation void is the "policy to foster and protect marriage, to encourage the parties to live together, and to prevent separation, marriage being the foundation of the family and of society, without which there would be neither civilization nor progress." *Shelton v. Stewart,* 193 Va. 162, 166, 67 S.E.2d 841, 843 (1951). Therefore, the law will examine a contract between spouses closely and if it appears that it was part of a scheme to effect a separation or obtain a divorce by agreement, where legal grounds therefor did not previously exist, the agreement will be declared a nullity. *Ryan v. Griffin,* 199 Va. 891, 896, 103 S.E.2d 240, 244 (1958).

Although generally speaking a valid separation agreement will preclude a spouse from suing for desertion, if one spouse knows that the other spouse dissents from the separation and he or she nevertheless is determined to continue it, the spouse desiring a reconciliation will not be precluded from obtaining a divorce for desertion. *Butler v. Butler,* 145 Va. 85, 133 S.E. 756 (1926).

## § 17.08 Approval by Court

The trial court may exercise its discretion in determining whether a property settlement agreement should be incorporated by reference into a final decree of divorce. *Doering v. Doering,* 54 Va. App. 162, 676 S.E.2d 353 (2009); see Va. Code § 20-109.1. In exercising its discretion, the court may incorporate all, none, or selected provisions of a property settlement agreement. *Owney v. Owney,* 8 Va. App. 255, 379 S.E.2d 745 (1989). In *Doering,* the trial court refused to incorporate the parties' property settlement agreement into their final divorce decree, explaining that the husband could not meet the support obligations imposed by the agreement, and that if the agreement were incorporated, the parties would be returning "on a weekly basis" for the wife to seek court-ordered support through contempt proceedings. The court of appeals upheld the trial court's exercise of discretion, stating that the trial court gave a reasonable explanation for its decision not to incorporate the property settlement agreement. Similarly, the Court of Appeals upheld a trial court's decision not to affirm, ratify and incorporate the child support provisions in a settlement agreement that obligated husband to pay wife child support to a date that preceded the entry of the divorce by almost three years. *Kumar v. Kumar*, 2016 Va. App. LEXIS 301 (Nov. 16, 2016). The Court of Appeals noted that the trial court found "that it would be inequitable to make the effective date of the obligation the date listed in the PSA, November 5, 2012, because husband had been making "significant financial expenditure[s]" under the *pendente lite* order that had benefitted wife and the children." *Id.*

If the court approves the agreement, but no order for payment of sums in lieu of alimony is made, then the obligation is not alimony but rather a private contractual agreement between the parties. *Shoosmith v. Scott,* 217 Va. 789, 232 S.E.2d 787 (1977). Compare *Durrett v. Durrett,* 204 Va. 59, 62, 63, 129 S.E.2d 50, 53 (1963) (order of payment as alimony).

In order for the court to have power to incorporate the parties' agreement. Va. Code § 20-109 requires the agreement to provide for incorporation. Language directing the court to "approve, ratify and confirm" an agreement is not the same as "incorporation," and the phrase that "it shall be enforceable otherwise" expresses the parties' intention that the agreements not be enforceable through the court's contempt power. *Hoffman v. Hoffman,* 1994 Va. App. LEXIS 137 (Mar. 15, 1994). An "outline" agreement does not have to be incorporated into the final divorce decree. *Brundage v. Brundage,* 1995 Va. App. LEXIS 521 (May 23, 1995).

Situations in which an agreement is affirmed, or incorporated into a decree, or "affirmed, ratified, incorporated, but not merged" into a decree are distinguishable. *Rubio v. Rubio,* 36 Va. App. 248, 549 S.E.2d 610 (2001). When a spousal support agreement is "incorporated but not merged" into a final decree, the agreement remains enforceable under either contract law or through the court's contempt power. *Hering v. Hering,* 33 Va. App. 368, 533 S.E.2d 631 (2000).

Merger prescribes the methods of enforcing entitlements created by contract, and the distinction between merged and nonmerged agreements is important in the context of enforcement. However, Va. Code § 20-109 limits the authority of a trial court to make or modify spousal support awards when an agreement between the parties exists. The statute was enacted to require divorce decrees to honor support agreements made by parties, and it "stands as a clarion pronouncement of the policy encouraging settlement by agreement." The statute does not employ the word "merge," but applies to "any valid agreement" affirmed by the court. Thus, when parties form a spousal support agreement, basic property rights that arise and limit judicial modification do *not* expire if the contract merges into the decree for enforcement purposes. *Smith v. Smith*, 41 Va. App. 742, 589 S.E.2d 439 (2003) (wife's support could *not* be terminated for cohabiting with another person, despite merger of parties' support contract into final decree, when parties had agreed that support would terminate only upon the death of a party or wife's remarriage).

Where the parties' agreement regarding spousal and child support and mortgage payments, inter alia, was modified by a consent decree before trial, it was proper for the court to enter the agreement filed with it, with modifications as allowed and provided for by the consent decree, as part of the final decree of divorce. *Lindsay v. Lindsay*, 218 Va. 599, 238 S.E.2d 817 (1977).

When nothing in the record indicated that a wife held out her attorney as having authority to execute a final property settlement agreement on her behalf, it was error for the court to find that the wife was bound by the agreement because of her attorney's apparent authority to sign, and to incorporate the agreement by reference into the wife's final decree of divorce. *Walson v. Walson*, 37 Va. App. 208, 556 S.E.2d 53 (2001).

The circuit court for the City of Fredericksburg has held that when a divorce decree affirms, ratifies, and incorporates the parties' separation agreement, it may also award the dependent spouse a judgment for support arrearages. *Adams v. Adams*, 24 Va. Cir. 380 (1991).

The agreement will be given full faith and credit if there is a foreign judgment of divorce with personal jurisdiction over both parties, approving and incorporating it. *Wallihan v. Hughes*, 196 Va. 117, 130–31, 82 S.E.2d 553, 561–62 (1954). Full faith and credit need not be given to child custody provisions, or executory child support, which are always subject to modification. Similarly, other states will enforce Virginia property settlement agreements for spousal support since they cannot be modified under Va. Code § 20-109. *Knodel v. Knodel*, 14 Cal. 3d 752, 122 Cal. Rptr. 521, 537 P.2d 353 (1975).

The agreement may be incorporated into the divorce decree either when it has been filed before the final decree of divorce, or when a separate decree is filed after entry of the final divorce decree. Va. Code § 20-109.1.

In the parties' final divorce decree, the court retained jurisdiction to determine spousal support and property rights. Thereafter, the parties entered into a settlement agreement pursuant to which the husband agreed to make annual payments to the wife, in return for which the wife agreed to "release and discharge . . . all claims which she might have for alimony." The trial court entered a decree that ratified and incorporated this settlement agreement. The court of appeals held that § 20-109.1 did not deprive the trial court of its power to incorporate a settlement agreement involving support in a decree following the entry of a decree of divorce. *Rogers v. Damron*, 23 Va. App. 708, 479 S.E.2d 540 (1997). It was therefore appropriate for the wife to use the court's contempt power to enforce the decree.

It was not appropriate to have the former husband sanctioned for appealing a second order of judgment for $45,000 based on an earlier separation agreement providing for child support and conveyance of property, since the appeal was not for improper purposes. *Wetstein v. Araujo-Wetstein,* 11 Va. App. 331, 398 S.E.2d 96 (1990).

A party's injury that arises from an attorney's malpractice in connection with a property settlement agreement occurs when the court enters a final decree of divorce that incorporates the property settlement agreement. *MacLellan v. Throckmorton*, 235 Va. 341, 367 S.E.2d 720 (1988). Thus, in *Van Dam v. Gay*, 280 Va. 457, 699 S.E.2d 480 (2010), the malpractice statute of limitations had already run with respect to a 1986 property settlement agreement, when a former wife discovered in 2006 that the agreement was insufficient, as a matter of federal law, to entitle her to survivor's benefits under her former husband's military and civil service retirement plans.

## § 17.09    Effect of Court Approval

[1]   *Termination at Remarriage.* Before the addition of Va. Code § 20-109, the obligation to pay under an incorporated agreement did not terminate at the dependent spouse's remarriage unless such termination was provided by its terms, *McLoughlin v. McLoughlin,* 211 Va. 365, 177 S.E.2d 781 (1970), since the court did not have jurisdiction to modify the contractual obligation. The converse is now true: the obligation will now cease upon remarriage unless otherwise provided in the agreement, Va. Code § 20-109.1. For example, in *Miller v. Hawkins,* 14 Va. App. 192, 415 S.E.2d 861 (1992), the parties' agreement provided that the spousal support should terminate when the minor child reached the age of 23 or graduated from college. In the same sentence, the parties agreed that "in the event Wife should pay in full the first lien deed of trust indebtedness owed against the above-described real estate prior to her remarriage," the weekly amount for

spousal support should be renegotiated. The wife remarried, and argued that the provisions, read together, were enough to show the parties' intent to continue spousal support notwithstanding her remarriage. Citing cases from other jurisdictions, the court held that in order for the spousal support obligation to survive remarriage of the dependent spouse, the agreement must contain clear and express language evincing the parties' intent that spousal support will continue after remarriage. See also *Baldwin v. Baldwin*, 44 Va. App. 93, 603 S.E.2d 172 (2004) (explaining operation of Va. Code § 20-109 with respect to agreements entered into before and after statute's enactment); *Hardesty v. Hardesty*, 40 Va. App. 663, 581 S.E.2d 213 (2003); *Gayler v. Gayler*, 20 Va. App. 83, 455 S.E.2d 278 (1995); *MacNelly v. MacNelly*, 17 Va. App. 427, 437 S.E.2d 582 (1993). In *Blakey v. Commissioner*, 78 T.C. 963 (1982), the court found that a unitary payment for alimony and child support under *Commissioner v. Lester*, 366 U.S. 299, 81 S. Ct. 1343, 6 L. Ed. 2d 306 (1961), still retains alimony characteristics for tax purposes despite the fact that alimony terminates by statute at remarriage.

**[2]**  *Termination at Death.* Unless husband and wife specify otherwise in the agreement, spousal support will terminate at the death of the payor. Va. Code § 20-107.1. Where husband and wife were separated with no possibility of reconciliation, and agreed that in exchange for all marital rights, save that of prosecuting for divorce, husband would pay wife a sum to discharge a debt secured by her home, his heirs after his death were obligated to continue the payments. *Higgins v. McFarland*, 196 Va. 889, 86 S.E.2d 168 (1955).

Where husband and wife's agreement was incorporated into a final decree that ordered payments as alimony, she could not recover from the husband's estate at his death. The duty to make alimony payments ceases upon the death of either husband or wife. *Durrett v. Durrett*, 204 Va. 59, 129 S.E.2d 50 (1963). Compare *Moore v. Crutchfield*, 136 Va. 20, 28, 116 S.E. 482, 484 (1923) (in lieu of alimony; no jurisdiction in court to enforce compliance).

**[3]**  *Reconciliation.* If the parties reconcile after they sign a separation or property settlement agreement, the agreement shall be abrogated unless it provides expressly to the contrary. Va. Code § 20-155.

Where the agreement was entered into prior to the enactment of Virginia's Premarital Agreement Act, a separation agreement is not abandoned by a mere conditional, experimental, and temporary living together of the parties, without any intention to abandon the agreement or return to their original situation as husband and wife. For example, in *Higgs v. Higgs*, 12 Va. Cir. 509 (Warren Co. 1983), the husband visited the home where his spouse lived as frequently and regularly as the schedule of the parties would permit. Although the parties had a property settlement agreement, the executory provisions were abrogated and were no longer effective and binding between the parties. See also *Knight v. Knight*, 22 Va. Cir. 485 (1981).

A valid reconciliation requires a mutual intention to resume the marital relationship absent bad faith; and the validity of a separation agreement is not affected by bad faith behavior. *Jacobsen v. Jacobsen*, 41 Va. App. 582, 586 S.E.2d 896 (2003). In *Jacobsen*, a husband continued an affair with another woman while engaging in a reconciliation with his wife that was motivated by his desire to defeat their separation agreement. Because the reconciliation was a sham, the separation agreement was valid, and a trial court did not err by ratifying, affirming, and incorporating the separation agreement into a final divorce decree.

Reconciliation of the parties for nearly four years terminated all executory portions of their separation agreement, including a waiver of spousal support. However, there was no abrogation for executed portions of the agreement. *Yeich v. Yeich*, 11 Va. App. 509, 399 S.E.2d 170 (1990). Although the parties resumed their marital relationship for four months after they signed a property settlement agreement, the wife filed for a fault divorce and later was awarded a no-fault divorce incorporating the agreement. The agreement provided: "In the event of a reconciliation and resumption of the marital relationship between the parties, all of the provisions of this Agreement . . . shall continue in full force and effect without abatement of any terms." The language of the Agreement demonstrated the parties' intent that it survive any reconciliation. *Jennings v. Jennings*, 12 Va. App. 1187, 409 S.E.2d 8 (1991). See also *Jevcak v. Jevcak*, 1994 Va. App. LEXIS 667 (Nov. 15, 1994) (not designated for publication), and *Smith v. Smith*, 19 Va. App. 155, 449 S.E.2d 506 (1994), where the agreement was enforceable because it was not revoked by a written agreement signed by the parties, as provided in the agreement. Similarly, when the parties agreed in a separation agreement that the husband would convey his rights in the marital residence to the wife, and that she would assume the mortgage, and this was assumed by a deed of assumption, the wife owned the property as feme sole. Although the parties reconciled, the property remained separate and not subject to equitable distribution when they later divorced. At the same time, the wife did not reacquire an interest in the husband's retirement benefits through the reconciliation, since they too had been a subject of the prior agreement. *Garland v. Garland*, 19 Va. Cir. 131 (1990).

In *Crenshaw v. Crenshaw*, 12 Va. App. 1129, 408 S.E.2d 556 (1991), the parties executed a property settlement that was approved and confirmed by a 1964 decree for a divorce *a mensa*. After obtaining the divorce *a mensa*, the parties reconciled for 21 years, believing they were married. They never revoked the 1964 decree. In 1974, without the parties' knowledge, the trial court dismissed the suit and removed it from the docket. In 1985, the parties again separated, and in 1986, the husband filed for divorce. The *a mensa* decree remained intact regardless of the intention of the parties, but dismissal of the case under Code § 8.01-335(B) terminated the decree of divorce from bed and board. It was therefore the agreement between the parties, and not the decree, that governed their property rights. The agreement was abrogated by the reconciliation, for when "the parties executed the separation agreement they intended to live separate and apart. When they reestablished a matrimonial home they thereby necessarily intended to void those portions of the agreement that remained executory."

**[4]  *Bankruptcy.*** The discharge in bankruptcy of the obligor spouse will not free the bankrupt from his duties to make spousal or child support payments even under a property settlement agreement. 11 U.S.C. § 522(d)(10)(D) allows the spouse to receive support payments. Section 523(a)(5) does not exempt them for the payor. *Douglas v. Douglas,* 17 Va. App. 380, 437 S.E.2d 244 (1993), concerned a divorce decree that required the husband to hold his wife harmless for a joint credit card debt. Although he paid off the balance, he then incurred a $5,000 additional debt for which the couple remained jointly responsible. He filed for bankruptcy, and failed to list the wife as a creditor or to notify her of the bankruptcy. The court of appeals held that the debt was not discharged in bankruptcy, and the husband was in contempt for failing to comply with the terms of the divorce decree. See also *Tankersley v. Tankersley,* 30 Va. Cir. 273 (1993); but see *Sexton v. Sexton,* 30 Va. Cir. 271 (1993) (no contempt since no order to comply with terms of agreement in final decree; wife still had remedy in assumpsit since debt not discharged). However, in *Carter v. Carter,* 18 Va. App. 787, 447 S.E.2d 522 (1994), the husband could discharge his obligation to pay his wife a monetary award to equalize their property distribution. However, by accepting discharge, the husband repudiated the agreement. He therefore gave the wife the right to seek rescission of the agreement. See also *Mosley v. Mosley,* 19 Va. App. 192, 450 S.E.2d 161 (1994) (trial court erred in attempting to hold husband financially responsible for one-half of all marital debts, circumventing the discharge granted him by the federal bankruptcy court). *Fleming v. Fleming,* 32 Va. App. 822, 531 S.E.2d 38 (2000) (trial court erred in awarding, in circumvention of discharge granted by federal bankruptcy court, lump sum spousal support that represented amount of debt that wife was discharged from paying; and trial court erred in awarding spousal support in violation of Va. Code § 20-109, which prohibits any spousal support award not in accordance with parties' contract agreement filed prior to entry of final divorce decree). See *In re Calhoun,* 715 F. 2d 1103 (6th Cir. 1983); *Poolman v. Poolman,* 289 F.2d 332 (8th Cir. 1961) (obligation to make payments on deed of trust for family home not dischargeable); see 11 U.S.C.A. § 35. According to the parties' property settlement agreement, incorporated into their final divorce decree, Mr. Tribby was to transfer his interest in the jointly owned marital residence to his wife within fifteen days. Although Mrs. Tribby occupied the house following the separation, and made payments on the deed of trust, Mr. Tribby never conveyed his interest to her. Instead, he failed to make payments on a bank loan to the National Bank of Fredericksburg, which obtained a judgment against him. In *Tribby v. Tribby,* 26 Va. Cir. 372 (1992), the circuit court found that the property settlement agreement and divorce decree, while binding on the Tribbys, had no effect on third parties. While they were married, the bank could not reach the home, which the parties owned as tenants by the entireties. After the divorce, however, the bank could extend their judgment lien to Mr. Tribby's interest in the home since the former spouses had become tenants in common.

Obligations arising out of property settlement agreements or equitable distribution awards are dischargeable in bankruptcy only if they are debts as defined in the Bankruptcy Code. A debtor's bankruptcy estate includes only property to which the debtor holds legal (as opposed to equitable) title; consequently, the nature of a former wife's interest in her former husband's pension or other property will govern whether the debtor husband's obligation is, or is not, a debt dischargeable in bankruptcy. *Brogan v. Brogan,* 31 Va. App. 769, 525 S.E.2d 618 (2000). In *Brogan,* a former husband's obligation, imposed by a final decree of divorce, to pay his former wife half of his federal civil service retirement pension was determined not to be a debt dischargeable in bankruptcy, because the wife's share of the pension was her sole and separate property, and was received by the husband only as a constructive trustee. Alternatively, the wife's interest in the husband's pension payments was not dischargeable because payments not yet due and payable at the time a bankruptcy petition is filed are not debts under the *Bankruptcy Code. Brogan v. Brogan,* 31 Va. App. 769, 525 S.E.2d 618 (2000).

If an agreement does not otherwise bar alimony, a court may modify alimony where one party discharged debt in bankruptcy that the other party was required to then pay. In *Rogers v. Rogers,* 51 Va. App. 261, 269, 656 S.E.2d 436, 439–40 (2008), the Virginia Court of Appeals stated:

A court may not order a lump sum spousal support award to compensate a non-debtor spouse for the other spouse's discharge of marital obligations in bankruptcy. This would "re-create a debt discharged under federal bankruptcy laws" and impermissibly intrude upon federal bankruptcy jurisdiction. Mosley, 19 Va. App. at 197, 450 S.E.2d at 164; Siragusa, 843 P.2d at 813. However, where a material change in circumstances due to bankruptcy otherwise occurs, a court may modify a spousal support order. Dickson, 23 Va. App. at 85–86, 474 S.E.2d at 171.

In their property settlement agreement, Audrey and Alvin Chattin agreed that he would pay her $1,200 per month spousal support for a six and one-half year period; that he would maintain an insurance policy on his life in the amount of $100,000, naming her as irrevocable beneficiary; and that he would provide health insurance for her. In *Chattin v. Chattin*, 245 Va. 302, 427 S.E.2d 347 (1993), the Virginia Supreme Court determined that the wife was entitled to specific performance of these provisions because she did not have an adequate remedy at law. In order to enforce the contractual provisions for spousal support, she either would have to sue on the contract each time the husband failed to make a payment or would have to wait until a significant arrearage had accumulated before filing suit. If he failed to pay premiums on either insurance policy, it could lapse, thereby requiring her to purchase similar coverage and to bring suit against him each time she paid a renewal premium. If the husband failed to cooperate in providing the necessary information for obtaining life insurance, the wife would be left with no remedy at law whatsoever.

For a discussion of how the 2005 amendments to the bankruptcy law prohibit certain debt from being discharged, see *Rogers v. Rogers*, 51 Va. App. 261, 269, 656 S.E.2d 436, 439–40 (2008).

**[5]** *Nonmodifiability.* Va. Code § 20-109 restricts the court's jurisdiction over the modification of alimony for any agreement that was entered before July of 2018. Therefore, where wife and husband had a property settlement agreement incorporated into a divorce decree providing for alimony and child support to be paid to the wife, the court was in error when it ordered an elimination of the duty to pay alimony for a month when the husband was unemployed. *Dienhart v. Dienhart*, 210 Va. 101, 168 S.E.2d 279 (1969). Va. Code § 20-109(C) was amended in July 2018, to provide that agreements must specifically state that the spousal support is not modifiable, and to preserve any non-modifiability, the agreement must contain the following specific language, *"The amount or duration of spousal support contained in this [AGREEMENT] is not modifiable except as specifically set forth in this [AGREEMENT]."* Additional discussion on this is located at § 20.22 of this treatise.

If the agreement so provides, the amounts payable may be modified based upon such factors as the consumer price index, the age of children, and the income of the spouses. The court may modify a support award in accordance with an agreement between the parties whether filed before or after entry of a final divorce decree. Va. Code § 20-109. See generally Wadlington, *Separation and Settlement Agreements in Virginia: Drafting for Future Modification,* 1976 Va. St. B.A.J. 4.

Va. Code § 20-109(C) (formerly Va. Code § 20-109) restricts a trial court's authority over awards of spousal support, suit money, or attorney's fees to the terms of any contract that is signed by the parties and incorporated into a final decree of divorce. *Rutledge v. Rutledge,* 45 Va. App. 56, 608 S.E.2d 504 (2005). In *Rutledge,* Va. Code § 20-109(C) precluded a trial court from awarding attorney's fees in a spousal support modification proceeding, because the parties' property settlement agreement authorized attorney's fees in only two situations, neither of which involved spousal support modification. In *Stacy v. Stacy,* 53 Va. App. 38, 669 S.E.2d 348 (2008), a trial court erred in treating a husband's mortgage payment obligation as spousal support and terminating the obligation on cohabitation grounds. Under the plainly stated terms of the parties' property settlement agreement, the mortgage payment obligation was an unconditional third-party obligation incurred by the husband as part of the parties' equitable distribution—with spousal support having been expressly waived. Thus, under Va. Code § 20-109(C), the trial court lacked authority to terminate the mortgage payment obligation. In *McCoy v. McCoy,* 55 Va. App. 524, 687 S.E.2d 82 (2010), a trial court was required, in accordance with a property settlement agreement incorporated into a final decree of divorce and Va. Code § 20-109(C), to order a husband to provide health insurance to his wife after their divorce and her remarriage.

Va. Code § 20-109(C) also restricts the court's jurisdiction in making an equitable distribution award under Va. Code § 20-107.3. To the extent that a husband and wife have already stipulated to a particular disposition of their property, the court may not decree inconsistent relief in an equitable distribution, because marital property settlements are favored in the law. *Campbell v. Campbell,* 32 Va. App. 351, 528 S.E.2d 145 (2000). In *Campbell,* a husband and wife executed a post-separation agreement that "voluntarily . . . waive[d] the right to have the court decree as to the property of the parties" and acknowledged their awareness of Virginia's equitable distribution law. Once incorporated into a divorce decree pursuant to Va. Code § 20-109.1, the agreement became a term of the decree, and the equitable distribution provisions of Va. Code § 20-107.3 became unavailable to remedy claims arising from the agreement. Instead, the husband and wife had elected to rely on the post-separation agreement to identify and establish their respective interests relative to the separate and marital estates, child custody, support, and myriad other issues incident to the marriage.

An amendment to a divorce decree could not be entered more than 21 days after the final distribution order. *Bogart v. Bogart*, 21 Va. App. 280, 464 S.E.2d 157 (1995).

**[6]** *Contempt.* Contempt is available once a property settlement agreement is incorporated into the divorce decree and the obligor is directed to pay a specified amount. *McLoughlin v. McLoughlin*, 211 Va. 365, 177 S.E.2d 781 (1970). See also *Adams v. Adams*, 24 Va. Cir. 380 (City of Fredericksburg 1991). It will be available even though, after the decree, the parties agree in writing to a lesser amount. *Capell v. Capell*, 164 Va. 45, 178 S.E. 894 (1935).

In the parties' final divorce decree, the court retained jurisdiction to determine spousal support and property rights. Thereafter, the parties entered into a settlement agreement pursuant to which the husband agreed to make annual payments to the wife, in return for which the wife agreed to "release and discharge . . . all claims which she might have for alimony." The trial court entered a decree that ratified and incorporated this settlement agreement. The court of appeals held in *Rogers v. Damron*, 23 Va. App. 708, 479 S.E.2d 540 (1997), that § 20-109.1 did not deprive the trial court of its power to incorporate a settlement agreement involving support in a decree following the entry of a decree of divorce. It was therefore appropriate for the wife to use the court's contempt power to enforce the decree.

When a husband sought a contempt order because his wife had not sold the marital home according to the terms of their modified settlement agreement, the trial court ruled that the combination of relevant terms in the modified and original agreement (which contained a numerical example) was ambiguous. The trial judge was not acting in error when he admitted parol evidence to establish the parties' real intention as expressed in the modified agreement. Once this amount was fixed at $475,000, the trial court could then enforce the personal obligations set forth in the agreement. *Shoup v. Shoup*, 31 Va. App. 621, 525 S.E.2d 61 (2000).

However, contempt will not be available as a remedy where the duty to provide some aspect of support under an agreement is not definite, but arises only by implication. *Winn v. Winn*, 218 Va. 8, 235 S.E.2d 307 (1977) (duty to maintain effective health insurance coverage following divorce). Nor was contempt available when the parties' divorce decree did not incorporate their settlement agreement nor order the husband to comply with its provisions regarding child support. In this case, the property settlement agreement constituted a private contract between the parties, and might not be enforced as part of the divorce suit. *Becerra-Cely v. Amick-Becerra*, 1997 Va. App. LEXIS 226 (Apr. 15, 1997).

Contempt will be available for any provision reasonably relating to maintenance and care of children that is incorporated into the decree. *Morris v. Morris*, 216 Va. 457, 219 S.E.2d 864 (1975) (custodial parent received residence, etc., and noncustodial parent ordered to keep life insurance policy for the benefit of each child). Whether to find a party in contempt lies within the sound discretion of the trial court. After the wife explained her conduct in *Clarke v. Clarke*, 1993 Va. App. LEXIS 113 (May 11, 1993), the court found that although she had breached the parties' separation agreement, her conduct did not deserve punishment. She had mistakenly thought that a camper would be conveyed to her along with property in North Carolina.

When seeking contempt, it is important to understand the distinction between civil and criminal contempt. *Mills v. Mills*, 70 Va. App. 362, 380–382, 827 S.E.2d 391, 399–401 (2019) explains how to determine if a contempt proceeding is civil or criminal. In *Mills*, the circuit court found Wife in civil contempt for violating the provision of the property settlement agreement requiring "the parties to 'foster love, affection, and respect between the children and both parents' and to refrain from doing 'anything to interfere with the love and affection of the children for the other party.'" *Mills*, 70 Va. App. at 362, 827 S.E.2d at 394. The court imposed a $1,000 fine against the wife and suspended its imposition conditioned upon wife not violating the provision in the future. Wife contended that the circuit court imposed a criminal contempt sanction, and she was not afforded the protections of that type of a proceeding. *Mills*, 70 Va. App. at 379–80, 827 S.E.2d at 399. The Court of Appeals agreed with the wife and in reversing the circuit court stated that the fine was not remedial, the fine was not owed to the husband, "the primary purpose was punitive," and that "contempt sanctions for violating prohibitory orders generally are considered criminal." *Mills*, 70 Va. App. at 380–81, 827 S.E.2d at 399–400.

The inability to pay a support award is a valid defense to a charge of contempt of court. *Street v. Street*, 24 Va. App. 14, 20–21, 480 S.E.2d 118, 121 (1997). Being charged with out-of-court contempt, a party "must be given the opportunity to present evidence in his defense, including the right to call witnesses." *Street v. Street*, 24 Va. App. 14, 20, 480 S.E.2d 118, 121 (1997). "The due process clause of the Fourteenth Amendment requires that alleged contemnors 'have a reasonable opportunity to meet [the charge of contempt] by way of defense or explanation.' " *Id.* (citations omitted).

**[7]** *Contractual Remedies.* Even though a child has reached majority, the contractual agreement between the parents, if it so provides, will still be in force. The divorce court will have jurisdiction to enforce the obligation after the child reaches majority. *Cutshaw v. Cutshaw,* 220 Va. 638, 261 S.E.2d 52 (1979). See also *Goldin v. Goldin,* 34 Va. App. 95, 538 S.E.2d 326 (2000) (when contract for post-minority child support was incorporated into divorce decree, court could modify support for minor child, but could only enforce contract terms for support of adult child).

Garnishment of a federal employee's wages or pension for arrearages of monies due under a support agreement incorporated into a final decree is proper. Although the payments are "alimony" within the federal statute since they are enforceable by contempt, they are not subject to the 25% limitation of the obligor's income since the judgment was not based upon a court order for support but rather upon a violation of a contractual obligation. *Butler v. Butler,* 221 Va. 1035, 277 S.E.2d 180 (1981). However, where yearly additional amounts for child support in a separation agreement were incorporated into a divorce decree, a consent order eliminated not only the effect of the decree but also any contractual obligations under the settlement agreement. The wife therefore had no contractual basis for recovery of the sums allegedly due for additional child support. *Anderson v. Van Landingham,* 236 Va. 85, 372 S.E.2d 137 (1988).

When an agreement is "filed with the papers in the cause," and never "affirmed, ratified, or incorporated" into the final divorce decree, the divorce court's acceptance of the agreement merely constitutes judicial approval of a private bilateral contract, and the court is constrained by Va. Code §§ 20-109.1 and 20-109 from entering any subsequent order in contravention of the contract agreement. *Bazzle v. Bazzle,* 37 Va. App. 737, 561 S.E.2d 50 (2002). In *Bazzle,* a husband and wife executed a property settlement agreement "filed with the papers in the cause," that required the husband to pay monthly spousal support. When the husband stopped paying, the wife sued for anticipatory breach of contract, and obtained a default judgment of $429,565 in satisfaction of the husband's remaining spousal support obligation. Later, the trial court enjoined the wife from collecting the judgment as long as the husband paid spousal support according to the contract agreement. After the husband's payments satisfied the judgment, he stopped paying spousal support, and the wife unsuccessfully sought a contempt order. The court of appeals held that the husband's future spousal support obligation had been quantified at $429,565 by the wife's election to obtain a judgment for anticipatory breach of contract, and that the wife was precluded from further spousal support litigation because the husband's spousal support obligation had been merged into the $429,565 judgment.

In *Brown v. Brown,* 244 Va. 319, 422 S.E.2d 375 (1992), according to the parties' separation agreement, Winfree Brown was to pay Angela a lump sum of $20,000, while Angela agreed to prepare and execute a deed conveying to him her interest in the family residence. In consideration of the lump sum payment, she also agreed to waive all claims in the husband's employment benefits, including pension plans, or to take property under the law of intestacy. Although the husband made plans to obtain the $20,000, and a check from the employer for nearly $16,000 was found in the glove compartment of his car, Winfree died in September of 1990, before the wife was paid or their divorce finalized. He died intestate, so that if the agreement was enforceable, the couple's two infant children would be his sole heirs at law. The co-administrators of Winfree's estate tendered the wife $20,000 in February, to be delivered to her upon execution of the documents terminating all her interests in the estate and employee benefits. The Virginia Supreme Court, in *Brown v. Brown,* 244 Va. 319, 422 S.E.2d 375 (1992), agreed with the trial court that tender was made within a reasonable time so that the separation agreement was binding upon the wife. Further, the wife's notarized signature of the separation agreement constituted a sufficient spousal consent to a change of beneficiary.

In *Kelley v. Kelley*, 248 Va. 295, 449 S.E.2d 55 (1994), the Virginia Supreme Court reversed an en banc court of appeals decision, *Kelley v. Kelley*, 17 Va. App. 93, 435 S.E.2d 421 (1993), which had concluded that a trial court lacked jurisdiction, after the 21-day period of Rule 1:1 had expired, to alter the terms of a divorce decree or the terms of a property settlement agreement that had been ratified, affirmed, and incorporated by reference into the decree. The incorporated property settlement included a provision which stated that (1) the husband would never be responsible for child support, (2) the wife would never seek court-ordered child support, and (3) consideration for the provision was the husband's relinquishment of his entire equity in the marital home. In reversing, the Virginia Supreme Court held that the provision was null and void as violative of established law, because the parties had contracted away the husband's duty to support his children. Moreover, the trial court had jurisdiction to declare the provision void and unenforceable, because (1) any contract purporting to impinge the rights of children to maintenance and support is facially illegal and void, (2) the portion of the decree that related to the void provision was void, and (3) it is well established that a void judgment may be attacked and vacated at any time. *Compare Rook v. Rook*, 233 Va. 92, 353 S.E.2d 756 (1987) (challenge to validity of property settlement agreement not involving child support should have been made prior to expiration of 21-day period after entry of judgment, pursuant to Rule 1:1).

Nevertheless, parties in a divorce can reach an agreement on child support without violating the *Kelley* principles. *Shoup v. Shoup*, 37 Va. App. 240, 556 S.E.2d 783 (2001). Thus, a final divorce decree incorporating an agreement that the wife waived her marital interest in her husband's military pension in exchange for a release from her obligation to pay child support was not void as against public policy. *Lehman v. Lehman*, 38 Va. App. 598, 567 S.E.2d 571 (2002). In *Lehman*, the parties did not contract away their children's right to support, because their agreement included a provision that the wife was to pay child support at her discretion; also, their agreement did not violate the *Shoup* directives.

A provision in a property settlement agreement which states that neither party can appeal a trial court's decision does not violate public policy, and is valid and binding on the parties. *Burke v. Burke*, 52 Va. App. 183, 662 S.E.2d 622 (2008). In *Burke*, a provision of the parties' property settlement agreement stated that each party agreed that any matter arising out of the agreement would be decided by a judge of the Circuit Court of the City of Portsmouth, Virginia, in a summary non-jury proceeding, and that the decision of the judge would be final, conclusive, and non-appealable, and binding upon the parties. In upholding the provision, the appellate court reasoned that the provision (1) did not waive the rights of anyone other than the parties, (2) allowed neutral review of the parties' dispute, and (3) did not violate any Virginia statute. The appellate court also observed that a no-appeal clause forces the parties to realize that the litigation must end; and that, given the contentious nature of some cases, protects the parties by resolving the dispute more quickly and minimizing costs.

Provisions of a property settlement agreement could not be specifically enforced by one spouse against the widow of the other. Specific performance is available only where there is privity of contract between plaintiff and defendant. The proper party defendant in such a suit is the executor, the deceased's legal representative. *Fisher v. Bauer*, 246 Va. 490, 436 S.E.2d 602 (1993).

Where one party was found to have intentionally misled the other party about the identity of the retirement plan in the Marital Settlement Agreement, the trial court reformed the parties' Agreement to name the correct retirement plan despite the fact that the divorce order, which affirmed, ratified and incorporated the agreement, had been entered more than ten years earlier. See *Ferry v. Beard,* 2020 Va. App. LEXIS 31 (February 4, 2020).

### § 17.10    Who May Sue

Children of parents who executed a property settlement have no ability to enforce it. *Buchanan v. Buchanan,* 170 Va. 458, 197 S.E. 426 (1938). See also *Yarborough v. Yarborough,* 290 U.S. 202, 54 S. Ct. 181, 78 L. Ed. 269 (1933). However, even if the provision for child support has not been incorporated into a final decree of divorce, the state retains the parents' patriae power to compel payment for a necessitous child.

All suits in Virginia must be prosecuted by and against living parties, either in their individual or representative capacity. *Loewinger v. Estate of Loewinger,* 64 Va. App. 1, 5, 763 S.E.2d 826, 828 (2014). After the trial court entered a divorce but before entering its final order dismissing the case, the husband passed away. Wife appealed the trial court's monetary award to her as being inconsistent with the terms of the parties' premarital agreement. In the appeal, wife improperly substituted husband's estate in the place of husband as the party in interest. Although a claim may be made against a decedent's estate, Va. Code § 8.01-229(B) requires that the decedent's personal representative defend any personal action which could have been brought against the decedent. *Id.,* 64 Va. App. at 5–6, 763 S.E.2d at 828.

### § 17.11    Spousal Support—Tax Consequences

For agreements entered into before July of 1985, unless an amount was specifically designated as child support, a sum payable "in lieu of alimony and for child support," or "for the care, support and maintenance of the spouse and the minor children" was entirely deductible by the obligor and taxable as income to the recipient spouse. *Commissioner v. Lester,* 366 U.S. 299, 81 S. Ct. 1343, 6 L. Ed. 2d 306 (1961).

If circumstances change so that, for instance, custody reverts to the obligor spouse, *Carter v. Carter,* 215 Va. 475, 211 S.E.2d 253 (1975), an allocation between child support and alimony will be made. This will not be necessary when one spouse seeks an increase in child support, however. *Wickham v. Wickham,* 215 Va. 694, 213 S.E.2d 750 (1975).

If the agreement provides that the unitary payments will continue despite the remarriage of the dependent spouse, the amounts received will still be treated for tax purposes as alimony despite Va. Code § 20-110. *Blakey v. Commissioner,* 78 T.C. 963 (1982).

Since the Domestic Relations Tax Reform Act of 1984, payments made that are contingent upon events relating to the child rather than the spouse will be treated as child support (not deductible nor taxable) rather than alimony. Section 422 of Title IV, Subtitle B., P.L. 98-369, amending I.R.C. § 71(c). Thus, there is currently no advantage to providing for unitary payments. As a result of the Tax Cuts and Jobs Act (TCJA), spousal support payments in any divorce or separation instrument that is entered after December 31, 2018, are not taxable, and accordingly, will neither be included within the payee's taxable income nor deductible from the payor's taxable income.

Another tax concern is the lump sum payment. Under the former § 71, the payment was required to be periodic to be classified as alimony. Under the revised § 71, there is no such requirement. However, § 71(f)(1) provides that payments in excess of $10,000 will not be treated as alimony unless made in each of six years, and will not be treated as alimony to the extent that they decrease by more than $10,000 over the previous taxable year. Section 71(f)(2). A lump sum would therefore be treated as alimony so long as paid out somewhat evenly over at least six years following the separation.

If spouses divorce after filing joint income tax returns, and return their refund check to the Commissioner, separate checks will be issued to husband and wife. Va. Code § 58.1-499.

Spousal support ends upon remarriage when a separation agreement states that there shall be weekly payments "until her death." In *Langley v. Johnson*, 27 Va. App. 365, 499 S.E.2d 15 (1998), the court found that these payments were indeed support payments despite the wife's arguments that these payments were really property division in disguise. They were to be adjusted annually according to the Consumer Price Index, and were to terminate at her death, indicating that these were traditional support and maintenance payments that would terminate at her remarriage.

### § 17.12 Termination at Death and Remarriage

If the agreement provides that support payments will terminate upon the dependent spouse's remarriage, the fact that the second marriage is voidable and annulled will not restore payment under the agreement. *McConkey v. McConkey*, 216 Va. 106, 215 S.E.2d 640 (1975). This is because the obligor spouse has the right to assume the validity of the second marriage and to so reorder his affairs. When the parties specified that the husband's payments of military income or retirement pay should terminate if the wife permanently "cohabited with a male as if to all appearances they were otherwise married," with "permanent" meaning "residence of more than thirty days," the wife's sharing a bedroom with another man for a substantial period of time since 1988 terminated the husband's support obligations under the agreement. *Schweider v. Schweider*, 243 Va. 245, 415 S.E.2d 135 (1992). *See*

*Stroud v. Stroud,* 49 Va. App. 359, 641 S.E.2d 142 (2007) (spousal support terminated pursuant to property settlement agreement because of wife's cohabitation with another woman); *Pellegrin v. Pellegrin,* 31 Va. App. 753, 525 S.E.2d 611 (2000) (spousal support not terminated under property settlement agreement because of wife's cohabitation, when husband failed to prove factors that demonstrated that wife and paramour had assumed mutual responsibilities of marital relationship); *Penrod v. Penrod,* 29 Va. App. 96, 510 S.E.2d 244 (1999) (spousal support terminated under separation agreement because of wife's cohabitation, when wife testified that she lived with one man over a period of four to five years, with conscious breaks to avoid 60-consecutive-day requirement in separation agreement). For further discussion of termination of spousal support because of cohabitation, *see* § 20.26.

If the parties do not clearly and expressly specify that spousal support obligations will survive the dependent spouse's remarriage, Va. Code § 20-109.1 requires that such an obligation will terminate. *Miller v. Hawkins,* 14 Va. App. 192, 415 S.E.2d 861 (1992). See also *MacNelly v. MacNelly,* 17 Va. App. 427, 437 S.E.2d 582 (1993) (spousal support terminated at remarriage when language of property settlement agreement and divorce decree stated that husband should pay $7,000 each month for seven years or until the death of either party, whichever occurred first); *Hardesty v. Hardesty, opn. on regh. en banc,* 40 Va. App. 663, 581 S.E.2d 213 (2003) (spousal support terminated at remarriage when property settlement agreement stated that support "cannot be terminated for any reason" but failed to include express provision that support would not terminate at remarriage).

Va. Code §§ 20-109(D) and 20-110, as amended in 2000, impose an affirmative duty on a supported spouse to immediately notify a payor spouse upon remarriage. Failure to notify the payor spouse will entitle the payor spouse to restitution in the amount of any current support paid after the date of remarriage, together with interest and attorney's fees and costs.

The trial court should have enforced an indemnification provision of the property settlement agreement that ordered the husband to reimburse the wife for paying his separate debt that had attached as a lien against the marital home. Shortly after the wife filed for divorce, the husband pled guilty to larceny of funds from his employer, and executed a judgment note for $45,000 plus interest secured by a deed of trust on the marital home. Under the parties' agreement, he was to hold her harmless for the debt and reimburse her when she refinanced the home and paid the employer the debt plus interest. This obligation to pay the wife was not in the nature of spousal support and therefore was not extinguished by the remarriage. *Guffey v. Guffey*, 1995 Va. App. LEXIS 819 (Nov. 7, 1995).

The Foreign Service Act of 1980, 22 U.S.C. § 4054(a)(2) gives no pension split to a wife who remarries before reaching age 53 (then 60) unless their agreement or court order expressly provides otherwise. Accordingly, the husband did not have to divide his pension with the ex-wife in *Wilson v. Collins*, 27 Va. App. 411, 499 S.E.2d 560 (1998). In contrast, when a property settlement agreement incorporated into a divorce decree specifically addressed a husband's Foreign Service Retirement and Disability System (FSRDS) pension, 22 U.S.C.A. § 4044 *et seq.*, and stated that the wife would be entitled to a pension split "regardless of her marital status to the extent allowable under federal law," the wife's pension split did not terminate upon her early remarriage. Existing federal law would have disqualified her from receiving a share of her ex-husband's pension benefits when she remarried before the age of 55, but the phrase in the property settlement agreement expressly waived the FSRDS's "marriage disqualifier" provision. *Allsbury v. Allsbury*, 33 Va. App. 385, 533 S.E.2d 639 (2000).

Where the parties contracted for spousal support in a marital agreement, the subsequent legislative amendment permitting termination of spousal support based on the payee's cohabitation did not apply as (1) the amendments affected substantive rights and are generally presumed to apply prospectively, and (2) applying the statutory amendments would amount to an unconstitutional impairment of the parties' contract. *Hering v. Hering*, 33 Va. App. 368, 533 S.E.2d 631 (2000).

Spousal support ends upon remarriage when a separation agreement merely states that there shall be weekly payments "until her death." In *Langley v. Johnson*, 27 Va. App. 365, 499 S.E.2d 15 (1998), the court found that these payments were indeed support payments despite the wife's arguments that these payments were really property division in disguise. They were to be adjusted annually according to the Consumer Price Index, and were to terminate at death.

A provision in a property settlement agreement that provides for termination of spousal support if the spouse cohabits with another in a relationship analogous to marriage is *not* self-executing. *Stroud v. Stroud*, 54 Va. App. 231, 677 S.E.2d 629 (2009). In *Stroud*, a husband was not entitled to unilaterally terminate spousal support payments on the basis of his wife's cohabitation with another woman without obtaining a proper court order. Furthermore, the husband was not entitled to attorney's fees pursuant to a provision in the settlement agreement, when his wife had no choice but to seek a judicial determination of whether she was cohabiting in a situation analogous to marriage.

## § 17.13    Modifiability—Change in Income, Custody, Etc.

A careful draftsman will consider how to best make the agreement modifiable in the event that various contingencies occur, since unless provided for in the agreement, there will be no modification if the agreement is incorporated into a final decree of divorce. Some possibilities for modification might include a sliding scale based upon the consumer price index, a change in the wages or health of either spouse, completion of a degree program and a change of custody. Another means of providing for contingencies is to say that if a contingency occurs, the agreement will be submitted for arbitration.

However, where yearly additional amounts for child support in a separation agreement were incorporated into a divorce decree, a consent order eliminated not only the effect of the decree but also any contractual obligations under the settlement agreement. *Anderson v. Van Landingham,* 236 Va. 85, 372 S.E.2d 137 (1988).

Pursuant to Va. Code § 20-109, an agreed upon amount of payments for spousal support cannot be modified except in accordance with the agreement, whereas the amounts for child support may always be modified, under Va. Code § 20-108. See, e.g., *Morris v. Morris,* 216 Va. 457, 219 S.E.2d 864 (1975); *Parrillo v. Parrillo,* 1 Va. App. 226, 230, 336 S.E.2d 23, 26 (1985) (where the parties' Agreement contained a unitary payment of spousal support and child support, the trial court had jurisdiction to modify child support). See also *Scott v. Scott,* 12 Va. App. 1245, 408 S.E.2d 579 (1991) (trial court not bound by the parties' Agreement regarding child support). Even if the award is a unitary sum made to effect tax savings under *Commissioner v. Lester,* 366 U.S. 299, 81 S. Ct. 1343, 6 L. Ed. 2d 306 (1961), the court may apportion such an award when necessary, *Carter v. Carter,* 215 Va. 475, 211 S.E.2d 253 (1975), such as after the transfer of custody to the obligor spouse. See also *Jarrell v. Jarrell,* 1994 Va. App. LEXIS 672 (Nov. 15, 1994). This does not mean that apportionment of a unitary award should be made without a showing of necessity. *Wickham v. Wickham,* 215 Va. 694, 213 S.E.2d 750 (1975). Necessity was not demonstrated when the dependent spouse merely sought an increase in child support.

Statutory modifications to Va. Code § 20-109(A) made in 2000 provide that absent an agreement, spousal support will terminate when the dependent spouse habitually cohabits with another in a marriage-like relationship unless termination would be unconscionable. Such statutory language has no effect on agreements entered into prior to the enactment of the statute, because otherwise the legislation would impair a pre-existing contractual obligation. *Rubio v. Rubio*, 36 Va. App. 248, 549 S.E.2d 610 (2001); *Hering v. Hering*, 33 Va. App. 368, 533 S.E.2d 631 (2000). See also *Baldwin v. Baldwin*, 44 Va. App. 93, 603 S.E.2d 172 (2004) (explaining operation of habitual cohabitation provisions of Va. Code § 20-109(A) with respect to agreements entered into before and after statute's enactment); *Smith v. Smith*, 41 Va. App. 742, 589 S.E.2d 439 (2003) (cohabiting wife's support could not be terminated when parties' support agreement, made prior to enactment of Va. Code § 20-109(A), provided that support would terminate only in the event of husband's death, wife's death, or wife's remarriage).

The provisions for spousal support may be modified in accordance with an agreement filed prior to or following entry of the final decree of divorce, as provided by Va. Code § 20-109.1. In order for spousal support provisions to be nonmodifiable under Va. Code § 20-109, the stipulation or contract must be signed by the party to whom relief might be awarded. *Lane v. Lane*, 32 Va. App. 125, 526 S.E.2d 773 (2000) (with respect to spousal support provisions, divorce decree signed by parties' counsel was modifiable, but subsequent consent decree signed by parties themselves was nonmodifiable). However, an attorney acting with actual authority may sign a consent decree on his client's behalf and thereby satisfy the signature requirement of Va. Code § 20-109(C). *Newman v. Newman*, 42 Va. App. 557, 593 S.E.2d 533 (2004) (holding that *Lane* court's distinction between consent decrees signed by attorneys on behalf of clients and those signed by clients personally was dicta that conflicted with settled principles of statutory construction). A fixed amount of spousal support provided for in an agreement will not be modified even if it requires the payor to reach his military disability payments as a source of funding. *Zabala v. Zabala*, 48 Va. Cir. 267 (1999). See also *Michael v. Michael*, 48 Va. Cir. 347 (1999) (spousal support set in the agreement was binding even when the husband's income was reduced).

The trial court did not err by awarding the wife with a set dollar amount of spousal support where the parties' agreement specified that the husband "shall support [w]ife in the manner to which she is accustomed and is currently being supported, recognizing the need of [w]ife to educate and nurture" their child. *Deluca v. Deluca*, 2015 Va. App. LEXIS 176 (May 19, 2015).

The court will not modify an agreement many years later when to do so would "render the property settlement agreement an absurdity." *Stevenson v. Stevenson*, 22 Va. Cir. 58 (1990). In this case, the wife was receiving 45% of the husband's military pension under the 1980 agreement as alimony, and wished 50% of the pension as a property distribution as well because of the enactment of the Uniform Services Former Spouses Protection Act.

Va. Code § 20-109(C) (formerly Va. Code § 20-109) restricts the court's jurisdiction in making awards of spousal support, suit money, or attorney's fees to the terms of any contract that is signed by the parties and incorporated into a final decree of divorce. *Rutledge v. Rutledge*, 45 Va. App. 56, 608 S.E.2d 504 (2005).

In *Rutledge*, Va. Code § 20-109(C) precluded a trial court from awarding attorney's fees in a spousal support modification proceeding, because the parties' property settlement agreement authorized attorney's fees in only two situations, neither of which involved spousal support modification.

Virginia Code § 20-109(C) also restricts the court's jurisdiction in making or modifying an equitable distribution award under Va. Code § 20-107.3. To the extent that a husband and wife have already stipulated to a particular disposition of their property, the court may not decree inconsistent relief. See *Campbell v. Campbell*, 32 Va. App. 351, 528 S.E.2d 145 (2000) (under Va. Code § 20-109(C), trial court could not depart from terms of husband and wife's post-separation agreement, incorporated into divorce decree, that waived their right to equitable distribution of property by court).

### § 17.14   Provisions for Security

Where the obligor agrees to pay the spouse an annuity, this will be a personal obligation of the obligor. There will not be a lien on the obligor's real estate unless the amount is reduced to judgment and recorded. Va. Code § 8-386. However, if the agreement is affirmed and incorporated into the divorce decree, amounts for spousal support will be considered alimony and constitute a lien upon the obligor's real estate as soon as the decree is recorded on the judgment lien docket. *Durrett v. Durrett*, 204 Va. 59, 129 S.E.2d 50 (1963).

In a case involving competing claims of an ex-wife and a current wife to a husband's pension plan, a circuit court ruled that when the language of the property settlement agreement between the parties to the first marriage is clear and unambiguous as to the intent of the parties, the ex-wife is entitled to an inclusion of that intent in the Qualified Domestic Relations Order (QDRO). *Riley v. Riley*, 1998 Va. Cir. LEXIS 409 (Aug. 14, 1998).

### § 17.15   Medical and Life Insurance

Husband and wife may contract that one of them will be required to maintain or pay for medical insurance that covers the other prior to divorce or their children at any time. See, e.g., *Morris v. Morris,* 216 Va. 457, 219 S.E.2d 864 (1975) (life insurance part of general alimony and child support scheme).

In *Chattin v. Chattin,* 245 Va. 302, 427 S.E.2d 347 (1993), the Virginia Supreme Court determined that the wife was entitled to specific performance of a contractual provision that the husband would provide medical insurance. If he failed to pay premiums on the insurance policy, it could lapse, thereby requiring the wife to purchase similar coverage and to bring suit against him each time she paid a renewal premium. Therefore, she did not have an adequate remedy at law. The court of appeals also enforced a contractual medical insurance provision in *Mackie v. Hill,* 16 Va. App. 229, 429 S.E.2d 37 (1993), even though specific language requiring the health insurance for the wife was not included in the divorce decree incorporating the property settlement agreement. In *McCoy v. McCoy,* 55 Va. App. 524, 687 S.E.2d 82 (2010), the court of appeals enforced a property settlement agreement that required a husband to provide health insurance to his wife after their divorce and her remarriage. In interpreting the agreement, the court rejected the husband's argument that his obligation to provide health insurance was a form of spousal support that should terminate upon the wife's remarriage.

When a husband and wife divorced, the husband agreed to make the children beneficiaries of his life insurance trust, formerly providing for the wife. Thirteen years later, he cancelled all the policies listed in the trust agreement, then totaling $70,000, and obtained other life insurance policies in which he named his second wife as beneficiary. His estate was insolvent, and the children sought to impose a constructive trust upon the proceeds of his life insurance policies. The court of appeals found that the husband breached the contract by canceling his life insurance coverage, and so established a constructive trust on the insurance proceeds, plus interest from the date of the husband's death. *Jones v. Harrison,* 250 Va. 64, 458 S.E.2d 766 (1995). See also *Faulknier v. Shafer,* 264 Va. 210, 563 S.E.2d 755 (2002) (remand for proof on issues of unjust enrichment and appropriateness of constructive trust when decedent designated second wife as life insurance beneficiary in contravention of separation agreement with first wife).

Under Va. Code § 20-107.3(G)(2), a trial court cannot order a person to obtain life insurance on himself or herself for the benefit of a former spouse, although a court can order that a person elect to have survivor's benefits on a pension or annuity. *Lewis v. Lewis,* 53 Va. App. 528, 673 S.E.2d 888 (2009). In *Lewis,* a trial court ordered a husband to obtain $200,000 in life insurance, naming his wife as beneficiary, as a remedy for the husband's destruction of the wife's right to a lifetime pension under the spouses' property settlement agreement. However, Va. Code § 20-107.3(G)(2) prohibited the trial court from ordering the husband to obtain life insurance for his wife's benefit, and the trial court could not derive authority to make the order from the spouses' property settlement agreement, because the agreement did not address the issue of life insurance in any way. See also *Lapidus v. Lapidus*, 226 Va. 575, 311 S.E.2d 786 (1984) (finding that trial court lacked statutory authority to order husband to contract for life insurance).

During the pendency of a divorce case, the court can "compel a party to maintain any existing policy owned by that party insuring the life of either party or to require a party to name as a beneficiary of the policy the other party or an appropriate person for the exclusive use and benefit of the minor children of the parties and . . . to allocate the premium cost of such life insurance between the parties, provided that all premiums are billed to the policyholder." Va. Code § 20-103.

Va. Code § 20-111.1 provides that any revocable beneficiary designation contained in a written contract owned by one party that provides for the payment of any death benefit to the other party is revoked upon the entry of a decree of annulment or divorce. "Death benefit" includes any payments under a life insurance contract, annuity, retirement arrangement, compensation agreement, or other contract that designates a beneficiary of a right, property, or money in the form of a death benefit. However, the statute does not apply: (1) to the extent that an annulment or divorce decree or a written agreement of the parties provides for a contrary result as to specific death benefits; or (2) to any trust or death benefit payable to or under any trust. After July 1, 2012, Va. Code § 20-111.1(E) mandates that every divorce order contain the following notice "in conspicuous, bold print":

> **Beneficiary designations for any death benefit, as defined in subsection B of § 20-111.1 of the Code of Virginia, made payable to a former spouse may or may not be automatically revoked by operation of law upon the entry of a final decree of annulment or divorce. If a party intends to revoke any beneficiary designation made payable to a former spouse following the annulment or divorce, the party is responsible for following any and all instructions to change such beneficiary designation given by the provider of the death benefit. Otherwise, existing beneficiary designations may remain in full force and effect after the entry of a final decree of annulment or divorce.**

Thus, Va. Code § 38.2-305(C) (added in 2000) requires that each life insurance policy for which the designated beneficiary is the spouse of the owner contain language stating that such designations become void upon entry of a divorce or annulment decree if they are revocable. If the parties intend to continue the beneficiary designation, they must either make it irrevocable, change the ownership of the policy to the designated beneficiary, establish their joint intention in a separate agreement or provide for the continuing designation in the divorce or annulment decree itself.

However, ERISA preempts state statutes that provide for the automatic revocation upon divorce of a designation of the divorced spouse as the beneficiary of a life insurance policy or pension plan, to the extent that the state statutes apply to ERISA-governed policies or plans. *Egelhoff v. Egelhoff*, 532 U.S. 141, 121 S. Ct. 1322, 149 L. Ed. 2d 264 (2001). Under Va. Code § 20-111.1(D), if federal preemption of the Virginia automatic revocation statute causes a former spouse who did not give value to receive payment of a death benefit that would have been revoked, the former spouse is personally liable to the person who would have been entitled to the death benefit except for the federal preemption.

Va. Code § 64.2-620 provides that a provision for a nonprobate transfer on death in certain specified types of written instruments, including insurance policies, pension plans, conveyances, and marital property agreements, is a nontestamentary transfer.

### § 17.16    Life Insurance and Federal Preemption

In the event of an annulment or divorce, any revocable beneficiary designation contained in a then existing written contract owned by one party that provides for the payment of any death benefit to the other party is revoked pursuant to Va. Code Ann. § 20-111.1(A). Conflict between the state statute and federal preemption became an issue in *Maretta v. Hillman*, 283 Va. 34, 722 S.E.2d 32 (2012). The decedent, a federal employee, named his first wife, Maretta, as the beneficiary of his Federal Employees' Group Life Insurance policy. They divorced in 1998 and the decedent married Hillman in 2002 but never changed the beneficiary designation in his policy. After her husband's death in 2008, Hillman filed a claim for benefits under the decedent's life insurance policy but was told the proceeds would be distributed to the decedent's designated beneficiary, Maretta, pursuant to the Federal Employees' Group Life Insurance Act (FEGLIA). 5 U.S.C. § 8701 et seq. Decedent's ex-wife, Maretta, filed a claim and received the insurance proceeds. Decedent's widow, Hillman, sued the ex-wife claiming that she was liable to her for the death benefits she received from the policy pursuant to state law. The ex-wife argued that the state law was preempted by FEGLIA. The circuit court found that the state law was not preempted by FEGLIA and awarded the widow $124,558.03. The ex-wife appealed.

FEGLIA contains an order of precedence for the payment of benefits under a FEGLIA insurance policy. Death benefits are first payable to the beneficiary or beneficiaries designated by the employee in a signed and witnessed writing received before death in the employing office. If there is no designated beneficiary, benefits are payable to the widow or widower of the employee. FEGLIA also states that its provisions, including payment of benefits, supersede and preempt any state law that is inconsistent with the Act.

On appeal, the Virginia Supreme Court recognized that the majority of state courts have generally held that FEGLIA does not preempt a state-law constructive trust on FEGLI proceeds for the benefit of someone other than the named beneficiary. Nevertheless, in an opinion that places Virginia in the minority of states, the Virginia Supreme Court reversed the circuit court's judgment, finding that the state law was subject to the doctrine of federal preemption under the United States Constitution's Supremacy Clause.

Subsequently, the following amendment to Va. Code Ann. § 20-111.1 passed the General Assembly of Virginia:

> *E. Every decree of annulment or divorce from the bond of matrimony entered on or after July 1, 2012, shall contain the following notice in conspicuous, bold print:*
>
> **Beneficiary designations for any death benefit, as defined in subsection B of Section 20-111.1 of the Code of Virginia, made payable to a former spouse may or may not be automatically revoked by operation of law upon the entry of a final decree of annulment or divorce. If a party intends to revoke any beneficiary designation made payable to a former spouse following the annulment or divorce, the party is responsible for following any and all instructions to change such beneficiary designation given by the provider of the death benefit. Otherwise, existing beneficiary designations may remain in full force and effect after the entry of a final decree of annulment or divorce.** Va. Code Ann. § 20-111.1(E)

The amendment was approved by the Governor and is effective as of July 1, 2012.

### § 17.17   Child Support, Tax of Unitary Payments, Exemptions

Generally speaking, child support is not taxable to the recipient spouse, nor deductible by the payor spouse. However, under the case of *Commissioner v. Lester,* 366 U.S. 299, 81 S. Ct. 1343, 6 L. Ed. 2d 306 (1961), if unitary payments were made to satisfy both spousal and child support obligations, and the exact amount of each was not stated in the agreement or decree, the total amount would be treated as alimony. This position has been removed by the amendments to § 71 found in the Domestic Relations Tax Reform Act of 1984.

If circumstances change so that, for instance, custody reverts to the obligor spouse, *Carter v. Carter,* 215 Va. 475, 211 S.E.2d 253 (1975), an allocation will be made between child support and alimony. This will not be necessary, however, when one spouse merely asks for an increase in child support. *Wickham v. Wickham,* 215 Va. 694, 213 S.E.2d 750 (1975).

The trial judge should not have at the same time incorporated the parties' separation agreement including the obligation to pay for health insurance and college tuition while increasing the agreed-upon amount to match the child support guidelines. *Spagnolo v. Spagnolo,* 20 Va. App. 736, 460 S.E.2d 616 (1995). When the trial judge severed the child support provision as if it were one of a series of separate and independent parts of the agreement, he both violated the parties' express agreement and adopted a remedy exceeding the statutory limitation requiring payments only during the children's minority. When he elected to disregard the agreement and proceed under his authority to make an award for child support, he should not have incorporated the child support provisions of the agreement. As the court noted, he was required to follow the agreement or the statutes, but not both.

The trial court has the authority, absent parental agreement, to order one party to execute all appropriate tax forms or waivers to grant the other party the right to take the income tax dependency exemption. Va. Code § 20-108.1(E) (amended 1998).

The parties' oral agreement to waive portions of a child support arrearage is unenforceable. *Smiley v. Erickson,* 29 Va. App. 426, 512 S.E.2d 842 (1999). The court noted: "No support order may be retroactively modified. Past due support installments become vested as they accrue and are thereafter immune from change. Parties cannot contractually modify the terms of a support order without the court's approval. Nor does a party's passive acquiescence in nonpayment of support operate to bar that party from later seeking support arrearages."

A court cannot retroactively increase child support, even if pursuant to an agreement of the parties incorporated into a final decree, unless that agreement is self-executing *Llerena v. Novak,* 1998 Va. Cir. LEXIS 450 (Nov. 17, 1998).

Where a separation agreement that was incorporated into the divorce decree was silent as to the matter of child support, but outlined that the parties had joint custody with the child residing with each parent for alternating two-week time periods, the court nevertheless ordered the father to pay child support so that the mother could be available after school to give ongoing, consistent parental care and supervision in the best interests of the child. The child had threatened to jump out a window because of a bad grade on his report card and was in therapy. During the marriage, the mother had been available for after-school care. *Hart v. Hodson*, 48 Va. Cir. 63 (1999). The presumptive guidelines were applied strictly according to shared custody support guidelines.

## § 17.18     Termination at Age of Majority of Child

If the parties agree in a contract modified and incorporated into their divorce decree that support of minor children shall be made, and at the time the agreement was written, the law provided that the age of majority was 21, the obligor's duty ceased at the time the child reached eighteen when the state law was changed during the child's minority. *Mack v. Mack*, 217 Va. 534, 229 S.E.2d 895 (1976). Compare *Paul v. Paul*, 214 Va. 651, 203 S.E.2d 123 (1974), where the agreement clearly contemplated that support payments might be made even after the children reached 21.

In *Virostko v. Virostko*, 59 Va. App. 816, 722 S.E.2d 678 (2012), the court of appeals held that, to be legitimately incorporated into a final decree, a child support provision in a Property Settlement Agreement (PSA) must satisfy three limitations:

(1)   Prior to approving the agreement's incorporation, the court must review the child support provisions for consistency with the child's or children's best interests;

(2)   The parties' agreement may not prevent the court from exercising its power to change, modify, or enforce its decree concerning child support; and

(3)   The parties may not use the agreement to terminate a parent's duty to support his or her child.

When the parties' property settlement agreement, incorporated into the final decree, required the father to pay child support until the younger child turned 18, the support obligation extended until the end of the month and did not end on the child's birthday. *Cory v. Cory*, 1993 Va. App. LEXIS 282 (July 20, 1993).

When they separated in Virginia, the spouses in *Saleem v. Saleem*, 26 Va. App. 384, 494 S.E.2d 883 (1998), executed a property settlement specifying that child support obligations would "terminate whenever a child dies, reaches the age of 18 years, or otherwise becomes emancipated, whichever comes first." They later amended their agreement by including language that specified child support "shall be determined on the basis of the laws of the jurisdiction(s) in which the children are residing at that time." Custody of the daughter eventually was given to the wife, while the sons remained with their father. The trial court erred in allowing New York guidelines to control the child support amounts or emancipation rules for the children living in that state. Although the children were living in New York, the parties had no power to govern these child support issues through their contract where Virginia retained jurisdiction.

In *Wilson v. Wilson*, 25 Va. App. 752, 492 S.E.2d 495 (1997), the father stopped paying child support when his daughter completed high school, five months before she turned 18. This violated the statutory scheme governing child support, which mandates the later of the two possible emancipating events.

### § 17.19 College Education

A provision that the husband would endeavor to provide a four-year college education for each child was enforced in *Barnes v. Craig*, 202 Va. 229, 117 S.E.2d 63 (1960). Although such provisions are enforceable, they will not be subject to the contempt power when suit is brought after the child reaches age eighteen. This is because the court's power to enforce the support ends with the child's reaching majority, and any action after that time must be based upon the contract.

The language of the contract will be enforced by the court. Thus, where the contract provided that the "father will participate in the decision making process as to the college to be attended," and he was consulted about college selection by his former wife and son, he was bound to pay support during the son's full-time attendance although he disapproved of the final choice of colleges. *Tiffany v. Tiffany*, 1 Va. App. 11, 15, 332 S.E.2d 796, 799 (1985).

The Circuit Court of Fairfax County determined in *Ackerson v. Ackerson*, 22 Va. Cir. 215 (1990), that a clause in a property settlement agreement providing that "Husband shall pay all reasonable expenditures for a college education for the minor children" should be construed under the circumstances as including the approximately $21,000 annual tuition at Duke University. The father contended that all he was required to pay was the approximately $10,000 for tuition at a state school. The court found that the school was a reasonable place for the daughter to attend college given the father's income and social circumstances. He is a partner at a Washington, D.C. law firm who attended graduate and law school at Harvard University. However, where the terms of the parties' agreement specified that the husband "shall agree on the college of attendance," his obligation to pay was conditioned on his agreement to the college the child attended. *Jones v. Jones*, 19 Va. App. 265, 450 S.E.2d 762 (1994).

A property settlement agreement provided that the parents "will in good faith negotiate mutual decisions" about the child's college education and also that the husband would pay tuition and book costs if the child was to attend a private school "suitable to both husband and wife." In this case, the father could successfully decline responsibility to pay tuition and books at Rice University even though he only declined to pay after she decided to attend the school. *Eissler v. Stange*, 1997 WL 92090 (Va. App.). In *Barnett v. Wampouille*, (Cir. Ct. Fairfax Co.), *aff'd*, 2000 Va. App. LEXIS 171 (Mar. 7, 2000), the husband breached the parties' property settlement agreement when he failed to transfer and maximize TIAA/CREF funds into a college fund for his daughter as agreed. He was therefore responsible for both his wife's and daughter's attorney's fees, and was ordered removed as trustee of the fund. He was further ordered to make up any difference in the value of what the fund should have rendered for his daughter's college expenses. In another case, *Douglas v. Hammett*, 28 Va. App. 517, 507 S.E.2d 98 (1998), it was not error for a court to award a wife reimbursement for son's college living and computer expenses when the separation agreement between the parties stated that "[t]he Husband agrees that he will pay the expenses of a college education for the child," even though the son had received a full athletic scholarship.

On the other hand, a father who promised to pay a pro-rata share of his children's college education if "each of the Parties decide[d] to send any or all of their children to college," would not necessarily have to pay a share of such expenses for his children not yet of college age, although he was responsible for his eldest child's expenses at the University of Virginia. He had no objections to her attending the college, but only to her beginning a year early and before graduating from high school. *Jackson v. Harley*, 1996 Va. App. LEXIS 357 (May 14, 1996).

The trial judge should not have at the same time incorporated the parties' separation agreement including the obligation to pay for health insurance and college tuition while increasing the agreed-upon amount to match the child support guidelines. *Spagnolo v. Spagnolo*, 20 Va. App. 736, 460 S.E.2d 616 (1995). When the father assumed responsibility for paying for the college education, the trial judge might well be justified in approving, ratifying, and incorporating an agreement to pay less than the presumptive guideline amount, so long as written reasons were given for the deviation. *Scott v. Scott*, 12 Va. App. 1245, 1250, 408 S.E.2d 579, 582 (1991).

## § 17.20     Attempt to Relieve Party of Duty of Support

A father who is a party to a divorce proceeding "cannot, by contract or otherwise, avoid, or relieve himself from, his primary obligation to maintain a minor child . . . . After submitting themselves to the jurisdiction of the court, the parents cannot by their agreement deprive it of power to control the custody and maintenance of the child." *Williams v. Woolfolk*, 188 Va. 312, 317, 49 S.E.2d 270, 272 (1948) (quoting from *Emrich v. McNeil*, 126 F.2d 841, 843, 75 U.S. App. D.C. 307 (1942)). See also *Buchanan v. Buchanan*, 170 Va. 458, 477, 197 S.E. 426, 434 (1938). See also *Brown v. Brown*, 22 Va. Cir. 263 (1990).

Some jurisdictions that apparently follow this rule have nevertheless held the custodial parent bound by the agreement, so that child support would be forfeited unless the child support was actually necessitous. See, e.g., *Pappas v. Pappas*, 247 Iowa 638, 75 N.W.2d 264 (1956). Virginia courts apparently take a stronger position. When the parties agreed that the wife would reimburse the husband for any court-ordered child support payments in exchange for his equity in the marital home, the husband was unable to enforce the covenant because it was against public policy. *Kelley v. Kelley*, 248 Va. 295, 449 S.E.2d 55 (1991). The children's rights to receive support from both parents were substantially abridged, and the court's power to decree support was diminished, violating clearly established law. See also *Lehman v. Lehman*, 38 Va. App. 598, 567 S.E.2d 571 (2002) (parties' agreement included provision waiving marital interest in military pension in exchange for release from obligation to pay child support). Nevertheless, parties in a divorce can reach an agreement on child support without violating *Kelley* principles. *Shoup v. Shoup*, 37 Va. App. 240, 556 S.E.2d 783 (2001); *Lehman v. Lehman*, 38 Va. App. 598, 567 S.E.2d 571 (2002).

Nor may parents condition receipt of child support upon the custodial mother's permission of visitation with the children or her sharing information about them. *Taxson v. Taxson*, 31 Va. Cir. 348 (1993).

## § 17.21   Large Expenditures

The careful attorney will address the subject of the responsibility for large expenditures in the property settlement agreement, in order to avoid resort to litigation at some future time when the parties might well be distracted. This would include unexpected large medical expenses, payment for orthodontic care, psychiatric services, and private schooling.

An obligation to pay mortgage payments does not amount to an order of spousal support. *White v. White*, 257 Va. 139, 509 S.E.2d 323 (1999). A husband agreed to make mortgage payments to the bank for the marital home. The wife sold the home and paid off the mortgage with the proceeds. The husband then stopped making monthly payments. The agreement did not obligate him to pay a fixed sum to the wife, and was therefore not an obligation for maintenance and support.

## § 17.22   Custody and Visitation in General

Although agreements between parents regarding custody and visitation may be accepted by a court and incorporated into a final decree, they are always subject to a modification based upon a showing of changed circumstances, which so affect the welfare of the child that a change should be made. *Crounse v. Crounse,* 207 Va. 524, 151 S.E.2d 412 (1966). The continuing jurisdiction of the court granting the divorce on the question of custody of minor children cannot be taken away by a contract made between their parents. *Williams v. Woolfolk,* 188 Va. 312, 317, 49 S.E.2d 270, 272 (1948) (citing *Gloth v. Gloth,* 154 Va. 511, 551, 153 S.E. 879, 893 (1930)). Moreover, a trial court must always consider the children's best interests in determining whether or not to affirm, ratify and incorporate a parenting agreement into a court order. The welfare of the children "is the primary, paramount, and controlling consideration of the court in all controversies between parents over the custody of their minor children. All other matters are subordinate." *Matthews v. Brinckhaus,* 2017 Va. App. LEXIS 181 (July 25, 2017). In the *Matthews* case, the trial judge abused its discretion by incorporating the Agreement without considering the best interest of the child statutory factors enumerated in Va. Code § 20-124.3.

The parents may not agree to condition payment of child support upon the custodial parent's allowing access to the children. *Taxson v. Taxson,* 31 Va. Cir. 348 (1993). The court noted that "the public policy articulated by Virginia law in favor of serving the best interests of the child would be reversed were the provisions in question treated as interdependent." *Id.* at 352.

Where a separation agreement that was incorporated into the divorce decree was silent as to the matter of child support, but outlined that the parties had joint custody while the child resided with each parent for alternating two-week time periods, the court ordered the father to pay child support so that the mother could be available after school to give ongoing, consistent parental care and supervision in the best interests of the child. During the marriage, the mother had been available for after-school care. The child was in therapy because he had threatened to jump out a window following receipt of a bad grade on his report card. *Hart v. Hodson,* 48 Va. Cir. 63 (1999). In *Austin v. Austin,* 47 Va. Cir. 525 (1999), the couple's property settlement agreement provided for joint legal custody, with the wife acting as primary physical custodian subject to the husband's liberal visitation. When they sought to ratify and incorporate the agreement into their final divorce decree, the husband attempted to modify the arrangement so that he would also have joint physical custody. The court declined to do this, noting that the agreement reflected "a thoughtful and caring" attitude, with detailed provisions reflecting the responsibilities of each parent in the nurturing of their son. Keeping the parties' autonomy and the public policy favoring settlements in mind, the court should not interfere.

## § 17.23   Marital Debts

The trial court should have enforced an indemnification provision of the property settlement agreement that ordered the husband to reimburse the wife for paying his separate debt that had attached as a lien against the marital home. Shortly after the wife filed for divorce, the husband pled guilty to larceny of funds from his employer, and executed a judgment note for $45,000 plus interest secured by a deed of trust on the marital home. Under the parties' agreement, he was to hold her harmless for the debt and reimburse her when she refinanced the home and paid the employer the debt plus interest. This obligation to pay the wife was not in the nature of spousal support and therefore was not extinguished by the remarriage. *Guffey v. Guffey*, 1995 Va. App. LEXIS 819 (Nov. 7, 1995).

An obligation to pay mortgage payments to a bank does not amount to an order of spousal support. *White v. White*, 257 Va. 139, 509 S.E.2d 323 (1999). A husband's agreement, incorporated into a final divorce decree, to make mortgage payments on the marital home did not obligate him to continue to make those payments as spousal support after the mortgage debt had been satisfied. See also *Stacy v. Stacy*, 53 Va. App. 38, 669 S.E.2d 348 (2008) (trial court erred by treating husband's mortgage payment obligation under property settlement agreement as spousal support and terminating obligation on cohabitation grounds).

## § 17.24   Tax Exemptions

Under the former tax law, the custodial spouse generally was entitled to the tax exemption for dependent minor children. However, if the noncustodial spouse provided more than one-half of the child's support, and this exceeded $1,200 per taxable year, under I.R.C. § 152(e)(2)(A), the noncustodial parent would receive the exemption.

The Domestic Relations Tax Reform Act of 1984, Title IV, Subtitle B, P.L. 98-369, § 152 was amended to provide that in all cases where the agreement occurred after July of 1984, the child living with the custodial parent (providing more than one-half the total support) should receive the deduction except when such parent filed a written release of the dependency exemption claim. I.R.C. § 152(e)(2).

Where child support is being ordered, and unless the parties have otherwise agreed, the court has the authority to allocate the child income tax dependency exemption and to order either parent to execute all appropriate tax forms. Va. Code § 20-108.1(E).

## § 17.25    Joint Custody

In many cases the parents may wish to consider an agreement to share custody of minor children. This option has been available in Virginia since the case of *Mullen v. Mullen,* 188 Va. 259, 49 S.E.2d 349 (1948), and may take several forms, all of which allow both parents to have a day-to-day role in child rearing, and simultaneously will permit the child to have a close relationship with both parents. Va. Code §§ 20-107.2; 20-108.1. Joint custody is most successful in cases where the parties enjoy good relationships with their children, and are able to agree on most issues surrounding their upbringing. If changes of custody are to be frequent, it is helpful if the parties plan to continue living near to each other, so that the children will not have to change schools and youthful companions. Cf. *Lundeen v. Struminger,* 209 Va. 548, 165 S.E.2d 285 (1969) (six months' alternating custody not in best interests of children).

## § 17.26    Visitation

Agreements regarding visitation are appropriate, and will be enforced as part of the custody mechanism by the trial court if the agreement is incorporated into the final decree of divorce. The parties may want to provide for specific hours of visitation, or that visitation will occur on a reasonable notice to the parent having custody. Some couples may wish to include a clause limiting visitation to the times when the noncustodial parent's companions of the opposite sex are not present.

## § 17.27    Keeping in State/Area

The Supreme Court of Virginia has approved an order requiring a child to be kept within the state when the custodial parent wished to move to New York, on grounds that the relationship with the parent making visitation would be weakened by such a move. *Carpenter v. Carpenter,* 220 Va. 299, 257 S.E.2d 845 (1979). See also *Gray v. Gray,* 228 Va. 696, 324 S.E.2d 677 (1985).

Couples may wish to include such a provision in their agreement, which would be enforceable as part of the custody provisions through the contempt power.

## § 17.28  Religious Training

A provision of a divorce decree that children would be reared in the Jewish faith and sent to weekly services and religious instruction was found unconstitutional under Va. Const. § 58 in *Lundeen v. Struminger,* 209 Va. 548, 165 S.E.2d 285 (1969). This was not a case where the parties had a contract that regulated religious upbringing of the children, however.

In *Finnerty v. Finnerty,* 22 Va. Cir. 523 (1982), the parties agreed to raise the children as Roman Catholics and to educate them in parochial schools. The agreement was not incorporated into the final decree of divorce, since to ratify and confirm it would violate Art. 1, § 16 of the Constitution of Virginia. The court noted: "If the parties inter se wish to agree that the one having custody will raise the children in a certain faith, the courts, again on grounds of religious freedom, could generally not interfere." *Id.* at 527. Further, the provision that the failure of the custodial parent to raise the children as Catholics would be grounds for termination of custody in such parent "violates the principle that primary consideration will be given to the welfare of the child."

## § 17.29  Property Division—General

In many situations, couples may find it desirable to include provisions pertaining to the division or distribution of marital property. These portions of the separation agreement may be enforceable by contempt, but other remedies may exist such as an action for breach of contract or specific performance. The parties may by agreement bind themselves to distribute property outside the state of Virginia, and such judgments, if the agreement is incorporated into a final divorce decree, will be given full faith and credit by other states. *Fall v. Eastin,* 215 U.S. 1, 30 S. Ct. 3, 54 L. Ed. 65 (1909).

When the parties agreed in a separation agreement that the husband would convey his rights in the marital residence to the wife, and that she would assume the mortgage, and this was assumed by a deed of assumption, the wife owned the property as feme sole. Although the parties reconciled, the property remained separate and not subject to equitable distribution when they later divorced. At the same time, the wife did not reacquire an interest in the husband's retirement benefits through the reconciliation, since they too had been a subject of the prior agreement. *Garland v. Garland,* 19 Va. Cir. 131 (1990). Mr. Tribby agreed to transfer his interest in the jointly owned marital residence to his wife within 15 days of the signing of the parties' property settlement agreement. Mrs. Tribby occupied the house following the separation, and made payments on the deed of trust. However, Mr. Tribby never conveyed his interest to her. Instead, he failed to make payments on a bank loan to the National Bank of Fredericksburg, which obtained a judgment against him. In *Tribby v. Tribby,* 26 Va. Cir. 372 (1992), the circuit court found that the property settlement agreement and divorce decree incorporating it, while binding on the Tribbys, had no effect on third parties. While they were married, the bank could not reach the home that they owned as tenants by the entireties. After the divorce, however, the bank could extend their judgment lien to Mr. Tribby's interest in the home since the former spouses had become tenants in common. The court noted that Mrs. Tribby could still pursue remedies of specific performance against Mr. Tribby for performance of the property settlement agreement. Mrs. Tribby might also be able to win damages in an amount equal to the amount of the judgment lien, plus attorney's fees and costs.

A term allowing the wife a portion of the wife's annuity described as $25,000 per year did not bind the husband to pay her the balance of what the employer actually paid, but was only descriptive. *Morris v. Chatman,* 1995 Va. App. LEXIS 361 (Apr. 18, 1995). The trial court could have awarded a wife a pro rata share of her husband's retirement payment representing the three days in March 1993, that preceded her remarriage. In the same case, *Gordon v. Whitt,* 1996 Va. App. LEXIS 43 (Jan. 23, 1996), the husband was required to pay the principal as well as the interest due on a home equity credit line when their property settlement agreement provided that he would be liable for the "current indebtedness" on this line of credit.

In *Hale v. Hale,* 42 Va. App. 27, 590 S.E.2d 66 (2003), a property settlement agreement contained a provision that divided a husband's "vested pension plan with his employer." The provision was interpreted to include all of the retirement plans that the husband's employer provided. When read in context with the rest of the property settlement agreement, the provision reflected the parties' intent to dispose of all of husband's vested retirement assets with his employer, which included both a defined benefit pension plan and a 401(k) employee contributions plan.

*Newcomb v. Newcomb,* 1995 Va. App. LEXIS 596 (July 25, 1995), involved payment of a lump sum due the wife "in lieu of alimony." The parties had a rather complex series of provisions in their agreement involving payment of $100,000 for the wife's interest in the parties' bed and breakfast inn, conveyance of the wife's interest to husband's assignee, and promise of a further payment of 20 percent of the difference between the gross sale price of husband's interest in the property and $250,000 if the inn were sold within fifteen years. Since the assignee had lent $150,000 to husband in consideration of the assignment of wife's share, the "gross sale price" was the stated amount ($470,000) less the $150,000 representing what had been wife's share. After deducting the $250,000 as provided in the agreement, twenty percent of the difference represented $14,000.

Although it may not be possible to have a spouse's professional degree distributed by court order under Va. Code § 20-107.3, obviously provisions may be made through a lump sum payment in a contract between separating spouses.

The agreement should provide that all necessary deeds, etc. will be executed to enable transfer of title as provided in the agreement. See, e.g., *Vellines v. Ely,* 185 Va. 889, 41 S.E.2d 21 (1947) (assignment of insurance proceeds).

Va. Code § 64.1-45.2, as enacted in 2001, provides that a provision for a nonprobate transfer on death in certain specified types of written instruments, including insurance policies, pension plans, conveyances, and marital property agreements, is a nontestamentary transfer.

### § 17.30   Tax Consequences of Property Distribution

Under *United States v. Davis,* 370 U.S. 65, 82 S. Ct. 1190, 8 L. Ed. 2d 335 (1962), *superseded by statute as stated in Polone v. Comm'r,* 505 F.3d 966 (2007), transfers of property in exchange for release of marital rights or obligations were held to be taxable events. This meant that appreciated property transferred was taxed as a capital gain to the transferor. The spouse receiving the property received an adjusted basis as of the time the property was transferred.

Transfers of property incident to divorce within one year after divorce, or within six years if pursuant to a divorce, will not be taxable events. The transferor will not be taxable, and the recipient spouse will have the original adjusted basis. I.R.C. § 1041. See, e.g., *Young v. Comm'r,* 240 F.3d 369 (4th Cir. 2001) (in post-divorce transfer of real property, no taxable event occurred and no gain or loss was realized by either spouse until property was conveyed to third party); *Pfister v. Comm'r,* 359 F.3d 352 (4th Cir. 2004) (transfer of property right pursuant to property settlement agreement which provides that wife will be owner of one-half of husband's "disposable retired or retainer pay" is nontaxable event, but income produced from property transferred is taxable distribution). If the parties specify that each will be responsible for paying taxes accrued on his or her respective income, there is no need for repayment of any "offset" if it turns out that no tax is owed. *Smith v. Smith,* 15 Va. App. 371, 423 S.E.2d 851 (1992).

If spouses divorce after filing joint income tax returns, and return their refund check to the Commissioner, separate checks will be issued to husband and wife. Va. Code § 58.1-499 (amended 1997).

In *Sharbutt-Ridge v. Ridge*, 1998 Va. App. LEXIS 106 (Feb. 24, 1998) (unpublished decision), a wife contended that the trial court erred in failing to assign her husband the duty of paying the federal income taxes due on her share of his pension. The parties' agreement omitted any discussion of paid income tax obligations in fixing the award to the wife of part of her husband's pension. The trial court was without authority to order a payment of over $6,000 in back income taxes by the husband to the wife when the IRS assessed her a portion of taxation of a pension. "Wife's remedy for overpayment of federal income taxes lies not in an appeal to the state courts, but in a prompt challenge to the IRS in the appropriate federal forum."

## § 17.31    Disclosure of Marital Property

As previously noted, the agreement may be found void if the parties did not adequately disclose the extent of their property at the time of its making. See, e.g., *Feinberg v. Feinberg,* 96 Misc. 2d 443, 409 N.Y.S.2d 365 (1978). However, where the parties had engaged in litigation, including extensive discovery, and subsequently read their agreement into the record in accordance with Va. Code § 20-155, the trial court had no authority to divide an IRA that was not addressed in the agreement and was not disclosed in discovery. *Eberhardt v. Eberhardt*, 2018 Va. App. LEXIS 343 (Dec. 11, 2018). On the other hand, more than ten years following the execution of the Marital Settlement Agreement and entry of the final order of divorce, the trial court reformed that retirement provision of the Marital Settlement Agreement to recite the proper retirement plan because the court found that Husband intentionally misled Wife as to the proper identity of the retirement plan. See *Ferry v. Beard*, 2020 Va. App. LEXIS 31 (February 4, 2020).

## § 17.32    Enforcement Provision

As previously noted, the property distribution portion of a separation agreement cannot be modified except by further contract. The defaulting party may be sued in an action on the contract for damages or specific performance. For example, in their property settlement agreement, Audrey and Alvin Chattin agreed that he would pay her $1,200 per month spousal support for a six and one-half year period, that he would maintain an insurance policy on his life in the amount of $100,000, naming her as irrevocable beneficiary, and that he would provide health insurance for her. In *Chattin v. Chattin,* 245 Va. 302, 427 S.E.2d 347 (1993), the Virginia Supreme Court determined that the wife was entitled to specific performance of these provisions because in order to enforce the contractual provisions for spousal support, she either would have to sue on the contract each time the husband failed to make a payment or would have to wait until a significant arrearage had accumulated before filing suit. If the husband failed to pay premiums on either insurance policy, it could lapse, thereby requiring the wife to purchase similar coverage and to bring suit against him each time she paid a renewal premium. If the husband failed to cooperate in providing the necessary information for obtaining life insurance, the wife would be left with no remedy at law whatsoever. Specific performance was therefore appropriate because she did not have an adequate remedy at law.

However, once a valid agreement between parties is affirmed, ratified, and incorporated by reference into a divorce decree, the agreement is deemed for all purposes to be a term of the decree, and the agreement can then be enforced by the trial court in the same manner as any other provision of the decree. Va. Code § 20-109.1. Although Va. Code § 20-109(C), formerly Va. Code § 20-109, restricts the trial court to enforcing the terms and conditions of an incorporated agreement, the parties are free to access the equitable powers of the court, including its contempt power, to enforce both the decree and the incorporated agreement. *Campbell v. Campbell*, 32 Va. App. 351, 528 S.E.2d 145 (2000). The non-payment of a monetary award can be pursued by a rule to show cause and the contempt powers of the court. *Kahn v. McNicholas*, 67 Va. App. 215 (2017).

Most parties will pursue a rule to show cause when the other party has breached an obligation arising under an agreement that was affirmed, ratified, and incorporated into a court order. However, the decision to pursue a rule to show cause as opposed to a contract action should be carefully examined. The findings from a final judgment on the merits from a show cause action or a contract enforcement action will be res judicata and can prevent additional proceedings on that issue. *Lee v. Spoden*, 290 Va. 235, 776 S.E.2d 798 (2015). However, where the court dismissed the show cause petition but there was no final determination adjudicating the claims on the show cause to enforce the terms of the parties' agreement, the wife's breach of contract claim was not barred by res judicata. *Kellogg v. Green*, 295 Va. 39, 46, 809 S.E.2d 631, 635 (2018).

Obligations arising out of property settlement agreements or equitable distribution awards are dischargeable in bankruptcy only if they are debts as defined in the Bankruptcy Code. Because a debtor's bankruptcy estate includes only property to which the debtor holds legal (as opposed to equitable) title, the nature of a former wife's interest in her former husband's pension or other property will govern whether the debtor husband's obligation is, or is not, a debt dischargeable in bankruptcy. *Brogan v. Brogan*, 31 Va. App. 769, 525 S.E.2d 618 (2000).

A no-appeal provision in a property settlement agreement that does not waive the rights of anyone other than the parties, allows neutral review of the parties' dispute, and does not violate any Virginia statute is valid and binding on the parties. *Burke v. Burke*, 52 Va. App. 183, 662 S.E.2d 622 (2008). See also *Kelley v. Kelley*, 248 Va. 295, 449 S.E.2d 55 (1994) (provision in property settlement agreement that restricts child's right to support or limits court's authority to order support is void as violative of public policy).

Whether to find a party in contempt lies within the sound discretion of the trial court. After the wife explained her conduct in *Clarke v. Clarke*, 1993 Va. App. LEXIS 113 (May 11, 1993), the court found that although she had breached the parties' separation agreement, her conduct did not deserve punishment. She had mistakenly thought that a camper would be conveyed to her along with property in North Carolina.

In *Tribby v. Tribby*, 26 Va. Cir. 372 (1992), the circuit court upheld a bank's judgment lien against the former marital home. According to the parties' property settlement agreement incorporated into their final divorce decree, Mr. Tribby was to transfer his interest in the jointly owned marital residence to his wife within fifteen days. Although Mrs. Tribby occupied the house following the separation, and made payments on the deed of trust, Mr. Tribby never conveyed his interest to her. Instead, he failed to make payments on a bank loan to the National Bank of Fredericksburg, which obtained a judgment against him. The court noted that Mrs. Tribby could seek specific performance against Mr. Tribby for performance of the property settlement agreement, and might win a judgment against him in an amount equal to the amount of the bank's lien, plus attorney's fees and costs.

According to their separation agreement, Winfree Brown was to pay Angela a lump sum of $20,000, while Angela agreed to prepare and execute a deed conveying to him her interest in the family residence. *Brown v. Brown*, 244 Va. 319, 422 S.E.2d 375 (1992). In consideration of the lump sum payment, she also agreed to waive all claims in the husband's employment benefits, including pension plans. She also agreed to waive her right to take property under the law of intestacy. The husband made plans to obtain the $20,000, and a check from the employer for nearly $16,000 was found in the glove compartment of his car. Winfree died in September of 1990, before his wife was paid or their divorce finalized. He died intestate, so that if the agreement was enforceable, the couple's two infant children would be his sole heirs at law. The co-administrators of Winfree's estate tendered the former wife $20,000 in February, to be delivered to her upon execution of the documents terminating all her interests in the estate and employee benefits. The Virginia Supreme Court agreed with the trial court that tender was made within a reasonable time so that the separation agreement was binding upon the wife and should be enforced as written. See also *Chattin v. Chattin,* 245 Va. 302, 427 S.E.2d 347 (1993), where Audrey and Alvin Chattin agreed that he would pay her $1,200 per month spousal support for a six and one-half year period, that he would maintain an insurance policy on his life in the amount of $100,000, naming her as irrevocable beneficiary, and that he would provide health insurance for her. The Virginia Supreme Court determined that the wife was entitled to specific performance of these provisions because she did not have an adequate remedy at law. In order to enforce the contractual provisions for spousal support, she either would have to sue on the contract each time the husband failed to make a payment or would have to wait until a significant arrearage had accumulated before filing suit. If he failed to pay premiums on either insurance policy, coverage could lapse, thereby requiring her to purchase similar coverage and to bring suit against him each time she paid a renewal premium. If the husband failed to cooperate in providing the necessary information for obtaining life insurance, the wife would be left with no remedy at law whatsoever.

In *Dziarnowski v. Dziarnowski,* 14 Va. App. 758, 418 S.E.2d 724 (1992), the wife failed to provide her former husband with the 1099 forms required by their property settlement by February 15. According to the agreement, she therefore waived her rights to receipt of spousal support. However, the husband made the next month's support payment and continued to insist that she proffer the income documents. He therefore waived the issue of her noncompliance. Similarly, a husband could not sue for breach of the parties' property settlement agreement, incorporated but not merged into their final divorce decree, unless he pleaded that he had upheld his portion of the contract or been excused for failure to perform. *Taxson v. Taxson,* 30 Va. Cir. 134 (1993). He was also unsuccessful in his suit for intentional infliction of emotional distress against the former wife because he failed to adequately allege facts supporting the cause of action.

A North Carolina property settlement agreement that was incorporated by references in the parties' divorce decree was registered and executed in *Sheppard v. Sheppard,* 1996 Va. App. LEXIS 261 (Apr. 9, 1996). The agreement required the husband to make payments on several loans encumbering the wife's residence, to pay her a monthly amount for utilities and an additional amount for spousal support. In another case, the trial court should have enforced an indemnification provision of the property settlement agreement that ordered the husband to reimburse the wife for paying his separate debt that had attached as a lien against the marital home. Shortly after the wife filed for divorce, the husband pled guilty to larceny of funds from his employer, and executed a judgment note for $45,000 plus interest secured by a deed of trust on the marital home. Under the parties' agreement, he was to hold her harmless for the debt and reimburse her when she refinanced the home and paid the employer the debt plus interest. This obligation to pay the wife was not in the nature of spousal support and therefore was not extinguished by the remarriage. *Guffey v. Guffey*, 1995 Va. App. LEXIS 819 (Nov. 7, 1995).

When a husband and wife divorced, the husband agreed to make the children beneficiaries of his life insurance trust, formerly providing for the wife. Thirteen years later, he cancelled all the policies listed in the trust agreement, then totaling $70,000, and obtained other life insurance policies in which he named his second wife as beneficiary. His estate was insolvent, and the children sought to impose a constructive trust upon the proceeds of his life insurance policies. The court of appeals found that the husband breached the contract by canceling his life insurance coverage, and so established a constructive trust on the insurance proceeds, plus interest from the date of the husband's death. *Jones v. Harrison*, 250 Va. 64, 458 S.E.2d 766 (1995).

In *Dugan v. Childers*, 261 Va. 3, 539 S.E.2d 723 (2001), a husband and wife stipulated in a property settlement agreement incorporated into a divorce decree that the husband would designate the wife as the beneficiary of his military survivor benefits plan, which was established by 10 U.S.C. §§ 1447–1455. Under the terms of the plan, the husband's surviving spouse would be his beneficiary, unless he submitted a written election to provide an annuity to his former spouse to his branch of the military service within one year of his divorce. Because the husband was required to make the election under an agreement incorporated into a court order, he would have been deemed to have made the election, if his former spouse had provided his branch of the military service with a written request and a copy of the court order within one year of the date of the court order. However, the former spouse failed to make the request, and as a result her claim for survivor's benefits was barred and could not form the basis for imposition of a constructive trust on the survivor annuity benefits under state law. Federal law expressed in 10 U.S.C. § 1450 preempts state law regarding a former spouse's entitlement to the survivor benefits of a military retiree.

## § 17.33   Appraisal and Valuation

It is appropriate before execution of the agreement to have a valuation of the parties' property made by an independent appraiser or accountant. This would be especially important in the case of a small business, a professional practice, or a closely held corporation, or when pension or retirement plans make up a portion of the marital assets. See, e.g., Troyan, *Divorce and the Valuation of a Disability Pension,* 10 Fam. L. Rep. 3043 (1984); Troyan, *Pension Evaluation and Equitable Distribution,* 10 Fam. L. Rep. 3001 (1984).

### § 17.34 Periodic Payment

Although the property may be conveyed in kind, spouses frequently contract to pay in cash over time. Although formerly such payments would not have been treated as alimony for tax purposes, since not in exchange for a marital right or obligation of support, under the Domestic Relations Tax Reform Act of 1984, I.R.C. § 71 provides that for agreements made after July 15, 1984, "alimony" need not be in exchange for a release of the duty to support. However, § 71 provides further that the payment must be made over a period of more than six years to be deductible, and that they not be "front-loaded" if in excess of $10,000 during any calendar year.

A spouse who agrees to assume a mortgage obligation has not been ordered to pay spousal support. *White v. White,* 257 Va. 139, 509 S.E.2d 323 (1999). A husband's agreement, incorporated into a final divorce decree, to make mortgage payments to the bank did not obligate him to pay the entire remaining amount of the original balance after the home had been sold.

### § 17.35 Security

Under Virginia law, since the divorce court lacked the power to transfer title, it could not affect the obligor's title to property even to guarantee security for making payments under a divorce decree. *Watkins v. Watkins,* 220 Va. 1051, 265 S.E.2d 750 (1980). This would, however, be entirely possible under a property settlement agreement executed by the parties.

### § 17.36 Effect of Separation Agreement on Workers' Compensation Death Benefits

A spouse's eligibility for benefits under Virginia's workers' compensation statute depends on the application of the statutory criteria set forth in the statute and not on a separate and unrelated agreement by the parties. Under the statute, death benefits are payable to those persons presumed to be wholly dependent upon the deceased employee, or to persons presumed to be partially dependent if there are no persons who are wholly dependent on the deceased employee.

In *Sifford v. Sifford,* 58 Va. App. 722, 716 S.E.2d 128 (2011), the wife appealed a decision by the Virginia Workers' Compensation Commission that found she was not entitled to death benefits because she was not an "actual dependent" of the decedent, having entered into a separation agreement that waived spousal support. The court of appeals held that the Commission erred in focusing on the purpose of the settlement agreement rather than on its effect. The overwhelming, uncontroverted evidence clearly demonstrated that the wife relied on the decedent for her reasonable necessities, that the decedent continued to support both the wife and their minor daughter on a regular basis, and that she relied on that support at the time of his death. Thus, the appellate court reversed the Commission's decision and concluded that the wife was an "actual dependent" under Va. Code Ann. § 65.2-515(A)(1), and was entitled to death benefits under Va. Code Ann. § 65.2-512.

## § 17.37   Repudiation

"[I]t is firmly established that for a repudiation of a contract to constitute a breach, the repudiation must be clear, absolute, unequivocal, and must cover the entire performance of the contract." *Sangaran v. Sachdeva* 2020 Va. App. LEXIS 178 (June 23, 2020) (citing *Bennett v. Sage Payment Sols., Inc.*, 282 Va. 49, 59, 710 S.E.2d 736 (2011)). If one party has anticipatorily repudiated a contract, the other party may rescind the contract, treat the repudiation as a breach and either bring a suit or seek a change, or wait until performance is required and then bring suit. *Id.* (citing *Simpson v. Scott*, 189 Va. 392, 398, 53 S.E.2d 21 (1949).

# CHAPTER 18

# Divorce from Bed and Board

## SYNOPSIS

## § 18.01 Introduction

At common law there was no absolute divorce, and the marriage continued until the death of one of the parties. In order to grant aid to cruelly treated, deserted, or abandoned wives, ecclesiastical courts first provided relief through the doctrine of necessaries, allowing third party creditors to recover, and later allowed more direct aid through the divorce from bed and board.

The alternate term *a mensa* divorce comes from the Latin words "divorce *a mensa et thoro*" or, literally, separation from table and pillow. The parties were no longer bound to live together. The first reported Virginia case to consider a divorce from bed and board is *Bailey v. Bailey,* 62 Va. (21 Gratt.) 43 (1871), a desertion case.

The limited divorce granted the woman a freedom from her consent to her husband's consortium, and allowed her financial relief through the court award of alimony, see, e.g., *Isaacs v. Isaacs,* 115 Va. 562, 79 S.E. 1072 (1913), as replacement for the spousal support to which she would otherwise have been entitled. See, e.g., *Carr v. Carr,* 63 Va. (22 Gratt.) 168, 173 (1872); *Bailey v. Bailey,* 62 Va. (21 Gratt.) 43 (1871).

Although able once more to handle her own property, see, e.g., *Myers v. Myers,* 83 Va. 806, 6 S.E. 630 (1887), *Marshall v. Baynes,* 88 Va. 1040, 1044, 14 S.E. 978, 979 (1892), the divorced wife was not able to marry again, since she was still married ("bound") to her original husband. In order to continue to receive alimony, she had the duty to remain his chaste and virtuous wife. *Courson v. Courson,* 213 Md. 183, 129 A.2d 917 (1957); *G. v. G.,* 67 N.J. Eq. 30, 41, 56 A. 736, 740 (1803). In *Crenshaw v. Crenshaw,* 12 Va. App. 1129, 408 S.E.2d 556 (1991), the parties executed a property settlement that was approved and confirmed by a 1964 decree for divorce *a mensa.* After obtaining the divorce *a mensa,* the parties reconciled for 21 years, believing they were married. They never revoked the 1964 decree. In 1974, without the parties' knowledge, the trial court dismissed the suit and removed it from the docket. In 1985, the parties again separated, and in 1986, the husband filed for divorce. The *a mensa* decree remained intact regardless of the intention of the parties, but dismissal of the case under Code § 8.01-335(B) terminated the decree of divorce from bed and board.

Because the law favored the continuance of marriages, no subsequent remarriage was necessary to terminate the divorce from bed and board, but merely a filing of a joint petition to the court granting the decree of divorce, which stated that there had been a reconciliation and that the parties wished to resume the status of husband and wife. In one case, *Carr v. Carr,* 63 Va. (22 Gratt.) 168 (1872), because the court felt that the parties might still reconcile, the judgment was suspended for six months to allow the wife to return to the husband she had deserted.

See generally 6A Michie's Jurisprudence *Divorce and Alimony* § 4.

## § 18.02  Reasons for Modern Action

Although the concept of the divorce from bed and board has changed so that it may now be granted to husbands as well as wives, it is still a viable cause of action in certain circumstances. The limited divorce is still used occasionally despite the existence of absolute divorces.

For religious reasons, some spouses are troubled by the idea of divorce, and are more comfortable with an action that will allow relative freedom, maintenance, and separate property while maintaining the marital status. See Va. Code § 20-118.

The divorce from bed and board may also be quicker to maintain. An *a mensa* divorce, unlike an absolute divorce for causes excluding adultery, may be brought as soon as the grounds appear. See Va. Code § 20-95; 6A Michie's Jurisprudence *Divorce and Alimony* § 19. No waiting period is involved, therefore, and after the expiration of a year the *a mensa* divorce may be converted by either spouse into an absolute divorce. Va. Code § 20-117. The decree for divorce *a mensa* is appealable and a final decree, so that the defendant could not afterwards file an answer, defensive pleadings, and a cross-bill. *Gordon v. Gordon,* 12 Va. Cir. 405 (City of Radford 1953).

## § 18.03  Requisites of Proof

In order to obtain a divorce from bed and board, counsel must establish three elements: (1) a valid marriage, see *Francis v. Francis,* 72 Va. (31 Gratt.) 283 (1879); see generally 6A Michie's Jurisprudence *Divorce and Alimony* § 29; (2) jurisdiction, *Blankenship v. Blankenship,* 125 Va. 595, 100 S.E. 538 (1919), which includes both domicile, *Chandler v. Chandler,* 132 Va. 418, 112 S.E. 856 (1922); *Howe v. Howe,* 179 Va. 111, 118, 18 S.E.2d 294, 297 (1942) (residence or domicile as used in the divorce statutes contemplates intention to live in adoptive home permanently or certainly for an indefinite period) and residence within the state; and (3) grounds.

The acts relied upon for the divorce must be alleged and proved to have occurred prior to the bringing of the suit, not while it is pending. *Beckner v. Beckner,* 204 Va. 580, 132 S.E.2d 715 (1963). A husband failed to overturn a five-year-old divorce from bed and board on grounds of fraud when the court of appeals found that the new evidence amounted at most to evidence of intrinsic fraud that could have been presented to the court in the original proceeding. *Will v. Will,* 1994 Va. App. LEXIS 100 (March 1, 1994). In the original divorce proceeding, husband's counsel cross-examined two psychologists who testified for the wife. On appeal, the husband sought to introduce affidavits from them stating that they had not been fully able to express their opinions that the wife had not been psychologically or physically abused. The trial judge correctly held that this issue regarding the wife's testimony was previously litigated and decided in the divorce proceeding.

The form for a decree of divorce from bed and board is found at Bean, *Domestic Relations Law Practice System* 177.

## § 18.04     Jurisdiction

In order to maintain a suit for divorce, Va. Code § 20-97 requires that at least one of the parties "was at the time of the filing of the suit and had been for at least six months preceding the filing of the suit an actual bona fide resident and domiciliary of this Commonwealth." If the spouse is a member of the armed forces stationed in Virginia, has lived with the spouse for six months before the separation in the state, and continues to live in the state until suit is filed, Virginia shall be presumed the state of domicile. If a serviceman or foreign service officer is stationed in another country or territory but was domiciled in Virginia for the six-month period immediately before he was stationed in that country or territory, he is deemed to have been domiciled in and a bona fide resident of Virginia for the period necessary for obtaining an annulment or divorce. Va. Code § 20-97(3).

Va. Code § 20-104 allows an order for publication to be entered after an affidavit is filed that the defendant is not a Virginia resident or cannot be located within the state. No deposition in such case can be heard until ten days after the making of the publication. The permissible form for such an order is set forth in Va. Code § 20-105. When a court obtains jurisdiction over a nonresident under the long-arm statute, such service shall have the same effect as service on the nonresident within Virginia. Va. Code § 8.01-320 (amended 1997). This statute specifically includes divorce and annulment cases.

A change of domicile must be clearly demonstrated. For example, in one case the husband's domicile of origin was in Virginia, and he also resided there for the one year prior to the complaint. The defendant wife was not then a resident of Virginia. The Virginia court had the power to decree a divorce even though the husband did for some years live in the District of Columbia with the wife. *Chandler v. Chandler,* 132 Va. 418, 112 S.E. 856 (1922).

The place where the parties last cohabited means the place where they last dwelled together as husband and wife with some degree of permanency, as opposed to the place where they last had sexual relations. *Colley v. Colley,* 204 Va. 225, 129 S.E.2d 630 (1963).

When the complaining spouse may have resided outside the state for a lengthy time, always with the intent to return to Virginia, more must be shown to indicate a bona fide actual residence. For example, the plaintiff might have left a wife or child in the state while continuing to support them, kept a house or room in the state ready for occupancy, or maintained a permanent mailing address within the state. *Hiles v. Hiles,* 164 Va. 131, 178 S.E. 913 (1935) (no residence shown where husband stationed in China for many years preceding suit).

Domicile and residency are distinct and separate issues, the determination of which present a mixed question of law and fact. *Adoteye v. Adoteye,* 32 Va. App. 221, 226, 527 S.E.2d 453, 456 (2000). Despite residing in Virginia for over 20 years, owning real property, maintaining financial accounts, and holding a valid Virginia driver's license, the wife was unable to prove both residency and domiciliary where she was in the United States based on a G-4 visa. *Id.,* 32 Va. App. at 227, 527 S.E.2d at 456. However, *In re Hanano,* 2001 Va. Cir. LEXIS 169 (Jan. 23, 2001), on a plea in bar, the husband was unable to prove that wife was not a resident and domiciliary of Virginia despite entering the United States on temporary visas.

See generally 6A Michie's Jurisprudence *Divorce and Alimony* § 36.

## § 18.05    Marriage

In order for there to be a divorce from bed and board, there must first be proof of a valid marriage.

In *Francis v. Francis,* 72 Va. (31 Gratt.) 283 (1879), the wife sought alimony from the husband after his desertion. He claimed that the parties had never married. The court discussed their relationship and found that they had in fact agreed to be married as required by a contemporary statute dealing with marriages between black people, and had held themselves out as married for many years. The wife was therefore entitled to relief.

## § 18.06    Grounds in General

Va. Code § 20-95 sets forth the grounds for a divorce from bed and board: cruelty, reasonable apprehension of bodily hurt, willful desertion, or abandonment.

## § 18.07    Desertion or Abandonment

Desertion is a breaking off of matrimonial cohabitation, combined with the intent to desert in the mind of the offender. *Bailey v. Bailey,* 62 Va. (21 Gratt.) 43, 48–49 (1871).

The mere unjustified refusal to have sexual relations will not constitute desertion, but withdrawal of the privilege plus such willful breach and neglect of other marital duties as to practically destroy home life in every true sense does afford grounds for divorce. Compare *Chandler v. Chandler,* 132 Va. 418, 112 S.E. 856 (1922) (absolute divorce); with *Goodwyn v. Goodwyn,* 222 Va. 53, 278 S.E.2d 813 (1981).

No desertion was shown where the wife moved the husband's things out of the marital bedroom and they thereafter ceased to have sexual intercourse, since there was no evidence of refusal to engage in sexual relations. The wife's departure to visit relatives on the day the divorce complaint was served was probably desirable to avoid another altercation, and in any event was not desertion. *Johnson v. Johnson,* 213 Va. 204, 191 S.E.2d 206 (1972); see also *Raiford v. Raiford,* 193 Va. 221, 68 S.E.2d 888 (1952) (husband ordered wife to leave after marital quarrel; she later refused to allow him in home although she had no grounds to fear him); compare *Tutwiler v. Tutwiler,* 118 Va. 724, 88 S.E. 86 (1916) (husband ordered or at least acquiesced to wife's leaving house, published notice that she had deserted so that he was not responsible for her debts, and refused to have her back; held desertion by husband).

The refusal by the wife to live with her husband in the home selected by him, without lawful justification, constitutes desertion. *Graves v. Graves,* 193 Va. 659, 70 S.E.2d 339 (1952).

Although the husband did not voice an objection to the wife's departure at that time, the circumstances showed her settled purpose and plan to leave him without just reason. *Miller v. Miller,* 196 Va. 698, 85 S.E.2d 221 (1955). This was desertion on the wife's part.

Desertion was shown where the wife voluntarily and wilfully left the marital home with the intention to permanently break off marital relations with her husband. She had no legal justification for her abandonment nor valid excuse for her failure to live with him. *Stolfi v. Stolfi,* 203 Va. 696, 126 S.E.2d 923 (1962). See also *Haynor v. Haynor,* 112 Va. 123, 127, 70 S.E. 531, 532 (1911); *Good v. Good,* 122 Va. 30, 94 S.E. 176 (1917).

When people understand that they must live together except for a few reasons known to the law, they learn to soften by mutual accommodation to that yoke which they know they cannot shake off. They become good husbands and wives for the necessity of remaining husbands and wives; for necessity is a powerful master in teaching duties which it imposes. *Evans v. Evans,* 1 Hogg. C.R. 35, 161 Eng. Rep. 466 (1790).

When the parties separate by consent, neither can complain of desertion in the other unless there is some desire expressed for reconciliation—some overture made in good faith for a restoration of the conjugal relation. *Latham v. Latham,* 71 Va. (30 Gratt.) 307, 326 (1878). However, Va. Code § 20-102 states that it shall not be necessary to prove an offer of reconciliation to show willful desertion.

Once the fact of desertion is proved, the complainant need not show that such desertion was without legal jurisdiction or excuse, *Graham v. Graham,* 210 Va. 608, 609–10, 172 S.E.2d 724, 725 (1970), since this would require proving that defendant was not entitled to any divorce on other grounds in addition to making out the primary cause of action. The duty of going forward with evidence of justification and excuse rests upon defendant unless such justification appears from plaintiff's case.

A desertion that is complete at the time, and gives no promise of a return within a reasonable time, certainly becomes permanent in the eyes of the law when the offending party refuses without cause to renew the marriage relation at the request in good faith of the other. *Ringgold v. Ringgold,* 128 Va. 485, 104 S.E. 836 (1920).

See generally 6A Michie's Jurisprudence *Divorce and Alimony* § 18.

## § 18.08 Cruelty

Mental anguish, repeated and unrelenting neglect and humiliation may be visited upon an unoffending spouse in such degree as to amount to cruelty, but it must be so serious that it makes the marriage relationship unendurable or intolerable. Mere coldness and denial of sexual intercourse, where other marital duties are performed, do not constitute cruelty. *Hoback v. Hoback,* 208 Va. 432, 158 S.E.2d 113 (1967). However, a refusal to permit the spouse sexual intercourse coupled with a general withdrawal from matrimonial cohabitation will constitute cruelty, *Ringgold v. Ringgold,* 128 Va. 485, 104 S.E. 836 (1920), where there is an element of danger to the spouse's health.

The wife was authorized a divorce from bed and board where the husband had over many years subjected her to coarse, vile, and abusive language including charges of prostitution and adultery, beaten her many times, failed to afford her proper support and maintenance, and finally deserted and abandoned her without just cause. *Prindes v. Prindes,* 193 Va. 463, 69 S.E.2d 332 (1952). See also *Myers v. Myers,* 83 Va. 806, 6 S.E. 630 (1887).

The wife was allowed an *a mensa* divorce on grounds of cruelty and constructive desertion where she left after the husband's attack. Although she provoked him by taking money from his wallet, the beating she received and that caused her to leave the marital home was out of proportion to this provocation. *Wimbrow v. Wimbrow,* 208 Va. 141, 156 S.E.2d 598 (1967).

Although some acts may be condoned and even forgiven for a time, cruelty is cumulative. Forgiveness will therefore not be a bar to bringing all the former acts out when continued cruelty has rendered the state of affairs intolerable. *Sollie v. Sollie,* 202 Va. 855, 120 S.E.2d 281 (1961). See also *Bennett v. Bennett,* 179 Va. 239, 18 S.E.2d 911 (1942).

See generally 43 Va. L. Rev. 125 (1957); 6A Michie's Jurisprudence *Divorce and Alimony* §§ 14 and 15.

### § 18.09    Pendente Lite Alimony

Va. Code § 20-103 provides that the court may order maintenance and support of the spouse and funds enabling the suit; and may restrain a spouse from interfering with the other; may allow custody and support of minor children; may order exclusive use and possession of the family residence and preservation of the spouse's estate; or may require security. There may also be an order restraining the spouse from entering the jointly owned family home for fifteen days from an ex parte order, where there has been a showing of a reasonable apprehension of bodily harm; or for longer after hearing or notice to the other party.

The court may also require the parties to attend courses in parenting responsibilities, conflict resolution, and financial responsibility, according to the amendments to Va. Code § 20-103 passed in 1997. For proceedings under Va. Code Title 16.1, a formula for a presumptively correct amount of pendente lite spousal support was enacted in 2007. Va. Code § 16.1-278.17:1.

### § 18.10    Attorney's Fees

Even though the wife is a defendant in a divorce action, in many cases it will be proper to award her attorney's fees and costs, where she has no separate estate. Va. Code § 20-103; *Rowlee v. Rowlee,* 211 Va. 689, 179 S.E.2d 461 (1971) (absolute divorce); *Hughes v. Hughes,* 173 Va. 293, 305, 4 S.E.2d 402, 407 (1939).

The amount of fees should be determined not only on the basis of the size of the party's estate, but in greater degree upon the difficulties of the litigation and the demands it makes upon the time, knowledge and skill of counsel. *Twohy v. Twohy,* 130 Va. 557, 565–66, 107 S.E. 642, 645 (1921).

Va. Code § 54.1-3932, as enacted in 2001, authorizes an attorney's lien on a cause of action for divorce or annulment, as security for attorney's fees for services rendered. However, the statute prohibits an attorney from exercising any claim until the divorce judgment is final and all residual disputes regarding marital property are concluded. Also, a trial court has discretion to exclude spousal and child support from the scope of the attorney's lien.

## § 18.11 Conduct of Hearing

Va. Code § 20-106 allows testimony to be heard orally *(ore tenus)* if required by the court; the testimony may be reduced to writing if either party desires it. Such testimony has the same weight as a deposition. No oral evidence may be taken without notice to the adverse party.

The facts must be clearly proved, independently of the admissions of either party in the pleadings or otherwise. *Prindes v. Prindes,* 193 Va. 463, 69 S.E.2d 332 (1952). Corroboration need only be slight where it is apparent that there is no collusion. *Graves v. Graves,* 193 Va. 659, 662, 70 S.E.2d 339, 340 (1952). The court has the duty "to see that the public policy of the State expressed in the statutes is not violated." *Raiford v. Raiford,* 193 Va. at 228, 68 S.E.2d at 893 (1952). The allegations need therefore be proved by full, clear, and adequate evidence. *Westfall v. Westfall,* 196 Va. 97, 102, 82 S.E.2d 487, 490 (1954).

The Chancellor, as in other suits in equity, may refer questions in a divorce from bed and board to a commissioner, who may prepare the cause and place it in a better position to enable the chancellor to decide it expeditiously and correctly. *Raiford v. Raiford,* 193 Va. 221, 224, 68 S.E.2d 888, 891 (1952).

The findings of the trial court, which had the opportunity to hear the witnesses, should be accorded great weight. *Barnard v. Barnard,* 132 Va. 155, 111 S.E. 227 (1922).

## § 18.12 Sexual Relations Following Decree

Va. Code § 20-117 provides that a divorce from bed and board shall not be a bar to either party's obtaining an absolute divorce unless grounds for such divorce were known to the party applying for the absolute divorce before the *a mensa* decree was entered.

Va. Code § 20-107.1 allows support following divorces for fault, except adultery, and even then when clear and convincing evidence shows that a denial of support would constitute a manifest injustice based upon the respective degrees of fault during the marriage and the relative economic circumstances of the parties.

Even though there were grounds obtained for a divorce from bed and board, since these were not also grounds for absolute divorce, they would not be sufficient to bar the right of the other spouse to an absolute divorce on grounds of adultery if proven. *Haskins v. Haskins,* 188 Va. 525, 50 S.E.2d 437 (1948).

See generally Wadlington, *Sexual Relations After Separation or Divorce: The New Morality and the Old and New Divorce Laws,* 63 Va. L. Rev. 249 (1977).

### § 18.13    Reconciliation—Effect

Va. Code § 20-120 provides that a decree of *a mensa* divorce may be revoked at any time upon the parties' joint application and satisfactory proof of reconciliation.

A mere cohabitation on a spasmodic basis on out of town trips cannot be dignified into the status of a reconciliation demanded by society of a husband and wife living with each other on a permanent basis. Although each of the parties may have unilaterally desired a reconciliation, their individual efforts were abortive and the decree *a mensa* was never revoked. *Roberts v. Pace,* 193 Va. 156, 161, 67 S.E.2d 844, 846 (1951).

### § 18.14    Merger into Absolute Divorce

Va. Code § 20-121 provides that after one year from the grounds for the bed and board decree, when the parties have been separated without interruption since the divorce, and no reconciliation is possible, the court may merge the decree into one for absolute divorce upon either party's application. No notice need be given the guilty party to the bed and board decree unless new matters are alleged, but ten days' notice is required to be given to the injured party. The absolute divorce shall not change prior orders for costs, counsel fees, spousal and child support, nor any restraining orders except as provided in the decree.

Merger may also take place after six months from the date of separation, where the divorce will be based upon the six month no-fault ground under amended Va. Code § 20-121.02. This portion of the no-fault ground is only effective where there are no children of the marriage, and where the parties have filed a separation agreement.

The court may itself enter an absolute divorce where desertion or cruelty is stated grounds for the divorce *a mensa* even though the prayer is for a bed and board divorce, under Va. Code § 20-121.02, so long as the statutory period has elapsed and the court is of the opinion that no reconciliation is possible.

There may not be any occupation of the marital bed during the separation period before merger, since in that event the "separation without interruption" is destroyed. Otherwise a man could "in effect make his wife his mere mistress until the final decree." *Anderson v. Anderson,* 196 Va. 26, 82 S.E.2d 562 (1954), *overruled, Petachenko v. Petachenko,* 232 Va. 296, 350 S.E.2d

600 (1986). This is to be distinguished from the conduct required to effect a reconciliation in order to change property rights, *id.* at 29–30, 82 S.E.2d at 565 (distinguishing the case from *Roberts v. Pace,* 193 Va. 156, 67 S.E.2d 844 (1951)), especially since in *Anderson,* in addition to three admitted acts of intercourse, the husband lived at home with the wife practically every weekend over a period of six months.

The *a mensa* decree will be superseded by the *a vinculo* decree. *Thomas v. Thomas,* 216 Va. 741, 222 S.E.2d 557 (1976). A property settlement agreement incorporated into the *a mensa* decree could not at that time be modified because of Va. Code § 20-109.

For forms see § 6527, *Petition for Merger of Decree from Bed and Board Into Decree from Bond of Matrimony,* Domestic Relations Law Practice System 179.

### § 18.15    Effect of Divorce from Bed and Board on Personal Marital Rights

Once the parties have separated, particularly if there has been a divorce *a mensa,* certain of the individual rights that are altered during the marital status again have independent significance. For example, when the parties have separated, one spouse no longer has a right of access to and consortium with the other. If the personal freedom and privacy of the spouse is invaded, a criminal cause of action may result. *Knox v. Commonwealth,* 225 Va. 504, 304 S.E.2d 4 (1983) (burglary from entry into estranged wife's apartment to engage in assault). Likewise, any consent to sexual relations by a wife that is normal during a marriage is revoked when the parties separate unequivocally, particularly if pursuant to a judicial decree, as in the divorce from bed and board. *Weishaupt v. Commonwealth,* 227 Va. 389, 315 S.E.2d 847 (1984).

### § 18.16    Change in Property Rights Following Divorce from Bed and Board

Va. Code § 20-116 provides that a divorce from bed and board operates upon property thereafter acquired and upon personal rights and legal capacities.

Where the parties' agreement following separation was in effect a divorce from bed and board, and the wife thereafter purchased property, the husband had no curtesy interest in the property. *Marshall v. Baynes,* 88 Va. 1040, 1044, 14 S.E. 978, 979 (1892). Where the property in question was acquired by the husband during the marriage, and the decree provided that "the marital rights of each party to the suit in and to any property owned by the other party be and the same are hereby extinguished," the divorce *a mensa* between the parties operated to extinguish the wife's dower rights. *Gum v. Gum,* 122 Va. 32, 94 S.E. 177 (1917).

See generally 6A Michie's Jurisprudence *Divorce and Alimony* § 52.

## § 18.17    Division of Property Following Divorce from Bed and Board

Division of the property is not possible under Va. Code § 20-107.3, which requires an absolute divorce or a dissolution of marriage.

There may of course be affirmation, ratification and incorporation of a property settlement or separation agreement under Va. Code § 20-109.1, which would include custody, child support, spousal support "or any other condition or consideration, monetary or nonmonetary."

Property settlement agreements are discussed in Chapter 17, *supra.*

## § 18.18    Alimony Following *A Mensa* Divorce

Alimony may be awarded according to the factors set forth in Va. Code § 20-107.1 unless the decree from bed and board is given against the party seeking alimony. Alimony may be made either in periodic payments, in lump sum, or both.

Since the marriage is still in existence, a decree of alimony could theoretically be made at any time following an *a mensa* divorce. Normally, however, if there was personal jurisdiction over the obligor spouse, the right to alimony will at least be reserved in the final decree.

Alimony in general is discussed in Chapter 19, *infra.* Personal jurisdiction must be obtained before an alimony award is made. *Osborne v. Osborne,* 215 Va. 205, 207 S.E.2d 875 (1974); *Bray v. Landergren,* 161 Va. 699, 172 S.E. 252 (1934).

## § 18.19    Custody

Va. Code § 20-107.2 provides jurisdiction to address custody issues in a divorce from bed and board. Custody and visitation are determined by analyzing the best interests of the child, and the factors for that determination are set forth in Va. Code § 20-124.3.

Child custody may be awarded following a divorce from bed and board, to either party, based upon the "best interests of the child" standard. *Fussell v. Fussell,* 182 Va. 720, 30 S.E.2d 555 (1944). Child custody in general is discussed in Chapter 23, *infra.*

## § 18.20    Child Support

Va. Code § 20-107.2 provides jurisdiction to (1) determine child support for a minor child or for an adult child who is disabled as set forth in Va. Code

§ 20-124.2, and (2) require that health insurance be provided for a child. Child support is governed by Va. Code §§ 20-108.1 and 20-108.2. Personal jurisdiction must be obtained before such an award is entered. See *Kulko v. Superior Court,* 436 U.S. 84 (1978); *Gramelspacher v. Gramelspacher,* 204 Va. 839, 134 S.E.2d 285 (1964). Child support and its enforcement are discussed in Chapter 22, *infra.*

## § 18.21 Termination of Alimony

The spouse's right to alimony terminates upon the death of the obligor spouse under Va. Code § 20-107.1, unless the decree incorporates a property settlement agreement specifically providing for nontermination upon death. See generally Chapter 20, *infra.*

Since the 1997 amendments to Va. Code § 20-109, if the dependent spouse has been cohabiting with another person in a relationship analogous to marriage for a year or more, the court may decrease or terminate spousal support or maintenance. This change may occur unless the divorcing parties' agreement otherwise provides, or unless the dependent spouse proves by a preponderance of the evidence that termination of support would constitute a manifest injustice. The cohabitation must be proved by clear and convincing evidence, and termination of support must follow a court order.

## § 18.22 Tax Aspects

The careful attorney must be aware of the tax implications of various financial aspects of the limited divorce. Parties may file as married persons filing separately, and for separation instruments and divorces entered on or before December 31, 2018, alimony may be deducted by the payor and taxable to the payee under 26 U.S.C. § 71. However, the Tax Cuts and Jobs Act (TCJA) upended the tax treatment of spousal support payments by declaring that spousal support payments will neither be included within the payee's taxable income nor deductible from the payor's taxable income for any divorce or separation instrument that is entered after December 31, 2018, are not taxable.

However, 1984 changes in the tax law limit the attractiveness of the "unitary award," which, according to *Commissioner v. Lester,* 366 U.S. 299, 81 S. Ct. 1343, 6 L. Ed. 2d 306 (1961), made a periodic payment for alimony and child support entirely treatable as alimony so long as the portions were not definitely fixed by the decree. The new law will not allow alimony treatment for any portion attributable to child support.

Transfers of property between spouses, even directly following a divorce or pursuant to a divorce, will no longer be taxable events as was required since *United States v. Davis,* 370 U.S. 65, 82 S. Ct. 1190, 8 L. Ed. 2d 335

(1962), for decrees rendered after July of 1984. The payment of money treated as alimony no longer need be solely in satisfaction of the support obligation, although the new provisions require payment for at least six years and a structure designed to prevent front-loading if payments are in excess of $10,000 yearly.

If spouses divorce after filing joint income tax returns, and return their refund check to the Commissioner, separate checks will be issued to husband and wife. Va. Code § 58.1-499 (amended 1997).

### § 18.23    Defenses to Action

*Res judicata.* If defendant demurred to plaintiff's complaint for an *a mensa* divorce, and the demurrer was sustained, defendant could success-fully plead res judicata when plaintiff brought an *a mensa* action for a second time, based upon the same grounds, and merely set forth the facts more specifically. *Griffin v. Griffin,* 183 Va. 443, 32 S.E.2d 700 (1945).

*Fraud and duress.* Although it was not shown by the facts in *Scott v. Scott,* 142 Va. 31, 128 S.E. 599 (1925), presumably fraud in procuring a divorce will be an affirmative defense causing the decree to be set aside. An absolute divorce was procured through fraud where the plaintiff husband failed to advise the court that his wife was insane and had been placed out of the state through his agreement. The pleadings stated that she was a nonresident, and she was served only by publication. *Taylor v. Taylor,* 159 Va. 338, 165 S.E. 414 (1932).

*Condonation.* This is a remission by one of the spouses of an offense the other has committed against the marriage, on condition that treatment will be with conjugal kindness thereafter. While the condition remains unbroken there can be no divorce, but a breach of it revives the original offense. *Owens v. Owens,* 96 Va. 191, 31 S.E. 72 (1898) (cruelty). See generally 6A Michie's Jurisprudence *Divorce and Alimony* § 25.

*Justifiable desertion.* Although one party can demonstrate that the other deserted, if that other can show that the leaving was without fault, even if not constituting separate grounds for divorce, no divorce for desertion will be granted. *Breschel v. Breschel,* 221 Va. 208, 269 S.E.2d 363 (1980) (*a vinculo* divorce); *Graham v. Graham,* 210 Va. 608, 172 S.E.2d 724 (1970) (*a mensa* divorce).

### § 18.24    Effect of Subsequent *Ex Parte* Divorce

Under Virginia law, a foreign *ex parte* divorce will not cut off a domiciliary spouse's right to alimony under an *a mensa* decree or otherwise. *Newport v. Newport,* 219 Va. 48, 245 S.E.2d 134 (1978); *Isaacs v. Isaacs,*

115 Va. 562, 79 S.E. 1072 (1913) (decided before "divisible divorce" concept of *Vanderbilt v. Vanderbilt,* 354 U.S. 416, 77 S. Ct. 1360, 1 L. Ed. 2d 1456 (1957)), and *Estin v. Estin,* 334 U.S. 541, 68 S. Ct. 1213, 92 L. Ed. 1561 (1948); Kentucky *ex parte* absolute divorce could dissolve marital status but not affect property rights under Virginia *a mensa* decree.

However, if there is personal jurisdiction over the dependent spouse in the foreign proceeding, the right to be awarded alimony will end unless there is a reservation of the right to seek alimony in the foreign final decree. *Ceyte v. Ceyte,* 222 Va. 11, 278 S.E.2d 791 (1981); *Osborne v. Osborne,* 215 Va. 205, 207 S.E.2d 875 (1974).

Full faith and credit has always been given a foreign judgment of a divorce based upon comity, where there was notice by publication plus personal service in Virginia, even though the grounds used for the foreign absolute divorce would only have been grounds for an *a mensa* decree in Virginia. *Humphreys v. Strong,* 139 Va. 146, 169–70, 123 S.E. 554, 561 (1924).

## § 18.25    Effect of Divorce from Bed and Board on Testimony

*Stewart v. Commonwealth,* 219 Va. 887, 252 S.E.2d 329 (1979), states the proposition that the wife will be competent to testify against her husband, and over his objection, following the parties' *a mensa* divorce.

> Her legal capacity to testify after the divorce from bed and board was no different from what it would have been if she had obtained a divorce from the bond of matrimony . . . . Whatever vestige of marital harmony might have remained to be protected by Stewart's exercise of his right to eliminate Mrs. Stewart as a witness against him had been thoroughly disrupted, if not totally destroyed, by the entry of the *a mensa* decree. Hence, the reason for the privilege no longer existed.

*Id.* at 892, 252 S.E.2d at 333. This limitation on competence has been abandoned by statute. Va. Code § 19.2-271.2. The privilege not to testify now belongs to the spouse witness.

Of course, the competence to testify, which is determined at the time of trial, should be distinguished from the privilege for confidential marital communications. Even though the parties are divorced at trial, the communication is privileged if made while the parties were married. See *Menefee v. Commonwealth,* 189 Va. 900, 55 S.E.2d 9 (1949).

See generally Friend, *Law of Evidence in Virginia* §§ 57 and 64 (2d ed. 1983).

# CHAPTER 19

# Absolute Divorce

## SYNOPSIS

## § 19.01    Introduction

Until the seventeenth century, it was impossible for a party to remarry unless a first marriage had been terminated by the death of a spouse. However, a divorce *a mensa,* or divorce from bed and board, could be decreed by the ecclesiastical court to protect the wronged wife after proof of her husband's desertion or abuse. In England, after the reign of Henry VIII, an absolute divorce, or divorce *a vinculo* (from the bonds of matrimony), allowing remarriage to another, could be obtained only by a special act of Parliament.

In Virginia, by statute of 1841, absolute divorces were obtainable through a judicial proceeding where the defendant was guilty of adultery. Act of Mar. 18, 1848, [1848–1849] Va. Acts ch. 122, § 2. The causes of action for absolute divorce were gradually augmented, so that they include imprisonment for a felony, cruelty and desertion after a one year period (also causes of action for divorces from bed and board), sodomy and buggery as well as adultery, and finally, since 1960, separation for a statutory period (now one year in most cases). Va. Code § 20-91.

Because divorce is not a common law action, the statutory requisites must all be closely followed. *White v. White,* 181 Va. 162, 24 S.E.2d 448 (1943). This is because courts are given the power to make divorce decrees by statute alone. See, e.g., *Johnson v. Johnson,* 224 Va. 641, 299 S.E.2d 351 (1983) (no power to divide joint checking account between the parties); *McCotter v. Carle,* 149 Va. 584, 592–94, 140 S.E. 670, 673–74 (1927).

Another way of looking at the law of divorce is to note that the state has an interest in the marriage relationship, and so may prescribe the conditions under which the parties may sever it. See, e.g., *McFarland v. McFarland,* 179 Va. 418, 19 S.E.2d 77 (1942); *Raiford v. Raiford,* 193 Va. 221, 68 S.E.2d 888 (1952).

The suit is an action in rem, binding upon parties who are privies and also upon strangers. See *Wills v. Spraggins,* 44 Va. 555 (1847) (probate proceeding).

## § 19.02    Elements of Proof

In order for a complainant to prevail in an action for absolute divorce, it is necessary to prove: (1) jurisdiction, achieved through domicile and residence of one of the parties in the state and the existence of a valid marriage; and (2) grounds for divorce under Va. Code § 20-91.

## § 19.03 Jurisdiction

Jurisdiction to grant divorces is statutory and strictly limited. *Chandler v. Chandler,* 132 Va. 418, 112 S.E. 856 (1922). Subject matter jurisdiction in a divorce proceeding requires a determination of both domicile and bona fide residency. *Blackson v. Blackson,* 40 Va. App. 507, 579 S.E.2d 704 (2003). In order to maintain a suit for divorce, Va. Code § 20-97 requires that at least one of the parties "was at the time of the filing of the suit and had been for at least six months preceding the filing of the suit an actual bona fide resident and domiciliary of this Commonwealth." If the spouse is a member of the armed forces stationed in Virginia, has lived with the spouse for six months before the separation in the state, and continues to live in the state until suit is filed, Virginia shall be presumed the state of domicile. Va. Code § 20-97(1). Being stationed or residing in the Commonwealth includes, but is not limited to, a member of the armed forces being stationed or residing upon a ship with a Virginia home port or at an air, naval, or military base located within the Commonwealth over which the United States enjoys exclusive federal jurisdiction. Va. Code § 20-97(2). If a serviceman or foreign service officer is stationed in another country or territory but was domiciled in Virginia for the six-month period immediately before he was stationed in that country or territory, he is deemed to have been domiciled in and a bona fide resident of Virginia for the period necessary for obtaining an annulment or divorce. Va. Code § 20-97(3).

In 2017, Va. Code § 20-97 was amended to specify that "any civilian employee of the United States, including any foreign service officer," was subject to the jurisdiction of the Commonwealth of Virginia provided that the civilian employee is "(i) at the time the suit is filed is, or immediately preceding such suit was, stationed in any territory or foreign country and (ii) was domiciled in the Commonwealth for the six-month period immediately preceding his being stationed in such territory or country." This amendment to Va. Code § 20-97 greatly expanded jurisdiction over federal government employees. Virginia's long arm statute, Va. Code § 20-328.1, was similarly amended in 2017 to provide jurisdiction over "civilian employees of the United States, including any foreign service officers."

In *Eddine v. Eddine,* 12 Va. App. 760, 406 S.E.2d 914 (1991), the husband and wife divorced in 1986. The husband was awarded the marital home as his separate property, and the wife appealed. The court of appeals reversed and remanded the case for further proceedings. At that point, the husband left the United States for Syria, closed his medical practice and stopped making child support payments. He failed to provide either the wife or the trial court with his new address. The wife moved under § 8.01-319(A) to dispense with any further notice to him. Notice of the hearing on her motion was posted on the door of the marital residence. The court entered an order granting the wife's motion, and four months later, in August of 1988, the trial court heard evidence and entered an order awarding her $289,500 as a monetary award and $3,000 in attorney's fees. The husband filed pro se to set aside this order, noting that he had received no notice of the August hearing, and that therefore § 8.01-319 violated his constitutional right to due process. The court of appeals held, one judge dissenting, that due process was not violated because the husband had a duty to advise the clerk of court of his address and any change in it. "To hold otherwise would allow a litigant disappointed in the direction litigation might be taking to thwart the authority of the court by leaving the area without notifying the court of his or her new address."

Similarly, a husband who refused to tell his wife where he was residing and prevented her being able to find him could not claim that the wife had not used due diligence. *Jennings v. Jennings*, 26 Va. App. 530, 495 S.E.2d 544 (1998). After he left the marital home in January 1990, the husband hid from his wife and creditors. He had no telephone service, no apartment lease, no utilities or "anything in [his] name . . . for the simple reason that [he] was involved in [a] . . . criminal case." A ruling on the legal question of the jurisdiction of the court in a divorce and child custody case is merely interlocutory and cannot be appealed. *Wells v. Wells*, 29 Va. App. 82, 509 S.E.2d 549 (1999).

If a serviceman or foreign service officer is stationed in another country or territory but was domiciled in Virginia for the six-month period immediately before he was stationed in that country or territory, he is deemed to have been domiciled in and a bona fide resident of Virginia for the period necessary for obtaining an annulment or divorce. Va. Code § 20-97(3). For example, Virginia did not have jurisdiction over the marriage of two German citizens who continued to own property in that country and where the wife was on leave of absence from her job there. *Kewisch v. Fliedner-Kewisch*, 1995 Va. App. LEXIS 265 (Mar. 21, 1995). See also *Adoteye v. Adoteye*, 32 Va. App. 221, 527 S.E.2d 453 (2000), in which citizens of Ghana resided in Virginia as employees of the World Bank for most of their 20-year marriage. They bought a home in Fairfax County, but the wife's visa was conditioned upon her World Bank employment. The husband obtained a divorce in Ghana, including a custody award prior to wife's Virginia divorce action. However, *In re Hanano*, 2001 Va. Cir. LEXIS

169 (Jan. 23, 2001), on a plea in bar, the husband was unable to prove that wife was not a resident and domiciliary of Virginia despite entering the United States on temporary visas. Domicile and residency are distinct and separate issues, the determination of which present a mixed question of law and fact. *Adoteye v. Adoteye*, 32 Va. App. 221, 226, 527 S.E.2d 453, 456 (2000).

When a court obtains jurisdiction over a nonresident under the long-arm statute, such service shall have the same effect as service on the nonresident within Virginia. Va. Code § 8.01-320. This statute specifically includes divorce and annulment cases.

The suit is brought in the circuit court, which has general equity jurisdiction. Va. Code § 20-96. Jurisdiction is based upon domicile, according to Va. Code § 20-97, for domicile of a party to the marriage relationship results in the presence of the status of marriage within the state. *Williams v. North Carolina*, 317 U.S. 287, 63 S. Ct. 207, 87 L. Ed. 279 (1942); *Howe v. Howe*, 179 Va. 111, 18 S.E.2d 294 (1942). Domicile requires residence in the state with the intent of remaining there for an indefinite period, if not permanently. *Humphreys v. Humphreys*, 139 Va. 146, 123 S.E. 554 (1924).

Statutes enacted in 1989 regarding experimental family courts were repealed in 1999, including Va. Code §§ 16.1-296.1, 20-96.1, and 20-96.2. There are no longer any such courts, and all appeals from such courts have been completed.

Juvenile and domestic relations district courts and circuit courts are vested with concurrent jurisdiction over matters of child and spousal support. Va. Code § 16.1-241(A)(3), (L); Va. Code § 16.1-244(A); Va. Code § 20-79; *Ipsen v. Moxley*, 49 Va. App. 555, 642 S.E.2d 798 (2007). However, when a district court has entered a child or spousal support order, its jurisdiction ceases and its orders become inoperative upon entry of a decree that provides for child or spousal support in a suit for divorce instituted in any circuit court having jurisdiction. Va. Code § 20-79. Thus, orders of a district court requiring child or spousal support remain in full force and effect until reversed or modified by a court to which an appeal has been perfected, or until entry of a decree that provides for child or spousal support in a suit for divorce instituted in a circuit court. *Martin v. Bales*, 7 Va. App. 141, 371 S.E.2d 823 (1988). Similarly, an order for *pendente lite* support issued by a circuit court divests a district court of jurisdiction. *Ipsen v. Moxley*, 49 Va. App. 555, 642 S.E.2d 798 (2007); Va. Code § 20-79; see Va. Code § 20-103.

In *Calfee v. Calfee*, 29 Va. App. 88, 509 S.E.2d 552 (1999), the Court of Appeals explained that a circuit court order in a divorce case can be transferred to juvenile and domestic relations (J&D) court, restoring concurrent jurisdiction. Specifically, "jurisdiction lost by the J&D court to the circuit court 'in any suit for divorce' may be resumed by 'transfer to the J&D court' by the circuit court for 'enforcement of its orders' or 'after the entry of a decree of divorce' for any other matters pertaining to 'support' pursuant to Code § 20-79(c)." *Calfee v. Calfee*, 29 Va. App. 88, 509 S.E.2d 552 (1999). In addition, if a district court exercises its jurisdiction over support issues and "loses" its jurisdiction upon entry of a temporary *pendente lite* support order in a proceeding that ends in a nonsuit, which places the parties back to where they were before the proceeding was filed, the district court's support order is automatically *resumed* upon entry of the nonsuit order. *Ipsen v. Moxley*, 49 Va. App. 555, 642 S.E.2d 798 (2007).

An appeal on a decree of divorce, however, is under the exclusive jurisdiction of the circuit court. Furthermore, when one parent wants to appeal the child support award, the divorce case cannot be reinstated for awards of attorney's fees. *Calfee v. Calfee*, 29 Va. App. 88, 94, 509 S.E.2d 552 (1999).

For any issue arising out of the suit for divorce and other child custody, support and visitation cases, the judge shall consider whether to refer the parties to mediation, and may do so sua sponte or on motion of one of the parties. Upon referral, the parties must attend one evaluation session during which they and the mediator assess the case and decide whether to continue with mediation or with adjudication. Va. Code § 8.01-576.4 et seq., 20-124.2, and 20-124.4. When the parties are referred to mediation, the court shall set a return date. The parties shall notify the court in writing if the dispute is resolved prior to this return date. The court may, in its discretion, incorporate any mediated agreement into the terms of its final decree. Only if the court order incorporates the mediated agreement will the terms of the voluntary settlement agreement affect any outstanding court order.

The court shall vacate a mediated agreement or an incorporating order where the agreement was procured by fraud or duress, where it is unconscionable, where there was inadequate disclosure of financial or property information, or where there was evident partiality or misconduct by the mediator that prejudiced the rights of a party. Misconduct includes failure of the mediator to inform the parties in writing at the beginning of mediation:

(1)   that the mediator does not provide legal advice;

(2)   that an agreement will affect the legal rights of the parties;

(3)   that each party to mediation has the opportunity to consult with independent legal counsel at any time and is encouraged to do so;

and

(4) that each party should have any draft agreement reviewed by independent counsel prior to signing the agreement, or should waive this opportunity. Va. Code § 8.01-576.12.

A motion to vacate an order or agreement must be made within two years after the agreement is reached. If the motion is based upon fraud, however, it shall be made within two years after these grounds are discovered or reasonably should have been discovered. Va. Code § 8.01-576.12.

In cases of divorce, annulment, and separate maintenance, disposition shall be governed by provisions of Title 20. Appeals from cases of divorce, annulment, or separate maintenance shall be to the court of appeals as provided in Va. Code § 17.1-405. Preliminary protective orders shall not normally be suspended during appeals to the court of appeals or subsequent petitions for appeal to the Supreme Court on writ of error.

A notice of appeal filed by an attorney with a suspended license is a nullity, and the court of appeals lacks jurisdiction to consider the appeal. *Jones v. Jones*, 49 Va. App. 31, 635 S.E.2d 694 (2006).

The court of appeals has subject matter jurisdiction over appeals (1) from any final judgment, order, or decree of a circuit court in a domestic relations case; and (2) from any interlocutory decree or order entered in a domestic relations case that grants, dissolves, or denies an injunction, or that adjudicates the principles of a cause. See *de Haan v. de Haan*, 54 Va. App. 428, 680 S.E.2d 297 (2009); Va. Code § 17.1-405. In *de Haan*, an appellate court lacked subject matter jurisdiction over an appeal from an interlocutory order marked "final order by judge *pro tempore*," because the order resolved only some of the main objects of the divorce case, and thus did not adjudicate "the principles of a cause." See also *Chaplain v. Chaplain*, 54 Va. App. 762, 682 S.E.2d 108 (2009) (interlocutory order adjudicated principles of a cause and was appealable, when divorce was uncontested and only issue decided by trial court was validity of premarital agreement).

The court of appeals may award attorney's fees for the cost of defending an appeal from a nonfinal or interlocutory order in a divorce case, even though the court has determined that it lacks subject matter jurisdiction over the appeal. See *Kotara v. Kotara*, 55 Va. App. 705, 688 S.E.2d 908 (2010).

If a case is filed in an improper venue but no objection or transfer motion is made by the parties, the divorce will be valid under Va. Code §§ 8.01-264 and 8.01-265. If the venue is not a preferred venue, the court, on its own motion and upon notice to all parties, may transfer the suit to the preferred venue so long as such transfer is implemented within sixty days after service upon all parties. Va. Code § 8.01-264(D). See *Ragouzis v. Ragouzis,* 10 Va. App. 312, 391 S.E.2d 607 (1990), where the husband unsuccessfully sought reversal of a divorce decree from Pulaski County to which the case had been transferred by the court in the City of Radford, where the wife thought he was residing and where she had him personally served.

Venue in divorce cases is no longer jurisdictional. Va. Code § 8.01-261(19) provides that venue for divorce cases may lie where (1) the parties last cohabited, (2) the defendant resides if elected by the plaintiff, and (3) the plaintiff resides when an order of publication against the defendant may be issued. The remainder of this paragraph discusses when venue was a jurisdictional requirement in divorce cases. Venue, which is also jurisdictional, *Blankenship v. Blankenship,* 125 Va. 595, 100 S.E. 538 (1919), is in the county in which the defendant resides, Va. Code § 20-98, or where the parties last cohabited. *Colley v. Colley,* 204 Va. 225, 129 S.E.2d 630 (1963), defines "cohabitation" for this purpose as living together as man and wife, rather than as an act of intercourse. See also *Netzer v. Reynolds,* 231 Va. 444, 345 S.E.2d 291 (1986). The husband failed to show that the parties last cohabited in the City of Richmond as alleged in his complaint. He did offer evidence providing that the defendant was a resident of that city, but her residence was not used as a basis for venue in his complaint. The husband was allowed to amend his Bill of Complaint and adopt all prior proceedings, but the court would not grant a divorce on the current pleadings, for there must be no variance between pleadings and proof. *Overby v. Overby,* 24 Va. Cir. 491 (1970).

Although the spouse need not have been physically present for every day of the statutory period of six months to afford the court jurisdiction, it is essential that during such part of the year as there was actual absence from the state that the spouse maintained in good faith at least a dwelling somewhere in Virginia as a permanent abode. The establishment of a sojourn or transitory abode outside the state will not end a person's bona fide residency. *Blackson v. Blackson,* 40 Va. App. 507, 579 S.E.2d 704 (2003) (military wife's absence from state was temporary sojourn). The requirement of actual residence within the state was not changed by the new language of Va. Code § 20-97, which gives jurisdiction to a person in the armed forces or the spouse of such person only when the person "has lived with his or her spouse for a period of six months or more in the Commonwealth," and when this residence continues "until and at the time a suit for divorce or legal separation is commenced." However, if the person is stationed outside the United States, but was domiciled in Virginia for the six months preceding being stationed in the foreign country or territory, he or she will be deemed to have been domiciled in and a bona fide resident of Virginia for purposes of annulment or divorce. Va. Code § 20-97(3) [added 1991]. In 2009, Va. Code § 20-97(3) was extended to apply to foreign service officers as well as members of the armed forces.

In *Barbero v. Barbero,* 23 Va. Cir. 301 (1991), the wife lived in Virginia during most of the marriage while the husband was in the Navy. When he retired from the Navy, he went to New York with the hope of beginning a job there. The wife and the parties' child joined the husband in April of 1990, after she quit the job she had in Virginia Beach. They leased a condominium in New York, opened a joint checking account there and began to receive mail at the New York address. They also put their Virginia Beach property on the market. In the summer of 1990, the parties separated. Mr. Barbero remained in New York until July 20, when he returned to Virginia to complete the sale of the marital home. He remained in Virginia thereafter, while Mrs. Barbero continued to reside in New York. The circuit court held that he had not reestablished domicile and residence for six months in Virginia when he filed for divorce in August of 1990.

After separation of husband and wife, the wife may establish her own separate domicile regardless of the circumstances of the separation. Va. Code § 20-97. See *Blackson v. Blackson,* 40 Va. App. 507, 579 S.E.2d 704 (2003) (military wife established Virginia as domicile, left Virginia only as temporary sojourn to accompany husband to next military duty station, then returned to domicile).

When a husband voluntarily nonsuited a divorce action he had brought in Switzerland (after his wife expended considerable sums in defending the Swiss action, and subpoenaed his former live-in paramour to testify), the trial court did not err by refusing to give extraterritorial recognition by way of comity to the Swiss procedural default doctrines. However, the court did err in granting the husband a final divorce and attempting to retain jurisdiction to later adjudicate the equitable distribution issues without having a joint motion of the parties or making a finding of clear necessity due to the complexity of the property issues. The final decree was vacated, and the case remanded for distribution of the property contemporaneous with the adjudication of the divorce. *Clark v. Clark,* 11 Va. App. 286, 398 S.E.2d 82 (1990).

See generally 6A Michie's Jurisprudence *Divorce and Alimony* § 36.

## § 19.04    Marriage

The use of domicile, or a status adjudication, rather than personal jurisdiction, for dissolution of marriage requires that the status existed in the first place. Thus it will be necessary to prove, usually by introduction of a marriage certificate or testimony of witnesses to a wedding ceremony, that the parties were in fact duly married. Accordingly, a woman could not obtain a declaration of the validity of her marriage necessary before she could proceed with an action for divorce, because the purported husband had been married to another at the time of the ceremony. The marriage was void *ab initio* even though the woman thought that the "husband" was divorced at the time of the ceremony. *Hager v. Hager,* 3 Va. App. 415, 349 S.E.2d 908 (1986).

Where the marriage was performed in Virginia, copies of the certificate furnished by the State Registrar of Vital Statistics are prima facie evidence of the facts set forth therein. Va. Code § 32-353.27.

If the validity of the marriage was determined in a prior proceeding, such as a separation action, even if the proceeding was in another state, the fact will be res judicata in a divorce action between the parties. *Romeo v. Romeo,* 218 Va. 290, 237 S.E.2d 143 (1977).

## § 19.05   Grounds for Divorce in General

Va. Code § 20-91 sets forth grounds for absolute divorce. These include adultery, sodomy and buggery outside the marriage, desertion or cruelty after a waiting period of a year, imprisonment for a felony and sentence to and service of term of imprisonment for a year or more, and living separate and apart for one year (or six months where there are no children and the parties have executed a property settlement agreement).

The no-fault provision, Va. Code § 20-91(A)(9), became effective on July 1, 1960, and was found constitutional in *Hagen v. Hagen,* 205 Va. 791, 139 S.E.2d 821 (1965), despite claims that it was retroactive legislation, since the defendant "had no vested right to prevent her husband from securing a divorce." *Id.* at 796, 139 S.E.2d at 825. The statute was also upheld in *Canavos v. Canavos,* 205 Va. 744, 139 S.E.2d 825 (1965), despite the fact that recrimination is not a bar to the no-fault section. The no-fault ground was a recognition that society was better off calling a legal end to marriages that had ceased to function in fact.

The court of appeals has indicated that a court may grant a no-fault divorce despite the parties' agreement not to divorce and the husband's objections to divorce on religious grounds. In *Terrell v. Hackett,* 1993 Va. App. LEXIS 487 (Oct. 12, 1993), the husband had not sufficiently raised the issue below, but the court noted that he probably would not have succeeded in any event.

When dual or multiple grounds for divorce exist, such as cruelty, desertion, and living separate and apart, the trial court may properly grant a divorce on any single ground. *Fadness v. Fadness*, 52 Va. App. 833, 667 S.E.2d 857 (2008). See, e.g., *Robertson v. Robertson*, 215 Va. 425, 211 S.E.2d 41 (1975) (separation, desertion, adultery); *Williams v. Williams*, 14 Va. App. 217, 415 S.E.2d 252 (1992) (separation, adultery); *Konefal v. Konefal*, 18 Va. App. 612, 446 S.E.2d 153 (1994) (separation, desertion).

## § 19.06 Adultery

The crime of adultery, which also constitutes grounds for divorce, occurs when "any person, being married, voluntarily [has] sexual intercourse with any person not his or her spouse." Va. Code § 18.2-365.

Adultery may be proven even though at that time of the intercourse the guilty party is armed with an *a mensa* divorce decree based upon the spouse's cruelty or desertion. The *a mensa* decree authorizes the parties to live apart, but does not finally sever the matrimonial bond, nor the obligations commensurate with it. *Haskins v. Haskins*, 188 Va. 525, 50 S.E.2d 437 (1948). Since this is true, even though the husband deserted the wife before he committed adultery, a divorce could be granted against him based upon the dual grounds, *Robertson v. Robertson*, 215 Va. 425, 211 S.E.2d 41 (1975); *Bennett v. Bennett*, 187 Va. 631, 47 S.E.2d 312 (1948).

The one question that apparently remains is the effect of adultery after the grounds of absolute divorce have already matured, as opposed to during the waiting period before divorce is granted on grounds of separation. *Coe v. Coe*, 225 Va. 616, 303 S.E.2d 923 (1983). Where the alleged adultery by his wife occurred more than 15 years after separation, and where it was the husband's own fault and misconduct that caused the termination of the marriage, his spousal support obligation continued. *Wallace v. Wallace*, 1 Va. App. 183, 336 S.E.2d 27 (1985). This parallels the development in other states. See also *Surbey v. Surbey*, 5 Va. App. 119, 360 S.E.2d 873 (1987) (both parties were at fault in causing separation and neither party was entitled to assert adultery as grounds for divorce because of the doctrine of recrimination). Divorce in such cases can still be obtained on the separate and apart ground. See generally Wadlington, *Sexual Relations Following Separation or Divorce*, 63 Va. L. Rev. 249 (1977). Post-separation adultery can be the ground for divorce even though it need not have caused the deterioration of the marriage, since the commission of adultery during the separation period is "the one act most likely to frustrate and prevent a reconciliation." *Derby v. Derby*, 8 Va. App. 19, 378 S.E.2d 74 (1989).

Proof in an adultery case must be strict, satisfactory and conclusive, *Phipps v. Phipps*, 167 Va. 190, 188 S.E. 168 (1936); *Throckmorton v.*

*Throckmorton,* 86 Va. 768, 11 S.E. 289 (1890), for "as the offense here is an unnatural one and involves the commission of a crime, the proof offered to establish it must be such as would 'lead the guarded discretion of a reasonable and just man to a conclusion of guilt.' " *Holt v. Holt,* 174 Va. 120, 123, 5 S.E.2d 504 (1939). Strongly suspicious circumstances are inadequate, and care and circumspection should accompany consideration of the evidence. *Painter v. Painter,* 215 Va. 418, 211 S.E.2d 37 (1975) (kissing and embracing not sufficient). See also *Romero v. Colbow,* 27 Va. App. 88, 497 S.E.2d 516 (1998); *Hughes v. Hughes,* 33 Va. App. 141, 531 S.E.2d 645 (2000) (wife living in same home with male co-worker not sufficient). However, the evidence of this particularly secret type of activity must of necessity be circumstantial in most cases. *Kirby v. Kirby,* 159 Va. 544, 166 S.E. 484 (1932) (husband spent many evenings taking other woman, with whom he engaged in dry cleaning business, out to dinner, going on drives, and staying alone with her in the apartment he rented for her). *Gamer v. Gamer,* 16 Va. App. 335, 429 S.E.2d 618 (1993) (the other woman had moved rugs, furniture, cookbooks, kitchen utensils, and home decorations into the Gamer home; a television and VCR were in the master bedroom; a closet contained her clothes and shoes; and the wife observed her checkbook and other items listing the Gamer address). See also *Davidson v. Davidson,* 1996 Va. App. LEXIS 130 (Feb. 20, 1996), where the wife's investigator observed him visiting a woman's apartment in the morning regularly and the husband knowingly executed an affidavit admitting that he committed adultery with her. Compare *Holt v. Holt,* 174 Va. 120, 5 S.E.2d 504 (1939) (though suspicious and perhaps improper, wife's conduct not sufficient to establish adultery). Testimony of private detectives is given little weight unless corroborated. *Dooley v. Dooley,* 222 Va. 240, 278 S.E.2d 865 (1981); *Martin v. Martin,* 166 Va. 109, 184 S.E. 220 (1936); *Colbert v. Colbert,* 162 Va. 393, 200, 174 S.E. 660 (1934). However, the husband's admission of adultery both to his wife and another, coupled with proof of his living arrangements with the other woman, were sufficient to support a charge of adultery. *Dodge v. Dodge,* 2 Va. App. 238, 343 S.E.2d 363 (1986). See also *Pommerenke v. Pommerenke,* 7 Va. App. 241, 372 S.E.2d 630 (1988) (wife testified that she and one VanWeel had an affair in Holland, and he later visited the Pommerenke's home for an extended period of time. Mrs. Pommerenke and VanWeel were seen in various stages of undress in the home. Husband was allowed to amend his complaint to add his count for adultery that he did not discover until after the parties had separated and filed for divorce on other grounds. Court found that adultery was proved). A divorce cannot be granted on the grounds of adultery when a married woman engages in sexual relations with another woman, because sexual intercourse cannot occur between them. *Glaze v. Glaze*, 46 Va. Cir. 333 (1998).

Two cases reflect the problems inherent in proof of an adultery case. Where a private investigator testified that the wife had been visited in her home until after midnight by the co-respondent, and where the husband's former attorney admitted to falling asleep on the wife's couch and therefore spending the night there, and visiting her on vacation where he stayed in the same motel but in a different room, adultery was not proven. *Dooley v. Dooley*, 222 Va. 240, 278 S.E.2d 865 (1981). In this case, the wife's explanation was that she was allowed to "date," and had done nothing improper. However, when the errant wife spent the entire night in the co-respondent's apartment, and offered no explanation for her conduct, adultery was proven. *Coe v. Coe*, 225 Va. 616, 303 S.E.2d 923 (1983). See also *Fu v. Fu*, 1994 Va. App. LEXIS 314 (May 24, 1994); *Watts v. Watts*, 40 Va. App. 685, 581 S.E.2d 224 (2003) (husband gave no explanation for covert, clandestine meetings with female coworker). But see *Seemann v. Seemann*, 233 Va. 290, 355 S.E.2d 884 (1987) (denial of sexual relations; wife's credibility supported by her religious convictions).

See generally 6A Michie's Jurisprudence *Divorce and Alimony* §§ 7–11.

## § 19.07  Desertion

The fault ground for desertion requires not only a willful separation by one spouse but also an intent carried through the statutory period of one year not to return to the unoffending spouse. *Markley v. Markley*, 145 Va. 596, 134 S.E. 536 (1926). There need not be an offer of reconciliation before a spouse can obtain a divorce based upon the other's desertion. Va. Code § 20-102; see *Colbert v. Colbert*, 162 Va. 393, 174 S.E. 660 (1934) (before statute). The intent of the non-deserting spouse is not relevant, and the deserted spouse need not make an offer of reconciliation upon the other spouse deserting the marriage. *Hill v. Thomas*, 2018 Va. App. LEXIS 102 (April 17, 2018).

If the deserting spouse was mentally ill during the time of separation, so that there could be neither intent to remain separate nor the desire to return, formerly there could be no cause of action for desertion. *Wright v. Wright*, 125 Va. 526, 99 S.E. 515 (1919) (decided when desertion required three years, and now rendered obsolete by Va. Code § 20-93). In such a case, there could also be a divorce under the no-fault separation ground, Va. Code § 20-91(9), since the insanity of the defendant does not preclude the running of the time required. Compare *Crittenden v. Crittenden*, 210 Va. 76, 168 S.E.2d 115 (1969), decided before amendment of this section.

When husband and wife married, the wife was a Baptist while her husband was Jewish. She converted to Judaism shortly thereafter. After the birth of the couple's son, however, the wife became intensely interested in and a convert to the Jehovah's Witnesses faith. The wife soon filed for separate maintenance while the husband sued for divorce on grounds of desertion and asked for custody of the child. The Circuit Court for the City of Richmond held in *Plotkin v. Plotkin,* 22 Va. Cir. 435 (1975), that the wife's religious persuasion, standing alone, was neither a ground for divorce nor the basis for an award of custody. Her behavior in pursuing the tenets of her new faith did not amount to an act of cruelty justifying the husband's turning her from the marital domicile nor refusing to reconcile unless she abandoned her religion. He was therefore guilty of constructive desertion, which barred his claim for divorce. However, he was successful in obtaining custody because "the zeal with which the defendant [wife] has and will continue to devote herself to the furtherance and advancement of her religious convictions will necessarily relegate the child to a place of secondary importance."

One spouse is not guilty of legal desertion in separating from the other after the institution of a suit for divorce or during its pendency. *Byrd v. Byrd,* 232 Va. 115, 348 S.E.2d 262 (1986) (no desertion although bill of complaint unsuccessful, since wife's suit was not frivolous); *Roberts v. Roberts,* 223 Va. 736, 292 S.E.2d 370 (1982); *Painter v. Painter,* 215 Va. 418, 211 S.E.2d 37 (1975); *Plattner v. Plattner,* 202 Va. 263, 117 S.E.2d 128 (1960).

There need not be a physical leaving of the marital home by the deserting spouse, but in such cases there must be more than an unjustified refusal to engage in sexual relations. There must be a complete abandonment of marital duties "to such an extent as to render the marriage state well nigh intolerable and impossible to be endured." *Chandler v. Chandler,* 132 Va. 418, 430–31, 112 S.E. 856, 861 (1922) (desertion). See also *Jamison v. Jamison,* 3 Va. App. 644, 352 S.E.2d 719 (1987) (willful withdrawal of sexual privileges without just cause or excuse and the willful breach and neglect of other marital duties; desertion). Compare *Goodwyn v. Goodwyn,* 222 Va. 53, 278 S.E.2d 813 (1981); *Preston v. Preston,* 1998 Va. App. LEXIS 17 (Jan. 20, 1998); *Davis v. Davis,* 1998 Va. App. LEXIS 307 (June 2, 1998). (no desertion).

An allegation, without more, that one spouse left without any reason and could not be found at time of trial will not constitute desertion. There must be evidence of the conduct of the parties prior to separation as well as testimony concerning the period since separation regarding any attempts at reconciliation. Without this, the departure would just as easily be consistent with a mutual separation as with desertion. *Walker v. Walker,* 120 Va. 410, 91 S.E. 180 (1917). See also *De Mott v. De Mott,* 198 Va. 22, 92 S.E.2d 342 (1956) (husband's witnesses only corroborated the fact that wife left the marital home). Compare *Pillow v. Pillow,* 13 Va. App. 271, 410 S.E.2d 407 (1991), where husband left the marital home to move in with another woman with whom he had been having romantic relations for several months, and refused his wife's invitation to move back to the marital home. The trial court correctly granted the wife a divorce on grounds of desertion rather than the no-fault ground; see also *Amos v. Amos,* 1993 Va. App. LEXIS 474 (Oct. 5, 1993) (credible evidence showing that husband left marital home, contacted a realtor to sell home, wrote utility companies seeking to discontinue service, signed a lease indicating that he and one son would be sole occupants, and moved out his furniture). There would also be no desertion where one party left the other to go into the armed services. *Moltz v. Moltz,* 182 Va. 737, 30 S.E.2d 561 (1944). However, long continued absence without detaining cause is the best proof of intent to desert. See *Dinsmore v. Dinsmore,* 128 Va. 403, 104 S.E. 785 (1920), where the husband indicated that "he did not intend to support or live any longer with his wife." See also *Collier v. Collier,* 2 Va. App. 125, 341 S.E.2d 827 (1986) (physical act of leaving the marital home, coupled with a letter showing the husband's intent to desert without legal justification, were sufficient to support the award of an absolute divorce). There will be no divorce based upon desertion where a mutually consented to separation agreement is in effect. Cf. *Barnes v. Barnes,* 16 Va. App. 98, 428 S.E.2d 294 (1993), (both parties had accepted that the marriage had ended, both intended to separate at some time in future, and the husband acquiesced in the separation); *Bryant v. Bryant,* 1994 Va. App. LEXIS 17 (Jan. 11, 1994). However, *Gerwe v. Gerwe,* 1996 Va. App. LEXIS 21 (Jan. 16, 1996), found that the husband had deserted the wife when he left the home and moved in with another woman, even though the marriage was "dead" since the spouses had had no relations, sexual or otherwise, for many years. But see *Kerr v. Kerr,* 6 Va. App. 620, 371 S.E.2d 30 (1988) (no desertion where wife refused to move with husband when transferred to another city by his employer; leaving marital home is justified when a spouse's conduct creates conditions so intolerable that the other spouse cannot reasonably be expected to remain in the home); *Rigsby v. Rigsby,* 13 Va. Cir. 86 (1987) (no desertion because wife free of legal fault for leaving marital home although evidence insufficient to support a finding of cruelty). *Butler v. Butler,* 145 Va. 85, 133 S.E. 756 (1926) (desertion shown where husband in fact wanted reconciliation but wife refused).

The husband generally has the duty of establishing the place of abode for the parties. The wife has a duty to acquiesce in his selection provided that it is not unreasonable, arbitrary or unjust, nor used to provoke a dissolution of the marriage. *Martin v. Martin,* 202 Va. 769, 120 S.E.2d 471 (1961) (desertion found where the wife insisted on moving to Florida); *Graves v. Graves,* 193 Va. 659, 70 S.E.2d 339 (1952) (desertion found where wife insisted upon living with her relatives in overcrowded conditions). This privilege of establishing domicile is of doubtful constitutional validity.

The husband told the wife to "get out" on two occasions after quarrels over financial matters. Without more, this did not constitute sufficient cause for a divorce on grounds of constructive desertion. *Rowand v. Rowand,* 215 Va. 344, 210 S.E.2d 149 (1974). See also *Brawand v. Brawand,* 1 Va. App. 305, 338 S.E.2d 651 (1986) (husband requested during arguments that wife leave the home).

A husband should not have been granted a divorce based upon his wife's desertion when she left the marital home in order to preserve her health. Remission of her condition of multiple sclerosis was threatened by the presence of the husband's son in the home, since he actively sought to get the wife to leave, and by the husband's refusal to obtain household help for the wife. *Breschel v. Breschel,* 221 Va. 208, 269 S.E.2d 363 (1980). She was free from legal fault and therefore could be awarded support. See also *Capps v. Capps,* 216 Va. 382, 219 S.E.2d 898 (1975).

These cases, where the wife was justified in leaving the marital home, should be compared to *D'Auria v. D'Auria,* 1 Va. App. 455, 340 S.E.2d 164 (1986) (wife's physician testified that her physical problems were the result of severe anxiety in contemplation of divorce; court found she was without legal justification for leaving marital home); and *Rexrode v. Rexrode,* 1 Va. App. 385, 339 S.E.2d 544 (1986). See also *Sprott v. Sprott,* 233 Va. 238, 355 S.E.2d 881 (1987); and *Reid v. Reid,* 7 Va. App. 553, 375 S.E.2d 533 (1989), where wife was not justified in removing herself from the marriage where there had been a gradual breakdown in the marriage, *Pillow v. Pillow,* 13 Va. App. 271, 410 S.E.2d 407 (1991); (case decided before Va. Code § 20-107.1 was amended to allow alimony in appropriate cases despite marital fault); *Garland v. Garland,* 19 Va. Cir. 131 (1990); *Hairfield v. Hairfield,* 18 Va. Cir. 256 (1989); and see *Dexter v. Dexter,* 7 Va. App. 36, 371 S.E.2d 816 (1988) (husband failed to prove that wife willfully breached and neglected significant marital duties where he made the decision to voluntarily leave the marital residence as the "gentlemanly thing" to do); *Kerr v. Kerr,* 6 Va. App. 620, 371 S.E.2d 30 (1988) (no desertion where wife refused to move with husband to another city when he came home intoxicated 4 or 5 times a week and frequently and profanely insulted her).

In order for there to be constructive desertion entitling the departing spouse to a divorce, the conduct of the other must amount to grounds for a divorce, usually based upon cruelty. *Ringgold v. Ringgold,* 128 Va. 485, 104 S.E. 836 (1920); *Ford v. Ford,* 200 Va. 674, 107 S.E.2d 397 (1959); *Baytop v. Baytop,* 199 Va. 388, 100 S.E.2d 14 (1957) (husband was unfaithful to wife; refused to make a home for her). Compare *Edwards v. Cuthbert,* 184 Va. 502, 36 S.E.2d 1 (1945) (no constructive desertion where wife unhappy in husband's family's home through no fault of husband). *Zinkhan v. Zinkhan,* 2 Va. App. 200, 342 S.E.2d 658 (1986) (husband established desertion on wife's part; although divorce was granted on one year separation ground, no spousal support could be awarded); *McLaughlin v. McLaughlin,* 2 Va. App. 463, 346 S.E.2d 535 (1986) (no spousal support where wife had previously expressed a desire to end the marriage and left after quarrel; cruelty claims not corroborated). However, the court of appeals affirmed a divorce granted on constructive desertion based on the husband's cross-dressing. See *Rakes v. Rakes,* 2019 Va. App. LEXIS 56 (March 12, 2019). When the husband always provided the wife with food, clothing, and a home, and never struck her or harmed her in any way, she was guilty of desertion in leaving the marital home because she had no legal justification for leaving. The wife argued that she was deprived of her station in the household and financial decisions because the parties' son had been given the sole responsibility of the checking account. *Lee v. Lee,* 13 Va. App. 118, 408 S.E.2d 769 (1991). Her desertion would be taken into account upon remand in determining the amount of spousal support to which she would be entitled. Compare *Johnson v. Johnson,* 1993 Va. App. LEXIS 214 (June 22, 1993), where the husband constructively deserted his wife. The wife testified that the husband continually sexually abused her, using sexual devices that caused her great pain. Her pleas to discontinue the practice were ignored, and she eventually had to undergo psychological counseling. Her sister and a son testified that the devices existed in the marital home, and she introduced a magazine addressed to the husband and offering similar devices for sale.

There should not be desertion if one spouse leaves to preserve the health or safety of a minor child of either spouse. Even an omission or refusal to provide necessary care, or permission for activity that allows a child's life or health to be seriously injured constitutes felony child abuse. Va. Code § 18.2-371.1 [amended 1988]. In cases involving child abuse, spouses are no longer disqualified from testifying. Va. Code § 19.2-271.2; and see *Osborne v. Commonwealth,* 214 Va. 691, 204 S.E.2d 289 (1974), discussed in § 11.03.

The fact that the plaintiff sought a reconciliation after a period of separation that defendant was not at fault in causing did not create desertion on defendant's part. *McDaniel v. McDaniel,* 175 Va. 402, 9 S.E.2d 360 (1940).

### § 19.08    Cruelty

Although normally the circumstances supporting a divorce for cruelty will involve physical violence or fear of violence, there are some cases in which marital misconduct is so severe that a divorce will be granted where there is no physical cruelty whatsoever. *Ringgold v. Ringgold,* 128 Va. 485, 104 S.E. 836 (1920) (husband continually abused wife by referring to incident in her childhood and, because of his religious fervor, refused to take her back into his home until she was "purged"). In another example, where the wife's alcohol problem caused her to neglect all the household duties and resulted in both public embarrassment of the husband and his continual stomach disorders, a divorce for cruelty was properly granted. *Hoffecker v. Hoffecker,* 200 Va. 119, 104 S.E.2d 771 (1958). See also *Taylor v. Taylor,* 1995 Va. App. LEXIS 51 (Jan. 17, 1995).

Mere coolness and denial of sexual intercourse, where other marital duties are performed, will not constitute cruelty or desertion. *Aichner v. Aichner,* 215 Va. 624, 626, 212 S.E.2d 278, 279 (1975) (wife refused husband sexual intercourse during last year of 25 year marriage when, she claimed, husband worked long hours, lacked affection for her, and displayed no warmth towards her). Mere problems between spouses, caused by unruly tempers, lack of patience, and uncongenial natures, do not require a court to grant a fault divorce. The cruelty must render the association intolerable. Although husband and wife in *Davis v. Davis,* 1994 Va. App. LEXIS 146 (Mar. 22, 1994) (not designated for publication), endured what the court characterized "a deplorable marital situation," the conditions did not substantiate either's claim that one spouse could not reasonably be expected to remain in the marriage due to the other's fault. Rather than one party's specific offense, the couple's drinking problems, constant bickering and lack of compassion caused the dissolution of their marriage. *Id.* at *6–*7.

In *Thomas v. Thomas,* 1996 Va. App. LEXIS 738 (Nov. 26, 1996), husband and wife had kept their money separate, each paying for specific expenses during the marriage. Mr. Thomas failed on numerous occasions to pay the expenses that he had accepted as his responsibilities. Mrs. Thomas, who was also employed throughout the marriage, also cared for the parties' children, maintained the home, and supported her husband's career by entertaining his colleagues. During the last ten years of the marriage, husband and wife had sexual relations only once. On that occasion, Mr. Thomas told his wife that he fantasized about being homosexual. She later found a register from a bed and breakfast establishment that caters to homosexuals, revealing that he had spent a weekend there with another man. She also found correspondence that he had received through a homosexual pen pal club, along with homosexual pornographic videos and paraphernalia. In November 1993, Mr. Thomas left the marital home and never returned. Mrs. Thomas sued for divorce on grounds of cruelty and constructive desertion, alleging particularly his homosexuality, which he admitted to under oath. Mrs. Thomas did not condone her husband's homosexuality. The evidence showed that at the time the parties had sexual relations, she believed that his homosexuality was a fantasy. When she discovered that it truly existed, she terminated marital relations. The wife was properly awarded 70% of the equity in the marital home.

However, in *Roberts v. Roberts*, 49 Va. Cir. 422 (1999), the wife's attempt to obtain a cruelty-based divorce failed when there was some evidence of "angry verbal confrontations, rudeness, vulgarity, snatching and slapping, pushing and shoving, and other sallies of passion." These incidents were infrequent, did not cause bodily harm, and "did not make family life well nigh intolerable." The parties were "quite young and very immature" and did date and have sexual relations after separation.

Although there may be provocation of acts of physical violence, these cannot be out of proportion to the other spouse's retaliatory conduct. *Graham v. Graham*, 210 Va. 608, 616, 172 S.E.2d 724, 729 (1970); see also *Wimbrow v. Wimbrow*, 208 Va. 141, 156 S.E.2d 598 (1967).

The acts of cruelty are cumulative, augmented by each additional act, although at first they are condoned to a certain point. *Miller v. Miller*, 140 Va. 424, 125 S.E. 220 (1924); see also *Wimbrow v. Wimbrow*, 208 Va. 141, 156 S.E.2d 598 (1967). A single act of violence will not constitute cruelty unless so atrocious as to endanger life, or unless it causes a reasonable apprehension of danger in the future. *De Mott v. De Mott*, 198 Va. 22, 92 S.E.2d 342 (1956) (no cruelty where husband grabbed wife, struck her, and threatened her with butcher knife on one occasion only, when wife stayed with husband for five days thereafter). The act must have occurred before institution of the divorce action. *Beckner v. Beckner*, 204 Va. 580, 132 S.E.2d 715 (1963) (shooting gun and throwing glass bottle during pendency of suit not cruelty).

A single act of cruelty was sufficient recrimination to bar husband from obtaining fault divorce on wife's prior desertion, when the conduct was so severe and atrocious that it endangered her life and caused her to sustain serious and permanent injuries (paralysis from waist down and confinement to a wheelchair as result of husband's shooting her). *Davis v. Davis,* 8 Va. App. 12, 377 S.E.2d 640 (1989).

The charges must be clearly proved by witnesses, stating the facts rather than their opinions. *Prindes v. Prindes,* 193 Va. 463, 69 S.E.2d 332 (1952). See also *Gottlieb v. Gottlieb,* 19 Va. App. 77, 448 S.E.2d 666 (1994). *Tucker v. Tucker,* 1993 Va. App. LEXIS 291 (July 20, 1993).

See generally 6A Michie's Jurisprudence *Divorce and Alimony* §§ 13–16.

### § 19.09    Imprisonment for Felony

This ground for divorce is allowed by Va. Code § 20-91 where a party subsequent to the marriage has been convicted of a felony and sentenced to confinement for more than one year, and has been confined for such felony. Cohabitation cannot have been resumed after knowledge of the confinement. The remaining question is whether parole after serving only a short portion of the sentence will affect the conjugal rights (as will a pardon, according to the statute).

In *Bandas v. Bandas,* 25 Va. Cir. 492 (1991), the husband, who had been convicted and sentenced for a felony in 1986, argued that the wife had resumed cohabitation when she visited him several times at the penitentiary. The court found that the parties did not resume cohabitation, for it implies a continuing condition of living together and carrying out of the marital responsibilities. Therefore, the husband was not faultless, and his fault was recrimination against the wife's proven adultery. In *Sealock v. Sealock,* 26 Va. Cir. 379 (1971), the wife obtained a divorce based on grounds of separation although the husband had been imprisoned for a parole violation.

### § 19.10    Living Separate and Apart

The no-fault ground does not take precedence over other causes of action for divorce. If other proven grounds exist, the court is not obliged to grant a divorce under the separation statute, Va. Code § 20-91(A)(9), to the exclusion of other fault grounds. *Robertson v. Robertson,* 215 Va. 425, 211 S.E.2d 41 (1975).

Amended Va. Code § 20-121.02 allows a cause of action for no-fault divorce to be brought without the filing of an amended bill of complaint, whatever the original grounds for divorce.

Amended Va. Code § 20-91(A)(9) allows a no-fault divorce when the parties have lived separate and apart for a period of one year. A bill of complaint for a no-fault divorce that is filed prior to expiration of the one-year separation period will be dismissed for failure to state a claim on which relief may be granted. *Harrell v. Harrell*, 272 Va. 652, 636 S.E.2d 391 (2006). However, this period is shortened to a six-month separation if the parties have entered into a written separation agreement and they have no minor children. A recent amendment to this section clarifies the word "children" to include children born of either party or adopted by one or both parties.

Va. Code § 20-121.02 provides that either party to a divorce sought on fault grounds or a divorce from bed and board may move the court for divorce under Va. Code § 20-91(A)(9) (the separate and apart section) once the statutory period has expired. In cases where there are no children born of either party or adopted by both or either, this would be six months; otherwise it would take one year. The complaint or cross bill need not be amended. The court did not err in granting a divorce on the no-fault ground even though the husband proved his wife's desertion and adultery. *Best v. Best,* 1993 Va. App. LEXIS 471 (Sept. 28, 1993). The conduct will, of course, be taken into account in determining spousal support.

When both parties are sane, there must be an intention to separate to establish the commencement of the statutory period. Thus, when the husband went overseas in connection with his employment, but wrote to an attorney two years later to institute divorce proceedings, the period of separation began at the later time, for "there must be proof of an intention on the part of at least one of the parties to discontinue permanently the marital cohabitation, followed by physical separation" without any cohabitation. *Hooker v. Hooker,* 215 Va. 415, 417, 211 S.E.2d 34, 36 (1975). Otherwise, many extended separations required for other reasons "could ripen into 'instant divorce' without the salutary period of contemplation required by the statute during which the parties have an opportunity for reconciliation." See also 24 Am. Jur. 2d *Divorce and Separation* § 184 at 305. In *Sealock v. Sealock,* 26 Va. Cir. 379 (1971), the wife obtained a divorce based on grounds of separation although husband had been imprisoned for a parole violation (decided at time when separation was required to be for two years without cohabitation). The parties' prenuptial agreement cannot substitute for the separation agreement required for the six-month separate-and-apart ground of Va. Code § 20-91(A)(9)(a). *McGee v. McGee,* 48 Va. Cir. 457 (1999).

The term "separate and apart" means more than mere physical separation. The separation must be coupled with the intention in the mind of at least one spouse to live separate and apart permanently. This intention must have occurred at the beginning of the one year period. *Hooker v. Hooker, supra.* This does not mean, however, that when the parties initially began living apart, they thought their separation was permanent. In reality, the parties usually separate on a trial or temporary basis at first. In *Andrews v. Creacey*, 56 Va. App. 606, 696 S.E.2d 218 (2010), an incapacitated husband, suffering from progressive dementia, was granted a divorce, when he formed an intent to divorce and then lived separate and apart from his wife without any cohabitation and without interruption for a period of more than one year. It did not matter whether the husband remained competent during the one-year period, in the absence of any evidence that he changed his mind or abandoned his intent to divorce.

Although apparently some judges have been granting divorces based upon this ground while the parties still reside under the same roof, see *Brightly v. Brightly,* C-68816 (1981), appeal denied, 82-0156 (Va. S. Ct. 1982), this seems to fly in the face of the *Hooker* statement that such situations might ripen into "instant divorce." *Doggett v. Doggett,* 5 Va. Cir. 349, 350 (1986) ("abandonment—desertion—[and thus, living separate and apart] may be as complete under the same shelter as if oceans rolled between"). See generally 20 U. Rich. L. Rev. 811, 823 (1986). But see *Reynolds v. Reynolds,* 9 Va. Cir. 423 (1977) (not sufficient to constitute living separate and apart if all marital duties and relations have not ceased); *Yane v. Yane,* 8 Va. Cir. 336 (1986) (cohabitation under Va. Code § 20-91(9)(a) means "having dwelled together under the same roof with more or less permanency," so there could be no divorce even though parties slept in different rooms and spent no time together as husband and wife); See also *Davis v. Davis*, 49 Va. Cir. 276 (1999), where the couple had not separated for purposes of the statute since they still functioned as a marital unit. *Hairfield v. Hairfield,* 18 Va. Cir. 256 (1989). See also *Brown v. Brown,* 12 Va. Cir. 525 (1983) (there was cohabitation where parties were staying in same household, wife occasionally prepared meals and husband did chores around the house and occasionally went shopping with wife); *Konefal v. Konefal,* 18 Va. App. 612, 446 S.E.2d 153 (1994); *Higgs v. Higgs,* 12 Va. Cir. 509 (1983) (cohabitation invalidating executory portions of separation agreement where parties lived together as frequently and regularly as their schedule would permit "in discharge of their mutual conjugal duties"). Cf. *Reel v. Reel,* 12 Va. Cir. 482 (1981) (alimony granted although parties still living under same roof; cohabitation "includes the idea of services rendered one to the other, mutual society and companionship, aid and comfort, protection and conjugal affection . . . . Sexual intercourse is a usual, important, but not necessarily required, element of the concept."). In *Bchara v. Bchara*, 38 Va. App. 302, 563 S.E.2d 398 (2002), a wife was granted a divorce on the basis of living separate and apart for one year, even though her husband remained in the family home during the period of separation. After discovering a videotape of the husband with another woman, the wife moved the husband's belongings to a guest bedroom, and stopped depositing money into a joint bank account, going to church with the husband, and attending the husband's family's functions, all with intent of remaining permanently apart from the husband. *Emrich v. Emrich,* 9 Va. App. 288, 387 S.E.2d 274 (1989) (The wife was justified in not filing an answer or appearing at deposition when her husband had resumed cohabitation with her and had told her that the divorce suit would be dismissed. The trial court should not have granted a divorce on grounds of living separate and apart without cohabitation and without interruption for more than one year.).

In addition to problems of collusion that are presented by such a situation, there is also absent a tangible sign of when the parties in fact entertained the intent to live separate and apart. A written agreement between them, or a judgment for nonsupport, might satisfy the evidentiary problems and afford the parties the ability to be free from the consortium of the other implied by the statute. See *Knox v. Commonwealth,* 225 Va. 504, 304 S.E.2d 4 (1983). Compare *Weishaupt v. Commonwealth,* 227 Va. 389, 315 S.E.2d 847 (1984) (rape conviction possible after separation for 11 months and consultation regarding divorce proceedings), with *Kizer v. Commonwealth,* 228 Va. 256, 321 S.E.2d 291 (1984) (no rape conviction possible where no clear intention that the marriage was at an end that was communicated to husband).

By statute, support may be awarded to either spouse after the decree for divorce under this section, unless there exists a fault cause of action against such party. Va. Code § 20-91(A)(9).

See generally 6A Michie's Jurisprudence *Divorce and Alimony* § 23.1.

## § 19.11 Defenses to the Action

Condonation, or resumption of cohabitation after learning of conduct constituting grounds for divorce, Va. Code § 20-94, is a matter of specific affirmative defense which must be specially pleaded, and the burden of proof of such defense is upon the defendant. *White v. White,* 121 Va. 244, 92 S.E. 811 (1917). The matter may be raised by the court on its own motion, denying divorce. *Martin v. Martin,* 166 Va. 109, 184 S.E. 220 (1936). A single act of intercourse after knowledge of adultery will suffice. *Tarr v. Tarr,* 184 Va. 443, 35 S.E.2d 401 (1945). However, the voluntary cohabitation need not be for a lengthy period. *Huddle v. Huddle,* 206 Va. 535, 145 S.E.2d 167 (1965) (ten days, husband continued to be suspicious that wife pregnant by another). Repetition of the misconduct revives the original ground of adultery. *McKee v. McKee,* 206 Va. 527, 145 S.E.2d 163 (1965). There must be an intent by the forgiving spouse to resume the marital relationship. For a modern example, see *Brundage v. Brundage*, 1995 Va. App. LEXIS 521 (May 23, 1995), where the court found that substantial evidence demonstrated that the husband knew of wife's ongoing adulterous relationship prior to the parties' reconciliation.

Cohabitation is more than sexual intercourse.

> Separate lives is the issue, not separate roofs. To continue to occupy the same marital home after several alleged acts of adultery; to partake of the hospitality, comfort, and satisfaction of enjoying the same shelter, its contents and surroundings; to accept the reputation, privileges, amenities and immunities of wedlock and apparent marital accord; the protection, security and safety of male companionship, or at least such presence, is enough to sustain the presumption of matrimonial cohabitation.

*Moran v. Moran*, 12 Va. Cir. 340 (1988). See also *Konicki v. Konicki*, 32 Va. Cir. 368 (1994). Similarly, cohabitation was found in *Emrich v. Emrich*, 9 Va. App. 288, 387 S.E.2d 274 (1989), where the wife failed to answer the complaint or to appear at deposition because the husband had moved back into the marital home for about one month following filing of the divorce complaint, and had told her that the action would be dismissed.

See generally 6A Michie's Jurisprudence *Divorce and Alimony* § 25.

In a desertion case brought against the husband, if he had repented and made any overture to his wife with the intention of ending the separation and if conduct on her part amounting to cruelty had prevented the cohabitation, that would have justified his continuing to live separate from her and *she* would have been guilty of desertion. *Cumming v. Cumming*, 127 Va. 16, 17, 102 S.E. 572 (1920) (dicta). However, an offer of reconciliation that contained no apology or excuse for the plaintiff's actions was not in the spirit of a bona fide offer. *McDaniel v. McDaniel*, 175 Va. 402, 9 S.E.2d 360 (1940).

Cohabitation between spouses during the pendency of the divorce suit is a sufficient reason for the defendant's belief that the plaintiff had abandoned the suit and a justification for not appearing to make a defense. The burden of proving such cohabitation and condonation rests upon the assailant of the decree. *Ware v. Ware*, 203 Va. 189, 193, 194, 123 S.E.2d 357, 360 (1962).

Res judicata will be a defense to all divorces except those based upon separation under Va. Code § 20-91(9). *Robinette v. Robinette*, 153 Va. 342, 149 S.E. 493 (1929); *McDaniel v. McDaniel*, 175 Va. 402, 9 S.E.2d 360 (1940). However, as in all cases of res judicata, the only issues barred will be those actually adjudicated in the first proceeding. For example, a divorce decree entered after publication was not a determination that the former spouse was alive at the time. *Simpson v. Simpson,* 162 Va. 621, 631, 175 S.E. 320, 324 (1934). However, when a complaint was demurred to and the demurrer sustained on the grounds that the allegations were indefinite and ambiguous, and a later complaint was filed based upon the same facts and allegations, the second bill was appropriately dismissed. *Griffin v. Griffin,* 183 Va. 443, 32 S.E.2d 700 (1945).

See generally 6A Michie's Jurisprudence *Divorce and Alimony* § 45.

The insanity of the defendant to a divorce proceeding was enough to invalidate the judgment of divorce (and plaintiff's subsequent remarriage) where plaintiff had not divulged to the trial court that defendant was insane and that he had agreed to her placement in West Virginia, where she was proceeded against by constructive service only. *Taylor v. Taylor,* 159 Va. 338, 165 S.E. 414 (1932). The failure to disclose her insanity amounted to fraud.

The fact that plaintiff has not complied with temporary alimony or child support orders should not result in dismissal of the divorce action. *Davis v. Davis,* 206 Va. 381, 143 S.E.2d 835 (1965). Other remedies, such as the requirement of Va. Code § 20-114 providing for the discretionary ordering of a recognizance, are appropriate in such cases.

Although there may be provocation of acts of physical violence that preclude an action for cruelty, these cannot be out of proportion to the other spouse's retaliatory conduct. *Graham v. Graham,* 210 Va. 608, 616, 172 S.E.2d 724, 729 (1970); see also *Wimbrow v. Wimbrow,* 208 Va. 141, 156 S.E.2d 598 (1967).

Collusion is a defense to a divorce, but the divorce procured through collusion cannot be attacked by either party. *Scott v. Scott,* 142 Va. 31, 39, 128 S.E. 599 (1925). There is no innocent party to be granted relief in such cases, because both are guilty of attempting to commit a fraud upon the court.

The defense of recrimination does not apply to the no-fault ground of separation, Va. Code § 20-91. In other cases, if plaintiff has also been guilty of conduct justifying a divorce, it may be recriminated as a defense and the suit dismissed. *Kirn v. Kirn,* 138 Va. 132, 120 S.E. 850 (1924) (wife guilty of desertion and adultery, husband of cruelty, no divorce to either). See also *Wallace v. Wallace,* 1 Va. App. 183, 336 S.E.2d 27 (1985) (recrimination would prevent husband's obtaining a divorce from wife based upon her adultery when his unjustified conduct had precipitated their separation 15 years before); *Surbey v. Surbey,* 5 Va. App. 119, 360 S.E.2d 873 (1987) (both parties were at fault in causing separation, and both committed adultery following separation so that recrimination barred either from using adultery as grounds for divorce); See also *Davis v. Davis,* 8 Va. App. 12, 377 S.E.2d 640 (1989) (recrimination barred husband's suit for desertion when he shot and seriously wounded wife following separation).

See 6A Michie's Jurisprudence *Divorce and Alimony* § 26.

In *Hollis v. Hollis,* 16 Va. App. 74, 427 S.E.2d 233 (1993), the court of appeals found that the husband had proved the wife's connivance, or prior consent to his adultery. The wife wrote several handwritten letters that were admitted into evidence, including one hoping that the husband and the other woman would "rent an apartment and live together for one year as man and wife everyday." When the husband and the other woman first had sexual relations at the Greenbrier Hotel, they received flowers and a card from Mrs. Hollis. The card said, "My very best wishes to you both today, to your new beginning." She therefore was not legally injured because she had consented to the misconduct alleged as grounds for divorce.

See generally C.J.S. *Divorce* §§ 208–212.

Estoppel or unclean hands will also be a defense to suits for divorce. *McNeir v. McNeir,* 178 Va. 285, 16 S.E.2d 632 (1941) (wife procured bilateral Nevada divorce but later sued husband for divorce in Virginia, stating that Nevada court did not have jurisdiction; wife also estopped by laches).

## § 19.12    Insane Person as Party to Suit

Even though the original separation took place while the defendant spouse was sane, formerly there could be no divorce on fault grounds requiring a period of separation when during that period the defendant became insane. The reason for this was because the cause of action required an intent to remain separate throughout the statutory period, which intent could not be entertained by the insane spouse. *Wright v. Wright,* 125 Va. 526, 99 S.E. 515 (1919). However, the fact that a defendant to a case of wilful desertion and abandonment became insane after her desertion is no longer a bar to suit. Va. Code § 20-93; *Pollard v. Pollard,* 204 Va. 316, 130 S.E.2d 425 (1963).

Originally the no-fault ground, Va. Code § 20-91(9) also required consciousness by the defendant of the separation. When that spouse was permanently insane, there could be no such knowledge, and the divorce could not be granted. *Crittenden v. Crittenden,* 210 Va. 76, 168 S.E.2d 115 (1969); see 4 U. Rich. L. Rev. 347 (1970). The legislature amended the statute in 1975 to provide that it shall not be a bar to a divorce under the section that either spouse has been adjudged insane before or after the one year period. The rationale for the amendment is set forth in the earlier case of *Gearheart v. Gearheart,* 21 Va. Cir. 447 (Roanoke Co. 1967). The husband was committed to a mental institution in 1941 after he attempted to kill the wife. The parties lived separate and apart for more than 25 years before the wife filed for a no-fault divorce.

When a couple divorces on grounds of insanity, the parties are not necessarily relieved of spousal support obligations. If the institutionalized spouse might be eligible for federal medical assistance services, the court shall first order the institutionalized spouse to make available the maximum income contribution to the other spouse. If the spousal support award exceeds the federally established monthly maintenance needs allowance, the court must find that the increase is necessary because of exceptional circumstances causing financial distress to the other spouse. These circumstances might include threatened loss of basic food, shelter, or medically necessary health care or the financial burden of caring for a disabled child, sibling, or other relative. Effective January 1994, the maximum spousal resource allowance is $72,660. Va. Code § 20-88.02:1.

The committee of the insane defendant shall be made a party to the case, or the court shall appoint a guardian ad litem to represent the insane defendant. Va. Code § 20-91(A)(9)(a).

The insanity of the defendant to a divorce proceeding was enough to invalidate the judgment of divorce (and plaintiff's subsequent remarriage) where plaintiff had not divulged to the trial court that defendant was insane and that he had agreed to her placement in West Virginia, where she was proceeded against by constructive service only. *Taylor v. Taylor,* 159 Va. 338, 165 S.E. 414 (1932). The failure to disclose her insanity amounted to fraud.

## § 19.13 Alimony *Pendente Lite*

Personal jurisdiction is required in order to enter decrees awarding alimony and child support pending litigation. Pendente lite alimony awards, under Va. Code § 20-103, terminate at the time the final judgment of absolute divorce is rendered, *Osborne v. Osborne,* 215 Va. 205, 207 S.E.2d 875 (1974), but child support may be continued or modified beyond this time. Pendente lite relief is not available on appeal, *Cralle v. Cralle,* 81 Va. 773 (1886), although attorney's fees may be. *Tarr v. Tarr,* 184 Va. 443, 35 S.E.2d 401 (1945).

Since 1998, the guidelines for award of permanent spousal and child support under § 20-108.2 are to be applied to compute *pendente lite* awards as well as permanent ones. Va. Code § 20-103. For proceedings under Va. Code Title 16.1, a formula for a presumptively correct amount of *pendente lite* spousal support was enacted in 2007. Va. Code § 16.1-278.17:1.

The usual form for pendente lite relief is through notice and motion rather than through a cross-bill. *Davis v. Davis,* 206 Va. 381, 143 S.E.2d 835 (1965). Such payments are tax deductible to the payor and taxable as income to the payee. I.R.C. § 71(a) (3).

Even though a person can support the divorce suit, he or she may still be entitled to sums sufficient for maintenance. The relief grows out of and is of the same nature as the duty of spousal support. *Eddens v. Eddens,* 188 Va. 511, 50 S.E.2d 397 (1948).

A lien upon the real estate of the defendant may be ordered to secure pendente lite allowances. Va. Code § 20-103; *Wilson v. Wilson,* 195 Va. 1060, 81 S.E.2d 605, 613 (1954).

Va. Code § 20-114 provides that the court may require the giving of recognizance, with or without surety, to insure compliance with child support orders, temporary as well as permanent. Contempt is available for violations of pendente lite orders. *McDaniel v. McDaniel,* 175 Va. 402, 9 S.E.2d 360 (1940).

A spouse may be ordered to provide health care coverage for the petitioning spouse, as well as for minor children, at any time pending the suit. Va. Code § 20-103.

The court may also require the parties to attend courses in parenting responsibilities, conflict resolution, and financial responsibility, according to the amendments to Va. Code § 20-103 passed in 1997.

In 2014, the Legislature amended Va. Code § 20-103 to provide that a court may, pending a suit for divorce, compel a party, or the parties together, to maintain any existing policy owned by that party insuring the life of either party or to require a party to name as a beneficiary of the policy the other party or an appropriate person for the exclusive use and benefit of the minor children of the parties. In addition, the court may allocate the premium cost of such life insurance between the parties, provided that all premiums are billed to the policyholder. Va. Code § 20-103(A)(ix).

*Pendente lite* support may not be modified because statutory support guidelines change. *Payne v. Payne,* 40 Va. Cir. 17 (1995).

## § 19.14   Complaint for Divorce

The pleadings in divorce cases are generally the same as in other equitable proceedings. Va. Code § 20-99.

The jurisdiction of a court to grant a divorce depends upon facts that must be pleaded. The bill of complaint must set forth in detail the specific facts as opposed to legal conclusions giving grounds for relief. *Haynor v. Haynor,*

112 Va. 123, 70 S.E. 531 (1911). Dates, places, and circumstances must be included, *Miller v. Miller,* 92 Va. 196, 23 S.E. 232 (1895), particularly in adultery cases. See generally 6A Michie's Jurisprudence *Divorce and Alimony* § 38.

Pleadings may be amended to state additional grounds for divorce: for example, adultery occurring after the original bill was filed. *Rosenberg v. Rosenberg,* 210 Va. 44, 168 S.E.2d 251 (1969) *Alphin v. Alphin,* 15 Va. App. 395, 424 S.E.2d 572 (1992). See Rule 1:8 of the Rules of the Supreme Court of Virginia. Amended Va. Code § 20-121.02 allows a party to seek a no-fault divorce under separate and apart grounds without filing an amended bill of complaint, notwithstanding the grounds for divorce originally asserted.

A suit for adultery must be instituted within five years of the act complained of under Va. Code § 20-94.

## § 19.15 Service of Divorce Complaint

According to Va. Code § 20-99.2, service in a divorce or annulment case may be made in any manner authorized under Va. Code § 8.01-296. Thus, process may be served by delivering a copy in writing to the party in person, or by substituted service. Service need no longer be made by a sheriff or other law enforcement officer since the 1986 amendment to Va. Code § 8.01-293, but may be made within Virginia by any person eighteen years of age or older who is not a party or otherwise interested in the action. Posting on the door of defendant's last known place of residence will suffice if the defendant has not abandoned the premises. Proof of abandonment lies with the defendant, and the defendant's failure to testify, taken together with circumstantial evidence from which conflicting inferences might be drawn, raised enough questions about abandonment to warrant denial of defendant's motion to quash a divorce complaint. *Wilson v. Wilson,* 9 Va. Cir. 508 (1982).

According to Va. Code § 20-99.1:1, a defendant in a divorce or annulment action may accept service by signing the proof of service before any officer authorized to administer oaths. Service may also have the effect of personal service by voluntary and notarized acceptance or waiver. If service is accepted outside the Commonweath by a nonresident pursuant to § 20-99.1:1, it will have the same effect as an order of publication.

Service may be accepted or waived by a defendant by the filing of an answer by counsel. The acceptance or waiver shall then have the same effect as personal service. Va. Code § 20-99.1:1. Alternatively, the attorney for either party may prepare a writing to be signed by a party before a notary that, when filed, shows the acceptance of service by the party. Va. Code § 20-99.1:1. Once the suit has been commenced and an appearance has been made on behalf of defendant by counsel, notices of depositions and other proceedings, but not contempt proceedings, may be served by delivering or mailing a copy to counsel for the opposing party. In such cases, the notices shall bear either acceptance of service or a certificate of counsel. Va. Code § 20-99(4).

Counsel for the opposing party includes a pro se party who has entered a general appearance in person or by filing a pleading or endorsing an order of withdrawal of that party's counsel, or who has signed a pleading in the case or who has notified the court clerk or the parties that he or she appears in the case. Va. Code § 20-99(4).

If a defendant cannot be found or served after due diligence, Va. Code § 8.01-316 provides that an order of publication may be entered by the clerk of the court, either stating the last known post office address of the party against whom publication is asked, or declaring that the last address is unknown. A husband who refused to tell his wife where he was residing and prevented her being able to find him could not claim that the wife had not used due diligence. *Jennings v. Jennings*, 26 Va. App. 530, 495 S.E.2d 544 (1998). After he left the marital home in January 1990, the husband hid from his wife and creditors. He had no telephone service, no apartment lease, no utilities or "anything in [his] name . . . for the simple reason that [he] was involved in [a] . . . criminal case." The order of publication shall give the abbreviated style of the suit, shall state its object, and require defendants to appear on or before the date stated in the order (no sooner than fifty-one days after entry of the order of publication). The order of publication shall be published once each week for four successive weeks in the newspaper prescribed by the court, or as directed by the clerk, shall be posted at the front door of the courthouse, and shall be mailed to defendant's last known address. Upon completion of the publication, the clerk shall file a certificate in the papers of the case that the requirements have been complied with. Va. Code § 8.01-317. The above Code provisions will be strictly construed and applied. *Robertson v. Stone*, 199 Va. 41, 97 S.E.2d 739 (1957); *Holcomb v. Holcomb*, 122 W. Va. 293, 8 S.E.2d 889 (1940).

When the defendant cannot be found within the state, and the matrimonial domicile was in Virginia at the time of separation, or at the time a cause of action for divorce arose, or at the time of commencement of the suit, the defendant may be reached personally under the longarm statute. Va. Code § 8.01-328.1(A)(9). See *Cabaniss v. Cabaniss*, 46 Va. App. 595, 620 S.E.2d 559 (2005) (sufficiency of pleadings). Jurisdiction under this provision depends upon proof of service of process on the nonresident party by a person authorized under Va. Code § 8.01-320. Thus, the person serving process need not be specifically authorized by the circuit court to serve process that commences divorce or annulment actions, but may be either (1) a person authorized to serve process in the jurisdiction where the party to be served is located, or (2) any person 18 years of age or older who is not a party or otherwise interested in the subject matter of the controversy. Va. Code § 8.01-320(A).

## § 19.16 Answer

An answer does not serve as evidence for the defendant, Va. Code § 8-123, but only admits or traverses the allegations of the complaint. *Hutcheson v. Savings Bank,* 129 Va. 281, 105 S.E. 677 (1921).

The defendant will be permitted to file a later answer with the court's permission even though Rule 3:8 of the Rules of the Supreme Court of Virginia provides for a responsive pleading or an answer to be filed within twenty-one days. This is because Va. Code § 20-99 separates divorce suits from other suits in equity by providing that the cause shall be heard independently of the parties' admissions and that a bill should not be taken for confessed. *Westfall v. Westfall,* 196 Va. 97, 82 S.E.2d 487 (1954).

Once an answer is filed, it confers jurisdiction notwithstanding the fact that the summons was not regularly reserved. *Scott v. Scott,* 142 Va. 31, 128 S.E. 599 (1925).

The defendant may accept service by signing the proof of service before an officer authorized to administer oaths, Va. Code § 20-99.1, or by having counsel prepare a writing to be signed before a notary, or by the filing of an answer by counsel.

In 2006, the rules pertaining to actions at law and those in equity were merged. Procedures for civil cases, both those at law and in equity, are now set forth in Part 3 of the Rules of the Supreme Court of Virginia. The prior rules pertaining to cases in equity were set forth at Part 2 of the Rules of the Supreme Court of Virginia. Rule 3:1 states that the rules apply to "all civil actions, whether the claims involved arise under legal or equitable causes of action, unless otherwise provided by law." However, for matters not covered by these Rules, "the established practices and procedures are continued." Va. Sup. Ct. R. 3:1. Therefore, the remainder of this paragraph will primarily have historical significance, but depending on the circumstance, it may provide guidance despite the merger of the equity and law procedures. Usually a cross-bill is filed separately to obtain affirmative relief. *Simpson v. Simpson,* 162 Va. 621, 175 S.E. 320 (1934) (cross-bill for divorce filed in annulment action). A cross-bill is not needed, however, for obtaining pendente lite relief. *Davis v. Davis,* 206 Va. 381, 143 S.E.2d 835 (1965). A cross-bill may be filed at any time when the defendant would not be in default for failure to file a pleading or thereafter by leave of court. Rule 2:13 of Virginia Equity Rules of Practice and Procedure. This period is 21 days after service, subpoena or acceptance of process, or after publication. Va. Equity Rule 2:7. If adultery is alleged in the cross-bill, it must have occurred within five years of the cross-bill, but before the filing of the cross-bill. *Willard v. Willard*, 98 Va. 465, 36 S.E. 518 (1900); *Rosenberg v. Rosenberg*, 210 Va. 44, 168 S.E.2d 251 (1969); Va. Code § 20-94.

Following the merger of law and equity procedure for civil cases, a defendant would assert a counterclaim against the plaintiff and a cross-bill is no longer the proper pleading. Va. Sup. Ct. R. 3:9. The counterclaim must generally be filed within 21 days of service of the summons and complaint, although 60 or 90 days is permitted when certain conditions are met. Va. Sup. Ct. R. 3:9(b). A counterclaim may state:

> any cause of action that the defendant has against the plaintiff or all plaintiffs jointly, whether or not it grows out of any transaction mentioned in the complaint, whether or not it is for liquidated damages, whether it is in tort or contract, and whether or not the amount demanded in the counterclaim is greater than the amount demanded in the complaint.

Va. Sup. Ct. R. 3:9(a).

Generally speaking, because of the importance of marriage and divorce and the desirability of having hearings on the merits, the courts are inclined to take a very liberal view of pleadings belatedly filed in divorce cases. *Willard v. Willard*, 98 Va. 465, 36 S.E. 518 (1900). See also *Westfall v. Westfall*, 196 Va. 97, 82 S.E.2d 487 (1954). Continuances are also granted with greater liberality because the state has an interest in seeing that everything is done to achieve a just and equitable result. *Gulland v. Gulland*, 62 W. Va. 671, 59 S.E. 612 (1907).

If a defendant fails to file an answer in a divorce suit or otherwise appear within the time allowed by law, after having been personally served with notice of the suit, no further notice to take depositions or conduct an ore tenus hearing is required to be served on the defendant, and the court may enter any order or final decree without notice to the defendant. Va. Code § 20-99(5). However, where a defendant has filed an answer, no order or decree may be entered without notice. *Zedan v. Westheim*, 60 Va. App. 556, 729 S.E.2d 785 (2012).

## § 19.17    Injunctive Relief Pending Decree

Va. Code § 20-103 provides that the court may enjoin a spouse from imposing any restraints on the personal liberty of the other, or for the exclusive use and possession of the marital home during suit or to preserve the estate of either. A spouse may be excluded from the jointly owned or rented family dwelling where the other spouse makes a showing of reasonable apprehension of physical harm.

*Brooks v. Brooks,* 201 Va. 731, 113 S.E.2d 872 (1960), is an example of such an injunction. The wife was restrained from going to the former husband's home or place of business while the husband was enjoined from going to her home, except, after appeal to the Supreme Court, to pick up or deliver their child for visitation.

In the case of *Vardell v. Vardell,* 225 Va. 351, 302 S.E.2d 41 (1983), the supreme court found that the husband had no case for constructive desertion where the wife obtained first an *ex parte* and then a contested injunction barring him from the marital home or contact with their child. In the divorce action brought by the wife, she was unable to corroborate her charges of cruelty by the husband.

### § 19.18  Discovery

Depositions may be taken in divorce actions in accordance with Va. Rule 4:5. Proper notice must be given under Va. Code § 20-99(5), Va. Code § 20-104 (after jurisdiction based upon order of publication), and Va. Sup. Ct. R. 4:1(f) (providing for methods of service of notice). These rules must be carefully followed. *Mackey v. Mackey,* 203 Va. 526, 125 S.E.2d 194 (1962). Types of discovery, as provided in Va. Rule 4:1(a), include depositions, interrogatories, admission of facts and documents, the subpoena duces tecum, physical and mental examinations, and motions to inspect.

Va. Sup. Ct. R. 4:1(b)(5) limits the scope of discovery to "matters which are relevant to the issues in the proceeding." However, given the broad scope of factors required by Va. Code § 20-107.1 (spousal maintenance), Va. Code § 20-107.2 (child custody and support), and Va. Code § 20-107.3 (property distribution), anything is apparently material.

Whether by contempt power authorized by Va. Rule 4:12, or by statutory authority provided by Va. Code § 20-103(A)(vii), the court has the power to appoint a conservator to determine information sought when a party repeatedly refuses discovery requests relating to asset identification, status, use/misuse, and dissipation. *Estate of Hackler v. Hackler,* 44 Va. App. 51, 602 S.E.2d 426 (2004).

### § 19.19  Commissioners and Judges *Pro Tempore*

In 2005, Va. Code § 8.01-607 was amended to limit the referral of cases to commissioners in chancery either when the parties agreed or the court found good cause. Prior to this statutory amendment, many jurisdictions in Virginia referred contested divorce matters to a commissioner in chancery for various reasons. The remainder of this paragraph is a historical discussion about the use of a commissioner in chancery (also note that the references to the Equity Rules are also no longer applicable). In some Virginia jurisdictions, as provided by local rule, the divorce action is referred to a commissioner in chancery by the chancellor (court) with a decree of reference directing the commissioner to require and report on the pertinent issues. *Moore v. Moore,* 218 Va. 790, 240 S.E.2d 535 (1978). In such case the procedure is set forth in Equity Rule 2:18. The commissioner is to determine such issues as: (1) whether the court has jurisdiction and venue; (2) whether the marriage ties should be severed; (3) the amount of alimony to be paid to the wronged spouse; and, where applicable, (4) child custody and maintenance. *Raiford v. Raiford,* 193 Va. 221, 68 S.E.2d 888 (1952). More recently, the duties have expanded to include equitable distribution under Va. Code § 20-107.3 as well. The commissioner's work is subject to the absolute review of the chancellor. *Shipman v. Fletcher,* 91 Va. 473, 476, 22 S.E. 458 (1895). In some counties, the work is handled by a judge *pro tempore.*

A judge pro tempore is authorized to act under Va. Code § 17.1-109 when the judge of the circuit court is disqualified or unable for any reason to try a matter. Va. Code § 17.1-110 defines a judge pro tempore's appointment and powers. The parties may be required to compensate the judge pro tempore. Va. Code § 17.1-111.

Once adopted by the chancellor, the commissioner's actions, findings, and recommendations become those of the supervising court. *Kelker v. Schmidt,* 34 Va. App. 129, 538 S.E.2d 342 (2000). In equitable distribution cases, the commissioner must report what was seen and heard concerning witness demeanor and appearance if the commissioner's decision is based even partly on those factors. When the commissioner's report is based on substance only, the chancellor is as competent as the commissioner to decide the facts; but the chancellor cannot give due regard to factual findings based on the commissioner's ability to see, hear, and evaluate witnesses' testimony unless the commissioner describes his or her observations in the report. *Kelker v. Schmidt,* 34 Va. App. 129, 538 S.E.2d 342 (2000).

Introduction of additional evidence after the filing of a commissioner's report generally requires a motion to receive after-discovered evidence. Four requirements must be met before the record can be reopened: (1) the evidence must have been discovered after the record was closed; (2) the evidence must not have been obtainable prior to the closing of the record through the exercise of reasonable diligence; (3) the evidence must not be merely cumulative, corroborative, or collateral; and (4) the evidence must be material, and, as such, should produce an opposite result from that contained in the commissioner's report. *Joynes v. Payne*, 36 Va. App. 401, 551 S.E.2d 10 (2001).

In *Morrill v. Morrill*, 45 Va. App. 709, 613 S.E.2d 821 (2005), a trial court properly reopened the record on a credit card forgery issue that had been heard by a commissioner in chancery, and allowed a party to present additional evidence. The trial court's general order of reference directed the commissioner (1) to answer whether the grounds of divorce alleged in the pleadings were proven, and (2) to state the factors and circumstances that might have contributed to the dissolution of the marriage. However, the general order specifically reserved to the trial court the authority to make findings and legal conclusions regarding the possible factors and circumstances and how the factors and circumstances affected the well-being of the family, the equitable distribution of the parties' property, and the allocation of debt. Therefore, the trial court reasonably interpreted the general order of reference as *not* invading its authority under Va. Code § 20-107.3(E) to examine evidence regarding the effect of a party's credit card forgery allegations on the marital property and equitable distribution award.

A nonsuit may be granted unless the action has been submitted to the court for decision. In divorce cases, where both parties have filed pleadings, this requires that both yield the issues to the court for consideration. *Moore v. Moore*, 218 Va. 790, 240 S.E.2d 535 (1978).

The finding of the chancellor after a hearing *ore tenus* will not be disturbed unless plainly wrong or without evidence to support it. *Alls v. Alls*, 216 Va. 13, 216 S.E.2d 16 (1975).

In *Brown v. Brown*, 11 Va. App. 231, 397 S.E.2d 545 (1990), a divorce decree was vacated when the wife's legal counsel contributed money to the commissioner's political campaign. The trial court erred in failing to set aside the commissioner's report, because although the court reviewed the commissioner's report, the review was insufficient to remove the taint caused by the suspicion of improper influence.

The trial judge's expression of "a serious concern" regarding the professional conduct of the father's attorney, standing alone, was not a basis for requiring that he recuse himself. *Buchanan v. Buchanan*, 14 Va. App. 53, 415 S.E.2d 237 (1992). The court noted that such a comment was less problematic than the formation of an opinion on a matter that might come before the judge later. The record reflected no indication that any bias affected the proceedings.

## § 19.20    Conduct of the Divorce Hearing

As set forth in the prior section, the use of commissioners in chancery was severely limited by the 2005 statutory amendments to Va. Code § 8.01-607. The discussions about commissioners hearing is retained largely for historical significance as well as for those cases that are referred to commissioners either upon the parties' agreement or when the court finds good cause. Any reference to Va. Rule 2 will no longer apply since the law and equity practice and procedure rules were merged into civil actions and are now set forth at Part 3 of the Rules of the Supreme Court of Virginia. The hearing may also be carried out by a commissioner, who is appointed to assist the chancellor (court), and whose work is subject to court review. The court shall confirm or reject the commissioner's report in whole or in part, according to the view that it entertains of the law and evidence. *Plattner v. Plattner,* 202 Va. 263, 117 S.E.2d 128 (1960).

Where the wife was proceeding pro se, after her counsel had withdrawn, mailing notice to her of the commissioner's hearing was insufficient service, so the final decree of divorce was vacated and the case remanded. *Soliman v. Soliman,* 12 Va. App. 234, 402 S.E.2d 922 (1991). However, after this case was decided, Va. Code § 20-99(5), which allows notices of hearings and other proceedings to be served by delivering or mailing a copy to counsel for opposing party, was amended to read that counsel for the opposing party shall include a pro se party who has entered an appearance by filing a pleading or endorsing an order of withdrawal of that party's counsel.

Evidence may be taken *ore tenus* or by depositions, whichever is determined by the court. Va. Rule 2:17. According to Va. Code § 20-104, evidence in actions where service was obtained by publication or mailing and posting cannot be taken until 10 days after the order was published or mailed and posted. In such cases, notice of depositions may be given to counsel of record within the state, under Va. Code § 20-99.1(5) and Va. Rule 1:12, except those of adverse witnesses, as provided under Va. Rule 4:2(a)(2).

A trial judge may not consider *ore tenus* testimony given in one proceeding when making a decision in another proceeding, even when the cases are between the same parties, unless the proceedings are put in evidence. *Hughes v. Hughes (Hughes Divorce),* 33 Va. App. 141, 531 S.E.2d 645 (2000). In *Hughes,* the trial judge erroneously weighed the wife's credibility in a divorce proceeding upon consideration of the wife's testimony at an *ore tenus* hearing in a separate custody proceeding. Compare with *Hughes v. Hughes (Hughes Custody),* 33 Va. App. 160, 531 S.E.2d 654

(2000), *aff'd after rehearing en banc*, 35 Va. App. 376, 545 S.E.2d 556 (2001) (petition for appeal to Va. Sup. Ct. pending) (related custody proceeding).

Va. Code § 20-124 provides that, upon motion of any party, the court may order the record or any agreement of the parties to be sealed and withheld from public inspection. The record and agreement shall thereafter be opened only to the parties, to their respective attorneys, and to such other persons as the judge in his discretion decides have a proper interest in the documents. A trial judge has discretion to vacate an order that seals the trial record pursuant to Va. Code § 20-124. *Shiembob v. Shiembob*, 55 Va. App. 234, 685 S.E.2d 192 (2009). In *Shiembob*, the court of appeals stated that a litigant's desire to seal the trial record, on the basis of an abstract claim of possible emotional damage, damage to professional reputation, or financial harm, is not a sufficient reason to override the Va. Code § 17.1-208 presumption of openness of judicial records. In order for a spouse to appeal from an adverse judgment, transcripts of all relevant hearings must be made part of the record. *Twardy v. Twardy*, 14 Va. App. 651, 419 S.E.2d 848 (1992). Because no party submitted transcripts from a hearing, the court was unable to determine if the wife presented the issue of estoppel to the trial court.

The court has authority pursuant to Va. Code § 20-103(A)(vii) to enter any order that may be proper during the pendency of a divorce suit in order to preserve the marital estate. *Estate of Hackler v. Hackler*, 44 Va. App. 51, 602 S.E.2d 426 (2004). In *Hackler*, the court properly appointed a conservator to manage marital assets controlled by a husband, when the husband continually violated the court's orders, refused to respond to discovery requests for financial information, and repeatedly dissipated the estate.

When a husband was in contempt of court for non-payment of support and his bill of complaint was dismissed for failure to comply with discovery requests, his due process rights were not violated when a final decree of divorce was entered in his absence. *Fox v. Fox*, 1998 Va. App. LEXIS 157 (Mar. 17, 1998), *aff'd*, 2000 Va. App. LEXIS 223 (Mar. 28, 2000). Dr. Fox had a history of non-appearance and an "utter and total disrespect and contempt for this Court and its orders."

### § 19.21 Testimony in Divorce Hearing

The statutes require that the cause of action be heard independently of the parties' admissions, in pleadings or otherwise. Va. Code § 20-99. The main object of this statute requiring corroboration of divorce testimony is to prevent collusion. *Forbes v. Forbes*, 182 Va. 636, 29 S.E.2d 829 (1944). Where it is apparent that there is no collusion, the corroboration only needs to be slight. *Graves v. Graves,* 193 Va. 659, 70 S.E.2d 339 (1952); *Collier v. Collier,* 2 Va. App. 125, 341 S.E.2d 827 (1986).

The burden of persuasion in desertion cases is that desertion must be shown by a preponderance of the evidence. *Bacon v. Bacon,* 3 Va. App. 484, 351 S.E.2d 37, 40–41 (1986). This is in contrast to the standard of persuasion in adultery cases, which requires that adultery be proved by clear and convincing evidence. *Coe v. Coe,* 225 Va. 616, 622, 303 S.E.2d 923, 927 (1983); *Dooley v. Dooley,* 222 Va. 240, 246, 278 S.E.2d 865, 868 (1981); *Hughes v. Hughes (Hughes Divorce),* 33 Va. App. 141, 531 S.E.2d 645 (2000). According to *Bacon,* the reason for the distinction is that the alleged conduct in desertion cases does not deviate from the norm as much as that in adultery cases, where a criminal offense is also being made out. 351 S.E.2d at 40 (citing *Haskins v. Haskins,* 188 Va. 525, 530–31, 50 S.E.2d 437, 439 (1948), and C. Friend, *The Law of Evidence in Virginia* § 86 (2d ed. 1983)).

Letters of the parties may be admitted in evidence in a divorce suit (except where written by collusion) just as in any other case for the purpose of providing or as tending to prove relevant facts. *Bailey v. Bailey,* 62 Va. 43, 51 (1871). See also *Holt v. Holt,* 174 Va. 120, 5 S.E.2d 504 (1939). Admissions of the parties are admissible and are highly credible evidence if corroborated. See, e.g., *Miller v. Miller,* 196 Va. 698, 85 S.E.2d 221 (1955); *Davis v. Davis,* 206 Va. 381, 143 S.E.2d 835 (1965).

The decree of a chancellor that is based upon depositions, while not as strong and conclusive as one based upon oral testimony, is presumed to be correct, and will not be disturbed unless manifestly wrong. *Martin v. Martin,* 202 Va. 769, 120 S.E.2d 471 (1961). Conclusions based upon testimony given *ore tenus* (orally) will not be set aside unless there is clear error. *Barnard v. Barnard,* 132 Va. 155, 111 S.E. 227 (1922). The right to require oral testimony is conferred upon the court, not the parties, to give it the advantage of seeing the witnesses and hearing them testify. *Id.*

The evidence of private investigators should be examined with greatest care and acted upon with great caution. *Dooley v. Dooley,* 222 Va. 240, 278 S.E.2d 865 (1981); *Colbert v. Colbert,* 162 Va. 393, 400, 174 S.E. 660, 662 (1934).

Husband and wife are competent to testify against each other in divorce cases, Va. Code §§ 8-82 and 8-287, but the divorce will not be granted on their uncorroborated testimony. *Black v. Black,* 134 Va. 246, 114 S.E. 592 (1922) (wife never appeared in case; evidence failed to corroborate husband's testimony regarding wife's reprehensible conduct that allegedly caused him to leave marital home); *Belle v. Belle,* 2016 Va. App. LEXIS 15

(Jan. 19, 2016) (trial court should not have entered a divorce where the evidence failed to corroborate the essential facts establishing the divorce grounds). The parties' child may also be a competent witness, *Hepler v. Hepler,* 195 Va. 611, 79 S.E.2d 652 (1954) (custody case; twelve year old child), but should seldom be used in adultery cases. *White v. White,* 121 Va. 244, 92 S.E. 811 (1917).

In 2014, the Legislature amended and reenacted Va. Code § 20-106 relating to oral testimony and evidence by affidavit in a divorce suit. (1) The legislation changed the requirements in affidavits for no-fault divorce relating to incarceration from affirming or verifying that neither party is incarcerated to affirming or verifying the incarceration status of both parties; limits the submission of evidence by affidavit where either party is incarcerated; and (2) replaces certain language in the statute, as follows:

> In any such suit, the trial court may require the testimony to be given orally in open court, and if either party desires it, the testimony and court rulings on exceptions, if any, shall be reduced to writing and certified by the judge. Once certified, the testimony shall stand on the same footing as a deposition, however, oral evidence cannot be given or heard unless and until notice to the adverse party has been given as required by law concerning the taking of depositions, or when there has been no service of process within this Commonwealth upon the defendant, or appearance by the defendant against whom such testimony is sought to be introduced. However, a party may proceed to take evidence in support of a divorce by deposition or affidavit without leave of court only in support of a divorce on the grounds set forth in Va. Code § 20-91(A)(9), where (i) the parties have resolved all issues by a written settlement agreement, (ii) there are no issues other than the grounds of the divorce itself to be adjudicated, or (iii) the adverse party has been personally served with the complaint and has failed to file a responsive pleading or to make an appearance as required by law. Va. Code § 20-106(A).

Pursuant to Va. Code § 20-106(B), the affidavit of a party submitted as evidence shall be based on the personal knowledge of the affiant, contain only facts that would be admissible in court, give factual support to the grounds for divorce stated in the complaint or counterclaim, and establish that the affiant is competent to testify to the contents of the affidavit. If either party is incarcerated, neither party shall submit evidence by affidavit without leave of court or the consent in writing of the guardian ad litem for the incarcerated party, or of the incarcerated party if a guardian ad litem is not required pursuant to Va. Code § 8.01-9. The affidavit shall:

1.   Give factual support to the grounds for divorce stated in the complaint or counterclaim, including that the parties are over the

age of 18 and not suffering from any condition that renders either party legally incompetent;

2. Verify whether either party is incarcerated;

3. Verify the military status of the opposing party and advise whether the opposing party has filed an answer or a waiver of his rights under the federal Servicemembers Civil Relief Act, 50 U.S.C. App § 501 *et seq.*;

4. Affirm that at least one party to the suit is, and has been for a period in excess of six months immediately preceding the commencement of the suit, a bona fide resident and domiciliary of the Commonwealth;

5. Affirm that the parties have lived separate and apart, continuously, without interruption and without cohabitation, and with the intent to remain separate and apart permanently, for the statutory period required by Va. Code § 20-91(A)(9);

6. Affirm the affiant's desire to be awarded a divorce pursuant to Va. Code § 20-91(A)(9);

7. State whether there were children born or adopted of the marriage and affirm that the wife is not known to be pregnant from the marriage; and

8. Be accompanied by the affidavit of a corroborating witness, which shall:

   a. Verify that the affiant is over the age of 18 and not suffering from any condition that renders him legally incompetent;

   b. Verify whether either party is incarcerated;

   c. Give factual support to the grounds for divorce stated in the complaint or counterclaim;

   d. Verify that at least one of the parties to the suit is, and has been for a period in excess of six months, a bona fide resident and domiciliary of the Commonwealth;

   e. Verify whether there were children born or adopted of the marriage and verify that the wife is not known to be pregnant from the marriage; and

   f. Verify the affiant's personal knowledge that the parties have not cohabitated since the date of separation alleged in the complaint or counterclaim, and that it has been the moving party's intention since that date to remain separate and apart permanently.

A verified complaint shall not be deemed an affidavit for purposes of this section. Va. Code § 20-106(C).

## § 19.22 Final Decree of Divorce

The decree must be appealed within the term of court to enable the court to have any further jurisdiction over the marriage relations, except to compel compliance with provisions of the decree. *Golderos v. Golderos,* 169 Va. 496, 194 S.E. 706 (1938) (alimony not modifiable after end of term of court; Va. Code § 20-109 permitting modification not then in effect). All final judgments, orders, and decrees, irrespective of terms of court, remain under the control of the trial court and are subject to modification, vacation, or suspension, for 21 days after the date of entry, and no longer. Va. Sup. Ct. Rule 1.1. A property settlement agreement that is affirmed, ratified, and incorporated into a final decree of divorce becomes a term of the decree, and becomes final within 21 days of entry of the decree. *Baker v. Baker,* 38 Va. App. 384, 564 S.E.2d 164 (2002).

In the parties' final divorce decree, the court retained jurisdiction to determine spousal support and property rights. Thereafter, the parties entered into a settlement agreement pursuant to which the husband agreed to make annual payments to the wife, in return for which the wife agreed to "release and discharge . . . all claims which she might have for alimony." The trial court entered a decree that ratified and incorporated this settlement agreement. The court of appeals held that § 20-109.1 did not deprive the trial court of its power to incorporate a settlement agreement involving support in a decree following the entry of a decree of divorce. *Rogers v. Damron,* 23 Va. App. 708, 479 S.E.2d 540 (1997). It was therefore appropriate for the wife to use the court's contempt power to enforce the decree.

The invalidation of an antenuptial agreement is not an appealable order because it will not necessarily affect the final disposition of the divorce. *Polumbo v. Polumbo,* 13 Va. App. 306, 411 S.E.2d 229 (1991). See also *Webb v. Webb,* 13 Va. App. 681, 414 S.E.2d 612 (1992).

If the parties' final divorce decree specified that the husband was to make spousal support payments, he could not receive restitution of payments made even when the court ultimately found that the wife had deserted him and therefore was not entitled to spousal support. *Reid v. Reid,* 245 Va. 409, 429 S.E.2d 208 (1993) (reversing 14 Va. App. 505, 419 S.E.2d 398 (1992)).

When a divorce decree is silent as to child support, except for transferring matters of support to the Juvenile and Domestic Relations District Court, the

Division of Child Support Enforcement has the administrative authority to issue a support order to establish a debt for public assistance paid on an order for child support. *Powers v. Commonwealth,* 13 Va. App. 309, 411 S.E.2d 230 (1991). In *Lehman v. Lehman,* 38 Va. App. 598, 567 S.E.2d 571 (2002), a final divorce decree was determined not to be void as against public policy because of its incorporation of arguably illegal child support provisions.

An affirmative statement that the trial court dispensed with the Rule 1:13 requirements for reasonable notice or endorsement by counsel is not required for the divorce decree to be valid. *Napert v. Napert,* 261 Va. 45, 540 S.E.2d 882 (2001) (divorce decree that contained neither endorsement of wife or counsel nor dispensation of endorsement by court was not facially void). A decree or order entered in violation of Rule 1:13 is merely voidable, not void. *Whiting v. Whiting,* 262 Va. 3 (2001). A voidable decree or order is not subject to collateral attack and must be challenged within 21 days of its entry pursuant to Rule 1:1, by a bill of review within the time prescribed by Va. Code § 8.01-623, or by an independent action pursuant to Va. Code § 8.01-428. *Whiting v. Whiting,* 262 Va. 3 (2001). See also *Hickson v. Hickson,* 34 Va. App. 246, 540 S.E.2d 508 (2001) (exceptions to Rule 1:1 requirement that decree be challenged within 21 days were inapplicable, when husband's counsel of record received notice, husband attended hearing by telephone, and circumstances did not justify bill of review); *De Avies v. De Avies,* 42 Va. App. 342, 592 S.E.2d 351 (2004) (consent decree signed by counsel but not client could not be set aside as void on basis of alleged violation of signature requirements of Va. Code §§ 20-109(C) and 20-149, because final decree could not be collaterally attacked). Until a party's counsel has formally withdrawn, service upon the party's counsel of record complies with Rule 1:13. *Francis v. Francis,* 30 Va. App. 584, 518 S.E.2d 842 (1999).

The statement of facts need not be signed by the trial judge for the decree to be valid if this omission is the fault of the judge. *Clary v. Clary,* 15 Va. App. 598, 425 S.E.2d 821 (1993). The divorce decree shall contain the parties' social security numbers under amended Va. Code §§ 20-91 and 32.1-268. However, Va. Code § 20-121.03, adopted in 2005, requires that the record of a divorce suit must not contain the social security number of a party or child, or any specifically identified financial information. Instead, such information should be submitted in a separate addendum, and the attorney or party who submits a petition, pleading, motion, agreement, order, or decree must ensure that protected information is removed prior to filing with the clerk.

Va. Code § 8.01-428 authorizes a trial court to correct clerical mistakes in judgments or other parts of the record and errors arising from oversight or inadvertent omission. When one provision of a divorce decree stated that the wife's spousal support would continue until the husband's remarriage, in conflict with two other provisions that stated that support would continue until the wife's remarriage, the trial court properly found there was a scrivener's error, and entered an amended final decree, *nunc pro tunc*, that made all three provisions state consistently that support would continue until the wife's remarriage. *White v. White*, 38 Va. App. 389, 564 S.E.2d 700 (2002). When the final decree of divorce did not reflect whether the spousal support payments were to continue from the date of entry of the decree or the execution of the couple's stipulation agreement, but the parties wanted the agreement approved by the trial court and made part of their final divorce decree, the trial court correctly amended the final decree nunc pro tunc. *Garrett v. Forbes-Garrett*, 1995 Va. App. LEXIS 860 (Nov. 28, 1995). Similarly, where the final order of divorce and subsequent retirement order inadvertently omitted awarding the retirement survivor benefits to the wife, Va. Code § 8,01-428(B) empowered the Court to amend the retirement order at any time in order to correct the inadvertent omission and award the survivor benefits to the wife. *Ruane v. Ruane*, 2017 Va. App. LEXIS (Oct. 31, 2017) (unpublished opinion).

### § 19.23   Counsel Fees and Costs

Like alimony, the award by a court of counsel fees and court costs will be enforceable through the use of the contempt power, *Eddens v. Eddens*, 188 Va. 511, 50 S.E.2d 397 (1948), the court reasoning that the fees are necessary to enforce the right to alimony.

In *Klein v. Klein*, 18 Va. Cir. 195 (1989), the husband failed to reimburse the wife for $5,000 she had paid in attorney's fees as he had been required by the divorce decree. This was held to be contempt of court.

The award of counsel fees is discretionary with the trial court, Va. Code § 20-103, and will not be disturbed unless there is an abuse of this discretion. *Wilkerson v. Wilkerson*, 214 Va. 395, 200 S.E.2d 581 (1973). Where one party has no separate estate and is the defendant in a divorce action, it is entirely proper for him or her to be allowed a reasonable sum for attorney's fees and costs, provided that the court does not ignore the financial condition of the plaintiff spouse. *Rowlee v. Rowlee*, 211 Va. 689, 179 S.E.2d 461 (1971) (no evidence showing abuse of discretion in failure to award fees to wife). A court may award counsel fees in an appropriate case even when grounds for divorce is not based upon fault. See, e.g., *Bandas v. Bandas*, 32 Va. Cir. 285 (1993).

The award of attorneys' fees and costs is personal to the parties. The attorney has no standing to seek relief under this section.

Va. Code § 54.1-3932, as enacted in 2001, authorizes an attorney's lien on a cause of action for divorce or annulment, as security for attorney's fees for services rendered. However, the statute prohibits an attorney from exercising any claim until the divorce judgment is final and all residual disputes regarding marital property are concluded. Also, a trial court has discretion to exclude spousal and child support from the scope of the attorney's lien.

## § 19.24    Resumption of the Maiden Name

Va. Code § 20-121.4 allows a party to be restored to a maiden name or a former name by an order entered in the divorce case. However, the name change is required to be in its own separate order and the order must meet the requirements of Va. Code § 8.01-217. This right would not go so far as to allow the custodial wife the ability to change the children's surnames to that of her new husband. *Flowers v. Cain,* 218 Va. 234, 237 S.E.2d 111 (1977). Whether it would extend to her right to have their names changed to her maiden name is questionable. See, e.g., *Lassiter-Geers v. Reichenbach,* 303 Md. 88, 492 A.2d 303 (1985).

## § 19.25    Effect on Dower and Curtesy

The absolute divorce destroys the contingent rights in the property of the other spouse that depend upon the continued existence of the marriage relationship. Va. Code § 20-111. This includes dower and curtesy, even if the divorce is obtained *ex parte. Simons v. Miami Beach First Nat'l Bank,* 381 U.S. 81, 85 S. Ct. 1315, 14 L. Ed. 2d 232 (1965). See also *Jones v. Kirby,* 146 Va. 109, 135 S.E. 676 (1926). Revocable beneficiary designations are rescinded by final divorces occurring on or after July 1, 1993, so that death benefits shall be paid as though the former spouse predeceased the decedent. Va. Code § 20-111.1.

## § 19.26    Effect on Ability to Testify

An absolute (or *a mensa*) divorce will make the former spouses competent to testify in all cases. The marital status at the time of trial determines whether or not the disability to testify is removed. *Menefee v. Commonwealth,* 189 Va. 900, 55 S.E.2d 9 (1949).

However, even though a person may testify against the former wife or husband, if a communication was made during the marriage and was made because of the marital relationship, it will be protected under the privilege for confidential marital communications. *Id.*

See generally Friend, *The Law of Evidence in Virginia* (2d ed. 1983).

## § 19.27 Ability to Remarry

In contrast to the *a mensa* divorce, the absolute divorce gives to each spouse, whether the divorce was awarded for or against that spouse, the ability to remarry. Until 1934, spouses were not allowed to remarry for a period of six months after the final decree to give them time to reconcile before a hasty remarriage made this action impossible and to remove the temptation for married spouses to divorce so that they might marry others. *Simpson v. Simpson,* 162 Va. 621, 633–34, 175 S.E. 320, 325–26 (1934). Since 1975, remarriage has been permissible even for persons divorced because of their adultery. Acts of 1975 c. 644. However, remarriage should not occur if exceptions are noted and a bond is given staying execution of the decree. Va. Code § 20-118. Fraud would certainly be sufficient grounds for vacating a decree. *Taylor v. Taylor,* 159 Va. 338, 165 S.E. 414 (1932). The divorce could be vacated although one party had remarried and had a child born of the second marriage. *Tarr v. Tarr,* 184 Va. 443, 35 S.E.2d 401 (1945) (defendant to divorce thought her conduct had been condoned by cohabitation following service of the complaint, so she failed to appear to make a defense).

## § 19.28 Effect on Property Held as Tenants by the Entirety or Joint Tenancy

By Va. Code § 20-111, property held as tenants by the entirety is converted to tenancy in common by the absolute divorce. This does not authorize the courts to allocate the property other than evenly between the spouses. *Smith v. Smith,* 200 Va. 77, 104 S.E.2d 17 (1958). Some financial compensation may be necessary if the funds that paid for the property were acquired by one party as a gift, and are therefore separate property under Va. Code § 20-107.3.

Joint property, such as that held in joint bank accounts, may only be changed to a tenancy in common, not distributed under the equitable distribution statute, Va. Code § 20-107.3. *Watkins v. Watkins,* 220 Va. 1051, 265 S.E.2d 750 (1980) (no jurisdiction to impair husband's personal property); *Johnson v. Johnson,* 224 Va. 641, 299 S.E.2d 351 (1983) (joint bank account).

The court of course does have the power to approve and confirm contracts between the parties concerning property division, support and maintenance. Va. Code § 20-109; *Gloth v. Gloth,* 154 Va. 511, 153 S.E. 879 (1930). See generally Chapter 17, *supra.*

## § 19.29    Other Financial Considerations

Alimony will be available to a dependent spouse despite the fact that the obligor was awarded the divorce, so long as the decree was based upon the "no-fault" ground of Va. Code § 20-91(9), and the dependent spouse was without fault or misconduct causing the separation. *Mason v. Mason,* 209 Va. 528, 165 S.E.2d 392 (1969). See also *Breschel v. Breschel,* 221 Va. 208, 269 S.E.2d 363 (1980); *Wallace v. Wallace,* 1 Va. App. 183, 336 S.E.2d 27 (1985). Unless alimony is provided for in the decree, or the right to modify it reserved, it cannot afterwards be awarded, since the decree is final. This does not apply to child support or custody, which are always subject to modification in the child's best interest. *Kern v. Lindsey,* 182 Va. 775, 30 S.E.2d 707 (1944).

If spouses divorce after filing joint income tax returns, and return their refund check to the Commissioner, separate checks will be issued to husband and wife. Va. Code § 58.1-499 (amended 1997).

## § 19.30    Full Faith and Credit for Judgments of Final Divorce

Virginia will give full faith and credit to judgments of absolute divorce rendered in other states, *Osborne v. Osborne,* 215 Va. 205, 207 S.E.2d 875 (1974), so long as domicile was validly obtained in the other state. The right to maintain or obtain alimony will not be terminated by an *ex parte,* as opposed to a bilateral, proceeding. *Id.; Ceyte v. Ceyte,* 222 Va. 11, 278 S.E.2d 791 (1981).

The divorce decree may also require that either party provide health care coverage for the children following a final divorce. Va. Code § 20-107.2.

## § 19.31    Effect on Death Benefits

In 2012, the Virginia legislature addressed the issue of beneficiary designation following a divorce. Under Va. Code § 20-111.1, a spousal beneficiary designation was automatically revoked upon divorce unless the divorce decree or agreement provided otherwise. However, in *Maretta v. Hillman,* 283 Va. 34, 722 S.E.2d 32 (2012), the Virginia Supreme Court found the law unconstitutional as it applies to federal employees, including military personnel and veterans. The court held that federal law preempted the state law under the Supremacy Clause of the United States Constitution. In response to *Maretta,* the legislature passed HB 282, which amended Va. Code § 20-111.1, by adding new subsection E:

> E. *Every decree of annulment or divorce from the bond of matrimony entered on or after July 1, 2012, shall contain the following notice in conspicuous, bold print:*
>
> *Beneficiary designations for any death benefit, as defined in subsection B*

*of § 20-111.1 of the Code of Virginia, made payable to a former spouse may or may not be automatically revoked by operation of law upon the entry of a final decree of annulment or divorce. If a party intends to revoke any beneficiary designation made payable to a former spouse following the annulment or divorce, the party is responsible for following any and all instructions to change such beneficiary designation given by the provider of the death benefit. Otherwise, existing beneficiary designations may remain in full force and effect after the entry of a final decree of annulment or divorce.*

# CHAPTER 20

# Spousal Support and Maintenance

## SYNOPSIS

## § 20.01   Introduction

The concept of spousal support was originally derived from the duty of the husband to support the wife during marriage. *Harris v. Harris,* 72 Va. (31 Gratt.) 13, 17 (1878). When, through the husband's fault, the parties were forced to live apart, the wife could collect alimony in order to continue to have the material things the husband was obliged to provide her. See *Capell v. Capell,* 164 Va. 45, 178 S.E. 894 (1935); *Purcell v. Purcell,* 14 Va. (4 Hen. & Mun.) 507 (1810). Since there was no absolute divorce, this duty continued until the death of either of the parties. See *Gloth v. Gloth,* 154 Va. 511, 537, 153 S.E. 879, 887 (1930) (case containing history of alimony in Virginia).

In Virginia, courts were empowered by statute to award alimony following divorces from bed and board, and, later, following absolute divorces where no-fault whatsoever existed against the dependent spouse. Law of March 18, 1848, ch. 122, p. 165, § 5; *Latham v. Latham,* 71 Va. (30 Gratt.) 307 (1878). As in the case of divorces, the entire subject, although in many respects equitable, is regulated by statute since this form of relief did not exist at common law. *Watkins v. Watkins,* 220 Va. 1051, 265 S.E.2d 750 (1980); *Bray v. Landergren,* 161 Va. 699, 172 S.E. 252 (1933) (citing cases). The term "support and maintenance" as used in the Virginia Code expresses this change from the original idea of alimony, since support does not necessarily depend upon the continued existence of marriage. See, e.g., Holt, *Support vs. Alimony in Virginia, It's Time to Use the Revised Statutes,* 12 U. Rich. L. Rev. 139, 139–40 (1977).

Alimony was allowed out of the husband's estate, but a specific piece of property could not be assigned the wife as alimony. *Lovegrove v. Lovegrove,*

128 Va. 449, 451, 104 S.E. 804 (1920). See also *Almond v. Almond,* 25 Va. (4 Rand.) 662 (1826).

In recent years, several more of the original concepts have changed. Since in the 1979 Supreme Court case of *Orr v. Orr,* 440 U.S. 268, 99 S. Ct. 1102, 59 L. Ed. 2d 306 (1979), support following divorce, if available to wives, must also be available to husbands. *Brooker v. Brooker,* 218 Va. 12, 235 S.E.2d 309 (1977). Additionally, with the growing financial independence of women, support has increasingly been awarded for limited time periods rather than for life or until remarriage, as was the former practice. *Thomas v. Thomas,* 217 Va. 502, 229 S.E.2d 887 (1976), suggested the requirement of evidence showing that the need of the wife or the ability of the husband would change in the immediate future before a two-year limitation was appropriate. Support may be used to compensate spouses for investments made that cannot be divided as marital property, or to allow the dependent spouse the opportunity to obtain an education or to raise a minor child. See Va. Code § 20-107.1(2); see generally Annot., Fineman, *Implementing Equality: Ideology, Contradiction and Social Change,* 1983 Wis. L. Rev. 789; Holt, *Support vs. Alimony in Virginia: It's Time to Use the Revised Statutes,* 12 U. Rich. L. Rev. 139 (1977); Krauskopf, *Recompense for Financing Spouse's Education: Legal Protection for the Marital Investor in Human Capital,* 28 Kan. L. Rev. 379, 411 (1980); O'Kelly, *Entitlements to Spousal Support After Divorce,* 61 N.D.L. Rev. 225 (1985); Weitzman, *The Economics of Divorce: Social and Economic Consequences of Property, Alimony and Child Support Awards,* 28 UCLA L. Rev. 1031, 1229 (1981).

The present support statute, Va. Code § 20-107.1, requires consideration of a number of factors before an award of alimony is made. *Bristow v. Bristow,* 221 Va. 1, 267 S.E.2d 89 (1980); *Brooker v. Brooker,* 218 Va. 12, 235 S.E.2d 309 (1977). Va. Code § 20-107.1 establishes the criteria to be used for the initial setting of spousal support, and the statute's language that "any maintenance and support shall be subject to the provisions of Code § 20-109" denotes only that a final support award properly calculated using Va. Code § 20-107.1 factors is subject to later modification under the criteria of Va. Code § 20-109. *Wright v. Wright,* 38 Va. App. 394, 564 S.E.2d 702 (2002). In *Wright,* a husband argued unsuccessfully that because Va. Code § 20-107.1 referenced Va. Code § 20-109, the legislature intended for courts to consider cohabitation as well as adultery to bar an initial award of spousal support.

Whether and how much spousal support will be awarded is a matter of discretion for the trial court. *Barker v. Barker,* 27 Va. App. 519, 500 S.E.2d

240 (1998). See, e.g., *Northcutt v. Northcutt,* 39 Va. App. 192, 571 S.E.2d 912 (2002) (parties with equivalent assets and earning capability denied spousal support).

Accrued alimony is not a provable debt in bankruptcy, nor is the obligor relieved from any future payments by a discharge in bankruptcy. *Eaton v. Davis,* 176 Va. 330, 338, 10 S.E.2d 893, 897 (1940).

The award of support should be made on the basis of presently available facts rather than speculation on future needs or incomes. *Jacobs v. Jacobs,* 219 Va. 993, 254 S.E.2d 56 (1979) (an escalator clause violated this policy). See also *Robertson v. Robertson,* 215 Va. 425, 211 S.E.2d 41 (1975).

The amount ordered by the chancellor will not be disturbed on appeal unless there is a clear abuse of discretion. *Lawrence v. Lawrence,* 212 Va. 44, 48, 181 S.E.2d 640, 643 (1971). But see, e.g., *Robbins v. Robbins,* 48 Va. App. 466, 632 S.E.2d 615 (2006) (circuit court abused its discretion in adopting commissioner's recommended spousal support award, because commissioner, in calculating spousal support, deducted child support award from wife's estimate of her financial needs).

Usually alimony is in the form of periodic payments. Va. Code § 20-107.1 also allows payment in the form of a lump sum. In some cases where there are equitable reasons for doing so, payment may be ordered to be both in lump sum and periodic. See *Turner v. Turner,* 213 Va. 42, 189 S.E.2d 361 (1972) (husband ordered to pay $16,000 in lump sum in addition to monthly payments since he had changed locks on marital home and wife owned no furniture).

Spousal support orders in which there are minor children whom the parties have a mutual duty to support must contain the provisions required in child support orders, including notice that payments may be withheld from earnings without filing an application. Va. Code § 20-60.3. This notice is not included in the less extensive set of provisions required in spousal support orders when there are no minor children whom the parties have a mutual duty to support. Va. Code § 20-107.1(h). In either case, orders will normally contain specified contact information for the parties, with instructions to report changes within specified times, but if a protective order has been issued or the court finds reason to believe that a party is at risk of physical or emotional harm from the other party, only the name of the party at risk will be included.

The juvenile and domestic relations court may require an obligor convicted of civil or criminal contempt to post a bond before an appeal is allowed. Va. Code § 16.1-296.

In determining whether to award support and maintenance for a spouse, the court is required to consider the circumstances and factors that contributed to the dissolution of the marriage. Va. Code Ann. § 20-107.1(E). Those circumstances and factors include adultery, cruelty, reasonable apprehension of bodily hurt, willful desertion, abandonment, and whether either of the parties subsequent to the marriage has been convicted of a felony, sentenced to confinement for more than one year and confined for such felony subsequent to such conviction, and cohabitation has not been resumed after knowledge of such confinement. See Va. Code Ann. § 20-91 and § 20-95.

In determining the nature, amount, and duration of an award pursuant to subsection (E), the court is required to consider the following:

1. The obligations, needs and financial resources of the parties, including but not limited to income from all pension, profit sharing or retirement plans, of whatever nature;

2. The standard of living established during the marriage;

3. The duration of the marriage;

4. The age and physical and mental condition of the parties and any special circumstances of the family;

5. The extent to which the age, physical or mental condition or special circumstances of any child of the parties would make it appropriate that a party not seek employment outside of the home;

6. The contributions, monetary and nonmonetary, of each party to the well-being of the family;

7. The property interests of the parties, both real and personal, tangible and intangible;

8. The provisions made with regard to the marital property;

9. The earning capacity, including the skills, education and training of the parties and the present employment opportunities for persons possessing such earning capacity;

10. The opportunity for, ability of, and the time and costs involved for a party to acquire the appropriate education, training and employment to obtain the skills needed to enhance his or her earning ability;

11. The decisions regarding employment, career, economics, education and parenting arrangements made by the parties during the marriage and their effect on present and future earning potential,

including the length of time one or both of the parties have been absent from the job market;

12. The extent to which either party has contributed to the attainment of education, training, career position or profession of the other party; and

13. Such other factors, including the tax consequences to each party and the circumstances and factors that contributed to the dissolution, specifically including any ground for divorce, as are necessary to consider the equities between the parties.

## § 20.02 Sufficiency of Written Findings and Conclusions in Contested Cases

In contested cases in the circuit courts, any order granting, reserving, or denying a request for spousal support shall be accompanied by written findings and conclusions of the court identifying the factors set forth in subsection (E) that support the court's order. Va. Code Ann. § 20-107.1(F). Failure to provide the required written findings constitutes reversible error. *Robinson v. Robinson*, 50 Va. App. 189, 648 S.E.2d 314 (2007), *appeal after remand*, 54 Va. App. 87, 675 S.E.2d 873 (2009) (mere confirmation of commissioner's report does not satisfy statutory mandate to identify Va. Code Ann. § 20-107.1(E) factors that support spousal support award).

In *Pilati v. Pilati*, 59 Va. App. 176, 717 S.E.2d 807 (2011), the circuit court awarded permanent spousal support of $600 per month to a wife in a divorce proceeding. The husband appealed claiming that the trial court did not provide sufficient written findings and conclusions, as required by subsection (F). The appellate court agreed, concluding that the trial court's letter opinion provided the litigants with an inadequate explanation of the circuit court's decision. The trial court paraphrased many of the statutory factors, but made only two specific findings of fact: The parties had been married "22 years" and enjoyed a "high middle class" standard of living.

The appellate court reversed and remanded, holding that, in contested cases, any order granting, reserving or denying a request for spousal support requires more than merely communicating the fundamental, predominating reasons for the decision. Instead, the order must be accompanied by written findings and conclusions that identify all relevant statutory factors supporting the court's decision and must also provide an explanation of the court's resolution of any significant underlying factual disputes.

## § 20.03 When May Support Be Awarded?

There must, of course, be some kind of marriage before the duty to support will attach. See *Purcell v. Purcell,* 14 Va. (4 Hen. & Mun.) 507, 515 (1810).

Following the reasoning of the other support cases involving void marriages, spousal support will apparently not be awarded to a person whose marriage was declared void by reason of insanity. *Somers-Shiflet v. Shiflet,* 29 Va. Cir. 206 (Fairfax Co. 1992). This situation is distinguishable from the case where one party becomes insane after the parties have been validly married, in which case the healthy spouse will be responsible if the other statutory factors are met.

Permanent spousal support may be awarded at the time an absolute or bed and board divorce is granted, if the court decrees that a divorce should be granted to neither party, or following dissolution of marriage. Va. Code § 20-107.1. Although "dissolution of marriage" is not defined in the statutes, it was construed in a child custody case to mean annulment of marriage. *Henderson v. Henderson,* 187 Va. 121, 46 S.E.2d 10 (1948). Dicta in an earlier case, *Bray v. Landergren,* 161 Va. 699, 172 S.E. 252 (1933), suggests that the right to alimony depends upon the existence of at least a voidable marriage. The reasoning of *Bray* was followed in *Mato v. Mato,* 12 Va. Cir. 153 (Spotsylvania Co. 1988), where wife sued husband for divorce for desertion and later adultery, and during deposition the attorneys discovered that the husband was married to someone else. Since the marriage to plaintiff was undoubtedly void as bigamous, no alimony could be awarded. In *Shoustari v. Zamani,* 39 Va. App. 517, 574 S.E.2d 314 (2002), which involved a bigamous marriage, the court of appeals held unequivocally that a trial court cannot award spousal support when a marriage is void ab initio, because a void marriage confers no legal rights to the parties. *Shoustari* distinguished *Henderson v. Henderson* as addressing only child support in the context of children of a void marriage.

Although *Bray v. Landergren* does not suggest this, in cases of some void marriages there may be an action in tort for damages for fraud and deceit. *Alexander v. Kuykendall,* 192 Va. 8, 63 S.E.2d 746 (1951).

At any time during the marriage an action may be brought for criminal nonsupport under Va. Code § 20-61 et seq. These suits should be brought in the juvenile and domestic relations court under Va. Code § 20-67. See *Heflin v. Heflin,* 177 Va. 385, 14 S.E.2d 317 (1941). The court in such cases may order temporary spousal support and may punish violation of such order by contempt. Va. Code § 20-71; *Wright v. Wright,* 164 Va. 245, 178 S.E. 884 (1935). The court may, after providing for support, garnish the wages of the obligor under Va. Code § 20-78.1, or order posting of recognizance under Va. Code § 20-72, or have payroll deductions made under Va. Code § 20-79.1. Support orders remain in effect unless removed by the original court, according to Va. Code § 20-74. These orders become inoperative once an order for support is entered by the circuit court in a divorce proceeding. Va. Code § 20-79.

Va. Code § 16.1-244 provides for concurrent jurisdiction of spousal support (as well as custody, visitation, and child support) in the juvenile and domestic relations district court and the circuit court. When a suit for divorce is filed in which "spousal support is raised by the pleadings and a hearing, including a pendente lite hearing, is set by the circuit court . . . for a date certain or on a motions docket to be heard within 21 days of the filing, the juvenile and domestic relations district courts shall be divested of the right to enter any further decrees or orders." Va. Code § 16.1-244. However, where both parties agree to a referral of the issue, the juvenile and domestic relations district court will continue to have jurisdiction to award spousal support.

Spousal support may be ordered to commence at any time including the date of commencement of the suit. The trial court has discretion to make the spousal support award retroactive to the date of filing. *Chaudhry v. Chaudhry*, 2020 Va. App. LEXIS 27 (January 28, 2020) (referring to Va. Code § 20-107.1(A)). The spousal support award can be effective at any time after the case has commenced. *Id.* (citing *Young v. Young*, 215 Va. 125, 126, 207 S.E.2d 825 (1974) (internal citation omitted); *Konefal v. Konefal*, 18 Va. App. 612, 614, 446 S.E.2d 153 (1994) (internal quotation omitted); *Weizenbaum v. Weizenbaum*, 12 Va. App. 899, 904, 407 S.E.2d 37 (1991)). In *Chaudhry*, the trial court's decision to award spousal support retroactive to the commencement of the case was affirmed even though no pendente lite support was requested.

The date as of which support is due is determined by the chancellor, and will not be disturbed unless there has been a clear abuse of discretion. *Lawrence v. Lawrence*, 212 Va. 44, 181 S.E.2d 640 (1971).

Spousal support must be requested in the original pleadings. Va. Code § 20-107.1(A) expressly requires that the party who is seeking support must properly plead his or her claim for support. A mere reference to "such other relief as may be just and equitable" does not give the court a basis for awarding spousal support. *Boyd v. Boyd*, 2 Va. App. 16, 18, 340 S.E.2d 578, 580–81 (1986). Thus there was no jurisdiction to grant a lump sum award of spousal support when there was no explicit reservation of jurisdiction to modify the periodic maintenance contained in the final decree. The wife therefore could not obtain the lump sum award even though the transcript of the hearing indicated that the trial court intended to make a lump sum award at a later time, but inadvertently failed to include the reservation in the final decree. *Dixon v. Pugh*, 244 Va. 539, 423 S.E.2d 169 (1992). Spousal support may be denied if a commissioner in chancery fails to recommend spousal support and no timely exceptions to the commissioner's report are filed. *Heath v. Heath*, 38 Va. App. 727, 568 S.E.2d 408 (2002).

The husband's divorce complaint, which prayed that the parties "be perpetually protected in their persons and property," was not sufficient to raise the issue of spousal support. The circuit court's divorce decree that revoked all prior support orders was therefore a nullity. *Reid v. Reid*, 24 Va. App. 146, 480 S.E.2d 771 (1997). See also *Harrell v. Harrell*, 272 Va. 652, 636 S.E.2d 391 (2006) (court erred in awarding wife a reservation of the right to request permanent spousal support, absent wife's specific prayer for that relief); *Fadness v. Fadness*, 52 Va. App. 833, 667 S.E.2d 857 (2008) (wife's request for "a periodic or lump sum monetary award" was sufficient to support award of spousal support).

Two appellate court cases affirmed the trial court awarding support where the recipient of support did not affirmatively request support in the pleadings. See *Ruane v. Ruane*, 2016 Va. App. LEXIS 320 (Nov. 22, 2016) and *Ozfidan v. Ozfidan*, 2017 Va. App. LEXIS 5 (Jan. 10, 2017). In both cases the husband's pleadings raised the issue of spousal support. Moreover, the opinions specified that Va. Code § 20-79 permits the award of spousal support when it is raised in either party's pleadings. However, following the *Ruane* and *Ozfidan* decisions, Va. Code § 20-107.1, which provides the statutory authority for courts to award support, was expressly amended in July 2017, to require that support could only be awarded to a spouse who made a request in his or her pleadings. Va. Code § 20-107.1(A) now mandates that support may only be awarded "provided that a claim for support has been properly pled by the party seeking support."

## § 20.04    Jurisdictional Problems in Obtaining Support

The award of spousal support creates a personal obligation on the part of the debtor. The adjudication therefore requires personal jurisdiction over the defendant, *Pennoyer v. Neff*, 95 U.S. 714, 24 L. Ed. 565 (1877); *Bray v. Landergren*, 161 Va. 699, 172 S.E. 252 (1933), and not merely personal service outside the state or notice by publication. *Minton v. First Nat'l Exchange Bank*, 206 Va. 589, 145 S.E.2d 139 (1965).

Va. Code § 8.01-328.1(a)(9) allows long-arm jurisdiction to be maintained when the marital domicile was in the state at the time of separation or when the cause of action for divorce arose or was commenced, and when there is personal service upon the nonresident. See *Cabaniss v. Cabaniss*, 46 Va. App. 595, 620 S.E.2d 559 (2005) (sufficiency of pleadings). When a court obtains jurisdiction over a nonresident under the long-arm statute, such service shall have the same effect as service on the nonresident within Virginia. Va. Code § 8.01-320 (amended 1997). This statute specifically includes divorce and annulment cases. However, personal jurisdiction is not obtained when a foreign divorce decree is registered in Virginia pursuant to the uniform acts discussed in § 20.05, and defendant is served in a third state. *Stephens v. Stephens,* 229 Va. 610, 331 S.E.2d 484 (1985). The fact that a settlement agreement including spousal support between the parties was entered into in the Commonwealth will not suffice to give Virginia courts personal jurisdiction for enforcement of a support order. *Morris v. Morris,* 4 Va. App. 539, 359 S.E.2d 104 (1987). For purposes of obtaining long-arm jurisdiction, the marital domicile cannot be unilaterally changed by one spouse. *Stellwagen v. Stellwagen*, 48 Va. Cir. 451 (Fairfax Co. 1999), involved a husband and wife who moved from Georgia, where they had been domiciled, to Virginia. They stayed for a year in Virginia, living on the lower floor of the wife's mother's home, intending to remain in the state, and receiving mail at the Virginia residence. Though the husband worked for a year in Virginia, in 1996 he left the state and moved first to New Hampshire and later to Florida. Although he claimed that his domicile had changed, "Husband and Wife never were present in any other place with the intent to live there indefinitely"; therefore, the Virginia court continued to have personal jurisdiction over him.

Where there is a valid separation agreement between the parties, jurisdiction by order of publication or by acceptance of service is sufficient to allow the agreement to be affirmed, ratified and incorporated into a final decree. Va. Code § 20-109.1; *Bray v. Landergren,* 161 Va. 699, 172 S.E. 252 (1933), (decided before the Supreme Court's decision of *Shaffer v. Heitner,* 433 U.S. 186, 97 S. Ct. 2569, 53 L. Ed. 2d 683 (1977), which restricts such quasi-in-rem jurisdiction to awards from property at issue in the instant proceedings).

Va. Code § 16.1-244 provides that once a divorce proceeding has begun in the circuit court, jurisdiction shall no longer lie in the juvenile and domestic relations district court unless both parties agree to the referral to juvenile court. See also Va. Code § 20-79 (district court's support orders become inoperative if decree providing for support is entered by circuit court). If a district court's support order is nullified by a subsequent *pendente lite* support order entered by a circuit court in a suit for divorce that ends in a nonsuit, the district court's support order is automatically resumed. *Ipsen v. Moxley*, 49 Va. App. 555, 642 S.E.2d 798 (2007). The circuit court's exercise of jurisdiction in entering a decree reducing the spousal support owed divested the juvenile and domestic relations court of jurisdiction to act further, according to *Romine v. Romine*, 22 Va. App. 760, 473 S.E.2d 99 (1996).

## § 20.05    Support Following a Foreign *Ex Parte* Divorce

The right to support is not extinguished by an *ex parte* decree rendered in another state, although the divorce itself will be given full faith and credit, *Newport v. Newport*, 219 Va. 48, 245 S.E.2d 134 (1978), so long as there was jurisdiction over the subject matter of the suit, obtained by domicile of the party seeking the divorce. *Williams v. North Carolina*, 325 U.S. 226, 65 S. Ct. 1092, 89 L. Ed. 1577, 31 Ohio Op. 83 (1945). The Supreme Court has not yet considered the effect of discrimination against the actions of other states, *Estin v. Estin*, 334 U.S. 541, 68 S. Ct. 1213, 92 L. Ed. 1561 (1948). The so-called divisible divorce concept changed the former rule in which alimony was extinguished with the severing of the marital bonds by the absolute divorce. See *Wright v. Wright*, 164 Va. 245, 178 S.E. 884 (1935) (husband's Nevada divorce precluded wife from later attacking the jurisdictional basis of the decree or seeking alimony). In *McClure v. McClure*, 1996 Va. App. LEXIS 639 (Oct. 8, 1996), the husband obtained an ex parte divorce in Guam. He later contended unsuccessfully that this removed the trial court's subject matter jurisdiction to rule on spousal and child support, child custody, and equitable distribution. A domestic *ex parte* decree must reserve the right to collect alimony. See, e.g., *Lenhart v. Burgett*, 1995 Va. App. LEXIS 300 (March 28, 1995), where the husband was served personally in Pennsylvania in the divorce action. The Virginia divorce decree reserved the issues of spousal support and equitable distribution. When the wife brought an action to reinstate the support and distribution matters, the husband appeared personally to contest the case.

If the dependent spouse appears in the foreign proceeding, the ability to later seek support in Virginia is lost, for the right to obtain support is extinguished. *Ceyte v. Ceyte*, 222 Va. 11, 278 S.E.2d 791 (1981); *Osborne v. Osborne*, 215 Va. 205, 207 S.E.2d 875 (1974).

The question remains whether an *ex parte* foreign divorce based upon fault will extinguish the Virginia spouse's support rights. Compare *Ceyte v. Ceyte*, 222 Va. 11, 278 S.E.2d 791 (1981) (personal jurisdiction since wife appeared in foreign proceeding to contest denial of support). The court of appeals held that a Tennessee decree rendered *ex parte* and finding the wife guilty of cruelty did not have to be given full faith and credit for purposes of barring a Virginia spousal support action, since "[a]ny decision or finding by the Tennessee court affecting the personal rights of support and property must be founded on in personam jurisdiction," even though such findings are sufficient to support the divorce award. *Gibson v. Gibson,* 5 Va. App. 426, 434, 364 S.E.2d 518 (1988).

## § 20.06     Revised Uniform Reciprocal Enforcement of Support Act and UIFSA

Va. Code § 20-88.12 et seq. set forth Virginia's enactment of the Revised Uniform Reciprocal Enforcement Act. This Act was repealed in 1994 and substituted with the enactment of the Uniform Interstate Family Support Act (see Va. Code § 20-88.32 et seq.). The remainder of this paragraph is retained primarily for historical significance. The act was designed to create an economical and expedient means of enforcing support for dependent Virginia children, *Scott v. Sylvester,* 220 Va. 182, 257 S.E.2d 774 (1979), and is also used for spousal support. *Alig v. Alig,* 220 Va. 80, 255 S.E.2d 494 (1979). The way that the statute works is to provide that the custodial spouse, or a legal custodian, Va. Code § 20-88.20-1, brings an action in the Juvenile and Domestic Relations Court, Va. Code § 20-88.2:2, where the obligee resides (rendering state), Va. Code § 20-88.21, showing that a duty to support exists, either under an existing court order or otherwise. Va. Code § 20-88.22. The court then forwards the petition to the state of the obligor, Va. Code § 20-88.22, called the responding state, which allows that party, in a full hearing, to present any defenses (Va. Code § 20-88.22) and also to demonstrate the extent of the ability to pay. The applicable law is that of the obligor's state at the time for which support is sought. This decision will then be binding upon the obligor. Va. Code § 20-88.15.

Where the obligation is under a foreign support order, the order may be registered in Virginia, Va. Code § 20-88.30:2 et seq., at which point it shall be treated as would be any Virginia support order. Va. Code § 20-88.30:6; *Alig v. Alig,* 220 Va. 80, 255 S.E.2d 494 (1979); *Scott v. Sylvester,* 220 Va. 182, 257 S.E.2d 774 (1979). Past due payments may be collected in Virginia even though accrued when the obligor was outside the state. However, in personam jurisdiction over the defendant is not obtained by registration of a foreign divorce decree pursuant to URESA, when the defendant is served in a third state. *Stephens v. Stephens,* 229 Va. 610, 331 S.E.2d 484 (1985). Enforcement then may be by way of recognizance, contempt, and payment through the court. Va. Code § 20-88.26. Federal legislation designed to aid in the enforcement of child support was enacted in 1984. The federal legislation required changes to various Virginia statutes providing methods of enforcement. The Virginia Dep't of Social Services is now authorized to contract with public or private entities for processing support payments. Va.

Code § 20-60.3. A localized system of collection and disbursement of support payments, with local accounting, has been reestablished. At the same time, a system of centralized accounting and enforcement with the Department will be maintained as required by federal law. Va. Code § 20-60.5. A dependent former wife may obtain an award for arrearages under a New Jersey divorce decree, although more than 10 years have elapsed after this foreign support order and eight years have passed since her remarriage. *Bennett v. Commonwealth, Dep't of Social Services,* 15 Va. App. 135, 422 S.E.2d 458. The court of appeals noted that a spousal support order adjudicates an ongoing indeterminate support obligation. *Koneczny v. Koneczny,* 1995 Va. App. LEXIS 914 (Dec. 19, 1995). However, when the husband's liability for sharing the repair costs was not conditioned on her presenting bills or documentation of the total repair costs. The court of appeals noted that a spousal support order adjudicates an ongoing indeterminate support obligation. The responsibility extends for the lifetime of the parties absent a stipulation or contract between them, and is subject only to termination by operation of law on the death of one of the parties or the remarriage of the obligee. The moment that each installment falls due and unpaid, it becomes a vested property right and is immune from modification. Because of the ongoing nature of the order, no time limitation is placed upon the obligee spouse within which to obtain a judgment for accumulated arrearages, and even the doctrine of laches may not defeat the arrearage claim. The court contrasted this situation with a URESA proceeding in which the foreign support order adjudicates a sum certain due and owing, in which Va. Code § 8.01-252 acts as a cutoff provision.

Virginia adopted the Interstate Family Support Act (UIFSA) in Va. Code § 20-88.32 et seq. (1994). The act is similar to the Uniform Reciprocal Support Act in many respects, but does not apply to alimony, as opposed to child support, according to Va. Code § 20-88.32. The support enforcement agency is not authorized to establish or enforce a support award for only spousal support. Va. Code § 20-88.39. Visitation issues cannot be raised in child support proceedings. Va. Code § 20-88.48.

### § 20.07   Role of Fault in Precluding Support

Until 1988, Va. Code § 20-107.1 specifically provided that if a cause of action for an absolute fault divorce under Va. Code § 20-91, or a bed and board divorce under Va. Code § 20-95 existed against a spouse, that spouse should not be awarded alimony. See, e.g., *Stolfi v. Stolfi,* 203 Va. 696, 126 S.E.2d 923 (1962). This included fault after the separation but before a cause of action accrues. *Haskins v. Haskins,* 188 Va. 525, 50 S.E.2d 437 (1948) (adultery after *a mensa* decree in favor of wife), see also *Gloth v. Gloth,* 154

Va. 511, 153 S.E. 879 (1930) (even though an *a mensa* divorce decree incorporated a separation agreement between the parties, it could be revoked when the wife subsequently committed adultery; before revision of § 20-109, which will not allow such an agreement to be modified except in accordance with its terms when filed with divorce pleadings). See generally Wadlington, *Sexual Relations After Separation or Divorce,* 63 Va. L. Rev. 249 (1977). The question of whether fault that occurs after the one-year separation period should negate the right to alimony remained, cf. *Coe v. Coe,* 225 Va. 616, 303 S.E.2d 923 (1983), as did the question of whether the dependent spouse's fault after conduct precipitating the marriage's demise on the part of the obligor should also be a bar. See *Wallace v. Wallace,* 46 Md. App. 213, 416 A.2d 1317 (1980). The court of appeals has determined that if the husband's conduct precipitated the parties' separation, and if the adulterous behavior occurred many years later, spousal support for the wife will not be precluded. *Wallace v. Wallace,* 1 Va. App. 183, 336 S.E.2d 27 (1985). See also *Surbey v. Surbey,* 5 Va. App. 119, 360 S.E.2d 873 (1987) (conduct of both parties caused separation, and no divorce could be granted to either on grounds of adultery because of recrimination).

The evolution of the standard for fault required to preclude support culminated in 1988 amendments to Va. Code § 20-107.1. The amendments provide that the court may make a spousal support award notwithstanding the existence of a fault ground for divorce, except in cases of adultery, sodomy or buggery. Even in adultery cases, the court may make an award if it determines from clear and convincing evidence that the denial of support and maintenance would constitute a manifest injustice, based upon the respective degrees of fault during the marriage and the relative economic circumstances of the parties. Fault must, nevertheless, be considered in determining whether to award support, and in deciding the amount to be awarded. See, e.g., *Williams v. Williams,* 14 Va. App. 217, 415 S.E.2d 252 (1992), where the wife was granted spousal support of $200 per month following a no-fault divorce despite the fact that the husband showed that she had become pregnant by another and had obtained a therapeutic abortion during the parties' separation. The trial judge had noted that he had considered factors set forth in § 20-107.1 although he did not elaborate on any specific factor. See also *Barnes v. Barnes,* 16 Va. App. 98, 428 S.E.2d 294 (1993), where both parties had accepted that the marriage had ended, both intended to separate at some time in future, and the husband acquiesced in the separation. Although the husband proved the wife had committed adultery, the court found that it would be manifestly unjust for her not to receive spousal support since the adultery had little, if anything, to do with the deterioration of the marriage and did not prevent a possible reconciliation. See also *Konicki v. Konicki,* 32 Va. Cir. 368 (Spotsylvania Co. 1994) (husband condoned wife's adultery); *Bandas v. Bandas,* 16 Va. App. 427, 430 S.E.2d 706 (1993), where husband divorced on grounds of his imprisonment for a felony had to pay spousal support despite his wife's subsequent adultery and cohabitation; and *Mullins v. Mullins,* 1994 Va. App. LEXIS 655 (Nov. 8, 1994), where parties were separated for fourteen years prior to divorce, and divorce was granted on that ground rather than the husband's adultery. He had lived with another woman for many years and had a child with her. Apparently his fault did not enhance her alimony award. See also *Calvin v. Calvin,* 31 Va. App. 181, 522 S.E.2d 376 (1999) (though fault weighed heavily in favor of the husband, denial of support to the wife would be a "manifest injustice given her health condition, her reliance during the marriage on the financial support" of the husband, and her inability to obtain insurance coverage); *Congdon v. Congdon,* 40 Va. App. 255, 578 S.E.2d 833 (2003) (respective degrees of marital fault of adulterous wife and verbally abusive husband, coupled with extreme economic disparities between them, supported finding that denying spousal support to wife would constitute "manifest injustice").

The manifest injustice is a narrow exception under the law and is synonymous with a miscarriage of justice. *Mundy v. Mundy,* 66 Va. App. 177, 181, 783 S.E.2d 535, 537 (2016) (the Wife was unable to prove a manifest injustice by clear and convincing evidence). Where the wife's adultery was proven, the trial court's award of a reservation of spousal support was overturned. *Giraldi v. Giraldi,* 64 Va. App. 676, 771 S.E.2d 687 (2015). However, where the circumstances were suspicious and the husband did not prove his wife's adultery by clear and convincing evidence, the trial court erred by refusing to grant Wife a reservation of alimony. *Romero v. Colbow,* 27 Va. App. 88, 497 S.E.2d 516 (1998). In addition, the trial court was upheld in finding a manifest injustice and awarding spousal support to the wife where the marriage broke down gradually over the years, the husband made most of the monetary contributions to the well-being of the family, and the wife made most of the non-monetary contributions. *Pattillo v. Pattillo,* 2018 Va. App. LEXIS 144 (May 29, 2018) (unpublished opinion).

It is significant to understand that when alimony is at issue, evidence regarding adultery on the part of the spouse seeking support can be presented even when the issue of adultery was not raised in any pleading or asserted as an affirmative defense. *Chaney v. Karabaic-Chaney,* 71 Va. App. 431, 837 S.E.2d 76 (2020). In response to Ms. Chaney's divorce complaint, Mr. Chaney filed a responsive pleading which neither asserted the affirmative defense of adultery nor included a counterclaim for divorce. *Id.* at 433. Since the Husband did not raise the issue of adultery, the trial court granted the Wife's motion in limine and prohibited the husband from introducing any evidence of the Wife's adultery. The Court of Appeals held that the trial court erred in granting the wife's motion in limine, and held that Va. Code § 20-107.1(E) "commands a court to consider evidence of adultery when awarding spousal support, even if the proponent of the evidence did not plead adultery as a ground for divorce or as an affirmative defense." *Id.* at 436. Nowhere does Va. Code § 20-107.1(E) "limit a court's consideration to the legal grounds actually pled for divorce when determining spousal support." *Id.* at 438.

Even though the husband succeeded in overturning the trial court's finding that there had been no desertion on the wife's part so that she was entitled to spousal support, the husband could not "equitably recoup" the $85,000 he had paid her pursuant to the erroneous decree. He could not recover the money under a theory of restitution, either, because the statutory scheme that allows a divorce court to grant alimony and later to modify that award does not expressly extend to the award of a judgment in favor of the payor spouse for previously paid amounts. Nor might the husband indirectly be reimbursed through a reduction in the monetary award given the wife as property distribution. *Reid v. Reid*, 245 Va. 409, 429 S.E.2d 208 (1993), reversing 14 Va. App. 505, 419 S.E.2d 398 (1992). Similarly, if one spouse is required to pay the other temporary alimony, the court may not order restitution of the amounts paid even though the payor obtains a divorce on fault grounds. *Hurt v. Hurt*, 16 Va. App. 792, 433 S.E.2d 493 (1993).

In accordance with Va. Code § 20-109(A), if the dependent spouse has been habitually cohabiting with another person in a relationship analogous to marriage for a year or more, the court must terminate spousal support or maintenance, unless the divorcing parties' agreement otherwise provides, or the dependent spouse proves by a preponderance of the evidence that termination of support would be unconscionable. The cohabitation must be proved by clear and convincing evidence, and termination of support must follow a court order. Post-separation cohabitation does not prohibit an award of spousal support under Va. Code § 20-107.1 if other evidence establishes that support was warranted.

It is common for a spouse who is seeking support to assert the privileges of the Fifth Amendment and refuse to testify to any information that may incriminate them being involved in an adulterous relationship. Until 2020, the assertion of the protections afforded by the Fifth Amendment were fairly absolute. However, as of July 1, 2020, Va. Code § 8.01-223.1 was amended to specify that in any civil proceeding for spousal support, custody or visitation, an adverse inference can be made against any party or witness who "refuses to answer a question about conduct described in subdivision A(1) of § 20-91 or in § 18.2-365." While the practical considerations of this amendment are debatable and are certainly favored by the party who may be subject to paying spousal support, the deprivation of constitutional protections is alarming and the constitutionality of this amendment is likely to be challenged.

### § 20.08  The Necessity for Showing Need

The need of each party must be considered in awarding alimony under Va. Code § 20-107.1(1). This principle is also reflected in Va. Code § 20-107.1(2), which lists the education and training, and ability to receive such, and § 20-107.1(5), which mentions the age and physical and mental condition of each party. For example, a wronged wife could show no need when she had supported herself (and the husband) throughout the marriage while he was in dental school. *Gagliano v. Gagliano,* 215 Va. 447, 211 S.E.2d 62 (1975). Her right to later receive alimony should have been reserved in the decree. The code sections referenced above are now located at Va. Code § 20-107.1(E)(1), (4) and (9). As a general rule, a spouse who seeks spousal support is obligated to earn as much as he or she reasonably can to reduce the amount of the support need. Thus, under appropriate circumstances, a court may impute income to a spouse seeking spousal support. *Srinivasan v. Srinivasan,* 10 Va. App. 728, 396 S.E.2d 675, 679 (1990). See *McKee v. McKee,* 52 Va. App. 482, 664 S.E.2d 505 (2008); *Brandau v. Brandau,* 52 Va. App. 632, 666 S.E.2d 532 (2008).

If a spouse works during the marriage, but stops working or accepts a job beneath his or her earning capacity after separation, income will be imputed to the spouse. See, e.g., *Baytop v. Baytop,* 199 Va. 388, 100 S.E.2d 14 (1957) (spouse worked during marriage but quit her employment prior to trial); *Butler v. Butler,* 217 Va. 195, 227 S.E.2d 688 (1976) (spouse could "double his income" by taking different job); *Poliquin v. Poliquin,* 12 Va. App. 676, 406 S.E.2d 401 (1991) (minimum lump sum support awarded to spouse with improved, rather than lessened, earning capacity); *O'Hara v. O'Hara,* 45 Va. App. 788, 613 S.E.2d 859 (2005) (wife's income ended when she was "terminated" by employer). See also *Joynes v. Payne,* 36 Va. App. 401, 551 S.E.2d 10 (2001) (when attorney wife had voluntarily terminated part-time employment with law firm, commissioner properly based determination of spousal support award on wife's demonstrated past earning capacity, rather than on testimony of husband's expert witness regarding wife's salary potential with her old law firm); *Bruemmer v. Bruemmer,* 46 Va. App. 205,

616 S.E.2d 740 (2005) (when wife had $2.3 million in assets and present ability to earn $89,000 a year, spousal support order providing for time-related decreases and termination of spousal support was proper, given wife's obligation to contribute to her own support, her earning capacity, and wide disparity in assets between parties).

In order to impute income based on past earnings, the evidence of the past earnings must be recent. *Collins v. Leeds,* 69 Va. App. 1, 9–10, 813 S.E.2d 902 (2018). In *Collins,* the former husband had voluntarily retired in 2013, and at wife's hearing in 2017 seeking to modify spousal support, she presented evidence only as to Husband's earnings from before his retirement in 2013. The evidence was too distant and failed to provide the court with credible information regarding the earnings that her former husband could reasonably expect at the time of the evidentiary hearing. *Id.*

However, income will not necessarily be imputed to a stay-at-home spouse with provable earning capacity who does not start work outside the home immediately upon entry of a divorce decree. See, e.g., *Srinivasan v. Srinivasan,* 10 Va. App. 728, 396 S.E.2d 675 (1990) (spouse who at time of divorce was leading life style she was accustomed to during marriage, and who had not unreasonably refused to accept employment, was entitled to reasonable time to secure employment); *Stubblebine v. Stubblebine,* 22 Va. App. 703, 473 S.E.2d 72 (1996) (spousal support awards must be made "upon the circumstances disclosed by the evidence at the time of the award"); *McKee v. McKee,* 52 Va. App. 482, 664 S.E.2d 505 (2008) (wife who could not legally work as respiratory therapist was not required to return to work immediately to avoid imputation of income); *Brandau v. Brandau,* 52 Va. App. 632, 666 S.E.2d 532 (2008) (support award was based on conditions existing at time of final divorce decree, including wife's heart condition, and left open possibility of recalibrating award at some later date if conditions changed). See also *Miller v. Cox,* 44 Va. App. 674, 607 S.E.2d 126 (2005) (wife was awarded $9,000 a month in spousal support, after successfully arguing that divorce should not require her to alter her standard of living or change her investment strategies, in that important goal during marriage was to accumulate sufficient assets to be able to retire at early age without financial concerns).

The trial court has discretion for determining whether or not to impute income. There is no "statutory preset requiring the imputation of income to a spouse seeking support if she has provable earning capacity at the time of divorce." *deCamp v. deCamp,* 64 Va. App. 137, 151, 765 S.E.2d 863, 870 (2014) (citations omitted). Neither "*Srinivasan* nor any other Virginia case has held that, for purposes of calculating spousal support, a stay-at-home spouse capable of working must go to work immediately after the divorce trial or face a judicially imposed imputation of income." *Id.* (internal citation omitted). Rather, income imputation cases have "involved spouses who worked during the marriage but, sometime after separation, either accepted a job beneath their earning capacity or stopped working altogether." *Id.* (internal citation omitted).

The burden is on the spouse seeking imputation of income to prove, either by producing evidence of a higher-paying former job or by showing that more lucrative work is currently available, that the other spouse is voluntarily foregoing more gainful employment. See *McKee v. McKee*, 52 Va. App. 482, 664 S.E.2d 505 (2008); *Joynes v. Payne*, 36 Va. App. 401, 551 S.E.2d 10 (2001).

The mere fact that a wife is entitled to support and the husband has the ability to pay does not mean that the court must award the wife attorney's fees. *Cirrito v. Cirrito*, 44 Va. App. 287, 605 S.E.2d 268 (2004).

The wife was entitled to spousal support where the parties had significant disparity in earning potential, where she was not at fault, and where the husband did not demonstrate any reason that she should not be entitled to support. *Via v. Via,* 14 Va. App. 868, 419 S.E.2d 431 (1992). See also *Simpson v. Simpson,* 1994 Va. App. LEXIS 123 (March 15, 1994), where the court affirmed an alimony award in a case where the husband earned $70,000 per year and wife $24,600. The court noted that the chancellor must consider the subjective needs of each spouse when examining the statutory factors of need and ability to pay, as well as the "station to which a party may have grown accustomed during marriage." *Id.* at *4. See also *Gelletly v. Gelletly*, 1996 Va. App. LEXIS 39 (Jan. 23, 1996), where the wife was working approximately 17 and a half hours a week, but was hampered by discomfort from two ruptured discs. *Kasprzak v. Kasprzak,* 1993 Va. App. LEXIS 284 (July 20, 1993); *Rein v. Rein,* 1994 Va. App. LEXIS 699 (Nov. 29, 1994) (wife was nurse who had not worked during the marriage; trial court to consider whether she unreasonably refused to seek employment or whether she needed additional time before she secured employment); *Hauger v. Hauger,* 1995 Va. App. LEXIS 206 (Feb. 28, 1995) (in January of 1990, husband agreed to pay wife sufficient temporary support to enable her to earn masters' degree; at the time of the hearing she still had completed only one-third of thesis research). A husband is not obliged to provide for the wife's expenditures on pet care, charitable contributions, cable television, AAA membership for adult children, and gifts. *Seidenberg v. Seidenberg,* 9 Va. Cir. 83 (Henrico Co. 1987); *Hodges v. Hodges,* 2 Va. App. 508, 347 S.E.2d 134 (1986), where the wife earned $145 weekly, had expended her inheritance during the marriage, and had no separate property of any significance, while the husband had income in excess of $64,000 per year and a net worth of between $167,000 and $189,000. She was appropriately awarded support for "[h]er need for support is clearly established." *Id.,* 347 S.E.2d at 138.

Although formerly the wife's personal estate had no bearing on the husband's obligation to pay alimony, *Ring v. Ring,* 185 Va. 269, 38 S.E.2d 471 (1946), the statute now requires that the financial resources of each be considered. Installment payments to complete property distribution should not have been considered as income to the recipient spouse. *Ray v. Ray,* 4 Va. App. 509, 358 S.E.2d 754 (1987). Both *Ray* and *Zipf v. Zipf,* 8 Va. App. 387, 382 S.E.2d 263 (1989), note that the law does not require the spouse who seeks support to exhaust his or her own estate in order to qualify. But see *McGuire v. McGuire,* 10 Va. App. 248, 391 S.E.2d 344 (1990), holding that it was permissible to consider wife's share of husband's monthly retirement pension as "income of whatever nature" reducing the husband's support obligation.

The wife provided an expert witness concerning her psychological condition and ability to work in *Umbarger v. Umbarger,* 1993 Va. App. LEXIS 132 (May 18, 1993). She had not been employed outside the home for 20 years, and the judge did not impute income to her based on her earning capacity.

All orders for spousal support shall contain a statement as to whether there is already an order requiring provision of coverage, or if the dependent spouse needs such an order, according to Va. Code § 20-60.3(6).

When a couple divorces on grounds of insanity, the parties are not necessarily relieved of spousal support obligations. If the institutionalized spouse might be eligible for federal medical assistance services, the court shall first order the institutionalized spouse to make available the maximum income contribution to the other spouse. If the spousal support award exceeds the federally established monthly maintenance needs allowance, the court must find that the increase is necessary because of exceptional circumstances causing financial distress to the other spouse. These circumstances might include threatened loss of basic food, shelter or medically necessary health care or the financial burden of caring for a disabled child, sibling or other relative. Effective January 1994, the maximum spousal resource allowance is $72,660. Va. Code § 20-88.02:1.

## § 20.09  Duration of Marriage

The duration of the marriage affects the right to support both directly, under Va. Code § 20-107.1(4), and indirectly, since frequently in marriages of long duration the spouses will have made many contributions to the family's well-being. Va. Code § 20-107.1(6). In marriages of long standing, one spouse may not have sought educational or other training or will have been removed from the job market for such an extended period of time that financial independence is not possible. See, e.g., *Reynolds v. Reynolds*, 9 Va. Cir. 423 (Henrico Co. 1977); see also Va. Code §§ 20-107.1(E)(3), (6), and (11).

There is no presumption in Va. Code § 20-107.1(C) that spousal support awards of limited duration will generally apply only to short term marriages. *Torian v. Torian*, 38 Va. App. 167, 562 S.E.2d 355 (2002). In *Torian*, an award of seven years of periodic spousal support following a 26-year marriage was proper, when the factors on which the award was premised (including the parties' ages; the amount, nature, and liquidity of assets they received in the equitable distribution; and the wife's ability to draw on her share of those assets at a specific age without incurring a tax penalty) were not so uncertain with respect to render the defined duration award speculative. Moreover, the trial court was justified in awarding spousal support for an undefined duration of time despite the marriage lasting only ten months. *Hyat v. Hina*, 2020 Va. App. LEXIS 179 (June 23, 2020).

The wife was awarded substantial alimony plus 40% of her husband's plastic surgery practice in *Silvester v. Silvester*, 1996 Va. App. LEXIS 774 (Dec. 31, 1996). The wife had managed the home and tended to the day-to-day duties of raising the children during the parties' 25-year marriage. On the other extreme, when the parties divorced after only a year of marriage, causing the wife to relocate twice in a short time, this should have a bearing on spousal support, but not equitable distribution of property. *Lightburn v. Lightburn*, 22 Va. App. 612, 472 S.E.2d 281 (1996).

## § 20.10  Reservation of Right to Support in Final Decree of Divorce

Once a decree for support has been rendered, it remains binding until a contingency occurs for which the decree provides, or until further order of the court. A subsequent contract between the parties will not prevent enforcement under the decree of the amount provided for in the agreement. *Capell v. Capell*, 164 Va. 45, 178 S.E. 894 (1935).

In order to preserve the right to have support, the decree should contain a proper reservation to that effect. *Brinn v. Brinn*, 147 Va. 277, 286, 137 S.E. 503, 505 (1927). If this is not done, the matter will be res judicata, and no support may later be awarded. Thus there was no jurisdiction to grant a lump sum award of spousal support when there was no explicit reservation of jurisdiction to modify the periodic maintenance contained in the final decree. The wife therefore could not obtain the lump sum award even though the transcript of the hearing indicated that the trial court intended to make a lump sum award at a later time, but inadvertently failed to include the reservation in the final decree. *Dixon v. Pugh,* 244 Va. 539, 423 S.E.2d 169 (1992). There was also no adequate reservation in a decree providing only for renegotiation of spousal support. *Sinnott v. Sinnott,* 1993 Va. App. LEXIS 151 (May 25, 1993). See, e.g., *Lauffer v. Lauffer,* 23 Va. Cir. 278 (Fairfax Co. 1991). There may be a reservation of a right to such future periodic support even after a limited lump sum award is made by the divorce court and even though the payee spouse does not request it. *Poliquin v. Poliquin,* 12 Va. App. 676, 406 S.E.2d 401 (1991); *Blank v. Blank,* 10 Va. App. 1, 389 S.E.2d 723 (1990).

The court may reserve the right of a party to receive support in the future in addition to or in lieu of an award for periodic payments, payments for a defined duration, or a lump sum award. Va. Code § 20-107.1(C). Pursuant to Va. Code § 20-107.1(D), there exists a rebuttable presumption that the reservation of spousal support will continue for half the length of time between the dates of marriage and separation. Once the reservation is granted, the duration of the reservation shall not be subject to modification. "Date of separation" means the earliest date at which the parties are physically separated and at least one intends the separation to be permanent, provided that the separation is continuous thereafter. Va. Code § 20-107.1(G).

The court may not grant a reservation of the right to request spousal support under Va. Code § 20-107.1(D) in the absence of a valid pleading that requests permanent spousal support. *Harrell v. Harrell,* 272 Va. 652, 636 S.E.2d 391 (2006). Va. Code § 20-107.1(A) expressly requires that the party who is seeking support must properly plead his or her claim for support. The trial court did not abuse its discretion in entering a reservation of spousal support where the wife expressly requested a reservation in her motion for reconsideration. *Wright v. Wright,* 61 Va. App. 432, 446–47, 737 S.E.2d 519, 525–26 (2013) (the Court of Appeals also noted that wife's divorce complaint contained a request for an award of spousal support). However, where Husband was able to prove Wife's adultery, the trial court's award of a reservation of spousal support was overturned. *Giraldi v. Giraldi,* 64 Va. App. 676, 771 S.E.2d 687 (2015). When a bar to the right to spousal support exists due to adultery, sodomy or buggery, the spouse cannot be awarded a reservation of spousal support. Va. Code § 20-107.1(B) (". . . no permanent maintenance and support shall be awarded from a spouse if there exists in such spouse's favor a ground of divorce under the provisions of subdivision A(1) of § 20-91."). Where each party was at fault of contributing to the dissolution of the marriage, a wife was entitled to a reservation of spousal support since no grounds for divorce under Va. Code § 20-91(A) were proven. *Wyatt v. Wyatt*, 70 Va. App. 716, 721, 833 S.E.2d 84 (2019).

## § 20.11    Contributions to the Marriage as Relevant to Support

Both monetary and nonmonetary contributions to the family's well-being are to be considered under Va. Code § 20-107.1(6). Although the length of the marriage is a relevant statutory factor for the court to consider in awarding alimony, it cannot be the only factor considered. *Bristow v. Bristow*, 221 Va. 1, 267 S.E.2d 89 (1980).

The wife was entitled to spousal support where the parties had significant disparity in earning potential, where she was not at fault, and where the husband did not demonstrate any reason that she should not be entitled to support. *Via v. Via*, 14 Va. App. 868, 419 S.E.2d 431 (1992). Further, she was entitled to attorney's fees because the husband's failure to provide discovery necessitated most of her litigation expenses.

When the parties divorced after only a year of marriage, causing the wife to relocate twice in a short time, this should have a bearing on spousal support, but not equitable distribution of property. *Lightburn v. Lightburn*, 22 Va. App. 612, 472 S.E.2d 281 (1996).

One important contribution that a spouse may make is in caring for a child, including an older child with special needs. This contribution is recognized in Va. Code § 20-107.1(4) and (5). Consider *Barker v. Barker*, 27 Va. App. 519, 500 S.E.2d 240 (1998). The Court of Appeals ruled that the husband's payments to his first wife constituted the use of marital funds to pay a separate debt. The trial judge was ordered to reconsider on remand the husband's positive contributions to the well-being of the family, which included support of his present wife's three children from a prior marriage whose father stopped paying child support.

The statutory factors listed in Va. Code § 20-107.1(E) for a trial court to consider in awarding spousal support include various contributions to earning capacity and marital well-being. For example: factor (9) considers each party's present earning capacity; factor (10) involves the question of whether additional education, vocational rehabilitation, or training is appropriate, given the parties' time and abilities as well as the costs of such training; and factor (11) requires the court to look at decisions regarding employment, career, education, and parenting the parties may have made during the marriage. Some of these choices may have affected current or future earning potential of one or both spouses. For example, this factor includes the length of time one or both has been absent from the job market. Finally, factor (12) requires consideration of the extent to which either party has contributed to the education, training, profession, or career position of the other. In contested cases in circuit court, any order granting, reserving, or denying spousal support shall be accompanied by written findings. The findings shall identify which of these factors buttress the court's order and which justify limiting support to a defined duration. Va. Code § 20-107.1(F).

These code sections are significant because they clarify Virginia's position on the important issue of career enhancement. Virginia will apparently join the states recognizing investments in the career of one spouse through alimony, rather than property, awards. The legislation also implicitly recognizes the concept of opportunity cost, the fact that investments in the earning capacity of one spouse come at a cost in terms of what either spouse could otherwise have done. For recent discussions of these topics, *see* Margaret F. Brinig, *Property Distribution Physics: The Talisman of Time and Middle Class Law*, 31 Fam. L.Q. 93 (1997); and Allen M. Parkman, *Human Capital as Property in Celebrity Divorces*, 29 Fam. L.Q. 141 (1995).

### § 20.12     Ability to Pay as Relevant to Support Award

The earning capacity and financial resources of each party are taken into account in determining alimony. Va. Code § 20-107.1(E)(1). This includes income from pension, profit sharing and retirement plans. It also includes the property possessed by each under Va. Code § 20-107.1(E)(7). For example, an unemployed husband was ordered to pay alimony where there was nothing to prevent him from renting his property or obtaining employment in order to have some visible means of income. *Canavos v. Canavos,* 205 Va. 744, 139 S.E.2d 825 (1965). See also *Hawkins v. Hawkins,* 187 Va. 595, 47 S.E.2d 436 (1948) (defendant able to work full-time but actually worked about three-quarters of the time). The court properly imputed income from a second job held regularly by the obligor, a school teacher, when this summer income was used to establish the standard of living during the marriage. *Cochran v. Cochran,* 14 Va. App. 827, 419 S.E.2d 419 (1992). See also *Gelletly v. Gelletly,* 1996 Va. App. LEXIS 39 (Jan. 23, 1996), where $85,000 income was imputed to the husband when he had "jumped from a place of safety into a dry hole," though he had voluntarily left his former employment for a lower paying job. His payments were reduced, but not eliminated, because "[t]he fact that the new job fell short of his expectations did not relieve him of his pre-existing spousal support obligations." The code sections referenced above are now located at Va. Code § 20-107.1(E)(1) and (7).

*Floyd v. Floyd,* 17 Va. App. 222, 436 S.E.2d 457 (1993), involved a husband in the construction business who systematically hid assets and income, according to the trial court. During one year, he cashed checks totaling almost $70,000 and received the proceeds in cash, while he claimed no income. The court of appeals affirmed the trial court's estimate of $45,000 in annual income for spousal and child support purposes. See also *Stubblebine v. Stubblebine,* 22 Va. App. 703, 473 S.E.2d 72 (1996). (Husband retired from the Army and worked for BDM Corporation, earning $90,000 annually. He resigned from this position, undertaking a variety of independent consulting jobs, and, although not gainfully employed, worked long hours for an organization involved in the study of parapsychology and psychic phenomena.). See also *Reece v. Reece,* 22 Va. App. 368, 470 S.E.2d 148 (1996). holding that when a supporting spouse refuses to accept an offer of comparable employment in another geographical location, there is no per se rule holding that the change in income constitutes voluntary unemployment or underemployment. *Leiffer v. Leiffer,* 1997 Va. App. LEXIS 134 (Mar. 18, 1997) (court imputed income where husband left a $100,000 a year job for a risky venture in a small company soon to be bankrupt).

In *Frazer v. Frazer,* 23 Va. App. 358, 477 S.E.2d 290 (1996), the husband made $30,000 in voluntary contributions to his retirement plan after the couple separated. The Court of Appeals found that these contributions should be included in his income for determining spousal support. But see *Bruemmer v. Bruemmer,* 46 Va. App. 205, 616 S.E.2d 740 (2005) (mandatory 401K retirement plan contributions determined by vote of law partnership were deductible from gross income of individual partner for child support purposes).

The income received by a spouse from the spouse's share of the distribution of a pension is a fungible asset that may be considered as a resource when determining the amount of an obligor's spousal support obligation, just as the other spouse's share of the pension is a resource that must be considered in determining need for support. *Moreno v. Moreno,* 24 Va. App. 190, 204, 480 S.E.2d 792 (1997); *to the contrary,* see *Cunningham v. Cunningham,* 1996 Va. App. LEXIS 524 (July 23, 1996) (unpublished). The *Moreno* court reasoned that although Va. Code § 20-107.3(G) limits the award a spouse can receive pursuant to the equitable distribution of marital property, no statutory language precludes that property from then being considered as income for purposes of calculation of spousal support.

It is imperative for the spouse seeking support to present evidence regarding the other party's ability to pay. *Robbins v. Robbins*, 48 Va. App. 466, 484, 632 S.E.2d 615, 624 (2006). Where a party relied solely on a pendente lite order at the final hearing, and did not offer any evidence of the spouse's earnings and ability to pay, the trial court's award of spousal support was reversed. *Collard v. Collins*, 2017 Va. App. LEXIS 281 (Nov. 14, 2017) (unpublished opinion).

In *Driscoll v. Hunter*, 59 Va. App. 22, 716 S.E.2d 477 (2011), the trial court denied the husband's motion to reduce or suspend his spousal support obligation and held that the payee spouse was not required to exhaust her share of the equitable distribution award in order to meet her needs. The 2018 amendment that added Va. Code § 20-109(F)(6) requiring the court to consider the assets and property interests of both parties where a request to modify spousal support is based on the payor's spouse's retirement, was intended to overrule *Driscoll*. The remaining portion of this section is left for historical purposes. The court of appeals affirmed the judgment finding that the trial court did not abuse its broad discretion in declining to reduce the amount of spousal support given the husband's considerable assets, his level of expenditures, and the relatively modest amount of spousal support of $2,100 per month. The evidence at trial showed that the husband owned an IRA worth approximately $1.376 million, investment accounts and stocks worth approximately $1.164 million, and additional checking, savings and money market accounts with a value estimated at $230,000. In addition, his home was insured for $800,000, with no outstanding mortgages on the house and he also received income from Social Security.

An award of 71 percent of the husband's income, leaving him with insufficient funds to pay for basic necessities, was erroneous according to *Justice v. Justice*, 1995 Va. App. LEXIS 212 (Feb. 28, 1995). Nor could a court impute income because the supporting father was one of four contingent beneficiaries of a trust established for his own mother and aunt. *Harrison v. Harrison*, 1996 Va. App. LEXIS 54 (Jan. 30, 1996). Likewise, spousal support should not have been awarded where the husband, a doctor, had no ability to pay after engaging in a series of unwise investment decisions, bad loans, and failed joint ventures. But the wife in *Masri v. Masri*, 48 Va. Cir. 5 (Chesterfield Co. 1999), was awarded the lion's share of the marital resources because of her "overwhelmingly greater monetary and non-monetary contributions to the marriage."

The ability to pay and need must be judged as of the time of the decree or modification. *Thomas v. Thomas*, 217 Va. 502, 229 S.E.2d 887 (1976); *Taylor v. Taylor*, 203 Va. 1, 121 S.E.2d 753 (1961). Therefore, it was erroneous for a court to include a clause escalating the amount of support payments based upon a percentage of increase in the husband's income, *Jacobs v. Jacobs,* 219 Va. 993, 254 S.E.2d 56 (1979), since this would be premised upon an uncertain future circumstance. See also *Robertson v. Robertson,* 215 Va. 425, 211 S.E.2d 41 (1975) (not proper to consider possible future receipt of trust fund).

A prior court order for support and maintenance of a previous spouse and child will clearly reduce the amount that would be available to pay a later one. *Id.* at 429.

When earning capacity, voluntary unemployment, or voluntary under-employment is at issue in determining support, the court may order a party to submit to an evaluation by a vocational expert employed by the other party. Va. Code § 20-108.1(H).

### § 20.13   *Pendente Lite* as Opposed to Permanent Support

Frequently, the first problem confronting an attorney in a divorce suit is the question of temporary spousal support. The pendente lite statute, Va. Code § 20-103, permits a trial court to award significant relief while a divorce case is pending. The relief includes such things as the payment of temporary spousal support, an obligation to maintain health care coverage, exclusive use of the family residence, the payment of secured and unsecured debts, and an obligation to maintain an existing life insurance policy. As of July 2016, any temporary spousal support has to be paid from the payor's post-separation income unless good cause exists to order otherwise. As of July 1, 2020, Va. Code § 20-103 was amended to specifically include statutory guidelines for pendente lite spousal support and child support in cases where the combined monthly gross income of the parties is $10,000 or less. Va. Code § 20-103(E)-(I).

In proceedings for *pendente lite* spousal support and maintenance under Va. Code Title 16.1 where the parties' combined monthly gross income is $10,000 per month or less, the presumptively correct amount of *pendente lite* spousal support is determined by the formula in Va. Code § 16.1-278.17:1(C), which compares percentages of the parties' respective incomes. A court may deviate from the presumptive amount for good cause shown, including evidence relating to the parties' current financial circumstances which indicates that the presumptive amount is inappropriate. Va. Code § 16.1-278.17:1(D). The 2007 legislation establishing this formula was introduced with the intent of making support cases more consistent state-wide, and would have applied both under Va. Code Title 16.1 and Va. Code Title 20, but the enacted version governs only proceedings under Va. Code Title 16.1. 2007 Va. Ch. 909; 2006 Va. SB 948. HB 1500 amended the percentage formulas as of July 1, 2020, in reaction to the TCJA which removed the tax deduction associated with spousal support. Where the parties do not have any children, the presumptive temporary spousal support guideline is now based on 27% of the payor's gross income (whereas prior to the 2020 amendment the formula was based on 30% of the payor's gross income) less 50% of the payee's gross income. When the parties have children, the presumptive temporary support amount now based on 26% of the payor's gross income (whereas prior to the 2020 amendment the formula was based on 28% of the payor's gross income) less 58% of the payee's gross income.

The Supreme Court of Virginia's decision in *Everett v. Tawes*, 833 S.E.2d 876 (2020) held that a trial court has the authority to retroactively modify a *pendente lite* support award. Whether or not a trial court was able to modify *pendente lite* support orders has been debated throughout the trial courts for years, especially since the evidence at a final hearing may demonstrate that the *pendente lite* support was based on faulty information. *Everett* provides a detailed analysis of this issue, and concludes that:

> . . . . a *pendente lite* order is interlocutory. A circuit court has the equitable power to retroactively correct errors in interlocutory orders during the pendency of a lawsuit. The divorce statutes are silent on retroactive modification of a pendente lite spousal support order, and the General Assembly has authorized circuit courts to fill statutory gaps in our divorce statutes by using common law equitable principles. Therefore, a circuit court may, in its discretion, retroactively modify a pendente lite spousal support order prior to the entry of a final decree in a case.

*Everett v. Tawes*, 833 S.E.2d at 884.

*Pendente lite* orders pursuant to divorce or annulment are enforceable through contempt proceedings. *Wright v. Wright,* 164 Va. 245, 178 S.E. 884 (1935). But see *Estate of Hackler v. Hackler*, 44 Va. App. 51, 602 S.E.2d 426 (2004) (court lost contempt jurisdiction when death of contemnor spouse abated divorce action and rendered underlying pendente lite orders void). The usual form is through notice of motion rather than a cross-bill. *Davis v. Davis,* 206 Va. 381, 143 S.E.2d 835 (1965). If a trial court makes a spousal support order pendente lite and the divorce decree is appealed, the court loses jurisdiction to increase or otherwise modify the award during the appeal. *Decker v. Decker,* 17 Va. App. 562, 440 S.E.2d 411 (1994). See also *Holden v. Holden*, 35 Va. App. 315, 544 S.E.2d 884 (2001) (trial court erred by modifying spousal support order during pendency of appeal of final property distribution order). The husband unsuccessfully appealed the trial court's orders denying his motion to modify *pendente lite* support and awarding equitable distribution, spousal support, and child support in his divorce. *Street v. Street*, 24 Va. App. 14, 480 S.E.2d 118 (1997).

In *Van Heuven v. Van Heuven*, 19 Va. Cir. 542 (Fairfax Co. 1988), the court held that absent fraud or bad faith on the wife's part, it should not vacate retroactively the pendente lite support award to a wife who unsuccessfully challenged a property settlement agreement in which she waived her right to support. The award of a "partial lump sum" alimony constitutes an appealable order, according to *Weizenbaum v. Weizenbaum*, 12 Va. App. 899, 407 S.E.2d 37 (1991). Similarly, the payor spouse could not retrieve money paid as temporary alimony even though he was ultimately awarded a divorce on fault grounds. *Hurt v. Hurt*, 16 Va. App. 792, 433 S.E.2d 493 (1993). However, where the marriage was void, the trial court did not abuse its discretion by ordering wife to reimburse husband for the pendente lite spousal support payments. *Naseer v. Moghal*, 2013 Va. App. LEXIS 220 (July 30, 2013).

### § 20.14   Standard of Living of the Marriage as Limitation on Amount of Support

Under Va. Code § 20-107.1(E)(2), the standard of living the parties established during their marriage shall be taken into consideration. A fair allotment is determined by balancing the needs of the dependent spouse against the ability of the obligor to pay, considering both actual earnings and capacity to earn. *Robertson v. Robertson*, 215 Va. 425, 427, 211 S.E.2d 41, 44 (1975); *Klotz v. Klotz*, 203 Va. 677, 680, 127 S.E.2d 104, 106 (1962). This will require some statement in the record of the computations used to reach the amount awarded. *Robertson, supra.*

The standard of living during the marriage affects both the initial setting of alimony, which should not relegate the dependent spouse to a standard far less than that enjoyed during the marriage, if the obligor can pay, and, in addition, the modification of alimony, since a drastic increase in the obligor spouse's income should not act to enable the dependent spouse to enjoy a higher standard of living than that established during the marriage. *Cole v. Cole*, 44 Md. App. 435, 409 A.2d 734 (1979); *Gagliano v. Gagliano*, 215 Va. 447, 211 S.E.2d 62 (1975). See also *Kasprzak v. Kasprzak*, 1993 Va. App. LEXIS 284 (July 20, 1993); and *Stubblebine v. Stubblebine*, 21 Va. App. 635, 466 S.E.2d 764 (1996) where the husband retired from the Army and worked for BDM Corporation, earning $90,000 annually. He resigned from this position, undertaking a variety of independent consulting jobs, and, although not gainfully employed, worked long hours for an organization involved in the study of parapsychology and psychic phenomena. The court found that he was capable of gainful employment, requiring continued support of his former wife. Theoretically, the divorce *a mensa* should not operate to so fix the standard of living since the marriage is continuing at that point. *Gloth v. Gloth,* 154 Va. 511, 153 S.E. 879 (1930).

Where the trial court concluded that the parties' extraordinary lifestyle "was maintained part through income, part through creative use of the tax laws, and part through the incurring of debt," and that an award of $10,000 per month permitted the wife to address "everyday needs," the decision would not be overturned on appeal. *McCombs v. McCombs,* 26 Va. App. 432, 494 S.E.2d 906 (1998). *See also West v. West,* 53 Va. App. 125, 669 S.E.2d 390 (2008) (wife was not entitled to spousal support that would maintain marital lifestyle, when marital lifestyle was subsidized by financial support from husband's parents); *Theismann v. Theismann,* 22 Va. App. 557, 573, 471 S.E.2d 809, 816, *aff'd en banc, Theismann v. Theismann,* 23 Va. App. 697, 479 S.E.2d 534 (1996) (alimony award permitted spouse to "address her everyday needs"). Also consider *Armistead v. Armistead,* 1998 Va. App. LEXIS 69 (Feb. 3, 1998). A wife was denied spousal support despite her showing that she was in poor health, had been unemployed for the past 30 years, and had become accustomed to having maids and other servants. She had admitted adultery which was corroborated by other witnesses.

## § 20.15    Distribution of Property as Affecting Support

The distribution of property under Va. Code § 20-107.3 will be taken into account when considering an award of spousal support. Va. Code § 20-107.1(E)(8). Although property owned by the dependent spouse should be taken into account, this does not require invasion of that estate to relieve the obligations of a former spouse whose actions have brought about the demise of the marriage. *Klotz v. Klotz,* 203 Va. 677, 127 S.E.2d 104 (1962) (wife received marital home, a payment in cash to dissolve the marital business partnership, but had only $90 income per month, with expenses of $400 per month). Nor are installment payments in lieu of support for property owned during marriage income that affects the amount of support. *Ray v. Ray,* 4 Va. App. 509, 358 S.E.2d 754 (1987).

A wife who supported her husband through medical school was entitled to reimbursement alimony in the amount of $75,000 to reflect her monetary contribution to his acquisition of the degree in the form of earnings and inheritance funds expended on his behalf during the period of his education and training, and substantial non-monetary contributions made. The degree itself was held to be the husband's separate property. *Palmer v. Palmer,* 21 Va. Cir. 112 (Fairfax Co. 1990).

Although an antenuptial agreement precludes the divorce court from equitably distributing the parties' property, it will not necessarily prohibit the court from making a spousal support award. *Hankins v. Hankins,* 1993 Va. App. LEXIS 317 (July 27, 1993); *Bracken v. Bracken,* 1993 Va. App. LEXIS 582 (Nov. 30, 1993). As *Bracken* noted, the trial court must make necessary findings under Code § 20-107.3 to determine which assets and debts are marital and separate, the values thereof, and the rights and equities of the parties in the properties and debts.

An agreed-upon obligation to pay mortgage payments does not amount to an order of spousal support. *White v. White,* 257 Va. 139, 509 S.E.2d 323 (1999). A husband's agreement incorporated into a final divorce decree, requiring him to make mortgage payments on the marital home, did not obligate him to continue to make those payments as spousal support after the wife sold the home, satisfying the mortgage.

A spouse who receives ownership of a marital home with an outstanding mortgage may seek support to pay the mortgage on that home. *McKee v. McKee,* 52 Va. App. 482, 664 S.E.2d 505 (2008). See also *Gamble v. Gamble,* 14 Va. App. 558, 421 S.E.2d 635 (1992) (in determining wife's need, chancellor properly considered wife's mortgage payments on marital home received in equitable distribution, but erred by misallocating wife's mortgage expenses).

## § 20.16    Fault Leading to Breakup of Marriage as Relevant

When considering spousal support, the statutory scheme requires that fault be considered two times: first, Va. Code § 20-107.1(E) mandates that fault be considered when determining whether or not to award support; and second, in determining the nature, amount and duration of an award, Va. Code § 20-107.1(E)(13) again requires the consideration of fault.

In *Hall v. Hall,* 9 Va. App. 426, 388 S.E.2d 669 (1990), the husband sought a divorce based upon the wife's desertion. Instead of appealing the divorce decree, he obtained a divorce based upon the separate and apart ground, and appealed the later award of spousal support to her based upon her alleged fault in deserting the marriage. The court of appeals held that res judicata barred reconsideration of the alleged misconduct at the spousal support and property distribution hearing, since the issue of fault had been finally and conclusively resolved by the trial court's ruling that the wife was justified in leaving the marital home.

"Although alimony is not to be used as a method of punishment, 'the court will not seek to find how light the burden may possibly be made, but what, under all the circumstances, will be a fair and just allotment.' " *Hawkins v. Hawkins,* 187 Va. 595, 601, 47 S.E.2d 436, 439 (1948) (quoting from *Bailey v. Bailey,* 62 Va. (21 Gratt.) 43, 58 (1871)).

Where the evidence showed that both parties had accepted that the marriage had ended, that both intended to separate at some time in the future, that the husband acquiesced in separation, and the divorce was granted upon the no-fault separation ground, the court found the wife "blameless for the marital breach," and awarded her spousal support. *Lamb v. Lamb,* 33 Va. Cir. 442 (Stafford Co. 1994).

If the dependent spouse has been cohabiting with another person in a relationship analogous to marriage for a year or more, the court may decrease or terminate spousal support or maintenance. Va. Code § 20-109(A). The court may not make the change where the divorcing parties' agreement otherwise provides, or unless the dependent spouse proves by a preponderance of the evidence that termination of support would be unconscionable. The cohabitation must be proved by clear and convincing evidence, and termination of support must follow a court order.

The husband's desertion decreased the share of the marital property awarded him in *Wilmott v. Wilmott,* 1997 Va. App. LEXIS 47 (Feb. 4, 1997). Additional factors were that the wife had controllable glaucoma, that the husband had a degree in business administration, and that her deferred compensation plan predated the parties' marriage. The wife's post-separation adultery justified making a larger award to the husband in *Mayhugh v. Mayhugh,* 1997 WL 92105 (Va. App.).

### § 20.17   Ability to Obtain Support Following No-Fault Divorce

The existence of fault on the part of the obligor is not necessary to obtain support. In fact, a dependent spouse may obtain support even though the obligor obtains a no-fault divorce against him or her. *Mason v. Mason,* 209 Va. 528, 165 S.E.2d 392 (1969). See also *Brooker v. Brooker,* 218 Va. 12, 235 S.E.2d 309 (1977); *Dukelow v. Dukelow,* 2 Va. App. 21, 25, 341 S.E.2d 208, 210 (1986).

### § 20.18   Lump Sum and Periodic Payments

Alimony may consist of lump sum or periodic payments, or both, under Va. Code § 20-107.1. The lump sum payment will not be treated as alimony for tax purposes unless paid over more than six years, under I.R.C. § 71. The rule until 1984 was that payment must occur over more than a 10-year period to be deductible by the payor. The code section referenced above is now located at Va. Code § 20-107.1(C). Periodic spousal support payment may be converted to a lump sum payment in an appropriate case. *Wheaton v. Wheaton,* 1997 Va. App. LEXIS 229 (Apr. 15, 1997).

The commissioner was in error when he determined that the wife was better served by filing for bankruptcy rather than increasing the amount of periodic spousal support, *Goetz v. Goetz,* 7 Va. App. 50, 371 S.E.2d 567 (1988), and also erred by assuming that the husband could pay a lump sum spousal support award of $15,000 that was premised on the belief that the husband continues to earn a significant amount of unreported cash income from "side jobs."

The obligation to pay lump sum alimony does not end with the wife's remarriage, even though payable in installments, since the obligation was fixed at the time of decree. *Mallery-Sayre v. Mallery,* 6 Va. App. 471, 370 S.E.2d 113 (1988).

It was reversible error for the court to award a lump sum for spousal support without reserving to the recipient the right to petition for further support upon a change of circumstances, where there was no showing that she would be otherwise provided for. *Blank v. Blank,* 10 Va. App. 1, 389 S.E.2d 723 (1990). See also *Weizenbaum v. Weizenbaum,* 12 Va. App. 899, 407 S.E.2d 37 (1991). Thus, in *Poliquin v. Poliquin,* 12 Va. App. 676, 406 S.E.2d 401 (1991), where the wife was a psychiatric nurse who was "in no worse financial situation now than she was either before or during the marriage" and the husband was a vascular surgeon who during the divorce proceedings left a position paying $80,000 per year to pursue his own practice, the wife was properly given a lump sum award of $6,000 payable over twelve months rather than periodic spousal support. However, the trial court should have reserved the right for her to petition the court for periodic spousal support based on changed circumstances.

The reasons for granting lump sum awards include a payor spouse's future unwillingness or potential inability to pay periodic payments, or a payee spouse's immediate need for a lump sum to maintain herself or himself or satisfy debts. *Blank v. Blank,* 10 Va. App. 1, 5, 389 S.E.2d 723, 725 (1990). When no such special needs or circumstances are shown, it is error to grant a lump sum. *Guilfoyle v. Guilfoyle,* 1995 Va. App. LEXIS 24 (Jan. 10, 1995); *Kaufman v. Kaufman,* 12 Va. App. 1200, 409 S.E.2d 1 (1991).

In *White v. White*, 257 Va. 139, 509 S.E.2d 323 (1999), husband agreed to pay the $30,000 mortgage remaining on the marital home. He made payments until the wife sold the home, paying off the mortgage from the proceeds of sale. He did not owe the remainder of the $30,000, since the debt had been satisfied.

Under amendments to Va. Code § 20-107.1, the court may award spousal support to be made in periodic payments for a specified duration (limited duration alimony), periodic payments for an undefined duration (permanent alimony), a lump sum, or in any combination of these. In addition to one or more of these awards, the court may reserve the right to reserve support in the future. The period for reservation shall be presumed to be 50% of the length of time between the date of the marriage and the date of separation. Once granted, the duration shall not be subject to a modification. Va. Code § 20-107.1(F) and (G). However, during the pendency of a defined duration support award, the court may consider modification according to the factors of subsection (E) of § 20-107.1, and may then increase, decrease, or terminate the amount or duration if the court finds that there has been a material change in the circumstances that could not have been reasonably in the contemplation of the parties, or if the parties anticipated the occurrence of some event that did not occur through any fault of the party seeking modification. Va. Code § 20-109.

A court may not order a lump sum spousal support award to compensate a spouse for the other spouse's discharge of marital obligations in bankruptcy because doing so would intrude upon federal bankruptcy jurisdiction by recreating a debt discharged under federal bankruptcy laws. However, a court may modify a spousal support order when a material change in circumstances occurs due to a spouse's bankruptcy. *Rogers v. Rogers*, 51 Va. App. 261, 656 S.E.2d 436 (2008) (reconciling *Mosley v. Mosley*, 19 Va. App. 192, 450 S.E.2d 161 (1994), and *Dickson v. Dickson*, 23 Va. App. 73, 474 S.E.2d 165 (1996)).

## § 20.19    Tax Consequences of Support Award

The tax consequences to each party are to be taken into consideration in determining support and maintenance. Va. Code § 20-107.1(E)(13) (formerly Va. Code § 20-107.1(9)).

The 2017 Tax Cut and Jobs Act, 131 Stat. 2054, Public Law 115-97, repealed the tax consequences related to spousal support. For any divorce or separation instrument executed after December 31, 2018, the spousal support can neither be deducted from the payor spouse's taxable income nor included in the payee's spouse's taxable income. The implications of the law can be far reaching. For instance, many antenuptial agreements executed prior to the enactment of the 2017 Tax Cut and Jobs Act may contain a spousal support award that is taxable to the payee and tax deductible to the payor. However, if the antenuptial agreement is not a divorce or separation instrument, the tax consequences may be disallowed. A similar issue may arise where spouses execute a written settlement agreement in 2018 but are not divorce until 2019. Internal Revenue Code § 71(b)(2) provides that a divorce or separation instrument can be either a written separation agreement or a divorce order. It is unclear if the IRS will treat the 2018 executed written agreement as a separation agreement and allow the spousal support tax consequences, or find that a 2019 divorce order nullifies the tax consequences associated with the spousal support obligation. As of mid-2018, the IRS has not published any guidance on how the 2017 Tax Cut and Jobs Act will apply to these situations.

In spite of the repeal of the tax deductibility/includability consequence of spousal support, the tax consequences will continue to be a significant factor for the court to consider in determining any award of spousal support. Knowing the overall tax liability for the payor spouse will be a significant factor in determining his/her ability to pay. Moreover, while the 2017 Tax Cut and Jobs Act eliminated the federal child dependency exemption, the allocation of child dependency exemption may provide a spouse with other tax benefits such as being able to file as the head of household or receive a child tax credit.

It should be noted that the tax impact of a past settlement agreement or support arrearages award do not need to be considered when determining the amount of future support. *Hoebelheinrich v. Hoebelheinrich*, 43 Va. App. 543, 600 S.E.2d 152 (2004).

The remainder of this section is retained for a historical perspective, and also will be useful when addressing issues related to pre-2019 divorces. Prior to the 2017 Tax Cut and Jobs Act, alimony, generally speaking, was deductible by the payor and taxable to the payee spouse. I.R.C. § 71. In order to qualify for this treatment, the payments must be made pursuant to court order or separation agreement and must be periodic: i.e., paid over more than six years, under the 1984 Domestic Relations Tax Reform Act, or 10 years under the former § 71.

The Tax Reform Act of 1986, in § 1843(c), amended this provision by eliminating the six-year minimum term rule under § 71(f)(1), and changing the six-year recapture rule of § 71(f)(2) into a new three-year rule. These changes affect any 1985 or 1986 instrument. The 1986 rule further provides that if alimony paid in the second year after divorce or separation exceeds payment in the following year (year three) by more than $15,000, the excess amount is recaptured in the following year (year three) as income to the payor and a credit to the payee. In addition, if the alimony paid in the first year (year one) exceeds the average annual alimony paid in years two and three by more than $15,000, the excess amounts are recaptured. These recapture rules do not apply if payments terminate because of the death of either spouse or the remarriage of the payee, nor do they apply to alimony pendente lite. This law applies to all orders beginning on or after January 1, 1987. I.R.C. § 71(f).

Prior to the Tax Reform Act of 1986, to constitute alimony the payments had to be in satisfaction of the spousal duty to support rather than as part of a division of property. The 1986 provision is not so limited. The other change is that formerly unitary payments of alimony and child support, so long as not divided specifically by the order or contract, were treated as alimony under the rule of *Commissioner v. Lester,* 366 U.S. 299, 81 S. Ct. 1343, 6 L. Ed. 2d 306 (1961). Agreements designed to obtain the favorable consequences of such unitary awards were recognized in the case of *Carter v. Carter,* 215 Va. 475, 211 S.E.2d 253 (1975). Payments made after remarriage and not under a separation agreement would not be in pursuance of the obligation of support and therefore would not be alimony. *Brown v. Commissioner of Internal Revenue,* 415 F.2d 310 (4th Cir. 1969). To be treated as alimony, payments must terminate upon the death of the payee spouse. I.R.C. § 71(b)(1). However, the instrument (decree or agreement) need not provide that alimony does not extend beyond the death of the payee.

The circuit court may order that alimony payments be non-taxable to the recipient and non-deductible by the payor under I.R.C § 91. *Hamilton v. Hamilton,* 19 Va. Cir. 241 (City of Alexandria 1990), because, the court reasoned, the Internal Revenue Code appears to allow the parties to agree which of them will bear the tax consequences of alimony payments.

See generally Podell, *The 1986 Tax Reform Act's Impact on Family Law: An Overview,* 13 Fam. L. Rep. 3001 (1986).

### § 20.20    Jurisdiction in Support Modification Cases

In a divorce case, the court retains jurisdiction to modify its award of spousal support. Va. Code § 20-109; *Thomas v. Thomas,* 217 Va. 502, 229 S.E.2d 887 (1976). The party reopening the matter must give notice to the other. Va. Code § 20-112. Publication will be sufficient. See also *State ex rel. Ravitz v. Fox,* 166 W. Va. 194, 273 S.E.2d 370 (W. Va. 1980); *Glading v. Furman,* 282 Md. 200, 383 A.2d 398 (1978); 24 Am. Jur. *Divorce & Separation* § 852 (1966). The juvenile and domestic relations court may require an obligor convicted of civil or criminal contempt to post a bond before an appeal is allowed. Va. Code § 16.1-296.

The trial court erred in refusing to reserve the right to spousal support in the final divorce decree when the wife implicitly requested reservation when she sought spousal support. *Vissicchio v. Vissicchio,* 27 Va. App. 240, 498 S.E.2d 425 (1998); *Blank v. Blank,* 10 Va. App. 1, 389 S.E.2d 723 (1990).

The parties must continue to make payments under the decree until modified by the court, and cannot elect not to comply because of a change in their circumstances. *Gloth v. Gloth,* 154 Va. 511, 554–55, 153 S.E. 879, 893 (1930).

Alimony decrees of other states are to be given full faith and credit only to the extent that installments are past due and are not subject to modification under the laws of the other state. *Sistare v. Sistare,* 218 U.S. 1, 30 S. Ct. 682, 54 L. Ed. 905 (1910).

A decree that schedules alimony to cease at a certain date may not be modified to extend the time of payments beyond that date without a reservation to that effect in the decree. *Losyk v. Losyk,* 212 Va. 220, 183 S.E.2d 135 (1971).

Cases involving spousal support may be heard in the juvenile and domestic relations court, or in circuit court if a divorce complaint has been filed. After the entry of a divorce decree, the court may transfer matters pertaining to spousal support to the juvenile and domestic relations court. The particular court to which the case is transferred may be in a different location within the state if a party or the court so moves and shows good cause. Va. Code § 20-79. After such a transfer, the circuit court will be divested of any further jurisdiction over the matter. Va. Code § 20-79(c).

In 1994, Virginia adopted the Interstate Family Support Act (UIFSA). Va. Code § 20-88.32 et seq. The act is similar to the Uniform Reciprocal Support Act in many respects. The Act does establish some new concepts. The UIFSA establishes uniform long-arm jurisdiction over nonresidents and provides for discovery and testimony once jurisdiction is obtained. Va. Code §§ 20-88.36, 20-88.59, 20-88.61. The UIFSA may only be used for child support proceedings not alimony under amended Va. Code Ann. § 20-88.32.

The only tribunal that can modify a support order is the one having continuing exclusive jurisdiction except in narrowly defined circumstances. If both parties no longer reside in the issuing state, a tribunal with personal jurisdiction over both or with power given by their agreement may modify. Va. Code §§ 20-88.39, 20-88.40, 20-88.68.

When the trial judge admitted on certification that he could not remember the facts of the case or what had prompted his order, the Court of Appeals could order a trial de novo over the wife's objection, according to *Kyhl v. Kyhl,* 32 Va. App. 53, 526 S.E.2d 292 (2000). In *Kyhl,* the parties differed over such basic facts as the value of the husband's realty, their respective incomes, and the facts supporting imputation of income to the wife.

The UIFSA authorizes establishment of parentage in interstate proceedings even when not accompanied by a support proceeding.

### § 20.21   Modification Under RURESA

This section is no longer applicable since the Revised Uniform Reciprocal Enforcement of Support Act was repealed.

## § 20.22    Inability to Modify if There is Property Settlement Agreement

In 2018, the legislature substantially amended Va. Code § 20-109(C) for situations involving spousal support agreement executed on or after July 1, 2018. Historically, and as set forth below, where an agreement provided for the payment of spousal support but failed to expressly state that the spousal support was modifiable, the spousal support award could not be modified by a court. The 2018 amendment to Va. Code § 20-109(C) reverses this long standing precedent as that sections now mandates that when there exists a material change of circumstances, a spousal support modification shall not be denied based on a written contract executed on or after July 1, 2018, unless the agreement affirmatively states that "The amount or duration of spousal support contained in this [AGREEMENT] is not modifiable except as specifically set forth in this [AGREEMENT]." Va. Code § 20-109(C) was again amended in 2020 by removing the requirement to the mandated language referenced in the preceding sentence. As of July 1, 2020, Va. Code § 20-109(C) states that:

> No request for modification of spousal support based on a material change in circumstances or the terms of stipulation or contract shall be denied solely on the basis of the terms of any stipulation or contract that is executed on or after July 1, 2018, unless such stipulation or contract expressly states that the amount or duration of spousal support is non-modifiable.

This provision will likely continue to add to the confusion and uncertainty regarding the modifiability of spousal support awards that are contained in prenuptial agreements and marital settlement agreements executed after July 1, 2018.

The pre-2018 statute and caselaw will remain relevant to spousal support agreements that were entered into before July 1, 2018. The practitioner needs to understand the application of Va. Code § 20-109 both before and after the 2018 amendment. Prior to the 2018 amendment, Va. Code § 20-109 provided that spousal support may be modified by the court at any time except when a stipulation or contract has been filed by the court. Modifications then may only be made in accordance with the terms of the contract. Accordingly, where a spousal support agreement recited the terms of the support to be paid and did not state that the support could subsequently be modified, the court had no authority to modify the support. *Pendleton v. Pendleton*, 22 Va. App. 503, 471 S.E.2d 783 (1996). When reading the following, be cognizant of the pre- and post-2018 amendment to 20-109(C), and understand that the analysis is based on the law that existed before the

2018 amendment. Va. Code § 20-109 and § 20-109.1, allow stipulations or contracts to be filed before or after entry of the final decree. See *Fleming v. Fleming*, 32 Va. App. 822, 531 S.E.2d 38 (2000) (separation agreement filed before entry of final divorce decree waived spousal support and precluded court from subsequently awarding lump sum spousal support); *Lane v. Lane*, 32 Va. App. 125, 526 S.E.2d 773 (2000) (with respect to spousal support provisions, divorce decree signed by parties' counsel was modifiable, but subsequent consent decree signed by parties themselves was nonmodifiable); *Smith v. Smith*, 41 Va. App. 742, 589 S.E.2d 439 (2003) (cohabiting wife's support could not be terminated when parties' support agreement, merged into final decree, provided that support would terminate only in the event of wife's death, husband's death, or wife's remarriage); *Newman v. Newman*, 42 Va. App. 557, 593 S.E.2d 533 (2004) (spousal support agreement was nonmodifiable (1) when signed by parties' counsel but not personally by clients, and (2) when oblique reference to Va. Code § 20-109 merely indicated that statute applied to consent decree); *Baldwin v. Baldwin*, 44 Va. App. 93, 603 S.E.2d 172 (2004) (explaining operation of Va. Code § 20-109 with respect to agreements entered into before and after statute's enactment); *Brown v. Brown*, 53 Va. App. 723, 674 S.E.2d 597 (2009) (consent decree incorporating spousal support agreement did *not* make spousal support nonmodifiable, when agreement was created in context of show cause petition rather than support modification motion, and considered *manner* of repayment of support arrears rather than *amount* of support to be paid). Va. Code § 20-109.1 permits modification even after the decree in accordance with agreements filed before or after the decree. Support still ceases under the decree at the death of either spouse, Va. Code § 20-110, although it may continue under the agreement if it specifically so provides. The Internal Revenue Code states that there must be no liability to make payments after death of the payee in order for payments to be considered alimony. I.R.C. § 71(b)(D).

Even when a divorce decree is seen, agreed on and endorsed, it will not change the terms of a property settlement agreement. *Enoch v. Enoch*, 45 Va. Cir. 530 (Roanoke 1998). The portion of the trial court's final decree allowing the court to modify the support obligation without the agreement of both parties was void *ab initio*.

## § 20.23   Substantive Standard: Material Change of Circumstances

The court has the inherent right, supplemented by Va. Code § 20-109, to modify an alimony award to meet the changed conditions of the parties and to attain the ends of justice. *Brinn v. Brinn*, 147 Va. 277, 287, 137 S.E. 503, 506 (1927). This is certainly true in cases of divorce *a mensa*. *Gloth v. Gloth*,

154 Va. 511, 535, 153 S.E. 879, 886 (1930). See also *Brown v. Brown,* 22 Va. Cir. 263 (Fairfax Co. 1990). Where the husband agreed to continue payments and was not compelled to do so, he could have ceased making non-obligatory payments at any time, but was required to continue to pay the amount required by the decree. *Buxbaum v. Buxbaum,* 20 Va. App. 181, 455 S.E.2d 752 (1995). See also *Sanford v. Sanford,* 19 Va. App. 241, 450 S.E.2d 185 (1994); and *MacNelly v. MacNelly,* 1995 Va. App. LEXIS 496 (June 6, 1995).

In 2018, Va. Code §§ 20-107.1 and 109 were amended to help address the uncertainty of a party's retirement and the impact on a possible modification of spousal support. When the court either grants or reserves any request for spousal support, the order "shall state whether the retirement of either party was contemplated by the court and specifically considered by the court in making its award, and, if so, the order shall state the facts the court contemplated and specifically considered as to the retirement of the party." This amendment is intended to aid the parties and the court in any future litigation regarding the modification of spousal support where a party has retired.

In addition, subsections (E), (F) and (G) were added to Va. Code § 20-109 in 2018. Va. Code § 20-109(E) provides that the spousal support payor's attainment of the "full retirement age" as defined by the federal Social Security Act (42 U.S.C. § 416, as amended), constitutes a material change of circumstance. The current maximum age is 67 years old. This provision is intended to allow the party seeking a modification to have a substantive hearing, but it does not mandate that the support award be modified.

Va. Code § 20-109(F) was added in 2018, and is intended to address the factors for the court to consider when a spouse seeks to modify support based on his/her retirement. First, the court may consider all of the factors listed in § 20-107.1(E). The inclusion of this reference is to clarify the confusion that had existed and instructs the courts that the factors that existed at the time of the prior award may be considered when a party seeks to modify support due to the payor spouse's retirement. Secondly, the court must consider the following factors when considering a request to modify spousal support based on the payor's retirement:

1.  Whether retirement was contemplated by the court and specifically considered by the court when the spousal support was awarded;

2.  Whether the retirement is mandatory or voluntary, and the terms and conditions related to such retirement;

3.  Whether the retirement would result in a change in the income of

either the payor or the payee spouse;

4. The age and health of the parties;

5. The duration and amount of spousal support already paid; and

6. The assets or property interest of each of the parties during the period from the date of the support order and up to the date of the hearing on modification or termination.

Subfactor (6) above is intended to overrule the ruling in *Driscoll v. Hunter*, 59 Va. App. 22, 716 S.E.2d 477 (2011). The factors set forth in Va. Code § 20-109(F)(1)–(6) do not apply are subject to the provisions in stipulations or contracts pursuant to Va. Code § 20-109(C), and do not apply to any situation where the spousal support is non-modifiable. Lastly, Va. Code § 20-109(F) applies to any spousal support modification/termination hearing regardless of when the suit for the initial support hearing was filed or the date that the initial support order was entered.

Va. Code § 20-109(G) was added in 2018, and states that in any hearing seeking an increase, decrease, or termination of spousal support, when there is a finding that a material change of circumstances has occurred, the court may consider the factors of Va. Code §§ 20-107.1(E) and (F), and shall consider (1) "the assets or property interest of each of the parties from the date of the support order and up to the time of the hearing", and (2) any income generated from the asset or property interest. Any order that grants or denies any motion to modify or terminate support must include the courts written findings and conclusions identifying the factors considered under Va. Code §§ 20-107.1(E) and (F).

The 2018 amendments to Va. Code §§ 20-107.1 and 20-109 establish substantive and significant changes to the law. The cases cited and discussed below must be read with the understanding that they were decided before these amendments, but that the reasoning and holdings of the cases may still apply to cases decided under these statutory changes.

The party seeking to modify alimony must bear the burden of showing there is a change of circumstances by a preponderance of the evidence. *Floyd v. Floyd*, 1 Va. App. 42, 45, 333 S.E.2d 364, 366 (1985) (defendant former husband did not sufficiently show that financial condition of business was deteriorating when there was also testimony that he had made cash withdrawals from company characterized as loans rather than as salary. The increase in expenses he proved may have occurred in large part because of second wife). A sufficient change in circumstances was demonstrated in *Wyatt v. Wyatt*, 19 Va. Cir. 49 (1989), where the wife chose to give up her job earning $20,000 annually, and had moved to North Carolina, and was sharing a condominium with a male friend and earning $320 per week. The Court found that she had shown the ability to earn more money than she was receiving in her current employment, and that her earning capacity exceeded that of her former husband.

Changes in circumstances include various changes in the financial condition of the dependent spouse. For example, one circumstance would be an increase in the needs of the dependent spouse, which might occur because of illness and a consequent increase in medical expenses, or a substantial increase in the cost of living. See, e.g., *Furr v. Furr,* 13 Va. App. 479, 413 S.E.2d 72 (1992) (as a consequence of significantly increased expenses, wife's standard of living declined). Another change would be a decrease in the dependent spouse's ability to provide financial independence. This might occur, again, because of illness or accident, an increase in general unemployment that affects the spouse, or reaching of retirement age. See, e.g., *Richards v. Richards,* 1994 Va. App. LEXIS 376 (June 14, 1994) (not designated for publication) (husband's employment terminated; income dropped from $154,000 to $90,000 per year). The amount owing to a dependent spouse might also decrease. For example, the needs of the spouse might become less over time as, for example, when education or vocational training is completed, or expenses are shared with another. Similarly, the dependent spouse may have a greater ability to pay upon becoming employed, or inheriting income-producing property. See, e.g., *Ward v. Ward,* 41 Or. App. 447, 599 P.2d 1150 (1979). However, a dependent spouse's receipt of passive income in the form of interest on the principal of an equitable distribution award will not constitute a change of circumstances, because that passive income was foreseeable when the trial court made the original spousal support award. *Barrs v. Barrs,* 45 Va. App. 500, 612 S.E.2d 227 (2005). For agreements entered into after amendments of Va. Code § 20-109(A) in 2000, if the dependent spouse has been cohabiting with another person in a relationship analogous to marriage for a year or more, the court may decrease or terminate spousal support or maintenance. The court may not make the change where the divorcing parties' agreement otherwise provides, or unless the dependent spouse proves by a preponderance of the evidence that termination of support would be unconscionable. The cohabitation must be proved by clear and convincing evidence, and termination of support must follow a court order.

Other changes involve the circumstances of the obligor spouse. Ordinarily, remarriage and acquisition of a second family will not constitute grounds for reduction in support. *Morris v. Morris,* 216 Va. 457, 219 S.E.2d 864 (1975) (child support). But see *Barton v. Barton,* 31 Va. App. 175, 522

S.E.2d 373 (1999), where the husband knew he had an obligation to support an additional illegitimate child before entry of the final decree setting spousal support, and *Zabala v. Zabala*, 48 Va. Cir. 267 (City of Norfolk 1999), where it was found that when a separation agreement awarded 50% of husband's military retirement benefits to wife, he could not later reduce wife's support by waiving the bulk of his retirement benefits in order to receive full disability benefits as a result of change in his disability status. However, a change in medical or other nonvolitional expenses might be sufficient to warrant a reduction in alimony. The obligor's ability to pay may also decrease if, for example, income is less in a particular year in a professional person's career, or retirement is mandated. The obligor's ability to pay may also increase to the point where a greater amount may be paid to the dependent spouse. See, e.g., *Gammell v. Gammell*, 90 Cal. App. 3d 90, 153 Cal. Rptr. 169 (1979). However, the dependent spouse must carry the burden of demonstrating a change of circumstances. The dependent spouse does not meet this burden merely by alleging an increase in the obligor's income and a decrease in expenses. *McElwrath v. McElwrath*, 1993 Va. App. LEXIS 133 (May 18, 1993). The husband's bankruptcy following his divorce was a sufficient change in circumstances to justify modification of the spousal support award, particularly since it discharged payments due the wife under equitable distribution. The payments of $1,000 per month for one year, $800 per month for the following year, and $600 per month for the third year were in the nature of periodic payments rather than a lump sum and therefore was modifiable. *Dickson v. Dickson*, 23 Va. App. 73, 474 S.E.2d 165 (1996). When the husband's bankruptcy proceedings after divorce were not yet concluded, it was error for the trial court to base its spousal support award in part upon the assumptions that (1) the husband's assigned joint credit card debt would be discharged in bankruptcy, and (2) the husband's creditor would pursue the wife for collection of the discharged debt. Spousal support must be determined on the basis of contemporary circumstances, and modified in the future as changes in circumstances occur. *Rogers v. Rogers*, 51 Va. App. 261, 656 S.E.2d 436 (2008). However, a reduction in spousal support payments will not be ordered where the payor suffered reduced income but failed to seek other employment commensurate with his background and training. *Smull v. Smull*, 45 Va. Cir. 336 (Fairfax Co. 1998). Likewise, spousal support should not have been awarded where the husband, a doctor, had no ability to pay after engaging in a series of unwise investment decisions, bad loans, and failed joint ventures. But the wife in *Masri v. Masri*, 48 Va. Cir. 5 (Chesterfield Co. 1999), was awarded the lion's share of the marital resources because of her "overwhelmingly greater monetary and non-monetary contributions to the marriage." Likewise in *Blackburn v. Michael*, 30 Va. App. 95, 515 S.E.2d 780 (1999), income should have been imputed to the wife, who had received diplomas certifying her as a "computer operations specialist" and a "legal secretary." The husband does not necessarily meet his burden of showing changed circumstances when he proves that the wife's income has increased since the original order. No reduction was required when his income had also increased. *Ragland v. Ragland*, 1993 Va. App. LEXIS 195 (June 22, 1993). See also *Norris v. Norris*, 1995 Va. App. LEXIS 237 (March 14, 1995), where a 66-year-old wife had waived any interest in husband's retirement benefits in exchange for $500 in spousal support, the husband could not allege that his retirement was a material change in circumstances. The court may refuse to hear a motion for reduction if the obligor has substantial arrearages in the amount he is to pay the wife for equitable distribution. *Bridgforth v. Bridgforth*, 1995 Va. App. LEXIS 258 (March 14, 1995). This cannot exceed the standard of living established during the marriage, however. See *Cole v. Cole*, 44 Md. App. 435, 409 A.2d 734 (1979).

A lowering of the husband's child support obligation was not a sufficient change in circumstances to justify a larger alimony award according to *Head v. Head*, 24 Va. App. 166, 480 S.E.2d 780 (1997).

Changes in circumstances that will allow modification of the duration of limited duration support are limited to those that could not reasonably have been contemplated at the time the award was made. Additionally, if the court anticipated that some event would occur during the duration of the award, and the event does not occur through no fault of the party seeking modification, the duration may be modified. Va. Code § 20-109(B). Such expected events might include emancipation of a child or employment of the dependent spouse.

### § 20.24    Change of Custody as Affecting Support

If custody is changed from the dependent to the obligor spouse, the amount awarded the dependent spouse may change. For instance, this would be a sufficient change in circumstance to require apportionment of a unified award for spousal and child support, *Carter v. Carter*, 215 Va. 475, 211 S.E.2d 253 (1975), since it was never contemplated by the parties when they entered into their settlement agreement. See, e.g., *Jarrell v. Jarrell*, 1994 Va. App. LEXIS 672 (Nov. 15, 1994); and *Tanger v. Tanger*, 1996 Va. App. LEXIS 297 (April 23, 1996).

### § 20.25    Death of Spouse

The death of the obligor spouse will signal the end of the obligation to pay support. This is because the obligation to support one's spouse ordinarily ceases at death. *Foster v. Foster,* 195 Va. 102, 77 S.E.2d 471 (1953); *Francis v. Francis,* 72 Va. (31 Gratt.) 283 (1879). A contract in lieu of alimony may specifically provide for continued payments, and then would survive the death of the obligor. *Durrett v. Durrett,* 204 Va. 59, 129 S.E.2d 50 (1963). Va. Code § 20-109.1. A property settlement agreement provision that requires a spouse to maintain a life insurance policy naming the other spouse as beneficiary is enforceable; the provision does not require the obligor spouse to pay spousal support after death, but only to honor the agreement to maintain life insurance during the obligor's life. *Sullivan v. Sullivan,* 33 Va. App. 743, 536 S.E.2d 925 (2000).

The death of the dependent spouse will cause support to cease. However, a contract for property settlement can be enforced by the decedent's estate. *Moore v. Crutchfield,* 136 Va. 20, 116 S.E. 482 (1923).

## § 20.26  Remarriage of Dependent Spouse

Remarriage of a dependent spouse causes support and maintenance to cease. Va. Code § 20-110. The only apparent exception to this rule is when an agreement between the parties relating to support allows it to continue after remarriage. Va. Code § 20-110. However, remarriage will not terminate unpaid installments of lump sum alimony, since this obligation becomes fixed at the time of decree. *Mallery-Sayre v. Mallery,* 6 Va. App. 471, 370 S.E.2d 113 (1988).

If the parties do not clearly and expressly specify that spousal support obligations will survive the dependent spouse's remarriage, Va. Code § 20-109.1 requires that such an obligation will terminate. *Miller v. Hawkins,* 14 Va. App. 192, 415 S.E.2d 861 (1992); *MacNelly v. MacNelly,* 17 Va. App. 427, 437 S.E.2d 582 (1993); *Radford v. Radford,* 16 Va. App. 812, 433 S.E.2d 35 (1993); *Hardesty v. Hardesty, opn. on regh en banc,* 40 Va. App. 663, 581 S.E.2d 213 (2003). Compare *Gayler v. Gayler,* 20 Va. App. 83, 455 S.E.2d 278 (1995) ("payments . . . . shall terminate only upon wife's death"). Spousal support ends upon remarriage when a separation agreement states that there shall be weekly payments, "until her death." In *Langley v. Johnson,* 27 Va. App. 365, 499 S.E.2d 15 (1998), the court found that these payments were indeed for her support despite the wife's arguments that they were really property division in disguise. They were to be adjusted annually according to the Consumer Price Index, and were to terminate at her death. Likewise, "remarriage" that is defined by a property settlement agreement to include "cohabitation, analogous to marriage, with another man" terminated spousal support in *Frey v. Frey,* 14 Va. App. 270, 416 S.E.2d 40 (1992). "Although matters relating to divorce are currently within the jurisdiction of circuits, they may be heard on the equity side, in the absence of a statutory grant cases." *MacNelly v. MacNelly*, 1995 Va. App. LEXIS 496 (June 6, 1995).

If the second marriage is voidable, and it is annulled, the dependent spouse is not entitled to a reinstatement of alimony. This is because the obligor spouse has a right to rely upon the remarriage and to rearrange his or her life and financial affairs, and the dependent spouse in remarrying assumes the risk of misfortune or mistake. The court has not yet expressed itself on the question of whether support would be provided where the second marriage was void. *McConkey v. McConkey*, 216 Va. 106, 215 S.E.2d 640 (1975).

Remarriage, although it signals the end of the duty to pay spousal support, may not signal the end of the tax treatment of payments as alimony. *Ensminger v. Commissioner*, 610 F.2d 189 (4th Cir.), *cert. denied*, 446 U.S. 941, 100 S. Ct. 2166, 64 L. Ed. 2d 796 (1979), if payable under a property settlement agreement; *McLoughlin v. McLoughlin*, 211 Va. 365, 177 S.E.2d 781 (1970) (alimony payments due under an incorporated separation agreement will not cease either; case decided before Va. Code § 20-110 required that the extension of the obligation to make payment after remarriage be explicit in contract).

If the dependent spouse remarries, he or she has an affirmative duty to notify the payor spouse immediately of remarriage. Failure to do so shall entitle the payor to restitution equal to the amount of any current support and maintenance paid after the date of remarriage, plus interest and reasonable attorney's fees and costs. Va. Code §§ 20-109(D) and 20-110.

Where the parties' settlement agreement stated that the spousal support immediately ceased forever upon Wife's remarriage and Wife had "an affirmative duty to advise Husband of her remarriage as soon as it occurs," the Wife was ordered to pay restitution of the spousal support payments Husband made to her following her remarriage. *Smith v. Smith*, 2020 Va. App. LEXIS 95 (April 7, 2020). The Court found that the property settlement agreement, as opposed to Va. Code § 20-110, controlled the outcome of the case. The parties' agreement communicated "a sense of urgency" in Wife's responsibility to inform Husband of her remarriage. Wife's mere mailing of notice to the Husband was deficient, especially since the parties communicated by email and they had also seen each other in person. The Court also held that the spousal support payments made after Wife's remarriage were not gifts to her since Husband had no knowledge of her remarriage.

## § 20.27 Cohabitation of Dependent Spouse

A trial court must terminate spousal support if there is clear and convincing evidence that a recipient spouse has been habitually cohabitating with another person in a relationship analogous to a marriage for one year or more commencing on or after July 1, 1997, unless (1) a stipulation or contract provides otherwise, or (2) the recipient spouse proves by a preponderance of the evidence that a termination of spousal support would be unconscionable. Va. Code § 20-109(A). However, this statutory language has no effect on agreements entered into prior to the enactment of Va. Code § 20-109(A), because otherwise, the legislation would impair a preexisting contractual obligation. *Rubio v. Rubio*, 36 Va. App. 248, 549 S.E.2d 610 (2001); *Hering v. Hering*, 33 Va. App. 368, 533 S.E.2d 631 (2000). See *Baldwin v. Baldwin*, 44 Va. App. 93, 603 S.E.2d 172 (2004) (explaining operation of habitual cohabitation provisions of Va. Code § 20-109(A) with respect to agreements entered into before and after statute's enactment).

The Virginia Court of Appeals addressed the question whether a sexual relationship is required to demonstrate that the cohabitation relationship is "analogous to a marriage" in *Brennan v. Albertson*, 2012 Va. App. LEXIS 240 (July 24, 2012). The court held that the absence of sexual intimacy or romance does not preclude a finding of a "relationship analogous to marriage" pursuant to Va. Code § 20-109(A). The court looked at the totality of the circumstances in making this determination. For example, the recipient spouse and her female friend shared a residence for a period of years. The couple functioned as a family unit and were interdependent financially. They shared in the childcare of each other's children. They vacationed together, attended each other's family reunions, attended church together, attended the activities of each other's children, and shared household chores. Based on these facts, the court held that their relationship was analogous to marriage and affirmed the trial court's decision terminating the ex-husband's obligation to pay child support.

As amended in 2001, Va. Code § 20-109(A) further provides that it applies to all orders and decrees for spousal support, regardless of the date of the suit for initial support, the date of entry of any support decree, or the date of any petition for modification of support. It also repeals the previous version of Va. Code § 20-109(A) retroactively to July 1, 1998. Va. Code § 20-109(A) was amended to nullify an unintended effect that was identified in *Rubio v. Rubio*, 33 Va. App. 74, 531 S.E.2d 612 (2000) (vacated and opinion withdrawn on rehearing en banc at *Rubio v. Rubio*, 36 Va. App. 248, 549 S.E.2d 610 (2001)), which held that the previous version of Va. Code

§ 20-109(A) was applicable only to spousal support orders obtained in suits commenced on or after July 1, 1998.

In 2016, the Virginia Supreme Court held that the cohabitation provision under Va. Code § 20-109(A) applied to same-sex couples. *Luttrell v. Cucco*, 291 Va. 308 (2016). The Court noted that the statute is gender neutral, reviewed the legislative history, and determined that same-sex marriages being illegal at the time that this code section was enacted was irrelevant.

Va. Code § 20-109(A) and its clear and convincing burden of proof is inapplicable to a case involving enforcement of a cohabitation provision in a negotiated property settlement agreement, because the negotiated agreement is a contract between the parties. The appropriate burden in an action to enforce a contract is proof by a preponderance of the evidence. *O'Hara v. O'Hara*, 45 Va. App. 788, 613 S.E.2d 859 (2005) (court incorrectly applied clear and convincing burden of proof in denying request to terminate spousal support pursuant to cohabitation provision of property settlement agreement).

In *Frey v. Frey*, 14 Va. App. 270, 416 S.E.2d 40 (1992), a case decided prior to the enactment of Va. Code § 20-109(A), the parties provided in their property settlement agreement that the husband's obligation to pay spousal support would terminate upon "her cohabitation, analogous to marriage, with another man." The court of appeals held that the phrase "cohabitation, analogous to a marriage" meant "a status in which a man and woman live together continuously, or with some permanency, mutually assuming duties and obligations normally attendant with a marital relationship." The phrase involved more than living together for a period of time and having sexual relations, but did *not* require that the other party assume the duty of providing some financial support. See also *Schweider v. Schweider*, 243 Va. 245, 415 S.E.2d 135 (1992) ("remarriage" in parties' agreement meant "permanent cohabitation with a male as if to all appearances they were otherwise married"; and "remarriage" terminating spousal support was found when wife shared bedroom with another man for substantial amount of time over period of years).

In *Penrod v. Penrod*, 29 Va. App. 96, 510 S.E.2d 244 (1999), the parties' separation agreement provided that the wife "shall be deemed to have 'remarried' in the event she cohabits and lives with a member of the opposite sex in a sexual relationship without the benefit of marriage for a period in excess of sixty (60) consecutive days." The agreement was enforced and spousal support was terminated after the wife admitted (1) to staying at one man's house three or four times a week over a period of several years, sleeping in the same room, and (2) to consciously causing breaks in the time she stayed at the man's home because of the "sixty consecutive days" requirement. The court of appeals found that this was in fact a long-term, intimate, and monogamous relationship that amounted to cohabitation and living in a sexual relationship for a period in excess of 60 consecutive days.

In *Pellegrin v. Pellegrin*, 31 Va. App. 753, 525 S.E.2d 611 (2000), the parties' agreement provided that spousal support would terminate if the wife "for any period of one month or more cohabits on a full-time or substantially full-time basis with a male non-relative." The court of appeals enunciated and applied four nonexclusive factors that demonstrated the mutual responsibilities of a marital relationship: (1) common residence, (2) intimate or romantic involvement, (3) provision of financial support, and (4) duration and continuity of the relationship and other indicia of permanency. However, although the evidence established that the wife had been romantically and sexually involved with a paramour for several years, the evidence failed to prove that the wife shared a common residence with the man, that the paramours had mutually assumed the duties and obligations normally associated with a marriage, or that the man financially contributed to her household in any significant way. Thus, the evidence failed to establish cohabitation as a matter of law.

In *Stroud v. Stroud*, 49 Va. App. 359, 641 S.E.2d 142 (2007), the parties' property settlement agreement provided that spousal support would terminate upon the death of either party, the remarriage of the wife, "and/or her cohabitation with any person to whom she is not related by blood or marriage in a situation analogous to marriage for a period of thirty (30) or more continuous days." Parol evidence and the parties' testimony established that the parties understood when the agreement was executed that "person" in the spousal support termination provision included individuals of *both* sexes. Applying the *Pellegrin* factors to the evidence, the court of appeals concluded that the wife (1) shared a common residence with another woman, (2) was involved in an intimate or romantic relationship with the woman, (3) was providing financial support to the woman, and (4) viewed her relationship with the woman as a durable, continuing, and permanent one that included the joint raising of the wife's children. Although the women did not present themselves to the public as a couple, their testimony explained that they did not do so for fear of adverse or terminal effects upon their jobs. Consequently, the evidence established, as a matter of law, that the wife's relationship with the other woman constituted cohabitation in a situation analogous to marriage, and that the spousal support termination requirement had been met. In *Stroud*, the court of appeals expressly rejected the wife's argument that people of the same sex could not cohabit in Virginia because marriage between persons of the same sex was barred. The court of appeals stated that its analysis of the phrase "analogous to marriage" in the property settlement agreement was based upon the *factual* relationship of the wife and the woman, and that it explicitly did not purport to grant, or comment on, the legal status of the relationship. Also, because the case involved an action to enforce a contract between parties, the clear and convincing standard of proof of Va. Code § 20-109(A) did not apply. See *O'Hara v. O'Hara*, 45 Va. App. 788, 613 S.E.2d 859 (2005) (standard of proof by a preponderance of the evidence). See also *Stroud v. Stroud*, 54 Va. App. 231, 677 S.E.2d 629 (2009) (provision for termination of spousal support if spouse cohabits is *not* self-executing, so that actual termination of spousal support payments requires court order).

In a 2011 case revisiting the issue of what constitutes "cohabiting in a situation analogous to marriage" so as to end alimony, the court of appeals set forth four factors to determine whether one party to a property settlement agreement has proved that the other party has "cohabited": (1) a common residence; (2) intimate or romantic involvement; (3) the provision of financial support; and (4) the duration and continuity of the relationship and other indicia of permanency. In *Cranwell v. Cranwell*, 59 Va. App. 155, 717 S.E.2d 797 (2011), the evidence showed that the ex-wife and her boyfriend did not share a residence. They had two residences, lived on opposite sides of the country, did not always stay with each other when in each other's home state, and neither had a key to the other's house. Thus, the court of appeals affirmed the trial court's ruling that the ex-wife was not cohabiting because cohabitation requires living together in the same house, as married persons live together, or in the manner of husband and wife.

In a case similar to *Cranwell*, the former spouse and her boyfriend lived next door to each other and constructed a path to connect their homes. However, based on the totality of the evidence, the trial court did not abuse its discretion in finding that wife and her boyfriend did not share a common residence, and Husband's motion to terminate spousal support due to his former wife's alleged cohabitation was properly denied. *Gobble v. Gobble*, 2019 Va. App. LEXIS 34 (Feb. 12, 2019).

### § 20.28    Jurisdiction for Enforcement Proceedings

Even though the defendant is in military service, the federal statute, 42 U.S.C. § 659(a), allows moneys due from the United States to be subjected to legal process for enforcement of alimony obligations in the same manner as for other private persons. This includes payments ordered under an incorporated separation agreement. *Butler v. Butler*, 221 Va. 1035, 277 S.E.2d 180 (1981).

Notice must be given if a foreign decree is to be enforced so that the defendant has the opportunity to raise defenses such as modification of accrued arrearages. *Griffin v. Griffin,* 327 U.S. 220, 233–34, 66 S. Ct. 556, 90 L. Ed. 635 (1946). This notice may be by constructive service where the defendant is now a nonresident. *Sheffield v. Sheffield,* 207 Va. 288, 148 S.E.2d 771 (1966). However, Virginia does not have personal jurisdiction needed for enforcement, although a property settlement agreement had been filed in case, where the defendant was now a nonresident. *Morris v. Morris,* 4 Va. App. 539, 359 S.E.2d 104 (1987).

The court has no power to sequester, for purposes of temporary alimony, property held by husband and wife as tenants by the entireties where the husband is outside the state, since such property could not be made subject to a debt because of the nature of the entireties estate. However, upon partition, the husband's share could be held as security for alimony. *Jenkins v. Jenkins,* 211 Va. 797, 180 S.E.2d 516 (1971).

In *M. Morgan Cherry & Assocs. v. Cherry,* 37 Va. App. 329, 558 S.E.2d 534, *aff'd,* 38 Va. App. 693, 568 S.E.2d 391 (2002), a trial court properly entered a $9,900 judgment against a corporation for its violation of an income deduction order that directed the corporation to withhold and pay $3,300 a month for spousal support out of a shareholder/employee's disposable income. When the shareholder/employee instructed the corporation to stop paying him a salary, and the corporation complied, the court entered judgment against the corporation for the amount that the court deemed was owed to the shareholder/employee's spouse over a three-month period.

## § 20.29    Modification of Arrearages

The courts are not given the power to modify amounts already accrued under a decree, see, e.g., *Carter v. Carter,* 215 Va. 475, 211 S.E.2d 253 (1975); *Cralle v. Cralle,* 84 Va. 198, 6 S.E. 12 (1887), since there is a vested property right in such installments, *Eaton v. Davis,* 176 Va. 330, 10 S.E.2d 893 (1940). This means that Virginia alimony arrearages must be given full faith and credit by other state courts. *Sistare v. Sistare,* 218 U.S. 1, 30 S. Ct. 682, 54 L. Ed. 905 (1910). If the parties' final divorce decree specified that the husband was to make spousal support payments, he could not receive restitution of payments made even when it turned out that the wife had deserted him and therefore was not entitled to spousal support. *Reid v. Reid,* 245 Va. 409, 429 S.E.2d 208 (1993) (reversing 14 Va. App. 505, 419 S.E.2d 398 (1992)). The wife was equitably estopped from claiming arrearage when she accepted lower payments for approximately four years when the husband left his law firm. In reliance on her representation that she would "just have to live" with those payments, the husband substantially changed his financial and personal positions. *Wheeler v. Wheeler,* 1994 Va. App. LEXIS 426 (July 5, 1994).

The entry of an order or decree of support for a spouse constitutes a final judgment for any sum or sums in arrears. The order must include an amount for interest on the arrearage at the judgment interest rate unless the obligee waives the collection of interest in a writing submitted to the court, and it may include reasonable attorney's fees if the amount of the arrearage, excluding interest, is equal to or greater than the amount of three months obligation. Va. Code § 20-78.2.

When a wife was awarded a final divorce judgment against her husband in 1973, and accumulated $84,000 in spousal support arrearages, she could not then file a motion to reopen the matter for entry of a QDRO that would allow garnishment of the husband's pension plan under ERISA.

*Hoy v. Hoy,* 29 Va. App. 115, 510 S.E.2d 253 (1999). A party to a divorce suit may not recast his or her claim as a judgment creditor via a QDRO, as would modify the terms of a final divorce decree.

Retroactive modification of a support order is prohibited by the Virginia Code, but support may be modified from the date of filing the petition for modification in any court. Va. Code § 20-112 (amended in 2004 to make clear that when a petition is filed in juvenile and domestic relations district court and then transferred to circuit court, the modification may take effect from the date of the original filing in juvenile court).

## § 20.30    Enforcement Under the Uniform Reciprocal Enforcement of Support Act and UIFSA

Virginia repealed the Revised Uniform Reciprocal Enforcement of Support Act in 1994. The portions of this section referring to the Act are retained primarily for historical analysis. A foreign decree registered in Virginia will be enforceable under the Revised Uniform Reciprocal Enforcement of Support Act. *Scott v. Sylvester,* 220 Va. 182, 257 S.E.2d 774 (1979) (child support). The entire amount owing will be collectible including portions that accrued while the defendant was outside Virginia. *Id.* at 187, 257 S.E.2d at 777. Amounts payable in the future may be treated with full force and effect under the doctrine of comity. *Alig v. Alig,* 220 Va. 80, 255 S.E.2d 494 (1979).

The registration of a foreign decree does not give in personam jurisdiction to Virginia courts where the defendant is served outside the state. *Stephens v. Stephens,* 229 Va. 610, 331 S.E.2d 484 (1985).

A Virginia judgment was enforced in a California order in *Harmon v. Harmon*, 160 Cal. App. 2d 47, 324 P.2d 901, *cert. denied*, 358 U.S. 881, 79 S. Ct. 120, 3 L. Ed. 2d 110 (1958).

Virginia adopted the Interstate Family Support Act (UIFSA) in new Va. Code § 20-88.32 et seq. (1994). The act is similar to the Uniform Reciprocal Support Act in many respects. The Act does establish some new concepts. The UIFSA establishes uniform long-arm jurisdiction over nonresidents and provides for discovery and testimony once jurisdiction is obtained. Va. Code §§ 20-88.36, 20-88.59, 20-88.61. The UIFSA may only be used for spousal and child support proceedings. Visitation issues cannot be raised in child support proceedings. Va. Code § 20-88.48.

The choice of law for interpretation of support orders registered under the UIFSA is that of the state issuing the underlying support orders, except that the longer of different statutes of limitation applies. Continuing exclusive jurisdiction is established, so that only one support order is normally effective at any given time.

The UIFSA provides that a support order may be mailed directly to an obligor's employer, triggering wage withholding without a hearing unless the employee objects. The obligor's state may administratively enforce the order, although all judicial enforcement begins with the registration of the existing order in the responding state.

The only tribunal that can modify a support order is the one having continuing exclusive jurisdiction except in narrowly defined circumstances. If both parties no longer reside in the issuing state, a tribunal with personal jurisdiction over both or with power given by their agreement may modify the order. Va. Code §§ 20-88.39, 20-88.40, 20-88.68.

The UIFSA authorizes establishment of parentage in interstate proceedings even when not accompanied by a support proceeding.

Under Va. Code § 20-88.43:2, a Virginia court issuing a spousal support order has continuing, exclusive jurisdiction to modify the order throughout the existence of the support obligation, and a Virginia court may not modify a spousal support order issued by a tribunal of another state having continuing, exclusive jurisdiction over that order under the law of that state. If an employer receives an order for income withholding from another state, under Va. Code § 20-88.64:1, the employer is to immediately forward a copy of the order to the obligor. After this, the order shall be treated as though it was a Virginia order.

In 2005, Virginia adopted most of the amendments proposed by the National Conference of Commissioners on Uniform State Laws in 2001 to clarify UIFSA and reflect changes in federal law. Among the changes was an expansion in the definition of "state" to allow foreign countries to have their orders enforced in the United States. See Va. Code § 20-88.32.

### § 20.31   Full Faith and Credit for Foreign Support Awards

A foreign decree for alimony is entitled to full faith and credit under Article IV, § 2 of the Constitution as to past due installments, if the right to the installments is not subject to modification in the state where the decree was rendered. *Sistare v. Sistare,* 218 U.S. 1, 30 S. Ct. 682, 54 L. Ed. 905 (1910). But if modifiable either for past due or future payments, the decree may be recognized nevertheless under principles of comity. *Alig v. Alig,* 220 Va. 80, 255 S.E.2d 494 (1979); *McKeel v. McKeel,* 185 Va. 108, 113, 37 S.E.2d 746, 749 (1946). During the enforcement proceeding, due process requires consideration of questions of modification which could have been presented to the court of the state where the decree was entered. *Griffin v. Griffin,* 327 U.S. 220, 233-34, 66 S. Ct. 556, 90 L. Ed. 635 (1946); *Alig v. Alig,* 220 Va. at 85, 255 S.E.2d at 498.

### § 20.32   Contempt

A decree for alimony is different from an ordinary judgment or debt.

It is an allowance in the nature of a partition of the husband's property, of which the wife is entitled to a reasonable share for her maintenance. It is an order compelling a husband to support his wife, and this is a public as well as a marital duty—a moral as well as a legal obligation. The liability is not based upon a contract to pay money, but upon the refusal to perform a duty. The imprisonment is not ordered simply to enforce the payment of the money, but to punish for the wilful disobedience of a proper order of a court of competent jurisdiction. *West v. West,* 126 Va. 696, 699, 101 S.E. 876, 877 (1920). Since imprisonment is a severe and harsh remedy, it should not be ordered except where the defendant is contumacious. *Id.* at 700, 101 S.E. at 878. The failure must therefore not stem from an inability to pay. *Branch v. Branch,* 144 Va. 244, 132 S.E. 303 (1926); *Lindsey v. Lindsey,* 158 Va. 647, 164 S.E. 551 (1932).

Contempt is available after a divorce decree providing for spousal support, or an award made independent of a proceeding for divorce. *Heflin v. Heflin,* 177 Va. 385, 14 S.E.2d 317 (1941).

Alimony is to be distinguished from breach of contract between the parties substituting for support, even if confirmed by the divorced couple, so long as the defendant was not ordered by the decree to make alimony payments. *Martin v. Martin,* 205 Va. 181, 135 S.E.2d 815 (1964). Once there is a court order for payment of the agreed upon amount, the decree will be enforceable by contempt. Va. Code § 20-109.1.

The proceeding to enforce spousal support is instituted by a written petition or motion. *Eddens v. Eddens,* 188 Va. 511, 50 S.E.2d 397 (1948). The contempt proceeding is captioned in the names of the parties or in the style of the original suit to be enforced. *Id.,* see also *Davis v. Davis,* 206 Va. 381, 143 S.E.2d 835 (1965) (enforcement of pendente lite order). Trial courts lack jurisdiction to dispose of contempt findings which are based on violations of *pendente lite* orders that have become void following abatement of divorce proceedings due to the death of a party. *Estate of Hackler v. Hackler,* 44 Va. App. 51, 602 S.E.2d 426 (2004).

If a recognizance is not complied with, or a party is found to be in contempt, he or she may be committed to an institution or work squad for a fixed or indeterminate sentence of not more than twelve months, with the county or city then paying support of five dollars to twenty-five dollars per week to the dependent spouse. Va. Code § 20-115.

The party seeking to have the obligor held in contempt may be entitled to attorney's fees. *McKeel v. McKeel,* 185 Va. 108, 116–17, 37 S.E.2d 746, 750 (1946). See also *Alig v. Alig,* 220 Va. 80, 86, 255 S.E.2d 494, 498 (1979). A defendant may be required to post a bond pending appeal of a contempt finding. *Adams v. El-Amin,* 31 Va. Cir. 451 (City of Richmond 1993).

The defendant in a contempt proceeding for failure to make support payments is entitled to the privilege against self-incrimination. *Gowen v. Wilkerson,* 364 F. Supp. 1043 (W.D. Va. 1973) (harmless error in this case). The husband's due process rights were violated when he was denied an opportunity to call a witness in support of his claim that he lacked money to pay court ordered spousal and child support. His voluntary reduction in income, following his sale of a carpet installation business in favor of working for someone else, did not in and of itself support a contempt finding. *Street v. Street,* 24 Va. App. 14, 480 S.E.2d 118 (1997).

### § 20.33   Laches

Acquiescence of nonpayment, even over an extended period of time, will not prevent a dependent spouse from bringing an action to collect the entire arrearages. *Richardson v. Moore,* 217 Va. 422, 229 S.E.2d 864 (1976) (twenty-six years after husband unilaterally reduced support payments, which reduced amount as accepted by wife). This would especially be true in a case where the dependent spouse at the time was mentally unstable and did not communicate with the obligor for three years. *Alig v. Alig,* 220 Va. 80, 255 S.E.2d 494 (1979). Interest and attorney's fees may be collected on unpaid installments, unless inequitable. *Id.* at 85, 255 S.E.2d at 497. See also *McKeel v. McKeel,* 185 Va. 108, 116, 37 S.E.2d 746, 750–51 (1946).

Husband was ordered by the juvenile and domestic relations court to pay spousal support. He perfected an appeal of this support order to the circuit court. A divorce decree, which was silent as to spousal support, was entered, and the husband stopped making payments. After an unsuccessful URESA proceeding in which the district court found that he was no longer bound to make payments, the wife eventually petitioned the district court requesting a hearing on the issue of husband's failure to make payments. An appeal was taken by the wife to the circuit court, which found that no payments had been made for nearly three years. When the husband appealed, arguing that wife was estopped from proceeding because she had not appealed from the district court URESA decision, the court of appeals held that he did not meet the requirements of estoppel because without legal excuse he had not complied with the lawful support decree. *Martin v. Bales,* 7 Va. App. 141, 371 S.E.2d 823 (1988).

Laches may bar a claim for overpayment of spousal support. *Bazzle v. Bazzle*, 37 Va. App. 737, 561 S.E.2d 50 (2002). In *Bazzle*, the court of appeals concluded that it would be prejudicial and inequitable to require a wife to repay thousands of dollars, after a husband took no action although he "knew or suspected" for 17 years that he was making spousal support overpayments.

## § 20.34   Other Defenses

The obligor must purge himself of contempt before the writ of execution is issued. Issuance of execution is regarded for this purpose as a new case. *Hall v. Hall,* 192 Va. 721, 66 S.E.2d 595 (1951) (husband had not filed his notice of appeal within time so could not appeal; court noted it would probably have affirmed case anyway on grounds that purging must commence before the court is required to entertain a motion to quash execution).

## § 20.35   Garnishment

Garnishment for past-due spousal support is authorized by Va. Code § 20-79.1. Orders entered after October 1, 1985, must give notice that arrearages may be withheld from income without amending the order. Va. Code § 20-60.3. Procedures are governed by Va. Code § 8.01-511.

If payment is to be made through the Department of Social Services, as provided since 1985 by Va. Code § 20-60.5, the parties must give the Department thirty days' written notice of changes of address. Further, if the Department does not pay an amount received within thirty days, it must also pay interest on the amount, if the account can be readily identified and the payee is not receiving public assistance.

A receiver may be appointed in the court's discretion to take possession of the property of a nonresident defendant and subject it to the payment of alimony. This would be in the nature of a writ of sequestration or injunction preventing alienation of or interference with the property without the court's consent. *Thornton v. Washington Savings Bank,* 76 Va. 432 (1882); See generally 2 Story's *Equity Jurisprudence* §§ 828–833. But cf. *Watkins v. Watkins,* 220 Va. 1051, 265 S.E.2d 750 (1980), disallowing a lien forbidding sale of the in-state husband's shares of stock in a closely-held family corporation on grounds that this procedure was outside the court's jurisdiction since it affected title to the property. Va. Code § 34-29 limits payroll deduction orders to no more than 50% of the payee's aggregate disposable earnings, which for purposes of Va. Code § 20-79.3 include retirement pay from former employers. *Donahue v. Donahue,* 28 Va. Cir. 70 (Fairfax Co. 1992).

A recognizance may be ordered under Va. Code § 20-114.

### § 20.36   Lien Against Property of Obligor Spouse

A decree for alimony is a lien upon the real estate of the obligor. *Isaacs v. Isaacs' Guardian,* 117 Va. 730, 86 S.E. 105 (1915). See, e.g., *Wilson v. Wilson,* 195 Va. 1060, 81 S.E.2d 605 (1954). Once recorded on the judgment lien docket, an execution of *fieri facias* on the decree becomes a statutory lien upon the obligor's intangible property, and when levied upon, an execution lien. *Harper v. Harper,* 159 Va. 210, 165 S.E. 490 (1932). If counsel obtains an order for a lien reduced to a docket judgment on the property, then the judge may require that a surety bond be posted against the sale of the property. Va. Code § 8.01-460.

The usual provision for a lien against the debtor's property within the state is a possible remedy. *Id.* (for sums already owed, and falling due after the decree). The lien should be registered in the city or county where the land is located. *Durrett v. Durrett,* 204 Va. 59, 62, 129 S.E.2d 50, 52 (1963). The court's jurisdiction is bounded by statute. Thus the court has no authority to enjoin a husband from selling his shares of stock in a closely-held family corporation in order to protect the wife or children's right to support. *Watkins v. Watkins,* 220 Va. 1051, 265 S.E.2d 750 (1980).

The order may be referred to the juvenile and domestic relations court for enforcement by the court entering the original order, either if the obligor fails to provide the ordered support or upon the court's own motion. Va. Code § 20-113.

The dependent spouse, as a lien creditor, may have partition of a jointly held estate if the other co-owner is not willing to take the whole property and the property is not susceptible of partition. In such case the property would be sold and the proceeds applied to discharge the lien. Va. Code § 8-690 et seq. See *Jenkins v. Jenkins,* 211 Va. 797, 180 S.E.2d 516 (1971).

### § 20.37    Posting of Bond of Recognizance

Va. Code § 20-114 provides that the court in its discretion may require a spouse to give a recognizance bond. See, e.g., *Canavos v. Canavos,* 205 Va. 744, 139 S.E.2d 825 (1965); *Lawrence v. Lawrence,* 212 Va. 44, 181 S.E.2d 640 (1971). This is also provided for in the Uniform Reciprocal Enforcement of Support Act, Va. Code § 20-88.22:1.

The section authorizing bond for release of a person accused of a crime was clarified in 2008 to provide that it does not prevent a court from imposing a recognizance or bond designed to secure a spousal or child support obligation. Va. Code § 19.2-123(E).

### § 20.38    Health Insurance

Based on a 2014 decision of the Court of Appeals, a spouse can now be ordered to pay for the former spouse's health insurance. *Wroblewski v. Russell,* 63 Va. App. 468, 480–82, 759 S.E.2d 1, 7 (2014). The wife had no claim for spousal support because her pleading was struck. Although no statutory provision exists that expressly confers the trial court with the authority to order one spouse to pay for the divorcing spouse's health insurance, the Court relied on the provisions of Va. Code §§ 20-108.1(C), 20-60.3(8), and 20-107.1(H) in reaching its decision. The opinion leaves open many issues, such as: the duration that a party will have to pay his former spouse's health insurance; the standard for modifying the obligation to pay the former spouse's health insurance; whether or not the payments are tax deductible; and whether or not the obligation will terminate upon the former spouse's remarriage.

### § 20.39    Life Insurance

Va. Code § 20-107.1:1 was enacted in July 2017, and authorizes a trial court to require a spouse who owes spousal support to maintain life insurance for the payee spouse upon the dissolution of the marriage, the entry of a divorce (be it absolute or from bed and board), or an order for separate maintenance. The following conditions must exist before a court can impose this obligation on the support payor: the life insurance policy must have existed during the marriage, whether it was purchased by either party or provided through the spouse's employment, or be within the effective control of the insured; the payor spouse must have the right to designate a beneficiary; the payee spouse must have been designated as a beneficiary during the marriage; and the payee spouse must have an insurable interest pursuant to Va. Code § 38.2-301(B). Va. Code § 20-107.1:1(A). The cost for the life insurance premiums can be allocated between the parties but all premiums must be billed to the policyholder. *Id.* The obligation to maintain any such life insurance ceases upon the termination of the spousal support. *Id.*

Pursuant to Va. Code § 20-07.1:1(B), in determining to require a payor spouse to maintain life insurance for the payee spouse, the court must consider the following factors:

- The age, health, and insurability of the insured party;

- The age and health of the payee spouse;

- The cost of the life insurance policy;

- The amount and term of the award of spousal support or separate maintenance;

- The prevailing insurance rates at the time of the order;

- The ability of either spouse to pay the premium cost of the life insurance; and

- Such other factors as the court deems necessary or appropriate to consider in order to arrive at a fair order.

# CHAPTER 21

## Property Distribution

### SYNOPSIS

## § 21.01    Overview

Historically, financial adjustment upon divorce in states following the common law tradition has occurred through alimony, almost always paid by the husband to the wife as the dependent spouse. See generally Vernier & Hurlbut, *The Historical Background of Alimony Law and Its Present Statutory Structure*, 6 Law & Contemp. Probs. 197 (1939). However, the real and personal property acquired during the marriage is not always held by the husband, nor have his efforts been the only ones instrumental in acquiring such property. See, e.g., *Hill v. Hill*, 227 Va. 569, 318 S.E.2d 292 (1984) (wife entitled to one half of shares of corporation because of her contributions during the marriage). The more modern rule, which among other advantages allows both spouses financial independence, allows marital property to be divided in some fashion upon divorce. In general, the equitable distribution of property represents an approach analogous to dissolution of a partnership. See, e.g., *Hinton v. Hinton*, 70 N.C. App. 665, 321 S.E.2d 161, 163 (1984); *Deering v. Deering*, 292 Md. 115, 122, 437 A.2d 883 (1981); see generally Krauskopf, *Theories of Property Division and Spousal Support: Searching for Solutions to the Mystery*, 23 Fam. L.Q. 253 (1989); Krauskopf & Thomas, *Partnership Marriage: The Solution to an Ineffective and Inequitable Law of Support*, 35 Ohio St. L.J. 558 (1974); Sharp, *The Partnership Ideal: The Development of Equitable Distribution in North Carolina*, 65 N.C.L. Rev. 197 (1987).

The value of services performed as a homemaker should be taken into account in determining the share of property accorded to each spouse. See, e.g., Va. Code § 20-107.3; *Gummow v. Gummow*, 356 N.W.2d 426 (Minn. App. 1984). Va. Code § 20-107.3 has been amended so that distribution now includes "all property, real and personal, tangible or intangible." Although practice goodwill is marital property and subject to division in equitable distribution, professional goodwill is a spouse's separate property. *Howell v. Howell*, 31 Va. App. 332, 344, 523 S.E.2d 514, 520 (2000).

A trial judge must follow three basic steps in making equitable distribution of property: (1) the court first must classify the property as either separate, marital, or hybrid (part separate and part marital property); (2) the court must assign a value to the property based upon evidence presented by both parties; and (3) the court must distribute the property to the parties after considering the statutory factors set forth in Code. Va. Code § 20-107.3(E). *Fox v. Fox*, 61 Va. App. 185, 193, 734 S.E.2d 662, 666 (2012) (citations omitted). When there was no marital property subject to equitable distribution, it was reversible error for the trial court to order the husband to pay the wife a $150,000 equitable restitution payment. *McGinnis v. McGinnis*, 69

Va. App. 572, 579–81, 821 S.E.2d 555, 559–60 (2018). For examples of how courts value nonmonetary contributions, see *Aidonis v. Brooks*, 1995 Va. App. LEXIS 471 (May 30, 1995); and *Graham v. Graham*, 1995 Va. App. LEXIS 811 (Nov. 7, 1995). For a case distinguishing between this determination and the considerations required for an award of spousal support, see, e.g., *Stumbo v. Stumbo*, 20 Va. App. 685, 460 S.E.2d 591 (1995).

The Virginia Bar Council has determined that it is ethically improper to represent a client in an equitable distribution case on a contingent fee basis. Op. No. 189, July 1, 1984. The property to be distributed is not a new asset as is a personal injury recovery, and to allow a contingent fee would be to encourage attorneys to concentrate on large monetary awards for the client at the possible expense of devoting time to other important areas of concern, and to minimize any possibility of reconciliation during the period of representation.

Although several states have adopted policies that presume that an equal division is equitable, see, e.g., *White v. White*, 64 N.C. App. 432, 308 S.E.2d 68, 71 (1983), Virginia has not adopted such a presumption of equal distribution, but instead requires consideration of specific factors set out in Va. Code § 20-107.3. *Papuchis v. Papuchis*, 2 Va. App. 130, 132, 341 S.E.2d 829, 830–31 (1986) (citing Report of the Joint Subcommittee Studying Section 20-107 of the Code of Virginia to the Governor and the General Assembly of Virginia, H. Doc. No. 32, at 8 (1982), which expressly rejected any such presumption). See also *Alphin v. Alphin*, 15 Va. App. 395, 424 S.E.2d 572 (1992); *Gaynor v. Hird*, 1995 Va. App. LEXIS 617 (Aug. 1, 1995); *Shackelford v. Shackelford*, 39 Va. App. 201, 571 S.E.2d 917 (2002). However, it is not wrong for the court to make such an award, dividing marital property equally. *Bentz v. Bentz*, 2 Va. App. 486, 345 S.E.2d 773 (1986) (down payment made by mother of husband; all payments made during marriage when each party had substantially the same income). However, once a trial judge makes the determination that the parties have equally contributed to the marriage, reasons must be stated for dividing the property unequally. *Artis v. Artis*, 10 Va. App. 356, 392 S.E.2d 504 (1990).

Conducting equitable distribution frequently presents the court with a difficult and complex challenge. The court needs to ensure that marital property is not distributed more than one time. In *Garza v. Garza*, 2018 Va. App. LEXIS 352 (Dec. 18, 2018), the trial court was reversed for "double-dipping." The husband had withdrawn funds from his retirement account to purchase a new residence. At trial, the wife's motion to value husband's retirement account on the date before he took the distribution was granted and the court ordered that Wife was to receive one-half of husband's retirement account valued at the date prior to Husband withdrawing funds. However, the court further awarded wife with an interest in the residence that Husband purchased with the distribution he took from his retirement account. The trial court erred by double counting the funds from Husband's retirement account.

A division of property, unlike spousal support, should not take into consideration the earning capacity of one spouse and the support needs of the other. *Reid v. Reid*, 7 Va. App. 553, 375 S.E.2d 533 (1989). As the court held in *Brown v. Brown*, 5 Va. App. 238, 246, 361 S.E.2d 364, 368 (1987): "Spousal support involves a legal duty flowing from one spouse to the other by virtue of the marital relationship. By contrast, a monetary award does not flow from any legal duty, but involves an adjustment of the equities, rights and interests of the parties in marital property." See also *Srinivasan v. Srinivasan*, 10 Va. App. 728, 396 S.E.2d 675 (1990). When the parties divorced after only a year of marriage, causing the wife to relocate twice in a short time, this should have a bearing on spousal support, but not equitable distribution of property. *Lightburn v. Lightburn*, 22 Va. App. 612, 472 S.E.2d 281 (1996). A monetary award issued pursuant to Va. Code § 20-107.3(D) shall neither be contingent upon the future continuity of spousal support payments or future circumstances. *Dixon v. Dixon*, 71 Va. App. 709, 719, 840 S.E.2d 1 (2020).

Va. Code § 8.01-382 provides that the judgment or decree of the court in any action at law or equity may provide for interest on any principal sum awarded, or any part thereof, and fix the period at which interest commences. The judgment or decree must provide for such interest until such principal sum is paid. This Code section is applicable in divorce cases. See, e.g., *Ragsdale v. Ragsdale*, 30 Va. App. 283, 516 S.E.2d 698 (1999) (interest on award of medical practice). However, under Va. Code § 20-107.3(D), the provisions of Va. Code § 8.01-382 apply "unless the court orders otherwise." Thus, in *Shackelford v. Shackelford*, 39 Va. App. 201, 571 S.E.2d 917 (2002), the wife was not entitled to interest on a monetary award that her husband had ten years to pay, because the court specified in the final divorce decree that interest on the monetary award was not awarded.

A pension payment to the wife in advance of the retirement of the husband as part of an equitable distribution, as opposed to alimony, was dischargeable in bankruptcy. *In re Lelak*, 38 B.R. 164 (S.D. Ohio 1984); cf. *In re Calhoun*, 715 F.2d 1103 (6th Cir. 1983) (joint debts dischargeable), superseded by statute, *In re Lewis*, 39 B.R. 842, 12 B.C.D. 279 (1984). Empirical studies of property distribution, the effect of fault, and the effect of litigation, include Eleanor Maccoby and Robert Mnookin, *Dividing the Child* Tables

6.1 and 7.7 (Harvard Univ. Press, 1992) (California litigated and settled divorces); Margaret Brinig & Michael V. Alexeev, *Trading at Divorce: Preferences, Legal Rules and Transaction Costs*, 8 Ohio St. J. on Disp. Res. 279 (1993) (Wisconsin and Virginia); Martha Garrison, *How Do Judges Decide Divorce Cases? An Empirical Analysis of Discretionary Decision-making*, 74 N.C. L. Rev. 403, 407 (1995) (no evidence of financial differences where custody threats were credible); Robert F. Kelly & Greer L. Fox, *Determinants of Alimony Awards: An Empirical Test of Current Theories and a Reflection on Public Policy*, 44 Syracuse L. Rev. 641, 696–97 & Table 3 (1993) (Michigan); Suzanne Reynolds, *The Relationship of Property Division and Alimony: The Division of Property to Address Need*, 56 Fordham L. Rev. 827, 854–55 (1988) (six states); and Yoram Weiss & Robert Willis, *Transfers among Divorced Couples: Evidence and Interpretation*, 11 J. Labor Econ. 629, 656 & Tab 4 (1993) (a national study).

## § 21.02 Ability to Transfer Title

Even with the equitable distribution statute, power does not lie to transfer title from one spouse to the other. Va. Code § 20-107.3C. For example, if property is owned as tenants by the entireties, more than a one-half share cannot be awarded to either spouse. *Ward v. Ward*, 48 Md. App. 307, 426 A.2d 443, appeal after remand, 52 Md. App. 336, 449 A.2d 443 (1982). Nor can a monetary sum be awarded without a prior determination of the value of all marital property. *Id.* (erroneous to award wife $10,000 in substitution of her one half interest when other property was also held by the couple). An important amendment to Va. Code § 20-107.3 that was made during the 1988 legislative session allows the court to order the division or transfer, or both, of jointly owned marital property or any part thereof. Va. Code § 20-107.3(C). This may, according to the statute, be accomplished by (1) ordering the transfer of real or personal property to one of the parties, permitting either party to purchase the interest of the other and directing the allocation of the proceeds, provided that the party purchasing the interest of the other agrees to assume any indebtedness secured by the property, or (2) ordering sale of the property through private or public sale, without the necessity for partition. This is in addition to the court's power to grant a monetary award. Va. Code § 20-107.3(C) contemplates that the court has the power to order the usual and necessary incidents requisite to transferring the property to reach an equitable distribution. *Bomar v. Bomar*, 45 Va. App. 229, 609 S.E.2d 629 (2005). In *Bomar*, the trial court erred by transferring the marital residence to the wife, who was to assume the mortgage debt, without ordering refinancing or other safeguards to ensure that the husband would not remain liable on the mortgage. The court may itself transfer an interest in property held jointly by the parties, even without a prior order that the parties make such a transfer, followed by a failure to comply. Va. Code § 20-107.3(C).

Case law decided before the enactment of this section recognized that a court may validly order payment of a mortgage pending the divorce and equitable distribution of the marital property, *Taylor v. Taylor*, 5 Va. App. 436, 440–41, 364 S.E.2d 244 (1988), and may validly order partition when the parties are unable to reach an agreed disposition. *Wagner v. Wagner*, 4 Va. App. 397, 406, 358 S.E.2d 407 (1987). Likewise, it may order satisfaction of an award by transfer of a particular piece of property, but only after exercising sound judicial discretion in light of the particular circumstances. *Payne v. Payne*, 5 Va. App. 359, 367, 363 S.E.2d 428 (1987) (error to satisfy award to wife by transfer of California property that husband had been unable to sell). See *Johnson v. Johnson*, 56 Va. App. 511, 694 S.E.2d 797 (2010) (court properly exercised discretion in approving husband's transfer of $120,000 share of retirement accounts to wife in satisfaction of $120,000 monetary award, even though transfer would net wife only $60,736 after taxes and early withdrawal penalties); Va. Code § 20-107.3(D). See also *Fitchett v. Fitchett*, 6 Va. App. 562, 370 S.E.2d 318 (1988) (trial court erred since it made no determination that partition could not be conveniently made before a partition sale was ordered). The trial court had no power to order the husband to convey his interest in the marital residence to the wife, while allowing her to make payments to him over time. *Stroop v. Stroop*, 10 Va. App. 611, 394 S.E.2d 861 (1990).

In *Stainback v. Stainback*, 11 Va. App. 13, 396 S.E.2d 686 (1990), the husband's father began Arlington Enterprises to help the husband toward a career in art. The husband was hired and worked for his father's firm as president and director. His duties included general management of a storage facility, management of various farms, and production of art works. The art works produced by the husband were the property of the firm, and all proceeds from the sale of the art work were deposited into the corporation's accounts. The court of appeals determined that the record supported the trial court's determination that the husband and Arlington Enterprises were alter egos, and therefore, since the paintings came into being because of the labors of the husband, the fruits of that labor were marital property. See also *Jacobs v. Jacobs*, 12 Va. App. 977, 406 S.E.2d 669 (1991), which concerned valuation of the wife's 32% interest in a closely held corporation. Accepting the figure presented by the husband was incorrect when it depended entirely upon what he or the corporation felt the stock was worth. Amendments to Va. Code § 20-107.3 allow for retention of jurisdiction on the motion of either party. However, the right to receive an equitable distribution of property pursuant to a divorce is lost if the party does not reserve such right in the final decree. *Toomey v. Toomey*, 251 Va. 168, 465 S.E.2d 838 (Va. 1996); see also *Lauffer v. Lauffer*, 23 Va. Cir. 278 (Fairfax Co. 1991); *Boyd v. Boyd*, 1996 Va. App. LEXIS 210 (March 26, 1996).

An example of a circumstance in which bifurcation was justified is *Tedesco v. Tedesco*, 1994 Va. App. LEXIS 103 (March 8, 1994). In this case, the husband had cancer and feared that a delay in obtaining the divorce might jeopardize his interests. Further, the property issues were complex. However, the trial court properly entered a final order of distribution when the husband was incarcerated, since he was present at the equitable distribution hearing and was represented by counsel. *Poppe v. Poppe*, 1995 Va. App. LEXIS 655 (Aug. 29, 1995).

The most common means of avoiding the necessity for transfers of title where there is no separation agreement is by the award of a sum payable by one spouse to the other in satisfaction of property interests. This may be payable in lump sum or over time. The advantage to the recipient spouse is that payment is not contingent upon nonremarriage of the recipient or survival of the obligor, as is alimony. These payments will not be taxable as alimony if made in less than six years. I.R.C. § 71.

The trial court did have the power to divide a large piece of jointly titled real property between the divorcing spouses, allowing the husband to continue living in the marital home while giving the wife her portion on the other side of the parcel, including a home that had been built for her parents. *Hart v. Hart*, 27 Va. App. 46, 497 S.E.2d 496 (1998). The case was remanded, however, because the court created an easement for ingress and egress over the husband's (dominant) parcels without apportioning the expenses for maintaining the easement. On remand, the trial court committed additional errors, resulting in a second appeal and a second remand with additional instructions for accomplishing the parties' property division. See *Hart v. Hart*, 35 Va. App. 221, 544 S.E.2d 366 (2001).

## § 21.03 Times Distribution is Available

Va. Code § 20-107.3 limits equitable distribution of property to occasions when the court decrees "the dissolution of a marriage, and also upon decreeing a divorce from the bond of matrimony." The court's jurisdiction to award equitable distribution is dependent on a timely "request" by a party; however, because the statute does not specify the form or substance of the "request," it is sufficient that a party make known to the court his or her desire that the court award equitable distribution. *Smith v. Smith*, 38 Va. App. 113, 562 S.E.2d 329 (2002). Because of confusion over whether jurisdiction to hear equitable distribution does continue subsequent to rendering a divorce decree (see *Parra v. Parra*, 1 Va. App. 118, 120, 336 S.E.2d 157, 158 (1985), and *Shaughnessy v. Shaughnessy*, 1 Va. App. 136, 140, 336 S.E.2d 166, 169 (1985)), the Legislature amended Va. Code § 20-107.3(A) in 1986 to enable the trial court to retain jurisdiction to equitably distribute the marital property following the entry of a divorce. Initially, in 1986, Va. Code § 20-107.3(A) required that both parties motioned the court to retain equitable distribution jurisdiction because of the complexities of the parties' property. This section now permits the court to retain equitable distribution jurisdiction upon motion of one party "when the Court determines that such action is clearly necessary." The section also validates all decrees where such reservations had been made. See *Christensen v. Christensen*, 26 Va. App. 651, 496 S.E.2d 132 (1998).

Several cases have involved situations in which the trial judge failed to find that it was necessary to reserve the issue of equitable distribution because of the complexity of the property. In such cases, the court of appeals has determined, for one reason or another, that jurisdiction was in fact retained. See *Erickson-Dickson v. Erickson-Dickson*, 12 Va. App. 381, 404 S.E. 2d 388 (1991) (husband did not make a timely objection to the trial court's ruling or its failure to make the required findings of fact); *Spriggs v. Spriggs*, 43 Va. App. 510, 600 S.E.2d 136 (2004) (court's decision to retain jurisdiction over equitable distribution could be challenged only by timely direct appeal); but see *Patel v. Patel*, 33 Va. App. 776, 537 S.E.2d 11 (2000) (language in final decree that retained case on docket until date certain "to perform equitable distribution" meant that court lost jurisdiction to adjudicate equitable distribution on date certain plus 21 days, under Rule 1:1). See also *Mina v. Mina*, 45 Va. App. 215, 609 S.E.2d 622 (2005) (jurisdiction retained over reserved issue of attorney's fees when court's order was not final for purposes of Rule 1:1). In the parties' final divorce decree, the court retained jurisdiction to determine spousal support and property rights. Thereafter, the parties entered into a settlement agreement pursuant to which the husband agreed to make annual payments to the wife, in return for which the wife agreed to "release and discharge . . . all claims which she might have for alimony." The trial court entered a decree that ratified and incorporated this settlement agreement. The court of appeals held that § 20-109.1 did not deprive the trial court of its power to incorporate a settlement agreement involving support in a decree following the entry of a decree of divorce. *Rogers v. Damron*, 23 Va. App. 708, 479 S.E.2d 540 (1997). It was therefore appropriate for the wife to use the court's contempt power to enforce the decree.

Under limited circumstances, a Virginia circuit court can conduct equitable distribution when a court outside of the Commonwealth granted a divorce. Specifically, Va. Code § 20-107.3(J) authorizes a court to conduct equitable distribution where a foreign court dissolved the marriage, and "(i) one of the parties was domiciled in this Commonwealth when the foreign proceedings were commenced, (ii) the foreign court did not have personal jurisdiction over the party domiciled in the Commonwealth, (iii) the proceeding is initiated within two years of receipt of notice of the foreign decree by the party domiciled in the Commonwealth, and (iv) the court obtains personal jurisdiction over the parties." Where a wife was divorced in Arizona and waited seven years to pursue equitable distribution in Virginia, which is where the husband resided, the court lacked jurisdiction since the matter had not been brought within two years of the divorce. *Campbell v. Altizer*, 19 Va. App. 553, 453 S.E.2d 570 (1995).

The court shall determine the value of marital property as of the date of the evidentiary hearing on the evaluation issue. *Rowe v. Rowe*, 33 Va. App. 250, 532 S.E.2d 908 (2000) (stating that 1998 amendments to Va. Code § 20-107.3(A) codified rule announced in *Mitchell v. Mitchell*, 4 Va. App. 113, 355 S.E.2d 18 (1987)). See *Thomas v. Thomas*, 40 Va. App. 639, 580 S.E.2d 503 (2003) (erroneous valuation of marital business at date of separation). Another date may be used for valuation, upon motion of either party and good cause shown. *Aster v. Gross*, 7 Va. App. 1, 371 S.E.2d 833 (1988) (husband's pension plan should have been valued at date nearest equitable distribution hearing rather than at date nearest filing of complaint). If an appellate court remands an equitable distribution award, the trial court should revalue the property to obtain the most accurate valuation and equitable distribution. *Wagner v. Tillman Wagner*, 15 Va. App. 120, 421 S.E.2d 218 (1992), *aff'd*, 16 Va. App. 529, 431 S.E.2d 77 (1993).

Except as authorized by statute, distribution of property is not available. Thus, the wife's dower rights should not have been extinguished in a decree for separate maintenance, as opposed to divorce. *Wilson v. Wilson*, 195 Va. 1060, 81 S.E.2d 605 (1954). In cases of divorce *a mensa*, property acquired during the relationship may be disposed of through a separation agreement between the spouses, see generally Chapter 17, or pursuant to a valid antenuptial agreement. Cf. *Burgess v. Burgess*, 123 Ill. App. 3d 487, 78 Ill. Dec. 345, 462 N.E.2d 203 (1984).

The parties must have final equitable distribution orders within 21 days of the divorce decree. Thus the court lacked jurisdiction to modify the order four years later. *Wilson v. Wilson*, 25 Va. App. 752, 492 S.E.2d 495 (1997).

If there is Virginia property, and if a former Virginia domiciliary obtains a foreign ex parte divorce, the "divisible divorce" doctrine of *Estin v. Estin*, 334 U.S. 541, 68 S. Ct. 1213, 92 L. Ed. 1561 (1948), should allow a later Virginia distribution proceeding. See *Newport v. Newport*, 219 Va. 48, 245 S.E.2d 134 (1978) (alimony). Rule 1:1 bars only further litigation of issues over which the court had power to adjudicate. *Hayes v. Hayes*, 3 Va. App. 499, 504, 351 S.E.2d 590, 592 (1986). When only in rem jurisdiction exists, the court is permitted only to dissolve the marriage and it cannot conduct equitable distribution. *Gibson v. Gibson*, 5 Va. App. 426, 429, 364 S.E.2d 518, 519 (1988). In *Lenhart v. Burgett*, 1995 Va. App. LEXIS 300 (March 28, 1995), wife brought an ex parte divorce action against her husband, who lived in Pennsylvania, reserving issues of support and equitable distribution. Later she had him served in Pennsylvania in connection with a spousal support and equitable distribution proceeding, and he appeared personally in Virginia. Once husband appeared personally in the divorce, the trial court was able to conduct equitable distribution. The court of appeals affirmed the trial court's award of 50% of the marital property. But see *Toomey v. Toomey*, 251 Va. 168, 465 S.E.2d 838 (1996), in which a husband brought a Virginia divorce action, serving his wife personally in Oregon. She filed no responsive pleadings, and the divorce decree was entered, making no provision for spousal support, child custody, or equitable distribution. The trial court granted the wife leave to file a cross-bill to seek equitable distribution of the husband's military retirement, and the court of appeals affirmed the decree. The Virginia Supreme Court reversed, stating that the wife failed to protect her interests in having the circuit court adjudicate her equitable distribution rights, because under Va. Code § 20-107.3 she could have asked the court to (1) adjudicate her rights before entering the divorce decree, or (2) retain its jurisdiction and adjudicate her rights after entering the divorce decree, but she did neither. In *Garrison v. Garrison*, 1994 Va. App. LEXIS 463 (July 12, 1994), the court gave full faith and credit to an ex parte Texas divorce but allowed the wife to bring a later Virginia action for child custody, child support, spousal support, and property distribution.

However, when the foreign court did have personal jurisdiction over both spouses, the wife could not later bring an equitable distribution action in Virginia. *Richardson v. Sass*, 49 Va. Cir. 242 (Fairfax Co. 1999).

## § 21.04   Jurisdiction

So long as marital property is within the state, the court will have in rem jurisdiction to divide it. There must be notice to the other spouse, particularly if out-of-state. This remains true despite the Supreme Court case of *Shaffer v. Heitner*, 433 U.S. 186, 97 S. Ct. 2569, 53 L. Ed. 2d 683 (1977), which restricts quasi-in-rem jurisdiction to controversies directly involving the property in the state, since by definition the parties to an equitable distribution proceeding are seeking to determine their interests in marital property. For example, although the husband died intestate during the couple's divorce proceedings, the fund made up of the proceeds from the sale of the marital home became a res over which the divorce court had jurisdiction. The wife could therefore seek a rule on the status of the funds the court held in escrow. *Sprouse v. Griffin*, 250 Va. 46, 458 S.E.2d 770 (1995). When one spouse is incarcerated at the time of the divorce proceedings, appointment of a committee is required under Va. Code § 53.1-223 before property can be distributed. *Mendes v. Mendes*, 1994 Va. App. LEXIS 182 (March 29, 1994).

When property is located outside the state, the court has no jurisdiction to transfer title. *Fall v. Eastin*, 215 U.S. 1, 30 S. Ct. 3, 54 L. Ed. 65 (1909); *Barber v. Barber*, 51 Cal. 2d 244, 331 P.2d 628 (1958); *Kaherl v. Kaherl*, 357 S.W.2d 622 (Tex. Civ. App. 1962). See *Beckwitt v. Beckwitt*, 1993 Va. App. LEXIS 457 (Sept. 28, 1993). However, where there has been personal jurisdiction over the absent spouse, the court may make an order to convey or to pay a sum that may be enforced in Virginia or the spouse's state of residence in another action. *Ivey v. Ivey*, 183 Conn. 490, 439 A.2d 425 (1981); cf. *Fall v. Eastin*, 215 U.S. 1, 30 S. Ct. 3, 54 L. Ed. 65 (1909).

If the property is located outside the state, the law to be applied in deciding whether or not title may be shifted is that of the state where the property is located. *Williams v. Williams*, 390 A.2d 4 (D.C. 1978). See also *Anderson v. Anderson*, 449 A.2d 334 (D.C. 1982).

When a spouse cannot be found within the state, and the matrimonial domicile was in Virginia, or the separation or facts giving rise to the cause of action for divorce took place within the state, the spouse may be reached personally under the longarm statute. Va. Code § 8.01-328.1(A)(9). See *Cabaniss v. Cabaniss*, 46 Va. App. 595, 620 S.E.2d 559 (2005) (court ordered equitable distribution after finding personal jurisdiction over non-resident husband pursuant to Va. Code § 8.01-328.1(A)(9), when husband and wife had maintained matrimonial domicile in Virginia at time when parties separated and cause of action for divorce arose).

The longarm statute was also applied in *Mock v. Mock*, 11 Va. App. 616, 400 S.E.2d 543 (1991). Husband and wife were married in Georgia and moved to Virginia shortly thereafter. They remained in Virginia for two years, and then were transferred to various other states pursuant to the husband's military orders. They returned to Virginia, purchased a home in Fairfax, and resided there until 1980. From 1980 to 1984 they lived in Ft.

Lewis, Washington, and in Turkey on military assignments. While still in Turkey, they separated, and the wife returned to the marital residence in Fairfax. In 1985, the husband returned to Nevada and obtained an ex parte divorce in which the court found that he was a bona fide resident and domiciliary of Nevada at the time of the divorce. The Virginia Court of Appeals determined that this finding was not binding on the Virginia court for purposes of determining whether it could exercise personal jurisdiction under Va. Code § 8.01-328.1(A)(9) for equitable distribution. The husband's course of conduct disclosed that he intended to make Virginia his permanent home: the couple purchased the Virginia residence, which they rented out when away on military assignments; the husband held a Virginia driver's license for 14 years, including the time of separation; some of his automobiles were registered in Virginia; and in March 1986, both parties signed a stipulation that they were residents of Virginia for the purposes of a partition suit. The court of appeals in *Mock v. Mock*, 11 Va. App. 616, 400 S.E.2d 543 (1991), found that the Mocks maintained a matrimonial domicile in Virginia at the time of their separation, so that the trial court was correct in asserting personal jurisdiction over the husband, a nonresident, under the long-arm statute. Likewise, the court could not order transfer of property located in Virginia where one of the spouses was domiciled outside of the state and was served only by publication. The court did have jurisdiction to adjudicate the ownership of the property as a proceeding in rem. *Jefferson v. Jefferson*, 27 Va. Cir. 184 (Fairfax Co. 1992).

Personal jurisdiction necessary for distribution of his military pension can be obtained over a serviceman stationed in Virginia through his entry of a general appearance and seeking of various forms of affirmative relief. *Kramer v. Kramer*, 19 Va. Cir. 231 (Fairfax Co. 1990). See also *Blackson v. Blackson*, 40 Va. App. 507, 579 S.E.2d 704 (2003) (serviceman entered special appearance but then sought affirmative relief, thus invoking court's jurisdiction and consenting to equitable distribution of marital estate including military pension). More generally, when a court obtains jurisdiction over a nonresident under the longarm statute, such service shall have the same effect as service on the nonresident within Virginia. Va. Code § 8.01-320 (amended 1997). This statute specifically includes divorce and annulment cases.

Death of either of the spouses would generally abate a claim for equitable distribution. *Sprouse v. Griffin*, 250 Va. 46, 50, 458 S.E.2d 770, 772 (1995). This is because the action is purely a personal one, and cannot be filed or maintained separate from divorce proceedings. However, when there is a bifurcated divorce proceeding in accordance with Va. Code § 20-107.3(A) which expressly retained the court's jurisdiction to conduct equitable distribution following a divorce, the trial court properly held the equitable distribution hearing despite one party dying after the divorce but prior to the equitable distribution hearing. *Brown v. Brown*, 69 Va. App. 462, 472–75, 820 S.E.2d 384, 389–90 (2018). The court in *Brown* recognized that a spouse's death during the pendency of the divorce litigation renders the divorce proceedings moot since the death terminates the marriage and leaves nothing to adjudicate. *Brown*, 69 Va. App at 471, 820 S.E.2d at 388. Nonetheless, when the trial court bifurcated the divorce proceeding from the equitable distribution issues, the trial court retained "jurisdiction until the matter before it has been fully adjudicated . . . 'so as to do complete justice between the parties.'" *Brown*, 69 Va. App at 472–73, 820 S.E.2d at 389 (internal citations omitted). Despite her former husband's death following the entry of the divorce, the bifurcated proceeding afforded the former wife the right to equitable distribution of marital property and "the trial court was obligated to complete the task of 'equitably distribut[ing] the material fruits of the marriage.'" *Brown*, 69 Va. App at 4773, 820 S.E.2d at 389 (internal citations omitted).

Moreover, once the court orders a distribution the decree survives the death of a spouse. *Fitzgerald v. Trueworthy*, 476 A.2d 183 (Me. 1984). See also *Byrne v. Byrne*, 19 Va. Cir. 357 (Chesterfield Co. 1990). Where a spouse dies and an appeal is taken, the proper party to substitute is the personal representative of the decedent as opposed to the estate of the decedent. *Loewinger v. Estate of Loewinger*, 64 Va. App. 1, 763 S.E.2d 826 (2014). Virginia requires that all actions be prosecuted by and against either living parties or their representative because a person must exist that "can be affected by the judgment and from whom obedience can be compelled." This is so because "[t]here must be such parties to the record as can be affected by the judgment and from whom obedience can be compelled." *Id.*, 64 Va. App. at 5, 763 S.E.2d at 828. In addition, Va. Code § 8.01-229(B) "allows claims to be filed against the property of the estate, but provides that actions may only be filed against the decedent's personal representative." *Id.*, 64 Va. App. at 6, 763 S.E.2d at 828.

The court may have jurisdiction to divide property following divorce without giving notice pursuant to Va. Code § 8.01-319(A) if a spouse departs the country without leaving any forwarding address with the court, counsel or opposing party. *Eddine v. Eddine*, 12 Va. App. 760, 406 S.E.2d 914 (1991). For any issue arising out of suits for divorce, annulment or affirmation of marriage, separate maintenance, or equitable distribution based on foreign decree, the judge shall consider whether to refer the parties to mediation, and may do so sua sponte or on motion of one of the parties. Upon referral, the parties must attend one evaluation session during which they and the mediator assess the case and decide whether to continue with mediation or with adjudication. Va. Code § 8.01-576.4 et seq., 20-124.2, and 20-124.4. The court may also require the parties to attend courses in parenting responsibilities, conflict resolution, and financial responsibility, according to Va. Code § 20-103. When the parties are referred to mediation, the court shall set a return date. The parties shall notify the court in writing if the dispute is resolved prior to this date. The court may in its discretion incorporate any mediated agreement into the terms of its final decree. Only if such an order is entered will the terms of the voluntary settlement agreement affect any outstanding court order.

The court shall vacate a mediated agreement or an incorporating order where the agreement was procured by fraud or duress, where it is unconscionable, where there was not adequate disclosure of financial or property information, or where there was evident partiality or misconduct by the mediator that prejudiced the rights of a party. Misconduct includes failure of the mediator to inform the parties in writing at the beginning of mediation:

(1)    that the mediator does not provide legal advice;

(2)    that an agreement will affect the legal rights of the parties;

(3)    that each party to mediation has the opportunity to consult with independent legal counsel at any time and is encouraged to do so; and

(4)    that each party should have any draft agreement reviewed by independent counsel prior to signing the agreement, or should waive this opportunity. Va. Code § 8.01-576.12.

A motion to vacate an order or agreement must be made within two years after the agreement is reached, except that if the motion is based upon fraud, it shall be made within two years after these grounds are discovered or reasonably should have been discovered. Va. Code § 8.01-576.12.

Under the facts of *Christensen v. Christensen*, 26 Va. App. 651, 496 S.E.2d 132 (1998), the trial court erred in bifurcating the equitable distribution and divorce proceedings. The trial court made no express finding that bifurcation of the proceedings was "clearly necessary." However, this did not warrant overturning the divorce decree and remanding. In *Horn v. Horn*, 28 Va. App. 688, 508 S.E.2d 347 (1998), the court ruled that when a trial court classifies certain business property as marital property without valuing or dividing it, that decree is interlocutory rather than final. Any appeal under these circumstances would be improper, and should be dismissed. The decision in *Christensen v. Christensen*, 26 Va. App. 651, 496 S.E.2d 132 (1998), is distinguishable from the decision in *Erickson-Dickson v. Erickson-Dickson*, 12 Va. App. 381, 404 S.E.2d 388 (1991), because *Christensen* involved a direct appeal from a divorce decree, and *Erickson-Dickson* involved a divorce decree that was not timely appealed. *Spriggs v. Spriggs*, 43 Va. App. 510, 600 S.E.2d 136 (2004).

### § 21.05  Gifts, Bequests, and Inheritance

Gifts by a third party to one spouse, or bequests to or inheritance by a spouse are not marital property according to Va. Code § 20-107.3(1); *see* current version at Va. Code § 20-107.3(A)(1). Compare *Lanier v. Lanier*, 1993 Va. App. LEXIS 246 (July 6, 1993), where husband and wife jointly purchased a home. The husband made the monthly interest payments, and his parents made the five annual $25,000 principal payments directly to the bank. In exchange for each payment, the husband executed a note for $25,000. Later each year, the parents forgave $20,000 of the note and filed a gift tax return for the $20,000. The notes were executed by the husband alone, and the gift tax returns designated him as the only donee. The property became marital property because each initial transaction was a loan from the parents to the husband that acted to relieve the wife of part of her mortgage obligation. Forgiveness of a portion, coming as a gift, could not change the initial character of the transaction.

The acquisition of a farm partnership during the marriage by sale, even though for less than full consideration, will result in its classification as marital property. *Brown v. Brown*, 5 Va. App. 238, 361 S.E.2d 364 (1987). See also *Wagner v. Wagner*, 4 Va. App. 397, 358 S.E.2d 407 (1987) (forgiveness of note to secure debt to father for purchase price did not alter character of property as marital). An acquisition by gift, even as an advancement on inheritance, will not be separate property if it is titled jointly, although consideration as to how and when the property was acquired will be appropriate in determining the amount of, and method for paying, a monetary award. *McClanahan v. McClanahan*, 19 Va. App. 399, 451 S.E.2d 691 (1994) (property was acquired in joint names as a gift from the husband's parents, and the orchard on the property was later sold to purchase other business property, so both became marital property); *Theismann v. Theismann*, 22 Va. App. 557, 471 S.E.2d 809 (1996) (The wife was awarded $950,000 of the marital property worth over $2.5 million, even though the marriage was of short duration and the husband brought the vast majority of financial contributions to the marriage. The husband had retitled the property from his own name to joint names.). *Brown v. Brown*, 1996 Va.

App. LEXIS 78 (Feb. 6, 1996) (husband's inherited insurance business became marital property when he used the property to form a new Virginia corporation in which he worked during the marriage. The wife worked in the business for some time as well.); *Cousins v. Cousins*, 5 Va. App. 156, 159, 360 S.E.2d 882 (1987). However, if stock is given in the husband's name only, and there is credible evidence that it was intended to be given individually, it remains separate property although the dividends are used for family purposes. *Rein v. Rein*, 1994 Va. App. LEXIS 699 (Nov. 29, 1994); *Stainback v. Stainback*, 11 Va. App. 13, 396 S.E.2d 686 (1990).

When husband and wife had transferred property to a revocable trust for estate purposes, it remained marital property though divided into separate shares for the trust. *Kelln v. Kelln*, 30 Va. App. 113, 515 S.E.2d 789 (1999). The court opined: "Under Virginia law, in the absence of clear and unambiguous intent to create a separate estate in the other party, an interspousal gift is ineffective as a device to transform an asset into separate property."

As noted in *Kelln*, marital property may become separate if there is a valid express agreement where one of the parties "has relinquished all right and interest in marital property and has transferred those rights unconditionally" to the other. *Kelln*, 30 Va. App. at 123, 515 S.E.2d at 793–94.

The Virginia Supreme Court held that spouses who own real property as tenants by the entirety successfully transferred all rights to the Wife even though the deed was only signed by the Husband. See *Evans v. Evans*, 772 S.E.2d 576 (2015).

Va. Code § 64.2-620, provides that a provision for a nonprobate transfer on death in certain specified types of written instruments, including insurance policies, pension plans, conveyances, and marital property agreements, is a nontestamentary transfer.

## § 21.06    Pensions and Retirement Plans

Under Va. Code § 20-107.3, after consideration of the statutory factors, the court may direct payment, in addition to a monetary award, of the marital share of any pension, profit-sharing or deferred compensation plan, or retirement benefits, but only as such benefits are payable. This may be direct assignment to a party from the employer trustee, plan administrator, or other holder of the benefits. Va. Code § 20-107.3(G). The court may order a party to designate a spouse or former spouse as an irrevocable beneficiary during the lifetime of the beneficiary of all or a portion of any survivor benefit or annuity plan, not including a life insurance policy. The court, in its discretion, shall determine as between the parties who shall bear the costs of maintaining the plan. Va. Code § 20-107.3(G)(2).

"Pensions" includes military pensions, *Sawyer v. Sawyer*, 1 Va. App. 75, 78–79, 335 S.E.2d 277, 278 (1985), when military service took place, at least in part, during the marriage. Further, if the statutory factors of Va. Code § 20-107.3 are taken into account, it is not incorrect to make a monetary award, payable in a lump sum or over a period of time, taking into account the present value of some percentage of military or other retirement benefits. *McGinnis v. McGinnis*, 1 Va. App. 272, 277, 338 S.E.2d 159, 161 (1985) (although case had to be remanded since court incorrectly awarded wife a portion of property titled in the husband's name, award of one-third of husband's federal retirement benefits was not incorrect). Provided that sufficient evidence is provided to the court regarding the spouse's participation in the retirement plan during the marriage as well as any participation that occurred prior to the marriage, present value evidence is not necessary as the court can divide the pension in accordance with the marital share definition at Va. Code § 20-107.3(G). *Mann v. Mann*, 22 Va. App. 459, 464–65, 470 S.E.2d 605, 607–08 (1996).

The Foreign Service Act of 1980, 22 U.S.C. § 4054(a)(2) gives no pension split to a wife who remarries before reaching age 53, unless their agreement or a court order expressly provides otherwise, and accordingly the husband did not have to divide his pension with the ex-wife. *Wilson v. Collins*, 27 Va. App. 411, 499 S.E.2d 560 (1998).

However, when a husband and wife's property settlement agreement incorporated into a divorce decree expressly stated that the wife was entitled to a share of the husband's foreign service retirement benefits "regardless of her marital status to the extent allowable under federal law," the wife's benefits did not terminate upon her early remarriage, even though existing federal law would have disqualified her from receiving benefits if she remarried before age 55, because the phrase in the agreement expressly waived the federal "marriage disqualifier" provision. *Allsbury v. Allsbury*, 33 Va. App. 385, 533 S.E.2d 639 (2000). Va. Code § 20-107.3(G) allows award, as marital property, of deferred compensation plans in addition to pension, profit sharing plans, and retirement benefits. Thus, in *Rigsby v. Rigsby*, 13 Va. Cir. 86 (Spotsylvania Co. 1987), the wife was awarded 25 percent of the husband's military pension as equitable distribution after a twenty-year marriage. Although the parties had been married only six years and the wife had voluntarily agreed to split the remainder of the couple's property evenly, it was error to exclude her from any share in the husband's pension from the government. *Cook v. Cook*, 18 Va. App. 726, 446 S.E.2d 894 (1994) (parties married seven years before separation); *Keyser v. Keyser*, 7 Va. App. 405, 374 S.E.2d 698 (1988). When the parties had executed a valid release of all property claims in a separation agreement, the subsequent enactment of the Uniform Services Former Spouses' Protection Act did not enable them to reopen the divorce proceeding. *Himes v. Himes*, 12 Va. App. 966, 407 S.E.2d 694 (1991). Retroactive application of the Act in this case resulting in the reclassification of the husband's military pension would impair the parties' contractual rights and obligations and disturb those rights that became vested by both the contract and the final divorce decree that incorporated it. See also *Nicholson v. Nicholson*, 21 Va. App. 231, 463 S.E.2d 334 (1995) (The terms of the parties' property settlement agreement were insufficient to support a finding that the wife had expressly waived her share in the husband's retirement annuity under the Foreign Service Act.).

In *Thomas v. Thomas*, 36 Va. Cir. 427 (Fairfax Co. 1995), the court found that "all of the benefits available to the Wife" in connection with the Uniformed Services Former Spouses' Protection act means medical and dental care but not the husband's military pension. "Pensions" also includes deferred compensation in the form of stock options, *Dietz v. Dietz*, 17 Va. App. 203, 436 S.E.2d 463 (1993), and a disability pension if the agreement specifies "benefits and pensions," *McGlathery v. McGlathery*, 1995 Va. App. LEXIS 297 (March 28, 1995). When a wife was awarded her pension as part of a separation agreement that anticipated that it would be $25,000, but upon retirement she actually received only half that amount from her employer, the court of appeals held that the amount included in the separation agreement was merely descriptive and did not constitute a guarantee by the husband. *Morris v. Chatman*, 1995 Va. App. LEXIS 361 (April 18, 1995).

It was permissible for a trial judge to reserve the power to reopen the suit at either party's death, although a pension award could not be charged against decedent's estate prior to the payment of the total award. *Holmes v. Holmes*, 7 Va. App. 472, 375 S.E.2d 387 (1988). After the decree was entered, the trial court could not validly change the order when to do so had the effect of delaying the wife's receipt of a share in the husband's retirement benefits. *Caudle v. Caudle*, 18 Va. App. 795, 447 S.E.2d 247 (1994). On the other hand, the wife could not receive more than 50 percent of the marital share of the husband's pension when the trial court required the husband to pay the cost of extending the wife's allowed benefit for her lifetime. *Gerwe v. Gerwe*, 1996 Va. App. LEXIS 21 (Jan. 16, 1996).

Retirement benefits are funds paid or to be paid upon cessation of employment to the employee by his or her employer as a means of deferred compensation. But once the recipient had deposited them in a bank account, although it was designated a "Retirement Plan," the funds were in the unrestricted control of the recipient, and they lost their character as "pension or retirement benefits" and therefore were not subject to the 50% limitation of the Code. *Robinette v. Robinette*, 10 Va. App. 480, 393 S.E.2d 629 (1990).

The federal Employee Retirement Income Security Act of 1974 (ERISA), 88 Stat. 829, 29 U.S.C. § 1001, does not preempt state laws regarding the division of retirement benefits. *Stone v. Stone*, 632 F.2d 740 (9th Cir. 1980); see also *In re Marriage of Lionberger*, 97 Cal. App. 3d 56, 158 Cal. Rptr. 535 (1979). ERISA does not invalidate a nonemployee spouse's waiver, in a divorce decree, of the spouse's interest in an employee spouse's ERISA pension plan benefits. *Kennedy v. Plan Adm'r for DuPont Sav. & Inv. Plan*, 555 U.S. 285, 129 S. Ct. 865, 172 L. Ed. 2d 662 (2009). Nor does ERISA preempt the garnishment of pension benefits to enforce post-divorce child and spousal support obligations. *Cody v. Riecker*, 594 F.2d 314 (2d Cir. 1979).

However, ERISA does preempt state statutes that provide for the automatic revocation upon divorce of any designation of the divorced spouse as the beneficiary of a life insurance policy or pension plan, to the extent that the state statutes apply to ERISA-governed policies or plans. *Egelhoff v. Egelhoff*, 532 U.S. 141, 121 S. Ct. 1322, 149 L. Ed. 2d 264 (2001). *Compare* Va. Code § 20-111.1 (designation of spouse as beneficiary of life insurance policy becomes void upon divorce or annulment if designation is revocable); Va. Code § 38.2-305(C) (formal statutory notice required in life insurance or annuity contracts that designate spouse of policy owner as beneficiary). Under Va. Code § 20-111.1(D), if federal preemption of the Virginia automatic revocation statute causes a former spouse who did not give value to receive payment of a death benefit that would have been revoked, the former spouse is personally liable to the person who would have been entitled to the death benefit except for the federal preemption.

The division of a police officer's pension rights is a judicial exception to the rule prohibiting alienation of pension benefits. "In the interest of protecting the State's broad public policy of protecting the employee and his family, the law allows family members to be treated differently than third-party creditors." *Barbee v. Barbee*, 23 Va. Cir. 68 (Fairfax Co. 1991). See also *Tenneco, Inc. v. First Va. Bank of Tidewater*, 698 F.2d 688 (E.D. Va. 1983); *Smith v. Mirman*, 749 F.2d 181 (E.D. Va. 1984). The court, in making a Qualified Domestic Relations Order, may direct a retirement system to make payments directly to a plan participant's spouse under 29 U.S.C. § 1001 et seq.

There should be no equitable distribution of a Veteran's Administration disability settlement, but such payments may be considered as income for spousal support purposes. *Lambert v. Lambert*, 10 Va. App. 623, 627, 395 S.E.2d 207 (1990) (noting that "V.A. benefits, unlike military disability retirement pay, are nonassignable, are exempt from the claims of creditors and are not liable to attachment, levy, or seizure under any legal or equitable process."). It was inappropriate for the court to award interest on the wife's share of her husband's pension benefits, which were not yet due. *Kaufman v. Kaufman*, 12 Va. App. 1200, 409 S.E.2d 1 (1991). However, in *Gamble v. Gamble*, 14 Va. App. 558, 421 S.E.2d 635, the court of appeals found that the trial court was correct in awarding the wife fifty percent of the husband's pension benefits, reduced to twenty percent to offset his interest in the marital home. In *Gamble*, the trial court did not order the transfer of pension property, but merely reduced the share the wife would otherwise have been entitled to receive. See also *Owen v. Owen*, 14 Va. App. 623, 419 S.E.2d 267 (1992) (federal law does not prevent a husband and wife from entering into an agreement to provide a set level of payments, the amount of which is determined by considering both disability and retirement benefits); *McLellan v. McLellan*, 33 Va. App. 376, 533 S.E.2d 635 (2000) (agreement that wife would receive a fixed percentage of husband's combined military disability and retirement benefits, by direct payment from husband rather than by direct assignment, was properly incorporated into divorce decree). For another case in which the wife received a portion of her husband's 60 percent disability-rated pension, see *Bullis v. Bullis*, 21 Va. App. 394, 464 S.E.2d 538 (1995) (Arizona community property award enforced in Virginia under Uniform Enforcement of Foreign Judgments Act); and *Gamble v. Gamble*, 14 Va. App. 558, 421 S.E.2d 635 (1992), where the wife was awarded the house while the husband received his entire pension, although distribution would not occur for some years.

It is important to understand the nature and origin of the disability payments. If the disability payments derive from a pension plan, the benefits may be subject to equitable distribution. In *Asgari v. Asgari*, 33 Va. App. 393, 533 S.E.2d 643 (2000), the court was correct in distributing a husband's Virginia Retirement System (VRS) disability benefit as a "pension" or "retirement benefit," when the VRS plan permitted "any member . . . [to] retire for disability," and the husband's benefit, which was based on his employment service, average wages, and age, was earned and accrued during his marriage. See also *Navas v. Navas*, 43 Va. App. 484, 599 S.E.2d 479 (2004) (discussed below in which the husband's disability payments under his employer pension were distributed to the wife); and *Henderson v.*

*Henderson*, 2018 Va. App. LEXIS 134 (May 15, 2018) (the husband's line of duty disability payments from his career as a professional athlete constituted retirement benefits that were marital property and subject to equitable distribution).

Where the husband continued to work at the job he held before divorce, the trial court did not have to "cap" the wife's share of the pension at its present value at the time of divorce. The husband unsuccessfully argued that the amount he would actually receive depended upon his highest five consecutive years of salary, which most likely would occur after the parties' divorce. The only limitation applicable to a pension award, according to Va. Code § 20-107.3, is the limitation that no payment shall exceed fifty percent of the cash benefits actually received. This was the amount the wife was awarded for the marital portion of the pension. *Dietz v. Dietz*, 17 Va. App. 203, 436 S.E.2d 463 (1993). See also *Havird v. Havird*, 1995 Va. App. LEXIS 19 (Jan. 3, 1995); *Herron v. Herron*, 1994 Va. App. LEXIS 208 (April 5, 1994); and *Banagan v. Banagan*, 17 Va. App. 321, 437 S.E.2d 229 (1993) (error to assume spouses would retire from state employment at age 55, because this would deny "to each party a full participation in the statutory marital share of the other's entire pension"). The court cannot indirectly exceed the 50% limitation on the equitable division of the marital share of retirement benefits by basing the spousal support award, in part, upon the marital share of the pension. When a wife was awarded a final divorce judgment against her husband in 1973, and accumulated $84,000 in spousal support arrearages, she could not file a motion to reopen the matter for entry of a QDRO that would allow garnishment of the husband's pension plan under ERISA, 29 U.S.C. § 1001 et seq. *Hoy v. Hoy*, 29 Va. App. 115, 510 S.E.2d 253 (1999). Under Virginia law, a former spouse may not recast his or her claim as a judgment creditor via a QDRO as that seeks to modify the terms of a final divorce decree.

When a husband elected to waive a portion of his military pension in exchange for disability pay, the amount his wife was to receive under their property settlement agreement should not be reduced. In *Owen v. Owen*, 14 Va. App. 623, 419 S.E.2d 267 (1992), the court of appeals held that federal law does not prevent a husband and wife from entering into an agreement to provide a set level of payments, the amount of which is determined by considering disability as well as retirement benefits. In *Boedeker v. Larson*, 44 Va. App. 508, 605 S.E.2d 764 (2004), the court of appeals held that a wife was entitled to a portion of a military "career status bonus" (CSB/Redux) that her husband elected to receive pursuant to 37 U.S.C. § 322. Under the parties' property settlement agreement, the wife was entitled to half of the marital share of her husband's military retirement benefits. The husband admitted that his election to receive the CSB/Redux bonus would reduce the amount of his military retirement benefits. Therefore, based on federal law, the parties' agreement, and the husband's admission, the wife was entitled to a portion of the CSB/Redux payments as "retirement" benefits rather than as post-separation "income."

Because an Individual Retirement Account (IRA) is merely a device by which the government gives a present tax advantage as an inducement to save, and does not require the owner to continue employment or attain a given age before withdrawal of the funds, it is not a pension, profit-sharing, or deferred compensation plan within the meaning of Va. Code § 20-107.3(G)(1). The husband's IRA in *Broom v. Broom*, 15 Va. App. 497, 425 S.E.2d 90 (1992), was subject to present equitable distribution because it was created with marital funds.

Severance pay awarded after the parties' final separation remains the separate property of the employee spouse. *Luczkovich v. Luczkovich*, 26 Va. App. 702, 496 S.E.2d 157 (1998). The key question is whether the severance pay was intended to compensate the employee for efforts made during the marriage or to replace post-separation earnings. *Cf. Cirrito v. Cirrito*, 44 Va. App. 287, 605 S.E.2d 268 (2004) ($1 million payment pursuant to noncompetition agreement that was negotiated before marriage was marital property when payment was earned by husband's forbearance from competition during marriage).

In a case involving competing claims of an ex-wife and a current wife to a husband's pension plan, a circuit court ruled that when the language of the property settlement agreement between the parties to the first marriage was clear and unambiguous as to the intent of the parties, the ex-wife is entitled to an inclusion of that intent in the QDRO. *Riley v. Riley*, 1998 Va. Cir. LEXIS 409 (Aug. 14, 1998). The specific language of the PSA and the implication of the entire agreement made it plain that the ex-wife was entitled to pension payments when the husband began to receive them at age 65. Because the pension plan permitted the husband to name his ex-wife as a surviving spouse, and the PSA stated she was entitled to receive "her marital share . . . as if the parties continued to live together as husband and wife," she was entitled to an order directing commencement of benefits to her upon age 65 or death. His current wife's benefits do not vest, under the husband's pension plan, until the death of the husband, and those benefits are conferred upon the person to whom he is married upon the earlier date of his retirement or his death.

Where the parties agreed that their children would be the beneficiaries of all 401(K) plans to be distributed upon the party's death, a wife was able to obtain a QDRO years after the death enforcing the distribution to the children despite the fact that husband designated his current wife as the beneficiary. *Griffin v. Griffin*, 62 Va. App. 736, 753 S.E.2d 574 (2014).

Federal law preempts state law on the subject of a former spouse's entitlement to the survivor benefits of a military retiree under the Survivor Benefit Plan established by 10 U.S.C. §§ 1447–1455. *Dugan v. Childers*, 261 Va. 3, 539 S.E.2d 723 (2001) (former spouse who was assigned military survivor benefits under property settlement agreement could not impose constructive trust under state law on survivor annuity benefits paid to former husband's surviving spouse under express terms of federal military survivor benefit plan).

Va. Code § 64.2-620, provides that a provision for a nonprobate transfer on death in certain specified types of written instruments, including insurance policies, pension plans, conveyances, and marital property agreements, is a nontestamentary transfer.

When entering a QDRO, the trial court may not modify a final divorce decree to adjust the terms of the decree in light of the parties' changed circumstances; rather, the QDRO must be consistent with the substantive provisions of the original decree. *Bradley v. Bradley*, 39 Va. App. 108, 570 S.E.2d 881 (2002). In *Bradley*, a QDRO that allowed a wife only postretirement survivor annuity benefits and that limited the marital share to one of two merged pension plans was consistent with the divorce decree. See *Prizzia v. Prizzia*, 58 Va. App. 137, 707 S.E.2d 461 (2011) (court's use of coverture fraction in QDRO impermissibly altered terms of final decree); *Turner v. Turner*, 47 Va. App. 76, 622 S.E.2d 263 (2005) (QDRO awarding 50% of marital share of pension was administrative mechanism that effectuated intent and purpose of award in final decree). See also *Fahey v. Fahey*, 24 Va. App. 254, 481 S.E.2d 496 (1997) (improper adjustment for appreciation and depreciation); *Hastie v. Hastie*, 29 Va. App. 776, 514 S.E.2d 800 (1999) (improper adjustment from percentage of present value); *Baker v. Baker*, 38 Va. App. 384, 564 S.E.2d 164 (2002) (improper adjustment for gains and losses).

However, the trial court may modify any order intended to affect or divide retirement benefits or any pension, profit-sharing, or deferred compensation plan, for the purpose of establishing or maintaining the order as a QDRO. Va. Code § 20-107.3(K). In *Williams v. Williams*, 32 Va. App. 72, 526 S.E.2d 301 (2000), a trial court properly modified a final divorce decree that had awarded a wife 50% of her husband's pension benefits, when the wife received a lesser amount after a QDRO went into effect. The trial court had the power to modify its divorce decree to effectuate the original order after the pension administrator did not effectively carry out the mandate of the decree. In *Navas v. Navas*, 43 Va. App. 484, 599 S.E.2d 479 (2004), a trial court erroneously refused to enter a QDRO after concluding that the QDRO was inconsistent with its final divorce decree. The decree awarded a wife one-half of the marital share of her husband's "WMATA pension," while the wife's motion for entry of the QDRO called for inclusion of the husband's WMATA disability allowance as part of the WMATA pension. The court of appeals held that under the express terms of the WMATA plan, the disability allowance was a retirement benefit. Therefore, the disability allowance was contemplated by the language "WMATA pension" in the final decree. See *Recker v. Recker*, 48 Va. App. 188, 629 S.E.2d 191 (2006) (QDRO restored wife's share of pension as measured by husband's retirement benefit before it was actuarially reduced by cost of second wife's survivor benefit). See also *Irwin v. Irwin*, 47 Va. App. 287, 623 S.E.2d 438 (2005) (trial court required to order husband to pay wife's one-half share of pension directly, to prevent delays in approval and entering of QDRO from operating to deny wife's property right in pension); *Cusack v. Cusack*, 53 Va. App. 315, 671 S.E.2d 420 (2009) (instruction in QDRO that husband was responsible for paying wife's share of pension benefits, to extent that designated agent was prohibited by law or regulation from paying wife's share, was proper to discourage delay in voluntary execution of QDRO-related documents).

Significant care must be taken when preparing the retirement orders as can be seen in *Jackson v. Jackson*, 69 Va. App 243, 817 S.E.2d 676 (2018). The January 3, 2011 final order of divorce awarded wife 50% the marital share of Husband's military pension which was already in pay status at the time of the divorce. On the same day, the court entered a pension order stating that wife was to receive $1,053.59 as her share of Husband's military annuity. Over the years, Wife did not receive any cost of living adjustments, and when she applied to modify the pension order in accordance with Va. Code § 20-107.3(K)(4), her motion was denied because the trial court determined she sought a substantive change that was not permitted, and that the pension order was consistent with the final order of divorce. *Jackson*, 69 Va. App at 246–47, 817 S.E.2d at 678. The Court of Appeals agreed with the trial court and denied wife's motion. *Jackson*, 69 Va. App at 252, 817 S.E.2d at 680. The Court of Appeals decision in *Jackson* was affirmed by the Virginia Supreme Court. *Jackson v. Jackson*, 298 Va. 132, 143, 835 S.E.2d 68 (2019). "[A]ny modification a court makes under the authority of [Va.] Code § 20-107.3(K)(4) must be limited to implementing the intent of the final decree or equitable distribution order, without affecting the substance of the division of property it awarded."

Va. Code § 20-107.3(K)(4) authorizes the court to make certain corrections to orders once they are final, but the modification must involve a "purely ministerial act." *Jackson v. Jackson*, 2019 Va. App. LEXIS 301 (December 17, 2019) (citing *Newsome v. Newsome*, 18 Va. App. 22, 26, 441 S.E.2d 346 (1994). In this case, the trial court properly amended the retirement order to identify the correct administrator of the retirement plan. The reader should be aware that this case of *Jackson v. Jackson* is not related to the *Jackson* matter case referenced above. The names of the two cases are purely coincidental.

Seeking amendments pursuant to Va. Code § 20-107.3(K)(4) to retirement orders after they become final is uncertain, and the result depends on whether a substantive modification to the rights in the retirement plan is being attempted. Framing that issue in the context of the court ruling or settlement terms is critically important. Two additional cases exemplify amendments to final retirement orders well after the 21 day period without utilizing Va. Code § 20-107.3(K)(4). In *Ferry v. Beard*, 2020 Va. App. LEXIS 31 (February 4, 2020), the trial court reformed the parties' Agreement to name the correct retirement plan despite the fact that the divorce order, which affirmed, ratified and incorporated the agreement, had been entered more than ten years earlier. The reformation was justified because the one party intentionally misled the other party about the identity of the retirement plan in the Marital Settlement Agreement. The case of *Highsmith v. Highsmith*, 2019 Va. App. LEXIS 278 (November 26, 2019), involves a tortured procedural history and correcting the trial court's error of awarding 100% of the marital share of Wife's military pension to Husband through a common law pleading of a bill of review. Va. Code § 20-107.3(G)(1) permits the court to award no more than 50% of the marital share of a pension to the non-owning spouse, and there was no dispute that the trial court erred by awarding Husband the entire marital share of the pension. However, this error was not raised before the entry of the final order of divorce or the expiration of the 21 day period provided for in Rule 1:1. Well after the trial court lost jurisdiction, the wife filed a second motion to reconsider, which on appeal the Court of Appeals, in a surprising manner, treated as a Bill of Review. The bill of review can correct errors in a circuit court's order outside of Rule 1:1's 21 day period provided the bill is filed within the limitations of Va. Code § 8.01-623. *Highsmith*, 2019 Va. App. LEXIS 278 (citing *De Avies v. De Avies*, 42 Va. App. 342, 346, 592 S.E.2d 351 (2004). The bill of review is a common law pleading that still exits, and can be used to reopen a suit in equity after the final order and used to correct an error of law that is apparent on the face of the record. *Id.* Therefore, based on *Ferry v. Beard* and *Highsmith v. Highsmith,* if amending a final retirement order pursuant to Va. Code § 20-107.3(K)(4) is not an option, the practitioner may want to see if filing a bill of review or seeking a contract reformation is a viable option.

### § 21.07     Valuation of Pensions

General principles for the valuation and division of property in equitable distribution proceedings apply to the valuation and division of retirement benefits, including the principle that the court must determine the value of property "as of the date of the evidentiary hearing on the evaluation issue." *Cusack v. Cusack,* 53 Va. App. 315, 671 S.E.2d 420 (2009); see Va. Code § 20-107.3(A); *McGinniss v. McGinniss,* 49 Va. App. 180, 638 S.E.2d 697, 701 (2006) (implicitly applying principle to deferred distribution of retirement benefits). In *Cusack,* a trial court erred by directing that a wife should begin receiving her share of her husband's military retirement benefits on the date of the husband's retirement, which occurred after the husband and wife separated, but almost a year before the wife filed for divorce, and more than two years before the equitable distribution evidentiary hearing.

It was erroneous for a court, in awarding the wife a 25 percent share of her husband's pension, to discount to present value the current value of the husband's share of the fund, when distribution was to be made only as the husband began receiving payments. A better method would be to calculate the present value of the pension for purposes of evaluating the entire marital estate and the wife's equitable share of the pension, and to allow her a percentage based upon this share upon the husband's retirement. *Zipf v. Zipf,* 8 Va. App. 387, 382 S.E.2d 263 (1989). See *McGinniss v. McGinniss,* 49 Va. App. 180, 638 S.E.2d 697 (2006), where trial court abused its discretion by limiting wife's share of husband's defined benefit pension plan to 50% of present value calculated as if husband had retired on date of separation, when (1) husband was not eligible to receive pension payment on that date, and (2) husband made no lump sum payment to wife of present value of 50% marital share. See also *Lewis v. Lewis,* 53 Va. App. 528, 673 S.E.2d 888 (2009) (court did not err in valuing and dividing husband's pension plan, because court's finding that plan was worth $3,719.82 per month as of parties' date of separation did not include credit for husband's months of service after that date).

Present value calculation is of use only when payment of portion of monetary award attributable to pension is to occur immediately rather than over period of time. If trial court orders deferred distribution of marital share of pension, it need not determine pension's present value. *Torian v. Torian,*

38 Va. App. 167, 562 S.E.2d 355 (2002). Limitation of a pension award that is payable in the future to a present value calculation denies the recipient the benefit of future earnings and adjustments that are attributable to the deferred share and its future appreciation. *Banagan v. Banagan*, 17 Va. App. 321, 437 S.E.2d 229 (1993). Compare *Steinberg v. Steinberg*, 11 Va. App. 323, 398 S.E.2d 507 (1990), where husband and wife stipulated to the value of the pension at the time of separation, and neither party indicated whether the stipulated value had been discounted either before or after it had been computed, and pension payments were not being received on the date of the last separation or when the divorce decree was entered. An award of a specified percentage of future pension benefits would have been to postpone the entry of an equitable distribution decree until such time as the pension payments were realized. When the parties' agreement did not specify a date for division of their pensions and IRAs, the date that should be used is the date of the parties' agreement. *Jones v. Jones*, 18 Va. App. 52, 441 S.E.2d 360 (1994). Once the trial court determined that the wife was entitled to a fifty percent marital share of her husband's pension, its current value became irrelevant. What was relevant was the value of the pension when due and owing, so that the parties share equally in any increases or decreases in the pension. *Barnes v. Barnes*, 1995 Va. App. LEXIS 319 (April 4, 1995). When the parties specified that the Commissioner should value the investment accounts as of a specific date, the wife was not entitled to prejudgment interest nor an increase in the value of the accounts that took place after that date but before trial. *Ragsdale v. Ragsdale*, 30 Va. App. 283, 516 S.E.2d 698 (1999).

Present value calculations for future pension payments are not necessarily required. A defined benefit pension plan can be divided pursuant to the statutory fraction set forth in Va. Code § 20-107.3(G). *Mann v. Mann*, 22 Va. App. 459, 464–65, 470 S.E.2d 605, 607–08 (1996). The statutory language found in Code § 20-107.3(G) "is mandatory and can be implemented through the use of a simple formula." *Mosley v. Mosley*, 19 Va. App. 192, 198, 450 S.E.2d 161, 165 (1994). Nonetheless, it has been held that, when payments are to be made in the future, the appropriate action is to determine the present value of the pension benefits in determining the total monetary award. However, the value of a retirement plan must be established by the party seeking a share, whether by expert witness or otherwise. *Bowers v. Bowers*, 4 Va. App. 610, 359 S.E.2d 546 (1987); *Torian v. Torian*, 38 Va. App. 167, 562 S.E.2d 355 (2002) (two methods recognized for valuing and dividing a defined benefit plan: (1) the "immediate offset" approach, and (2) the "deferred distribution" approach). See also *Gamer v. Gamer*, 16 Va. App.

335, 429 S.E.2d 618 (1993), where the wife claimed a portion of Mr. Gamer's military retirement benefits, but did not produce sufficient evidence of the present value of the pension to demonstrate the marital share. The court of appeals held that the trial court did not err when it allowed both parties to retain their respective pensions. Similarly, in *Brundage v. Brundage*, 1995 Va. App. LEXIS 521 (May 23, 1995), the marital share of the husband's pension could not be calculated at the time of divorce, since the husband continued to be employed. The court should have awarded the wife a thirty-five percent portion of the marital share of the pension, to be paid at the time the husband began to receive it. The wife did not present sufficient evidence to enable to the court to segregate proper expenditures from improper ones in *Harvey v. Harvey*, 1995 Va. App. LEXIS 928 (Dec. 29, 1995), where the husband used his pension payments, at least in part, to abide by the *pendente lite* decree's support order.

The award of 40 percent of a husband's disposable military pension meant the amount due him before tax deductions. *Lovell v. Lovell*, 18 Va. Cir. 64 (Fairfax Co. 1988).

The trial court transferred to the wife "one half of each of three Keogh accounts," valued by the agreement at $214,000. More than a year later, the plan administrator divided one account in-kind rather than in accordance with the agreed value as expressed in a QDRO. The account had increased in value by one-third since the date of the parties' agreement. At the wife's request, the court issued an amended QDRO for one-half of the accrued shares of the plan as of the agreement date, together with any subsequently accrued appreciation or depreciation. However, the manifest intent of the original order was to allot the wife one-half of the value of the account at that date. The court was without authority to substantively modify its order to redress the change in value. *Fahey v. Fahey*, (1997). See also *Baker v. Baker*, 38 Va. App. 384, 564 S.E.2d 164 (2002) (QDRO that allocated gains and losses attributable to wife's share of husband's profit-sharing plan was inconsistent with final divorce decree incorporating parties' agreement that wife's share would be one-half of profit-sharing plan valued as of date of agreement); *Lewis v. Lewis*, 53 Va. App. 528, 673 S.E.2d 888 (2009) (under property settlement agreement that awarded wife half of marital share of profit-sharing account, rather than half of marital share of account as of a particular date, interest that accrued on wife's portion of marital share belonged to wife).

In 2016, the definition of disposable pay set forth at 10 U.S.C. § 1048 of the Uniformed Services Former Spouses' Protection Act was amended for military members who are not retired at the time of divorce. When dividing the member's military pension prior to his/her retirement, "the total monthly retired pay to which the member is entitled shall be . . . the amount of retired pay to which the member would have been entitled using the member's retired pay base and years of service on the date of the decree of divorce, dissolution, annulment or legal separation [computed with appropriate cost of living adjustments]. 10 U.S.C. § 1408(a)(4)(B). This division materially alters the traditional coverture fraction that is used under Virginia's equitable distribution law. See *Starr v. Starr*, 70 Va. App. 486, 488–91 828 S.E.2d 257 (2109). To address the inconsistency in Virginia law and the amended federal law, Va. Code § 20-107.3(G)(1) was amended in July 2019 to provide that "Any determination of military retirement benefits shall be in accordance with the federal Uniformed Services Former Spouses' Protection Act (10 U.S.C. 1408 et seq.)." The decision in *Starr* is enlightening and provides a thorough analysis of calculating the marital share within the restrictions implemented by the Uniformed Services Former Spouses' Protection Act. The date of divorce is used as the date of the service member's hypothetical retirement, and the court cannot include the service member's post-divorce service "as a component of the total interest in the service member's military retirement." *Starr*, 70 Va. App. at 491. While "federal law determines the total interest in a military member's retired pay that is distributable to a spouse at the time of divorce," the method for determining the marital share is an issue of state law. *Id.* at 495–96. Therefore, denominator of the coverture fraction can be limited to the length of the member's military service through the date of divorce, as opposed to the member's entire military service. *Id.* at 496. "The denominator of that fraction is the time of military service until the date of divorce because that is the date of hypothetical retirement. Any other denominator would not render an accurate marital-share determination as required by Code § 20-107.3." *Id.*

## § 21.08  Stock Options

An employee may be given stock options as a form of compensation. A stock option is the right to purchase a certain number of shares of a company's stock at a pre-set price, usually the price of the shares on the date of issuance, at some future date. If a spouse earned stock options during the marriage, most courts will award at least a portion of the options, or the value of the options, to the other spouse in the event of a divorce. Because stock options are potentially valuable, their allocation as marital or separate property often becomes an issue in a divorce. However, there are certain conditions that often accompany stock options, such as vesting, which became an issue in *Schuman v. Schuman*, 282 Va. 443, 717 S.E.2d 410 (2011).

In *Schuman*, the husband challenged a judgment of the court of appeals which affirmed the trial court's finding that the wife's stock awards were her separate property. The court of appeals found that the stock awards were not marital property under Va. Code Ann. § 20-107.3 because they did not vest during the marriage. The Supreme Court held that the stock awards were improperly classified as the wife's separate property and that the court of appeals erred in its classification of the stock awards based solely on the date of vesting. The stock awards were payment for work already performed as well as the work the wife performed until the date of vesting.

The Supreme Court found that the stock awards were a form of deferred compensation and that the inclusion of the phrase "whether vested or nonvested" in Va. Code Ann. § 20-107.3(G)(1) indicated that the date of vesting was not, by itself, dispositive of whether the deferred compensation was marital or separate property. The Supreme Court reversed the judgment of the court of appeals.

### § 21.09    Degrees and Other Enhancements of Earning Capacity

An important addition to Va. Code § 20-107.1(E) lists among the factors the court should consider in making spousal support awards various contributions to earning capacity and marital well-being. For example, new factor (9) considers each party's present earning capacity. Factor (10) involves the question of whether additional education, vocational rehabilitation, or training is appropriate, given the parties' time and abilities as well as the costs of such training. Factor (11) requires the court to look at decisions regarding employment, career, education, and parenting the parties may have made during the marriage. Some of these choices may have affected current or future earning potential of one or both spouses. For example, this factor includes the length of time one or both has been absent from the job market. Scholars estimate that for each year a person does not participate in the paid labor force there is a permanent loss of 1.5% of lifetime earning capacity. Finally, factor (12) requires consideration of the extent to which either party has contributed to the education, training, profession, or career position of the other. In contested cases in circuit court, any order granting, reserving, or denying spousal support shall be accompanied by written findings identifying which of these factors support the court's order, and which support limiting support to a defined duration. Va. Code § 20-107.1(F).

These new code sections are significant because they clarify Virginia's position on the important issue of career enhancement. Virginia will apparently join the states recognizing investments in the career of one spouse through alimony, rather than property, awards. The new legislation also implicitly recognizes the concept of opportunity cost, the fact that investments in the earning capacity of one spouse come at a cost in terms of what either spouse could otherwise have done. See Margaret F. Brinig, *Property Distribution Physics: The Talisman of Time and Middle Class Law*, 31 Fam. L.Q. 93 (1997), and Allen M. Parkman, *Human Capital as Property in Celebrity Divorces*, 29 Fam. L.Q. 141 (1995).

The majority rule is that degrees earned by either spouse are nondivisible. See, e.g., *Graham v. Graham*, 194 Colo. 429, 574 P.2d 75 (1978); *In re Weinstein*, 128 Ill. App. 3d 234, 83 Ill. Dec. 425, 470 N.E.2d 551 (1984); 11 Fam. L. Rep. (BNA) 1015 (and cases cited therein); *Wright v. Wright*, 469 A.2d 803 (Del. Fam. 1983). Some cases support the prevailing view that degrees are not marital property. See, e.g., *Hodge v. Hodge*, 513 Pa. 264, 520 A.2d 15 (1986); *Drapek v. Drapek*, 399 Mass. 240, 503 N.E.2d 946 (1987). The most frequently cited exception is *O'Brien v. O'Brien*, 66 N.Y.2d 576, 498 N.Y.S.2d 743, 489 N.E.2d 712 (1985). Goodwill, but not a professional degree, was included as marital property in *Gold v. Gold*, 1 Va. Cir. 390, 396, 397–98 (Roanoke Co. 1983). One alternative solution that gives credit to contributions during the earning of a degree is to award restitution alimony. See *Mahoney v. Mahoney*, 91 N.J. 488, 453 A.2d 527 (1982). Mahoney was followed in the case of *Palmer v. Palmer*, 21 Va. Cir. 112 (Fairfax Co. 1990), which gave the wife reimbursement alimony but held that the husband's medical degree was not marital property.

Useful articles include Krauskopf, *Recompense for Financing Spouse's Education: Legal Protection for the Marital Investor in Human Capital*, 28 Kan. L. Rev. 379, 411 (1980), and Mullinex, *The Valuation of an Educational Degree at Divorce*, 16 Loy. L.A.L. Rev. 227 (1983).

## § 21.10 Professional Corporations and Goodwill

Several cases have noted that the goodwill belonging to a small corporation or a professional practice is distributable as marital property. For example, the goodwill included in the value of a doctor's professional practice was marital property, with valuation by the percentage of gross income approach being particularly appropriate since the doctor kept the profit from his practice at an artificially low margin. *Russell v. Russell*, 12 Va. Cir. 326 (Henrico Co. 1988), *aff'd*, 11 Va. App. 411, 399 S.E.2d 166 (1990). See also *Gold v. Gold*, 1 Va. Cir. 390 (Roanoke Co. 1983). When the value of the corporation for which the husband worked increased dramatically during the marriage, the increase in value of its stock, which he held separately, was marital property to the extent that his efforts contributed to the increase. *Decker v. Decker*, 17 Va. App. 12, 435 S.E.2d 407 (1993) (Here, 20 percent, since he was one of five key executives and "first among equals."). See also *Stewart v. Stewart*, 1994 Va. App. LEXIS 88 (Feb. 22, 1994). The value of husband's dental practice should not have been discounted by estimating the capital gains taxes on a hypothetical sale as opposed to the present fair market value of the property. *Arbuckle v. Arbuckle*, 22 Va. App. 362, 470 S.E.2d 146 (1996). This case was revisited in 1998 in *Arbuckle v. Arbuckle*, 27 Va. App. 615, 500 S.E.2d 286 (1998). The court noted that although the tax consequences were "hypothetical" in the 1996 case, that "valuation cannot be mere guesswork." It also stated that on the other hand, "a certain degree of imprecision will be inevitable in applying the factors" in distribution. The parties were to share equally in the marital property; the husband was awarded the value of his practice while the wife received oil company stock.

In *Shooltz v. Shooltz*, 27 Va. App. 264, 498 S.E.2d 437 (1998), the court of appeals ruled that it was error for the trial court to refuse to reopen the matter of a business valuation a year and four months after the first Equitable Distribution hearing. The wife argued that since that time the husband's business had turned from a beginning and struggling one to a profitable one. Va. Code § 20-107.3 does indeed give the trial court discretion to value a business as of a date other than the hearing date, particularly when the valuation was not based on any earnings history.

Virginia's equitable distribution law employs the concept of "intrinsic value" in determining the value of certain types of marital assets, including business goodwill and stock in a family owned company. See, e.g., *Hoebelheinrich v. Hoebelheinrich*, 43 Va. App. 543, 600 S.E.2d 152 (2004) (valuation of goodwill in medical practice); *Owens v. Owens*, 41 Va. App. 844, 589 S.E.2d 488 (2003) (valuation of stock in closely held corporation); *Howell v. Howell*, 31 Va. App. 332, 523 S.E.2d 514 (2000) (valuation of goodwill of law firm).

An appellate court views the evidence in the light most favorable to the prevailing party as to the classification of property in a divorce proceeding. In *Sfreddo v. Sfreddo*, 59 Va. App. 471, 720 S.E.2d 145 (2012), the appellate court reversed the circuit court's ruling classifying the husband's interest in a family-owned company as marital.

There is a rebuttable presumption that property acquired during the marriage is marital property. Va. Code Ann. § 20-107.3(A)(2). The party claiming property as separate has the burden to produce satisfactory evidence to rebut this presumption. Gifts from others to a party represent separate property. Va. Code Ann. § 20-107.3(A)(1). When in the case of a gift there is credible evidence presented to show that the property was intended by the donor to be separate property the presumption is overcome.

In *Sfreddo*, the board of directors included the husband, his mother, and his brother. All three directors testified they understood the transaction of shares of stock in the corporation to represent a gift. The husband testified that neither he nor his brother paid anything for their shares. The husband's brother also testified that he never paid for his shares and had no knowledge of husband paying for the shares. The mother testified she intended to give her two sons stock in the corporation. The appellate court held that where the surrounding circumstances of a contract demonstrate a gift rather than a bargained for sale, the transaction constitutes a gift, and the evidence in this case plainly demonstrated a gift from the company to the husband.

## § 21.11 Transfers of Property to Third Party

Transfers of real or personal property made "with intent to delay, hinder, or defraud creditors, purchasers, or other persons of, or from what they are, or may be lawfully entitled to" are void. Va. Code § 55-80. The "entitlement" of a spouse who alleges a fraudulent conveyance need not be judicially established or reduced to judgment at the time the challenged conveyance takes place. *Buchanan v. Buchanan*, 266 Va. 207, 585 S.E.2d 533 (2003). In *Buchanan*, a couple had been separated for eleven months when the husband obtained a loan and a line of credit secured by marital property. After using the funds to repay loans allegedly made by relatives, he filed for divorce on the grounds of separation in excess of one year. In consolidated divorce and fraudulent transfer proceedings, the husband's transfers of the borrowed funds were voided. Although the transfers took place before the divorce was filed, the husband had made them with the intent to delay, hinder, or defraud his wife's ability to recover property she might be entitled to.

Should one spouse attempt to transfer what would otherwise be marital property to a third party in order to avoid equitable distribution, the courts will include such property or its value in the marital estate. See, e.g., *Muehlenthaler v. De Bartolo*, 347 N.W.2d 688 (Iowa 1984); *Abraham v. Abraham*, 203 Neb. 384, 279 N.W.2d 85 (1979). However, the fraud must be proved. *Hofmann v. Hofmann*, 99 Ill. App. 3d 526, 54 Ill. Dec. 712, 425 N.E.2d 577 (1981) (mortgage foreclosed by relative; fraud not proved); *Ellington v. Ellington*, 8 Va. App. 48, 378 S.E.2d 626, 5 V.L.R. 2100 (1989) (appreciated value of husband's stock in closely held corporation could be marital property). See *Davis v. Davis*, 239 Va. 657, 391 S.E.2d 255 (1990) (fraud when husband conveyed real property to friend after shooting and paralyzing wife. She could be awarded spousal support and the property conveyed was subject to her lien despite a valid antenuptial agreement).

An appreciation in value of separate property is generally the separate property of a spouse. Va. Code § 20-107.3(1). See, e.g., *In re Marriage of Komnick*, 84 Ill. 2d 89, 49 Ill. Dec. 291, 417 N.E.2d 1305 (1981); *Painter v. Painter*, 65 N.J. 196, 320 A.2d 484 (1974), *superseded by statute as stated in Landwehr v. Landwehr*, 111 N.J. 491, 545 A.2d 738 (1988); *Dillingham v. Dillingham*, 434 S.W.2d 459 (Tex. Civ. App. 1968). But see *Gravenstine v. Gravenstine*, 58 Md. App. 158, 472 A.2d 1001, 1009 (1984), where the parties were able to purchase additional shares of stock because of both parties' contribution.

If the parties agree to divide the proceeds from sale of the marital home, and before the sale one of them remains in the home, the nonpossessor is entitled to half the reasonable rental value for the property. *Gaynor v. Hird*, 15 Va. App. 379, 424 S.E.2d 240 (1992); see also *Cole v. Cole*, 27 Va. Cir. 225 (Loudoun Co. 1992). When a marital home is conceded to be marital property, the trial court may consider fair rental value or actual rental income from the home, along with associated expenses of the home, in fashioning an equitable distribution award. *Anderson v. Anderson*, 42 Va. App. 643, 593 S.E.2d 824 (2004). In *Anderson*, a wife moved out of the marital home and conveyed title to her husband, who rented the home to third parties during the 42 months that preceded the couple's divorce. In calculating the equitable distribution award, the trial court credited the husband with an amount for mortgage payments, taxes, insurance, and repairs on the property during the 42-month period, and offset that amount by crediting the wife with her share of the fair rental value during the same period. See *McIlwain v. McIlwain*, 52 Va. App. 644, 666 S.E.2d 538 (2008) (in crafting overall equitable distribution of marital property, court did not abuse discretion by awarding wife an amount equal to one-half of fair market rental value of marital home from date of parties' separation, after considering and weighing Va. Code § 20-107.3(E) factors).

## § 21.12   Property Acquired in Part Before Marriage

In 1990, the Virginia legislature made significant amendments to Va. Code § 20-107.3, providing that property may be part separate and part marital property. These amendments have the effect of overriding the Virginia Supreme Court's decision in *Smoot v. Smoot*, 233 Va. 435, 357 S.E.2d 728 (1987). According to the amended statute, income received from separate property during the marriage shall be marital property only to the extent due to the personal efforts of either party. Increases in value of separate property during the marriage shall be marital property only to the extent that marital property or the personal efforts of either party have contributed to such increases. Va. Code § 20-107.3(A)(3)(a). See, e.g., *Robinson v. Robinson*, 46 Va. App. 652, 621 S.E.2d 147 (2005) (wife's personal efforts to control parties' finances did not increase value of husband's separate property trust income); *Courembis v. Courembis*, 43 Va. App. 18, 595 S.E.2d 505 (2004) (increase in value of husband's separate property real estate was marital property to extent that increase was due to significant personal efforts of either husband or wife during marriage); *Congdon v. Congdon*, 40 Va. App. 255, 578 S.E.2d 833 (2003) (appreciation in value of husband's stock in his family's business was 90% separate property, 10% marital property, considering efforts of family members other than husband). The Virginia Supreme Court clarified though that under Va. Code § 20-107.3(A)(3)(a), the non-owning spouse does not have the initial burden to prove that significant personal efforts or marital contributions caused the substantial increase in value of the separate property. *David v. David*, 287 Va. 231, 241, 754 S.E.2d 285, 291 (2014).

When marital property and separate property are commingled by contributing one category of property to another, resulting in the loss of identity of the contributed property, the classification of the contributed property shall be transmuted to the category of property receiving the contribution. Va. Code § 20-107.3(A)(3)(d). See, e.g., *Duva v. Duva*, 55 Va. App. 286, 685 S.E.2d 842 (2009) (marital funds used to pay bulk of mortgage on property acquired by husband before marriage were transmuted to husband's separate property); *Robinson v. Robinson*, 46 Va. App. 652, 621 S.E.2d 147 (2005) (absent evidence of value of wife's contributions in managing husband's trust income, her contributions were transmuted into husband's separate property).

However, to the extent that contributed property is retraceable by a preponderance of the evidence and was not a gift, such contributed property shall retain its original classification. Va. Code § 20-107.3(A)(3)(d). See, e.g., *Moran v. Moran*, 29 Va. App. 408, 512 S.E.2d 834 (1999) (husband successfully traced marital funds used to reduce principal of mortgage on wife's separate property, so that wife's property was properly classified as part marital, part separate, or "hybrid" property); *Asgari v. Asgari*, 33 Va. App. 393, 533 S.E.2d 643 (2000) (when funds from sale of husband's separate property home were deposited into joint checking account and partially withdrawn, months later, to purchase marital home, trial court was unable to trace and preserve husband's separate property); *McIlwain v. McIlwain*, 52 Va. App. 644, 666 S.E.2d 538 (2008) (when husband proved that separate funds from sale of separate property homes were deposited in bank account, but failed to trace those funds directly to withdrawals from bank account, commingled funds in bank account were marital property).

When marital and separate property are commingled into newly acquired property resulting in the loss of identity of the contributing properties, the commingled property shall be deemed transmuted to marital property. However, to the extent the contributed property is retraceable by a preponderance of the evidence and was not a gift, the contributed property shall retain its original classification. Va. Code § 20-107.3(A)(3)(e).

When separate property is retitled in the joint names of the parties, the retitled property shall be deemed transmuted to marital property. However, to the extent the property is retraceable by a preponderance of the evidence and was not a gift, the retitled property shall retain its original classification. Va. Code § 20-107.3(A)(3)(f). See, e.g., *Robinson v. Robinson*, 46 Va. App. 652, 621 S.E.2d 147 (2005) (all assets acquired during marriage were retraceable to husband's separate property trust income); *Bchara v. Bchara*, 38 Va. App. 302, 563 S.E.2d 398 (2002) (jointly titled home built during marriage was retraceable to wife's separate property inheritance); *Von Raab v. Von Raab*, 26 Va. App. 239, 494 S.E.2d 156 (1997) (husband's separate property home was transmuted to marital property by his wife's contributions, refinancing of home, and retitling of home to husband and wife as tenants by the entirety, so that husband's separate interest was not retraceable, and entire property was classified as marital property).

When the separate property of one party is commingled into the separate property of the other party, or the separate property of each party is commingled into newly acquired property, to the extent the contributed property is retraceable by a preponderance of the evidence and was not a gift, each party shall be reimbursed the value of the contributed property. Va. Code § 20-107.3(A)(3)(g). If retraceable separate property is used to purchase a gift, it does not retain its classification as separate property. *Watts v. Watts*, 40 Va. App. 685, 581 S.E.2d 224 (2003).

The "source of funds" rule is a vehicle to determine whether property has been transmuted into part separate and part marital, or "hybrid," property. *Duva v. Duva*, 55 Va. App. 286, 685 S.E.2d 842 (2009); see *Srinivasan v. Srinivasan*, 10 Va. App. 728, 396 S.E.2d 675 (1990). The source of funds is a factor that the court should consider in making an equitable distribution award, and is a particularly significant factor when funds have been transmuted. See Va. Code § 20-107.3(E)(6). However, the source of funds does *not* determine the initial classification of property, because one acquires property either as separate or marital. *Duva v. Duva*, 55 Va. App. 286, 685 S.E.2d 842 (2009); see Va. Code § 20-107.3(A)(3). Any analysis of "hybrid" property requires the court to determine, first, whether the property is separate or marital, and then to determine, second, what portion of the separate property or marital property is "hybrid" by applying Va. Code § 20-107.3(A)(3). *Duva v. Duva*, 55 Va. App. 286, 685 S.E.2d 842 (2009).

Refinancing does not necessarily preclude the possibility of tracing separate property, or constitute an independent transmutation, even if the proceeds of refinancing may become marital property. *Wiese v. Wiese*, 46 Va. App. 399, 617 S.E.2d 427 (2005). In *Wiese*, a husband applied the proceeds from the sale of his separate property home to the purchase of a marital home that was titled in his and his wife's names. Subsequently, the couple refinanced the marital home three times. The third time they treated the refinancing proceeds as marital property and divided the proceeds evenly by mutual agreement. Because the wife failed to show that the separate property funds used to acquire the marital home were a gift, the marital home was, prior to the refinancings, part marital and part separate property, or "hybrid" property. However, neither the refinancings nor the equal division of proceeds from the third refinancing transmuted the equity in the marital home entirely into marital property. Therefore, equitable distribution under a *Brandenburg* or similar analysis was required. See *Brandenburg* discussion *below*.

No presumption of gift arises from the fact that property is conveyed or retitled into joint ownership. Va. Code § 20-107.3(A)(3)(h). Thus, when separate property that has been transferred into joint title is shown to be retraceable, the party seeking to retain the marital property classification must prove the property was a gift. *Utsch v. Utsch*, 266 Va. 124, 581 S.E.2d 507 (2003). In *Utsch*, a husband executed a "deed of gift" conveying his separate property residence to himself and his wife as tenants by the entirety "for and in consideration of the love and affection of [husband] for [wife]." On its face, the deed was clear and unambiguous both as to the husband's intent to jointly title the marital residence, and as to his donative intent in making the transfer. See *Prizzia v. Prizzia*, 58 Va. App. 137, 707 S.E.2d 461 (2011) (husband's retraceable separate interest in marital home was marital property when wife demonstrated husband's intent to make gift, gift's delivery or transfer, and wife's acceptance of gift); *Robinson v. Robinson*, 46 Va. App. 652, 621 S.E.2d 147 (2005) (assets retraceable to husband's separate property trust income were not marital property absent finding that husband gifted wife with share of assets); *Cirrito v. Cirrito*, 44 Va. App. 287, 605 S.E.2d 268 (2004) (real estate purchased with separate funds but jointly titled in husband's and wife's names for protection against creditors was not marital property absent proof of donative intent).

Where there is no commingling, the property acquired prior to marriage remains separate property. *Atkinson v. Atkinson*, 19 Va. Cir. 340 (1990). See also *Fowlkes v. Fowlkes*, 42 Va. App. 1, 590 S.E.2d 53 (2003) (before enactment of Va. Code § 20-107.3(A)(3)(g) concerning commingling of separate property with separate property of other party, addition to wife's separate property home, built with husband's and wife's separate property funds, was *not* part marital and part separate property under Va. Code § 20-107.3(A)(3)(d), because parties never commingled separate property with marital property). The court must determine first the value of the marital portion of the property and then make an equitable distribution of the newly established value of the property. *Gravenstine v. Gravenstine*, 58 Md. App. 158, 472 A.2d 1001, 1007 (1984). Payment of taxes is not a part of the on-going process of payment for property fully purchased prior to the marriage. *Id.* at 171, 472 A.2d at 1007–08. However, the contribution of joint funds to the mortgage may result in its being marital property. *Stallings v. Stallings*, 75 Ill. App. 3d 96, 30 Ill. Dec. 718, 393 N.E.2d 1065 (1979).

Placing separately acquired assets in a joint bank account before using them to purchase another asset results in the transmutation of the new property into marital property. *Taylor v. Taylor*, 9 Va. App. 341, 387 S.E.2d 797 (1990); *Lassen v. Lassen*, 8 Va. App. 502, 383 S.E.2d 471 (1989).

When funds are acquired prior to marriage but contributions to them are made during the marriage, the party claiming the funds as separate property must overcome the presumption that they are marital property. *Rexrode v. Rexrode*, 1 Va. App. 385, 394, 339 S.E.2d 544, 548–49 (1986). Where a spouse fails to segregate and instead commingles separate property with marital property, the chancellor must classify the commingled property as marital property subject to equitable distribution. *Smoot v. Smoot*, 233 Va. 435, 442, 357 S.E.2d 728, 731 (1987). See also *Price v. Price*, 4 Va. App. 224, 236, 355 S.E.2d 905, 912 (1987) (parties commingled separate and marital property to create a "new" piece of property); *Westbrook v. Westbrook*, 5 Va. App. 446, 364 S.E.2d 523 (1988) (parties agreed that separate property would be marital property); *Rudisill v. Rudisill*, 1995 Va. App. LEXIS 404 (May 2, 1995); and *Walker v. Walker*, 19 Va. Cir. 390 (Clarke Co. 1990) (property purchased prior to marriage, but payments made to purchase price from owner's salary during marriage). In all these cases, however, the original owner's contributions will be considered in determining the final award. Property will be presumed to be marital property unless there is a deed, title, or other clear indication that it is not jointly owned. Va. Code § 20-107.3(A)(2).

To overcome the marital property classification, the spouse seeking a "part-separate" or "hybrid" property classification has the burden of producing evidence to establish, by a preponderance of the evidence, that the claimed separate portion of the commingled property is identifiably derived from a separate asset. *Rahbaran v. Rahbaran*, 26 Va. App. 195, 209, 494 S.E.2d 135, 142 (1997). See *Robbins v. Robbins*, 48 Va. App. 466, 632 S.E.2d 615 (2006) (when stock shares had source classification 60% marital, 40% separate, and husband sold more than half of shares to accommodate incoming shareholders, husband's tracing evidence failed to prove he intended to sell only marital shares, with result that all shares were marital property); *Ranney v. Ranney*, 45 Va. App. 17, 608 S.E.2d 485 (2005) (wife's evidence was insufficient to prove that an identifiable portion of her separate funds was used to purchase either a SeaRay boat or certain unimproved real property in South Carolina). Cf. *Barker v. Barker*, 27 Va. App. 519, 500 S.E.2d 240 (1998). There must be an identifiable asset, and a proved contribution to its acquisition or to the raising of its value, not just payments made on marital bills to distribute assets. See also *Holden v. Holden*, 31 Va. App. 24, 520 S.E.2d 842 (1999), (*Holden I*), where the husband successfully claimed some real property was hybrid, consisting of $17,000 that was his alone (coming from the sale of individually owned comic books, with bank deposits traceable to their sale); and *Holden v. Holden*, 35 Va. App. 315, 544 S.E.2d 884 (2001) (*Holden II*), where the court of appeals concluded that on remand the trial court correctly distributed the hybrid real property by awarding the husband $23,500 of the value ($17,000 as his separate property interest and $6,500 as his half of the marital property interest).

Before the marriage, the husband acquired the home. With the exception of the first four years of the marriage, during which the wife was completing college, both parties worked and contributed to a joint account from which the mortgage was paid. Additionally, proceeds from the sale of a jointly held home in Pennsylvania were used to construct an addition to the home. The trial court appropriately found that the home was an asset deriving value from commingled marital and separate property, and awarded the husband 75% of its equity. *Pembelton v. Pembelton*, 1996 Va. App. LEXIS 771 (Dec. 17, 1996). *See also Hart v. Hart*, 27 Va. App. 46, 497 S.E.2d 496 (1998) (*Hart I*); *Hart v. Hart*, 35 Va. App. 221, 544 S.E.2d 366 (2001) (*Hart II*).

In *Keeling v. Keeling*, 47 Va. App. 484, 624 S.E.2d 687 (2006), a husband made substantial separate property contributions to the purchase and maintenance of the marital residence. He challenged the trial court's equitable distribution, arguing that the court, by failing to apply the formula adopted in *Brandenburg v. Brandenburg*, 617 S.W.2d 871 (Ky. Ct. App.

1981), had calculated the marital share of home equity at too high a figure. The court of appeals reasoned that strict application of the Brandenburg formula would yield an unfair result, because (1) the hybrid property had been obtained by both a significant separate property down payment and a significant joint mortgage, (2) the hybrid property equity had significantly increased primarily due to market forces, and (3) neither the down payment nor the mortgage had contributed disproportionately to the husband and wife's ability to acquire and hold the property. Therefore, in calculating the marital contributions and total contributions to acquisition of the marital residence, the trial court did not abuse its discretion by considering the parties' joint loan obligation as a creditable contribution to acquiring and maintaining the property long enough to enjoy a significant increase in equity due primarily to market forces. *See Rinaldi v. Rinaldi*, 53 Va. App. 61, 669 S.E.2d 359 (2008) (when equitable result was achieved, trial court did not abuse discretion by using *Keeling* method to calculate separate and marital shares of hybrid riverfront property, while using *Brandenburg* formula to calculate marital equity in hybrid marital home).

In *Dehaven v. Dehaven*, 1997 Va. App. LEXIS 208 (Apr. 8, 1997), the couple constructed a family residence on land belonging to the husband's father. The husband received financial assistance from his father and labor from his father's plant nursery business when constructing the residence. Several years later, the husband's parents deeded the property by deeds of gift to both husband and wife. The wife worked for the family nursery business for 15 years, until the parties separated. The husband worked for the business throughout the parties' married life, and by the time the parties separated, owned 95% of the corporation as a result of gifts of stock made to him by his parents. In contrast to the wife, he was paid a substantial salary during this time period. The trial court found that the first shares, given to the husband in 1986, were marital property, and found that the increase in value of the husband's shares were due to the personal efforts of the parties, and therefore were marital property. Holding that any part of the stock itself was marital property was erroneous, according to the court of appeals, for all the shares of stock were gifted solely to him from his parents and retained in his name throughout the marriage. The court of appeals agreed with the trial court that the increase in value of the corporate stock, other than from inflation, was due to the efforts of both parties, and that the home was entirely marital property. See also *Congdon v. Congdon*, 40 Va. App. 255, 578 S.E.2d 833 (2003) (increase in value of husband's stock in his family's business was 90% separate property, ten percent marital property, when personal efforts of family members other than husband were taken into consideration); *Gilman v. Gilman*, 32 Va. App. 104, 526 S.E.2d 763 (2000) (shares of stock in Overnite Transportation stock were husband's, as were shares in Dow-Gil, the husband's business, and stock pledges used to purchase other stock); *Challoner v. Challoner*, 1997 Va. App. LEXIS 202 (Apr. 1, 1997); *Rowe v. Rowe*, 24 Va. App. 123, 480 S.E.2d 760 (1997) (*Rowe I*) and *Rowe v. Rowe*, 33 Va. App. 250, 532 S.E.2d 908 (2000) (Rowe II) (increase in value of husband's stock in newspaper could be attributable to husband's efforts, to passive factors, or to the efforts of third parties such as the husband's fellow editor); *Moran v. Moran*, 29 Va. App. 408, 512 S.E.2d 834 (1999) (increase in husband's separate share of a defined contribution pension plan was passive income that belonged to husband).

It is not error to award one party, whose premarital savings were used to make it, the entire value of a down payment on the property titled in joint names, so long as the court finds that equity dictates such a result upon consideration of all the factors of Va. Code § 20-107.3(E). *Pommerenke v. Pommerenke*, 7 Va. App. 241, 372 S.E.2d 630 (1988). See also *Hauger v. Hauger*, 1995 Va. App. LEXIS 206 (Feb. 28, 1995) (not designated for publication). Further, appreciation of stock acquired prior to marriage by the husband in a closely held corporation may have been marital property, where the wife's affirmative actions may have led in part to the appreciation. *Ellington v. Ellington*, 8 Va. App. 48, 378 S.E.2d 626 (1989). Compensation for improvements (heating, air conditioning, and trim) would be limited to the amount by which the value of the home was enhanced. The husband would also be credited with the mortgage payments made since the wife left the marital home and he assumed the mortgage payments. *Lee v. Lee*, 13 Va. Cir. 239 (Henrico Co. 1988). Because Va. Code § 20-107.3(E)(2) requires the trial court to consider the monetary and nonmonetary contributions of each party in the acquisition, care, and maintenance of marital property, a trial court did not abuse its discretion in awarding a wife 95% of the marital share of equity in a home that was purchased with a substantial down payment from her husband's separate property. The husband made negative contributions to the marital estate by making "improvements" to the home that actually decreased the value of the home. *Mir v. Mir*, 39 Va. App. 119, 571 S.E.2d 299 (2002).

The income received from separate property during the marriage is separate property as well if it does not result from the significant personal efforts of either party. The increase in value of separate property during the marriage is separate property unless marital property or the significant and effective personal efforts of either party have contributed to such increases, and then only to the extent of the increases in value attributable to such contributions. The burden of proof is on the nonowning party to prove that his or her personal efforts were significant and resulted in substantial appreciation of separate property. *Gilman v. Gilman*, 32 Va. App. 104, 526 S.E.2d 763 (2000). See also *Robinson v. Robinson*, 46 Va. App. 652, 621 S.E.2d 147 (2005) (wife's personal efforts to control parties' finances did not increase value of husband's separate property trust income); *Cirrito v. Cirrito*, 44 Va. App. 287, 605 S.E.2d 268 (2004) (discussion of three-tiered burden of proof applicable to part separate, part marital property); *Bchara v. Bchara*, 38 Va. App. 302, 563 S.E.2d 398 (2002) (husband's construction labor did not increase value of wife's separate property, and his contract negotiations were not type of "personal efforts" required for transmutation of separate property to marital property); *Hart v. Hart*, 27 Va. App. 46, 497 S.E.2d 496 (1998) (wife's improvements made by painting and wallpapering were not contributions that demonstrated added value to marital property); *Martin v. Martin*, 27 Va. App. 745, 501 S.E.2d 450 (1998) (error not to apply *Brandenburg* formula to give husband back his down payment contribution plus appreciation). However, in 2015, the Supreme Court of Virginia found that the non-owning spouse did not have the burden to prove causation between the significant personal efforts and the substantial appreciation in value. *David v. David*, 287 Va. 231, 239, 754 S.E.2d 285 (2014).

Property that was jointly held at one point during the marriage may become separate property if the parties expressly agree to do so. For example, in *Garland v. Garland*, 19 Va. Cir. 131 (Spotsylvania Co. 1990), husband and wife had separated and the wife received the marital home under their written agreement. They then reconciled, but divorced some years later. The property, still in the wife's name as feme sole, was now her separate property.

In *Amburn v. Amburn*, 13 Va. App. 661, 414 S.E.2d 847 (1992), the husband became a partner in Thomson Instrument Company shortly before the parties' marriage in 1978. He was the president of the company and oversaw its day-to-day operations. In 1979, the wife left her full-time employment to work for the corporation, eventually becoming the full-time office manager. At trial, the parties stipulated that the value of husband's interest in the corporation was $90,000. The court of appeals held that "it is not clear that the trial court abused its discretion by finding that the wife expended labor in the appreciation of the company's value," so that an equal division of the husband's interest was well within the fact finder's discretion. Likewise, in *Barnes v. Barnes*, 16 Va. App. 98, 428 S.E.2d 294 (1993), the husband owned a 40 percent interest in an insurance adjustment business at the time of the marriage. However, he worked to support the family in the adjusting business during the eight-year marriage, while the wife made substantial nonmonetary contributions to the marriage, including entertaining his business associates and accompanying him to business conventions and other business-related functions. The contributions of both parties during the marriage transmuted his interest, which had been separate property, into marital property. It was therefore proper to award the wife 5 percent for her interest in that marital asset.

In *Theismann v. Theismann*, 22 Va. App. 557, 471 S.E.2d 809 (1996), the wife was awarded $950,000 of the marital property worth over $2.5 million, even though the marriage was of short duration and the husband brought the vast majority of financial contributions to the marriage.

### § 21.13 Marital Debts

For equitable distribution purposes, marital debt must be considered as well as marital property. Va. Code § 20-107.3(A). Before enactment of specific statutory rules for debt in 2011, debt was regarded as included within the definition of "marital property." See *Stumbo v. Stumbo*, 20 Va. App. 685, 460 S.E.2d 591 (1995).

*Separate debt* is defined by statute to include (1) debt incurred by either party before the marriage, (2) debt incurred by either party after separation, and (3) that part of otherwise marital debt designated by the court as separate. The court may designate otherwise separate debt as marital to the extent that a party can show by a preponderance of the evidence that the debt was incurred for the benefit of the marriage or family. Va. Code § 20-107.3(A)(4).

*Marital debt* is defined to include (1) debt incurred in the joint names of the parties before separation, whether incurred before or after the date of the marriage, and (2) debt incurred in either party's name after marriage and before separation. However, the court may designate the entire debt as separate or a portion of the debt as marital and a portion of the debt as separate to the extent that a party can show by a preponderance of the evidence either that debt was incurred for a nonmarital purpose, or that the proceeds secured by incurring debt were used for a nonmarital purpose. Va. Code § 20-107.3(A)(5).

The court may divide or transfer jointly owed marital debt according to the factors set forth in Va. Code § 20-107.3(E), but it may not divide or transfer separate debt or debt that is not jointly owed. Va. Code § 20-107.3(C).

In *Gilliam v. McGrady*, 279 Va. 703, 691 S.E.2d 797 (2010), the court held that the marital property presumption normally applicable to assets received or accumulated during the marriage did not apply to the husband's trust fund tax debt that he incurred alone during the marriage. The court found that instead of imposing the burden on the wife to show that the debt was the husband's separate liability, the lower court should have placed the burden on the husband to show that the tax liability was a marital debt to be divided equally. The evidence demonstrated that the husband incurred the debt fully on his own, despite the wife's monthly requests that the husband resolve the matter with the Internal Revenue Service.

The enactment of statutory definitions for marital and nonmarital debt was the legislature's response to *Gilliam*'s holding that there was no presumption that debts incurred by spouses during marriage were marital. According to the *Gilliam* court, proof that a debt was jointly incurred would constitute a prima facie showing that the debt was marital, and shift the burden of persuasion to the spouse contending that the debt was separate. Conversely, proof that a debt was incurred by a single spouse would constitute a prima facie showing that the debt was separate, and shift the burden of persuasion to the spouse contending that the debt was marital. In classifying a debt incurred during marriage, the trial court would be guided by the factors set forth in Va. Code § 20-107.3(E).

While the Virginia Supreme Court in *Gilliam* rejected the appellate court's application of a presumption for debt incurred during marriage, it approved the appellate court's approach in determining classification of debt as separate or marital depending on the purpose of the debt, which in most cases can be determined by evaluating who benefited from the debt. See *Gilliam v. McGrady*, 53 Va. App. 476, 673 S.E.2d 474 (2009) (appellate court's analysis on this point affirmed in *Gilliam v. McGrady*, 279 Va. 703, 691 S.E.2d 797 (2010)). The trial court had decided that a debt owed to the federal government for a husband's unpaid business payroll taxes was a marital debt, because the funds that the husband might have used to pay the taxes were used instead to meet the husband's and wife's living expenses. However, the trial court erred by using the concepts of *purpose* of the debt and *effects of the failure to pay* the debt interchangeably. By considering only who benefited from the *failure to pay* the debt, the trial court failed to consider who *benefited* from the original debt, and also failed to consider the *purpose* of the original debt. In addition, the trial court failed to consider the criminal implications of the husband's nonpayment of his business payroll taxes. By characterizing the tax debt as marital debt, the trial court created an anomalous situation that allowed the husband to better his position by violating federal law. Therefore, the appellate court remanded the case for further consideration by the trial court.

Despite filing separate tax returns for years that occurred during the marriage, the trial court did not abuse its discretion in ordering the wife to pay a portion of the liability resulting from the husband's separately filed tax returns during the same years. *Wroblewski v. Russell*, 63 Va. App. 468, 488–89, 759 S.E.2d 1, 11 (2014). The parties had not filed tax returns for a number of years, and the wife filed separate tax returns for 2005–2010. By refusing to file joint income tax returns, husband owed approximately $300,000 in taxes, and his liability was $92,400 more than it would have been if the parties filed joint income tax returns. The husband's tax liability was found to be a marital debt pursuant to Va. Code § 20-107.3(A)(5). *Id.* "The fact that a spouse has the right under federal law to file separately does not in any way foreclose a state court, in the context of adjudicating a divorce, from considering the deleterious effect of this decision on the marriage." *Id.*

In *Booth v. Booth*, 7 Va. App. 22, 371 S.E.2d 569 (1988), the husband successfully argued that the trial court had erred in failing to consider the wife's "waste" of the marital assets. "Waste" was characterized as the dissipation of marital funds "in anticipation of divorce or separation for a purpose unrelated to the marriage and in derogation of the marital relationship at a time when the marriage is in jeopardy"; and was viewed as a negative contribution in the form of squandering and destroying marital resources. The trial court should have included the wasted assets as marital property and should have considered the waste as a factor in determining the monetary award. In *Budnick v. Budnick*, 42 Va. App. 823, 595 S.E.2d 50 (2004), the payment of costs to defend criminal charges in order to protect marital assets was distinguished from the payment of costs resulting from criminal convictions in order to accomplish purposes unrelated to the welfare of the marriage and family. Thus, a husband's withdrawal of funds from a retirement account acquired during marriage, in order to pay court-ordered fines and victim restitution resulting from his criminal activities, constituted a substantial waste of marital assets.

Similarly, if an encumbrance on marital property is created in anticipation of divorce, deliberately to reduce the value of the marital property and the amount of the monetary award, then the trial court may include the unencumbered value of the marital property within the pool of the marital wealth from which the court determines the amount of the monetary award. *Trivett v. Trivett*, 7 Va. App. 148, 371 S.E.2d 560 (1988). In *Trivett*, the trial court failed to consider whether a previously unsecured indebtedness was converted to indebtedness on specific marital property deliberately to frustrate equitable distribution.

There is a presumption that if marital funds are spent after separation, they are being dissipated. *Clements v. Clements*, 10 Va. App. 580, 397 S.E.2d 257 (1990). However, the expenditure of marital funds for living expenses or voluntary spousal support after separation is for a valid marital purpose, and does not constitute dissipation of marital assets in a deliberate attempt to affect a monetary award. *Alphin v. Alphin*, 15 Va. App. 395, 424 S.E.2d 572 (1992). See also *Northcutt v. Northcutt*, 39 Va. App. 192, 571 S.E.2d 912 (2002) (proceeds from husband's business loan and property sale used for valid marital purposes). Likewise, the expenditure of marital funds after separation for court-ordered *pendente lite* spousal support is for a valid marital purpose, and does not constitute marital waste. *Thomas v. Thomas*, 40 Va. App. 639, 580 S.E.2d 503 (2003). Despite having a high income and the ability to make the payments from his earnings or other assets, husband did not commit waste when he diminished the value of marital assets by $1,400,000 to pay income taxes, real estate taxes, tuition, and other school expenses for the minor child, *pendente lite* spousal support, and his legal fees and expert fees related to the divorce. *Wright v. Wright*, 61 Va. App. 432, 462–65, 737 S.E.2d 519, 533–35 (2013). However, where the husband spent marital funds to pay for college and graduate school expenses for parties' adult son, he was held to have committed waste of marital property. *Hvozdovic v. McGuire*, 2018 Va. App. LEXIS 51 (Feb. 27, 2018) (unpublished opinion).

The court, however, had no authority to require one party to pay specific debts incurred during the marriage at the time of *Day v. Day*, 8 Va. App. 346, 381 S.E.2d 364 (1989). A helpful discussion of these issues appears in McHenry & Sweeny, *Anderson v. Anderson: The Court of Appeals and the Role of Debt*, 11 Fam. L. News 8 (1990). See *Anderson v. Anderson*, 9 Va. App. 446, 389 S.E.2d 175 (1990) (loan of money from father of husband was payable at partition proceeding before distribution of proceeds as marital estate; wife bound by this determination that had been made at equitable distribution proceeding). The court now has authority under 20-107.3 to require one party to pay specific debts incurred during the marriage, *Hayes v. Hayes*, 21 Va. App. 515, 465 S.E.2d 590 (1996), although it did not at the time of the trial of *Gaynor v. Hird*, 1995 Va. App. LEXIS 617 (Aug. 1, 1995), involving some $36,457 of debts in both parties' names and $9,000 in the name of the husband alone.

The party requesting apportionment of marital debts was required to establish the amount of the outstanding marital debts by a preponderance of the evidence. *Kelker v. Schmidt*, 34 Va. App. 129, 538 S.E.2d 342 (2000) (decided before 2011 enactment of statutory definitions of marital and nonmarital debt). In *Kelker*, a chancellor properly rejected a commissioner's unexplained finding that alleged loans to a wife were marital debts, when the wife produced no documentary evidence that the loans were made, e.g., promissory notes or deposit slips, or that the loan money was used for household expenses, e.g., statements, receipts, or cancelled checks.

The trial court should have enforced an indemnification provision of the property settlement agreement that ordered the husband to reimburse the wife for paying his separate debt that had attached as a lien against the marital home. Shortly after the wife filed for divorce, the husband pled guilty to larceny of funds from his employer and executed a judgment note for $45,000 plus interest secured by a deed of trust on the marital home. Under the parties' agreement, he was to hold her harmless for the debt and reimburse her when she refinanced the home and paid the employer the debt plus interest. This obligation to pay the wife was not in the nature of spousal support and therefore was not extinguished by the remarriage. *Guffey v. Guffey*, 1995 Va. App. LEXIS 819 (Nov. 7, 1995). Marital debts and capital gains tax consequences were factors considered in the equitable distribution award affirmed in *Nigh v. Nigh*, 1995 Va. App. LEXIS 830 (Nov. 14, 1995).

In *Hall v. Hall*, 1998 Va. App. LEXIS 589 (Nov. 24, 1998) (unpublished decision), it was not error for the wife to be awarded 60% of the marital property when she demonstrated she contributed funds to pay closing costs and purchase appliances for the home, and made additional contributions to it, and the husband presented no evidence.

## § 21.14  Property Titled in One Spouse's Name

Under the 1988 amendments to Va. Code § 20-107.3, the court has the authority to allot, apportion, or transfer specific property titled jointly. There is no authority, however, to transfer or divide separate property or marital property not jointly owned, absent agreement of the parties. See, e.g., *McGinnis v. McGinnis*, 1 Va. App. 272, 276, 338 S.E.2d 159, 161 (1985); *Taylor v. Taylor*, 5 Va. App. 436, 442–43, 364 S.E.2d 244 (1988) (automobile); *Ellington v. Ellington*, 8 Va. App. 48, 378 S.E.2d 626, 5 V.L.R. 2100 (1989).

For example, it was permissible for the trial court to distribute property in the wife's name, but error to require her to buy out the husband's interest in the marital home over time, since there is no provision in the statute allowing delay in payments to the transferor of monies due for the interest one spouse is required to convey. *Stroop v. Stroop*, 10 Va. App. 611, 394 S.E.2d 861 (1990).

It was a reversible error for a trial court to make a final award requiring husband to pay a sum equal to half the value of the marital property (jewelry) given to the wife when she retained ownership of the items during the marriage. *Kaufman v. Kaufman*, 7 Va. App. 488, 375 S.E.2d 374 (1988). Wife was held entitled under the parties' property settlement agreement to a fifty percent interest in the husband's royalties from books he wrote or was writing during the marriage in *Jennings v. Jennings*, 12 Va. App. 1187, 409 S.E.2d 8 (1991).

In several recent cases, the court of appeals has dealt with the increasingly common problem of distributing shares in a closely held family corporation. In *Roane v. Roane*, 12 Va. App. 989, 407 S.E.2d 698 (1991), the husband was the sole owner of Dave's Cabinet Shop., Inc., and asserted that the wife made no contribution to the appreciated value of the stock. The husband had, however, obtained a Small Business Administration loan using the wife's signature. The case was remanded for consideration in light of the fact that her nonmonetary contributions were sufficient to meet the test of *Smoot v. Smoot*; she was not foreclosed from asserting that ownership of the stock had been transmuted to marital property, his intent not to give her an interest in the corporation was not controlling, and her efforts contributed to the appreciation in value of the stock. In *Jacobs v. Jacobs*, 12 Va. App. 977, 406 S.E.2d 669 (1991), the parties established International Diversified Products Corporation during the marriage. The corporation was financed from marital funds and funds provided by the husband's father. After a brief separation in 1976, the husband placed fifty percent of his shares of the corporation (32 percent of the outstanding stock) in the wife's name. The issue in the case was how to value the stock. The commissioner found that International Diversified Products had a value of $500,000, so that the wife's share was $175,000. The wife challenged the valuation because Mr. Jacobs and his father together controlled the business. In fact, the court noted, the value of the wife's stock interest depended entirely on what husband or the corporation felt her stock was worth. He had also used a substantial amount of the corporation's assets for his own personal benefit. Upon remand, the circuit court was ordered to take the nonliquid nature of Mrs. Jacob's interest into consideration. See also *Stainback v. Stainback*, 11 Va. App. 13, 396 S.E.2d 686 (1990); *Decker v. Decker*, 17 Va. App. 12, 435 S.E.2d 407 (1993) (one-fifth of increase in value of corporate shares due to efforts of husband, one of five key employees, and therefore marital property); *Hurt v. Hurt*, 16 Va. App. 792, 433 S.E.2d 493 (1993) (earned income received by husband and deposited into personal ledger caused transmutation into marital property); *Reynolds v. Reynolds*, 1994 Va. App. LEXIS 10 (Jan. 18, 1994) (husband's astute management of company transmuted stock that was wife's separate property into marital property); *Bonner v. Bonner*, 1993 Va. App.

LEXIS 361 (Aug. 17, 1993) (home originally wife's separate property was transmuted into marital property when the parties used it to procure a home equity loan, most of which paid for improvements on it); *Cirrito v. Cirrito*, 44 Va. App. 287, 605 S.E.2d 268 (2004) ($1 million payment pursuant to noncompetition agreement that was negotiated before marriage was marital property when payment was earned by husband's forbearance from competition during marriage); *Ranney v. Ranney*, 45 Va. App. 17, 608 S.E.2d 485 (2005) (stock options were marital property when condition for vesting of husband's right to exercise options was fulfilled by husband's continued employment during marriage); *Shiembob v. Shiembob*, 55 Va. App. 234, 685 S.E.2d 192 (2009) (when husband's right to restricted stock shares was conditioned on his continued employment but right to shares did not vest until after husband and wife separated, shares were husband's separate property). Compare *Huger v. Huger*, 16 Va. App. 785, 433 S.E.2d 255 (1993) (value of stock received as gifts from husband's family was not enhanced because of the parties' efforts).

In *Bartlett v. Rennier*, 1996 Va. App. LEXIS 503 (July 16, 1996), the husband and two of his colleagues established a software development company called Blacksmith. Creation of the company was made possible by a $100,000 investment by the wife's father, Mr. Bartlett. Mr. Bartlett was willing to invest in the venture with no requirement of a business plan because he intended to benefit his daughter by making the investment. In return for his investment, Mr. Bartlett received Blacksmith stock, and was retained as corporate counsel. During the marriage, Mr. Rennier drew a $30,000 salary from Blacksmith, approximately half of what he was making at the time of the marriage. Ms. Bartlett encouraged her husband in the new undertaking and participated in the discussions with her father that culminated in the $100,000 investment. She also provided limited assistance in forming the business and getting it off the ground, and served as corporate secretary. The trial court erred in awarding Ms. Bartlett no share in Blacksmith, instead awarding her only 100% of her own defunct and failed business and a rental dwelling not worth the debt against it and with a negative cash flow inadequate to pay its mortgage. The court of appeals found that both parties pursued business interests with the approval and support of the other. It does not follow that the more successful partner should obtain all the profits, leaving nothing to the partner who worked at an unsuccessful part of the endeavor. See also *Matthews v. Matthews*, 26 Va. App. 638, 496 S.E.2d 126 (1998) (wife heavily involved in husband's commodities trading business during its first two years); and *Rahbaran v. Rahbaran*, 26 Va. App. 195, 494 S.E.2d 135 (1997), which involved a husband who began a shoe business with separate funds received as gifts from his father. Because these were commingled with marital funds, its successor, Kami, Inc., ultimately became marital property.

A court may properly consider the parties' premarital contributions, both monetary and nonmonetary, that enhance the value of marital property. Cohabitation that does not have an impact on the marital property values will not justify consideration. *Floyd v. Floyd*, 17 Va. App. 222, 436 S.E.2d 457 (1993). See also *Ingram v. Snarr-Ingram*, 1994 Va. App. LEXIS 437 (July 5, 1994) (husband purchased home in 1978, before couple met. They married in 1983, when the value of the home had increased from $42,000 to $64,500. The husband deeded the house to himself and his wife as tenants by the entirety in 1986. Husband should have been allowed premarital appreciation of property found to be separate property.)

The husband's separate property did not become marital assets when the wife was compensated for her renovation and sales efforts according to the parties' marital agreements. *Cummings v. Cummings*, 1996 Va. App. LEXIS 72 (Feb. 6, 1996). Similarly, property purchased by the husband and carefully segregated throughout the marriage remained his separate property, though he was responsible to repay $11,000 remaining on loans made to him by the wife. *Baer v. Baer*, 1996 Va. App. LEXIS 73 (Feb. 6, 1996).

## § 21.15  Compensation for Personal Injuries

Courts have disagreed as to whether monies paid to compensate one spouse for a personal injury suffered during the marriage is marital property. See, e.g., *Bywater v. Bywater*, 128 Mich. App. 396, 340 N.W.2d 102 (1983) (holding that compensation for pain and suffering was a divisible asset); *Van de Loo v. Van de Loo*, 346 N.W.2d 173 (Minn. 1984) (holding that funds were not divisible as marital property); *Amato v. Amato*, 180 N.J. Super. 210, 434 A.2d 639 (1981) (not divisible; like replacement of separate property).

Two Virginia Circuit Court cases have considered compensation for personal injuries that occurred during the marriage as marital property. *Mabe v. Mabe*, 8 Va. Cir. 339 (Wise Co. 1987) (workers' compensation award to husband for personal injuries suffered after separation was marital property; personal injury award to wife for her pain and suffering due to accident before separation was separate property); *Seidenberg v. Seidenberg*, 9 Va. Cir. 83 (Henrico Co. 1987) (husband shot by spouse of person with whom he was having an affair; marital property unless proved to be separate property, although occurrence, settlement, and payment all occurred after parties had separated). Compare *Lambert v. Lambert*, 10 Va. App. 623, 395 S.E.2d 207 (1990) (disability retirement benefits from employment prior to work were separate property, although the payments might be considered as sources of income for spousal and child support).

In *Thomas v. Thomas*, 13 Va. App. 92, 95, 408 S.E.2d 596 (1991), the court of appeals held that (1) a lump sum personal injury settlement that a spouse receives during the course of marriage for injuries also incurred during marriage is presumptively marital property subject to equitable distribution at divorce; and (2) the presumption may be rebutted by a showing that settlement funds consist only of noneconomic damages personal to the injured spouse.

In 1990, the Virginia Legislature amended Va. Code § 20-107.3 to expressly state that the "marital share" of a personal injury or worker's compensation recovery by either party, as defined by Va. Code § 20-107.3(H), constitutes marital property. As of 2008, Va. Code § 20-107.3(H) defines the "marital share" as "that part of the total personal injury or workers' compensation recovery attributable to lost wages or medical expenses to the extent not covered by health insurance accruing during the marriage and before the last separation of the parties." Va. Code § 20-107.3(H) also provides that upon consideration of the factors set forth in Va. Code § 20-107.3(E), a trial court "may direct payment of a percentage of the marital share of any personal injury or workers' compensation recovery . . . whether such recovery is payable in a lump sum or over a period of time." See Va. Code §§ 20-107.3(A)(3)(c), (H).

In *Chretien v. Chretien*, 53 Va. App. 200, 670 S.E.2d 45 (2008), divorcing spouses disputed the character of $129,000 of the wife's personal injury recovery for injuries she received in a motorcycle accident caused by the husband. The wife argued that because Va. Code § 20-107.3 states that the marital share of a personal injury recovery is marital property, all proceeds that are not part of the marital share are separate property. The husband argued that nothing in the statute mandates that the non-marital share of the personal injury recovery is separate property. The court of appeals explained that Va. Code § 20-107.3(H) expressly provides that a personal injury recovery is part marital and part separate property. The statute identifies the part of a personal injury recovery that is marital property, and makes it clear that the remainder of the recovery is separate property. Under the statutory scheme, the court of appeals said, the trial court must divide the recovery into its marital and separate parts, by (1) determining what part of the recovery is attributable to lost wages and medical expenses not covered by health insurance, and classifying that portion as marital property; and (2) classifying the remaining portion as separate property. However, because the wife failed to show that any portion of the recovery was attributable to things other than lost wages or uncompensated medical expenses, the wife failed to overcome the presumption in favor of marital property. Nevertheless, the trial court did not abuse its discretion by awarding the entire personal injury recovery to the wife. The trial court (1) considered all of the Va. Code Ann. § 20-107.3(E) factors, and (2) reasonably concluded that factor 11 was controlling, because the husband had negligently caused the accident that led to the wife's serious injuries.

## § 21.16   When Does Time Run?

Property acquired before the parties marry, even during a period they are living together, will not be marital property. *Cotter v. Cotter*, 58 Md. App. 529, 473 A.2d 970 (1984), *superseded by statute as stated in Flanagan v. Flanagan*, 181 Md. App. 492, 956 A.2d 829 (2008); *Wilen v. Wilen*, 61 Md. App. 337, 486 A.2d 775, 780–81 (1985).

Va. Code § 20-107.3 specifies that the period within which acquisition of property will make it marital property expires upon the filing of the complaint for divorce. The question still arises, however, whether property acquired when the parties have been separated for an extended period of time ought to be divisible. Where the marriage relationship is not at an end because of continued contact between the parties, property obtained should be marital property. *Brandenburg v. Brandenburg*, 83 N.J. 198, 416 A.2d 327 (1980) (presumption in state that the marital partnership continued until the divorce complaint was filed); *Wilen v. Wilen*, 61 Md. App. 337, 486 A.2d 775 (Md. App. 1985); cf. *Di Giacomo v. Di Giacomo*, 80 N.J. 155, 402 A.2d 922 (1979) (oral agreement plus division of property sufficient). The situation has been clarified somewhat by the 1986 amendment to Va. Code § 20-107.3(A)(2), which now defines marital property as all property acquired by either spouse during the marriage "and before the last separation of the parties, if at such time or thereafter at least one of the parties intends that the separation be permanent." By amendment to Va. Code § 20-107.3, the court shall determine the value of marital property as of the date of the evidentiary hearing on the evaluation issue, or some other date upon motion of either party and where good cause is shown. See *Aster v. Gross*, 7 Va. App. 1, 371 S.E.2d 833 (1988) (military pension of husband). The value of the property at the time of the equitable distribution proceeding is only res judicata as to its value on that date, rather than at a later partition proceeding. *Anderson v. Anderson*, 9 Va. App. 446, 389 S.E.2d 175 (1990). Severance pay awarded after the parties' final separation remains the separate property of the employee spouse. *Luczkovich v. Luczkovich*, 26 Va. App. 702, 496 S.E.2d 157 (1998). The key question is whether the severance pay was intended to compensate the employee for efforts made during the marriage or to replace post-separation earnings.

In *Shooltz v. Shooltz*, 27 Va. App. 264, 498 S.E.2d 437 (1998), the court of appeals ruled that the trial court should have reopened the matter of a business valuation a year and four months after the first equitable distribution hearing. The wife argued that since that time the husband's business had turned from a beginning and struggling one to a profitable one. Va. Code § 20-107.3 does indeed give the trial court discretion to value a business as of a date other than the date of the hearing, particularly when the valuation was not based on any earnings history.

In *Martin v. Martin*, 27 Va. App. 745, 501 S.E.2d 450 (1998), it was error not to apply the *Brandenburg* formula to give the husband back his down payment contribution plus appreciation. Similar to the "added value" discussed in *Hart v. Hart*, 27 Va. App. 46, 497 S.E.2d 496 (1998), painting and wallpapering done by the wife were not significant personal efforts for home improvements.

However, when the parties specified that the Commissioner should value the investment accounts as of a specific date, the wife was not entitled to prejudgment interest nor to an increase in the value of the accounts that took place after that date but before trial. *Ragsdale v. Ragsdale*, 30 Va. App. 283, 516 S.E.2d 698 (1999).

When the couple's pattern was to take out equity loans during the year which would be paid back when the husband received his law firm bonus, he could not alter that pattern after separation, leaving the loans as marital debt while retaining the bonus as his separate property. The entire debt was properly allocated to him. *Howell v. Howell*, 31 Va. App. 332, 523 S.E.2d 514 (2000).

In *Taylor v. Taylor*, 23 Va. Cir. 133 (Fairfax Co. 1991), the trial court found in 1988 that 22,000 shares of the Marriott Corporation were separate property of the husband. At this time the stock was valued at $644,000. The court of appeals found that the stock was in fact marital property (9 Va. App. 341, 387 S.E.2d 797 (1990). Upon remand in 1991, the court held that the wife was entitled to receive six and one-half percent of the value of the Marriott stock, or nearly $42,000. The husband claimed that it would be inequitable to require him to pay a monetary award based upon the value the stock had more than two years earlier, since it had declined in value by approximately two-thirds. The court of appeals held that a monetary award including the interest in the Marriott stock must be determined as of December 13, 1990, the date of the final evidentiary hearing. Similarly, if a court remands an equitable distribution award, a second evaluation should establish the value of the property. *Wagner v. Wagner*, 15 Va. App. 120, 421 S.E.2d 218 (1992), *aff'd*, 16 Va. App. 529, 431 S.E.2d 77 (1993). See also *Robbins v. Robbins*, 48 Va. App. 466, 632 S.E.2d 615 (2006) (commissioner abused discretion by relying on inapplicable law-of-the-case doctrine when declining to revalue marital home that had increased greatly in value); *Holden v. Holden*, 35 Va. App. 315, 544 S.E.2d 884 (2001) (Holden II) (on remand, trial court erred by arbitrarily assigning stock and all of its loss of value to husband, contrary to holding of *Wagner v. Wagner*, 16 Va. App. 529, 431 S.E.2d 77 (1993) (en banc), which requires a revaluation on remand to obtain the most accurate valuation and equitable distribution); *Rowe v. Rowe*, 33 Va. App. 250, 532 S.E.2d 908 (2000) (on remand, trial judge erred and abused discretion by failing to revalue stock that had been held by one party for lengthy period of time, when value of stock, including value of wife's portion, had greatly changed).

If the court makes a monetary award where one marital asset is a pension, it need not wait until distribution of the pension before making an offsetting award. Thus in *Gamble v. Gamble*, 14 Va. App. 558, 421 S.E.2d 635 (1992), the wife was awarded the house, while the husband received his entire pension. In *Walls v. Walls*, 1993 Va. App. LEXIS 329 (Aug. 10, 1993), the court of appeals reversed the trial court for finding the two pensions were equal and offsetting. The wife had cashed in her pension, while the husband's continued to accumulate. Based upon values paid in and expected to be paid, the husband's pension was a significant asset.

## § 21.17   Fault as a Factor

In Virginia, fault may be considered in making equitable division of property. Va. Code § 20-107.3(E)(5). Fault was apparently considered in the case of *Bentz v. Bentz*, 2 Va. App. 486, 345 S.E.2d 773 (1986), although the husband was not allowed to amend his complaint to include grounds of adultery. The court was required to consider fault by Va. Code § 20-107.3, and, for this purpose, fault need not be pled nor be sufficient to constitute grounds for divorce. *Id.* at 774. Other Virginia cases holding that fault in breaking up the marriage should be considered include *Robbins v. Robbins*, 48 Va. App. 466, 632 S.E.2d 615 (2006) (wife's romantic involvement with co-worker was major contributing factor and precipitating event in her decision not to continue marriage, justifying 65/35 division of assets when husband made most monetary contributions); *Westbrook v. Westbrook*, 5 Va. App. 446, 364 S.E.2d 523 (1988) (husband's desertion of wife to resume his relationship with his paramour considered; wife's untruthfulness regarding her sexual relations after separation had no bearing upon the division of property); *Cousins v. Cousins*, 5 Va. App. 156, 360 S.E.2d 882 (1987) (husband's adulterous behavior that contributed to dissolution of marriage properly considered even though divorce granted on no fault grounds); *Seidenberg v. Seidenberg*, 9 Va. Cir. 83 (Henrico Co. 1987) (husband was shot by spouse of woman with whom he was having affair). Cf. *Marion v. Marion*, 11 Va. App. 659, 401 S.E.2d 432 (1991) (no showing that husband spent significant amount of marital assets on vacations with woman with whom he was having an affair). Even though one spouse obtains a fault divorce, if the fault has no economic impact on the value of the marital assets, it will not affect the equitable distribution award. *Donnell v. Donnell*, 20 Va. App. 37, 455 S.E.2d 256 (1995); *Gamer v. Gamer*, 16 Va. App. 335, 429 S.E.2d 618 (1993). See also *Barden v. Barden*, 1995 Va. App. LEXIS 200 (Feb. 28, 1995). However, fault was properly considered when the wife received approximately two-thirds of the marital estate, including the marital home. In *Crump v. Crump*, 1993 Va. App. LEXIS 404 (Sept. 7, 1993), the husband had earned the bulk of the family's income during the 30-year marriage, but had also engaged in a long-term extramarital affair that ultimately broke up the marriage. See also *Lamb v. Lamb*, 33 Va. Cir. 442 (Stafford Co. 1994); *Major v. Major*, 36 Va. Cir. 190 (Pittsylvania Co. 1995) (husband convicted of "several horrible felonies" and divorced for cruelty and imprisonment; wife, who "suffered a disastrous financial setback as a result of his cruel and inhumane treatment," was awarded all the marital property). In *Ranney v. Ranney*, 45 Va. App. 17, 608 S.E.2d 485 (2005), a wife's "fraudulent inducement of marriage" by representing that the marriage would be her second rather than her fifth was properly considered as a factor contributing to the dissolution of the marriage under Va. Code § 20-107.3(E)(5). However, the wife's fraudulent inducement did not act as a complete bar to her receipt of marital assets in an equitable distribution.

In *O'Loughlin v. O'Loughlin*, 20 Va. App. 522, 458 S.E.2d 323 (1995), the husband not only committed adultery but also spent over ten thousand dollars on his paramours, thus affecting the marriage partnership's economic condition. Further, the husband made no nonmonetary contributions to the well-being of the family. The court stated, "Fault is not a 'wild card' that may be employed to justify what otherwise would be an arbitrary or punitive award. When fault is relevant in arriving at an award, the trial judge is required to consider it objectively, and how, if at all, it quantitatively affected the marital estate or well being of the family." See also *Joynes v. Payne*, 36 Va. App. 401, 551 S.E.2d 10 (2001) (attorney wife's unilateral decision to terminate part-time employment with law firm was negative nonmonetary contribution to marriage that factored into marital breakup and impacted marital property); *Watts v. Watts*, 40 Va. App. 685, 581 S.E.2d 224 (2003) (husband's actions in meeting with female co-worker after work and staying out late prejudiced well-being of family and constituted serious negative nonmonetary contributions that justified unequal division of marital property); *Budnick v. Budnick*, 42 Va. App. 823, 595 S.E.2d 50 (2004) (husband's criminal business activities and convictions that irreparably harmed marriage and negatively impacted well-being of family constituted negative monetary contributions that justified wife's award of 90% of marital property). This property distribution rule was established in *Aster v. Gross*, 7 Va. App. 1, 371 S.E.2d 833 (1988).

In *Thomas v. Thomas*, 1996 Va. App. LEXIS 738 (Nov. 26, 1996) (unpublished opinion), husband and wife had kept their money separate, each paying for specific expenses during the marriage. Mr. Thomas failed on numerous occasions to pay the expenses that he had accepted as his responsibilities. Ms. Thomas, who was also employed throughout the marriage, also cared for the parties' children, maintained the home, and supported her husband's career by entertaining his colleagues. Ms. Thomas eventually sued for divorce on grounds of cruelty and constructive desertion. She was properly awarded 70% of the equity in the marital home because she made all the non-monetary and many of the monetary contributions to the marital residence. She saved the home from foreclosure and maintained it for the family.

See also *Masri v. Masri*, 48 Va. Cir. 5 (Chesterfield Co. 1999), in which the wife was awarded the lion's share of the marital resources because of her "overwhelmingly greater monetary and non-monetary contributions to the marriage." The wife not only supported the husband during medical residency, but also supported the family when he made a series of disastrous financial investments, filed for bankruptcy and lost his medical license following a conviction for mail fraud.

There is a presumption if marital funds are spent after separation that they are being dissipated. *Clements v. Clements*, 10 Va. App. 580, 397 S.E.2d 257 (1990). Dissipation occurs when one spouse uses marital property for personal benefit and for a purpose unrelated to the marriage at a time when the marriage is undergoing an irreconcilable breakdown. It does not include the use of funds for living expenses while the parties are separated. *Id.* In 2004, the statutory property division factors were amended to add the use, expenditure or dissipation of marital property for a nonmarital separate purpose in anticipation of divorce or after the last separation. Va. Code § 20-107.3(E)(10). Despite having a high income and the ability to make the payments from his earnings or other assets, husband did not commit waste when he diminished the value of marital assets by $1,400,000 to pay income taxes, real estate taxes, tuition, and other school expenses for the minor child, pendente lite spousal support, and his legal fees and expert fees related to the divorce. *Wright v. Wright*, 61 Va. App. 432, 462–65, 737 S.E.2d 519, 533–35 (2013).

The husband had no right to introduce evidence of marital fault at the trial court proceeding involving equitable distribution when he did not object to the commissioner's awarding of a no-fault divorce, and no evidence of fault was preserved in the record. *Klein v. Klein*, 11 Va. App. 155, 396 S.E.2d 866 (1990).

Va. Code § 20-107.3(E) allows a trial court to determine the method of payment of an equitable distribution award, but the statute does *not* permit a court to set conditions of payment that are unrelated to the award itself. *Prizzia v. Prizzia*, 58 Va. App. 137, 707 S.E.2d 461 (2011). In *Prizzia*, a trial court erred by ordering a former wife's equitable distribution award to be held in escrow until she complied with a child visitation order issued by a Hungarian court.

## § 21.18   Custody of Children

The party granted custody of the children may need a sizable share of the marital estate in order to provide them a home and perhaps to remain home in order to care for them if they are small. See *Wiese v. Wiese*, 46 Va. App. 399, 407–08, 617 S.E.2d 427 (2005) (the trial court did not err in granting Wife the right of refusal to purchase Husband's interest in the marital home by considering that she had custody of the children and the children would benefit by remaining in the only home they had ever known). It is important to note however that the custody of the minor children is not an expressed factor for the court to consider under Va. Code § 20-107.3(E) when determining equitable distribution.

## § 21.19   Age, Income, Education and Potential

One of the justifications for an equitable distribution of property is to reward a homemaker spouse for contributions to the marital estate through performance of services that allowed the family unit to accumulate wealth. An award of property may give such a spouse financial independence without the continued dependence and contact resulting from an alimony award. Such contributions are less likely to have occurred in a marriage of short duration. See, e.g., *Duffy v. Duffy*, 94 A.D.2d 711, 462 N.Y.S.2d 240 (1983). The trial court did not err in determining that the primary factor establishing the marital standard of living was the husband's completion of his education before marriage rather than the non-monetary contributions of the wife. An award of 25 percent of the marital property was thus not an abuse of discretion. *Zipf v. Zipf*, 8 Va. App. 387, 382 S.E.2d 263 (1989).

Other equitable considerations such as the health of a party may also be factors. See, e.g., *Campbell v. Campbell*, 554 S.W.2d 10 (Tex. Civ. App. 1977) (husband was 100 percent disabled with severe emphysema and only income Social Security disability; wife was employed and had rental income from separate property). Va. Code § 20-107.3(E)(4) mandates consideration of the ages and physical and mental condition of the parties in fashioning an equitable distribution award. Furthermore, age is a valid indicator of need, because older parties generally have less income and more medical expenses. *Ay Hwa White v. White*, 56 Va. App. 214, 692 S.E.2d 289 (2010). In *White*, a trial court properly took a husband's future needs into account, to the extent they related to his age and health, when the husband suffered from Parkinson's disease, a condition that would likely continue into the future.

Where one spouse not only makes the majority of financial contributions towards acquisition of property but also performs most of the normal marital duties, the division of property need not be even. *Stallings v. Stallings*, 75 Ill. App. 3d 96, 30 Ill. Dec. 718, 393 N.E.2d 1065 (1979).

A nonmarital debt of a party, while not property to be distributed, does impact the economic circumstances of the parties and their ability to meet financial obligations. *Schweizer v. Schweizer*, 301 Md. 626, 484 A.2d 267, 272 (1984). The portion of an acquisition that remains unpaid does not constitute marital property. *Id.*

The fact that a party's financial condition is no worse when the marriage is dissolved than when the party entered the marriage is not a proper basis for denying an award based upon property acquired during the marriage. *Keyser v. Keyser*, 7 Va. App. 405, 374 S.E.2d 698 (1988).

See generally June Carbone and Margaret F. Brinig, *Rethinking Marriage: Feminist Ideology, Economic Change and Divorce Reform*, 65 Tul. L. Rev. 953 (1991).

## § 21.20   Use of Expert Testimony

Usually an accountant or actuary will be needed to evaluate pension plans. See, e.g., *Axtell v. Axtell*, 482 A.2d 1261 (Me. 1984); *Bloomer v. Bloomer*, 84 Wis. 2d 124, 267 N.W.2d 235 (1978); *Nisos v. Nisos*, 60 Md. App. 368, 483 A.2d 97 (1984); Troyan, *Pension Evaluation and Equitable Distribution*, 11 Fam. L. Rep. (BNA) 301 (1984). For the interest in a corporation, see, e.g., *Gorman v. Gorman*, 90 Cal. App. 3d 454, 153 Cal. Rptr. 479 (1979). See also *Jacobs v. Jacobs*, 12 Va. App. 977, 406 S.E.2d 669 (1991).

Such expert services may be necessary for any property whose fair market value is difficult to ascertain; for example, interests in works of art or in patent or copyright rights. See, e.g., *Donley v. Donley*, 83 Ill. App. 3d 367, 38 Ill. Dec. 733, 403 N.E.2d 1337 (1980). Frequently, the present value of future payments in distribution of a marital estate must be calculated since the value of the property might increase while the buying power of installments would substantially decrease. See, e.g., *Pankow v. Pankow*, 347 N.W.2d 566 (N.D. 1984). See also *Douty v. Douty*, 1994 Va. App. LEXIS 196 (April 5, 1994) (valuation of car wash business). Expert testimony may also resolve difficulties in tracing funds. *Dewitt v. Dewitt*, 1996 Va. App. LEXIS 561 (Aug. 6, 1996).

An accountant may be necessary for valuation of a small business. For example, the husband in *Bosserman v. Bosserman*, 9 Va. App. 1, 384 S.E.2d 104 (1989), was a 25 percent owner of a closely held family corporation. The bylaws provided for buy-out of stock based upon the "true book value" of the corporation, $28,032 at the time of divorce. The wife's accountant, however, placed the true market value of the farm owned by the corporation at $174,600. The court of appeals followed the majority rule that a buy-out provision does not control the determination of value when the other spouse did not consent or was not otherwise bound by its terms. The reasoning behind this rule is that buy-out provisions do not necessarily reflect the intrinsic worth of the stock to the parties. However, the limitation of alienability created by the restricting agreement necessarily affects the actual marketability of the stock, and thus its value. The valuation accepted by the court of appeals was based upon the corporation's net assets, the farm. See also *Owens v. Owens*, 41 Va. App. 844, 589 S.E.2d 488 (2003) (despite expert testimony, 50% owner of family corporation was not entitled to "minority interest" discount in valuation of stock holdings); *Howell v. Howell*, 31 Va. App. 332, 523 S.E.2d 514 (2000) (experts using "excess earnings" and "capitalized historic earning" approaches to valuing goodwill of law firm gave conflicting testimony).

Although accountants are commonly used at experts to value a business, this is not always the case. In *Shuler v. Shuler*, 2016 Va. App. LEXIS 243 (Sept. 13, 2016), the wife was allowed to testify as to the value of the husband's business. Wife was familiar with the business, as she had worked there, had done some accounting work for the business, and she provided the accountant with quarterly and year-end reports. Wife testified that she was "intimately familiar with the business and the value of the business assets." Since husband did not present any evidence of the business' value, the trial court did not err by accepting the wife's valuation that the business was worth $750,000.

Properly qualified evidence of comparable sales of other real property may be admissible to prove the value of the real property at issue. See, e.g., *In re Marriage of Smith*, 79 Cal. App. 3d 725, 145 Cal. Rptr. 205 (1978). If an equitable distribution award is remanded or the matter is reheard, a second evaluation should establish the value of the property, whether separately or jointly titled. *Wagner v. Wagner*, 15 Va. App. 120, 421 S.E.2d 218 (1992) (second evaluation in 1988 needed when original award was entered in 1984); *Gaynor v. Hird*, 11 Va. App. 588, 400 S.E.2d 788 (1991). The value of the husband's dental practice should not have been discounted by estimating the capital gains taxes on a hypothetical sale as opposed to the present fair market value of the property. *Arbuckle v. Arbuckle*, 22 Va. App. 362, 470 S.E.2d 146 (1996). The parties were to share equally in the marital property; the husband was awarded the value of his practice while the wife received oil company stock. There were no tax consequences to be determined here, as any such consequences would be merely hypothetical in nature. The more recent opinion in *Arbuckle v. Arbuckle*, 27 Va. App. 615, 500 S.E.2d 286 (1998), noted that while "valuation cannot be mere guesswork," but on the other hand, "a certain degree of imprecision will be inevitable in applying the factors" in distribution.

Although a trial court may appropriately limit cross-examination, subject to the rules of evidence, it is an abuse of trial court discretion, as a matter of law, for the court to prevent a party from cross-examining a material witness on a relevant matter solely because of previously announced time limits imposed on the presentation of evidence and the cross-examination of witnesses. *Campbell v. Campbell*, 49 Va. App. 498, 642 S.E.2d 769 (2007). In *Campbell*, court-imposed time limits prevented a husband from cross-examining his wife's handwriting expert and one factual witness about the authenticity of the husband's signature on a disputed marital agreement that the husband claimed was a forgery written by his wife. See Va. Code § 8.01-401(A).

## § 21.21   Tax Consequences of Distribution

Since 1984, I.R.C. § 1041 provides that transfers between spouses, or immediately after separation or divorce, are treated as gifts for income tax purposes. This means that they are not taxable, and the spouse receiving the property or interest in property takes the transferor's basis. Installments made by the payor may not be deducted as is alimony. *Slawski v. United States*, 6 Cl. Ct. 433 (1984). In order to receive this tax treatment, the transfer must be before divorce or within one year of divorce, or pursuant to a settlement agreement made in connection with a divorce. The transfers may be treated as alimony even if the decree or agreement does not provide that they will terminate at the death of the payee. I.R.C. § 71(b)(1).

Changes made in the treatment of capital gains affects the 1984 Tax Reform Act's effective elimination of the holding of *United States v. Davis*, 370 U.S. 65, 82 S. Ct. 1190, 8 L. Ed. 2d 335 (1962). Capital gains are now taxed as ordinary income for the most part. However, they will now be paid by the transferee rather than by the transferor, as had been true under Davis. I.R.C. § 1202. When formulating an equitable distribution award, a trial court is not required to reduce the award to account for potential capital gains tax consequences, no matter how certain or uncertain they may be. Va. Code § 20-107.3(E)(9) only requires that the court *consider* tax consequences. *Owens v. Owens*, 41 Va. App. 844, 589 S.E.2d 488 (2003).

In *Shooltz v. Shooltz*, 27 Va. App. 264, 498 S.E.2d 437 (1998), the trial court should have reopened the matter of a business valuation a year and four months after the first equitable distribution hearing under Va. Code § 20-107.3. The wife argued that since that time the husband's business had turned from a beginning and struggling one to a profitable one. It was also not error to reopen the case six months after the equitable distribution hearing to allow the husband to pay taxes, thus reducing the wife's award by the amount of the taxes.

The award to the wife of 50 percent of the husband's royalties under a property settlement agreement meant net royalties, since otherwise the husband would be required to bear the entire tax burden. *Jennings v. Jennings*, 12 Va. App. 1187, 409 S.E.2d 8 (1991). If the parties specify that each will be responsible for paying taxes accrued on his or her respective income, there is no need for repayment of any "offset" if it turns out that the parties do not owe any tax. *Smith v. Smith*, 15 Va. App. 371, 423 S.E.2d 851 (1992). Tax liability may be allocated but need not be. *Alphin v. Alphin*, 15 Va. App. 395, 424 S.E.2d 572 (1992).

Calculations of probable taxes must be estimated based on expert opinions. *Mains v. Mains*, 1993 Va. App. LEXIS 362 (Aug. 17, 1993).

### § 21.22 Effect on Dower and Curtesy, Use of Marital Home, Title

The husband as well as the wife is now able to acquire a sole and separate equitable estate in real property. *Jacobs v. Meade*, 227 Va. 284, 315 S.E.2d 383 (1984).

If the property was held as a married person, even though titled in the name of only one spouse, the other spouse historically had a dower or curtesy interest in the property. For a conveyance in fee simple to a third party, the spouse with the contingent interest must also join in the deed. Contingent property interests such as dower were extinguished by the divorce decree. Va. Code § 20-111.

There is no need for a specific claim in an equitable distribution proceeding, in contrast to a partition suit. Compensation for improvements to the marital home will be limited to the increase in its value plus mortgage payments made after the separation. *Lee v. Lee*, 13 Va. Cir. 239 (Henrico Co. 1988).

In *Martin v. Martin*, 27 Va. App. 745, 501 S.E.2d 450 (1998), it was error not to apply the *Brandenburg* formula to give the husband back his down payment contribution plus appreciation. Similar to the "added value" discussed in *Hart v. Hart*, 27 Va. App. 46, 497 S.E.2d 496 (1998), the painting and wallpapering done by the wife were not significant personal efforts resulting in a substantial increase in the home's value.

### § 21.23  Finality

A judgment for equitable distribution is a final order, and is not modifiable. See, e.g., *Boschee v. Boschee*, 340 N.W.2d 685 (N.D. 1983). It therefore will be given full faith and credit by other states under U.S. Const. art. IV, § 2. *Varone v. Varone*, 359 F.2d 769 (7th Cir. 1966).

### § 21.24  *Res Judicata*

Res judicata will be a defense to a second litigation concerning the same parties and property, even though the legal theories used change in each suit. *Whitaker v. Whitaker*, 60 Md. App. 695, 484 A.2d 314 (1984).

Under the law of the case doctrine, when there have been two appeals in the same case, between the same parties, and the facts are the same, nothing decided on the first appeal can be reexamined on the second appeal. Right or wrong, for the purpose of that case, the decision on the first appeal is law and is binding on both the trial court and the appellate court. *Rowe v. Rowe*, 33 Va. App. 250, 532 S.E.2d 908 (2000). The law of the case doctrine applies both to issues that were actually decided by the court and also to issues necessarily involved in the first appeal, whether actually adjudicated or not. *Guan v. Ran*, 2020 Va. App. LEXIS 122 (April 28, 2020) (citing to *Miller-Jenkins v. Miller-Jenkins*, 276 Va. 19, 26, 661 S.E.2d 822 (2008)). "[W]hen a party fails to challenge a decision rendered by a court at one stage of litigation, that party is deemed to have waived the right to challenge that decision during later stages of the 'same litigation.'" *Id.* In *Guan*, the accounting methodology employed by the expert was not challenged and upon the remand hearing the trial court properly utilized the expert's methodology.

In the absence of an identity of claims or issues, the defenses of res judicata and collateral estoppel will fail. *Wright v. Eckhardt*, 267 Va. 24, 591 S.E.2d 668 (2004). In *Wright*, a Texas divorce decree awarded a portion of a husband's military retirement benefits to his wife upon retirement. After the husband retired from the military, the wife sought enforcement in Virginia, where the husband resided. Giving full faith and credit to a Texas court's clarifying order that decided the wife was not entitled to payments because the husband was not yet retired, a Virginia court ruled against the wife. Later, the Texas court reversed the clarifying order, and the wife again sought enforcement in Virginia. The wife's second action based on the reversed clarifying order was *not* precluded by res judicata. In both of the wife's actions, the issue was whether a judgment of a foreign jurisdiction should be given full faith and credit by a Virginia court, *not* whether she was entitled to the retirement payments.

Res judicata does not apply unless there is a final judgment. *Stiles v. Stiles*, 48 Va. App. 449, 632 S.E.2d 607 (2006). In *Stiles*, a trial court issued a "Final Order" relating to spousal support, when issues relating to child and spousal support were before the court. Because the order adjudicating spousal support was not a final judgment regarding child support, res judicata did not bar a subsequent order modifying child support.

## § 21.25   Use of Contempt Power

Va. Code § 20-107.3(K)(2) expressly authorizes the court to "[p]unish as contempt of court any willful failure of a party to comply with the provisions of any order made by the court under this section." Monetary awards are therefore fully enforceable through the court's contempt powers. *Kahn v. McNicholas*, 67 Va. App. 215 (2017). Moreover, when marital settlement agreements are affirmed ratified and incorporated into a court order, they become part of the order, and pursuant to Va. Code § 20-109.1, are "enforceable in the same manner as any provision of such decree." *Kahn*, 67 Va. App. at 227 (citing Va. Code § 20-109.1). In *Kahn*, the Court of Appeals noted that while Va. Code § 20-107.3(D) permits a monetary award to be enforced in the same manner as any other money judgment, that remedy is not exclusive and the monetary award can also be enforced through a contempt proceeding. *Kahn*, 67 Va. App. at 230. Lastly, the *Kahn* opinion explains how the ruling of *Brown v. Brown*, 5 Va. App. 238 (1987), which held that monetary awards must be enforced as monetary judgments, is inapplicable due to the statutory amendments following the *Brown* decision which permit monetary awards to be pursued by contempt proceedings.

Moreover, Va. Code § 20-115 provides that a party who has been convicted of contempt for "willfully failing or refusing to comply with any order entered pursuant to" Va. Code § 20-107.3, may be committed and sentenced to a local correctional facility for a fixed or indeterminate period of time not to exceed 12 months.

In addition to contempt, an award entered pursuant to § 20-107.3 constitutes a judgment within the meaning of § 8.01-426, so that provisions of § 8.01-382 relating to interest on judgments shall ordinarily apply.

### § 21.26    Attorney's Fees

The Virginia Bar Council has determined that it is ethically improper to represent a client in an equitable distribution case on a contingent fee basis. Op. No. 189, July 1, 1984. The property to be distributed is not an asset as is a personal injury recovery, and to allow a contingent fee would be to encourage attorneys to fix large monetary awards for the client at the possible expense of other areas of disagreement, and to minimize any possibility of reconciliation during the period of representation.

# CHAPTER 22

# Child Support

## SYNOPSIS

## § 22.01    Introduction

The duty of a parent to support a minor child was considered in general in Chapter 15. The present chapter concerns child support as one of the economic consequences of dissolution or termination of marriage.

Generally speaking, child support can be distinguished from other financial considerations because the relationship of parent and child does not

22-1

end with the judicial termination of marriage. Although spousal support is fixed by the standard of living enjoyed during the marriage, children are entitled to whatever financial advantages they would have enjoyed had the family remained intact. See, e.g., *Conway v. Conway*, 10 Va. App. 653, 395 S.E.2d 464 (1990). Although a contract between the parties regarding spousal support will, if filed with the pleadings in a divorce action, be nonmodifiable, child support can always be modified by the court in the child's best interest. *Featherstone v. Brooks*, 220 Va. 443, 446, 258 S.E.2d 513, 515 (1979); *Carter v. Carter*, 215 Va. 475, 481, 211 S.E.2d 253, 258 (1975).

Because of problems in the collection of child support from noncustodial parents, a uniform act has been adopted by all states, including Virginia. Va. Code § 20-88.12 et seq. In 1984, Congress passed the Child Support Enforcement Assistance Amendments to the Social Security Act that balance the less favorable tax consequences of child support mandated by the Domestic Relations Tax Reform Act of 1984. The amendments require states, as a condition of receiving federal funds under the Act, to provide for mechanisms for enforcement such as withholding from the obligor's income, imposition of liens against real property, posting of security or bonds if support is overdue, and withholding from state or federal income tax refunds. 42 U.S.C. § 658(a) et seq. They also require the establishment of guidelines for the amount of support, now found in Va. Code § 20-108.1.

Both parents owe a duty of support. *Featherstone v. Brooks*, 220 Va. 443, 448, 258 S.E.2d 513, 516 (1979). This case preceded the establishment of the child support guidelines and remains included for historical purposes.

Liability for child support is determined retroactively for the period measured from the date the proceeding was commenced by the filing of the action with the court. Va. Code § 20-108.1(B). Thus a child support award must be made retroactive to the date the child support action was commenced. *Cirrito v. Cirrito*, 44 Va. App. 287, 605 S.E.2d 268 (2004). See *Asgari v. Asgari*, 33 Va. App. 393, 533 S.E.2d 643 (2000).

In *Pittman v. Pittman*, 2019 Va. App. LEXIS 216 (October 1, 2019), approximately three years had passed between the commencement of the suit and the final order, and during the pendency of the case the husband had been ordered to pay the mortgage, the utilities, HOA dues, real estate taxes, and *pendente lite* spousal support. However, there was no order for *pendente lite* child support. The trial court was found to have erred by not making the child support retroactive to the commencement of the proceeding.

Va. Code § 20-108 allows a trial court to modify child support awards with respect to any period during which there is a pending petition for modification, but only from the date that notice of the petition was given to the responding party. *Stiles v. Stiles*, 48 Va. App. 449, 632 S.E.2d 607 (2006).

Clerical mistakes in judgments or other court records may be corrected by a nunc pro tunc order. *Cutshaw v. Cutshaw*, 220 Va. 638, 261 S.E.2d 52 (1979) (failure to prepare order for entry by court); *Dorn v. Dorn*, 222 Va. 288, 279 S.E.2d 393 (1981) (correction of ambiguity as to whether the word "biweekly" inserted by attorney into incorporated stipulation agreement referred to time of payment or frequency of payment). Va. Code § 8.01-428B.

Child support orders and spousal support orders in which there are minor children whom the parties have a mutual duty to support must contain notice that payments may be withheld from earnings without filing an application. Va. Code § 20-60.3. Orders will normally contain specified contact information for the parties, with instructions to report changes within specified times, but if a protective order has been issued or the court finds reason to believe that a party is at risk of physical or emotional harm from the other party, only the name of the party at risk will be included.

Under Virginia law, a court lacks authority to relieve a delinquent spouse of the obligation to pay accrued installments of child support. The reasoning underlying this rule is that each installment becomes a vested property right the moment it falls due, and therefore is immune from modification. *Taylor v. Taylor*, 14 Va. App. 642, 418 S.E.2d 900 (1992).

Attorney's fees may be awarded to the custodial spouse who is forced to litigate delinquent child support or child custody. *Burke v. Burke*, 25 Va. Cir. 446 (Spotsylvania Co. 1991). Custody orders may be entered even when no divorce is pending. In such cases, orders pendente lite may be directed to any person with a legitimate interest who is a party. The custody and visitation orders in these non-divorce proceedings shall be made in accordance with Va. Code § 20-124 et seq. (1994). Pendente lite orders shall have no presumptive effect and shall not determine the ultimate outcome of the case.

When the custodial father gave the mother $1,000 per month so that she could maintain housing and visit the children, and the mother did not use the support for those purposes, the court was justified in obligating the mother to pay him $242.83 a month in child support. The amount she was to pay deviated from the guideline presumptions, but the variation was justified to provide the mother with funds to be used in her attempt to repair the relationship with that child. *Collins v. Alexander*, 1995 Va. App. LEXIS 768 (Oct. 24, 1995).

The trial court's discretion will not be interfered with unless some injustice has been done. *Gramelspacher v. Gramelspacher*, 204 Va. 839, 846, 134 S.E.2d 285, 290 (1964).

An appeal bond is required for an appeal from a juvenile and domestic relations district court order or judgment establishing support arrearages or suspending payment of support during the pendency of an appeal; and may be required for an appeal from a conviction for failure to support or from a finding of civil or criminal contempt involving a failure to support. Va. Code § 16.1-296(H). In *Mahoney v. Mahoney*, 34 Va. App. 63, 537 S.E.2d 626 (2000), a father's failure to post an appeal bond was fatal to his appeal challenging a juvenile court's jurisdiction to enter orders, even though the father specifically excluded the juvenile court's establishment of a support arrearage and its finding of contempt from his notice of appeal. The court of appeals reasoned that the substantive issue of support arrearages was logically related to, and inherent in, the father's challenge to the juvenile court's jurisdiction. In *Virginia Dep't of Soc. Servs., Div. of Child Support Enforcement, ex rel. May v. Walker*, 253 Va. 319, 485 S.E.2d 134 (1997), an unwed father, who was found by the district court to be in contempt for child support arrearages, had filed an appeal but had not posted an appeal bond. The court of appeals ruled that it had jurisdiction to hear the case even though the father had not posted the bond. The Virginia Supreme Court ruled that the court of appeals did not have jurisdiction to hear the appeal because failure to post an appeal bond is a fatal jurisdictional defect that cannot be cured. Consequently, the Supreme Court reinstated the district court's judgment that became final when the father failed to perfect his appeal. See also *Hutchins v. Carrillo*, 27 Va. App. 595, 500 S.E.2d 277 (1998) (when father's appeal regarding custody and child support was dismissed for untimely filing due to early closing of court clerk's office, father's due process rights were violated and he was entitled to have his appeal proceed as if appeal bond requirement had been timely satisfied).

Under Va. Code § 16.1-296(H), a judgment may have a component that requires an appeal bond (e.g., support arrearages) and a component that does not. In such a case, an appeal bond is required only for the portion of the judgment that requires a bond (e.g., the portion establishing support arrearages). *Avery v. Department of Soc. Servs., Div. of Child Support Enforcement ex rel. Clark*, 22 Va. App. 698, 472 S.E.2d 675 (1996). In *Sharma v. Sharma*, 46 Va. App. 584, 620 S.E.2d 553 (2005), a father filed a notice of appeal from a juvenile and domestic relations district court order that increased his child support and established a child support arrearage. A court clerk completed the appeal bond portion of the notice of appeal form, and set the appeal bond amount at "0." A circuit court subsequently dismissed the father's appeal on the basis that he had failed to post an appeal bond as required by Va. Code § 16.1-296(H). The court of appeals affirmed the dismissal, reasoning that (1) the circuit court lacked jurisdiction to hear the appeal because an appeal bond set at "0" did not comply with Va. Code § 16.1-296(H); (2) the child support and child support arrearages components of the court order could not be separated to permit the father to appeal only the child support component; and (3) an appeal bond set at "0" had a jurisdictional defect that could not be cured by increasing the bond amount pursuant to Va. Code § 16.1-109.

Child support payments received by a custodial parent, including arrears, are not subject to garnishment, and a depository in which child support payments have been deposited may not be required to determine the portion of deposits subject to garnishment. Va. Code § 20-108.1(G).

If a military parent is being deployed to active service where the parent cannot bring his or her child, a petition to establish custody, visitation, or support for the child must be identified at the time of filing by the deploying parent to ensure that the deploying parent has access to the child, and that reasonable support and other orders are in place for the protection of the parent-child relationship. Va. Code § 20-124.9(A). The court may conduct a hearing using a telephonic or electronic communication system if a deploying parent is reasonably unable to appear as a result of his deployment. Va. Code § 20-124.9(B).

See Margaret F. Brinig & F.H. Buckley, *The Market for Deadbeats*, 25 J. Legal Stud. 201 (1996) (discussing why some states might be more successful at collecting child support than others); David L. Chambers, *Fathers, the Welfare System, and the Virtues and Perils Of Child-Support Enforcement* 81 Va. L. Rev. 2575 (1995). See also Krause, *Child Support Reassessed: Limits of Private Responsibility and the Public Interest*, 1989 U. Ill. L. Rev. 367 (1989).

## § 22.02  Who May Bring Action?

Although child support is for the benefit of the child, in this context it arises from the jurisdiction over the parents' divorce action. In consequence, only a parent may bring an action for enforcement of a child support obligation. *McClaugherty v. McClaugherty*, 180 Va. 51, 21 S.E.2d 761 (1942). See also *Yarborough v. Yarborough*, 290 U.S. 202, 54 S. Ct. 181, 78 L. Ed. 269 (1933) (father satisfied obligation under divorce decree; daughter in another jurisdiction could not sue on own behalf for additional funds including college expenses); *Kelleher v. Kelleher*, 21 Ill. App. 3d 601, 316

N.E.2d 212 (1974) (after custodial wife died, grandmother could not bring action on child's behalf to collect arrearages under divorce decree).

In *Shelton v. An Infant*, 12 Va. App. 859, 406 S.E.2d 421 (1991), the court of appeals held that a child, suing through her next friend, was not barred from filing an action against her natural father. Her natural mother had previously been divorced from another man, with the court awarding "custody of the children of the parties" to the mother. The child is not a party to the divorce decree and therefore is not bound by a paternity determination in it unless formally made a party and represented by a guardian ad litem and given the right to litigate. See also *Commonwealth ex rel. Gray v. Johnson*, 7 Va. App. 614, 376 S.E.2d 787 (1989) (divorce decree asserted that there were no children born of the marriage).

However, a separation agreement that acknowledged that the husband was not the father of his wife's child, born during the marriage, waived her right to enforce express promises made prior to and after the birth to support the child as if it were his own. The agreement allowed the wife to remain in the marital residence for a year and gave her $6,500 to cover the birth expenses and care of the infant. *Mills v. Mills*, 36 Va. Cir. 351 (Fairfax Co. 1995).

When Dinkum was identified as the father of Gifford's child, the trial court should have ordered retroactive child support from the date she filed her petition. *Gifford v. Dunkum*, 1996 Va. App. LEXIS 114 (Feb. 13, 1996).

Once the child reaches the age of majority, the nature of the support obligation changes, and such child must bring an action independently of a parent to enforce the statutory obligation to support a necessitous child. *Harmatz v. Harmatz*, 457 A.2d 399 (D.C. 1983) (brain-damaged child; recovery sought by parent under common law duty to support necessitous adult child; parent found not automatically the most suitable guardian).

Arrearages may also be collected at this time by the parent if due under a divorce action.

See generally 6A Michie's Jurisprudence Divorce and Alimony § 57.

## § 22.03    Jurisdiction

Jurisdiction in child support actions depends wholly upon statute. *Jackson v. Jackson*, 211 Va. 718, 180 S.E.2d 500 (1971) (no jurisdiction to award custodial wife use of marital home as part of alimony and child support provisions); *Buchanan v. Buchanan*, 170 Va. 458, 197 S.E. 426 (1938) (no jurisdiction to award child support as part of habeas corpus proceeding). Further, the mother of a 16-year-old girl could not obtain child support from the father when, though their divorce was pending, they continued to live in the same house. *Patron v. Patron*, 40 Va. Cir. 379 (City of Richmond 1996). However, child support may be awarded following annulment of the parent's void marriage under the present Va. Code § 20-107.2, which allows support following "dissolution of marriage." *Henderson v. Henderson*, 187 Va. 121, 46 S.E.2d 10 (1948). The court found in this case that the legislature did not intend to make ineligibility to marry the ground upon which the support of children of the marriage should be denied. Courts may make child support or custody orders and decrees in suits for annulment or separate maintenance. Va. Code Ann. § 20-107.2 [amended 1996].

An agreement between the parents that one will not pay support, or as to a specific amount of payment, will not bind the court. *Featherstone v. Brooks*, 220 Va. 443, 258 S.E.2d 513 (1979). See also *Pilson v. Salvoni*, 79 F.2d 411, 65 App. D.C. 55 (1935); *Weaver v. Garrett*, 13 Md. App. 283, 282 A.2d 509 (1971).

Also, courts have equity jurisdiction to award child support when a case is originally filed as a divorce proceeding and the court has jurisdiction to determine child custody, even if the court does not end up exercising jurisdiction over the divorce itself. *Prizzia v. Prizzia*, 58 Va. App. 137, 707 S.E.2d 461 (2011).

Once a divorce judgment has been rendered, the court maintains continuing jurisdiction over the matter of child support throughout the child's minority. Because there had been no hearing on the matter nor due process provided to the wife prior to the judge's closing the file, the husband's duty to pay child support was not terminated by the judge's notation that the file was closed, even though thereafter the husband obtained a divorce decree not mentioning support. *Brown v. Brown*, 240 Va. 376, 397 S.E.2d 837 (1990).

The parties were divorced *a mensa et thoro* in Virginia in 1973, and their property settlement agreement was ratified and confirmed. At that time, the husband signed a notarized waiver of services providing in part that he waived "notice of any further proceedings held in this matter" and "consented to the validity of all proceedings held in this matter." The couple obtained an absolute divorce a year later. Both parties had substantial contact with Virginia, where their son was born and they lived for the last three years of their marriage. After the divorce, however, the wife moved to California and the husband to South Carolina. The wife filed a request to withhold wages through the California child support agency. The South Carolina family court order stayed implementation of a wage withholding petition, noting that there was a dispute concerning the existence of the arrearage. The wife, again through the California agency, sought to recover the alleged support arrearages through a Virginia action, and in 1992 registered the original Virginia order in California. By 1995, the Department of Child Support Enforcement filed a motion for judgment and interest in Fairfax County Circuit Court. The husband appeared specially to register the 1992 South Carolina family court order. On appeal from the circuit court, which had ruled that it was bound by the South Carolina order and dismissal for lack of jurisdiction, the Court of Appeals found that the South Carolina order was not one that could be registered under the provisions of the UIFSA. Virginia thus had continued jurisdiction and the right to enforce its own decrees under UIFSA even if all the parties were no longer residents. The Court of Appeals therefore remanded to determine what arrearages, if any, existed. *Division of Child Support Enforcement v. Richter*, 23 Va. App. 186, 475 S.E.2d 817 (1996).

Virginia is not a convenient forum when both the obligor and the obligee are residents of California as are the children whose support is in issue. *Roche v. Roche*, 45 Va. Cir. 525 (Fairfax Co. 1998). Based on considerations of judicial administration and convenience to the parties, even when Virginia has jurisdiction over the arrearage issue, it no longer has exclusive jurisdiction under the Uniform Interstate Family Support Act (Va. Code. Ann. § 20-88.39(C)).

When they separated in Virginia, the spouses in *Saleem v. Saleem*, 26 Va. App. 384, 494 S.E.2d 883 (1998), executed a property settlement specifying that child support obligations would "terminate whenever a child dies, reaches the age of 18 years, or otherwise becomes emancipated, whichever comes first." They later amended their agreement by including language that specified child support "shall be determined on the basis of the laws of the jurisdiction(s) in which the children are residing at that time." Custody of the daughter eventually was given to the wife, while the sons remained with their father. The trial court erred in allowing New York guidelines to control the child support amounts or emancipation rules for the children living in that state. The parties could not enlarge the jurisdiction of the Virginia courts nor depart from the public policy of Virginia's guidelines through their contract.

A decree for child support is an in personam action. *Gramelspacher v. Gramelspacher*, 204 Va. 839, 842, 134 S.E.2d 285, 288 (1964). The children need not be present or domiciled in the state for the decree to be effective. *Id.* at 843, 134 S.E.2d at 289. Because of the personal nature of the obligation, the requirement of a divorce action that one spouse be domiciled within the forum jurisdiction will not suffice for the financial obligation of child support. It will be necessary in such cases to acquire jurisdiction over the absent spouse either through personal service within Virginia, or through the Virginia long-arm statute, Va. Code § 8.01-328.1. However, the long-arm statute, by its plain language, does *not* reach persons who have conceived or fathered children outside Virginia, even if the persons later acknowledge parentage while in Virginia. *Bergaust v. Flaherty*, 57 Va. App. 423, 703 S.E.2d 248 (2011). In *Bergaust*, the long-arm statute, Va. Code § 8.01-328.1, was *not* satisfied in a child support action, and did *not* confer *in personam* jurisdiction over an expatriate father who was living in France, when the father's child had been conceived in France.

Acquisition of *in personam* jurisdiction by personal service within Virginia or by means of the Virginia long-arm statute will allow the action to be maintained in Virginia if the marital domicile had been within the state for six months next preceding the complaint or cause of action, so long as there was service over the absent spouse in the manner prescribed by the foreign state. In other words, service by publication will not suffice. The United States Supreme Court has indicated that the type of transitory contacts such as marriage in the state, presence there for a total of six days, and presence of the wife and children in the state would not constitute the type of "taking advantage of the privileges of doing business in the state" as to give jurisdiction for this personal obligation. *Kulko v. Superior Court of California*, 436 U.S. 84, 98 S. Ct. 1690, 56 L. Ed. 2d 132 (1978). Service under the long-arm statute, Va. Code §§ 8.01-328.1(8) and (9), must be made, must be made personally by a person authorized to make such service by § 8.01-320. Posting will not confer in personam jurisdiction in a child support action. *Prillaman v. Prillaman*, 29 Va. Cir. 441 (Warren Co. 1992). When a court obtains jurisdiction over a nonresident under the long-arm statute, such service shall have the same effect as service on the nonresident within Virginia. Va. Code § 8.01-320. This statute specifically includes divorce and annulment cases.

No personal service was given to the husband when a summons was "posted" on his door rather than mailed to him as provided by statute. The default judgment entered against him for support was therefore invalid. *Garrity v. Virginia Dep't of Social Services*, 11 Va. App. 39, 396 S.E.2d 150 (1990).

Statutes enacted in 1989 regarding the experimental family courts were repealed in 1999, including Va. Code §§ 16.1-296.1, 20-96.1, and 20-96.2. There are no longer any such courts, and all appeals from such courts have been completed.

For any issue arising out of suits for divorce, annulment or affirmation of marriage, separate maintenance, and other child custody, support, and visitation cases, the judge shall consider whether to refer the parties to mediation, and may do so sua sponte or on motion of one of the parties. Upon referral, the parties must attend one evaluation session during which they and the mediator assess the case and decide whether to continue with mediation or with adjudication. Further participation in the mediation shall be by consent of all parties, and attorneys for either may be present during mediation. Va. Code § 16.1-272.1. When the parties are referred to mediation, the court shall set a return date. The parties shall notify the court in writing if the dispute is resolved prior to this return date. The court may, in its discretion, incorporate any mediated agreement into the terms of its final decree. Only if such an order is entered will the terms of the voluntary settlement agreement affect any outstanding court order.

In 2013, Va. Code §§ 8.01-576.10 and 8.01-581.22 were amended to ensure the confidentiality of child support guideline worksheets prepared during mediation. The child support guideline worksheets may not be introduced in court if the parties were unable to reach a settlement agreement. However, if the parties settle child support in mediation then the requirements for submitting and attaching the agreement to the court's order are unchanged. The legislation was needed to close a loophole in the prior language that appeared to allow litigants to use child support guideline worksheets against one another in court even though the worksheets were prepared for the purpose of negotiation.

The Division of Child Support Enforcement had no standing in a child support case where the parties settled between themselves the issue of child support and the custodial parent was not receiving public assistance, even though the settlement was for less than the statutory guideline amount. *Kuser v. Kuser*, 40 Va. Cir. 217 (Warren Co. 1996). In a child support proceeding, service by posting at the last known address of the respondent must be accompanied by service by mail as well, pursuant to Va. Code § 8.01-296(20)(b). *Martin v. McGee*, 46 Va. Cir. 87 (Fairfax Co. 1998).

An acknowledgment of the relationship between a child and a man may be established by a subsequent voluntary written statement made under oath. This may be rescinded by either within 60 days of its signing or within the time period in an administrative or judicial proceeding relating to the child.

If a juvenile and domestic relations district court has entered a child or spousal support order, its jurisdiction ceases and its orders become inoperative upon entry of a decree that provides for child or spousal support in a suit for divorce instituted in any circuit court having jurisdiction. *Ipsen v. Moxley*, 49 Va. App. 555, 642 S.E.2d 798 (2007); Va. Code § 20-79. However, the circuit court may transfer enforcement of divorce decrees, including *pendente lite* orders, to the juvenile and domestic relations district court. Va. Code § 20-79(c). An appeal from a juvenile and domestic relations court lies in

The wife appealed the family court's order reducing the husband's child support payment, claiming that the family court had no jurisdiction to make the reduction. The circuit court ruled in her favor. The husband in *Kiss v. McDonald*, 1993 Va. App. LEXIS 196 (June 22, 1996), unsuccessfully claimed that he should not be found in arrears for paying only the abated amount. The court of appeals reasoned that the family court's order was ineffective, so the circuit court had no authority to make any changes on past-due installments under Va. Code § 20-108. The circuit court could have made changes had there been a pending petition in a court with jurisdiction. In another appeal from the juvenile court, the father claimed the circuit court lacked jurisdiction to hear the matter because the child Christopher's maternal grandparents had been named his guardians, replacing the mother. The court found that the mother was a proper party to the litigation since when the father filed his petition, she was the custodial parent. *Evans v. Division of Child Support Enforcement ex rel. Light*, 1996 Va. App. LEXIS 93 (Feb. 6, 1996).

According to legislation adopted in 1995, foreign orders under the Uniform Interstate Enforcement of Support Act should be registered in the juvenile and domestic relations district court, not the circuit court. Va. Code § 20-88.32.

An alternative way of bringing an action is through the Uniform Reciprocal Enforcement of Support Act, Va. Code § 20-88.12 et seq. This allows a petition to be filed in Virginia establishing the duty to support and the need therefor. The state where the absent spouse resides (responding state) allows the spouse to contest the duty to support and the ability to make payments. Once a valid order is obtained, either through a divorce action or through URESA, it will be enforced in Virginia exactly as is a Virginia order. *Scott v. Sylvester*, 220 Va. 182, 185, 257 S.E.2d 774, 776 (1979). URESA is remedial in nature and should be liberally construed so that its purpose of providing support for dependent children is achieved. *Scott v. Sylvester*, 220 Va. at 185, 257 S.E.2d at 776. Thus a foreign order for child support will be given comity and enforced "with the same force and effect as if it had been entered in Virginia." *Id.* (quoting from *Alig v. Alig*, 220 Va. 80, 84, 255 S.E.2d 494, 497 (1979)). Enforcement will proceed in Virginia even though the defendant was only present in the state for a portion of the time during which the arrearage accrued. Va. Code § 20-88.30:6(1); *Scott v. Sylvester*, 220 Va. at 187, 257 S.E.2d at 777. However, Virginia does not obtain in personam jurisdiction over a defendant when the Virginia resident registers a foreign decree under RURESA and serves the defendant in another state. *Stephens v. Stephens*, 229 Va. 610, 331 S.E.2d 484 (1985) (spousal support). This method will be supplanted by the UIFSA, discussed in § 22.20.

The court does not possess the power to relieve an obligor parent of accrued payments of support money. *Cofer v. Cofer*, 205 Va. 834, 838, 140 S.E.2d 663, 666 (1965). This means that arrearages will be final judgments that must be given full faith and credit by other states. Cf. *Griffin v. Griffin*, 327 U.S. 220, 66 S. Ct. 556, 90 L. Ed. 635 (1946).

The wife obtained a pendente lite unitary award for spousal and child support that was to continue until further order of the court, and the husband later obtained a final divorce. The decree reserved custody, support, and property division for later decision. The husband died eight years later, and his estate was subject to a lien for unpaid payments under the temporary support order. *Duke v. Duke*, 239 Va. 501, 391 S.E.2d 77 (1990).

Child support orders and spousal support orders in which there are minor children whom the parties have a mutual duty to support must contain notice that payments may be withheld from earnings without filing an application. Va. Code § 20-60.3. Orders will normally contain specified contact information for the parties, with instructions to report changes within specified times, but if a protective order has been issued or the court finds reason to believe that a party is at risk of physical or emotional harm from the other party, only the name of the party at risk will be included.

## § 22.04  Proving Parentage

A divorcing spouse need only make payments for the support of his or her own children. Some recent cases have found that a stepparent assumed the responsibility of providing for children of the former spouse, and therefore should be estopped from asserting parenthood as a ground for avoiding such payments after the spouses separate. See, e.g., *In re Marriage of Johnson*, 88 Cal. App. 3d 848, 152 Cal. Rptr. 121 (1979). The duty of support would turn upon whether the spouses had acted in loco parentis during the marriage.

If the parentage of the child is in question, the earlier discussion in Chapters 3 and 16 should be consulted. Where the parents were married at the time of the child's likely conception or birth, the very strong presumption of legitimacy applies. See, e.g., *Landes v. Landes*, 1 N.Y.2d 358, 153 N.Y.S.2d 14, 135 N.E.2d 562 (1956). Whenever parentage of any child is in doubt, the court may require the alleged father, mother, and child to submit to blood grouping tests. The court may order the costs to be borne by the person requesting such tests, unless indigent, and the results of such blood grouping tests shall be admitted in evidence when contained in a written report prepared and sworn to by a duly licensed physician. Blood grouping tests must be ordered during paternity proceedings where child support is in issue under revised Va. Code § 20-49.3.

A child was not barred by res judicata by a previous finding against his mother in a paternity action, since the two were not in privity, or so identified in interest that she represented his legal rights, and the child was not formally named as a party, represented by a guardian ad litem nor given an adequate opportunity to litigate the issue. *Commonwealth ex rel. Gray v. Johnson*, 7 Va. App. 614, 376 S.E.2d 787 (1989). See also *Shelton v. An Infant*, 12 Va. App. 859, 406 S.E.2d 421 (1991) (child not barred by finding that she was "child of the parties" in divorce action between her natural mother and another man). On the other hand, a prior finding that a man was the father of a child in a divorce proceeding acts to collaterally estop him from establishing through conclusive blood testing that he was not the biological parent. *Slagle v. Slagle*, 11 Va. App. 341, 398 S.E.2d 346 (App. 1990). Similarly, in *Aviles v. Aviles*, 14 Va. App. 360, 416 S.E.2d 716 (1992), the husband filed for divorce, alleging that the child in question was born of the marriage. He testified that he had heard rumors both before and during the divorce proceedings that he might not be the child's father, but did not inform his attorney of this issue. Further, he treated the child as his own and supported the child during the marriage. The Virginia Supreme Court held that the trial court did not err in ruling both that the husband had not proved by clear and convincing evidence that the wife committed fraud on the court and that the evidence did not justify terminating the husband's child support obligation. See also *McFadden v. McFadden*, 1995 Va. App. LEXIS 878 (Dec. 5, 1995); *Dunnaville v. Virginia Dep't of Social Servs., Div. of Child Support Enforcement ex rel. Comptroller of Virginia*, 1995 Va. App. LEXIS 222 (Mar. 7, 1995); *Hartman v. Hartman*, 33 Va. Cir. 373 (Fairfax Co. 1994).

However, when the husband had no knowledge prior to the final decree that he was not the father of Natalie, he was not bound, *Batrouny v. Batrouny*, 13 Va. App. 441, 412 S.E.2d 721 (1991), so that the final decree would be corrected to reflect that one child, Ashley, was born to the parties. See also *Schalton v. Schalton*, 31 Va. Cir. 47 (Fairfax Co. 1993). However, a separation agreement that acknowledged that the husband was not the father of his wife's child, born during the marriage, waived her right to enforce express promises made prior to and after the birth to support the child as if it were his own. The agreement allowed the wife to remain in the marital residence for a year and have $6,500 to cover the birth expenses and care of the infant. *Mills v. Mills*, 36 Va. Cir. 351 (Fairfax Co. 1995). Compare

*Rose v. Rose*, 1993 Va. App. LEXIS 375 (Aug. 24, 1993) (husband knew he was not the father of the child before entry of the final decree, and agreed to make child support payments anyway); and *Bromley v. Bromley*, 30 Va. Cir. 83 (Fairfax Co. 1993) (after 21 days expired, decree could not be modified to change the statement of child's parentage. However, when another man admitted paternity and DNA testing revealed a 99.3% probability of his parentage, there was a change in circumstances warranting elimination of the husband's duty to pay child support.).

Under amended Va. Code § 20-61.1, fathers between the ages of fourteen and sixteen who are represented by a guardian ad litem may testify and may be required to provide for support and maintenance just as they would be if adult.

### § 22.05     Custody as Relieving Duty

A custodial spouse may fulfill the duty of support by providing shelter and day-to-day care for the child. See, e.g., *Suire v. Miller*, 363 So. 2d 945 (La. App. 1978). Thus the mother, who left her paid employment to care for the parties' son before and after school (even on days when the father had custody under their shared custody arrangement) was not voluntarily underemployed. The son had once threatened to jump from a second-story window when he received a B on his report card, and his therapist recommended that the mother provide after-school care. *Hart v. Hodson*, 48 Va. Cir. 63 (Loudoun Co. 1999). (adult necessitous child). If the custodial spouse is a person of means, however, the duty will extend to the provision of necessaries or even luxuries for the child. The noncustodial parent should also bear part of the burden to the extent of that spouse's ability.

Under equitable and limited circumstances, a court may allow a party credit for nonconforming child support payments, provided that the payments substantially satisfy the purpose and function of the support award in the court decree, and that the allowance of credit does not vary the support award. *Department of Soc. Servs., Div. of Child Support Enforcement ex rel. Comptroller of Virginia v. Skeens*, 18 Va. App. 154, 158, 442 S.E.2d 432, 434–435 (1994). Generally, credit will not be given for nonconforming payments unless there is (1) an agreement by the parties modifying the terms or method of payment, and (2) there is no adverse effect on the support award. If an agreement establishes or modifies the support obligation itself, credit will not be given. *Wilderman v. Wilderman*, 25 Va. App. 500, 506, 489 S.E.2d 701, 705 (1997). However, as one limited exception to the rule, parties may agree to eliminate a noncustodial parent's child support obligation by transferring full custody of a child to the obligor parent. See *Acree v. Acree*, 2 Va. App. 151, 152, 342 S.E.2d 68, 69 (1986). In *Acree*, the

Court of Appeals held that if the custodial parent has by his or her own volition entered into an *Acree v. Acree*, 2 Va. App. 151, 342 S.E.2d 68 (1986). See also *Lipscomb v. Lipscomb*, 18 Va. Cir. 244 (Chesterfield Co. 1989) (relinquishment for two years and three months).

However, *Acree's* holding applies only to cases in which the parent receiving child support has relinquished physical custody entirely to the other parent. *Gallagher v. Gallagher*, 35 Va. App. 470, 546 S.E.2d 222 (2001). Thus, in *Gallagher*, when the parents entered mediation and renegotiated a settlement agreement incorporated into their divorce decree to reduce the father's child support payments to reflect custodial time that had been increased to fifty-fifty joint custody, the renegotiated agreement was unenforceable absent court approval, and the father was liable for child support arrearages. The *Gallagher* court concluded that to permit parties to modify a decree when there was only a partial change in custody would invite "continuous trouble and turmoil," because a determination of whether an agreed-upon reduction in support payments properly corresponded to a greater burden assumed as a result of increased custodial time would not be easily susceptible of proof.

The *Acree/Gallagher* rule was invoked in a case with unusual facts, *Miederhoff v. Miederhoff*, 38 Va. App. 366, 564 S.E.2d 156 (2002), to permit a trial court to allow a party credit for nonconforming child support payments as an offset against child support arrearages. In *Miederhoff*, a minor child's parents agreed that the mother would not seek child support arrearages if the father would pay the child's college expenses. After the child reached the age of majority and the father's child support obligation ceased, and after the father had paid $11,611 in college expenses, the mother filed a claim for $16,650 in unpaid child support. The father was allowed an offset of $11,611 against the $16,650 in support arrearages, because (1) the parties had an agreement, (2) the child's reaching the age of majority amounted to a complete change of custody, (3) the parties' agreement did not alter the child support provision of the custody decree, in that the accrued arrearages were enforced in full, and (4) the parties' agreement merely altered the method of payment, by authorizing payment to the college instead of to the mother.

The *Acree/Gallagher* rule was ruled inapplicable to another case, *Jones v. Davis*, 43 Va. App. 9, 595 S.E.2d 501 (2004). In *Jones*, a father took *de facto* custody of a child at a mother's request. Nevertheless, the parents disputed custody until the father obtained a custody modification order, and they could not agree on child support. After the father unilaterally adjusted his child support, arrearages accrued. Eventually, a trial court awarded the father credits for nonconforming support supplied in-kind to his child. However, although the father's custody order substituted for a custody agreement between the parents, the absence of any child support agreement was fatal to the father's claim for credits against child support arrearages. The trial court erred in allowing the credits when no agreement as to child support existed between the parties and no petition for modification of support was pending during the period for which the credits were awarded.

If the custodial parent refuses to abide by a court decree, such as a visitation provision, the court may order payment of child support contingent upon the posting of a bond to guarantee compliance. *Kern v. Lindsey*, 182 Va. 775, 30 S.E.2d 707 (1944). Refusal also may be grounds for a change in custody. Va. Code § 20-108. However, parents may not agree between themselves that one should be relieved of paying support for a minor child. *Kelley v. Kelley*, 248 Va. 295, 449 S.E.2d 55 (1994) (wife agreed to hold husband harmless for child support in exchange for his share of marital home; this did not preclude later action for child support). See also *Department of Social Servs., Div. of Child Support Enforcement ex rel. Sparks v. Mavis*, 1995 Va. App. LEXIS 82 (Jan. 31, 1995).

An award of sole legal custody to one parent does not relieve the other parent of responsibility for supporting the children. In sole legal custody cases, the noncustodial parent's child support obligation is determined under the "sole custody support" provision of Va. Code § 20-108.2(G)(1). *Barrett v. Va. State Bar ex rel. Second Dist. Comm.*, 277 Va. 412, 675 S.E.2d 827 (2009).

In *Vissicchio v. Vissicchio*, 27 Va. App. 240, 498 S.E.2d 425 (1998), the trial court did not err in strictly calculating child support according to guidelines and determining the child's primary physical custody would be with the mother, when the father lived in New York and was granted visitation of one-fourth of the child's time, plus alternating holidays.

## § 22.06   Split Custody, Shared Custody, or Multiple Custody Arrangements

In 2018, Va. Code § 20-108.2 was amended, and in addition to split custody and shared custody, which had already been included in the statue, subsections (G)(4)–(6) were included to address multiple custody arrangements.

Shared custody may relieve a portion of the child support necessary, according to Va. Code § 20-108.2. For an application of this principle, see *Ewing v. Ewing*, 1995 Va. App. LEXIS 192 (Feb. 28, 1995), where a husband argued unsuccessfully that partial days (so long as more than half days) could be counted toward meeting the 110-day requirement of the statute; see also *Steinberg v. Steinberg*, 1996 Va. App. LEXIS 57 (Jan. 30, 1996); *Laverty v. Laverty*, 1995 Va. App. LEXIS 750 (Oct. 17, 1995) (same).

The shared custody formula of Va. Code § 20-108.2(G)(1)(3) requires that the non-primary custodial parent has "more than 90 days of the year." When a determination has been made that a party has custody or visitation for more than 90 days of the year, a shared custody child support obligation will be ordered. For purposes of calculating shared custody support, a "day" means 24 hours. Where the parent who has fewer overnight periods during the year has an overnight period with the child, but has physical custody of the shared child for less than 24 hours during such an overnight period, there is a presumption that each parent shall be allocated one-half of a day of custody.

There are alternative bases for determining child support obligations. Where a shared custody child support calculation shall be made, the presumptive support to be paid shall be the shared custody support amount. If a party affirmatively shows, however, that the sole custody support amount is less than the shared custody support amount, the lesser amount shall be the support to be paid. Furthermore, the multiplier used in the shared custody child support calculation was changed from 1.25 to 1.4 to reduce the "cliff effect" and allow a more gradual decrease in child support for any given number of days of visitation or custody.

Although the parties' separation agreement provided for joint legal and physical custody of the children, in fact it also provided for "visitation" by the husband one day every weekend, on one day each week, and for six weeks in the summer. The final divorce decree did not include language of the agreement which had limited the husband's obligation to the period in which the children were in the wife's custody, but just awarded her a flat amount per month. The Court of Appeals agreed with the trial court's interpretation of the final decree, finding that the husband was to pay child support every month without interruption. The court found also that he could not unilaterally reduce his support payments without supplying the wife "independently verifiable evidence that his income had been reduced" to justify modification according to the agreement. *Schlenk v. Schlenk*, 1996 Va. App. LEXIS 813 (Dec. 10, 1996).

In cases involving split custody, the amount of child support paid shall be the difference between the amounts owed by each parent as a noncustodial parent with the noncustodial parent owing the larger amount paying the difference to the other parent. In shared custody cases, the Virginia Code provides that the amount of child support to be paid is the difference between the amounts owed by each parent to the other parent. The parent owing the larger amount is to pay the difference to the other, not to the child. *Ingram v. Snarr-Ingram*, 1996 Va. App. LEXIS 373 (May 21, 1996). Split custody shall be limited to those situations where each parent has physical custody of a child or children born of the parents, born of either parent and adopted by the other, or adopted by both parents. For purposes of calculating a child support obligation in such cases, a separate family unit exists for each parent, and the amount of child support is based upon the number of such children that reside with the parent. The parent is considered a noncustodial parent to the children in the other parent's family unit. Va. Code § 20-108.2(G)(2).

The 2018 amendments addressed multiple custodial arrangements as more fully set forth in Va. Code §§ 20-108.2(G)(4), (5) and (6). Va. Code § 20-108.2(G)(4), referred to as "Multiple shared custody support," applies where the parties have two or more children, the parties exercise a shared custody schedule, but not all of the children follow the same arrangement. Va. Code § 20-108.2(G)(5), referred to as "Sole and shared custody support," applies where the parties have two or more children, one or more of the children are subject to the sole custody guideline, and one or more of the children are subject to the shared custody guideline. Lastly, Va. Code § 20-108.2(G)(6), referred to as "Split and shared custody support," applies where the parties have three or more children, at least two are subject to the sole custody guideline split custody guideline, and shared custody guideline is used for the other child(ren). The application of these guidelines is highly technical and will require the use of multiple sheets when addressing these complex situations.

The parents cannot contract away their duties to pay child support. However, when they agreed to amend the divorce decree, which had given the mother sole custody and provided for child support, so that the father became the physical custodian, he was entitled to a credit for child support payments made after he assumed custody. *Reinaldo v. Reinaldo*, 40 Va. Cir. 340 (Loudoun Co. 1996).

When they separated in Virginia, the spouses in *Saleem v. Saleem*, 26 Va. App. 384, 494 S.E.2d 883 (1998), executed a property settlement specifying that child support obligations would "terminate whenever a child dies, reaches the age of 18 years, or otherwise becomes emancipated, whichever comes first." They later amended their agreement by including language that specified child support "shall be determined on the basis of the laws of the jurisdiction(s) in which the children are residing at that time." Custody of the daughter eventually was given to the wife, while the sons remained with their father. The trial court erred in allowing New York guidelines to control the child support amounts or emancipation rules for the children living in that state. The parties could not by their contract enlarge the Virginia court's jurisdiction or depart from the public policy reflected in the guidelines of Va. Code § 20-108.2.

### § 22.07    Amount Necessary

Va. Code § 20-108.1 prohibits the courts from utilizing a mathematical formula for computing child support as the sole determinative basis for an award and encourages a complete hearing, stating that any such formula may only be used as a guideline. In 1988, guidelines were added to § 20-108.2. These include a basic support obligation involving gross income subject to reasonable business expenses. To this basic amount is added any extraordinary medical and dental expenses and any child-care costs incurred on behalf of the child or children due to employment. In 2014, the Legislature updated the child support guidelines. Va. Code § 20.108.2(B). The 2014 amendments provide that if the gross income of the obligor is equal to or less than 150 percent of the federal poverty level promulgated by the U.S. Department of Health and Human Services from time to time, then the court, upon hearing evidence that there is no ability to pay the presumptive statutory minimum, may set an obligation below the presumptive statutory minimum provided doing so does not create or reduce a support obligation to an amount which seriously impairs the custodial parent's ability to maintain minimal adequate housing and provide other basic necessities for the child. The statutory child support guideline set forth at Va. Code § 20-108.2 establishes the presumptively correct amount of child support, but at every child support hearing the court is required to "consider all evidence presented relevant to any issues joined in that proceeding" and render a decision "upon the evidence relevant to each individual case." Va. Code § 20-108.1. To rebut the presumption, the court must make written findings in the order that the application of the guidelines would be unjust or inappropriate in a particular case as determined by relevant evidence pertaining to the factors set forth in Va. Code § 20-108.2.

This total child support obligation is to be divided between the parents in the same proportion as their gross incomes bear to their combined gross income.

In 2013, the Legislature amended Va. Code § 20-108.1 to allow the court to consider the reasonableness of a parent's voluntary unemployment or underemployment when the parent decides to attend and complete an educational or vocational program that is likely to maintain or increase the parent's earning potential. This does not prevent the court from imputing income to the parent while attending such a program, but it is one of the relevant factors the court may consider in determining child support. In addition, the new legislation allows the court to consider child care costs associated with the parent's participation in an educational or vocational program. Previously, courts could only consider work-related child care costs in computing child support.

In determining these amounts, gross income of the obligor shall not include amounts actually paid for spousal support under a preexisting order or written agreement. Va. Code § 108.1(C). The Circuit Court for the City of Charlottesville has held that child support may be increased based upon the percent increase in income when the parties' combined gross income exceeds the statutory guidelines. *May v. May*, 24 Va. Cir. 407 (City of Charlottesville 1991) (husband unemployed but has a net worth in excess of $3,000,000; income increased from $85,000 in 1984 to $154,000 in 1990). This decision is affected by recent additions to § 20-108.2(B), which provide for much lower percentage increases for gross monthly incomes exceeding those in the guideline tables. However, the guidelines may be exceeded if the parties have a written property settlement agreement that specifies the way the amounts will be modified. *Scott v. Scott*, 12 Va. App. 1245, 408 S.E.2d 579 (1991); *Watkinson v. Henley*, 13 Va. App. 151, 409 S.E.2d 470 (1991) (amount agreed to in consent decree exceeded guidelines). See also *Jordan v. Jordan*, 23 Va. Cir. 470 (Fairfax Co. 1991). In *Watkinson*, the court of appeals held that where parents have agreed upon an amount, or agreed upon other provisions, for the support and maintenance of a child, the trial court must consider the provisions of the agreement that relate to the factors in Code §§ 20-107.2 and 20-108.1. Further, if the trial court finds that the presumptive amount is unjust or inappropriate because the provisions in a separation agreement serve the best interest of the child, the court may vary from the guidelines by ordering that support be paid in an amount equal to the benefits provided for in the contract. *Id.* at 159, 409 S.E.2d at 480–81. However, the trial court may not depart from the statutory guidelines because "use of the guidelines would seriously impair [wife's] ability to maintain minimal adequate housing and provide other basic necessities for the child." *Pharo v. Pharo*, 19 Va. App. 236, 450 S.E.2d 183 (1994). *Compare Looney v. Looney*, 32 Va. App. 134, 526 S.E.2d 777 (2000) (amount in guidelines was $548, but parents' agreement on $200 per month upheld).

In *Milligan v. Milligan*, 12 Va. App. 982, 407 S.E.2d 702 (1991), the court of appeals held that if the parties' income changes so that the amount awarded is no longer within the statutory guidelines, the material or substantial change of circumstance rule is no longer required as a condition precedent to obtaining a modification of child support.

Amendments to Va. Code § 20-108.2 made in 1991 include the addition of new factors to be considered in assessing the obligation and ability to pay child support. These are the age, physical, and mental condition of the child or children, including extraordinary medical or dental expenses, and child-care expenses; independent financial resources of the child or children; the standard of living for the family established during the marriage; the earning capacity, obligations and needs, and financial resources of each parent; education and training of the parties and the ability and opportunity of the parties to secure such education or training; contributions, monetary and nonmonetary, of each party to the family's well-being; provisions made with regard to the marital property; tax consequences to the parties regarding claims for dependent children and child care; and such other factors including tax consequences to each party, as are necessary to consider the equities for the parents and children. Another consideration is a written agreement between the parties that includes an amount for child support. Va. Code § 20-108.1(B)(16).

The court's authority to award child support under Title 20, Title 16.1, or Title 63.2 includes the power to order either party or both parties to provide health care coverage or cash medical support for dependent children if reasonable under all the circumstances. Va. Code § 20-108.1(C). The extra costs of health care coverage and dental coverage for the children that are actually being paid by either a parent or a parent's spouse must be added to the basic child support obligation, but only to the extent that the costs are directly allocable to the children and are beyond the costs of the coverage the parent or parent's spouse would otherwise have. Va. Code § 20-108.2(E). In each support order, the court must include an order for health care coverage if available at reasonable cost. Va. Code § 20-60.3(8). See, e.g., *Albert v. Albert*, 38 Va. App. 284, 563 S.E.2d 389 (2002) (father was obligated to reimburse mother for children's medical bills, despite mother's failure to notify him of appointments and to use only doctors listed by his insurance provider).

The starting point in determining the monthly child support obligation is the amount as computed by the schedule found in Va. Code § 20-108.2(B). This amount is determined according to a schedule that varies according to the combined gross income of the parents and the number of children involved. No additions or subtractions from the parents' gross income, as defined in Va. Code § 20-108.2(C), even if otherwise valid considerations, may be made before this figure is determined. However, after determining the presumptive amount of support according to the schedule, the amount may be adjusted in accordance with the factors found in Va. Code §§ 20-108.2 and 20-108.1. *Richardson v. Richardson*, 12 Va. App. 18, 401 S.E.2d 894 (1991).

The child support amount must be based on the parents' actual gross income. See, e.g., *West v. West*, 53 Va. App. 125, 669 S.E.2d 390 (2008) (court's failure to recalculate child support obligations using father's increased annual income constituted reversible error). In determining the statutory presumptively correct amount of child support, the statute requires that the court use each party's current income. *Tidwell v. Late*, 67 Va. App. 668, 679–80 (2017). However, after calculating the guideline child support, the trial court could consider whether a deviation from the guideline was warranted based on a party's earning capacity. *Id.* at 680. Only actual income, rather than imputed income, may be used in determining the presumptive child support amount. Imputed income is a factor which may be used to rebut the presumptive amount after the presumptive amount is determined. *Farley v. Liskey*, 12 Va. App. 1, 401 S.E.2d 897 (1991). A parent who is already paying child support or spousal support is entitled to an appropriate deduction from actual gross income when the presumptive amount is determined. See Va. Code § 20-108.2(C). Otherwise, a parent's actual monetary support for other children, family members, or former family members is a factor which may be used to rebut the presumptive amount after the presumptive amount is determined. *Farley v. Liskey*, 12 Va. App. 1, 401 S.E.2d 897 (1991); see Va. Code § 20-108.1(B). The presumptive child support amount must be determined before the amount of child support contained in a property settlement agreement may be awarded. *Watson v. Watson*, 17 Va. App. 249, 436 S.E.2d 193 (1993).

Deviations from the presumptive support amount must be supported by written findings which state why the application of the guidelines in the particular case would be unjust or inappropriate. *Richardson v. Richardson*, 12 Va. App. 18, 21, 401 S.E.2d 894 (1991); see Va. Code § 20-108.2(A). The written findings must (1) state the amount of support that would have been required under the guidelines, (2) give a justification of why the order varies from the guidelines, and (3) be determined by relevant evidence pertaining to various enumerated statutory factors that affect the child support obligation, each parent's ability to provide child support, and the child's best interests. Va. Code § 20-108.1(B). See *Mayers v. Mayers*, 15 Va. App. 587, 425 S.E.2d 808 (1993) (court's failure to make written findings to justify deviation from guidelines constituted reversible error, because review of court's support determination and alleged deduction for wife's expenses incurred during visitation was impossible); *Herring v. Herring*, 33 Va. App.

281, 532 S.E.2d 923 (2000) (court's deviation from guidelines without first calculating and stating presumptive amount of support constituted reversible error, because support order that does not expressly determine presumptive amount or fully explain reasons for deviation from that amount does not provide adequate basis for future support modifications); *Princiotto v. Gorrell*, 42 Va. App. 253, 590 S.E.2d 626 (2004) (short paragraph in court order satisfied requirement for written findings by providing sufficient detail and exactness to allow for appellate review).

Written findings are required to justify an increase in child support to an amount less than the guideline support amount. See *Richardson v. Richardson*, 12 Va. App. 18, 21, 401 S.E.2d 894 (1991). Similarly, written findings are required to justify a decrease in child support to an amount less than the guideline support amount. See *Alexander v. Alexander*, 12 Va. App. 691, 406 S.E.2d 666 (1991). When no material change in circumstances has occurred after a modification hearing that has considered a child support award that deviates from the support guidelines, so that a court at a subsequent hearing cannot modify the nonconforming award, the court at the subsequent hearing is not required to make written findings explaining the nonconforming award. *Hiner v. Hadeed*, 15 Va. App. 575, 425 S.E.2d 811 (1993).

New shared custody guidelines adopted in July 1992 justify a modification proceeding when the child support amount under the new guidelines varies significantly from the child support amount determined under the earlier guidelines. *Slonka v. Pennline*, 17 Va. App. 662, 440 S.E.2d 423 (1994). Amended guidelines, effective in July 1995, that limit the incremental amount for monthly gross incomes over $50,000 to one percent, constitute a material change in circumstances requiring that deviation from the presumptive amount be justified with a written explanation. *Cooke v. Cooke*, 23 Va. App. 60, 474 S.E.2d 159 (1996).

It is erroneous to reduce the child support owed by normal expenses the noncustodial parent incurs in visiting the child, or by the amount the noncustodial parent spends during visitation, unless the custodial spouse's expenses are reduced thereby. *Baumgartner v. Moore*, 14 Va. App. 696, 419 S.E.2d 291 (1992).

It is erroneous to reduce the child support owed by normal expenses the noncustodial parent incurs in visiting the child, or by the amount the noncustodial parent spends during visitation, unless the custodial spouse's expenses are reduced thereby. *Baumgartner v. Moore*, 14 Va. App. 696, 419 S.E.2d 291 (1992).

The parent has the duty to support the child in accordance with this obligor's fortune and station in life, and not only with the child's needs. This clearly includes education for the children. *Conway v. Conway*, 10 Va. App. 653, 395 S.E.2d 464 (1990) A father could be asked to pay private school tuition when the child's expenses were calculated to determine child support. *Newland v. Newland*, 1997 Va. App. LEXIS 218 (Apr. 8, 1997). The father had not objected to the wife's choice of schools and had attended events at the school since the child's enrollment there. A noncustodial parent may not voluntarily stay home in order to care for the child or children of a second marriage, and therefore avoid a child support obligation. *Horn v. Horn*, 19 Va. Cir. 73 (Henrico Co. 1989).

Even though the child was only two years old, alimony and child support payments of $1,200 monthly were not sufficient where the husband's business earned him $100,000 per year. *Ingram v. Ingram*, 217 Va. 27, 225 S.E.2d 362 (1976).

*Bennett v. Division of Child Support Enforcement*, 22 Va. App. 684, 472 S.E.2d 668 (1996), involved a husband's appeal from the trial court's refusal to modify his monthly support obligation. He claimed, unsuccessfully, that her circumstances had changed because the couple's severely disabled child was now in school each weekday and that his former wife was now "home schooling" the two oldest children. He asked that the trial court impute income to her, and that it include in her income government housing and disability benefits she received. The Court of Appeals agreed with the trial court's decision not to impute income to her because she needed to remain available to "intervene" in the disabled child's classroom or take him home. Once the child came home from school, she had to devote her full time and attention to caring for him. Although both parents bear the responsibility of supporting their dependent children, and the mother could not absolve herself of this obligation by voluntarily home schooling the children, income need not be imputed when she was caring for the profoundly disabled child as well. Moreover, she had not worked for over ten years and no evidence was introduced regarding the availability of jobs for her or the amount of income she could earn. See also *Rinaldi v. Dumsick*, 32 Va. App. 330, 528 S.E.2d 134 (2000) (SSI benefits received by custodial parent do not affect noncustodial parent's child support obligation, but SSI benefits received by adult disabled child may be considered as child's independent financial resources in determining amount of continuing support award).

Va. Code § 20-108.2(B), as amended in 2000 and 2008, provides exemptions from the presumptive minimum monthly child support amount of $65 for parents who are unable to pay child support because they lack assets and are (1) institutionalized in a psychiatric facility, (2) imprisoned for life with no chance of parole, (3) medically verified to be totally and permanently disabled with no evidence of potential for paying child support, or (4) otherwise involuntarily unable to produce income.

Va. Code § 20-108.2(C), as amended in 2001, adjusts the child or spousal support guideline to provide that (1) spousal support received is included in gross income and spousal support *paid* is deducted from gross income, (2) child support paid for a party's other children who are not the subject of the current proceeding is deducted from the party's gross income, (3) any adjustment to gross income under the subsection must not create or reduce a support obligation to an amount that seriously impairs the custodial parent's ability to maintain minimal adequate housing and provide other basic necessities for the child, and (4) the existence of a party's financial responsibility for another child who is not the subject of the current proceeding does not of itself constitute a material change in circumstances for modifying a previous child support order. Compare *Frazer v. Frazer*, 23 Va. App. 358, 477 S.E.2d 290 (1996) (holding that, under prior version of statute, spousal support should be calculated before child support and included or deducted from gross income when calculating child support). Va. Code § 20-108.2(C)(4), added in 2004, provides that income from secondary employment obtained to discharge a child support arrearage is not counted in "gross income," and cessation of such income upon payment of the arrearage is not the basis for a material change in circumstances warranting a modification of support.

Va. Code § 20-108.2(D), as amended in 2004, provides that except for good cause shown or the agreement of the parties, child support orders will require that unreimbursed medical and dental expenses over a specified dollar threshold will be paid by the parents in proportion to their income.

Va. Code § 20-108.2(F), as amended in 2004, provides that the tax savings a party derives from child-care cost deductions or credits will be factored into the calculation of child-care costs to be added to the basic child support obligation. The work-related child-care costs incurred by either custodial parent are to be added to the presumptive child support calculation. *Tidwell v. Late*, 67 Va. App. 668, 682 (2017).

Va. Code §§ 20-60.3 and 20-108.2(G), as amended in 2000, make technical changes under the shared custody and support guidelines regarding (1) net support calculated as owed by a primary custodian, (2) payment or reimbursement of children's extraordinary medical expenses, and (3) the presumptively correct support amount if either party's income is at or below 150% of the federal poverty level. Further changes to Va. Code § 20-108.2(G) in 2004 added identical provisions for determining responsibility for unreimbursed medical and dental expenses for sole custody, split custody, and shared custody, respectively.

Va. Code § 20-108.2(H), as amended in 2000 and again in 2004, requires review of the child support guidelines every four years by the Child Support Guidelines Review Panel.

### § 22.08  Limitation of Parental Ability to Pay

The amount required for child support is limited by the noncustodial spouse's ability to pay. *Taylor v. Taylor*, 203 Va. 1, 121 S.E.2d 753 (1961).; A voluntary relinquishment of a higher paying position will not change the ability to pay for these purposes. 203 Va. at 5, 121 S.E.2d at 756. But compare *Payne v. Payne*, 5 Va. App. 359, 363 S.E.2d 428 (1987) (no evidence of how much husband could earn in counseling business that had been entered into with wife's support; nor suggestion that he could seek other fields of employment that would yield a higher income).

The ability to pay includes not only the parent's salary, but also the ability to earn and assets generally. *Hawkins v. Hawkins*, 187 Va. 595, 600–01, 47 S.E.2d 436, 439 (1948). See also *Hur v. Commonwealth Dep't of Social Services Div. of Child Support Enforcement ex rel Klopp*, 13 Va. App. 54, 409 S.E.2d 454 (1991) (a parent does not have the unfettered right to remain unproductive under the shelter of college enrollment so as to avoid support obligations); *Hamel v. Hamel*, 18 Va. App. 10, 441 S.E.2d 221 (1994) (trial court should have imputed income to a noncustodial wife who voluntarily quit her job and had no income at the time of the hearing); *Will v. Will*, 1994 Va. App. LEXIS 100 (Mar. 1, 1994) (guideline amount of zero would not be followed when noncustodial father was voluntarily unemployed); *Brody v. Brody*, 16 Va. App. 647, 432 S.E.2d 20 (1993) (income imputed where wife left $54,000 per year job to stay home with children and care for child of second marriage); *O'Brien v. Rose*, 1994 Va. App. LEXIS 97 (Mar. 1, 1994) (income imputed when wife quit teaching position to move with new husband to Thailand, then returned to the United States where she needed to renew her teacher certification); *Auman v. Auman,* 21 Va. App. 275, 464 S.E.2d 154 (1995) (When a family breaks up, "a party is not free to make career decisions that disregard the needs of his dependents and his potential obligation to them, and 'the risk of his success at his new job [is] upon him and not upon [his child].' "); *Calvert v. Calvert*, 18 Va. App. 781, 447 S.E.2d 875 (1994); *Floyd v. Floyd*, 17 Va. App. 222, 436 S.E.2d 457 (1993) (husband hiding income, so $45,000 yearly income imputed to him). But see *Belke v. Belke*, 1994 Va. App. LEXIS 461 (July 12, 1994) (husband who resigned from the Navy for a job earning two percent less because he was scheduled to go to sea for a fourth submarine tour was not underemployed);

*L.C.S. v. S.A.S.*, 19 Va. App. 709, 453 S.E.2d 580 (1995) (no imputed income where husband was legally barred from the practice of law due to the loss of his license); *Mir v. Mir*, 39 Va. App. 119, 571 S.E.2d 299 (2002) (court erred in imputing income to husband absent evidence of higher-paying former job, or of more lucrative jobs that were currently available); *Budnick v. Budnick*, 42 Va. App. 823, 595 S.E.2d 50 (2004) (no imputed income when wife declined job transfer to different geographical area after employer relocated offices); *Bruemmer v. Bruemmer*, 46 Va. App. 205, 616 S.E.2d 740 (2005) (no imputed income when mandatory 401K retirement plan contributions were determined by vote of law partnership, not individual partner). A noncustodial parent may not voluntarily stay home in order to care for the child or children of a second marriage and thereby avoid a child support obligation. *Horn v. Horn*, 19 Va. Cir. 73 (Henrico Co. 1989). However, the fact that a father had two legitimate children must be taken into account in determining the amount of support due to his illegitimate children. *Zubricki v. Motter*, 12 Va. App. 999, 406 S.E.2d 672 (1991). Reduction would not be justified where the noncustodial parent voluntarily contributed to the support of two adult children from a prior marriage. *Lewis v. Lewis*, 1993 Va. App. LEXIS 354 (Aug. 17, 1993).

It is erroneous to reduce the child support owed by the normal expenses the noncustodial parent makes in visiting the child, or by the amount the noncustodial parent spends during visitation, unless the custodial spouse's expenses are reduced thereby. *Baumgartner v. Moore*, 14 Va. App. 696, 419 S.E.2d 291 (1992). A noncustodial parent's payments to third party vendors do not constitute nonconforming child support payments for which the noncustodial parent is entitled to receive credit. *Gallagher v. Gallagher*, 35 Va. App. 470, 546 S.E.2d 222 (2001) (clarifying holding of *Wilderman v. Wilderman*, 25 Va. App. 500, 489 S.E.2d 701 (1997)).

The court may impute income from a second job held regularly by the obligor. In *Cochran v. Cochran*, 14 Va. App. 827, 419 S.E.2d 419 (1992), the obligor was a school teacher, and the summer income was used to establish the standard of living during the marriage.

When a husband received a personal injury settlement embracing his claims for lost earnings and earning capacity, this amount as well as his social security disability benefits should have been included in the computation of his income. The amount that the children independently received from Social Security as dependents of their disabled father should be included in his income as well, but should be credited toward his child support obligation. The court reasoned that the benefits derived from his employment, and offset his incapacity to provide for his children normally.

*Colbert v. Whitaker*, 18 Va. App. 202, 442 S.E.2d 429 (1994). See also *Department of Social Servs., Div. of Child Support Enforcement ex rel. Comptroller of Virginia v. Skeens*, 18 Va. App. 154, 442 S.E.2d 432 (1994) (Social Security disability benefits, although constituting an independent entitlement, are in the nature of support made in lieu of a disabled employee's earnings, but the extent to which they should be credited against child support arrearage depends upon the circumstances of each case); but see *Defebo v. Defebo-Carpini*, 1993 Va. App. LEXIS 470 (Sept. 28, 1993) (disability payments made to children should not have been included in either custodial mother's or father's income to determine guideline amount) Under Va. Code § 20-108.2(C) as amended in 1998, if a parent's gross income includes disability insurance benefits, it also includes benefits for the child derived from the parent's entitlement to disability insurance benefits, but the amount of the child's benefits is credited against the parent's support obligation.

Deviation from the guideline amounts was justified when both parties enjoyed substantial incomes, and testimony showed that "these people have taken great pride in giving their children a lot of the better things in life." *Wilson v. Wilson*, 18 Va. App. 193, 196, 442 S.E.2d 694, 696 (1994).

The events leading to husband's conviction and incarceration were entirely voluntary, and he committed destructive acts against the mother knowing of the probable consequences. Therefore, he should be considered "voluntarily unemployed" within the meaning of § 20-108.2(B)(3), and income should be imputed to him for purposes of child support. The amount of the income imputed to him would be based upon his most recent employment at $1,745 per month rather than the job of $32,000 a year he had previously left voluntarily. *Major v. Major*, 36 Va. Cir. 190 (Pittsylvania Co. 1995).

When earning capacity, voluntary unemployment, or voluntary underemployment is at issue in determining support, the court may order a party to submit to an evaluation by a vocational expert employed by the other party. Va. Code § 20-108.1(H).

For discussion of whether loss of income resulting from voluntary unemployment or voluntary underemployment justifies modification of existing child support orders, see §§ 22.16 and 22.17.

## § 22.09   Age Limitation

Generally speaking, a parent has the legal obligation to support his or her children only through their minority. Va. Code § 20-61. However, Va. Code § 20-124.2(C) and former Va. Code § 20-107.2 provide that the court may also order that support be paid for any child who is a full-time high school senior, not self-supporting, and living in the home of the parent seeking or receiving child support, until such child reaches the age of nineteen or graduates from high school, whichever first occurs. See, e.g., *Goldin v. Goldin*, 34 Va. App. 95, 538 S.E.2d 326 (2000) (court had jurisdiction to modify child support until child graduated from high school or reached age 19). The jurisdiction of a court to provide for child support pursuant to a divorce is purely statutory. *Jackson v. Jackson*, 211 Va. 718, 719, 180 S.E.2d 500 (1971). After the age of majority is reached, the court's jurisdiction ceases, and the only form of relief is in cases where an agreement extends the liability. See *Eaton v. Eaton*, 215 Va. 824, 213 S.E.2d 789 (1975). However, if the obligee parent obtains a child support order from another state, e.g., New York, where the duty of support is extended beyond Virginia's duty of support, e.g., until the child reaches age twenty-one, then the obligor parent residing in Virginia must pay child support until the child is emancipated under the law of the other state. *Robdau v. Dep't of Soc. Servs., Div. of Child Support Enforcement ex rel. Robdau*, 35 Va. App. 128, 543 S.E.2d 602 (2001) (decided under Uniform Interstate Family Support Act (Va. Code § 20-88.32 et seq.)). If the obligor parent moves to another state where the duty may be extended past the child's reaching the age of majority, and the Virginia child support obligation is nonfinal and modifiable, then the Virginia decree need not be given full faith and credit and the duty may be extended through college. *Oman v. Oman*, 333 Pa. Super. 356, 482 A.2d 606 (1984) (enforcement of Virginia child support order by Pennsylvania court, decided under Revised Uniform Reciprocal Enforcement of Support Act (former Va. Code § 20-88.12 et seq.)).

In 2015, the legislature amended the child support statute for those who are over the age of majority but meet the disability criteria. Under Va. Code § 20-124.2, child support can either be paid initially or continue to be paid for any child over the age of 18 who is (a) severely and permanently mentally or physically disabled, and such disability existed prior to the child reaching the age of 18 or the age of 19 if the child met the requirements of clauses (i), (ii), and (iii); (b) unable to live independently and support himself; and (c) residing in the home of the parent seeking or receiving child support. Va. Code §§ 16.1-287.15, 20-60.3, 20-103, and 20-107.2 were also amended.

A written agreement that extends payments past the age of majority will not be enforceable through the divorce court after the child reaches eighteen. In *Cutshaw v. Cutshaw*, 220 Va. 638, 261 S.E.2d 52 (1979), the parties' agreement requiring the father to pay $25 per week for child support until modified by a court or until such time as the last child left home or completed an undergraduate education was incorporated into the divorce decree. The amount was increased in a modification proceeding in 1974, and the same year was reduced again to $35. After the youngest child reached majority the wife sought enforcement of the arrearages. Although the contractual obligation to pay continued, the court lacked the jurisdiction to enforce the support obligation for any amount payable after the child turned 18. See also *Hosier v. Hosier*, 221 Va. 827, 273 S.E.2d 564 (1981) (no jurisdiction to award even temporary support for adult son in college). Compare *Fry v. Schwarting*, 4 Va. App. 173, 355 S.E.2d 342 (1987) (agreement incorporated and never modified).

Nevertheless, a property settlement agreement for post-minority child support that is incorporated into a divorce decree will be enforceable by a divorce court after the children reach the age of majority. In *Goldin v. Goldin*, 34 Va. App. 95, 538 S.E.2d 326 (2000), a property settlement incorporated into a divorce decree provided that the parties "shall, each year . . . re-apply the Virginia child support formula to determine the appropriate amount of child support due," and that the "[h]usband's obligation to pay child support for each child shall continue until such time as each child reaches the age of twenty-three (23) or twenty-two (22) years and graduates from college." Under this language, the husband was obligated to pay child support at Virginia child support guideline levels from the time each child reached the age of majority until the child reached age 22 or 23 and graduated from college. This language also obligated the husband to pay child support at the guideline level for an adult child who had left the custodial parent's home. However, an agreement incorporated into a divorce decree does not affect a trial court's jurisdiction to modify child support for minor children. See *Edwards v. Lowry*, 232 Va. 110, 112, 348 S.E.2d 259, 261 (1986). Thus, in *Goldin*, the trial court had the power to reduce the child support amount for one child who was still a minor, and it could also deviate from the child support guidelines as long as it provided a written explanation pursuant to Va. Code §§ 20-108.1(B) and 20-124.2(C). Also, the trial court had jurisdiction to modify child support until the minor child graduated from high school or reached age 19, pursuant to Va. Code § 20-124.2(C) and former Va. Code § 20-107.2.

Where the parties' agreement incorporated into the final decree of divorce provided for child support until the children reached age twenty-one or were otherwise emancipated, the obligor husband had a duty to continue making the payments after the children reached eighteen. *Paul v. Paul*, 214 Va. 651, 203 S.E.2d 123 (1974). This is to be contrasted with *Eaton v. Eaton*, 215 Va.

824, 213 S.E.2d 789 (1975), where the parties were operating under a court-ordered modification of the agreement at the time the age of majority was changed.

The court was willing to extend the noncustodial father's child support obligations past the age set by the parties' separation agreement, when the child remained in high school after reaching age 18 due in part to a learning disability. *Arnold v. Royall*, 28 Va. Cir. 405 (City of Richmond 1992). See also *Frey v. Frey*, 33 Va. Cir. 191 (Loudoun Co. 1994) (totally disabled adult child). The duty to pay while the child completes high school or reaches age 19 is now included in Va. Code Ann. §§ 16.1-278.5 and 20-107.2.

A required clause in support orders provides that if arrearages for child support exist at the time the youngest child emancipates, payments continue until all arrearages are paid. The amount of this continuing payment will be the total amount payable for current support plus arrearages at the time of emancipation. Va. Code § 20-60.3(16).

### § 22.10    Emancipation

Emancipation may occur by operation of law when the child reaches the age of majority, see *Eaton v. Eaton*, 215 Va. 824, 213 S.E.2d 789 (1975), or when the parent accepts the child's independence from familial obligations. See, e.g., *Penn et al. v. Whitehead et al.*, 58 Va. (17 Gratt.) 503, 522 (1867). This de facto emancipation usually occurs when the child is married. See *Bennett v. Bennett*, 179 Va. 239, 243, 18 S.E.2d 911, 913 (1942); see also *Corbridge v. Corbridge*, 230 Ind. 201, 102 N.E.2d 764 (1952). In some cases, emancipation will occur when the child moves away from home and begins supporting himself or herself. *Buxton v. Bishop*, 185 Va. 1, 37 S.E.2d 755 (1946). In such cases the child will no longer have the obligation of giving the parent control over earnings, and the parent will have no corresponding duty of support.

Virginia Code § 8.01-229 and §§ 16.1-331 to 16.1-334 define emancipation according to these common law concepts. The statutes allow a minor who has attained the age of sixteen to petition for emancipation to the Juvenile and Domestic Relations Court. The court is to appoint a guardian ad litem for the child, and is authorized to issue an order of emancipation if the minor: (1) is validly married; (2) is on active duty in the armed forces; or (3) willingly lives apart from parents or guardians with their consent and is able to support himself or herself. Va. Code § 16.1-333.

A case decided before this section was enacted found that the minor in question, who was employed full-time but living at home, was emancipated. *Ware v. Ware*, 10 Va. App. 352, 391 S.E.2d 887 (1990).

See generally Katz, *Emancipating Our Children—Coming of Legal Age in America*, 7 Fam. L.Q. 211 (1973).

## § 22.11   Death of Parent

Va. Code § 64.2-528 lists child support arrearages as one of the priority of debts paid from a decedent's estate.

When the spouses were divorced, the husband was ordered to pay child support until further order of the court. The husband conveyed his property to his father despite an injunction restraining him from disposing of it, and died intestate. The father brought suit asking that the real estate conveyed to him be declared free from any encumbrance. The court found that the lien so created was intended to and did by the decree continue after the death of the husband and until the child reached majority. *Morris v. Henry*, 193 Va. 631, 70 S.E.2d 417 (1952):

> To deny a court of equity, sitting as a court of divorce, the power to make the estate of a parent liable for the support of infant children, would in some cases make that court helpless to discharge the function of a guardian in the protection of the rights and interests of infant children of divorce . . . .

## § 22.12   Method of Payment

In *Fearon v. Fearon*, 207 Va. 927, 931, 154 S.E.2d 165, 167 (1967), the husband was ordered to pay $400 per month for his wife and the children as part of a divorce decree. He paid money directly to the children, and then sought credit for these amounts in defense of the wife's contempt action. The supreme court found that he must pay the specified amount in accordance with the decree. Likewise, payments made to third parties to provide necessaries for the children could not be credited. *Id.* at 931, 154 S.E.2d at 168 (citing *Bradley v. Fowler*, 30 Wash. 2d 609, 192 P.2d 969 (1948)). The disbursement of the funds paid to provide a home and support for the wife and the children was her privilege and responsibility. 207 Va. at 932, 154 S.E.2d at 168. In *Gagliano v. Gagliano*, 215 Va. 447, 211 S.E.2d 62 (1975), the Virginia Supreme Court, with apparent reluctance, allowed checks made payable to the parties' son to be credited to the father's child support obligation. The court distinguished *Fearon* on the ground that this decree did not specifically require that the payments be made to the custodial mother. In *Lipscomb v. Lipscomb*, 18 Va. Cir. 244 (Chesterfield Co. 1989), the husband stopped making child support payments pursuant to an agreement with the wife under which, at her request, he assumed custody of the children for more than two years. Although he had not sought relief from the court, to award the wife arrearages would be inequitable since it was her desire that he take and support the children, and the father performed his portion of the agreement.

However, should the custodial parent refuse to use the child support for the children's benefit, and instead appropriate it to his or her own use, a constructive trust might be established for the children. *Rosenblatt v. Birnbaum*, 16 N.Y.2d 212, 264 N.Y.S.2d 521, 212 N.E.2d 37 (1965). If the custodial parent is shown to be financially irresponsible, then the trial court may order the noncustodial parent to make direct payments of the children's expenses, rather than direct child support payments to the custodial parent. *Princiotto v. Gorrell*, 42 Va. App. 253, 590 S.E.2d 626 (2004).

Legislation in 1985 and 1986 has changed the method of payment to custodial parents on public assistance, which since October 1, 1985, has been made to conform to federal provisions under the Social Security Act, 42 U.S.C. §§ 651–667. Va. Code § 20-60.5(F) provides that if the custodial parent is receiving public assistance, the Department of Social Services shall be the payee of child support. The custodial parent shall become the payee upon request that support services no longer be provided by the Department.

In 2017, Va. Code §§ 16.1-278.15(A) and 20-124.2 (C) were amended to authorize the court to order that child support payments, upon the request of either party, could be ordered to be paid to "a special needs trust or an ABLE savings trust account as defined in § 23.1-700."

According to Va. Code § 63.2-1923, income withholding can be initiated through an administrative order sent by first class or certified mail, or by electronic means. In either case the obligor's employer receives the notice, and is to promptly inform the obligor under Va. Code § 20-79.3.

## § 22.13    Need for Schedule

The need for an itemized statement of expenses as opposed to mere nebulous allegations of where money is spent is demonstrated in the case of *Crosby v. Crosby*, 182 Va. 461, 29 S.E.2d 241 (1944), where the husband was unsuccessful in reducing his large alimony and support obligations despite the fact that his net income had been cut in half. See also *Conway v. Conway*, 10 Va. App. 653, 395 S.E.2d 464 (1990) (mother capable of obtaining increase when she could itemize expenses). A mother seeking an increase in child support was entitled to a discovery of documentation needed to calculate the father's current monthly gross income as well as the parties' combined monthly gross income. The father was therefore not entitled to a protective order even though he admitted that he had the ability to pay. *Harding v. Harding*, 21 Va. Cir. 130 (Fairfax Co. 1990).

Va. Code § 20-108.2 was amended to provide that the court may require the custodial parent, upon the request of the non-custodial parent, to present documentation to verify the costs incurred for child care due to employment.

## § 22.14    Parent as Witness

Any spousal incompetency to testify remaining after Va. Code § 8.01-398 (1996) does not extend to proceedings between them concerning child support. See, e.g., Va. Code § 20-88.29 (URESA action).

## § 22.15    Tax Aspects of Child Support

The tax consequences of child support payments upon the parties are among the factors to be considered in determining the amount of child support. In particular, tax savings a parent derives from child-care cost deductions or credits will be factored into the calculation of child-care costs to be added to the basic child support obligation. Va. Code § 20-108.2(F). In addition, "[t]ax consequences to the parties including claims for exemptions, child tax credit, and child care credit for dependent children," are factors to consider in determining if a deviation from the child support guideline is warranted. Va. Code § 20-108.1(B)(13).

In general, child support payments are not deductible by the payor nor taxable to the payee as income. The exception to this rule was that if the amount of a sum paid for spousal and child support actually attributable to child support was not expressly stated in the decree or agreement, the entire amount would be taxable as alimony under I.R.C. § 71. *Commissioner v. Lester*, 366 U.S. 299, 81 S. Ct. 1343, 6 L. Ed. 2d 306 (1961). However, this exception was abrogated in the Domestic Relations Tax Reform Act of 1984, which treats as child support all amounts dependent upon contingencies associated with the child rather than the spouse receiving support: for example, emancipation or reaching the age of majority.

The other major tax consideration involving child support payments is the dependency exemption. For tax years after 2004, a child is normally the "qualifying child" of the custodial parent, who is thus entitled to claim the exemption. 26 U.S.C. §§ 152(a) and (c). The exemption may be transferred to the noncustodial parent if the parents together provide more than one-half the child's support, the child is in the custody of one or both parents for more than half the year, and the noncustodial parent attaches to his or her tax return an IRS form signed by the custodial parent declaring that the custodial parent will not claim the exemption for that year. 26 U.S.C. § 152(e). In the normal case the child will then be treated as the "qualifying child" of the noncustodial parent, and in any event the noncustodial parent will be entitled to the exemption without regard to the portion of the child's support that he or she personally provides. 26 U.S.C. § 152(e)(1). Under the 1984 Tax Reform Act, the custodial parent will normally receive the dependency exemption. The exception to this rule will occur when the decree or agreement says that the other spouse is to receive it, and the noncustodial spouse actually contributes more than half the dependent's support.

The trial court has the authority, absent parental agreement, to order one party to execute all appropriate tax forms or waivers to grant the other party the right to take the income tax dependency exemption. Va. Code § 20-108.1(E) (amended 1998).

The 1986 Tax Reform Act allows unearned income of children under age fourteen to be taxed at the same rate as the custodial parent's income. I.R.C. § 1411; I.R.C. § 1(i), 1986 Tax Reform Act § 1411.

### § 22.16   Modification of Support—General

Child support may be modified when a material change in circumstances and conditions has occurred. In such cases, the burden rests upon the party seeking to alter the decree to establish such a change. *Morris v. Morris*, 216 Va. 457, 219 S.E.2d 864 (1975). The change must be shown by a preponderance of the evidence. *Hammers v. Hammers*, 216 Va. 30, 31, 216 S.E.2d 20, 21 (1975). Because of the requirement of a change in circumstances, a court order establishing an automatic yearly adjustment tied to the percentage increase or decrease in salaries at the payor's Virginia workplace was improper. *Keyser v. Keyser*, 2 Va. App. 459, 461, 345 S.E.2d 12, 14 (1986).

In a modification proceeding, written reasons need to be given for deviation from the guidelines established in Va. Code § 20-108.2. *Richardson v. Richardson*, 12 Va. App. 18, 401 S.E.2d 894 (1991). See also *Maya v. Maya*, 1996 Va. App. LEXIS 8 (Jan. 11, 1996); *Jordan v. Jordan*, 23 Va. Cir. 470 (Fairfax Co. 1991); and *May v. May*, 24 Va. Cir. 407 (City of Charlottesville 1991). In *Milligan v. Milligan*, 12 Va. App. 982, 407 S.E.2d 702 (1991), the court of appeals held that if the parties' income changes so that the amount awarded is no longer within the statutory guidelines, the material or substantial change of circumstance rule is no longer required as a condition precedent to obtaining a modification of child support. See also *Kaplan v. Kaplan*, 21 Va. App. 542, 466 S.E.2d 111 (1996) (father's employer ceased its business operations in Virginia; bankruptcy of corporation and financial difficulties that caused the father to renegotiate the arrangement supported the finding that the reduction was involuntary); *Rawlings v. Rawlings*, 20 Va. App. 663, 460 S.E.2d 581 (1995) (father's participation in his trade union's strike did not constitute voluntary underemployment, and thus was grounds for warranting a reduction in child support); *In re Gregory*, 22 Va. Cir. 173 (City of Charlottesville 1990).

In *Virginia Dep't of Social Servs., Div. of Child Support Enforcement ex rel. Ewing v. Ewing*, 22 Va. App. 466, 470 S.E.2d 608 (1996), the court of appeals reversed court's elimination of the husband's child support obligation. The father, a registered pharmacist earning $79,000 in 1991, entered medical school in 1992. Although he could elect to become unemployed because of his class responsibilities, he might not terminate his employment to the detriment of support obligations to his child. To do so, even to secure a possible future reward, overlooked the child's current needs and gave priority to his own ambition. Similarly, the Court of Appeals found that his decision to quit his employment and begin a new business constituted either purposeful evasion of his support obligations or such callous disregard for the obligation as to require that income be imputed. A trial court's imputation of income to a mother was reversed when a mother had not worked as a day-care provider since 1996 even though she was still licensed as a day-care provider. *Niemiec v. Department of Soc. Servs., Div. of Child Support Enforcement ex rel. Niemec*, 27 Va. App. 446, 499 S.E.2d 576 (1998).

In *Mansfield v. Taylor*, 24 Va. App. 108, 480 S.E.2d 752 (1997), the father was unable to show that his career change was made in good faith and without disregard for his support obligation. On the other hand, in *Commonwealth, Dep't of Soc. Servs., Division of Child Support Enforcement v. Bowyer*, 1997 Va. App. LEXIS 213 (Apr. 8, 1997), a father was allowed a temporary abatement of his child support obligation when he resigned from his regular employment because of "life-threatening" medical problems, including migraine headaches and high blood pressure. When the father's mental health significantly worsened in the months following the divorce decree, and affected his business operations, he was able to modify child support and spousal support. *Street v. Street*, 24 Va. App. 2, 480 S.E.2d 112 (1997).

In *Payne v. Payne*, 1998 Va. Cir. LEXIS 525 (Aug. 3, 1998), a divorce decree ordered the mother, who had joint legal custody, to pay child support to the primary custodian father. Her voluntary unemployment was due to her choice to tutor her daughter from a prior marriage at home. The court stated that she cannot choose to benefit one child at the expense of the other three children. Her prior income of $34,000 per year was imputed to her in determining her child support obligation.

The parties' agreement to waive portions of a child support arrearage is unenforceable. *Smiley v. Erickson*, 29 Va. App. 426, 512 S.E.2d 842 (1999).

"No support order may be retroactively modified. Past due support installments become vested as they accrue and are thereafter immune from change. Parties cannot contractually modify the terms of a support order without the court's approval. Nor does a party's passive acquiescence in nonpayment of support operate to bar that party from later seeking support arrearages."

If a parent seeks a change in a child support obligation set by a trial court before July 1, 1989, the party need only establish a "significant variance" between the presumptive amount of child support under Code § 20-108.2 and the amount originally awarded. If a modification is ordered, the Code states that the modification will not be retroactive, but will date only from the time that notice of petition has been given to the responding party. *O'Brien v. Rose*, 14 Va. App. 960, 420 S.E.2d 246 (1992). See also *Herbert v. Herbert*, 33 Va. Cir. 155 (Fairfax Co. 1994).

However, the dependent spouse must carry the burden of demonstrating a change of circumstances. The dependent spouse cannot merely allege an increase in the obligor's income and a decrease in expenses. *McElwrath v. McElwrath*, 1993 Va. App. LEXIS 133 (May 18, 1993).

An agreement between the parents cannot prevent the court from modifying a support award. In *Hogge v. Hogge*, 1993 Va. App. LEXIS 121 (Apr. 20, 1993), the trial court first established the guideline amount, and then considered whether the amount agreed upon by the parents would better serve the interests of the parties. The court did not commit error when it settled on the presumptive sum found in the guidelines. However, the trial court could calculate an increase beginning with the formula included in the parties' separation agreement. *Claytor v. Suter*, 1995 Va. App. LEXIS 507 (June 13, 1995).

An agreement between parents that is incorporated into a divorce decree and provides for "renegotiation" of child support on the happening of certain future events, such as the emancipation of a child, is not void, although the parents' renegotiation of child support must be submitted to the divorce court for approval. *Riggins v. O'Brien*, 263 Va. 444, 559 S.E.2d 673 (2002). *Compare Gallagher v. Gallagher*, 35 Va. App. 470, 546 S.E.2d 222 (2001) (parents' renegotiation of child support to reflect noncustodial parent's increased custodial time is valid only if custodial parent entirely relinquishes physical custody of child).

In contrast, a "self-executing" agreement incorporated into a divorce decree that provides for child support adjustments without further court action on the happening of certain future events, such as fluctuation in child care costs or the emancipation of a child, will be valid and enforceable if it (1) is consistent with the children's best interests, (2) does not circumvent the divorce court's jurisdiction to enforce or modify support, (3) does not "contract away" the children's right to support from either parent, and (4) has been determined by the divorce court to be consistent with the children's best interest and not void as against public policy. Such self-executing agreements promote the public policies that favor the amicable resolution of support issues and the prompt resolution of child care and maintenance disputes. *Shoup v. Shoup*, 37 Va. App. 240, 556 S.E.2d 783 (2001). Under Va. Code § 20-109.1 as amended in 2003, an agreement between the parties regarding modification of child support that is incorporated in a decree is valid and enforceable without a further court decree, but the court retains the power to revise the decree under Va. Code § 20-108.

When the spouses' property settlement agreement provided that child support could be modified "by mutual consent . . . in writing and executed with the same formality as this Agreement," the parties could lower the amount of payments without resorting to the divorce court. *Twinam v. Twinam*, 1996 Va. App. LEXIS 699 (Nov. 12, 1996).

A court cannot retroactively increase child support, even if pursuant to an agreement of the parties incorporated into a final decree, unless that agreement is self-executing. In *Llerena v. Novak*, 1998 Va. Cir. LEXIS 450 (Nov. 17, 1998), the parties entered into a separation agreement in West Virginia which was incorporated into a final order, and registered in the J&DR court in Fairfax County pursuant to the UCCJA, Va. Code § 20-139. The agreement had triggering points for reevaluation of child support. However, the agreement was not self-executing. The custodial parent failed to pursue the action at one point, or to present evidence of triggering points at this trial.

In a modification proceeding, the trial judge is not required to specify in writing why an earlier award of child support should continue to deviate from the guidelines when there has been no material change justifying a modification of the earlier award. *Crabtree v. Crabtree*, 17 Va. App. 81, 435 S.E.2d 883 (1993).

A noncustodial parent may have to reimburse the other parent for extraordinary medical expenses incurred after the original award and before a modification petition has been filed, including amounts for personal expenses the custodial parent incurred during a minor child's illness. *Carter v. Thornhill*, 19 Va. App. 501, 453 S.E.2d 295 (1995). The change from one private school to a more expensive one did not constitute an adequate reason to increase the noncustodial father's child support obligation. *Solomond v. Ball*, 22 Va. App. 385, 470 S.E.2d 157 (1996).

However, the child support award may exceed the presumptive guidelines in order to continue the parties' practice of sending their children to private school. *Ragsdale v. Ragsdale*, 30 Va. App. 283, 516 S.E.2d 698 (1999).

A court order incorporating a settlement agreement was amended to reflect the larger payments already being made voluntarily by the noncustodial father. Modifications as each child reached majority should still affect the amount due. The reductions, made according to the plan of the original agreement, should simply be subtracted from the revised as opposed to the original amount. *Schmidt v. Schmidt*, 6 Va. App. 501, 370 S.E.2d 311 (1988).

For example, additional costs of orthodontic care, day camp and music lessons are all expenses attributable to the increased needs of growing children, which, without a substantial change in the custodial spouse's income, warranted a modification of the original decree so that the wife was required for the first time to make support payments. *Id.* See also *Barnes v. Craig*, 202 Va. 229, 117 S.E.2d 63 (1960).

The court may not cancel or modify arrears in support money, but only may change future installments. *Cofer v. Cofer*, 205 Va. 834, 839, 140 S.E.2d 663, 667 (1965). Past-due installments are vested and are immune from change. Nor will laches bar collection of a unitary sum awarded for alimony and child support. The court also found that the requirement that a decree-based modification be based upon a change of circumstances under *Jacobs v. Jacobs*, 219 Va. 993, 254 S.E.2d 56 (1979), should not be applied retroactively. *Barnett v. Barnett*, 24 Va. Cir. 282 (Campbell Co. 1991). In a contempt proceeding, a trial court exceeded its authority by retroactively modifying child support, when it deleted an "unduly burdensome" child health care coverage provision from an underlying support order, absent any petition for child support modification. *Commonwealth ex rel. Graham v. Bazemore*, 32 Va. App. 451, 528 S.E.2d 193 (2000). No support order may be retroactively modified, but a support order may be modified with respect to any period during which there is a pending petition for modification in any court, but only from the date that notice of the petition is given to the responding party. Va. Code §§ 20-108; 20-112. See *Stiles v. Stiles*, 48 Va. App. 449, 632 S.E.2d 607 (2006) (child support modified "retroactively" when mother's motion for modification was served on father but not adjudicated for four years). Va. Code § 20-112 was amended in 2004 to make clear that when a petition is filed in juvenile and domestic relations district court and then transferred to circuit court, a child or spousal support modification may take effect from the date that notice of the petition was given to the responding party.

Va. Code Ann. § 20-109.1 allows parties to contract for future modifications without returning to the trial court for approval in certain cases. But, the ability to do so depends on the language of the modification provision. If the modification provision is self-executing, the parties do not need to obtain court approval for the modification to legally take effect. A modification provision is considered self-executing if it refers to objective standards for calculating support, such as the Child Support Guidelines. If the modification provision is not self-executing, the parties must return to court to obtain approval of the modification.

In *Virostko v. Virostko*, 59 Va. App. 816, 722 S.E.2d 678, (2012), the father argued that the trial court disregarded the terms of the parties' Separation and Property Settlement Agreement (PSA) in both determining the child support owed to the mother and the prescribed methodology by which child support was to be calculated. The appellate court affirmed the judgment of the trial court. The court held that although the modification provision in the PSA was valid, it was not self-executing because there was no objective standard by which the parties could determine a new amount of child support. The court further restated the long-settled principle that a trial court retains jurisdiction over child support modification despite any agreement between the parents.

### § 22.17    Change of Circumstances

The father seeking a reduction in his child support obligation must make a full and complete disclosure relating to his ability to pay, and must show that his lack of ability is not voluntary or due to his neglect. *Hammers v. Hammers*, 216 Va. 30, 216 S.E.2d 20 (1975). See also *Broadhead v. Broadhead*, 51 Va. App. 170, 655 S.E.2d 748 (2008) (husband's leaving company after being involuntarily transferred to position for which he was not qualified did not support finding of voluntary unemployment); *Hatloy v. Hatloy*, 41 Va. App. 667, 588 S.E.2d 389 (2003) (husband not voluntarily underemployed after losing job in "hi-tech industry"); *Ryan v. Kramer*, 21 Va. App. 217, 463 S.E.2d 328 (1995) (income imputed to airline pilot father who accepted early retirement from airline, then earned nothing as real estate agent); *Barnhill v. Brooks*, 15 Va. App. 696, 427 S.E.2d 209 (1993) (obligor's underemployment was voluntary, but obligor's being in arrears in making payments did not prevent modification); *Buland v. Buland*, 25 Va. Cir. 280 (Loudoun Co. 1991) (father's child support arrearage did not prevent court from proceeding on motion to modify child support obligation in accordance with child support guidelines); *Division of Child Support Enforcement v. Huddleston*, 42 Va. Cir. 443 (City of Salem 1997) (incarcerated father was voluntarily unemployed because he had voluntarily committed crime that caused his incarceration).

A reduction in income that results from a parent's voluntary employment decision may not justify a reduction in the parent's support obligation even if the parent's decision was reasonable and in good faith. When a parent had changed from a salaried position to one compensated on a commission basis, it was within the circuit court's discretion to place the risk of success in the new endeavor on the parent rather than the children. *Antonelli v. Antonelli*, 242 Va. 152, 409 S.E.2d 117 (1991).

The determination of whether a parent seeking a child support modification is voluntarily underemployed, which justifies the imputation of income to the parent, involves not only a determination of whether the parent left previous employment voluntarily, but also an examination of the parent's efforts to find new employment at a comparable level of income. A parent can be involuntarily terminated from a high-paying job, but still be voluntarily underemployed in his or her current job. *Broadhead v. Broadhead*, 51 Va. App. 170, 655 S.E.2d 748 (2008). *See Hatloy v. Hatloy*, 41 Va. App. 667, 588 S.E.2d 389 (2003).

The Virginia Court of Appeal explained that there is no mandatory rule requiring the imputation of income where a party is voluntarily unemployed or under-employed when that party has acted in good faith and reasonably in employment decisions. *Murphy v. Murphy*, 65 Va. App. 581, 586, 779 S.E.2d 236, 238 (2015). The legislature expressly granted the trial court with discretion in this matter. Nonetheless, where a parent has not acted reasonably in his employment, the trial court is required to consider imputing income. *Niblett v. Niblett*, 65 Va. App. 616, 628, 779 S.E.2d 839, 845 (2015).

The fact that the husband has remarried and has another family dependent upon him for support is entitled to little, if any consideration. *Hammers v. Hammers*, 216 Va. 30, 32, 216 S.E.2d 20 (1975); see also *Morris v. Morris*, 216 Va. 457, 219 S.E.2d 864 (1975); cf. *Treger v. Treger*, 212 Va. 538, 186 S.E.2d 82 (1972) (sufficient change when income decreased from $28,000 to $12,000). However, it was error for a court ordering support for a father's two illegitimate children to ignore the existence of the two children born of his current marriage. *Zubricki v. Motter*, 12 Va. App. 999, 406 S.E.2d 672 (1991). A father's income should be reduced by obligations to his other children. *Hallman v. Hallman*, 25 Va. Cir. 144 (Fairfax Co. 1991). A noncustodial father could also seek a deviation from guideline amounts based upon the birth of his new child. *Evans v. Division of Child Support*

*Enforcement*, 1996 Va. App. LEXIS 93 (Feb. 6, 1996). But see *May v. May*, 31 Va. Cir. 480 (Clarke Co. 1982) (second family, investments, and lower level of unemployment).

*Bennett v. Division of Child Support Enforcement*, 22 Va. App. 684, 472 S.E.2d 668 (1996), involved a husband's appeal from the trial court's refusal to modify his monthly support obligation. He claimed, unsuccessfully, that her circumstances had changed because the couple's severely disabled child was now in school each weekday and that his former wife was now "home schooling" the two oldest children. He asked that the trial court impute income to her, and that it include as income government housing and disability benefits she received. The Court of Appeals agreed with the trial court's decision not to impute income to her because she needed to remain available to "intervene" in the disabled child's classroom or take him home. Once the child came home from school, she had to devote her full time and attention to caring for him. Although both parents bear the responsibility of supporting their dependent children, and the mother could not absolve herself of this obligation by voluntarily home schooling the children, income need not be imputed when she was caring for the profoundly disabled child as well. Moreover, she had not worked for over ten years and no evidence was introduced regarding the availability of jobs for her or the amount of income she could earn.

Proof of a change in circumstances was not required in order to have support adjusted to conform to the guidelines of Va. Code § 20-108.2, which was enacted following the parties' divorce. *Milligan v. Milligan*, 12 Va. App. 982, 407 S.E.2d 702 (1991). See also *Hiner v. Hadeed*, 15 Va. App. 575, 425 S.E.2d 811 (1993).

In *Cooke v. Cooke*, 23 Va. App. 60, 474 S.E.2d 159 (1996), the custodial wife had received an increase in the husband's monthly child support obligation from $2,420 to $3,845.66, the amount presumed by guidelines effective in 1992. Effective July 1, 1995, the statutory guidelines limited the incremental amount for monthly gross incomes over $50,000 to one percent. This guideline change constituted a material change in circumstances requiring that deviation from the presumptive amount (after the effective date of the statute) be justified with a written explanation. However, when the parties had made a written child support agreement, the trial court was not obligated to determine the presumptive guideline amount. *Moreno v. Moreno*, 24 Va. App. 227, 481 S.E.2d 482 (1997). The trial court properly recalculated the former husband's child support obligation pursuant to guideline amendments. However, a decrease of 6.5 percent in the husband's income was not a material change in circumstances. *Head v. Head*, 24 Va. App. 166, 480 S.E.2d 780 (1997).

When a trial court terminated the father's child support obligation based on the fact that the child moved from Virginia to India and no court of competent jurisdiction assumed jurisdiction or established support for the child, the case was reversed and remanded as a clear abuse of discretion. *Karimi v. Karimi*, 1998 Va. App. LEXIS 349 (June 16, 1998). Until another court of competent jurisdiction supplants the trial court's original continuing jurisdiction, that trial court retains jurisdiction even though the parties no longer reside in Virginia. The best interests of the child rule is still controlling for support needs under these circumstances.

In *Layman v. Layman*, 25 Va. App. 365, 488 S.E.2d 658 (1997), the court of appeals determined that an obligor cannot avoid child support because of his or her imprisonment. An obligor's incarceration is considered "voluntary unemployment."

If there is a change of custody, child support may be modified even though the original payments were structured for tax purposes as a unitary sum in lieu of child support and alimony. *Carter v. Carter*, 215 Va. 475, 481, 211 S.E.2d 253, 258 (1975) (decided before Domestic Relations Tax Reform Act of 1984 removed the tax advantage to the obligor presented by *Commissioner v. Lester*, 366 U.S. 299, 81 S. Ct. 1343, 6 L. Ed. 2d 306 (1961)). In a case where there has been a change of custody, the unitary sum will be apportioned between spousal and child support. See, e.g., *Jarrell v. Jarrell*, 1994 Va. App. LEXIS 672 (Nov. 15, 1994). However, a mere increase in child support engendered by a change in financial circumstances would not require such an apportionment. *Wickham v. Wickham*, 215 Va. 694, 213 S.E.2d 750 (1975). When a husband paid child and spousal support as a lump sum, with no method for determining how it was to be allocated, the husband was required to continue paying until relieved of this responsibility by a court. *Taylor v. Taylor*, 10 Va. App. 681, 394 S.E.2d 864 (1990).

A mother's letter waiving the husband's child support obligation while she and the child were in Louisiana did not relieve the husband of his duty to make the payments, even though he believed that she had to petition the court upon her return to Virginia to reinstate payments. *Goodpasture v. Goodpasture*, 7 Va. App. 55, 371 S.E.2d 845 (1988).

The intentional withholding of visitation of a child from the other parent without just cause may constitute a material change in circumstances justifying a change of custody in the discretion of the court. Va. Code § 20-108. The statute does not provide that withholding of visitation would be a reason for decreasing or terminating child support. As the court reasoned in *Commonwealth v. Hogge*, 16 Va. App. 520, 431 S.E.2d 656 (1993):

> Child support provides for the economic best interest of a dependent child; it is not a weapon with which to punish a parent. Accordingly, we hold that a trial court may not deviate from the presumptive amount of child support because a custodial parent has denied a noncustodial parent visitation with their child.

However, where the parties divorced when the child was three years old, the wife concealed him until he was in college, and she then sought arrearages in child support, no arrearages will be ordered paid. *Hartman v. Hartman*, 33 Va. Cir. 373 (Fairfax Co. 1994).

See generally Czapanskiy, *Child Support and Visitation: Rethinking the Connections*, 20 Rutgers L.J. 619 (1989).

### § 22.18   Jurisdiction for Modification

The court in a divorce action retains continuing jurisdiction to modify the portions of its decree dealing with child support during the minority of the child. Va. Code § 20-108.2. Since personal jurisdiction was already obtained in the divorce action, notice only need be given in the modification proceeding. See, e.g., *Glading v. Furman*, 282 Md. 200, 383 A.2d 398 (1978); *State ex rel. Ravitz v. Fox*, 166 W. Va. 194, 273 S.E.2d 370 (1980).

Under the Uniform Reciprocal Enforcement of Support Act, Va. Code § 20-88.12 et seq., a valid order of a foreign court must be given comity and recognized as a Virginia decree. *Scott v. Sylvester*, 220 Va. 182, 257 S.E.2d 774 (1979). However, if the foreign court gives no consideration or effect to a prior Virginia decree, and, more importantly, if the foreign proceedings were uncontested, the foreign decree may be modified as to child support provisions without a showing of changed circumstances. *Osborne v. Osborne*, 215 Va. 205, 207 S.E.2d 875 (1974). However, the registration of a foreign order in Virginia, with service upon the obligor outside the state, will not give Virginia in personam jurisdiction. *Stephens v. Stephens*, 229 Va. 610, 331 S.E.2d 484 (1985) (spousal support).

In *Rippy v. Rippy*, 13 Va. Cir. 188 (Caroline Co. 1988), the court held that a father was under continuing obligation to support his child, which could not be satisfied by payments made directly to the child.

A transfer of a child support case to the juvenile and domestic relations court for enforcement purposes does not divest the circuit court of jurisdiction to modify the child support and visitation. *Crabtree v. Crabtree*, 17 Va. App. 81, 435 S.E.2d 883 (1993). The court of appeals would not adopt a construction of the statutes "that would needlessly require issues to be remanded to a court not of record before they can be heard in the circuit court." *Id.* at 886.

### § 22.19    Jurisdiction for Enforcement

The divorce decree shall contain the parties' social security numbers under amended Va. Code § 20-91. If an obligor has not complied with an order for payment of child support, the Department of Motor Vehicles may refuse to grant an application for a driver's license, under Va. Code § 46.2-320. The posting of a bond before an appeal from the juvenile and domestic relations court is entertained by the circuit court is a jurisdictional requirement. *Division of Child Support Enforcement v. Walker*, 253 Va. 319, 485 S.E.2d 134 (1997).

In *Franklin v. Dep't of Soc. Servs., Division of Child Support Enforcement ex rel. Franklin*, 27 Va. App. 136, 497 S.E.2d 881 (1998), a family had sought help from the American Embassy by returning to the United States from Africa, entering into Virginia, and remaining residents since that time. Service of process on the husband via service on his company's United States office and several mailed notices were sufficient to generate jurisdiction over him for enforcing child support. The court also had authority to affirm an ex parte emergency custody order preventing either parent from removing the children from Virginia. When the husband requested a show cause ruling on the issue of visitation, he automatically waived any jurisdictional objection. This case, however, is most significant because it analyzed the scope of Va. Code § 20-88.35(5). The section provides that jurisdiction may be obtained over an individual who has performed an affirmative act in the state or invoked the laws of the state. The husband stated that he never directed his wife to move to Virginia, but the court found that in ordering the family to leave the marital home in Africa, his children did become residents of Virginia. This allowed Virginia to exercise personal jurisdiction over him.

Because additional defenses may be involved in a support proceeding, the defendant must be given an opportunity to appear and to contest the judgment. *Sistare v. Sistare*, 218 U.S. 1, 30 S. Ct. 682, 54 L. Ed. 905 (1910). Long-arm jurisdiction may be appropriate. For example, the husband in *Bosserman v. Bosserman*, 9 Va. App. 1, 384 S.E.2d 104 (1989), was a 25 percent owner of a closely-held family corporation. The bylaws provided for buy-out of stock based upon the "true book value" of the corporation, $28,032 at the time of divorce. The wife's accountant, however, placed the true market value of the farm owned by the corporation at $174,600. The court of appeals followed the majority rule that a buy-out provision does not control the determination of value when the other spouse did not consent or was not otherwise bound by its terms. The reasoning behind this rule is that buy-out provisions do not necessarily reflect the intrinsic worth of the stock to the parties. However, the limitation of alienability created by the restricting agreement necessarily affects the actual marketability of the stock, and thus its value. The valuation accepted by the court of appeals was based upon the corporation's net assets, here the farm.

When the divorce court did not have personal jurisdiction over the husband, who was served in another state, it could incorporate the parties' agreement. However, the court did not have power to enter an enforceable support order, so the husband could not be held in contempt for violating the support provisions of the decree. *Price v. Price*, 17 Va. App. 105, 435 S.E.2d 652 (1993). For in personam jurisdiction permitting enforcement, the pleadings must at least allege a connection to Virginia recognized by the long-arm statute. However, the husband could register a foreign state's support order obtained under URESA where his "duty of support" arose from the parties' separation agreement.

### § 22.20    Uniform Reciprocal Enforcement of Support Act and UIFSA

The Uniform Reciprocal Enforcement of Support Act, Va. Code § 20-88.12 et seq., provided that a foreign judgment of support may be registered in Virginia and enforced exactly as though it were a Virginia decree. This Act was repealed in 1994 and replaced by the Uniform Interstate Family Support Act.

Virginia adopted the Interstate Family Support Act (UIFSA) in Va. Code § 20-88.32 et seq. (1994). The Act is similar to the Uniform Reciprocal Support Act in many respects. The Act does establish some new concepts. The UIFSA establishes uniform long-arm jurisdiction over nonresidents and provides for discovery and testimony once jurisdiction is obtained. Va. Code §§ 20-88.36, 20-88.59, 20-88.61. The UIFSA may only be used for spousal and child support proceedings. Visitation issues cannot be raised in child support proceedings. Va. Code § 20-88.48.

UIFSA may be used by the Department of Social Services to collect a debt owed to another state that paid public assistance to a custodial parent. *Commonwealth ex rel. Gagne v. Chamberlain*, 31 Va. App. 533, 525 S.E.2d 19 (2000).

The choice of law for interpretation of support orders registered under UIFSA is that of the state issuing the underlying support orders, except that the longer of different state statutes of limitations applies. See, e.g., *Robdau v. Dep't of Soc. Servs., Div. of Child Support Enforcement ex rel. Robdau*, 35 Va. App. 128, 543 S.E.2d 602 (2001) (under UIFSA, Virginia must enforce New York child support order that remains in effect beyond Virginia's age of majority, until child reaches 21 years of age).

Under UIFSA, continuing exclusive jurisdiction is established so that only one support order is effective at any given time. Under the version of Va. Code § 20-88.39 applicable from 1994 to 2005, if the parties and the child left the state and took up residence elsewhere after a Virginia court issued a child support order, the Virginia court retained continuing, exclusive jurisdiction to modify that order until all parties consented in writing to allow another state to assume continuing, exclusive jurisdiction to modify the order. *Nordstrom v. Nordstrom*, 50 Va. App. 257, 649 S.E.2d 200 (2007). For example, in *Virginia Dep't of Social Servs., Div. of Child Support Enforcement, ex rel. Kenitzer v. Richter*, 23 Va. App. 186, 475 S.E.2d 817 (1996), a wife and husband divorced *a mensa et thoro* in Virginia, then relocated to California and South Carolina, respectively. Acting for the wife, a California agency filed a wage withholding petition in a South Carolina court, which issued an order staying the petition because support arrearages were disputed. Subsequently, the wife registered the original Virginia support order in California, and the California agency filed an action in Virginia to recover the alleged support arrearages. After the Department of Child Support Enforcement filed a motion for judgment and interest in Virginia circuit court, the husband appeared specially to register the South Carolina court's order. The Virginia court ruled that it was bound by the South Carolina order, and dismissed the arrearages action. However, the Virginia Court of Appeals concluded that the South Carolina order could *not* be registered under UIFSA; that under Va. Code § 20-88.39(A)(1), Virginia had continuing jurisdiction and the right to enforce its own decrees even if all parties were no longer residents. Therefore the Virginia circuit court was required to resolve the arrearages dispute.

In 2005, Virginia adopted most of the amendments proposed by the National Conference of Commissioners on Uniform State Laws in 2001 to clarify UIFSA and reflect changes in federal law. Among the changes was an expansion in the definition of "state" in Va. Code § 20-88.32 to allow foreign countries to have their orders enforced in the United States. Also, the crucial Va. Code § 20-88.39 was reorganized for greater clarity, while retaining the basic concept that the tribunal issuing a child support order retains continuing, exclusive jurisdiction to modify that order except in narrowly defined circumstances.

However, a substantive 2005 change in Va. Code § 20-88.39(A)(2) provides that the issuing tribunal may continue to exercise continuing, exclusive jurisdiction to modify a prior child support order after all the parties and the child have left Virginia *only if* the parties "consent in a record." Absent the parties' recorded consent, the issuing tribunal lacks continuing, exclusive jurisdiction to *modify* the order, which is contrary to the prior rule; although the issuing tribunal retains jurisdiction to *enforce* the order, pursuant to Va. Code § 20-88.40. *Nordstrom v. Nordstrom*, 50 Va. App. 257, 649 S.E.2d 200 (2007).

The UIFSA provides that a support order may be mailed directly to an obligor's employer, triggering wage withholding without a hearing unless the employee objects or the parties agree to an alternative payment agreement, or one of the parties demonstrates good cause why there should not be immediate withholding. The employer forwards payments to the department for recording and disbursement to the obligee. The obligor's state may administratively enforce the order, although all judicial enforcement begins with the registration of the existing order in the responding state. See Va. Code § 20-79.2.

The only tribunal that can modify a support order is the one having continuing exclusive jurisdiction except in narrowly defined circumstances. If both parties no longer reside in the issuing state, a tribunal with personal jurisdiction over both or with power given by their agreement may modify. Va. Code §§ 20-88.39, 20-88.40, 20-88.68.

The UIFSA authorizes establishment of parentage in interstate proceedings even when not accompanied by a support proceeding. Registration of foreign child support orders under UIFSA takes place in the juvenile and domestic relations district court. Va. Code §§ 20.88.32 and 20.88.67(A).

## § 22.21     Enforcement of Child Support

Recent legislation puts Virginia in conformance with federal statutes. The statutes provide for collection of arrearages through garnishment, and requires that all payors be notified that payroll deductions may be made without amending the order. Va. Code §§ 20-60.3, 20-79.1.

At the birth of a child, the social security number of each parent shall be reported in the manner prescribed and on forms furnished by the state registrar. 42 U.S.C. § 405; Va. Code § 32.1-257.1.

Likewise, the parents' divorce decree must contain their social security numbers under Va. Code § 20-91. Va. Code § 63.2-1937 provides that applications for issuance or renewal of a license to engage in a business, trade, profession, recreational activity, or occupation must include the applicant's social security number or a control number issued by the Department of Motor Vehicles.

Suspension of certain licenses issued by the commonwealth may be employed as a means of enforcing child support obligations. The Department of Motor Vehicles may suspend or refuse to renew the driver's license of an obligor who is delinquent in the payment of child support by 90 days or more or in an amount of $5,000. Va. Code § 46.2-320. The obligor is entitled to a judicial hearing if timely requested, and suspension or refusal to renew the driver's license will be authorized only if the court finds that the obligor's noncompliance was willful.

An authorization to engage in a business, trade, profession or occupation, or recreational activity may be suspended for failure to comply with child support obligations on petition by either the obligee or the Department of Social Services under Va. Code § 63.2-1937. Under this provision, suspension may be ordered if the obligor is 90 days delinquent or owes at least $5,000, and if other remedies are not likely to result in collection of the delinquency. A court may refuse to order suspension if it would result in irreparable harm to the obligor or the obligor's employees, if it would not result in collection of the delinquent amount, or if the obligor has made a demonstrated, good faith effort to reach an agreement. The license or certificate will be reinstated if the obligor complies or reaches an agreement with respect to the delinquency and makes at least one payment pursuant to such an agreement. Support orders (1) must include a notice that upon a delinquency for a period of 90 days or more or in an amount of $5,000 or more, a petition may be filed for suspension of any license, certificate, registration, or other authorization to engage in a profession, trade, business, occupation, or recreational activity issued to a parent, and (2) must indicate any such authorizations currently held by either parent. Va. Code § 20-60.3.

Va. Code § 20-108.2, as amended in 1999, allows garnishments for child and spousal support when the United States is the third party. The amended statute eliminates the automatic lapse after 180 days, and allows for garnishments to take place until modified by the issuing court, or in the case of the arrearage, until the arrearage is paid in full.

The Department of Social Services may withhold child support payments from banks, savings institutions, other financial institutions, or broker-dealers where the support debtor has an individual or joint account. Va. Code § 63.2-1931. Virginia Code § 20-79.3 sets forth the necessary contents for orders for withholding a support debtor's earnings as an employee. At the time of employment, the employer shall ask each new employee whether there is an outstanding child support order. If the answer is yes, then the employer is to begin withholding. Va. Code § 60.2-114.1.

In cases transferred from the courts to the Department of Social Services, the payee shall be deemed to have executed an authorization to seek or enforce a support obligation with the Department's Division of Child Support Enforcement unless the payee specifically indicates that the Division's services are not desired. Va. Code § 20-65.5.

The Department of Social Services is to pay interest at the legal rate on support payments it receives, where the recipient is not on public assistance, if the amount received is not paid out within thirty days of the end of the months in which received, and the accrued interest exceeds five dollars. Va. Code §§ 20-60.5, 20-78.2, Va. Code § 63.2-1951. Amendments to Va. Code § 16.1-279(F) provide that in any determination of a support obligation, the support obligation as it becomes due and unpaid creates a judgment by operation of law. Such judgment becomes a lien against real estate only when docketed in the county or city where the real estate is located.

The entry of an order or decree of support and maintenance for a child constitutes a final judgment for any sum or sums in arrears. The order must include an amount for interest on the arrearage at the judgment interest rate unless the obligee waives the collection of interest in a writing submitted to the court, and it may include reasonable attorney's fees if the amount of the arrearage, excluding interest, is equal to or greater than three months of support and maintenance. Va. Code § 20-78.2.

The Department of Child Support Enforcement shall have the authority to assess and recover attorneys' fees from the absent responsible parent when the Department has had a proceeding to enforce the child support obligations. It shall also have the authority to assess and recover the actual costs of blood testing against the absent responsible parent, and the actual costs of intercept programs. The fees and costs may be collected using any mechanism provided by Chapter 19 of Title 63.2. Va. Code § 63.2-1960.

An attorney representing a husband in a claim against the Division of Child Support Enforcement should not accept or continue representation of the ex-wife, who was petitioning for child support against a man who allegedly fathered her two younger children. The conflict of interest arose because of the substantial relatedness of each client's matter, together with the fact that the paternity issue had not yet been fully resolved. Virginia State Bar Ethics Opinion No. 1279 (September 21, 1989).

An attorney may not advertise that he would represent clients in need of legal advice for the collection of child or spousal support arrearages on a contingent fee basis, unless the advertisement clearly indicated that such an arrangement is only permissible where the child support arrearages have been reduced to judgment. The attorney must still explain to individual clients before accepting employment that the costs and expenses of litigation and the case file remain the client's responsibility. Virginia State Bar Ethics Opinion No. 1229 (April 25, 1989).

Section 20-87 provides that when a chief of police or sheriff becomes satisfied that a person is violating the directions given by a judge for his or her conduct, such officer shall have the authority to arrest such person after issuance of a proper capias or warrant. Another possible remedy is the addition in Va. Code § 20-79.2 of the immediate payroll deduction unless the obligee and obligor agree to an alternative arrangement. Income, under Va. Code § 63.2-1900, means any periodic form of payment due an individual from any source, including salaries, wages, commissions, royalties, bonuses, dividends, severance pay, pension or retirement payments, interest, trust income, annuities, capital gains, social security benefits, workers' compensation benefits, unemployment insurance benefits, disability insurance benefits, veterans' benefits, spousal support, net rental income, gifts, prizes or awards. See also Va. Code § 20-108.2(C) (definition of "gross income" for purposes of child support guidelines). The procedure for obtaining immediate withholding is set forth in Va. Code § 63.2-1923. After issuance of an order under § 20-79, as amended in 1988, the court may upon the motion of any party or on its own motion transfer any matters covered by the decree to any juvenile and domestic relations district court that constitutes a more appropriate forum.

Although a responsible parent need not be present in order for reimbursement to the state of child support payments to be determined, there can be no collection of the money prior to notice and a right to hearing and appeal. *Commonwealth v. Broadnax*, 18 Va. Cir. 276 (City of Richmond, 1989) (due process was provided in this case).

As with spousal support, since a duty is involved, enforcement of child support obligations may be through special remedies, such as contempt, see, e.g. *Boaze v. Commonwealth*, 165 Va. 786, 793, 183 S.E. 263, 266 (1935), or sanctions, see, e.g., *Fox v. Fox*, 41 Va. App. 88, 581 S.E.2d 904 (2003) ("nonparticipation sanction" imposed on husband found in contempt, prohibiting husband from filing pleadings until he personally appeared and posted bond); and also through the more traditional remedies of garnishment, see, e.g., *In re Marriage of Stutz*, 126 Cal. App. 3d 1038, 179 Cal. Rptr. 312 (1981). See generally attachment of property; see also Va. Code § 20-114 (recognizance for compliance with support order in divorce action), Va. Code § 19.2-123(E) (recognizance or bond to secure support obligation in addition to recognizance or bond to assure appearance in criminal action), and Va. Code § 8.01-460 (lien on support obligor's real property).

In 2013, the Legislature amended Va. Code §§ 60.2-114 and 63.2-1946 to require employers to report information about newly hired employees to the Virginia New Hire Reporting Center, Division of Child Support Enforcement, within 20 days of the employment of the newly hired employee. This information is used to locate individuals for the purpose of establishing paternity, and establishing, modifying, and enforcing child support obligations.

At the time defendant is found in contempt, there must be an ability to pay, or there will be imprisonment for debt. *Barrett v. Barrett*, 470 Pa. 253, 368 A.2d 616 (1977). However, the inability to pay must be involuntary. See, e.g., *Branch v. Branch*, 144 Va. 244, 132 S.E. 303 (1926) (defendant husband able to work as laborer since healthy and young); *D. v. M.*, 107 Misc. 2d 217, 433 N.Y.S.2d 715 (1980). Where the court may hold a parent guilty of criminal contempt for failure to pay child support, a jury trial is required. *Kessler v. Commonwealth*, 18 Va. App. 14, 441 S.E.2d 223 (1994).

The husband's due process rights were violated when he was denied an opportunity to call a witness in support of his claim that he lacked money to pay court-ordered spousal and child support. His voluntary reduction in income, following his sale of a carpet installation business in favor of working for someone else, did not in and of itself support a contempt finding. *Street v. Street*, 24 Va. App. 14, 480 S.E.2d 118 (1997).

Contempt may result in commission to a correctional facility, to a work release program, or to perform public service work. Va. Code § 20-115. If a noncustodial parent in arrears fails to post an appeal bond, the circuit court is not required on its own motion to bifurcate the issues and determine whether he intended to separately pursue an appeal from a civil contempt citation. *McCall v. Department of Social Servs., Div. of Child Support Enforcement ex rel. Ware*, 20 Va. App. 348, 457 S.E.2d 389 (1995).

The lien made by a decree, order, or judgment for support and maintenance of a child may be released upon agreement of all obligees, provided they are adults and agree to the release of the specified real property. Va. Code § 8.01-460.

The wife obtained a pendente lite unitary award for spousal and child support that was to continue until further order of the court, and the husband later obtained a final divorce. The decree reserved custody, support, and property division for later decision. The husband died eight years later, and his estate was subject to a lien for unpaid payments under the temporary support order. *Duke v. Duke*, 239 Va. 501, 391 S.E.2d 77 (1990).

An appeal bond is required for an appeal from a juvenile and domestic relations court order or judgment establishing support arrearages or suspending payment of support during the pendency of an appeal; and may be required for an appeal from a conviction for failure to support or from a finding of civil or criminal contempt involving a failure to support. Va. Code § 16.1-296(H). See *Sharma v. Sharma*, 46 Va. App. 584, 620 S.E.2d 553 (2005) (trial court properly dismissed father's appeal of child support order establishing support arrearages, when appeal bond had incurable jurisdictional defect); *Mahoney v. Mahoney*, 34 Va. App. 63, 537 S.E.2d 626 (2000) (law governing appeals from courts not of record provides well established legal foundation for imposition of bond). Posting of an appeal bond is required in proceedings from the juvenile and domestic relations court, even if the responsible parent is found in civil contempt of court. *Scheer v. Isaacs*, 10 Va. App. 338, 392 S.E.2d 201 (1990); see also *Virginia Dep't of Social Servs., Div. of Child Support Enforcement, ex rel. May v. Walker*, 253 Va. 319, 485 S.E.2d 134 (1997) (when juvenile and domestic relations court fails to set appeal bond as required, circuit court is deprived of jurisdiction).

Defenses might be based upon a nonability to pay, see, e.g., *Branch v. Branch*, 144 Va. 244, 132 S.E. 303 (1926) (defendant husband unsuccessful in defense since healthy and able to work as day laborer), or satisfaction of the original order. The failure of the custodial spouse to abide by other portions of the decree will not allow the noncustodial spouse to cease making payments. For example, although the husband argued that since the wife refused him visitation, he was not liable for amounts payable for her support, the court construed the payments required by an incorporated property settlement agreement to be in fact child support rather than alimony. In any event, the parties should comply with the terms of a divorce decree until modified by the court's further order. It was for the court, not the husband, to determine whether the payment of the "household maintenance" item had been forfeited by the alleged breach of the terms of the settlement agreement and the decree by the wife. *Newton v. Newton*, 202 Va. 515, 118 S.E.2d 656 (1961).

Nor could overpayments be set off against any required future payments for child support. *Id.* at 518–19, 118 S.E.2d at 658–59 (citing 17A Am. Jur. Divorce and Separation § 876 at 65). His remedy if the circumstances varied was to apply to the court for a change in the terms of the decree.

A parent who willfully fails to provide support for his or her child under the age of 18 years who is "then and there in necessitous circumstances" is guilty of a misdemeanor that is punishable by fine, imprisonment, or both. Va. Code § 20-61. See *Williams v. Commonwealth*, 57 Va. App. 750, 706 S.E.2d 530 (2011) (Commonwealth is not required to show that parent *caused* child's "necessitous circumstances").

A party who is incarcerated by conviction of non-payment of child support is exempt from the bond requirement under Va. Code § 16.1-296(H). *Frazier v. Department of Soc. Servs., Division of Child Support Enforcement ex rel. Sandridge*, 27 Va. App. 131, 497 S.E.2d 879 (1998).

The Child Support Recovery Act of 1992 (CSRA), 18 U.S.C. § 228, amended by the Deadbeat Parents Punishment Act (DPPA), 18 U.S.C. § 228 (Supp. 1999), makes the willful failure to pay a past due child support obligation for a child residing in a different state into a federal offense. The obligation must be for court-ordered child or family support, and must have remained unpaid for longer than one year or be greater than $5,000 (if the obligor travels in interstate commerce intending to evade the support obligation, or if the child lives in another state), or must have remained unpaid for longer than two years or be greater than $10,000 (if the child lives in another state). The offense is either a misdemeanor or a felony, depending on the amount and length of time that the obligation has remained unpaid. See 18 U.S.C. § 228 (Supp. 1999).

Several federal Circuit Courts of Appeals have held that the CSRA and the DPPA do not violate the Ex Post Facto Clause of the United States Constitution, U.S. Const. art. I, § 9, cl. 3, which prohibits the application of laws that retroactively alter the definition of a crime or retroactively increase the punishment for criminal acts; and that both acts are therefore constitutional. See, e.g., *United States v. Wilson*, 210 F.3d 230 (4th Cir. 2000). The CSRA and DPPA apply only to a parent's illegal conduct (the parent's willful failure to pay a past due child support obligation) that occurs after their enactment, on October 25, 1992, and June 24, 1998, respectively. See *United States v. Mussari*, 152 F.3d 1156 (9th Cir. 1998). However, when a parent is prosecuted under the CSRA and DPPA, the relevant fact is not when the debt in excess of $5,000 or $10,000 accrued, but when the willful failure to pay occurred. See *United States v. Wilson*, 210 F.3d 230 (4th Cir. 2000). Thus, in *Wilson*, a parent charged with a felony under the DPPA, who had accrued more than $10,000 in unpaid support obligations prior to, but not after, the date of the DPPA's enactment, was properly charged, because he had committed the crime of willful failure to pay a child support obligation after the date of the DPPA's enactment.

The CSRA includes a venue provision which provides that a prosecution under 18 U.S.C. § 228 may be brought in, among other places, "the district in which the obligor resided" during the time the obligor willfully failed to meet the child support obligation. 18 U.S.C. § 228(e). The term "resided" is defined as "the act or fact of living in a given place permanently or for an extended period of time," and does *not* include an intent by the obligor to remain in, or be domiciled in, the district. See *United States v. Novak*, 607 F.3d 968 (4th Cir. 2010).

Under the Employee Retirement Income Security Act (ERISA), 29 U.S.C. § 1001 et seq., the funds of an employee benefit plan generally may not be assigned or alienated. However, this prohibition does not apply when a state domestic relations order is determined to be a qualified domestic relations order (QDRO). 29 U.S.C. § 1056(d)(3). ERISA states that each pension plan shall provide for the payment of benefits in accordance with the applicable requirements of any qualified domestic relations order. 29 U.S.C. § 1056(d)(3).

Under ERISA, the term *"domestic relations order"* is defined as any judgment, decree, or order that (1) relates to the provision of child support, alimony payments, or marital property rights to a spouse, former spouse, child, or other dependent of a participant, and (2) is made pursuant to a state domestic relations law. 29 U.S.C. § 1056(d)(3)(B)(ii). One of the main reasons for enacting the ERISA amendments that created the QDRO feature was to give enhanced protection to plan beneficiaries such as dependent children in the event of divorce or separation.

In *Nkopchieu v. Minlend*, 59 Va. App. 299, 718 S.E.2d 470 (2011), the mother made a motion to the circuit court requesting a qualified domestic relations order (QDRO) to permit her to attach the father's retirement account to pay a child support arrearage. The father argued that a QDRO could not be entered because the mother had expressly disavowed any property interest in her husband's retirement account assets in the parties' premarital agreement. The trial court denied the mother's motion, and the mother appealed.

The appellate court held that the parties' premarital agreement did not bar the QDRO because the mother sought no personal interest in the account but only sought to pursue child support for the parties' children. The court held that the mother could seek a QDRO making the children the account's alternate payees because: (1) the purpose of 29 U.S.C. § 1056(d)(3) was to protect dependent children in a divorce; and (2) her request related to providing child support, which satisfies a condition for the entry of a QDRO, under 29 U.S.C. § 1056(d)(3)(B)(ii)(I). The appellate court reversed the trial court decision and remanded the case, stating that the trial court could enforce the father's duty to support his children because: (1) neither parent could abridge their rights to receive support from him; and (2) the law allowed the attachment of his only known asset to satisfy this duty. Subsequently, an amendment to Va. Code Ann. § 20-113 passed the General Assembly of Virginia, codifying the holding in the *Nkopchieu* case:

> [T]he court may enter a qualified domestic relations order or other order for the purpose of enforcing a support order by attaching or garnishing any pension, profit-sharing, or deferred compensation plan or retirement benefits pursuant to the United States Internal Revenue Code or other applicable federal laws.

This amendment was approved by the Governor and is effective as of July 1, 2012.

### § 22.22    Laches

Laches is an omission to assert a right for an unreasonable and unexplained length of time, under circumstances prejudicial to the adverse party. *Stiles v. Stiles*, 48 Va. App. 449, 632 S.E.2d 607 (2006). In *Stiles*, a former wife asserted her right to a child support modification by filing a petition for modification and serving it on her former husband. Although the wife's claim for a child support modification was not adjudicated for more than four years, the doctrine of laches was inapplicable, because the husband had notice and was not prejudiced.

A custodial parent's passive acquiescence in an obligor parent's noncompliance with a support order, even for a very long period of time, will not preclude support enforcement by the appropriate court. See *Richardson v. Moore*, 217 Va. 422, 229 S.E.2d 864 (1976) (twenty-five years after husband unilaterally reduced child support payments, wife was able to enforce support order). See also *Johnson v. Johnson*, 1 Va. App. 330, 338 S.E.2d 353 (1986) (wife's 10-year delay in seeking support arrearages did not bar recovery because laches is not a defense to noncompliance with a lawful decree); *Carter v. Hall*, 42 Va. Cir. 437 (City of Roanoke 1997) (neither laches nor 20-year statute of limitations nor children's emancipation barred mother's recovery of child support arrearages).

In *Adcock v. Dep't of Soc. Servs. Div. of Child Support ex rel. Houchens*, 56 Va. App. 334, 693 S.E.2d 757 (2010), *rev'd*, 282 Va. 383, 719 S.E.2d 304 (2011), the circuit court found that the 20-year statute of limitations under Va. Code Ann. § 8.01-251 did not bar a wife's recovery of child support arrearages, even though she waited 30 years to seek enforcement of a 1966 child support order, and even though the husband's child support obligation had ended more than 20 years earlier with the youngest child's emancipation. On appeal, the Supreme Court reversed, holding that the payments that the father was ordered to pay pursuant to the divorce decree, as they became due and were unpaid, created judgments. The youngest child for whom the father owed support reached the age of 18 on June 24, 1982, and all judgments were created on or before that date. Thus, the action to collect past due child support obligations, based upon the 1966 decree, was filed more than 20 years after any payments ordered by the decree became judgments by operation of law and was barred pursuant to § 8.01-251(A).

# CHAPTER 23

# Child Custody

## SYNOPSIS

## § 23.01    Introduction

In Virginia, "the welfare of the infant is the primary, paramount, and controlling consideration of the court in all controversies between parents over the custody of their minor children." *Mullen v. Mullen*, 188 Va. 259, 269, 49 S.E.2d 349, 354 (1948). See also *Coffee v. Black*, 82 Va. 567, 569

(1866). In fact, "the right of a parent to custody of its minor child is subordinate to the right of a child to a custodial care of a parent." *McCreery v. McCreery*, 218 Va. 352, 237 S.E.2d 167 (1977). This emphasis runs contrary to the perception of many clients that it is the parents' rights that are of concern during custody litigation. The emphasis upon the children, as opposed to the parents, colors many recent substantive and procedural developments in the law of custody. A recently reported circuit court decision outlines the problems the court faces in custody cases:

> A heavy responsibility rests on the court whenever it must make a decision which will sever for one parent or the other the "tender ties of affection," but when this unfortunate necessity arises, neither sentimentality nor sympathy for either parent should alter a course directed to promoting the rights of children to have the more proper award of their custody made. *Shockey v. Shockey*, 30 Va. Cir. 493, 498 (Frederick Co. 1979).

Guardianship is distinguished from custody in *In re O'Neil*, 18 Va. App. 674, 446 S.E.2d 475 (1994). According to that case, guardianship of the person and estate of a child entails a broader power to have custody of the ward and the right to take possession of the ward's estate to pay for the ward's maintenance and education. Unlike the legal custodian, the guardian is a fiduciary or guarantor of the child.

This "best interests" standard does not require a showing of unfitness on the part of a parent, although cases certainly refer to unfitness and in fact state that evidence of unfitness must be clear and convincing. See, e.g., *Moore v. Moore*, 212 Va. 153, 156, 183 S.E.2d 172, 174 (1971).

The weight to be placed on the fitness factor, *i.e.*, the physical and mental health of a parent, is within the discretion of the trial court. *Joynes v. Payne*, 36 Va. App. 401, 551 S.E.2d 10 (2001). In *Joynes*, a parent's bulimia, standing alone, did not support an award of sole custody to the other parent.

Originally, a father was entitled to the custody of his child when a fit and suitable person, unless custody was voluntarily relinquished. *Coffee v. Black*, 82 Va. 567 (1866) (action against sister-in-law); *Latham v. Latham*, 71 Va. (30 Gratt.) 307 (1878) (husband given custody when no divorce granted to wife). After this, the mother for many years was found to be "the natural custodian of her child of tender years," *Mullen v. Mullen*, 188 Va. 259, 270–71, 49 S.E.2d 349, 354 (1948), and thus was given custody if she was fit and all other things were equal. However, Va. Code § 20-107.2 now provides that there is no legal presumption in favor of either parent. See also *Wince v. Wince*, 26 Va. Cir. 420 (Henrico Co. 1978). The principle of *Moore v. Moore*, 212 Va. 153, 183 S.E.2d 172 (1971), is that a rebuttable inference exists that when the mother is fit, and other things are equal, she should have custody of a child of tender years. See *Harper v. Harper*, 217 Va. 477, 229 S.E.2d 875 (1976) (custody awarded to mother when both parents were fit and proper persons to have custody). In fact, therefore, although the statute has eliminated any conclusive presumption based upon the gender of the parent and the child's age, a strong preference for the mother exists in many cases where the children are very young, particularly if they are girls. This preference of course may be overcome by evidence showing that all things are not equal and that in fact the child would be better off in the custody of the father.

There is no legal presumption of custody that favors a biological parent over an adoptive parent. *Carter v. Carter*, 35 Va. App. 466, 546 S.E.2d 220 (2001). In *Carter*, a husband adopted his wife's biological child, and the husband and wife together had a biological child. After the couple separated, a trial court awarded custody of both children to the husband, in the best interests of the children. The Court of Appeals affirmed, stating that once a stepparent adoption is final, there is no distinction in law between the adoptive parent and the biological parent. Both parents are equally charged with the adopted child's care, nurture, welfare, education and support, and both parents are equally entitled to consideration as the adopted child's custodial parent. *Carter v. Carter*, 35 Va. App. 466, 546 S.E.2d 220 (2001).

The parties' contract regarding custody will not prevent the court from exercising its power to alter custody. See, e.g., *Hammers v. Hammers*, 216 Va. 30, 31, 216 S.E.2d 20, 21 (1975) (child support); *Campbell v. Campbell*, 203 Va. 61, 64, 122 S.E.2d 658, 661 (1961). See generally Sharp, *Modification of Agreement-Based Custody Decrees: Unitary or Dual Standard?*, 68 Va. L. Rev. 1263 (1982).

The decision of the trial judge, who has had the opportunity to see the parties and hear witnesses testify, is entitled to great respect, *Brown v. Brown*, 218 Va. 196, 200–01, 237 S.E.2d 89, 92 (1977), and will not be reversed unless there has been an abuse of discretion. A parent may appeal an order entered by a lower court even though counsel has "seen and agreed to" the order, according to *Cox v. Cox*, 16 Va. App. 146, 428 S.E.2d 515 (1993). In *Cox*, the appeal was from the juvenile and domestic relations district court and the Court interpreted Va. Code § 16.1-296 which permitted an appeal from *any* final order of the juvenile court.

The factors involved in custody cases, and definitions of joint and shared custody, appear in Va. Code Ann. §§ 20-124.1–20-124.3. Although a trial court must examine all of the factors set out in Va. Code Ann. § 20-124.3, the court is not required to quantify or elaborate exactly what weight or consideration it has given to each of the statutory factors. *Kane v. Szymczak*, 41 Va. App. 365, 585 S.E.2d 349 (2003); *Sargent v. Sargent*, 20 Va. App. 694 (1995).

Va. Code § 20-124.3 requires the trial court to consider the following factors in a custody dispute:

1.  The age and physical and mental condition of the child, giving due consideration to the child's changing developmental needs;

2.  The age and physical and mental condition of each parent;

3.  The relationship existing between each parent and each child, giving due consideration to the positive involvement with the child's life, the ability to accurately assess and meet the emotional, intellectual, and physical needs of the child;

4.  The needs of the child, giving due consideration to other important relationships of the child, including but not limited to siblings, peers, and extended family members;

5.  The role that each parent has played and will play in the future, in the upbringing and care of the child;

6.  The propensity of each parent to actively support the child's contact and relationship with the other parent, including whether a parent has unreasonably denied the other parent access to or visitation with the child;

7.  The relative willingness and demonstrated ability of each parent to maintain a close and continuing relationship with the child, and the ability of each parent to cooperate in and resolve disputes regarding matters affecting the child;

8.  The reasonable preference of the child, if the court deems the child to be of reasonable intelligence, understanding, age, and experience to express such a preference;

9.  Any history of (i) family abuse as that term is defined in § 16.1-228; (ii) sexual abuse; (iii) child abuse; or (iv) an act of violence, force, or threat as defined in § 19.2-152.7:1 that occurred no earlier than 10 years prior to the date a petition is filed. If the court finds such a history or act, the court may disregard the factors in subdivision 6; and

10.  Such other factors as the court deems necessary and proper to the determination.

A trial judge's discretion is broad when evaluating and weighing the evidence, and determining the credibility of the witnesses. *Wynnycky v.*

*Kozel,* 71 Va. App. 177, 192, 834 S.E.2d 512 (2109); *Street v. Street,* 25 Va. App. 380, 387, 448 S.E.2d 665 (1997).

To satisfactorily communicate the basis of the decision, as required by Va. Code § 20-124.3, the trial court must provide a case-specific explanation of the fundamental, predominating reason or reasons for the decision. The court is *not* required to address all aspects of the decisionmaking process, as would be expected from comprehensive findings of fact and conclusions of law. *Kane v. Szymczak,* 41 Va. App. 365, 585 S.E.2d 349 (2003) (insufficient communication). However, communicating the basis of the decision does require the trial court to provide the parties with more than boilerplate language or a perfunctory statement that the statutory factors have been considered. *Lanzalotti v. Lanzalotti,* 41 Va. App. 550, 586 S.E.2d 881 (2003) (insufficient communication). See *Artis v. Jones,* 52 Va. App. 356, 663 S.E.2d 521 (2008) (insufficient communication through combined oral and written statements).

On February 27, 2012, the legislature passed HB 84, which amended Va. Code § 20-124.3 and codified the level of communication required. The trial court must provide the basis for its decision regarding child custody or visitation, except in cases of a consent order for custody or visitation, and must set forth the judge's findings regarding the relevant statutory factors used to determine the best interests of the child.

Va. Code § 20-124.3(6) provides that the trial court must consider whether a parent has unreasonably denied the other parent access to or visitation with the child as a factor in determining custody or visitation arrangements. However, that factor may be disregarded if the court finds a history of (1) family abuse, (2) sexual abuse, (3) child abuse, or (4) an act of violence, force, or threat as defined in Va. Code § 19.2-152.7:1 that occurred no earlier than 10 years prior to the date a petition is filed.

In any appropriate case, the trial court may refer the parents to a dispute resolution evaluation session to be conducted by a mediator. Va. Code § 20-124.4.

Va. Code § 20-124.6 provides that neither a custodial nor a noncustodial parent may be denied access to his or her child's academic records, health records or child day care center or family day home records.

The parties to any petition for custody, visitation or support, regardless of whether contested, must show proof that they have attended a court-approved parent education program within 12 months before their first court appearance or that they will attend a program within 45 days after their appearance. This program must be at least four hours long and must address the effects of separation or divorce on children, parenting responsibilities, options for conflict resolution and financial responsibilities. Va. Code § 20-103(A).

The Virginia Military Parents Equal Protection Act is set forth at Va. Code §§ 20-124.7 through 20-124.10. If a military parent is being deployed to active service where the parent cannot bring his or her child, a petition to establish custody, visitation, or support for the child must be identified at the time of filing by the deploying parent to ensure that the deploying parent has access to the child, and that reasonable support and other orders are in place for the protection of the parent-child relationship. Va. Code § 20-124.9(A). The court may conduct a hearing using a telephonic or electronic communication system if a deploying parent is reasonably unable to appear as a result of his deployment. Va. Code § 20-124.9(B). The trial court improperly applied the Virginia Military Parents Equal Protection Act where the father's prior orders for assignment in Bahrain permitted his family to deploy with him, as did his current orders for assignment in Virginia Beach. *Rubino v. Rubino*, 64 Va. App. 256, 262–63, 767 S.E.2d 260, 263 (2015). In Va. Code § 20-124.7, deployment is defined as compliance with military orders "for which the deploying parent or guardian is required to report unaccompanied by any family member." *Id.*, 64 Va. App. at 263, 767 S.E.2d at 263.

See generally Robert Cochran, *The Search for Guidance in Determining the Best Interests of the Child at Divorce*, 20 U. Rich. L. Rev. 1 (1985); Martha Fineman, *Dominant Discourse, Professional Language and Legal Change in Child Custody Decisionmaking*, 101 Harv. L. Rev. 727 (1988); Jerry McCant, *The Cultural Contradiction of Fathers as Nonparents*, 21 Fam. L.Q. 127 (1987); Robert Mnookin, *Child Custody Adjudications: Judicial Functions in the Fact of Indeterminacy*, 39 Law & Contemp. Probs. 226 (1975); John Murray, *Improving Parent-Child Relationships Within the Divorced Family: A Call for Legal Reform*, 19 U. Mich. J. Law Reform 563 (1986). See also Stephen B. Bershing, *"Entreat Me Not to Leave Thee": Bottoms v. Bottoms and the Custody Rights of Gay and Lesbian Parents*, 3 Wm. & Mary Bill Rts. J. 289 (1994); Barry M. Parsons, Note, *Bottoms v. Bottoms: Erasing the Presumption Favoring a Natural Parent Over Third Parties—What Makes This Mother Unfit?* 2 Geo. Mason Independent L. Rev. 457 (1994).

## § 23.02    Who May Seek Custody?

At common law, the mother of an illegitimate child was its natural custodian, and frequently the unwed father was presumed unfit as a matter of law and therefore was given no notice when the mother's rights were terminated before adoption. The United States Supreme Court, in *Stanley v.*

*Illinois*, 405 U.S. 645, 92 S. Ct. 1208, 31 L. Ed. 2d 551 (1972), held that such presumptions violated the fourteenth amendment, and that hearings would be required where a substantial relationship existed between parent and child. Later cases suggested that where such a relationship existed, the father could veto an attempted adoption by a stepparent and seek adoption himself, *Caban v. Mohammed*, 441 U.S. 380, 99 S. Ct. 1760, 60 L. Ed. 2d 297 (1979), but that an unwed father could not seek to block a stepparent adoption without such a relationship. *Quilloin v. Walcott*, 434 U.S. 246, 98 S. Ct. 549, 54 L. Ed. 2d 511 (1978). See also *Michael H. v. Gerald D.*, 491 U.S. 110, 109 S. Ct. 2333, 105 L. Ed. 2d 91 (1989), where the Court held that a married woman's lover was not entitled to a paternity hearing although blood tests showed that in all probability he was the child's father. There have been many Virginia cases dealing with custody disputes other than those between husband and wife pursuant to divorce. In *Commonwealth v. Hayes*, 215 Va. 49, 205 S.E.2d 644 (1974), the Supreme Court of Virginia heard a case considering an unwed father's fitness to take custody when the mother put the child up for adoption. Since the father had never taken any prior interest in the child nor had contact with her, and since his plans for the future were unsatisfactory and speculative, his rights in the child were terminated. The Court found him unfit to have custody. See also *In re Custody of Sloan*, 25 Va. Cir. 227 (Amherst Co. 1991) (father found unfit since he had abandoned children, had disobeyed court orders and exhibited a very unstable lifestyle, including at least two concurrent marriages; custody was awarded to foster parents, and father denied visitation rights). In *Wadford v. Wadford*, 1998 Va. App. LEXIS 342 (June 16, 1998) (unpublished decision), a custody order granted to the mother and Redford, her boyfriend during a separation, was affirmed upon an appeal brought by the husband. The husband and wife resumed cohabitation after the separation, and a daughter was born. The husband was awarded custody of the children after the second separation. Later DNA tests proved Redford was the daughter's father. The trial court awarded custody of the son to the husband, and custody of the daughter to the wife and Redford. Upon the husband's appeal, the Court of Appeals held that the trial court used the proper standard of best interests of the child in determining that the daughter be placed in the custody of her natural mother and father. The evidence in the record showed that Redford filed for custody promptly upon learning that he was the child's father, asserting his custody interest without delay. The record also showed that he was a fit and good parent and that he established a good relationship with the daughter.

The right of the natural father of an illegitimate child was also superior to that of the child's maternal grandparents. *Hayes v. Strauss*, 151 Va. 136, 144 S.E. 432, 434 (1978). But see *Forbes v. Haney*, 204 Va. 712, 133 S.E.2d 533 (1963), where the maternal grandparents of an illegitimate child were given custody when the natural father was "immoral," since the grandparents were fit and "the welfare of the child is to be regarded more highly than the technical legal rights of the parent." *Id.* at 716, 133 S.E.2d at 536. See also *Patrick v. Byerley*, 228 Va. 691, 325 S.E.2d 99 (1985) (holding that former stepmother ought to be awarded custody since natural mother had abandoned child).

In *Bailes v. Sours*, 231 Va. 96, 340 S.E.2d 824 (1986), the natural mother was a virtual stranger to her child, who had lived with his father and stepmother for eight years before his father's death. In a psychologist's opinion, a change of custody would have had a significant harmful impact on the child, who strongly desired to remain with his stepmother. In leaving custody with the stepmother, the *Bailes* court held that the presumption favoring a parent over a nonparent was not conclusive, but could be rebutted by clear and convincing evidence of: (1) parental unfitness; (2) a previous divestiture order; (3) voluntary relinquishment; (4) abandonment; or (5) a finding of "special facts and circumstances constituting an extraordinary reason for taking a child from his parent, or parents." See *Florio v. Clark*, 277 Va. 566, 674 S.E.2d 845 (2009) (totality of evidence supported trial court's conclusion that presumption favoring parent over nonparent was rebutted by "special facts and circumstances," even though natural father and son shared affectionate relationship). Once the presumption favoring parental custody is rebutted, a natural parent who seeks to regain custody must bear the burden of proving that custody with the natural parent is in the child's best interests. See *Shortridge v. Deel*, 224 Va. 589, 299 S.E.2d 500 (1983).

In *Bottoms v. Bottoms*, 249 Va. 410, 457 S.E.2d 102 (1995), a child's grandmother was awarded custody in a contested dispute with the child's natural mother. Among other things, the child had spent 70 percent of his time with the grandmother and 30 percent with his mother. Further, the mother "refused to subordinate her own desires and priorities to the child's welfare." She moved frequently, misused welfare funds, and participated in illicit relationships with both men and the woman with whom she presently lived. See also *In re O'Neil*, 18 Va. App. 674, 446 S.E.2d 475 (1994) (private petition for transfer of guardianship; action between parents and grandparents).

Where no special facts and circumstances existed, although the child had resided for some time in the home of her maternal great aunt, when the parents were able to resume custody of the child, "there was nothing to justify a finding that the best interest of [the child] would be served" by separating her from her parents and siblings. *Smith v. Pond*, 5 Va. App. 161, 360 S.E.2d 885 (1987).

After the custodial mother died, the maternal grandparents were success-ful in contesting a change of custody to the father, since the child's best interests were paramount, and the child would be a complete stranger to the father's new wife and her teenage children, with whom the child would have to share a room. *In re Custody of Forrest*, 13 Va. Cir. 424 (City of Roanoke 1970). However, even though the child was in the physical custody of the paternal grandmother, custody was given to a now more adult and remarried mother. *Cunningham v. Crummett*, 13 Va. Cir. 495 (Bath Co. 1980). Further, in *Mason v. Moon*, 9 Va. App. 217, 385 S.E.2d 242 (1989), custody was awarded to the natural mother over the paternal grandmother with whom the custodial father and child had lived since the child's parents separated. The natural mother was favored despite the fact that only thirteen days after the father's death she had married the man who had killed the child's father. See also *Elder v. Evans*, 16 Va. App. 60, 427 S.E.2d 745 (1993), where the natural father sought custody from people with whom mother had placed the child. He was granted custody since despite a number of problems at the beginning, he was now a caring and loving parent, his family life was appropriate, and the child showed an ability to adapt to the family. Likewise, in *Roberts v. Williams*, 1996 Va. App. LEXIS 103 (Feb. 13, 1996), the natural father was able to obtain custody since he had made efforts to gain custody despite placement of the child with the mother's first cousin. In *Bonds v. Anderson*, 1996 Va. App. LEXIS 504 (July 16, 1996), a child's parents were never married, and the child lived with the mother after the couple separated, while the father never provided any financial assistance or attention and eventually relocated to Florida. Shortly before the child's second birthday, the mother was killed in an automobile accident. Both the father and the maternal grandmother sought custody. The trial court awarded custody to the father, finding that he had obtained employment in Florida while pursuing education as a "pharmacist assistant," and that he provided an adequate home and attendant support for his son. Although the grand-mother initially assumed custody, the father was awarded custody by the trial court. The grandmother complained unsuccessfully that the father had once "picked the child up from the floor" and "slammed him up against the corner of a door and a wall" and that he was living in a "meretricious relationship" with his fiancée. responsibility of the natural father even if handicapped.

convincingly rebut the presumption that the father's custody best served the child's interests.

In *Boyce v. Bush*, 1997 Va. App. LEXIS 270 (Apr. 29, 1997), the child's mother and grandparents sued the child's former stepfather, who had been awarded temporary custody. The identity of the child's natural father was unknown, and the mother had left the child to move in with her parents when she left the marital home to move in with a friend, later relinquishing custody to the parents. The stepfather, who was 23 and seven years older than the mother, petitioned for custody of the child following the parties' separation. Although both the stepfather's and the grandparents' homes were suitable, the mother had voluntarily relinquished custody to a third party, her father, rebutting the statutory presumption of parental preference. At that point, the best interests of the child standard came into play, and under this standard, award of custody to the former stepparent was appropriate. Compare *Tanner v. Price*, 48 Va. Cir. 314 (City of Richmond 1999), where an 8-year-old girl had lived with her mother and her maternal grandmother for most of her life, and with her grandmother alone after her mother began experiencing mental problems. Her father nonetheless was awarded custody because of the parental preference rule; and *Barker v. Barker*, 49 Va. Cir. 403 (City of Richmond 1999), where the father owed $450 in back child support for the children in question, had a longstanding problem with drugs and lived with his parents, his fiancée, their son, and two of the fiancée's daughters. The children had been living with their maternal aunt and uncle, who had no children of their own, were devoted to the children, and were eager to continue their custodial relationship. The court found that the "Hillises made a stronger impression that the best interest of the children would be served by having custody remain with them."

A natural parent may not seek to terminate his own parental rights, even if the custodial parent has actively encouraged the children to be alienated from their father. *Tallent v. Rosenbloom*, 32 Va. Cir. 61 (Fairfax Co. 1993). See also *Walker v. Fagg*, 11 Va. App. 581, 400 S.E.2d 208 (1991), where the father was awarded custody over both sets of grandparents despite the fact that he had killed the children's mother and was previously an unfit parent. The award of custody to the father was on the basis that his life "had experienced a complete turnaround," and was tentative, subject to vacation should his change of lifestyle prove not to be permanent. Visitation may be extended to stepparents and former stepparents under Va. Code §§ 16.1-241(A)(6) and 16.1-278.15(B) (juvenile and domestic relations district courts) and § 20-107.2 (circuit courts). For a case before the new provisions in which a stepparent was allowed visitation rights, see *Arnold v. Newberry*, 24 Va. Cir. 431 (Washington Co. 1991).

When, after blood tests, DNA testing excluded Mr. Vaughan as the biological father, he sought continued visitation privileges. The trial court held that the Code does not grant visitation privileges to persons other than "family members." *In re Jones*, 26 Va. Cir. 165 (Amherst Co. 1991).

When a child is adopted after his parents' rights are terminated involuntarily, the natural parent may not seek custody or visitation rights. Nor may a person convicted of sexual assault seek custodial or visitation privileges with a child conceived as the result of the assault. Va. Code §§ 16.1-241 and 20-107.2. Custody orders may be entered even when no divorce is pending. In such cases, there may be orders pendente lite directed to any person with a legitimate interest who is a party. The custody and visitation orders in these non-divorce proceedings shall be made in accordance with § 20-124 et seq. Pendente lite orders shall have no presumptive effect and shall not determine the ultimate outcome of the case.

Where the parties were friends, and the female became pregnant by inseminating herself with the use of an ordinary turkey baster, the natural father had the right to pursue visitation. *Bruce v. Boardwine*, 64 Va. App. 623, 770 S.E.2d 774 (2015). The parties never entered into any contract, and the Virginia Assisted Conception statute at Va. Code § 20-156 et seq. did not apply since "assisted conception" was defined by Va. Code § 20-156 to involve medical technology. The use of an ordinary kitchen implement used at home was not analogous to the medical technologies listed in the statute. *Id.*, 64 Va. App. at 630–31, 770 S.E.2d at 776–77.

Current Virginia statutes allow "persons with a legitimate interest" to seek custody, visitation, support, or control of a child. This standing requirement is to be liberally construed, and includes, but is not limited to, grandparents, stepparents, former stepparents, blood relatives and family members. It does not include (1) any person whose parental rights have been terminated by court order (either voluntarily or involuntarily); or (2) any person whose interest in the child derives from or through a parent whose rights have been terminated, such as relatives of a child who has been legally adopted (unless the adoption was a stepparent adoption); or (3) persons involved in rape or statutory rape when the child was conceived as a result of the crime. Va. Code §§ 16.1-241(A) and 20-124.1. See *Surles v. Mayer*, 48 Va. App. 146, 628 S.E.2d 563 (2006) (individual who acted as child's surrogate father for four years was "functional equivalent" of former stepparent, and qualified as "person with legitimate interest" under Va. Code § 20-124.1). See also *Damon v. York*, 54 Va. App. 544, 680 S.E.2d 354 (2009) (former girlfriend of child's mother, who married mother in Canada under law authorizing same-sex marriage, was not "functional equivalent" of child's stepparent who could qualify as "person with legitimate interest" to seek visitation under Va. Code § 124.1); *Yokshas v. Bristol Dep't. of Soc. Servs.*, 2017 Va. App. LEXIS 286 (Nov. 14, 2017) (unpublished opinion) (finding that foster parents who cared for the child for nine months constituted persons with a legitimate interest despite the child being placed back with the custodial parent and the foster care contract being terminated, and therefore had standing to petition for custody and for adoption).

Virginia does not adhere to a de facto parent doctrine. *Hawkins v. Grese*, 68 Va. App. 462, 472, 809 S.E.2d 441, 445 (2018) (citing *Stadter v. Siperko*, 52 Va. App. 81, 661 S.E.2d 494 (2008)). In *Hawkins*, same sex partners intentionally decided to have a child, Grese became pregnant through artificial insemination, and she gave birth to a son in 2007. The child was raised by both parties and considered them to be his parents. However, Hawkins never adopted the child, and the parties neither married nor formed a civil union. When their relationship ended, Hawkins petitioned for custody. The court analyzed the concept of parent and found that "by looking to other areas within the Code of Virginia where parent is used, it is clear that the term "parent" contemplates a relationship to a child based upon either the contribution of genetic material through biological insemination or by means of legal adoption." *Hawkins*, 68 Va. App. at 462, 809 S.E.2d at 445. The case resulted in a devastating impact for Hawkins, and likely the child, as Hawkins' claim for custody was denied since she was unable to rebut the fundamental rights of the biological parent and presumptions respecting the rights of the biological parent against claims made by a third party. *Hawkins*, 68 Va. App. at 486, 809 S.E.2d at 452.

A parent may be enjoined from filing a petition relating to custody and visitation of a child for up to 10 years if the parent has been convicted of certain serious offenses where the victim was the parent's child, a child residing with the parent, or the other parent. A petition for such an order may be brought by a person with legal custody of the child, and the court will determine whether granting the petition is in the best interest of the child. The court must appoint a guardian ad litem for the child when such a petition is filed. Va. Code § 20-124.2(E).

Although a court may order delegation of visitation rights to a family member of a deploying military parent, that family member does not obtain a separate right to visitation. The delegation order terminates by operation of law upon the return of the deploying parent. Furthermore, the deploying parent may file a motion to rescind the order at any time, and the nondeploying parent or guardian may file such a motion on a showing of a material change in circumstances. Va. Code § 20-124.8(B).

## § 23.03   Jurisdiction

One of the jurisdiction questions in custody cases concerns subject matter jurisdiction. In extreme circumstances, such as when both parents had died in a car accident, custody jurisdiction may attach when the child is present even though both parents are absent. *Falco v. Grills*, 209 Va. 115, 161 S.E.2d 713 (1968). See *Spinner*, 1997 Va. App. LEXIS 200 (Apr. 1, 1997) (unpublished opinion) (when child's custodian died unexpectedly after surgery, Virginia court awarded custody to child's established Virginia guardians, despite competing custody petition filed by natural mother in District of Columbia). See also *Scott v. Rutherfoord*, 30 Va. App. 176, 516 S.E.2d 225 (1999) (when (1) parents divorced in Virginia, (2) mother obtained Virginia custody order after relocating to District of Columbia, (3) father relocated to District of Columbia to facilitate visitation, and (4) District of Columbia court declined jurisdiction, it was proper for Virginia court to exercise continuing custody modification jurisdiction pursuant to UCCJA and PKPA); *Franklin v. Department of Soc. Servs., Division of Child Support Enforcement ex rel. Franklin*, 27 Va. App. 136, 497 S.E.2d 881 (1998) (under Va. Code § 20-88.35(5), which provides that jurisdiction may be obtained over person who has performed affirmative act in Virginia or has invoked laws of Virginia, Virginia court had jurisdiction over nonresident husband whose actions included causing wife and children to take up residence in Virginia by ordering wife to leave marital home in Africa, and using husband's employer's Virginia field office to distribute husband's mail); *Khilji v. Khilji*, 49 Va. Cir. 294 (Fairfax Co. 1999) (when husband petitioned for divorce in Pakistan but wife and child resided in Virginia, Virginia court had custody jurisdiction under UCCJA because mother and child had significant contacts with Virginia and because evidence regarding child's "best interests" was in Virginia). The presence of both parents within the state, or at any rate, personal jurisdiction over them, is necessary for a valid custody decree under *May v. Anderson*, 345 U.S. 528, 73 S. Ct. 840, 97 L. Ed. 1221, 52 Ohio Op. 45, 67 Ohio Law Abs. 468 (1953). This is because a custody decree concerns personal rights (of the parents) at least as important as the property rights that undoubtedly require personal jurisdiction. To the same effect, see *Bailey v. Bailey*, 172 Va. 18, 21, 200 S.E. 622, 623 (1939). Nor will an uncontested foreign decree be given full force and effect. *Osborne v. Osborne*, 215 Va. 205, 207 S.E.2d 875 (1974) (child support).

Personal jurisdiction may be obtained under the long-arm statute, §§ 8.01-328.1(8) and (9), but only if service is made personally by a person authorized to make such service by Va. Code § 8.01-320.

When a court obtains jurisdiction over a nonresident under the long-arm statute, such service shall have the same effect as personal service on the nonresident within Virginia. Va. Code § 8.01-320. This statute specifically includes divorce and annulment cases.

Va. Code § 20-146.8 provides immunity from personal service for persons who are in Virginia solely to participate in child custody proceedings. *Harrison v. Harrison*, 58 Va. App. 90, 706 S.E.2d 905 (2011). In *Harrison*, a trial court lacked *in personam* jurisdiction over a wife who was personally served in Virginia after she returned to Virginia to be physically present at a child custody hearing.

When a father's appeal regarding custody and child support was dismissed from circuit court for untimely filing due to early closing of juvenile court clerk's office, his due process rights were violated and he was entitled to have his appeal proceed as if the bond requirement had been timely satisfied. *Hutchins v. Carrillo*, 27 Va. App. 595, 500 S.E.2d 277 (1998).

A court having in personam jurisdiction over both parents may enter a child custody order in the absence of the child. *Gramelspacher v. Gramelspacher*, 204 Va. 839, 134 S.E.2d 285 (1964) (mother and children remained in Indiana, the marital domicile, while defendant husband eventually settled in Virginia, where the action was brought). However, as has been discussed, the Virginia cases indicate that it is the child's right to custody, rather than the parents' that is the heart of custody adjudications. *McCreery v. McCreery*, 218 Va. 352, 237 S.E.2d 167 (1977).

Several cases from other states note that when there is no foreign court asserting jurisdiction, custody may be decided on the basis of the presence of the child and a parent domiciled within the state, since the dispute concerns a family status. See, e.g., *McAtee v. McAtee*, 174 W. Va. 129, 323 S.E.2d 611(W. Va. 1984) (custody is a status exception under *Shaffer v. Heitner*, 433 U.S. 186, 97 S. Ct. 2569, 53 L. Ed. 2d 683 (1977), that may be determined in the absence of personal jurisdiction); *In re Marriage of Myers*, 92 Wash. 2d 113, 594 P.2d 902 (1979); *Perry v. Ponder*, 604 S.W.2d 306 (Tex. Civ. App. 1980). The parent-child relationship would, under this theory, be similar to the marital res necessary for divorce. *Williams v. North Carolina*, 317 U.S. 287, 63 S. Ct. 207, 87 L. Ed. 279 (1942). Support for this argument may also be found in the case of *Falco v. Grills*, discussed above. See generally *Developments in the Law—The Constitution and the Family*, 93 Harv. L. Rev. 1156, 1246 (1980).

In 2001, Virginia repealed the Uniform Child Custody Jurisdiction Act (UCCJA), Chapter 7 of Title 20 of the Virginia Code (Va. Code §§ 20-125 through 20-146), and replaced it with an updated version, the Uniform Child Custody Jurisdiction and Enforcement Act (UCCJEA), Chapter 7.1 of Title 20 of the Virginia Code (Va. Code §§ 20-146.1 through 20-146.38). The UCCJEA is intended to eliminate the problems created by the issuance of competing child custody orders in different states. The UCCJEA became effective on July 1, 2001; however, any motion or other request for relief made in a child custody proceeding or child custody enforcement proceeding, that was commenced before July 1, 2001 is governed by the law in effect at the time the motion or other request was made. Va. Code § 20-146.37.

Under the UCCJEA, Virginia courts have jurisdiction to make initial child custody determinations only if one of the following conditions is met:

(1) Virginia is the child's home state on the date the proceeding is commenced, or Virginia was the child's home state within six months before the proceeding was commenced, and the child is absent from the state, and a parent or person acting as a parent continues to live in Virginia. Va. Code § 20-146.12(A)(1). See *O'Rourke v. Vuturo*, 49 Va. App. 139, 638 S.E.2d 124 (2006) (definition of "person acting as a parent"). See also *Prizzia v. Prizzia*, 58 Va. App. 137, 707 S.E.2d 461 (2011) (Virginia, not Hungary, was child's home state when child's residence was changed to Hungary within six months before proceeding was commenced).

(2) No other state court has jurisdiction as the child's home state, or a court of the child's home state has declined to exercise jurisdiction on the basis that Virginia is a more appropriate forum, and (i) the child and the child's parents, or the child and at least one parent or person acting as a parent have a significant connection with Virginia other than mere physical presence, and (ii) substantial evidence is available in Virginia concerning the child's care, protection, training, and personal relationships. Va. Code § 20-146.12(A)(2). See also Va. Code § 20-146.18 (inconvenient forum).

(3) All courts having jurisdiction under either of the two preceding conditions have declined to exercise jurisdiction on the basis that Virginia is the more appropriate forum. Va. Code § 20-146.12(A)(3).

(4) No court of any other state would have jurisdiction under the criteria specified under the three preceding conditions. Va. Code § 20-146.12(A)(4).

The UCCJEA is the exclusive jurisdictional basis for child custody determinations made by Virginia courts. Va. Code § 20-146.12(B). Physical presence in Virginia or personal jurisdiction over a party or child is not necessary, or sufficient, for a Virginia court to make a child custody determination. Va. Code § 20-146.12(C). However, once a Virginia court makes a child custody determination that is consistent with the UCCJEA, that court has exclusive, continuing jurisdiction over child custody orders for as long as the child, the child's parents, or any person acting as a parent continues to live in Virginia. Va. Code § 20-146.13(A).

Conversely, once an out-of-state court makes a child custody determination consistent with the UCCJEA, that court will have exclusive and continuing jurisdiction over custody matters relating to the child. Thus, Virginia courts will generally lack jurisdiction to modify child custody determinations made by out-of-state courts. See Va. Code §§ 20-146.13 and 20-146.14. See also Va. Code § 20-146.17 (simultaneous proceedings).

Nevertheless, a Virginia court may exercise temporary emergency jurisdiction over a child who is present in Virginia and has been abandoned, or if it is necessary in an emergency to protect the child because the child, or a sibling or parent of the child, is subject to or threatened with mistreatment or abuse. Va. Code § 20-146.15.

A Virginia court may decline to exercise jurisdiction if it determines that it is an inconvenient forum under the circumstances and that a court of another state is a more appropriate forum. Va. Code § 20-146.18. See *Swalef v. Anderson*, 50 Va. App. 100, 646 S.E.2d 458 (2007) (when Minnesota court refused to exercise custody jurisdiction absent decline of jurisdiction by Virginia court, Virginia court properly declined to exercise jurisdiction upon finding that children's best interests dictated that custody issue be resolved by White Earth Tribal Court located in Minnesota). See also *Foster v. Foster*, 52 Va. App. 523, 664 S.E.2d 525 (2008) (Virginia court was *not* an "inconvenient forum" when (1) Virginia court considered statutory factors and mother's assertion of domestic violence; and (2) Maine court concurred with Virginia court's determination and declined to continue to exercise temporary emergency jurisdiction). A Virginia court may also decline to exercise jurisdiction if a person seeking to invoke its jurisdiction has engaged in unjustifiable conduct. See Va. Code § 20-146.19. However, in declining to exercise jurisdiction, a Virginia court must comply with the specific statutory requirements of Va. Code §§ 20-146.18 and 20-146.19, as applicable. *Prizzia v. Prizzia*, 58 Va. App. 137, 707 S.E.2d 461 (2011) (court erred by failing to find it was an inconvenient forum and by not allowing parties to present evidence).

The UCCJEA broadens the UCCJA, because it covers enforcement of out-of-state custody and visitation orders, as well as jurisdiction to make and modify custody and visitation orders. See Va. Code § 20-146.22 et seq. The UCCJEA includes a procedure for registration of out-of-state custody orders, and requires Virginia courts to enforce registered child custody orders made by out-of-state courts. See Va. Code § 20-146.26 (registration); Va. Code § 20-146.27 (enforcement); *Morrison v. Morrison*, 57 Va. App. 629, 704 S.E.2d 617 (2011) (Va. Code § 20-146.24(A) does not permit registration and enforcement of another state's *modified* custody determination); *Prashad v. Copeland*, 55 Va. App. 247, 685 S.E.2d 199 (2009) (registration of custody orders issued by North Carolina court that exercised jurisdiction in substantial conformity with UCCJEA). The UCCJEA also authorizes Virginia courts to make temporary orders enforcing visitation schedules or visitation orders made by out-of-state courts. See Va. Code § 20-146.25.

The UCCJEA authorizes an award of attorney's fees and costs to the prevailing party in a UCCJEA proceeding to enforce a child custody determination or to challenge an improper invocation of jurisdiction. See Va. Code § 20-146.33(A); *Tyszcenko v. Donatelli*, 53 Va. App. 209, 670 S.E.2d 49 (2008) (authority provided by Va. Code § 20-146.33(A) to award attorney's fees to prevailing party is inapplicable to parent's motion under Va. Code § 20-146.18 to change jurisdiction).

Cases decided under Virginia's former law, the UCCJA, serve to illustrate the jurisdictional problems that used to arise in connection with child custody. One jurisdictional concern was related to conflict of laws. That is, even when Virginia courts possessed jurisdictional power under at least one of the traditional rules (e.g., presence of a child and a parent domiciled in the state), and even though there had been personal service or notice, another state might be better able to litigate the custody question. When the child's "home state" under the UCCJA was Virginia, even though the parent contesting custody or even the child was outside the state, Virginia would nonetheless have jurisdiction to decide the custody issue under former Va. Code § 20-125 et seq., the Uniform Child Custody Jurisdiction Act. This is because the sources of information relative to a determination of the best interests of the child would be located within the state. *Middleton v. Middleton*, 227 Va. 82, 314 S.E.2d 362 (1984).

Where Virginia was the home state of the children at the start of the proceedings, and the father continued to live in the state, and Virginia courts have ruled on visitation motions throughout the intervening period, Virginia had jurisdiction under the UCCJA although the mother and children had lived in California since 1986. *Musser v. Musser*, 1995 Va. App. LEXIS 463

(May 30, 1995). While the children's residence in California might merit a future determination that Virginia is an inconvenient forum, the court did have jurisdiction to rule on the father's rule to show cause for violation of existing visitation orders. See also *Osborne v. Osborne*, 215 Va. 205, 207 S.E.2d 875 (1974) (continuing jurisdiction from *pendente lite* proceeding).

If the child is taken in violation of a Virginia custody order, the Parental Kidnapping Prevention Act, 28 U.S.C. § 1738A is also violated. Va. Code § 18.2-49.1. Of course, the reciprocal is true for proceedings and court orders in other states. See, e.g., *Middleton v. Middleton*, 227 Va. 82, 314 S.E.2d 362 (1984). See also *Johnson v. Johnson*, 26 Va. App. 135, 493 S.E.2d 668 (1997), where Virginia exercised its continuing jurisdiction over a case involving two lawyers, one of whom worked for the Swedish foreign service. The father, who remained in Virginia, sought to prevent the mother's relocation to Sweden, since the parties had exercised joint custody, with physical custody alternating every two weeks. The mother nonetheless relocated to Sweden and wrongfully withheld the child from visitation with the father. The Virginia court granted the father sole physical custody and found the mother in contempt.

Similarly, in *Wheaton v. Wheaton*, 42 Va. Cir. 139 (Fairfax Co. 1997), Virginia never lost jurisdiction to determine custody under the UCCJA or the PKPA even though there were custody proceedings pending in Guam. The parties had lived and been divorced in Virginia, but sent the children to live in Guam with his parents after the divorce. Since the children had left Virginia on June 9, 1996, and the Guam proceeding commenced on October 30 of that year, the "home state" of the children was still Virginia, which therefore possessed jurisdiction while the Guam proceeding was not consistent with the PKPA. On the other hand, where both parties, who shared joint legal custody, moved out of Virginia after their 1996 divorce, the state retained no jurisdiction to hear the father's contempt motion against the mother for denying him visitation with his daughter. *Taylor v. Taylor*, 42 Va. Cir. 190 (Fairfax Co. 1997). A ruling on the legal question of the jurisdiction of the court in a divorce and child custody bill of complaint is merely interlocutory and cannot be appealed. *Wells v. Wells*, 29 Va. App. 82, 509 S.E.2d 549 (1999).

If a party contends violation of the Rehabilitation Act, 29 U.S.C. § 794(a), or the Americans with Disabilities Act, 42 U.S.C. § 12132, there must be evidence supporting the assertion of the disability to make out a prima facie case of discrimination under these acts. *Plotkin v. Fairfax County Dep't of Family Servs.*, 1998 Va. App. LEXIS 535 (Oct. 13, 1998) (unpublished decision). In a proceeding to remove a mother's children from her custody, her claims of discrimination against her "multiple chemical sensitivity" impairment were without merit, as there was neither a medical report nor any evidence whatsoever of this disability.

When, on the other hand, the best sources of information lie outside the state, even if they are outside the United States, Virginia will not exercise jurisdiction. *Oehl v. Oehl*, 221 Va. 618, 272 S.E.2d 441 (1980). See also *Barnes v. Barnes*, 1995 Va. App. LEXIS 319 (April 4, 1995). Similarly, it was appropriate to transfer jurisdiction from Virginia to South Carolina under the Uniform Child Custody Jurisdiction Act where there might be adverse publicity in Virginia because of acts of child sexual abuse that allegedly occurred in the state. Transfer was appropriate because the children's home state was South Carolina. Further, the witnesses available to testify about the circumstance, particularly the children and mental health experts, were in South Carolina. *Farley v. Farley*, 9 Va. App. 326, 387 S.E.2d 794 (1990). The court did not abuse its discretion when it transferred jurisdiction over all custody and visitation issues to South Carolina when the legal custodians, the child's paternal grandparents, moved to a retirement community in that state. *Hale v. Hale*, 1994 Va. App. LEXIS 35 (Feb. 1, 1994).

Nor did the grandparents exhibit contemptuous behavior when they failed to obtain court approval prior to relocating, when the noncustodial mother was incarcerated and the child was never comfortable with the infrequent visits with her.

See generally Brinig, *Interstate Child Custody Disputes: The Uniform Child Custody Jurisdiction Act in Virginia*, 10 Va. B.A.J. 17 (1984); Comment, 14 U. Rich. L. Rev. 435 (1979).

## § 23.04    Where is the Action Brought, and When is it Appropriate?

For cases filed before January 1, 1996, the circuit court may transfer enforcement of divorce decrees, including pendente lite orders, NOTE: In 1999, the statutes enacted in 1989 regarding the experimental family courts were repealed, including Va. Code §§ 16.1-296.1, 20-96.1, and 20-96.2. After such a transfer, the circuit court is divested of any further jurisdiction over the matter. Va. Code § 20-79(c). Final orders involving the division or transfer of real property between the parties to divorce or annulment, or following a foreign divorce, shall, if the decree so directs, be transmitted to the circuit court named in the order or decree for docketing on the judgment lien index. Va. Code § 20-107.3.

Appeals from juvenile and domestic relations court decisions are taken to the circuit court. Va. Code §§ 16.1-136, 16.1-296. See also *Loudoun County*

*Dep't of Social Servs. v. Etzold*, 245 Va. 80, 425 S.E.2d 800 (1993) (appeals from juvenile and domestic relations courts that had become "experimental family courts" were taken to the circuit court). A party appealing to the circuit court has the right to a *de novo* trial on appeal. Va. Code §§ 16.1-136, 16.1-296. Once the trial *de novo* commences in the circuit court, the juvenile and domestic relations court judgment is annulled, and is not available thereafter for any purpose. See *Turner v. Commonwealth*, 49 Va. App. 381, 641 S.E.2d 771 (2007). At the trial *de novo*, the circuit court must consider all relevant evidence: the parties are neither restricted to the evidence presented before the juvenile court, nor are they required to present new evidence to the circuit court. *Alexander v. Flowers*, 51 Va. App. 404, 658 S.E.2d 355 (2008). No appeal bond is required of a party appealing from an order of a juvenile and domestic relations district court, except for that portion of any order or judgment establishing a support arrearage or suspending payment of support during the pendency of an appeal. Va. Code § 16.1-296(H). The requirement that an appealing party post a bond under § 16.1-107 is jurisdictional, so that failure to post such a bond requires dismissal of the appeal. *Shurm v. Shurm*, 27 Va. Cir. 255 (Chesterfield Co. 1992).

Virginia adopted the Interstate Family Support Act (UIFSA) in Va. Code § 20-88.32 et seq. (1994). The Act is similar to the Uniform Reciprocal Support Act in many respects. The Act does establish some new concepts. The UIFSA establishes uniform long-arm jurisdiction over nonresidents and provides for discovery and testimony once jurisdiction is obtained. Va. Code §§ 20-88.36, 20-88.59, 20-88.61. The UIFSA may only be used for child support proceedings. Visitation issues cannot be raised in child support proceedings. Va. Code § 20-88.48.

The UIFSA authorizes establishment of parentage in interstate proceedings even when not accompanied by a support proceeding. Custody orders may be entered even when no divorce is pending. In such cases, there may be orders pendente lite directed to any person with a legitimate interest who is a party. The custody and visitation orders in these non-divorce proceedings shall be made in accordance with § 20-124 et seq. (1994). Pendente lite orders shall have no presumptive effect and shall not determine the ultimate outcome of the case.

Courts may make child support or custody orders and decrees in suits for annulment or separate maintenance. Va. Code Ann. § 20-107.2 [amended 1996]. After the entry of a divorce decree, the court may transfer matters pertaining to child custody to the juvenile and domestic relations court, which may be in a different location within the state if a party or the court so moves, and shows good cause. Va. Code § 20-79. Va. Code § 16.1-243(B)(2) provides that any juvenile and domestic relations district court to which a suit is transferred for enforcement of orders pertaining to custody may transfer the case to a city or county that is the most appropriate of several in which venue lies. The best interests of the child shall determine the most appropriate forum.

According to Va. Code § 20-107.2, an award of custody may be made upon divorce; a declaration that neither party is entitled to divorce, *Latham v. Latham*, 71 Va. (30 Gratt.) 307 (1878); or upon dissolution of marriage. "Dissolution of marriage" was interpreted to include annulment of a marriage void as bigamous where the parties had married before the date permitted by the wife's decree in her divorce from her first husband. *Henderson v. Henderson*, 187 Va. 121, 46 S.E.2d 10 (1948). Since the children were legitimated by statute, the father had the same right to their custody, control, and maintenance as if they were the issue of a valid marriage. "The right of a father to have his marriage annulled permits him to be relieved of his obligation as a husband, but does not permit him to rid himself of his obligations as a father." *Id.* at 129, 46 S.E.2d at 14.

The parties' reconciliation did not abrogate their preceding custody order, though the three-year reconciliation was itself a material change of circumstances. *In re Green*, 48 Va. Cir. 170 (City of Richmond 1999). The parents were awarded joint legal custody of their son, while the mother was awarded physical custody because she had more space for him and would be able to see him daily.

## § 23.05   *Pendente Lite* **Award of Custody**

An award of temporary custody may be made under Va. Code § 20-103 when a party has applied for a divorce or annulment. In a custody or visitation dispute, the juvenile and domestic relations district court may order a custody or psychological evaluation of a parent or custodian, or it may order drug testing. Va. Code § 16.1-278.15.

Effective July 1, 2003, through July 1, 2008, former Va. Code § 20-124.3:1 provided that a licensed mental health care provider's records concerning a parent, and information obtained from therapy, were privileged and confidential, and that a mental health care provider could not be required to testify for or against a parent or any of the parent's adult relatives except with the advance written consent of the parent. Those restrictions did not apply to a mental health care provider conducting an independent mental health evaluation at the court's order. See *Rice v. Rice*, 49 Va. App. 192, 638 S.E.2d 702 (2006) (trial court properly restricted mental health provider's testimony, sought by grandparents, regarding how children's therapy had gone); *Schwartz v. Schwartz*, 46 Va. App. 145, 616 S.E.2d 59 (2005) (trial court violated Va. Code § 20-124.3:1 by allowing children's therapist to testify about parent without parent's advance written consent). However, Va. Code § 20-124.3:1 was repealed in 2008.

The usual factors that would be taken into account in determining the child's best interest are the same as those that are required for a permanent custody decision. A decree of temporary custody is not entitled to conclusive weight at a final custody hearing. It was therefore error to refuse to admit any relevant evidence including depositions taken before the temporary hearing. *Armistead v. Armistead*, 228 Va. 352, 322 S.E.2d 836 (1984). Va. Code § 20-103(E) provides that a pendente lite order entered under this code section "shall have no presumptive effect and shall not be determinative when adjudicating the underlying cause."

## § 23.06  Attorney for Child

Although an attorney in a divorce proceeding has been hired to represent one of the spouses, in a certain sense the interests of the child must be represented as well, even though these are not necessarily the same. Virginia Informal Ethics Opinion 345 (December 4, 1979) states that an attorney representing one of the spouses at a child custody proceeding should disclose to the court both favorable and unfavorable medical reports pertaining to the client's fitness as a custodial parent, since the child's best interest is paramount.

A guardian ad litem may be appointed for the child in contested custody proceedings. *Verrocchio v. Verrocchio*, 16 Va. App. 314, 429 S.E.2d 482 (1993). See also *Ferguson v. Grubb*, 39 Va. App. 549, 574 S.E.2d 769 (2003) (court with custody jurisdiction over children has authority to order continued appointment of guardian ad litem until children reach age of majority). Attorneys for children appointed under Va. Code § 16.1-266(D) are not subject to the maximum fee limitations for court-appointed counsel set forth in Va. Code § 16.1-267. *Kaplan v. Kaplan*, 1993 Va. App. LEXIS 420 (Sept. 14, 1993).

An attorney for the child or a guardian ad litem will not necessarily be appointed when each party claiming custodial rights is represented by counsel. In accordance with Va. Code § 16.1-266(F), where the parties to a custody dispute each have counsel, "the court shall not appoint counsel or a guardian ad litem to represent the interests of the child or children unless the court finds, at any stage in the proceedings in a specific case, that the interests of the child or children are not otherwise adequately represented."

See generally *Lawyering for the Child: Principles of Representation in Custody and Visitation Disputes Arising from Divorce*, 87 Yale L.J. 1126 (1978).

## § 23.07  Psychiatric Reports

Any reports must be subject to cross-examination and rebuttal. See, e.g., *Collins v. Collins*, 283 S.C. 526, 324 S.E.2d 82 (1984).

An independent mental health or psychological evaluation to assist the court in determining the best interests of the child may be ordered by the court in any case in which custody or visitation is at issue. Va. Code § 20-124.2(D). See *O'Rourke v. Vuturo*, 49 Va. App. 139, 638 S.E.2d 124 (2006) (independent psychological evaluation properly ordered to assist trial court in determining (1) potential psychological consequences of severing long-term relationship between presumed father and child, and (2) whether actual harm to child would result). Rule 4:10 of the Rules of the Supreme Court of Virginia also authorize a judge to order a physical or mental examination. The Rule is fairly technical and contains many requirements. Good cause must be shown and notice must be provided to "specify the time, place, manner, conditions, and scope of the examination and the person or persons by whom it is to be made." Va. Sup. Ct. R. 4:10. The order must also fix the time for filing the report and furnishing the copies. *Id.*

Some commentators conclude that psychiatric and psychological experts have little to contribute to a best interests determination and that they interfere with the judicial function. See, e.g., Robert Cochran, *The Search for Guidance in Determining the Best Interests of the Child at Divorce*, 20 U. Rich. L. Rev. 1 (1985); Martha Fineman, *Dominant Discourse, Professional Language and Legal Change in Child Custody Decisionmaking*, 101 Harv. L. Rev. 727 (1988); Ohpaku, *Psychology: Impediment or Aid in Child Custody Cases?*, 29 Rutgers L. Rev. 1117 (1976). On the other hand, others suggest that judges may not be well-equipped to handle the developmental issues posed by custody cases. See, e.g., Watson, *The Children of Armageddon: Problems of Custody Following Divorce*, 21 Syracuse L. Rev. 55 (1969–1970); Batt, *Child Custody Disputes—A Developmental-Psychological Approach to Proof and Decisionmaking*, 12 Willamette L.J. 491 (1976). The classic work in the field is J. Goldstein, A. Freud & A. Solnit's *Beyond the Best Interests of the Child* (1973).

## § 23.08  School Reports; Siblings and Friends

In representing a parent seeking custody, the attorney must show that the client's home would be "best" for the child. This is done by examining the physical situation, but also the affection each parent has for the child, the school environment, siblings or playmates in the neighborhood, child care for young children, and the plans for religious upbringing. This is sometimes done through a series of photographs or through depositions from the persons who will be providing services.

Va. Code § 20-124.6, as amended in 2000 and 2005, provides that neither a custodial nor a noncustodial parent may be denied access to his or her child's academic or health records.

A mother whose concern for her job and her employer were stronger than her concern for the children, while the father was willing to place the welfare of the children above all else, and was a "very nurturing parent," was denied custody after testimony by a babysitter, a psychiatrist, and some neighbors. *McCreery v. McCreery*, 218 Va. 352, 237 S.E.2d 167 (1977). See also *Peple v. Peple*, 5 Va. App. 414, 423, 364 S.E.2d 232 (1988) (father had become an "exceptionally attentive parent, actively involved in the physical, mental, and religious guidance of the child," and the mother, "while a loving and fit parent, was more occupied by her employment and not able to provide the same quality of care").

Similarly, a father was awarded custody on the basis of changed circumstances when the mother seemed overly concerned with the child's medical problems. He had retired and could devote his full energies to rearing his daughter, while there was also evidence that the mother had interfered with visitation. *Grubb v. Grubb*, 1994 Va. App. LEXIS 92 (March 1, 1994). Where a father was imprisoned for sexually abusing children, including his own son, and was ordered not to have any contact with the son during his minority, there was "good cause" for limiting dissemination of the child's medical, psychiatric, and school records. *L.C.S. v. S.A.S.*, 19 Va. App. 709, 453 S.E.2d 580 (1995).

> The court's desire to award custody to the parent with the "best" situation does not necessarily mean the most expensive home, or the one with the prettiest furnishings, or the one with the greatest number of "creature comforts." For we are firmly of the view that a house is not a home, that a home is more than bricks and mortar. "Best" to us is the home that will provide the children the greatest opportunity to fulfill their potential as individuals and as members of society. *Keel v. Keel*, 225 Va. 606, 613, 303 S.E.2d 917, 922 (1983).

Where the two parents' homes in a custody dispute were similar, and both parents were employed full-time so that they could spend the same amount of time with the boy, the choice to award custody to the father was made on the basis of companionship of other children in the neighborhood and the affectionate interest of the child's relatives who lived in the area and who were alienated from the mother. *White v. White*, 215 Va. 765, 213 S.E.2d 766 (1975).

The fact that four siblings were already in the custody of the natural parents was an important consideration in the case of *Smith v. Pond*, 5 Va. App. 161, 360 S.E.2d 885 (1987), where the court wrote that "the trial judge is not required to disregard the fact that familial bonds may be a significant factor in a child's life," so that there was nothing that "would justify a finding that the best interest of [the child] would be served by separating her from her siblings."

### § 23.09   Stability of Situation

Once the child has been in a custodial situation for an extended period of time, courts will be reluctant to change the arrangement. See *Bailes v. Sours*, 231 Va. 96, 340 S.E.2d 824 (1986) (though both mother and stepmother were fit, child had been with stepmother for so long that for him, she was his mother. *Id.* at 100–01, 340 S.E.2d at 827). Likewise, where the noncustodial mother made no effort to obtain custody until the children had been living with their father for nearly three years, nor had she seen them until testifying in the custody case, to require a change of custody "would be a painful disruption" to the children's lives. *Hall v. Hall*, 210 Va. 668, 672, 173 S.E.2d 865, 868 (1970). See also *Patrick v. Byerley*, 228 Va. 691, 325 S.E.2d 99 (1985) (former stepmother who had cared for child for five years awarded custody when to do otherwise would "be highly disruptive to Chris and not in his best interest").

When the aunt and uncle of the child in question, who had previously been awarded custody by the Juvenile and Domestic Relations Court after a voluntary relinquishment by the mother, sought to adopt the child, they were not permitted to do so because they were separated. Nor would custody be returned to the natural mother because her life was still unstable and the child was fast friends with her cousin who was nearly the same age. *Watson v. Shepard*, 217 Va. 538, 229 S.E.2d 897 (1976). Cf. *Lundeen v. Struminger*, 209 Va. 548, 165 S.E.2d 285 (1969) (two children not separated in modification of alternating custody award since not in their best interests). The natural father's lifestyle, attitude, behavior, instability, living circumstances, personal habits, and emotional status made him unfit in *In re Custody of Sloan*, 25 Va. Cir. 227 (Amherst Co. 1991), so that foster parents who had assumed the child's care at the mother's request were entitled to custody. However, in *Terrell v. Hackett*, 1993 Va. App. LEXIS 487 (Oct. 12, 1993), the trial court was in error to grant custody to the mother's foster parents when the father was fit and wanted custody. This was despite testimony from the child's social worker that she was comfortable living with the foster parents and uncomfortable seeing her father.

## § 23.10    Fault

Historically the party not at fault was usually awarded custody. *Owens v. Owens*, 96 Va. 191, 196, 31 S.E. 72, 74 (1898). However, the custody of minor children has never been given to one parent to punish the other. *Rowlee v. Rowlee*, 211 Va. 689, 690, 179 S.E.2d 461, 462 (1971) (citing cases). The rule favoring the "innocent" spouse most often obtains where the fault itself has a deleterious effect on the child. For example, where the mother continued an adulterous relationship during the time she was separated, and one of the children developed a hyperactive condition and was obviously disturbed about the other man sleeping with his mother, custody was transferred to the father, since the relationship had an adverse impact on the children. *Brown v. Brown*, 218 Va. 196, 237 S.E.2d 89 (1977). See also *Keel v. Keel*, 225 Va. 606, 303 S.E.2d 917 (1983) (relationship of custodial mother with married man relevant in change of custody); *Miller v. Miller*, 22 Va. Cir. 470 (Henrico Co. 1981).

However, in several cases, the mother was awarded custody despite the existence of adultery, since the child had not been exposed to the immoral relationship. *Brinkley v. Brinkley*, 1 Va. App. 222, 336 S.E.2d 901 (1985) (no showing of improper conduct in the presence of the child); *Venable v. Venable*, 2 Va. App. 178, 342 S.E.2d 646 (1986) (although trial court attempted to restrict children's contact with mother's lover until such time as he and the mother might marry; father had also committed adultery). See also *Sutherland v. Sutherland*, 14 Va. App. 42, 414 S.E.2d 617 (1992) (wife awarded custody although she began live-in, adulterous relationship with man she intends to marry when he obtains his divorce, and children are often present in the house when the adultery occurs); and *Ford v. Ford*, 14 Va. App. 551, 419 S.E.2d 415 (1992) (father and companion not only went to great lengths to shield daughter from their adultery, they were also open with her about their ultimate intentions with regard to one another, telling her that they intended to marry); *Lewis v. Lewis*, 1993 Va. App. LEXIS 632 (Dec. 7, 1993) (custody awarded to mother where both parents guilty of adultery but planning to marry respective companions, child well-established in school and preferred to live with mother).

The adverse impact of extramarital sexual conduct is also related to the parent's fitness as a custodian. The Virginia Supreme Court recently reversed a custody award made by a circuit court to a homosexual father with a live-in male companion. Finding that the case was controlled by *Brown*, the court noted that the harm to the child could be presumed since the homosexual acts were illegal and the child would also suffer from ostracism by his peers and the larger community. The father's unfitness was manifested by his willingness to impose this burden upon her in exchange for his own gratification. *Roe v. Roe*, 228 Va. 722, 324 S.E.2d 691 (1985). Cf. *Doe v. Doe*, 222 Va. 736, 284 S.E.2d 799 (1981), where the Supreme Court refused to terminate all the parental rights of a lesbian mother who was otherwise very fit. In *Doe* the issue was visitation, which could take place when the lover was not present. In the day-to-day living situation posed by *Roe*, the child would of necessity be exposed to the homosexual lifestyle of the father.

In the nationally publicized case of *Bottoms v. Bottoms*, 249 Va. 410, 457 S.E.2d 102 (1995), a maternal grandmother was awarded custody of her daughter's child. The court wrote that "living daily under conditions stemming from active lesbianism practiced in the home may impose a burden upon a child" because of the condemnation of others "which will inevitably afflict the child's relationships." *Id.*, 249 Va. at 420. See Stephen B. Bershing, *"Entreat Me Not to Leave Thee": Bottoms v. Bottoms and the Custody Rights of Gay and Lesbian Parents*, 3 Wm. & Mary Bill Rts. J. 289 (1994); Barry M. Parsons, Note, *Bottoms v. Bottoms: Erasing the Presumption Favoring a Natural Parent Over Third Parties—What Makes This Mother Unfit?* 2 Geo. Mason Independent L. Rev. 457 (1994).

The court of appeals affirmed a recent decision denying a lesbian mother custody of her child based on the stability of the father's home and his schedule compared with the instability of the mother's day-to-day schedule, living arrangements, and relationships. *Piatt v. Piatt*, 27 Va. App. 426, 499 S.E.2d 567 (1998). Numerous factors were cited regarding the mother's inappropriate behavior for maintaining continuity and stability for her child and the child's routine, including the mother's promiscuity and experimentation with sexual preference. A dissent in this case cites promiscuity on the part of both mother and father while they were still married.

In *Hughes v. Hughes (Hughes Custody)*, 33 Va. App. 160, 531 S.E.2d 654 (2000), *aff'd after reh'g en banc*, 35 Va. App. 376, 545 S.E.2d 556 (2001) a trial judge ordered a change in custody from a wife to a husband, based upon a finding in a separate divorce proceeding that the wife committed adultery. In the divorce proceeding, the facts indicated that the wife was abused, that she and the children vacated the family home and lived for a time with relatives and in shelters, and that they eventually moved into the home of a male coworker of the wife, to whom the wife was not married. The trial judge found that both husband and wife were fit parents, but relied on the finding of adultery in the divorce proceeding as the material change in circumstances that justified the change in custody. After reversing the divorce decree for lack of evidence of adultery, the Court of Appeals reversed the change of custody decree as well, holding that the trial judge erred in finding that the husband carried his burden of proving a change in circumstances. Compare with *Hughes v. Hughes (Hughes Divorce)*, 33 Va. App. 141, 531 S.E.2d 645 (2000) (related divorce proceeding).

The fact that a parent was involved in family abuse, will be a factor in determining child custody under Va. Code § 20-124.3. See, e.g., *L.C.S. v. S.A.S.*, 19 Va. App. 709, 453 S.E.2d 580 (1995). However, a spouse should not file a malicious or knowingly unfounded report of child abuse or neglect, for he or she may then be subject to criminal action. The first such conviction is a Class 4 misdemeanor; a subsequent conviction is a Class 2 misdemeanor. *Id.* Va. Code § 5:101 [added 1996]. Further, a court has found that a custodial mother's persistent questioning of her three children concerning her allegations of the father's sexual abuse was a negative change in the mother's circumstances, amounting to emotional abuse of the children, and clearly not in their best interests. The mother was denied all visitation until a plan for supervised visitation could be approved. *Juarez v. Juarez*, 1996 Va. App. LEXIS 108 (Feb. 13, 1996). See generally Katharine A. Salmon, Note, *Child Custody Modification Based on a Parent's Non-Marital Cohabitation: Protecting the Best Interests of the Child in Virginia*, 27 U. Rich. L. Rev. 915 (1993).

In *D'Ambrosio v. D'Ambrosio*, 45 Va. App. 323, 610 S.E.2d 876 (2005), a trial court entered an injunction prohibiting a former husband with joint child custody from making "defamatory comments" about his former wife to "any third parties." During a dispute over his child's medical care, the husband allegedly informed a pediatrician that he thought the wife had borderline personality disorder. The Court of Appeals reversed and vacated the injunction, holding that the trial court had failed to make the necessary findings for injunctive relief.

### § 23.11 Religion and Morality

The concept of morality is closely related to that of fault, although the presence of grounds for divorce will require a higher degree of proof. The morality of a would-be custodial parent is important for:

> The moral climate in which children are to be raised is an important consideration for the court in determining custody, and adultery is a reflection of a mother's moral values. An illicit relationship to which minor children are exposed cannot be condoned. Such a relationship must necessarily be given the most careful consideration in a custody proceeding.

*Brown v. Brown*, 218 Va. 196, 199, 237 S.E.2d 89, 91 (1977). For example, custody of two teenaged boys was awarded to the mother, a Jehovah's

Witness, whose religion did not interfere with her duties as a parent and who was a fit and suitable person, in *Crute v. Crute*, 12 Va. Cir. 190 (Henrico Co. 1988). The father had been involved in psychotherapy for seven years and had been treated for depression, and had never taken an active role in the boys' activities. In *Plotkin v. Plotkin*, 22 Va. Cir. 435 (City of Richmond 1975), the wife converted to the Jehovah's Witnesses faith during the marriage. The husband was successful in obtaining custody because "the zeal with which the defendant [wife] has and will continue to devote herself to the furtherance and advancement of her religious convictions will necessarily relegate the child to a place of secondary importance." See also *Petersen v. Petersen*, 13 Va. Cir. 216 (City of Norfolk 1988), where the mother had "dated" while still married and worked in a bar, while the father of the nine-year-old boy was stable, mature, and hardworking, and had "immediately accepted the pleasures and responsibilities of fatherhood." See generally Walter Wadlington, *Sexual Relations After Separation or Divorce: The New Morality and the Old and New Divorce Laws*, 63 Va. L. Rev. 249 (1977).

In *Roberts v. Roberts*, 41 Va. App. 513, 586 S.E.2d 290 (2003), a trial court terminated a father's in-person visitation, limiting him to telephonic visits, after the children feigned illness before visits and complained that their father told them their mother was a fornicator who was going to hell and threatened them with punishment if they did not obey his religious teachings. The trial court's decision did *not* violate the father's constitutionally protected religious rights by infringing on his "free exercise" right to contribute to his children's religious instruction. The father's "unconscionable" conduct was contrary to the children's best interests, and the compelling state interest in protecting the children's welfare and best interests was controlling. Also, the father was only barred from threatening the mother and children, and remained free to instruct the children regarding his religious beliefs.

## § 23.12 Joint Custody

Virginia was one of the first states to endorse the practice of joint custody.

> The advisability of dividing or alternating the custody of the child has been seriously considered. While there are certain disadvantages in such division, ere are also important advantages and benefits. It gives the child the experience of two separate homes. The child is entitled to the love, advice and training of both her father and her mother. Frequent associations, contact, and friendly relations with both of her parents will protect her future welfare if one of her parents should die. It gives recognition to the rights of parents who have performed obligations as parents.

*Mullen v. Mullen,* 188 Va. 259, 272–73, 49 S.E.2d 349, 355 (1948) (mother awarded custody during school year; father in summer). Cf. *Andrews v. Geyer,* 200 Va. 107, 104 S.E.2d 747 (1958) (substantial visitation by mother continued); *Parrish v. Parrish,* 116 Va. 476, 82 S.E. 119 (1914) (boy's custody awarded to father, but because of his delicate health and tender years he was to live with mother in Virginia during school year).

The concept of joint custody, as defined below, was explicitly recognized in Va. Code § 20-107.2. The first type of joint custody is joint legal custody, where both parents retain joint responsibility for the care and control of the child and joint authority to make decisions concerning the child, even though the child's primary residence may be with only one parent. The second is joint physical custody, where both parents share physical and custodial care of the child. The section now provides in part that:

> In awarding the custody of the child or children, the court may give consideration to joint custody or to sole custody, but shall give primary consideration to the welfare of the child or children, and, as between the parents, there shall be no presumption or inference of law in favor of either.

Definitions for sole custody and joint custody are located at Va. Code § 20-124.1. In 2018, Va. Code § 20-124.2(B) was amended to specify that there is no legal presumption favoring any form of custody and that the court "shall consider and may award joint legal, joint physical, or sole custody." Split custody is also discussed in Va. Code § 20-108.1. Split custody is limited to those situations where each parent has physical custody of a child or children born of the parents, born of either parent and adopted by the other, or adopted by both parents. Although it has certain benefits for the child, joint custody is not always appropriate. One of the problems stems from frequent moving of the child between the two parents. For example, in *Brooks v. Brooks,* 201 Va. 731, 113 S.E.2d 872 (1960), the court disapproved of an arrangement giving the wife custody but allowing the father visitation from Friday afternoon to Monday morning, since the frequent shifting of custody between the parents for short periods would be detrimental to his welfare, and would result in his having no real home and no permanent environment and associations. Instead, the arrangement was changed to allow visitation for the month of July and each weekend. See also *Lundeen v. Struminger,* 209 Va. 548, 165 S.E.2d 285 (1969) (modifying alternate six months' arrangement so that children would be with one parent during the school year).

Joint custody with unsupervised visitation should not have been continued when the father violated court orders that he not feed the son with a baby bottle, that the son be in charge of his own body for bathing and cleaning purposes, and that the son sleep in his own bed. *Wilson v. Wilson*, 12 Va. App. 1251, 408 S.E.2d 576 (1991). Custody was awarded to the mother and the case was remanded for establishment of visitation subject to appropriate safeguards. Joint custody requires cooperation, open communication and mutual respect between the parents. Therefore, it should not be awarded where there is conflict and enmity between the parents and they are unable to communicate effectively with one another. *Gonella v. Gonella*, 1994 Va. App. LEXIS 183 (March 29, 1994).

In *Ewing v. Ewing*, 22 Va. App. 466, 470 S.E.2d 608 (1996), the father appealed the trial court's continuation of the mother's sole legal custody of the parties' son. The court of appeals affirmed, mentioning the parties' lack of communication concerning the child. The parents had resorted to use of the mother's sister as a neutral third party for delivery of the child, and this neutral testified that communication with the father was nonexistent during the exchanges.

Even with poor communications, a tumultuous relationship and a protective order being entered against the mother, the trial court was affirmed when it ordered that the parents would have joint legal custody of their daughter. *Armstrong v. Armstrong*, 71 Va. App. 97, 106, 834 S.E.2d 473 (2019).

In *Jones v. Jones*, 26 Va. App. 689, 496 S.E.2d 150 (1998), the parties married on September 25, 1988. A son was born of the marriage in 1989, and the husband adopted his wife's daughter, who was four years older. The parties agreed that the wife should stay home to care for the children rather than work during the marriage. The parties separated in the fall of 1995. Pursuant to a pendente lite order entered March 11, 1996, and a revised decree pendente lite entered March 22, 1996, the parties exercised joint legal custody of the children, with the wife having primary physical custody. The commissioner recommended an award of joint legal custody, but the trial court instead awarded sole custody to the father. The trial court should not have done this without first considering all the factors in Va. Code § 20-124. No trial court is required to adopt a recommendation made by an expert witness according to *Summers v. Summers*, 1998 Va. App. LEXIS 566 (Nov. 10, 1998) (unpublished decision). When the parents' battles caused confusion in the care of the children, it was not improper to award sole custody to the mother, rather than continuing the unsuccessful attempt at joint custody, amply supported by the evidence.

In *In re Green*, 48 Va. Cir. 170 (City of Richmond 1999), the child's parents had reconciled after an original award of joint custody with primary residence of the child with the mother. The father was awarded physical custody after the parties' second separation. The mother appealed to the circuit court. Based on the best interests of the child and living arrangements rather than the argument's proffered by the parents, all other things being equal, the court granted joint custody to the parties with physical custody awarded to the mother. See also *Austin v. Austin*, 47 Va. Cir. 525 (Loudoun Co. 1999), where the parties' agreement specified joint legal custody but physical custody with the mother. This arrangement was continued in the divorce decree over the father's objection since the arrangement reflected a "thoughtful and careful agreement" with detailed provisions outlining the responsibilities of each; agreement, rather than litigation, is the goal of Va. Code § 20-124(2).

When the parties agreed to joint custody of their children, one party's repeated refusal to abide by the agreement, participate in mediation, speak with the other party or communicate other than by message, fax or mail were enough to constitute changed circumstances justifying sole custody in the other party, even though contrary to the recommendation of the expert custody evaluator. *Etter v. Etter*, 1998 Va. App. LEXIS 276 (May 5, 1998). See also Va. Code § 124.3(6) (amended 2000), which lists unreasonable interference with access as one of the factors in determining what is in the child's best interests.

Compare *Pope v. Pope*, 1994 Va. App. LEXIS 52 (Feb. 8, 1994), where the court of appeals affirmed an order for joint custody. In *Pope*, both parents enjoyed good relationships with the child and played an equal role in her upbringing. Sole custody is defined in Va. Code § 20-124.1 as a court award to one person of primary responsibility for making decisions affecting the child. This parent retains responsibility for the child's care and control. Shared custody, which triggers allocation of child support responsibilities, is described in Va. Code § 20-108.2. See, e.g., *Ewing v. Ewing*, 1995 Va. App. LEXIS 192 (Feb. 28, 1995); *Laverty v. Laverty*, 1995 Va. App. LEXIS 750 (Oct. 17, 1995); *Hiner v. Hadeed*, 31 Va. Cir. 193 (City of Richmond 1993).

## § 23.13   Evidence in Custody Hearings

The wishes of the minor concerning which parent the minor would prefer to be the custodian will be considered if the child is of the age of discretion. See Va. Code § 20-107.2. In each such case, the court looks to the capacity, information, intelligence, and judgment of the child to determine competency. The wishes of the minor should be given great weight, although they will not be conclusive. *Hall v. Hall*, 210 Va. 668, 672, 173 S.E.2d 865, 868 (1970) (citing cases). Testimony in these cases is usually taken in camera. For example, the wishes of an intelligent, sensitive, eight-year-old were the primary reason custody was transferred from the father to the mother, who had remarried. *Turner v. Turner*, 3 Va. App. 31, 348 S.E.2d 21 (1986). One of the factors a court shall consider in granting custody is the "reasonable preference of the child, if the court deems the child to be of reasonable intelligence, understanding and experience to express such a preference." Va. Code § 20-124.3. See, e.g., *Schalow v. Schalow*, 1993 Va. App. LEXIS 212 (June 22, 1993) (opinions of eight- and ten-year-old children considered); *Sargent v. Sargent*, 20 Va. App. 694, 460 S.E.2d 596 (1995) (nine-year-old child was not of sufficient age to decide with whom he should live, while other factors favored the mother's retaining custody). However, the chancellor did not err in refusing over the mother's objection to receive testimony from the couple's children where expert testimony suggested that requiring them to testify would be detrimental to their welfare. Instead, the commissioner correctly proceeded to receive the children's testimony in an informal proceeding in camera without counsel or the parties present. *Haase v. Haase*, 20 Va. App. 671, 460 S.E.2d 585 (1995).

When the court conducts an in camera interview of a minor whose custody or visitation is at issue without the presence of the parties or their counsel, a record of the interview will be prepared unless the parties agree otherwise, and this record will become part of the record in the case unless that would endanger the safety of the child. Va. Code § 20-124.2:1.

If a party contends violation of the Rehabilitation Act, 29 U.S.C. § 794(a), or the Americans with Disabilities Act, 42 U.S.C. § 12132, there must be evidence supporting the assertion of the disability, whatever that disability may be, to make out a prima facie case of discrimination under these acts.

In *Fanning v. Fanning*, 1999 Va. Cir. LEXIS 684 (Jan. 21, 1999), although the father made considerable constitutional arguments to win "equal" custody of his child, he offered no evidence or applicable law upon which the court could render a decision in his favor. The best interests of the child standard is "the most important legal principle" in custody and visitation decisions, rather than the fourteenth amendment requirement of equal protection for citizens under the law. The evidence showed that the child was doing fine living with her mother, and that any change would bring instability to her.

In order for a parent to obtain custody solely on the basis of the other parent's physical condition, e.g., bulimia, the evidence must demonstrate that the other parent is not consistently alert to symptoms of relapse, does not fully understand the illness, or is unwilling to seek immediate treatment upon signs of relapse. See *Joynes v. Payne*, 36 Va. App. 401, 551 S.E.2d 10 (2001).

After a commissioner has filed a report, the introduction of additional evidence requires a motion to receive after-discovered evidence. Four requirements must be met before the record can be reopened: (1) the evidence must have been discovered after the record was closed; (2) the evidence must not have been obtainable prior to the closing of the record through the exercise of reasonable diligence; (3) the evidence must not be merely cumulative, corroborative, or collateral; and (4) the evidence must be material, and, as such, should produce an opposite result from that contained in the commissioner's report. *Joynes v. Payne*, 36 Va. App. 401, 551 S.E.2d 10 (2001).

In *Travis v. Finley*, 36 Va. App. 189, 548 S.E.2d 906 (2001), the court of appeals held that a father's discovery requests regarding a mother and child's whereabouts at a certain time and the mother's method of removing the child from the United States were relevant to child support and custody proceedings. The fact that the child might have been removed to another country and secreted was relevant to whether the father's failure to pay child support was in "bad faith" or in "willful disobedience," and the child's whereabouts were relevant to the conditions to which the child was subjected and to the mother's efforts to separate the child and father.

In *Surles v. Mayer*, 48 Va. App. 146, 628 S.E.2d 563 (2006), a trial court in a child custody proceeding properly admitted evidence that a father had been involved in relationships with other women while cohabitating with his child's mother. The evidence was relevant to the child's best interests, because the father's affairs (1) created hostility between the parents, (2) precipitated a breakup that removed the child from a two-parent to a one-parent home, and (3) had bearing on the future stability and moral climate of the father's home.

Effective July 1, 2003, through July 1, 2008, former Va. Code § 20-124.3:1 provided that a licensed mental health care provider's records concerning a parent, and information obtained from therapy, were privileged and confidential and that a mental health care provider could not be required to testify for or against a parent or any of the parent's adult relatives except with the advance written consent of the parent. Those restrictions did not apply to a mental health care provider conducting an independent mental health evaluation at the court's order. See *Rice v. Rice*, 49 Va. App. 192, 638 S.E.2d 702 (2006) (trial court properly restricted mental health provider's testimony, sought by grandparents, regarding how children's therapy had gone); *Schwartz v. Schwartz*, 46 Va. App. 145, 616 S.E.2d 59 (2005) (trial court violated Va. Code § 20-124.3:1 by admitting testimony from children's therapist regarding parent's behavior without parent's consent).

## § 23.14 Agreements Between Parties to Mediation

This amendment further provides that in assessing the appropriateness of a referral, the court shall ascertain upon motion of a party whether there is a history of family abuse.

In recent years, an agreement frequently is reached by the spouses after mediation pursuant to Va. St. Bar Ethics Opinion of April 28, 1983, and attachment. Since the mediator does not represent either spouse, and the parties are concerned with their own interests, although they may couch their arguments in terms of what is best for the children, the question arises whether there is any representative of the children's interests. In litigated custody cases, the judge will decide which parent will be "best" for the child. In mediation, the parties themselves reach an agreement, which merely requires approval by the court. See, e.g., John Murray, *Improving Parent-Child Relationships Within the Divorced Family: A Call for Legal Reform*, 19 U. Mich. J. Law Reform 563 (1986). On the other hand, parties to mediation will have increased communications skills and will presumably be able to better cooperate on custody and visitation arrangements. See generally Pearson and Thoennes, *Mediation of Divorce: The Benefits Outweigh the Costs*, 4 Fam. Advocate 26 (1984).

Court-directed mediation has been sanctioned by Va. Code § 16.1-274, which provides that when the court services unit is directed to provide mediation services in matters involving a child's custody, visitation, or support, the court shall assess a fee against the petitioner, the respondent, or both, in accordance with regulations and fee schedules established by the State Board of Social Services. Similarly, when requested by another court services unit or by a similar entity in another state to conduct an investigation or to provide mediation services or supervised visitation, the local department or the court services unit performing the service may require payment of fees prior to conducting the investigation or providing mediation services or supervised visitation. For any issue arising out of suits for divorce, annulment or affirmation of marriage, separate maintenance or equitable distribution based on foreign decree, termination of residual parental rights, and other child custody, support, and visitation cases, the judge shall consider whether to refer the parties to mediation, and may do so sua sponte or on motion of one of the parties. Upon referral, the parties must attend one evaluation session during which they and the mediator assess the case and decide whether to continue with mediation or with adjudication. Further participation in the mediation shall be by consent of all parties, and attorneys for any party may be present during mediation. Va. Code § 16.1-272.1; Va. Code § 20-124.4.

When the parties are referred to mediation, the court shall set a return date. The parties shall notify the court in writing if the dispute is resolved prior to this date. The court may in its discretion incorporate any mediated agreement into the terms of its final decree disposing of a case. Only if such an order is entered will the terms of the voluntary settlement agreement affect any outstanding court order. The court shall vacate a mediated agreement or an incorporating order where the agreement was procured by fraud or duress, where it is unconscionable, where there was not adequate disclosure of financial or property information, or where there was evident partiality or misconduct by the mediator that prejudiced the rights of a party.

Va. Code § 20-124.2 was also amended and reenacted to provide that when mediation is used in custody and visitation matters, the goals of the mediation may include development of a proposal addressing the child's residential schedule and care arrangements, and determining how disputes between the parents will be handled in the future. Mediators are to be certified according to standards promulgated by the Judicial Council, according to Va. Code § 20-124.4, which also sets their fees at $1,000 per appointment. For an example of the preference for agreed-upon outcomes, see *Austin v. Austin*, 47 Va. Cir. 525 (Loudoun Co. 1999), where the parties' agreement specified joint legal custody but physical custody in the mother. This arrangement was continued in the divorce decree over the father's objection since the arrangement reflected a "thoughtful and careful agreement" with detailed provisions outlining the responsibilities of each. Agreement, rather than litigation or "micromanagement," is the goal of Va. Code § 20-124(2).

Misconduct includes failure of the mediator to inform the parties in writing at the beginning of mediation that (1) the mediator does not provide legal advice; (2) an agreement will affect the legal rights of the parties; (3) each party to mediation has the opportunity to consult with independent legal counsel at any time and is encouraged to do so; and (4) each party should have any draft agreement reviewed by independent counsel prior to signing the agreement, or should waive this opportunity. Va. Code § 16.1-272.2. A motion to vacate an order or agreement must be made within two years after the agreement is reached, except that if the motion is based upon fraud, it shall be made within two years after these grounds are discovered or reasonably should have been discovered.

## § 23.15   Removal of Child from State

In Virginia, the "best interests of the child" controls the issue of removal of a child to another state by a custodial parent, and the court may consider a benefit to the parent from relocation only if the move independently benefits the child. *Goodhand v. Kildoo*, 37 Va. App. 591, 560 S.E.2d 463 (2002). See also *Petry v. Petry*, 41 Va. App. 782, 589 S.E.2d 458 (2003) (relocation permitted when both children and parents had substantial contacts with New York locale). In cases involving relocation and joint or shared custody, there is no presumption of harm that requires the court to consider the harmful impact on the child that would be caused by the relocation. To the contrary, Virginia simply requires the court to consider and weigh the factors set out in Va. Code § 20-124.3 to determine whether a change in custody is in the best interest of the child, and whether relocation is in the best interest of the child. *Goodhand v. Kildoo*, 37 Va. App. 591, 560 S.E.2d 463 (2002).

In determining whether to permit a custodial parent to relocate with a child to another state, the trial court must find (1) a material change in circumstances since the prior decree; (2) that the relocation would be in the child's best interests; and (3) that the child's relationship with the noncustodial parent will be substantially maintained. *Wheeler v. Wheeler*, 42 Va. App. 282, 591 S.E.2d 698 (2004). In *Wheeler*, a mother and her children were permitted to relocate to Florida to improve their deteriorating economic situation, when the bond between the children and their father was so strong that their relationship could be maintained even though distance might cause some inconvenience. As a general rule, the added difficulty in maintaining a relationship between a child and a noncustodial parent should *not* be the sole basis for restricting a custodial parent's residence, unless the benefits of the relationship cannot be substantially maintained if the child moves away from the noncustodial parent. *Scinaldi v. Scinaldi*, 2 Va. App. 571, 347 S.E.2d 149 (1986).

The court may require that the custodial parent keep the child within the state, see, e.g., *Carpenter v. Carpenter*, 220 Va. 299, 257 S.E.2d 845 (Va.1979), unless the child's best interest would be served elsewhere. In *Carpenter*, a custodial mother sought to move from the Tidewater area to New York, where she felt employment opportunities might be better and she would live near her mother. Noting that any job prospects were speculative at the time of the decision, the court refused to approve the move, stating that the cultural and social advantages of the Tidewater area were not less than those found in New York, and that visitation by the father would be more difficult. However, when removal to Arizona was found to be in the children's best interest, the trial court was in error in denying the mother's request to move with them out of Virginia. *Gray v. Gray*, 228 Va. 696, 324 S.E.2d 677, 678 (1985). See also *Simmons v. Simmons*, 1 Va. App. 358, 339 S.E.2d 198 (1986).

After a trial court's order allowing a parent to relocate with a child to South Carolina was reversed for being solely in the parent's best interests, the parent was successful in arguing that it was in the child's best interests to remain in South Carolina, due to the changed circumstances that had occurred since the child's relocation (e.g., the child's bonds formed with South Carolina friends and neighbors). *Sullivan v. Jones*, 42 Va. App. 794, 595 S.E.2d 36 (2004). See *Surles v. Mayer*, 48 Va. App. 146, 628 S.E.2d 563 (2006) (relocation served child's best interests, when child was happy, adjusted, and well-settled in new Florida environment).

Removal of the children to another state may not be allowed if maintaining the status quo custody arrangement, as established by the parents, is found to be in the children's best interest. *Cloutier v. Queen*, 35 Va. App. 413, 545 S.E.2d 574 (2001). In *Cloutier*, a trial court initially issued an order allowing a mother and children to relocate to Pennsylvania. However, upon reconsideration of the order within the 21-day period allowed by Rule 1:1, the trial court concluded that it had wrongly equated the mother's best interest with the children's best interest, and that the children's best interest required a continuation of the parents' existing, working joint custody arrangement, including the physical proximity that the parents had gone to great lengths to establish. Consequently, the trial court reversed itself and refused to allow the removal of the children to Pennsylvania. On appeal, the mother objected to the trial court's imposition of a remedy that neither parent had requested. However, the Court of Appeals affirmed, noting that it would circumvent the trial court's statutory obligation to determine custody based only on the children's best interests, if the trial court's options and remedies were limited only to custody arrangements requested by parents. *Cloutier v. Queen*, 35 Va. App. 413, 545 S.E.2d 574 (2001). See also against the wishes of a fit custodial *Sullivan v. Knick*, 38 Va. App. 773, 568 S.E.2d 430 (2002) (trial court's decision to disturb the "status quo" by allowing mother to relocate with child to another state was plainly wrong, when evidence clearly established that move would disrupt father's positive involvement in child's life, a result at odds with child's best interests).

The child's best interest apparently does not extend to movement within the state, perhaps because the problems of full faith and credit then do not apply. Failure to return a child to the state in violation of a court order may result in loss of custody. The custodial parent would not then be a fit and proper person to have custody. *Rowlee v. Rowlee*, 211 Va. 689, 179 S.E.2d 461 (1971). See also Va. Code § 20-108.1, explicitly mentioning that intentional denial of visitation may constitute a change in circumstances justifying modification of custody. Another consequence may be restraint on visitation. For example, a father's visitation privileges could only be exercised within Dickenson County, Virginia, where the trial court found that he would not return the children to the county if permitted to take them therefrom. *Branham v. Raines*, 209 Va. 702, 167 S.E.2d 355 (1969). Va. Code § 18.2-49.1 makes parental abduction a class six felony and therefore subject to the provisions of the federal Parental Kidnapping Prevention Act, 28 U.S.C. § 1738A. The Virginia statute proscribes any person from knowingly, wrongfully, and intentionally withholding a child from the child's custodial parent in a clear and significant violation of a court order respecting the custody or visitation of such child, so long as such child is withheld outside the Commonwealth.

In *Wilson v. Wilson*, 12 Va. App. 1251, 408 S.E.2d 576 (1991), the trial court erred in ordering that the father should become the primary physical custodian of the son should the wife ever move from her current residence of Nashville, Tennessee. The court of appeals found that a "predetermined automatic reversal of primary custody, based on an undetermined move in the future, is clearly an abuse of discretion." While a move from Nashville to another location at some time in the future might prove to be in the son's best interest, this could not be determined until the move was contemplated and all the circumstances associated with it known. Although the unknown potential future relocation in *Wilson* was too speculative of a basis to award a future custody modification, a child entering first grade within one year of the custody ruling was found not to be speculative. In *Wynnycky v. Kozel*, 71 Va. App. 177, 192, 834 S.E.2d 512 (2109), the trial judge ordered an equal shared physical custody schedule until the child entered first grade in approximately two years, and then the mother was to have primary physical custody and the father was given visitation every other weekend. The Court of Appeals affirmed the trial court's prospective future change of custody. Unlike *Wilson* which premised a future custody modification on a speculative unknown potential future event, "it was all but certain that the child would enter first grade at some point in the relatively near future," the circuit court made a contingency plan in the event the child did not enter first grade in September 2019, and "there was little to no evidence to suggest that there would be any other significant changes in the time from the circuit court's order to the child starting first grade," *Id.* at 195–96. In addressing prospective events when making custody determinations, the Court held that:

> In fact, it would be error for the circuit court not to consider future events in crafting a custody decree. After all, the custody determination is to be

made for the best interests of the child going forward, not merely the best interests of the child on the day of entry of the order. Accordingly, the statutory factors explicitly require the circuit court take the future into account. *See, e.g.,* Code 20-124.3(1) (requiring a court to consider "the age and physical and mental condition of the child, *giving due consideration to the child's changing developmental needs*" (emphasis added)); Code § 20-124.3(5) (requiring a court to consider "[t]he role that each parent has played *and will play in the future,* in the upbringing and care of the child" (emphasis added))

*Id.* at 196. A "circuit court does not necessarily abuse its discretion in basing its custody decision on future events so long as the future events are viewed as they appear at the time the decision is made." *Id.* at 197. Despite affirming the prospective custody change two years after court's ruling, the Court of Appeals cautioned that "the opinion should not be taken as a wholesale endorsement of 'automatic' changes in custody arrangements based on the occurrence of a future event." *Id.* at 199.

See also *Laing v. Walker*, 1995 Va. App. LEXIS 592 (July 18, 1995), where the mother proposed a move to Egypt. Although she canceled her plans to move, the trial court entered a final decree awarding the father sole legal and physical custody of the children, subject to her visitation rights; and *DeCapri v. DeCapri*, 1996 Va. App. LEXIS 36 (Jan. 23, 1996) (mother's move to Cleveland to attend community college resulted in a change from joint to sole custody in the father; father had a very close relationship with his daughter and maintained an active role in her care, education, and development). A custodial father was not allowed to relocate to North Carolina with the child, where the divorce court had been undecided about which parent would be the best custodian, and where the father's efforts were focused on curtailing the mother's access to the child. The mother had recently remarried and her spouse was a marine stationed at Quantico, Virginia, where they expected to reside for the foreseeable future. She testified that she was pregnant, and that her life "really has become much more stable." The Court of Appeals found that the evidence supported the conclusion that the beneficial relationship between the child and her mother would not be maintained and would be placed at risk were the father allowed to remove the child to *North Carolina. Bostick v. Bostick-Bennett*, 23 Va. App. 527, 478 S.E.2d 319 (1996). However, in *Parish v. Spaulding*, 26 Va. App. 566, 496 S.E.2d 91 (1998), the court found a change of circumstances in a case in which a sole custodial mother had remarried and moved to Indiana without prior court approval. The changed circumstances were of her making, but the move with the necessary change in visitation schedule was in the children's best interests since the mother's new husband had lost his Virginia employment, the parties could live rent-free in Indiana, and the reconstituted family unit contained both an adult male and female, as well as the children from both marriages. The mother had a close relationship with the children. The Supreme Court appeal, *Parish v. Spaulding*, 257 Va. 357, 513 S.E.2d 391 (1999), did not challenge the best interests ruling, but rather the procedure. The Court explained that *Gray v. Gray*, 228 Va. 696, 698, 324 S.E.2d 677, 678 (1985) ("before a court permits a custodial parent to remove children from the Commonwealth it must determine that removal is in the children's best interests") doesn't mean that the court cannot decide the question after the move. The Court also reasoned that it was not error to fail to enforce the order, because the kids already had been moved outside Virginia. The fact that the custodial mother was transferred overseas pursuant to her military assignment did not constitute a change in circumstances where there was testimony that her duties at the base would most likely require only regular daytime work hours and the base had all standard facilities, including a new child care center. *Lee v. Lee*, 1994 Va. App. LEXIS 206 (April 5, 1994). See also *Mortimer v. Mortimer*, 1995 Va. App. LEXIS 930 (Dec. 29, 1995) (mother retained custody although moved to California without giving notice to husband, who had joint legal custody); *Boyles v. Boyles*, 1996 Va. App. LEXIS 318 (April 30, 1996) (mother permitted to move from Virginia Beach to Charlottesville, where she had siblings and family support; father continued to contact and harass her despite prior court orders requiring no contact, and made derogatory comments to the children about her).

Under Va. Code § 20-124.5, a court shall require in all custody and visitation orders that a custodial parent give 30 days' notice to the court and the other party of an intent to relocate or any intended change of address. This is not necessary in cases where the court finds that there is good cause for omitting such an order. See *Judd v. Judd*, 53 Va. App. 578, 673 S.E.2d 913 (2009) (implicit finding of good cause).

In relocation cases, the burden of proof is on the moving party to prove by a preponderance of the evidence that the relocation is in the child's best interest. However, once a *prima facie* case for relocation has been made, any subsequent misallocation of the burden of proof by the trial court is harmless error. *Stockdale v. Stockdale*, 33 Va. App. 179, 532 S.E.2d 332 (2000).

See generally Comment, *Residence Restrictions on Custodial Parents*, 12 Rutgers L.J. 341 (1980).

## § 23.16    Visitation

In accordance with Va. Code § 20-124(B)(1) and 16.1-278.15(G), the use of the phrase "parenting time" in any custody or visitation proceeding is synonymous with the term "visitation."

The visitation rights of a noncustodial parent are subordinate to the welfare of the infant. *Oehl v. Oehl*, 221 Va. 618, 272 S.E.2d 441 (1980) (citing *Branham v. Raines*, 209 Va. 702, 167 S.E.2d 355 (1969)). In *Roberts v. Roberts*, 41 Va. App. 513, 586 S.E.2d 290 (2003), a trial court terminated a father's in-person visitation after the father's religious beliefs motivated him to threaten his children with punishment if they did not obey his teachings and to denounce the children's mother as a fornicator who was going to hell. The children feigned illness before visits, and their school performance suffered before and after visits. The father's behavior was found to be "unconscionable," and the state's compelling interest in protecting the children's welfare and best interests was controlling. Many of the decided cases involve issues of parental morality. Where there was no harm shown to the son of a lesbian mother by her unconventional lifestyle, and in all other respects she was shown to be a fit parent, her parental rights could not be terminated, and visitation privileges were continued. There might be a future time when it would become necessary to sever her relationship with the woman with whom she lived. *Doe v. Doe*, 222 Va. 736, 284 S.E.2d 799 (1981). In *Roe v. Roe*, 228 Va. 722, 324 S.E.2d 691 (1985), custody of the girl child was changed from the homosexual father who lived with another man to the mother, and visitation by the father was restricted to places outside the home and times when his homosexual lover was not present. Cf. *Brown v. Brown*, 218 Va. 196, 237 S.E.2d 89 (1977) (heterosexual lover not to be present while wife visited with children).

Even though the mother was living in Arizona in a house occupied by two males, psychiatrists testified that the children would be adversely affected if they were prohibited from visiting her in Arizona in her home. In addition, the children wished to visit with her at her Arizona residence. Therefore, it was improper for the trial judge to decree that visitation between the mother and her children was to take place only in Virginia. *Robinson v. Robinson*, 5 Va. App. 222, 361 S.E.2d 356 (1987). However, it was permissible to order that the noncustodial wife have no overnight guests of the opposite sex during the child's visitation. *Carrico v. Blevins*, 12 Va. App. 47, 402 S.E.2d 235 (1991). The wife lived with a man to whom she was not married and his two daughters. The husband testified that sometimes after the child visited with his mother he was difficult and did not mind well, and that on one occasion he returned home upset that the wife's male companion had walked into the bathroom while he was naked. The husband had strong religious and moral views against the child being in the home with the mother and her boyfriend, which should have been considered in imposing visitation restraints.

Joint custody with unsupervised visitation should not have been continued when the father violated court orders that he not feed the son with a baby bottle, that the son be in charge of his own body for bathing and cleaning purposes, and that the son sleep in his own bed. *Wilson v. Wilson*, 12 Va. App. 1251, 408 S.E.2d 576 (1991). Custody was awarded to the mother and the case was remanded for establishment of visitation subject to appropriate safeguards. See also *Hale v. Hale*, 1994 Va. App. LEXIS 35 (Feb. 1, 1994) (supervised visitation appropriate); *Smith v. McPeak*, 1993 Va. App. LEXIS 241 (July 6, 1993) (contact restricted to letters screened by guardian ad litem). Denial of visitation is not itself a material change in circumstances warranting a change in custody, in a case where the noncustodial parent moved from Spotsylvania County to Maryland. *Covington v. Covington*, 1996 Va. App. LEXIS 775 (Dec. 17, 1996). However, an amendment to the Virginia Code suggests that it certainly is one of the factors to be considered in making a "best interests" determination. Va. Code § 20-124.3(6) adds to the "best interests" factors the fact that "a parent has unreasonably denied to the other parent access to or visitation with the child."

Current Virginia statutes permit grandparents, step-grandparents, stepparents, former stepparents, and other relatives to seek visitation through the juvenile and domestic relations courts, which are to determine custody and visitation according to the best interests of the child. Va. Code §§ 16.1-241(A), 16.1-278.15(B), 20-107.2, 20-124.1, 20-124.2(B). However, these statutes must be analyzed for constitutionality if the nonparents are seeking visitation against the wishes of a fit custodial parent or parents. See *Troxel v. Granville*, 530 U.S. 57, 120 S. Ct. 2054, 147 L. Ed. 2d 49 (2000). In *Troxel*, the United States Supreme Court found that a Washington state visitation statute was unconstitutional as applied to a fit mother and her children in a grandparent visitation context. The "breathtakingly broad" Washington statute permitted "any person" to petition for visitation rights "at any time" and authorized Washington trial courts to grant visitation rights whenever "visitation may serve the best interest of the child." The Supreme Court reasoned that application of the statute to the fit mother violated her fundamental due process right to make decisions concerning the care, custody, and control of her children, because the statute authorized a trial court to disregard *any* decision by a fit custodial parent regarding third-party visitation, solely on the basis of the *trial court's* determination of a child's best interest. Thus, in *Troxel*, grandparents who sought more visitation time with their deceased son's children than the children's mother was willing to allow were unable to obtain court-ordered visitation under the Washington statute, because the statute unconstitutionally interfered with the fundamental right of parents to rear their children. After *Troxel*, a key question for determining the constitutionality of state statutes authorizing third-party visitation, at least in situations involving fit parents, seems to be whether the statute authorizes a trial court to freely substitute its own judgment regarding a child's best interest for the fit parent's judgment regarding the child's best interest.

In *Williams v. Williams*, 256 Va. 19, 501 S.E.2d 417 (1998), which was decided before *Troxel v. Granville*, 530 U.S. 57, 120 S. Ct. 2054, 147 L. Ed. 2d 49 (2000), the Virginia Supreme Court held that Virginia statutes permitting visitation by grandparents and other nonparents do *not* violate federally protected parental rights by interfering with the constitutional right of parents to autonomy in child-rearing. The Court reasoned that the statutes satisfy federal constitutional requirements because Virginia courts must find "an actual harm to the child's health or welfare without [nonparent] visitation" *before* ordering such visitation over the objections of the child's parents. Thus, in determining nonparent visitation when parents oppose it, a trial court may consider the "best interests of the child" standard only *after* it considers the "actual harm" standard and makes a finding that actual harm will occur if nonparent visitation is *not* ordered. See also *Griffin v. Griffin*, 41 Va. App. 77, 581 S.E.2d 899 (2003) (trial court erred by collapsing "actual harm" and "best interests" standards). In *Williams*, a trial court was found to lack the authority to allow visitation by grandparents against the wishes of a child's parents, because the child's intact family unit was fit and capable of meeting all of the child's needs. The Virginia Supreme Court's holding in *Williams* was cited in *Troxel*, and is apparently consistent with the *Troxel* holding. Once a non-biological parent has satisfied the actual harm test and been awarded custody, any subsequent proceeding to modify custody or visitation is based on the existence of a material change of circumstances and the best interests of the child, and there is no obligation by the non-biological parent to satisfy the actual harm standard. *Rhodes v. Lang,* 66 Va. App. 702, 709 (2016).

Before the enactment of the statutes that allow grandparents and other relatives to seek visitation through the juvenile and domestic relations courts, a stepparent who had lived with a child for seven years was able to obtain visitation over the objection of the natural father of the child, who then had custody. *Arnold v. Newberry*, 24 Va. Cir. 431 (Washington Co.

1991). In *Joseph v. Portsmouth Dep't of Soc. Servs.*, 2006 Va. App. LEXIS 264 (June 13, 2006), a paternal great great step-aunt was determined to be a person "with a legitimate interest" within the meaning of the statute permitting an individual who is not a biological parent of a child to petition for visitation with child.

After the enactment of the statutes that allow grandparents and other relatives to seek visitation, and after the decision in *Williams v. Williams*, 256 Va. 19, 501 S.E.2d 417 (1998), but before the decision in *Troxel v. Granville*, 530 U.S. 57, 120 S. Ct. 2054, 147 L. Ed. 2d 49 (2000), grandparents were allowed to visit, with the court setting visitation at one Saturday per month, after their son died and over the mother's objection to court interference. The paternal grandparents had been the child's primary child care providers since both parents worked. *Decatur v. Eskam*, 49 Va. Cir. 357 (Spotsylvania Co. 1999). See also *Dotson v. Hylton*, 29 Va. App. 635, 513 S.E.2d 901 (1999), where the mother, who objected to the paternal grandmother's visits, had been awarded sole custody by the divorce court and the father, who encouraged the visitation, was confined to the penitentiary.

After the decisions in both *Troxel v. Granville*, 530 U.S. 57, 120 S. Ct. 2054, 147 L. Ed. 2d 49 (2000), and *Williams v. Williams*, 256 Va. 19, 501 S.E.2d 417 (1998), an estranged husband was denied visitation with his wife's child, who was fathered by another man, when his estranged wife objected to the nonparent visitation. Although the trial court found that visitation would be in the child's best interests, the "actual harm" standard took precedence over the "best interests" standard; and thus the trial court was required to make a finding that actual harm to the child's health or welfare would occur if the nonparent visitation did *not* occur, *before* the trial court could consider the child's best interests. *Griffin v. Griffin*, 41 Va. App. 77, 581 S.E.2d 899 (2003). The *Griffin* court distinguished *Dotson v. Hylton*, 29 Va. App. 635, 639, 513 S.E.2d 901, 903 (1999), which held that the "actual harm" standard need not be followed when one parent objects to nonparent visitation but the other parent requests the visitation, by noting that the dispute before it was only between the estranged wife (a fit parent) and the estranged husband (a nonparent) because the child's father had *not* requested the visitation. See *Stadter v. Siperko*, 52 Va. App. 81, 661 S.E.2d 494 (2008) (former lesbian cohabitant with legitimate interest in child under Va. Code § 20-124.1 must show that child will suffer actual harm if visitation does not occur, when child's fit biological parent objects to visitation); *Surles v. Mayer*, 48 Va. App. 146, 628 S.E.2d 563 (2006) (surrogate father required to show that child would suffer actual harm if visitation did not occur, when neither biological parent requested visitation with surrogate father).

In *Yopp v. Hodges*, 43 Va. App. 427, 598 S.E.2d 760 (2004), a child's grandparents were awarded visitation absent any finding that denial of the nonparent visitation would be harmful or detrimental to the child's welfare, when only one of the child's parents objected to the visitation. The court of appeals held that the "best interests" standard of *Dotson v. Hylton*, 29 Va. App. 635, 640, 513 S.E.2d 901 (1999), controls custody and visitation disputes between two fit parents.

In *Albert v. Ramirez*, 45 Va. App. 799, 613 S.E.2d 865 (2005), a child's mother and stepfather shared joint legal and physical custody pursuant to a trial court's consent decree. After the mother relocated from Arlington to Bentonville, she sought sole physical custody with no visitation. The trial court denied her request, and she appealed. A circuit court found that the stepfather was a nonparent, applied the *Griffin* court's "actual harm" standard in determining custody, and ruled that the mother's custody modification request should be granted because the stepfather had not shown by clear and convincing evidence that his stepdaughter would suffer actual harm if there were to be no visitation. The stepfather appealed, and the court of appeals reversed. The court of appeals concluded that the *Troxel* and *Griffin* decisions were inapplicable, because they both involved third-party requests to *establish* custody or visitation. Although the stepfather was a nonparent, the trial court's consent decree had already established his custody and visitation rights. Therefore, because the matter did not involve an initial custody or visitation determination, the mother bore the burden of proving that a material change of circumstances had occurred, and that a change in visitation would be in the child's best interests pursuant to Va. Code § 20-108. Consequently, the circuit court should have applied the "best interests" standard, rather than the *Griffin* "actual harm" standard, in resolving the custody dispute between the mother and stepfather.

In *Denise v. Tencer*, 46 Va. App. 372, 617 S.E.2d 413 (2005), a trial court approved a custody agreement forged by a child's terminally ill mother, her father, and the child's biological father. The agreement provided that after the mother's death the child's grandfather and father would share joint legal custody, and the child's primary residence would be with the grandfather. When the custodial arrangement proved untenable, the father sought sole legal and physical custody. Applying the "best interests" standard, the trial court concluded that changed circumstances did not warrant modification of the custodial arrangement at that time. On appeal, the father argued, citing *Troxel*, *Williams*, and *Griffin*, that the trial court's award of joint legal custody to the grandfather contravened his own constitutionally protected fundamental liberty interest to raise his child without interference from a third party or the state, in the absence of clear and convincing evidence of his unfitness as a parent. In affirming the trial court's order, the court of appeals stated that the decisions in *Troxel*, *Williams*, and *Griffin* were inapplicable to the father's case, because they all involved situations in which nonparents without custodial rights were seeking visitation with children against the wishes of fit parents who were possessed of their constitutional rights to child-rearing autonomy. In the father's case, the grandfather's status as the child's legal custodian gave him the same child-rearing autonomy as that of a parent. Therefore, the situation was analogous to a custody dispute between two fit parents who were both deemed to be acting in the children's best interests, and the "best interests" standard, rather than the "actual harm" standard, was applicable to the custody dispute between the father and grandfather. See also *Stadter v. Siperko*, 52 Va. App. 81, 661 S.E.2d 494 (2008) (declining to recognize former lesbian cohabitant as *de facto* parent with same rights as biological parent and to whom "best interests" standard would have applied in determining visitation over objection of child's fit biological parent); *Surles v. Mayer*, 48 Va. App. 146, 628 S.E.2d 563 (2006) (citing *Denise* for proposition that "actual harm" standard is inapplicable when third party already possesses joint legal and sole physical custody of child through valid consent order).

In *Rice v. Rice*, 49 Va. App. 192, 638 S.E.2d 702 (2006), a trial court properly denied visitation to the paternal grandparents of a child who had been sexually abused by her father in the grandparents' home. The trial court found that the child "is suffering at this time and has problems and difficulties," and ruled that giving the child's mother "the right to make the decision about how things are handled with this child" was in the child's best interests. In making its ruling, the trial court properly considered the evidence and the "best interests of the child" factors of Va. Code § 20-124.3. The court of appeals declined to determine whether the trial court erred by applying the "best interests of the child" standard rather than the "actual harm" standard articulated in *Williams* and *Griffin*. Because the trial court denied the grandparents' petition for visitation under the more lenient of the two standards, the result would be the same, even if the trial court erred by not first finding actual harm.

In the juvenile and domestic relations courts, persons with legitimate interests may file petitions involving custody, visitation, support, or control of a child. This standing requirement is to be liberally construed, and includes, but is not limited to, grandparents, stepparents, former stepparents, blood relatives and family members. It does not include (1) any person whose parental rights have been terminated by court order (either voluntarily or involuntarily); or (2) any person whose interest in the child derives from or through a parent whose rights have been terminated, such as relatives of a child who has been legally adopted (unless the adoption was a stepparent adoption); or (3) persons involved in rape or statutory rape when the child was conceived as a result of the crime. Va. Code §§ 16.1-241(A) and 20-124.1. See *Surles v. Mayer*, 48 Va. App. 146, 628 S.E.2d 563 (2006) (individual who acted as child's surrogate father for four years was "functional equivalent" of former stepparent, and qualified as "person with legitimate interest" under Va. Code § 20-124.1).

Va. Code § 20-124.2(B) requires a showing of "clear and convincing evidence" before visitation may be awarded to a nonparent. Griffin v. Griffin, 41 Va. App. 77, 581 S.E.2d 899 (2003). See, e.g., *O'Rourke v. Vuturo*, 49 Va. App. 139, 638 S.E.2d 124 (2006) (expert testimony established that denying visitation would cause actual harm to child, and that visitation was in child's best interests).

Birth parents and parents by previous adoption, as well as other persons whose interest in the child derives from or through them, lose their visitation and other familial rights after all final adoptions except when the adopting parent is a stepparent. Va. Code § 63.2-1215.

Some cases involve other restrictions the custodial parent has wished to place on the other. The custodial parent may not force the noncustodial parent to dispose of recreational vehicles the custodial parent does not approve of, so long as they are not dangerous or do not affect the child's welfare. *Eichelberger v. Eichelberger*, 2 Va. App. 409, 345 S.E.2d 10 (1986). Nor may the custodial parent force the children to attend religious services during the time spent with the noncustodial parent. *Carrico v. Blevins*, 12 Va. App. 47, 402 S.E.2d 235 (1991). The trial court had the authority to require the custodial mother's husband to refrain from making derogatory comments about the noncustodial father in the presence of the children. *Forrest v. Ruhlin*, 1995 Va. App. LEXIS 579 (July 18, 1995).

An award of overnight, out-of-state visitation one weekend a month could satisfy the requirement of Va. Code § 20-124.2 that trial courts "assure minor children of frequent and continuing contact with both parents, . . . and encourage parents to share in the responsibilities of rearing their children." Although a three-day visitation every third weekend might better accommodate both father and daughter, the trial court did not abuse its discretion by refusing to modify the visitation schedule for the second time in a year.

*Crisco v. Sorensen*, 1997 Va. App. LEXIS 272 (Apr. 29, 1997). See also *Goldhamer v. Cohen*, 31 Va. App. 728, 525 S.E.2d 599 (2000), where wife's midweek overnight visitation was eliminated when evidence showed that it "disrupted the child's schedule for 'normal sleeping and waking, homework and other activities,' " according to the child's treating psychologist.

In *Franklin v. Department of Soc. Servs., Division of Child Support Enforcement ex rel. Franklin*, 27 Va. App. 136, 497 S.E.2d 881 (1998), a family had sought help from the American Embassy by returning to the United States from Africa, entering into Virginia, and remaining residents since that time. Service of process on the husband via service on his company's United States office and several mailed notices were sufficient to generate jurisdiction over him for enforcing child support. The court also had authority to affirm an ex parte emergency custody order preventing either parent from removing the children from Virginia. When the husband requested a show cause ruling on the issue of visitation, he automatically waived any jurisdictional objection. This case, however, is most significant because it analyzed the scope of Va. Code § 20-88.35(5). The section provides that jurisdiction may be obtained over an individual who has performed an affirmative act in the state or invoked the laws of the state. The husband stated that he never directed his wife to move to Virginia, but the court found that in ordering the family to leave the marital home in Africa, his children did become residents of Virginia. This allowed Virginia to exercise personal jurisdiction over him.

## § 23.17  Powers in Joint Custody

In the divorce decree, husband and wife were awarded alternate custody of their two children. Later, each moved for sole custody. The arrangement was modified so that the mother was awarded custody during the school year, so that the situation would be less disruptive to the child. Moreover, a portion of the decree requiring that the children be reared in the Jewish faith and that they attend religious school each week violated the free exercise clause of the Virginia Constitution. *Lundeen v. Struminger*, 209 Va. 548, 165 S.E.2d 285 (1969).

Where the parents had joint legal custody, it was not error for the trial court to give the father "ultimate decision-making authority over the child's education and day care issues." *Tucker v. Clarke*, 2011 Va. App. LEXIS 68, at *11 (Feb. 22, 2011).

## § 23.18  Name Change

Even though a mother has sole custody of the children and remarries, she cannot have the children's surname changed to that of her new husband. This is because the father's rights were not terminated, and, more important still, the already strained bond between the noncustodial parent and child should not be further weakened. Unless the child is being adopted, the effect of a change of name would be to deprive the child of the one father known to him or her. *Flowers v. Cain*, 218 Va. 234, 237 S.E.2d 111 (1977). However, in *Rowland v. Shurbutt*, 259 Va. 305, 525 S.E.2d 917 (2000), the father did not file the name change petition until the child was nearly seven, although the parents litigated custody, visitation and support issues "most of the child's life." Although the mother and father had joint legal custody of the child, the child resided with the mother and her husband since birth. Citing *Flowers v. Cain*, the court reasoned that the burden of proving that a name change "is in the best interests" of a minor rests upon the petitioning parent. The father's evidence in *Rowland* rested upon the deposition of a psychiatrist who had never met the child's mother or her husband, and who concluded that "a child should be able to carry the name of both his parents" and that the father "has been extensively involved with the child." The court noted that the psychiatrist's opinions focused mainly on the father's "rights" and "only tangentially" addressed the child's best interests. The court concluded that the child's best interests would be served without the name change, since with his present name he is "healthy, happy, developing normally in school and socially, and is the best balanced of all the parties." See also *Spero v. Heath*, 267 Va. 477, 593 S.E.2d 239 (2004) (unwed father failed to offer evidence showing any of *Flowers* criteria, and thus failed to show that name change was in child's best interest). However, when the mother and the father never married, and the child from birth bore his mother's surname, the mother could change the name to that of her new husband despite the natural father's opposition. *In re Change of Name of O.*, 27 Va. Cir. 260 (Loudoun Co. 1992). Although the father was a loving parent who had made substantial commitments to the child's well-being, the strong bond between parent and child had never before been in any way dependent upon his use of the surname.

Further, when a child was born to unmarried parents, the mother later married, the birth father had not visited the child for two and one-half years "because of his work schedule," and the child, now eight years old, wanted to change her last name to that of her stepfather, her best interests were served by allowing the name change. The mother testified that she sought to encourage a "healthy relationship" between the child and her father, and he admitted that with the exception of one occasion she had never "hindered or stopped him from seeing his daughter." *May v. Grandy*, 259 Va. 629, 528 S.E.2d 105 (2000).

A living parent who does not join in a child's application for change of name must be served with notice of the application unless the court waives notice after an ex parte hearing; if the parent objects to the change of name, the court will hold a hearing to determine whether the change is in the best interest of the child. Va. Code § 8.01-217.

## § 23.19    Modification

The standard in a modification proceeding is also the welfare, or "best interests," of the child. The cases require a "change in circumstances," which may be due to a change in either parents' condition or simply a change in the child's needs or situation. Although stability in the custodial relationship is important, it is simply another factor to be considered in determining the best interests of the child. There is no requirement that the current environment actually be harmful to the child. *Keel v. Keel*, 225 Va. 606, 607, 303 S.E.2d 917, 920 (1983). See also *Turner v. Turner*, 3 Va. App. 31, 348 S.E.2d 21 (1986); *Peple v. Peple*, 5 Va. App. 414, 364 S.E.2d 232 (1988). Because of the trial court's statutory obligation to determine child custody based only on the best interests of the child, the court's options and remedies are not limited to custody arrangements specifically requested by one parent. *Cloutier v. Queen*, 35 Va. App. 413, 545 S.E.2d 574 (2001).

The intentional withholding of visitation of a child from the other parent without just cause may constitute a material change of circumstances justifying a change of custody in the discretion of the court. Va. Code § 20-108. Va. Code § 20-124.3, as amended in 2000, provides that the court must consider whether a parent has unreasonably denied the other parent access to or visitation with the child, as a factor in determining custody or visitation arrangements. The inquiry, then, is twofold: (1) has there been a change in circumstances; and (2) would a change in custody be in the child's best interests? *Id.* at 611–12, 303 S.E.2d at 921; *Collins v. Collins*, 183 Va. 408, 32 S.E.2d 657 (1945). However, denial of visitation was not itself a material change in circumstances warranting a change in custody, in a case where the noncustodial parent moved from Spotsylvania County to Maryland. *Covington v. Covington*, 1996 Va. App. LEXIS 775 (Dec. 17, 1996) (it should be noted that this case was decided before the amendments to Va. Code § 20-124.3(6), which now lists among the "best interests" factors unreasonable denial of access to or visitation with the child). In *Petrova v. Leach*, 2019 Va. App. LEXIS 310, custody was modified where the mother refused to return the child to the United States. The mother was limited to having supervised visits until she submitted the child's Bulgarian passport to the clerk of the circuit court. The court noted that the father had been deprived of several moths of visitation when the mother kept the child in Bulgaria.

In a case decided before the amendment to the statute, *Parish v. Spaulding*, 26 Va. App. 566, 496 S.E.2d 91 (1998), the court found a change of circumstances in a case in which a sole custodial mother had remarried and moved to Indiana without prior court approval. The changed circumstances were of her making, but the move with the necessary change in visitation schedule was in the children's best interests since the mother's new husband had lost his Virginia employment, the parties could live rent-free in Indiana, and the reconstituted family unit contained both an adult male and female, as well as the children from both marriages. The mother had a close relationship with the children.

The Supreme Court appeal, *Parish v. Spaulding*, 257 Va. 357, 513 S.E.2d 391 (1999), did not challenge the best interests ruling, but rather the procedure. The Court explained that *Gray v. Gray*, 228 Va. 696, 698, 324 S.E.2d 677, 678 (1985) ("before a court permits a custodial parent to remove children from the Commonwealth it must determine that removal is in the children's best interests"), doesn't mean that the court cannot decide the question after the move. The Court also reasoned that it was not error to fail to enforce the order, because the kids already had been moved outside Virginia. See *D'Ambrosio v. D'Ambrosio,* 45 Va. App. 323, 610 S.E.2d 876 (2005) (father had notice regarding issue of modification of parents' medical decision-making authority).

In *In re Green*, 48 Va. Cir. 170 (City of Richmond 1999), the child's parents had reconciled after an original award of joint custody with primary residence of the child with the mother. When they separated again, the father was awarded physical custody. The court held that the first order was no longer binding once the parties reconciled. The court then reconsidered the evidence presented at the hearing in Juvenile and Domestic Relations District Court. Based on the best interests of the child and the parties' living arrangements rather than the arguments proffered by the parents, the court granted joint custody to the parties with physical custody awarded to the mother.

In *Albert v. Albert*, 38 Va. App. 284, 563 S.E.2d 389 (2002) a trial court properly denied a father's request for modification of a visitation schedule in order to reduce child care expenses. The father did not demonstrate changed circumstances or that a change would be in the children's best interests; instead, he demonstrated only that a change would be in his own best interest.

A noncustodial parent does not establish a prima facie case for a change in custody based solely on an affidavit. *Ohlen v. Shively*, 16 Va. App. 419, 430 S.E.2d 559 (1993). By accepting an affidavit as the only substantive evidence required to establish father's prima facie case, the trial judge improperly shifted to the custodial mother the burden of proving the absence of a change in circumstances. However, the parent seeking a change in custody need not prove by clear and convincing evidence that a change was in the child's best interests. *Newland v. Neal*, 1996 Va. App. LEXIS 105 (Feb. 13, 1996). The preponderance of the evidence standard is appropriate for a change in custody motion. A noncustodial father, as a defense in a civil contempt proceeding for failure to pay spousal support, contested the validity of a consent order granting his wife custody on grounds that she testified falsely about the children and their relationship with their parents. In *Peet v. Peet*, 16 Va. App. 323, 429 S.E.2d 487 (1993), the court of appeals held that this was an allegation of intrinsic fraud. Fraud must be addressed either during cross-examination and impeachment, or in a separate proceeding directly attacking the decree. See also *Ohlen (Shively) v. Shively*, 16 Va. App. 419, 430 S.E.2d 559 (1993) (error to change custody on father's deposition alone).

In *Travis v. Finley*, 36 Va. App. 189, 548 S.E.2d 906 (2001), the court of appeals held that Va. Code § 8.01-223.1 barred a court from dismissing a mother's custody modification petition because of her failure to answer discovery requests, when the mother clearly exercised a constitutional protection in a civil action by invoking her Fifth Amendment privilege against self-incrimination.

The trial court appropriately ordered a change of custody from mother to father in *Schalow v. Schalow*, 1993 Va. App. LEXIS 212 (June 22, 1993). The mother frequently interfered with the father's court-ordered visitation, while her boyfriend, who had been ordered by the trial court to stay away from her home, engaged the father in a fight in the presence of at least one child. Finally, the parties' children preferred to live with their father. See also *Flinchum v. Flinchum*, 1993 Va. App. LEXIS 207 (June 22, 1993), where the children were frequently absent or late arriving at school, and lacked stability and security while in their mother's custody. Further, the mother attempted to interfere with the love and affection between the children and their father and intentionally impeded his visitation with them.

Allowing a child to remain in his mother's sole custody was not an abuse of discretion even when the child stayed in day-care before and after school. The trial court noted that evidence indicated that the boy's "experience in day care has been a good one and a positive one." *Lewis v. Callahan*, 1997

Va. App. LEXIS 105 (Feb. 18, 1997). Nor did the father convince the court that the mother's smoking contributed to the child's respiratory problems.

If a nonparent has obtained custody or visitation rights pursuant to a valid court order, then any subsequent modification of custody or visitation will require application of the "material change and best interests" standard under Va. Code § 20-108, rather than the "actual harm" standard articulated in *Griffin v. Griffin*, 41 Va. App. 77, 581 S.E.2d 899 (2003). See *Albert v. Ramirez*, 45 Va. App. 799, 613 S.E.2d 865 (2005) (stepfather); *Denise v. Tencer*, 46 Va. App. 372, 617 S.E.2d 413 (2005) (grandparent). See also *In re Morris*, 40 Va. Cir. 413 (City of Richmond 1996) (grandparents).

An order limiting previously ordered custodial or visitation rights of a military parent due to the parent's deployment must be entered as a temporary order. Va. Code § 20-124.8(A). This temporary order must require the nondeploying parent to reasonably accommodate the leave schedule of the deploying parent, and to facilitate opportunities for telephonic and electronic mail contact with the child. Va. Code § 20-124.10. When the parent returns from deployment, he or she can obtain an expedited hearing on a petition to modify the order that was based on the deployment, and the nondeploying parent bears the burden of showing that reentry of the prior custody or visitation order is no longer in the child's best interests. Va. Code § 20-124.8(C). However, modification of custody or visitation on the basis of changed circumstances is not precluded. Va. Code § 20-124.8(D). Until the deploying parent's return, visitation may be delegated to a family member with whom the child has a close and substantial relationship, including a stepparent. Va. Code § 20-124.8(B).

## § 23.20   Jurisdiction in Modification Proceedings

Jurisdiction in modification proceedings is governed by the Uniform Child Custody Jurisdiction and Enforcement Act (UCCJEA), Chapter 7.1 of Title 20 of the Virginia Code (Va. Code §§ 20-146.1 through 20-146.38), which replaced the Uniform Child Custody Jurisdiction Act (UCCJA), Chapter 7 of Title 20 of the Virginia Code (Va. Code §§ 20-125 through 20-146). The UCCJEA became effective on July 1, 2001; however, any motion or other request for relief made in a child custody proceeding or child custody enforcement proceeding, that was commenced before July 1, 2001 is governed by the law in effect at the time the motion or other request was made. Va. Code § 20-146.37.

Under the UCCJEA, discussed at the beginning of this chapter, a child custody or visitation order must usually be modified by the court that issued the order, because that court has exclusive and continuing jurisdiction over child custody matters as long as the child, the child's parents, or any person acting as a parent continues to live in that court's state. See Va. Code §§ 20-146.13 and 20-146.14. When all of the parties have left a state, so that the issuing court loses jurisdiction, or in certain other specific circumstances, then child custody orders may be modified pursuant to Va. Code § 20-146.14.

Under Virginia's former law, the UCCJA, some cases allowed modification of custody awards when the children and one parent were within the state even though there was no in personam jurisdiction over the absent parent. See, e.g., *Ben-Levi v. Ben-Levi*, 87 N.J. 308, 434 A.2d 63, dismissed for want of jurisdiction, 8 Fam. L. Rep. (BNA) 2016 (1981). The UCCJA required that the child's "home state" retain jurisdiction unless at some time another state assumed it. Former Va. Code § 20-126. A husband and wife separated in Texas, where they had been living. The father took the children to Virginia, while the mother remained in Texas. In 1976, the Arlington County, Virginia, Juvenile and Domestic Relations Court awarded the father custody and ordered the mother to pay child support. The mother was to visit with the child only in Arlington. Later the father threatened the mother that she would never see the children again if she disobeyed his wishes. When she took them to Texas for a visit, she unsuccessfully petitioned the Texas court for custody. She then returned the children to the father and procured a Texas divorce. While the custody matter was under appeal, the father took the children overseas where he had been stationed by the military. The mother then tried unsuccessfully for three years to obtain visitation. She finally petitioned Arlington County Circuit Court for a change in custody based on his noncompliance with the visitation order. After she was granted custody, the father appealed, alleging lack of jurisdiction. In *Lutes v. Alexander*, 14 Va. App. 1075, 421 S.E.2d 857 (1992), the court of appeals affirmed the change of custody, finding that the Virginia courts had continuing jurisdiction over the matter. The mother, through her attorney, had attempted to serve the father "in every conceivable manner." The service was unsuccessful only because Major Lutes refused to accept it. To allow the father to defeat jurisdiction by refusing to accept service is "tantamount to granting anyone the right to avoid the valid jurisdiction of our courts based on a personal whim."

Thus in *Wheaton v. Wheaton*, 42 Va. Cir. 139 (Fairfax Co. 1997), Virginia never lost jurisdiction to determine custody under the UCCJA or the PKPA even though there were custody proceedings pending in Guam. The parties had lived and been divorced in Virginia, but sent the children to live in Guam with his parents after the divorce. Since the children had left Virginia on June 9, 1996, and the Guam proceeding commenced on October 30 of that year, the "home state" of the children was still Virginia, which therefore possessed jurisdiction while the Guam proceeding was not consistent with the PKPA. See also *Johnson v. Johnson*, 26 Va. App. 135, 493 S.E.2d 668 (1997); *Gardner v. Fore*, 49 Va. Cir. 38 (Washington Co. 1999) (after obtaining Virginia divorce with a decree giving her joint legal and primary physical custody, mother and children moved to North Carolina).

On the other hand, where both parties, who shared joint legal custody, moved out of Virginia after their 1996 divorce, the state retained no jurisdiction to hear the father's contempt motion against the mother for denying him visitation with his daughter. *Taylor v. Taylor*, 42 Va. Cir. 190 (Fairfax Co. 1997).

## § 23.21    Enforcement of Custody Decrees

If a parent fails to abide by court orders relating to custody, several remedies are available. The most obvious, of course, is contempt. If the parent fails to afford visitation to the noncustodial parent, custody may be changed since such conduct shows that the custodial parent is not fit. The intentional withholding of visitation of a child from the other parent without just cause may constitute a material change of circumstances justifying a change of custody in the discretion of the court. Va. Code § 20-108. See, e.g., *Rowlee v. Rowlee*, 211 Va. 689, 179 S.E.2d 461 (1971).

The aggrieved parent or other legal guardian may bring charges under Va. Code § 18.2-49.1, which makes parental abduction from the state in violation of a custody or visitation order a felony. Compare Va. Code § 18.2-47 (abduction of child by parent from state is a felony; abduction of child by parent, if punishable by contempt, is Class 1 misdemeanor). See also *Taylor v. Commonwealth*, 260 Va. 683, 537 S.E.2d 592 (2000) (general abduction statute contains no exception for parent of abducted person). The Parental Kidnapping Prevention Act, 28 U.S.C. § 1738A, is only available where the crime is a felony in Virginia: where the child is removed from the Commonwealth. A parent, or one assisting a parent, is immune from prosecution under the federal kidnapping statute (as opposed to the Parental Kidnapping statute). *United States v. Boettcher*, 780 F.2d 435 (4th Cir. 1985). The first time that a parent knowingly, wrongfully, and intentionally commits a clear and significant violation of a custody or visitation order, the parent is guilty of a Class 3 misdemeanor. A second violation within twelve months is a Class 2 misdemeanor, and a third violation within twenty-four months is a Class 1 misdemeanor. Va. Code § 18.2-49.1. These cases are in the jurisdiction of the juvenile and domestic relations district court regardless of which court issued the original custody or visitation order. Va. Code § 16.1-241(J).

The criminal abduction and custodial interference case of *Foster-Zahid v. Commonwealth*, 23 Va. App. 430, 477 S.E.2d 759 (1996) involved a father who did not return the parties' son to the mother, who was joint custodian and was to have physical custody during the school year. On appeal, the father claimed that he had not violated the abduction statutes because the abduction was accomplished outside Virginia. The Court of Appeals disagreed, stating that the statute had been enacted to prevent exactly the sort of behavior that the father had exhibited, and that the conduct out of state had clear Virginia effects.

One other possibility for relief lies in a tort action for intentional infliction of emotional distress. See *Womack v. Eldridge*, 215 Va. 338, 210 S.E.2d 145 (1974). The specific tort might be interference with familial relationships or kidnapping. See, e.g., *Kajtazi v. Kajtazi*, 488 F. Supp. 15 (E.D.N.Y. 1978); *Bennett v. Bennett*, 682 F.2d 1039, 221 U.S. App. D.C. 90 (D.C. Cir. 1982); *Bartanus v. Lis*, 332 Pa. Super. 48, 480 A.2d 1178 (1984). The action might be brought either in federal court, *Lloyd v. Loeffler*, 694 F.2d 489 (7th Cir. 1982),where the child has been taken outside the state, or in Virginia. The Fourth Circuit, using the lines of reasoning in both *Lloyd v. Loeffler* and *Kajtazi* (although neither was cited), has found both that recovery would lie for intentional infliction of emotional distress despite Virginia's abolition of the alienation of affections action and that such a proceeding could be brought in federal court despite the "domestic relations exception" to federal jurisdiction. *Raftery v. Scott*, 756 F.2d 335 (4th Cir. 1985).

The trial court has discretionary power to make an award of attorney's fees that are incurred by an aggrieved parent in a contempt proceeding for a parent's violation of a child custody or visitation order. See *Carswell v. Masterson*, 224 Va. 329, 295 S.E.2d 899 (1982). A parent's debt for attorney's fees awarded in a contempt proceeding arising from the parent's violation of a visitation order is nondischargeable in bankruptcy under U.S.C. § 523(a)(5), because the debt is "in the nature of support of the child or the child's parent," and thus fits within the definition of "domestic support obligation" that is contained in 11 U.S.C. § 101(14A). *Marvin v. Marvin*, 51 Va. App. 619, 659 S.E.2d 579 (2008).

## § 23.22 Enforcement of Foreign Custody Judgments

A child custody order is never final. Therefore res judicata would not apply, and the decision would not be entitled to full faith and credit absent the Parental Kidnapping Prevention Act, which provides that full faith and credit must be given to other states' valid custody orders. 28 U.S.C. § 1738A. Because courts were quick to find "changed circumstances" immediately after entry of a foreign decree if one of their domiciliaries was involved, see, e.g., *Webb v. Webb*, 451 U.S. 493, 101 S. Ct. 1889, 68 L. Ed. 2d 392 (1981); *Borys v. Borys*, 76 N.J. 103, 386 A.2d 366 (1978), Congress enacted the Parental Kidnapping Prevention Act, 48 U.S.C. § 1738A, which mandates full faith and credit for a valid foreign order. In order to enjoin a foreign proceeding under this action in federal court, there must be two judgments in conflict. In *Middleton v. Middleton*, 227 Va. 82, 314 S.E.2d 362 (1984), the Virginia Supreme Court noted that the U.C.C.J.A. must be followed, absent emergency allowing cases involving foreign custody awards to be decided in Virginia only when Virginia was the child's "home state," i.e., the state where the child resided for the six months preceding the action or where removal from Virginia occurred in defiance of a court order. This result is mandated because of the need for the forum court to have the most substantial connection with information concerning the child. Clearly, no full faith and credit need be given a foreign custody decision where there was no personal jurisdiction over the absent spouse. *May v. Anderson*, 345 U.S. 528, 73 S. Ct. 840, 97 L. Ed. 1221, 52 Ohio Op. 45, 67 Ohio Law Abs. 468 (1953). More recently, courts have questioned whether this jurisdiction might be acquired by the long-arm statute, Va. Code § 8.01-328.1(9), plus personal service in the foreign state, see, e.g., *Commonwealth ex rel. Taylor v. Taylor*, 332 Pa. Super. 67, 480 A.2d 1188 (1984) (citing cases), or through the domicile of one parent plus the presence of the other in the state as a family status to be adjudicated. See, e.g., *McAtee v. McAtee*, 174 W. Va. 129, 323 S.E.2d 611 (1984).

Foreign child custody orders may now be enforced under the Uniform Child Custody Jurisdiction and Enforcement Act (UCCJEA), Chapter 7.1 of Title 20 of the Virginia Code (Va. Code §§ 20-146.1 through 20-146.38), which replaced the Uniform Child Custody Jurisdiction Act (UCCJA), Chapter 7 of Title 20 of the Virginia Code (Va. Code §§ 20-125 through 20-146), and is discussed at the beginning of this chapter. The UCCJEA became effective on July 1, 2001; however, any motion or other request for relief made in a child custody proceeding or child custody enforcement proceeding, that was commenced before July 1, 2001 is governed by the law in effect at the time the motion or other request was made. Va. Code § 20-146.37.

Where multiple states or foreign countries have potential initial jurisdiction over child custody, the UCCJEA dictates where actual jurisdiction shall be exercised. In *Prizzia v. Prizzia*, 58 Va. App. 137, 707 S.E.2d 461 (2011), the husband and wife were married in Hungary and their child was born in Hungary. They subsequently moved to Virginia, and in December 2002, they returned to Hungary for the Christmas holidays. Following the visit, the husband returned to Virginia, but the wife remained with the child in Hungary. In February 2003, the wife filed for divorce and custody in Hungary. In May 2003, the husband filed for divorce and custody in Virginia. The court determined that Virginia had jurisdiction pursuant to Va. Code § 20-146.12(1), which provides that Virginia has jurisdiction to make an initial child custody determination if:

> [t]he Commonwealth is the home state of the child on the date of the commencement of the proceeding, or was the home state of the child within six months before the commencement of the proceeding and the child is absent from this Commonwealth but a parent or person acting as a parent continues to live in this Commonwealth.

The court reversed the trial court's decision to decline to exercise its jurisdiction, stating that the trial court failed to follow the applicable statute. In order to decline to exercise its jurisdiction, the court must have specifically determined that: (1) Virginia was an inconvenient forum under the circumstances; and (2) Hungary was a more appropriate forum. The court is also required to allow the parties to present evidence to support their positions. The appellate court held that the trial court failed to make the statutory determinations and further did not allow the parties to present evidence on this issue. The appellate court reversed the trial court decision and remanded the case for the trial court to decide whether to exercise its jurisdiction or properly decline to exercise its jurisdiction pursuant to the statute.

When a parent wrongfully removes a child under the age of 16 to a foreign country, or wrongfully retains a child in a foreign country after visitation, the other parent may be able to bring an action for the return of the child under the Hague Convention on the Civil Aspects of International Child Abduction. See 42 U.S.C. § 11601 et seq. United States District Courts and state courts have concurrent original jurisdiction over actions brought under the Hague Convention. See 42 U.S.C. § 11603(a). Because the Hague Convention is a treaty, both countries must be signatories. In adopting the Hague Convention, the signatory nations have sought "to protect children internationally from the harmful effects of their wrongful removal or retention and to establish procedures to ensure their prompt return to the State of their habitual residence, as well as to secure protection for rights of access." The primary purpose of the Hague Convention is to preserve the custody status quo and to prevent international forum-shopping; therefore, the scope of a court's inquiry under the Hague Convention is limited to the merits of the child abduction claim. *Miller v. Miller*, 240 F.3d 392 (4th Cir. 2001).

In *Miller v. Miller*, 240 F.3d 392 (4th Cir. 2001), two children who had lived with their mother in Canada for most of their lives were removed to the United States by their father. Seeking the children's return under the Hague Convention, the children's mother was required to establish that the children were "wrongfully removed or retained within the meaning of the Convention." See 22 U.S.C. §§ 9001–9011 (formerly 42 U.S.C. § 11603(e)(1)(A)). Thus, the mother had to prove that: (1) the children were "habitually resident" in Canada at the time of their removal, (2) the removal was in breach of her custody rights under Canadian law, and (3) she was exercising her custody rights at the time of the removal. Once the mother established that the children's removal was wrongful, the father was required to establish one of four defenses, by showing that: (1) there was a grave risk that the children's return would expose them to physical or psychological harm or otherwise place them in an intolerable situation, (2) the return of the children to Canada would not be permitted by the fundamental principles of the United States relating to the protection of human rights and fundamental freedoms, (3) the action was not commenced within one year of the abduction, and the children were well-settled in their new home, or (4) the mother was not actually exercising custody rights at the time of removal or had consented to or subsequently acquiesced in the removal. Eventually, a federal District Court ordered the children's return to Canada, and the Fourth Circuit Court of Appeals affirmed. The Virginia Court of Appeals adopted the *Miller* standard for determining a child's habitual residence under the International Child Abduction Remedies Act. *Coe v. Coe*, 66 Va. App. 457, 476 (2016).

A parent must establish the children's "habitual residence" by a preponderance of the evidence. *Humphrey v. Humphrey*, 434 F.3d 243 (4th Cir. 2006). Federal courts have developed a two-part framework for determining the children's "habitual residence," asking (1) whether the parents shared a settled intention to abandon their former country of residence; and (2) whether there was a geographical change coupled with the passage of sufficient time for the children to become acclimatized to their new environment. See *Maxwell v. Maxwell*, 588 F.3d 245 (4th Cir. 2009). In *Maxwell*, a father failed to prove by a preponderance of the evidence that his quadruplets' habitual residence was Australia, when the children's mother did *not* intend to abandon the United States as the children's residence, and the quadruplets did not become acclimatized to Australia during their two-month stay.

A parent possessing a *ne exeat* right, the right to consent before the other parent may take the child to another country, has a "right of custody" under the Hague Convention. *Abbott v. Abbott*, 560 U.S. 1, 130 S. Ct. 1983, 176 L.

Ed. 2d 789 (2010) (overruling *Fawcett v. McRoberts*, 326 F.3d 491 (4th Cir. 2003), which held that a Scottish *ne exeat* law did *not* confer "rights of custody"). However, although a parent with a *ne exeat* right has a right of custody and may seek return of a child, a return order is not automatic. Return is *not* required if an abducting parent can establish that a Convention exception applies. Thus, for example, return is *not* required if there is a grave risk of physical or psychological harm to the child, or if a child who is of sufficient age and maturity objects to the return. *Abbott v. Abbott*, 560 U.S. 1, 130 S. Ct. 1983, 176 L. Ed. 2d 789 (2010).

In *Bader v. Kramer*, 484 F.3d 666 (4th Cir. 2007) (*Bader II*), the Court of Appeals affirmed a District Court's decision that a father was exercising his custody rights under German law and the Hague Convention when his child was removed from Germany to the United States by the child's mother. The Court of Appeals adopted the "nearly-universal" approach of liberally finding "exercise" of custody rights under the Hague Convention whenever a parent with *de jure* custody rights keeps, or seeks to keep, any sort of regular contact with his or her child. Because the father did not clearly and unequivocally abandon the child, but had physical custody on at least three occasions before the removal, he exercised his custody rights, rather than a mere right of "access" or visitation. Thus, the child was wrongfully removed from Germany, and return of the child was required, because the child's mother failed to establish a defense that would preclude the child's return.

Federal courts are not required to abstain from deciding Hague Convention cases while state custody proceedings are pending. *Hazbun Escaf v. Rodriguez*, 52 Fed. Appx. 207, 2002 U.S. App. LEXIS 25292 (4th Cir. Dec. 11, 2002). Return of a child to another country in compliance with a federal District Court's order under the Hague Convention does not moot a parent's appeal of the order. *Fawcett v. McRoberts*, 326 F.3d 491 (4th Cir. 2003). A child is not an indispensable party who must be joined in a lawsuit under the Hague Convention, although the child's rights and wishes may be taken into account. *Hazbun Escaf v. Rodriguez*, 52 Fed. Appx. 207, 2002 U.S. App. LEXIS 25292 (4th Cir. Dec. 11, 2002).

Under the International Child Abduction Remedies Act (ICARA), 42 U.S.C. §§ 11601–11610, which implements the Hague Convention in the United States, federal courts lack jurisdiction to hear "access claims" (claims involving visitation rights). Under the Hague convention, a parent with an access claim must either (1) petition the Central Authority (e.g., the U.S. Department of State) to address the claim, or (2) petition a state court to address the claim under the state's visitation law. *Cantor v. Cohen*, 442 F.3d 196 (4th Cir. 2006).

In *Sasson v. Shenhar*, 276 Va. 611, 667 S.E.2d 555 (2008), the Virginia Supreme Court held that the "Fugitive Disentitlement Doctrine" may be applied in appropriate cases whenever a Virginia court in the exercise of sound judicial discretion deems it necessary to protect the court's dignity and power from abuse by a litigant. The Fugitive Disentitlement Doctrine may be applied to bar a litigant's appeal if three required elements are present: (1) the appellant must be a fugitive; (2) there must be a nexus between the current appeal and the appellant's status as a fugitive; and (3) dismissal must be necessary to effectuate the policy concerns underlying the doctrine. Guided by these principles, the Virginia Supreme Court affirmed the decision of the Court of Appeals in *Moscona v. Shenhar*, 50 Va. App. 238, 649 S.E.2d 191 (2007), that a litigant forfeited his right to appeal from a circuit court's judgments by willfully becoming a fugitive.

In *Moscona v. Shenhar*, 50 Va. App. 238, 649 S.E.2d 191 (2007), affirmed by the Virginia Supreme Court in *Sasson v. Shenhar*, 276 Va. 611, 667 S.E.2d 555 (2008), the Court of Appeals applied the "fugitive disentitlement doctrine" in a proceeding under the Hague Convention, and dismissed a father's appeals (1) from a trial court's rulings that the father failed to prove either that his child's mother had "wrongfully removed" his child from Spain or that Spain was the child's habitual residence; and (2) from the trial court's orders that the father must return the child to the United States, that he must pay attorney's fees, and that he was in contempt of court. The Court of Appeals explained that the "fugitive disentitlement doctrine" is appropriately applied when (1) an appellant's fugitive status impacts the case on appeal, (2) the record contains no indication that the appellant will respond to a judgment except one favorable to him, and (3) the appellant's conduct will render the judgment unenforceable against him, so that application of the doctrine is the only means of minimizing prejudice to the appellee. As to the first element, the Court of Appeals noted that the father, after receiving an unfavorable ruling on his Hague Convention petition, had failed to comply with a court order to return his child to Virginia, and had also failed to appear at a hearing on his noncompliance, with the result that the trial court found him in contempt of court and issued a capias for his arrest. As to the second element, the father only appealed from the trial court's orders, thus demonstrating by his conduct that he would submit to judgments of the Virginia judicial system only if the judgments were favorable to him. As to the third element, if the father's appeals were dismissed, then the goals of the "fugitive disentitlement doctrine" would be furthered by discouraging flight from justice, encouraging compliance with court orders, and promoting the efficient, dignified operation of the courts. Consequently, the Court of

Appeals dismissed the father's appeals without considering any other issues, stating that "[i]n light of [the father's] refusal to recognize the authority of the Virginia judicial system and to comply with the trial judge's order, we hold he cannot seek relief from the same judicial system whose authority he evades."

In *Morrison v. Morrison*, 57 Va. App. 629, 704 S.E.2d 617 (2011), the Court of Appeals refused to apply the fugitive disentitlement doctrine to a mother who was a fugitive from a bench warrant in Michigan but *not* a fugitive from any judgment entered in Virginia. The Court reasoned that the fugitive disentitlement doctrine should be used only sparingly in cases involving child custody, and only when there is no significant negative impact on the children's best interests. See also *Prizzia v. Prizzia*, 58 Va. App. 137, 707 S.E.2d 461 (2011) (fugitive entitlement doctrine does not apply if remedy other than dismissal or complete bar to participation is appropriate).

### § 23.23   Power of Attorney

In 2019, Va. Code §§ 20-166 and 167 were enacted, which authorize parents or legal custodians to execute a power of attorney that delegate the custody, care and control of a child's property for a period not to exceed 180 days. The delegation can exceed 180 days in the case of a service member who is on active duty for more than 180 days. Va. Code § 20-166(a). Expressly exempted from the delegable powers are the ability to change custody, "the power to consent to marriage or adoption of the child, the performance or inducement of an abortion on or for the child, or the termination of parental rights to the child." *Id*. The power of attorney must be signed by "all persons with authority to make decisions concerning the child," the person to whom the powers are being delegated, and a representative of the" a licensed child-placing agency that assists parents and legal guardians with the process of delegating parental and legal custodial powers of their children, including assistance with identifying appropriate placements for their children and providing services and resources to support children, parents and legal guardians, and persons to whom parental or legal custodial powers are delegated pursuant to this chapter." Va. Code § 20-166(B). The power of attorney must also be filed with the local department of social services. *Id*.

# Appendix

# Forms

## SYNOPSIS

## Form 1  Complaint for divorce.

**NOTE:** These forms have been designed to make the production of the complaint, and various other documents, a matter of selecting from alternative paragraphs. Here those paragraphs that might appear in a Complaint for divorce are set forth, with a cover sheet that can be copied so that the complaint may be customized easily. Each complaint for divorce must allege (1) marriage, (2) domicile, (3) grounds, and (4) relief sought. It should be reemphasized that the matters set forth in the complaint are those which must be proved at the divorce hearing. Within each of these four categories, variations are possible. Optional paragraphs are indicated by bracketed numbers. Applicable Virginia Code sections (as of the date of publication) appear in parenthesis.

The complaint for annulment will be similar, except that the grounds for annulment (paragraph 31 et seq. for divorce) should be drawn from Va. Code §§ 20-38.1, or 20-89.1 (voidable marriages). Several of the paragraphs may also be used in the filing of counterclaims for divorce or for answers.

§ 20-45.1 (void marriages)

*Alternative Paragraphs for Complaint for Divorce*

| Marriage 10 | Domicile 20 | Grounds 30 | Relief 40 |
|---|---|---|---|
| | (Code § 20-97) | (Code § 20-91) | (Code §§ 20-107.1 to 20-109.1) |
| 11 Ceremonial marriage | 21 Domicile and residence in Virginia | 31 No fault separation (6 months) | 41 Divorce |
| OR | OR | OR | [42] Separation Agreement |
| 12 Common law marriage in another state | 22 Military and stationed in state | 32 No fault separation (12 months) | [43] Custody of children |
| [13] Minor children | OR | OR | [44] Spousal Support |
| [14] Separation Agreement | 23 Military, | 33 Adultery | [45] Child Support |

| Marriage 10 | Domicile 20 | Grounds 30 | Relief 40 |
|---|---|---|---|
| | domiciled in Virginia, now stationed abroad | | |
| [15] No military service | 24 Plaintiff and defendant last cohabited at [address] in [city or county], Virginia | *OR* | [46] Property Distribution |
| | | 34 Cruelty | [47] Resumption of maiden or former name |
| | | *OR* | [48] Fees and costs |
| | | 35 Desertion | [49] Other relief |
| | | *OR* | |
| | | 36 Imprisonment | |

VIRGINIA:

IN THE CIRCUIT COURT FOR THE COUNTY (CITY) OF [NAME]

| | |
|---|---|
| [Name of plaintiff] | |
| v. | In Case No. _____ |
| [Name of defendant] | |

### *COMPLAINT FOR DIVORCE*

The plaintiff respectfully represents as follows:

11 Plaintiff and defendant were married on [date] in [locality].

12 On or about [date, plaintiff and defendant, being then domiciliaries of the state of [name], which recognizes common law marriage, entered into a present agreement to be husband and wife on or about [date]. They cohabited as husband and wife and held themselves out to the community as husband and wife.

13 [Number]children were born of this marriage (have been adopted by

the parties), namely: [name, date of birth, and age of each child].

14 Since the separation, the parties, while each was represented by counsel of his or her own choosing, entered into a separation agreement dated [date]concerning [custody, support, child support, property division, and other matters relating to the marriage.] A copy of this agreement is attached as Exhibit A.

15 Plaintiff and defendant are over the age of 18 years, and neither of them is in the military service of the United States.

21 Plaintiff and defendant (plaintiff is) (defendant is) are domiciled in and have been bona fide residents of the State of Virginia for more than six months next preceding the commencement of this suit.

22 Plaintiff (defendant) is in the military service of the United States. For the six months next preceding the complaint, plaintiff (defendant) was stationed at [name of base], [name of city or county], Virginia. Plaintiff (defendant) continues to live in this state.

23 Plaintiff is in the military service of the United States. Plaintiff is now stationed outside the United States in [locality in foreign country or territory]. For the six months before being stationed in [country], plaintiff was domiciled in and a bona fide resident of Virginia.

24 Plaintiff and defendant last cohabited at [address] in [city or county], Virginia.

31 The plaintiff and defendant have lived separate and apart, without any cohabitation and without interruption for a period exceeding six months. Plaintiff (defendant) had the intention to remain permanently separated from defendant (plaintiff) since [date]. There are no minor children of the marriage, and plaintiff and defendant have entered into a separation agreement dated [date], a copy of which is attached as Exhibit A.

32 The plaintiff and defendant have lived separate and apart, without any cohabitation, and without interruption, for a period exceeding twelve months. Plaintiff (defendant) had the intention to remain permanently separated from defendant (plaintiff) since [date].

33 On or about [date], and on various other occasions, defendant committed adultery (sodomy or buggery) with [name or names].

34 On or about [date], defendant committed the following acts of cruelty toward the plaintiff (caused plaintiff reasonable apprehension of bodily hurt), namely [state actions].

35 On or about [date], defendant willfully deserted and abandoned

plaintiff, without just cause or excuse, and the parties have lived separate and apart since that date.

36 On [date], defendant was sentenced to [name of prison] for a term of [state term] for the crime of [state felony]. Defendant began service of this sentence on [date of incarceration for felony]. Plaintiff and defendant have not resumed cohabitation since plaintiff has known of this confinement.

41 WHEREFORE, plaintiff prays that she/he be awarded a divorce from the bond of matrimony from defendant.

42 that the agreement dated [date] between the parties be affirmed and ratified by this Court and incorporated as a part of any decree entered herein, pursuant to § 20-109.1, Code of Virginia.

43 that the plaintiff (and defendant) be awarded joint legal custody and that plaintiff (defendant) be awarded primary physical custody) of the minor children born of this marriage. ( *or* that the best interests of the minor children of the parties require that plaintiff (defendant) be awarded responsibility for their care and custody).

44 Defendant is gainfully employed as [job] at [place of employment]. Plaintiff is not gainfully employed. ( *or* Plaintiff is gainfully employed as [job] at [place of employment]). The earning capacity, obligations, and financial training of each, require that the defendant be ordered to pay for the maintenance and support of the plaintiff pursuant to Virginia Code § 20-107.1.

45 Defendant is gainfully employed as [job] at [place of employment]. Plaintiff is not gainfully employed. ( *or* Plaintiff is gainfully employed as [job] at [place of employment]). The earning capacity, obligations, and financial training of each require that the defendant be ordered to pay for the maintenance, education, and support of the minor children of the marriage, pursuant to Virginia Code § 20-107.2.

46 Pursuant to § 20-107.3, Code of Virginia, plaintiff moves that the court determine legal title as between the parties and the ownership and value of all real and personal property of the parties, and that the court classify such property into separate and marital property categories, and order the division or transfer of jointly owned marital property (order that plaintiff be granted a monetary award based upon the rights and equities in such property).

47 that plaintiff (defendant) be allowed to resume her maiden (his former) name.

48 that plaintiff be awarded attorneys' fees and court costs expended in this suit.

49 and for such other and further relief as may be just and equitable.

_____ [Signed by plaintiff]
_____ [Name and address of plaintiff's counsel]

**Form 2   Affidavit for service by publication.**

VIRGINIA:
IN THE CIRCUIT COURT FOR THE COUNTY (CITY) OF [NAME]

[Name of plaintiff]

v.                                    In Case No. _____

[Name of defendant]

### *AFFIDAVIT FOR SERVICE BY PUBLICATION*

Comes now [name], plaintiff herein, and being first duly sworn, upon oath deposes and states that [name], defendant in the above cause, is not a resident of the State of Virginia (defendant's residence cannot be found after diligent search), his last known post office address or place of abode being, to the best of plaintiff's knowledge, information and belief, [address], and further states upon oath that to the best of her knowledge, information and belief that said defendant is not a member of the Armed Forces of the United States, nor has he been such within the past thirty (30) days, nor is he a member of the United States Public Health Service.

_____
[Signed by plaintiff]

_____
Subscribed and sworn to before me this [date]

_____
[Signed by notary public]

My commission expires:

**Form 3  Order of publication.**

VIRGINIA:
IN THE CIRCUIT COURT FOR THE COUNTY (CITY) OF [NAME]

| | |
|---|---|
| [Name of plaintiff] | |
| v. | In Case No. _____ |
| [Name of defendant] | |

### ORDER OF PUBLICATION

The object of this suit is for the plaintiff to obtain a divorce from the defendant on the ground that [specify grounds].

An affidavit having been filed that the defendant is a nonresident of the State of Virginia (defendant's whereabouts cannot be ascertained after diligent search), the Clerk enters this order of publication this [date].

UPON CONSIDERATION WHEREOF, it is ordered that the defendant appear here within ten (10) days after due publication of this order of publication and do what is necessary to protect his interest in this suit.

_____ [Signed by clerk or deputy clerk]

_____ [Name and address of plaintiff's counsel]

**Form 4  Answer.**

VIRGINIA:
IN THE CIRCUIT COURT FOR THE COUNTY (CITY) OF [NAME]

| | |
|---|---|
| [Name of plaintiff]<br><br>        v.<br><br>[Name of defendant] | In Case No. _____ |

*ANSWER*

Defendant answers the complaint filed against him (her) and states as follows:

1. He admits the allegations contained in paragraphs [number] through [number] of the complaint.

2. He denies the allegations contained in paragraphs [number] through [number] of the complaint.

[3.] Defendant asserts that plaintiff and defendant have resumed cohabitation, and that therefore plaintiff has no cause of action for divorce.

[4.] Even if plaintiff proves that defendant was involved in certain of the conduct alleged in his (her) complaint, by continuing to live as husband and wife with defendants after the date such conduct allegedly occurred, plaintiff has condoned any such conduct by the defendant.

[5.] Defendant was required to leave the marital residence because the conduct of plaintiff threatened defendant's health and well-being.

WHEREFORE, defendant prays that his interests in this matter be protected.

_____ [Signed by defendant]
_____ [Name and address of defendant's counsel]

## CERTIFICATE OF SERVICE

This is to certify that a copy hereof was mailed, first class postage prepaid, to [name and address of plaintiff's counsel], as counsel for Plaintiff, on [date].

_____

[Signed by defendant's counsel]

**Form 5    Counterclaim for divorce.**

VIRGINIA:
IN THE CIRCUIT COURT FOR THE COUNTY (CITY) OF [NAME]

| | |
|---|---|
| [Name of plaintiff]<br><br>v.<br><br>[Name of defendant] | In Case No. _____ |

### COUNTERCLAIM FOR DIVORCE

Comes now the defendant, and for his (her) Counterclaim for Divorce, states as follows:

1. He (she) incorporates by reference the allegations contained in paragraphs [number] through [number] of the complaint.

2. On or about [date], the plaintiff [set out grounds for divorce, from Form 1, paragraphs 31–36, and supporting allegations].

3. Defendant alleges he (she) was always a good and faithful husband (wife) to plaintiff and gave her (him) no just cause for her (his) actions.

WHEREFORE, defendant prays that he (she) be granted a divorce from the bond of matrimony from plaintiff on the grounds of [specify grounds]; [*add as applicable* prayers for relief, as found in Form 1, paragraphs 41–49].

_____ [Signed by defendant]
_____ [Name and address of defendant's counsel]

**Form 6   Answer to counterclaim.**

VIRGINIA:
IN THE CIRCUIT COURT FOR THE COUNTY (CITY) OF [NAME]

| | |
|---|---|
| [Name of plaintiff]<br><br>v.<br><br>[Name of defendant] | In Case No. _____ |

### ANSWER TO COUNTERCLAIM FOR DIVORCE

Comes now plaintiff, by counsel, and for her (his) answer to the counterclaim for divorce filed against her (him), states as follows:

1. She (he) admits the allegations contained in paragraphs [number] and [number] of the counterclaim for divorce.

2. She (he) denies the allegations of paragraphs [number] and [number] of the counterclaim for divorce.

[3.] She (he) affirmatively defends against the divorce sought by plaintiff as follows [insert applicable affirmative defenses as in Form 5, paragraphs 3–5].

WHEREFORE, plaintiff moves that the prayers of her bill of complaint be granted.

_____ [Signed by plaintiff's counsel]
_____ [Name and address of plaintiff's counsel]

### CERTIFICATE OF SERVICE

This is to certify that a copy hereof was mailed, first class postage prepaid, to [name and address of defendant's counsel], as counsel for Defendant, on [date].

_____ [Signed by plaintiff's counsel]

**Form 7**    **Request for production of documents.**

VIRGINIA:

IN THE CIRCUIT COURT FOR THE COUNTY (CITY) OF [NAME]

| | |
|---|---|
| [Name of plaintiff] <br><br>        v. <br><br> [Name of defendant] | In Case No. _____ |

*REQUEST FOR PRODUCTION OF DOCUMENTS*

TO: _____ [Name of defendant]
c/o [Name and address of defendant's counsel]

Plaintiff, by counsel, pursuant to Rule 4:9 of the Rules of the Supreme Court of Virginia, requests that the defendant [name] produce at the Law Offices of [name and address of plaintiff's counsel] on [date] the following documents for inspection and/or copying:

1. All of his (her) bank statements and canceled checks of each and every one of his (her) checking bank accounts, from January 1, [year], to the date of production, including individual accounts and those held in trust by him (her) or for his (her) benefit.

2. All statements of each and every savings account, money market account, mutual fund, stock and/or bond account, and any other account of value of _____ [name of defendant] from January 1, [year], to the date of production, including individual accounts and those held in trust by him (her) or for his (her) benefit.

3. Documentary evidence of any and all business enterprises, including but not limited to, partnerships, corporations or syndicates, in which he (she) has or had a financial interest from January 1, [year], to the date of production.

4. A statement of all earnings of _____ [name of defendant] for the period January 1, [year], to the date of production, whether by wages, dividends, interest or other income, whether reportable for income tax purposes or not.

5. Documentary evidence of all gifts received from any person, firm, corporation, trust or other entity for the period January 1, [year] to the date of production.

6. Signed copy of his (her) [year] federal income tax return.

_____ [Signed by plaintiff's counsel]

### CERTIFICATE OF SERVICE

I, the undersigned, hereby certify that a true copy of the foregoing Request for Production of Documents was mailed, first class postage prepaid, this [date] to _____ [name and address of defendant's counsel], counsel for defendant.

_____ [Signed by plaintiff's counsel]

**Form 8**   **Notice of taking discovery deposition.**

VIRGINIA:

IN THE CIRCUIT COURT FOR THE COUNTY (CITY) OF [NAME]

| | |
|---|---|
| [Name of plaintiff] | |
| v. | In Case No. _____ |
| [Name of defendant] | |

### NOTICE OF TAKING DISCOVERY DEPOSITION

TO: _____ [Name of defendant]
c/o[Name and address of defendant's counsel]

PLEASE TAKE NOTICE that on the _____ [day] day of [month], [year], at [time] o'clock a.m./p.m., at the offices of [name and address of plaintiff's counsel], the undersigned will, pursuant to Rule 4:5 of the Supreme Court of Virginia, take the discovery deposition of [name], defendant herein.

If said deposition is commenced but not concluded, the taking thereof shall be continued to such date and time as shall be mutually agreed by counsel for the parties.

_____ [Signed by plaintiff's counsel]

### CERTIFICATE OF SERVICE

This is to certify that a copy hereof was mailed, first class postage prepaid, to _____ [name and address of defendant counsel], as counsel for defendant, on [date].

_____ [Signed by plaintiff's counsel]

**Form 9   Notice of motion for decree of reference.**

VIRGINIA:
IN THE CIRCUIT COURT FOR [Jurisdiction]

---

[Name of plaintiff]

                    v.                    } In Case No. _____

[Name of defendant]

*NOTICE OF MOTION FOR DECREE OF REFERENCE*

TO: _____ [Name of defendant]
_____ [Defendant's address]

   PLEASE TAKE NOTICE that on the _____ [day] day of [month], [year], at [time] o'clock a.m./p.m., or as soon thereafter as I can be heard, I will move in the Circuit Court of [Jurisdiction], that the court refer this case to one of the duly appointed commissioners in chancery. The commissioner will have the authority to hear the evidence I present and to report his or her findings and recommendations to the Court.

_____ [Plaintiff's counsel, or Plaintiff if pro se]
_____ [Counsel's address]

**Form 10    Motion for decree of reference.**

VIRGINIA:
IN THE CIRCUIT COURT FOR [Jurisdiction]

| | |
|---|---|
| [Name of plaintiff]<br><br>v.<br><br>[Name of defendant] | In Case No. _____ |

### MOTION FOR DECREE OF REFERENCE TO COMMISSIONER

On [month] [day], [year], I filed a Complaint for Divorce in this Court. A copy of this was duly served upon the defendant by the Sheriff of [Jurisdiction] on [month] [day], [year]. Defendant did not file an answer to the Complaint. More than twenty-one (21) days have passed since defendant was served. The cause is therefore ready to be heard.

I THEREFORE MOVE that this cause be referred to one of the duly appointed commissioners in chancery of this Court, to convene the parties, supervise the taking of evidence, and to report his/her findings and recommendations to the Court respecting the issues raised.

Made this _____ [day] day of [month], [year].

I ASK FOR THIS:

_____

_____


_____

[Plaintiff's counsel, or Plaintiff, pro se]

**Form 11    Decree of reference.**

VIRGINIA:
IN THE CIRCUIT COURT FOR [Jurisdiction]

| | |
|---|---|
| [Name of plaintiff] | |
| v. | In Case No. _____ |
| [Name of defendant] | |

## DECREE OF REFERENCE TO COMMISSIONER

THIS CAUSE was heard based upon the Complaint for Divorce previously filed. A copy of this was duly served upon the defendant by the Sheriff of [Jurisdiction] on [month] [day], [year]. Defendant did not file an answer to the Complaint. More than twenty-one (21) days have passed since defendant was served. The cause is therefore ready to be heard. It is therefore, upon motion of the Plaintiff,

ADJUDGED, ORDERED AND DECREED that this cause be, and the same hereby is, referred to one of the duly appointed commissioners in chancery of this Court, to convene the parties, supervise the taking of evidence, and to report his/her findings and recommendations to the Court respecting the issues raised.

Entered the _____ [day] day of [month], [year].

**Form 12   Notice of pendente lite hearing.**

VIRGINIA:
IN THE CIRCUIT COURT FOR THE COUNTY (CITY) OF [NAME]

[Name of plaintiff]

v.                              In Case No. _____

[Name of defendant]

### NOTICE OF PENDENTE LITE HEARING

TO: _____ [Name of defendant]
     c/o [Name and address of defendant's counsel]

PLEASE TAKE NOTICE that on the _____ [day] day of [month], [year], at [time] o'clock a.m./p.m., or as soon thereafter as she may be heard, the undersigned will, by her counsel, petition for the following Pendente Lite relief:

[1] Spousal support or maintenance.

[2] Child custody.

[3] Child support for minor children of the marriage.

[4] Support for a child who is under the age of nineteen and a full-time high school student.

[5] Health insurance coverage for plaintiff and the children of the parties.

[6] An order restraining the defendant from harassing plaintiff or from imposing any restraint on plaintiff's physical liberty.

[7] An award of the exclusive use and possession of the family residence.

[8] An order excluding defendant from the jointly owned (rented) family dwelling.

[9] An order restraining defendant from disposing of his (her) personal or the marital estate pending the suit for divorce, and to furnish security against disposing of the same.

[10] Preliminary counsel fees and court costs.

[11] Reimbursement for Clerk's and Sheriff's Fees.

_____ [Signed by plaintiff's counsel]

## CERTIFICATE OF SERVICE

This is to certify that a copy hereof was mailed, first class postage prepaid, to _____ [name and address of defendant's counsel], as counsel for defendant, on _____ [date].

_____ [Signed by plaintiff's counsel]

**Form 13    Pendente lite decree.**

VIRGINIA:
IN THE CIRCUIT COURT FOR THE COUNTY (CITY) OF [NAME]

[Name of plaintiff]

         v.           In Case No. _____

[Name of defendant]

*PENDENTE LITE DECREE*

[specify applicable relief from Form 12, paragraphs 1-11]

This cause came on this day to be heard on motion of the plaintiff for after notice duly and timely served upon the defendant, and after the taking of the sworn testimony of the parties.

UPON CONSIDERATION WHEREOF, and the Court having considered the evidence of both the plaintiff and the defendant, and being of the opinion that the plaintiff is entitled to the relief prayed for, it is accordingly adjudged, ordered, and decreed that the defendant pay to the plaintiff the sum of _____ [amount] per _____ [time period] as support for the [number] minor children of the parties, commencing on [date], and a like sum on [future installment information] until further decree of this Court, and it is further ordered, adjudged, and decreed that the defendant shall within [number] days pay to [name], counsel for plaintiff, the sum of [amount] as preliminary attorneys' fees and [amount], reimbursement of Clerk's and Sheriff's service fees.

ENTER:

DATE:


SEEN:

_____ p.q.
SEEN AND OBJECTED TO:
_____ p.d.

**Form 14 Notice of entry of final decree.**

VIRGINIA:
IN THE CIRCUIT COURT FOR THE COUNTY (CITY) OF [NAME]

| | |
|---|---|
| [Name of plaintiff] | |
| v. | In Case No. _____ |
| [Name of defendant] | |

*NOTICE OF ENTRY OF DECREE*

TO: _____ [Name of defendant]
       c/o [Name and address of defendant's counsel]

   PLEASE TAKE NOTICE that on the _____ [day] day of [month], [year], at [time] o'clock a.m./p.m., or as soon thereafter as she may be heard, the plaintiff will, by counsel, move for entry of a Final Decree of Divorce, copy of which is attached hereto.

_____ [Signed by plaintiff's counsel]

I ASK FOR THIS:
_____ p.q.

SEEN AND NO OBJECTION:
_____ p.d.

**Form 15    Decree of divorce.**

VIRGINIA:
IN THE CIRCUIT COURT FOR THE COUNTY (CITY) OF [NAME]

| | |
|---|---|
| [Name of plaintiff] | |
| v. | In Case No. _____ |
| [Name of defendant] | |

### DECREE OF DIVORCE FROM BOND OF MATRIMONY

This cause came to be heard upon the complaint, service of process upon the defendant, (*add as applicable:* defendant having neither appeared and answered nor otherwise responded, answer filed by the defendant, answer and counterclaim filed by the defendant, plaintiff's answer to the cross-bill, decree of reference appointing [name], Commissioner in Chancery, depositions taken before the same commissioner in chancery after due notice to defendant and the commissioner's report recommending that the plaintiff be awarded a divorce from the bond of matrimony from the defendant, upon a hearing *ore tenus,* upon depositions duly taken before [name], notary public, and was argued by counsel).

The court finds from the evidence, independently of the admissions of the parties in the pleadings or otherwise, that the plaintiff has been a bona fide resident of and actually domiciled in the Commonwealth of Virginia for more than six months next preceding the filing of this suit; that the defendant was a resident of [locality], Virginia when this suit was filed and that the parties last cohabited as man and wife in [locality], Virginia, and that this Court has jurisdiction to hear and determine this cause; that plaintiff and defendant were lawfully married to each other on [date], in [locality], and are both over the age of eighteen years and neither is a member of the Armed Forces of the United States; that [number] children were born of this marriage, and that the defendant [set out facts supporting grounds for divorce].

Accordingly, it is adjudged, ordered and decreed that plaintiff [name] be, and she (he) hereby is, granted a divorce from the bond of matrimony from the defendant [name] on the ground of [set out grounds for divorce]; [ *add as applicable:* relief from Form 1, paragraphs 41-49]; that this cause be, and hereby is, transferred to the Juvenile and Domestic Relations District Court of the City (County) of [name] for such further proceedings as may be from time to time required on all matters pertaining to support and maintenance and to the care and custody of the minor children of the parties; that the

Separation Agreement dated [date] by and between the parties hereto, and introduced into evidence as Plaintiff's Exhibit A, be, and hereby is, affirmed, ratified and incorporated by reference in this decree, pursuant to § 20-109.1, Code of Virginia (1950), as amended.

And nothing further remaining to be done in this case, it is ordered stricken from the docket and filed among the ended causes.

ENTER:

DATE:

I ASK FOR THIS:

_____ p.q.

I HAVE SEEN THIS:

_____ p.d.

**Form 16     Final decree for divorce (no answer).**

VIRGINIA:
IN THE CIRCUIT COURT FOR [Jurisdiction]

[Name of plaintiff]

        v.                    In Case No. _____

[Name of defendant]

## *DECREE OF DIVORCE FROM BOND OF MATRIMONY*

Plaintiff filed a complaint, and served process upon the defendant. Since the defendant neither appeared, answered nor otherwise responded, the court issued a decree of reference appointing [name] as Commissioner in Chancery. After a hearing, the Commissioner's report recommended that the plaintiff be awarded a divorce from the bond of matrimony from the defendant. The court has considered these pleadings and the commissioner's report.

The court makes findings from the evidence independent of the admissions of the parties in the pleadings or otherwise. The court finds that the plaintiff has been a bona fide resident of and actually domiciled in the Commonwealth of Virginia for more than six months next preceding the filing of this suit; that the defendant was a resident of [town], when this suit was filed and that the parties last cohabited as man and wife in [town, Virginia], and that this Court has jurisdiction to hear and determine this cause. Further, the court finds that plaintiff and defendant were lawfully married to each other on [date] in [city, state], and are both over the age of eighteen years. On [date], the parties separated, and since then, and for a period in excess of six months, they have lived separate and apart, without any cohabitation and without interruption. No children were born of this marriage. On [date], the plaintiff and defendant entered into a separation agreement.

Accordingly, it is adjudged, ordered and decreed that plaintiff [name] be, and [he or she] hereby is, granted a divorce from the bond of matrimony from the defendant [name] on the ground of living separate and apart for a period in excess of six months; and that the Separation Agreement dated [date] between the parties, and introduced into evidence as Plaintiff's Exhibit A, be, and hereby is, affirmed, ratified and incorporated by reference in this decree, pursuant to § 20-109.1, Code of Virginia (1950) as amended.

Since nothing further remains to be done in this case, it is ordered stricken from the docket and filed among the ended causes.

s/_____
[Circuit Judge]

I ASK FOR THIS:
_____

_____ [Name of plaintiff's counsel]

**Form 17    Petition for custody and support.**

VIRGINIA:
IN THE CIRCUIT FOR THE COUNTY (CITY) OF [NAME]

| | |
|---|---|
| [Name of plaintiff] <br><br> v. <br><br> [Name of defendant] | In Case No. _____ |

### PETITION FOR CUSTODY AND SUPPORT

The plaintiff respectfully represents as follows:

(1) Plaintiff and defendant were married on [date] in [locality].

(2) [Number] children were born of this marriage, namely: [name, date of birth, and age of each child].

(3) Plaintiff and defendant are domiciled in and have been bona fide residents of the State of Virginia for more than six months next preceding the commencement of this suit and their minor children, now residing with plaintiff, are also domiciliary residents of the state.

(4) The parties hereto have been living separate and apart, since on or about [date], when defendant left the parties' home in [locality].

(5) Defendant has recently advised plaintiff that he (she) intends to move to [locality] and to take said children with him (her). Plaintiff wishes the children to remain with her (him), which she (he) considers to be in their best interest. Plaintiff feels that such a move would be detrimental to the children, who are happy and well adjusted residing with plaintiff.

WHEREFORE, plaintiff prays, that she (he) be awarded custody of the parties' minor children, [names of children], and support for said children, subject to rights of reasonable visitation with said children by defendant, a reasonable award of counsel fees and reimbursement for court costs and for such other and further relief as may seem just and equitable.

_____ [Signed by plaintiff]
_____ [Name and address of plaintiff's counsel]

**Form 18   Decree for custody and support.**

VIRGINIA:
IN THE CIRCUIT FOR THE COUNTY (CITY) OF [NAME]

| | |
|---|---|
| [Name of plaintiff] | |
| v. | In Case No. _____ |
| [Name of defendant] | |

### DECREE FOR CUSTODY AND SUPPORT

THIS CAUSE came to be heard on [date] upon the bill of complaint, (*add as applicable:* service of process upon the defendant in person, maturity of the cause for hearing by the Court after defendant failed to file response in pleadings herein, upon due notice of said hearing served upon defendant in person by [name and address of process server], answer filed by the defendant, upon a hearing *ore tenus,* and was argued by counsel).

The Court finds from the sworn testimony of plaintiff and her (his) witnesses, and that of defendant, and his (her) witnesses, that plaintiff and the [number] minor children of the parties have been bona fide residents of, and actually domiciled in, the Commonwealth of Virginia for more than six months immediately preceding the filing of this suit; that the defendant was a resident of [locality], Virginia when this suit was filed and that the parties last cohabited in [locality], Virginia; that the parties hereto were lawfully married to each other on [date] in [locality]; and that the [number] minor children aforesaid were born of the marriage.

The Court further finds, from the evidence taken and considered, that the Court has jurisdiction of this cause, that all parties are properly before the Court, and that the plaintiff is entitled to the custody of and support from defendant for the [number] said minor children, subject to defendant's right to reasonable visitation with said children.

Accordingly, it is adjudged, ordered and decreed that the plaintiff [name] be, and hereby is, awarded custody of [names of children], the [number] minor children of the parties, that the defendant pay to plaintiff [amount] on [date] and on the 1st day of each month thereafter, as support for said minor children, until further decree of this Court, subject to reasonable visitation with said children reserved to defendant, at such reasonable times and places as the parties may from time to time mutually agree, and that defendant shall pay to plaintiff's counsel, [name], the sum of [amount], on or before [date], as counsel fees due for said counsel's representation of plaintiff in this proceeding.

ENTER:
DATE:

SEEN:
_____ p.q.

**Form 19 Petition for rule to show cause.**

VIRGINIA:
IN THE CIRCUIT COURT FOR THE COUNTY (CITY) OF [NAME]

| | |
|---|---|
| [Name of plaintiff]<br><br>       v.<br><br>[Name of defendant] | In Case No. _____ |

### PETITION FOR RULE TO SHOW CAUSE

Comes now [name], plaintiff in the above action, by her (his) counsel, and in support of her (his) affidavit heretofore filed herein, petitions pursuant to § 20-113 et seq., Code of Virginia (1950), as amended, for the issuance of a rule to show cause, returnable [date], to be personally served upon the defendant herein, [name], to show cause, if any he (she) may, why he (she) should not be adjudged in contempt of this Court for his alleged failure to have complied with this court's decree entered on [date]. Plaintiff respectfully prays for:

(1) Issuance of a rule to show cause why defendant should not be held in contempt of this Court and for award of counsel fees and Court costs.

(2) Such other relief as to the Court may seem just and equitable.

_____ [Signed by plaintiff's counsel]
_____ [Name and address of plaintiff's counsel]

**Form 20   Affidavit for rule to show cause.**

VIRGINIA:
IN THE CIRCUIT COURT FOR THE COUNTY (CITY) OF [NAME]

[Name of plaintiff]

v.                                    In Case No. _____

[Name of defendant]

*AFFIDAVIT*

STATE OF VIRGINIA

COUNTY (CITY) OF [name], to wit:

I, [name], plaintiff herein, having been first duly sworn, upon oath depose and state that the defendant herein, [name], has failed and refused to abide by the Court's decree, entered herein on [date], in that he (she) has not paid plaintiff the sum of [amount] now due her (him) under the terms of said decree.

WHEREFORE, plaintiff prays that a rule to show cause be issued, returnable [date], whereby said defendant is summoned to appear before this Court to show cause, if any he (she) can, why he (she) should not be adjudged in contempt of this Court for such nonpayment and for counsel fees and Court costs.

_____
[Signed by plaintiff]

_____
[Subscribed and sworn to before me this date].

_____
[Signed by notary public]

My commission expires:

_____
[Signed by plaintiff's counsel]

**Form 21 Rule to show cause.**

VIRGINIA:
IN THE CIRCUIT COURT FOR THE COUNTY (CITY) OF [NAME]

| | |
|---|---|
| [Name of plaintiff] | |
| v. | In Case No. _____ |
| [Name of defendant] | |

### RULE TO SHOW CAUSE

This cause came to be heard upon the affidavit of plaintiff and plaintiff's petition for rule to show cause, and the Court that there is cause to grant the prayer of plaintiff's petition for rule to show cause, based upon her (his) affidavit filed herein.

Accordingly, it is adjudged, ordered and decreed that the defendant, [name], be, and hereby is, directed to appear before this Court on [date] to show cause, if any he (she) may, why he (she) should not be adjudged in contempt of this Court for his (her) alleged failure to comply fully with the terms of this Court's decree, entered herein on [date], and it is further adjudged, ordered and decreed that plaintiff cause to be served upon [name of defendant], whose last known address is [address], a certified copy of this rule to show cause.

ENTER:

DATE:

I ASK FOR THIS:
_____ p.q.

**Form 22  Income and expense summary.**

INCOME AND EXPENSE SUMMARY

MONTHLY INCOME:

Name:

Occupation:

Employer's name and address:

Pay period:

Rate of Pay:

Average gross pay per pay period:

Average net pay per pay period:

Other income (specify):

Average monthly net income:

MONTHLY EXPENSES: (Indicate self and/or children)

*Household*

Mortgage/rent:

Maintenance of residence and grounds (specify):

Property taxes:

Reserve for major repairs:

Furniture/appliance repair/replacement:

House cleaning:

*Utilities*

Electricity:

Fuel oil/gas:

Telephone:

Water/sewer:

Garbage:

Cable television:

*Food*

Groceries:

Lunches:

*Automobile*

Payment/depreciation:

Gas and oil:

Repair/maintenance/tires:

License tags/inspection/local registration:

Other transportation:

Personal property taxes:

Parking:

Reserve for replacement:

*Insurance*

Automobile liability:

Health:

Home owners:

Life:

*Clothing and shoes*

New:

Dry cleaning, laundry:

Special/uniforms:

*Health expenses*

Doctor:

Dentist:

Eye glasses:

Hospital:

Clinic membership:

Medicines, vitamins:

Other (specify):

*Gifts*

Church/charity:

Holidays/birthdays:

*Entertainment/recreation*

*Vacations*

*Dues*

Professional:

Social clubs:

Pool:

Other (specify):

*Sundries*

Newspapers:

Magazines:

Personal grooming:

Hair care:

Other (specify):

*Children's special expenses*

School supplies:

Nursery school or day care:

School tuition:

Extended day fees:

Lunch money:

Allowance:

Additional health insurance to provide coverage for children:

Medical expenses not covered by insurance:

Sports, musical, etc., equipment/supplies:

Lessons-music, art, etc.:

Special education:

Transportation:

Camp:

Other (specify):

*Pets*

Vet:

Other (specify):

*Miscellaneous*

Legal expenses:

Taxes:

Hobbies:

Other (specify):

*Fixed debts with interest*

For each credit provide name and address, monthly payment amount, and balance due:

*Current debts* (over and above monthly expenses)

For each creditor provide name and address, minimum or usual monthly payment amount, and balance due:

MONTHLY EXPENSE SUMMARY:

Self and children:

Fixed debts:

Current debts:

Total:

TOTAL AVERAGE MONTHLY NET INCOME:

TOTAL MONTHLY EXPENSE:

BALANCE (+ or -):

Signed:
Date:

**Form 23   Assets and liabilities disclosure statement.**

DISCLOSURE
Party Making Disclosure:

*Separate property*

ASSETS

Cash on hand:

Real property (describe; specify when and how acquired, source of purchase price, legal title and/or ownership interest; give estimated value and offset any liens to give net value):

Personal property (identify specific items and for each: specify when and how acquired, source of purchase price), title and/or ownership interest; give estimated value and offset any liens to give net value):

*Marital property*

ASSETS

Cash on hand:

Real property (describe; specify when and how acquired, source of purchase price, legal title and/or ownership interest; give estimated value and offset any liens to give net value):

Personal property (identify specific items and for each: specify when and how acquired, source of purchase price), title and/or ownership interest; give estimated value and offset any liens to give net value):

LIABILITIES

Joint debts (for each list name and address of creditor, amount currently due, date incurred, and purpose for incurring):

Separate debts of husband (for each list name and address of creditor, amount currently due, date incurred, and purpose for incurring):

Separate debts of wife (for each list name and address of creditor, amount currently due, date incurred, and purpose for incurring):

**Form 24    Premarital agreement.** (Va. Code § 20-147 et seq.)

**NOTE:** Like the Complaint for Divorce, the Premarital Agreement Form consists of a group of numbered paragraphs which may be selected as desired to fit the individual needs and desires of the client. Numbered paragraphs without brackets must be included in order to comply with Va. Code § 20-147 et seq. Those with brackets are optional, although the subjects of the suggested paragraphs are usually included in premarital agreements.

Numbering is according to subject matter, as follows:

01–09 *Recitals*

    01    General purpose of agreement

    02    Intent that agreement govern classification of property

    [03]    Acknowledgement of property acquired prior to marriage

    [04]    Acknowledgement that separate assets may increase in future

    [05]    Acknowledgement of previous marriage and children by such marriage

    06    Understanding of legal rights in property that would accrue absent agreement

    07    Review by separate counsel

    08    Acknowledgement of disclosure of property

    09    Voluntary nature of agreement

10–19 *Separate property*

    [11]    Separate property, income from, and appreciation of separate property

    [12]    Control and disposition of separate property

    [13]    Additions to separate property

    [14]    Gifts, conveyances, and bequests between the parties

20–29 *Marital property*

    [21]    Property titled jointly

    [22]    Income earned through gainful employment during marriage

    [23]    Contributions for spousal support from separate property

    [24]    Support during marriage

30–39 *Individual obligations and liabilities*

   [31]   Debts and tortious liability

   [32]   Voluntary contributions to individual obligations or liabilities

40–49 *Disposition of property at death of spouse*

   [41]   Release of marital interests in property that would otherwise accrue

   [42]   Waiver of ability to claim against estate

   [43]   Joinder in instruments needed by personal representative

   [44]   Waiver of right to claim as beneficiary of life insurance

50–59 *Disposition of property in event of divorce*

   [51]   Waiver of equitable distribution of property

   [52]   Waiver of spousal support or maintenance

60–69 *Taxation*

   [61]   Filing of income tax returns; tax liability

   [62]   Refunds from tax returns

70–79 *Personal matters*

80–89 *Concluding paragraphs*

   81   Construction according to Virginia law

   82   Amendment or modification of agreement

   83   Agreement is entire understanding of parties

   84   Voluntary nature of agreement

### PREMARITAL AGREEMENT

THIS AGREEMENT is made and entered into between [name] and [name] (sometimes referred to as the parties) in contemplation of their marriage. It is to become effective upon their marriage to each other. The purpose of this agreement is to settle the rights and obligations of each of them, during their marriage, upon the death of either or both of them, or in case of dissolution of the marriage.

*RECITALS:*

01 [Name] and [name] have entered into this agreement through their mutual discussions. The parties desire to contract with each other concerning

matters of the classification and disposition of the parties' property in the event of their death or divorce.

02 It is the intention of both parties that the classification of each other's property and estate during their lifetime, in the event of the death of either of them, or in the event of divorce, shall be determined solely by this Agreement.

03 Both parties as of this date are individually possessed of certain separate property, and both acknowledge that they played no role in the accumulation of the other's separate property.

[04] Each party understands that the assets of the other may be increased in the future by reason of inheritances, gifts, business profits, realized or unrealized appreciation, accumulated income, and other increases or additions, and each acknowledges that he or she is entering into this Agreement regardless of the value thereof.

[05] Each party has previously been married to another, and each party has children (and grandchildren) by that previous marriage, all of whom are each individual party's presumptive heirs-at-law.

06 Each party fully understands that, in the absence of this agreement, the law would confer upon him or her certain property rights and interests in the assets and property owned, received, or acquired by the other presently or in the future; and it is the intent of each party, by this agreement, to relinquish certain of such property rights and interests in such assets as specified herein.

07 This agreement has been reviewed by the separate legal counsel of each party.

08 Each party is aware of the nature and extent of their separate and joint income, real and personal property, and any outstanding debts or other liabilities. Both parties affirm that they have, in negotiating this agreement, fairly disclosed to the other all their respective incomes and expenses, assets and liabilities, all of which are set forth in the Appendices to this Agreement to the best of each parties' knowledge and ability.

09 [Name] and [name] have entered into this agreement freely and voluntarily. No coercion or undue influence has been used by or against either party in making this agreement.

*AGREEMENT:*

The parties agree as follows:

[11] The property currently belonging to each party and titled in his or her name shall remain his (her) separate property. All income, dividends, rents

or profits from this property shall also remain separate property. All appreciation in value of the separate property, whether attributable to market conditions or the application of the skills or efforts of the owner thereof or any other party, shall be separate property. Any property purchased from the proceeds of the management or sale of such separate property shall also be considered separate property.

[12] Each party shall have the right to sell, rent, use, or otherwise manage and control this separate property, with the same effect as if no marriage had occurred between them. The other party hereby ratifies and consents on his or her part to any such management and control. Notwithstanding anything contained herein, each party agrees that, if asked by the other party or by any grantee or donee, he or she will join in any deed, mortgage, or other conveyance of such property by the other for the purpose of divesting any such rights, claims, or property interests, whether actual or apparent, or perfecting a clear record title to the property.

[13] Any property coming to either party during the marriage through gift, bequest, or inheritance shall be considered separate property and shall be treated as set forth above.

[14] Notwithstanding any other provision of this agreement, either party may, by appropriate written instrument, transfer, give, convey, devise, or bequeath any property to the other. Neither party intends by this agreement to limit or restrict the right to receive any such transfer, gift, conveyance, devise, or bequest from the other.

[21] Assets titled in the names of both parties shall be classified as marital property, and shall be held as tenants in common unless expressly stated to be owned or titled as joint tenants or tenants by the entireties.

[22] The parties agree that income earned from the gainful employment of either of them shall be considered marital property, and shall be used to meet household and other expenses.

[23] Should this income be inadequate to meet household or other expenses, the parties agree that they shall contribute equally (or in some other proportion) to their joint account in order to meet these obligations.

[24] The parties agree that each is currently physically, emotionally, and financially capable of providing for his or her own support at an appropriate standard of living. The parties may contribute in agreed upon proportions to provide for their mutual support and the household in which they reside in the form of food, clothing, transportation, and other necessities consistent with a reasonable and appropriate standard of day-to-day living of the parties. The parties realize that they cannot abrogate the duty to support each other under Virginia law.

[31] All liabilities or obligations of any nature or description, including without limitation, those for torts, punitive damages, penalties, fines or forfeitures, which either party has incurred or hereafter incurs, including the parties' respective shares of liabilities or obligations which have been incurred jointly, either with each other or with third persons, shall be the individual liabilities and obligations of the incurring party as though he or she were an unmarried person. Unless prohibited by law, any such liability or obligation shall be satisfied exclusively out of the incurring party's separate property.

[32] Notwithstanding the foregoing paragraph, either party may, at his or her sole option, voluntarily contribute toward the payment of the individual liabilities or obligations of the other. However, such payment shall not constitute an assumption of the individual liabilities by the contributing party, nor shall such payment constitute an admission of liability therefore by the contributing party.

[41] Each party waives, discharges, and releases all rights, claims, or property interests, of whatever nature, which he or she might otherwise have in the event of the death of the other in or to all or any part of the separate property of the other under any law nor or hereafter in effect in the state of Virginia or in any other jurisdiction in which the parties may be domiciled, whether by way of homestead, curtesy, dower, election against the will, spousal allowances, intestate succession, marital property, community property, or otherwise.

[42] Each party agrees that he or she will not, in the event of the death of the other, make or assert any claim or ownership right of any kind whatsoever in or to the individual property, estate or assets of the other, other than for a bona fide debt. In the event that either party dies leaving any property, or estate, or assets to be administered intestate, the same shall be inherited by and distributed to the heirs at law of the decedent (excluding the other party) with the same force and effect as if they had not been married.

[43] Each party shall join in the execution and filing of any instrument or conveyance, and in the taking of any other action necessary to abrogate or otherwise avoid the effect of the law of any jurisdiction conferring any such right or interest, if the legal representative or successor in interest of the other party so requests.

[44] Each party agrees that he (she) will make no claim as beneficiary of any insurance policy upon the life of the other.

[51] In the event of the dissolution of their marriage, a vinculo or a mensa, the parties acknowledge that this agreement constitutes a written agreement

recognized and enforceable under Va. Code § 20-107.3(H). In the event of the dissolution of the marriage of the parties, each party waives, discharges and releases all rights, claims, or property interests, of whatever nature, which he or she might otherwise have in or to all or any part of the individual property of the other under Va. Code § 20-107.3; and each party agrees that he or she will not, in the event of the dissolution of the marriage of the parties, make or assert any claim or ownership right of any kind whatsoever in or to the separate property of the other, other than for a bona fide debt.

[52] Each party agrees that he (she) will make no claim for spousal support or maintenance in the event of the dissolution of their marriage.

[61] The parties will file a joint federal and state income tax return for each year in which filing such a joint return will result in less aggregate federal and/or state income tax obligations than would result from their filing separate returns. The federal and state income tax liability due with respect to any such joint return shall be allocated between the parties and paid by each of them out of his or her separate property in a manner such that the amount paid out by each shall bear the same ratio to the total tax payable with respect to such joint return as the federal gross income of each bears to the total federal gross income. Any additional assessments or costs of taxation by audit or other adjustment shall be similarly allocated between the parties.

[62] Any refund resulting from joint federal and state declarations and returns shall be shared between the parties in the same proportion as their respective contributions to the tax payments. The parties agree to consult and cooperate in obtaining any refund to which they may be entitled and agree to share the reasonable expenses of obtaining a refund in the same proportion as their respective contributions to the tax payments.

[71] Other matters, such as support of children of either of the parties from prior relationships; the payment of debts generated prior to the marriage; or personal rights and obligations, such as religious instruction of children that might be born to the marriage, plans for education of the parties or relationships with friends or family of either party may be included here. [Note that such provisions must not be in violation of public policy or criminal statutes.]

81 The parties agree that this Agreement shall be governed by the laws of the state of Virginia [or other state]. This agreement shall at all times be construed in accordance with the laws of the state of Virginia, notwithstanding the establishment of a domicile elsewhere by either or both of the parties at any time subsequent to the execution of this agreement.

82 This agreement shall be amended only by a written agreement signed

by both parties. No modification or waiver of any of the terms of this agreement shall be valid unless in writing and executed with the same formality as this agreement.

83 The parties intend this agreement to set forth their present understanding in its entirety. If any of the provisions of this agreement shall for any reason become invalid or otherwise cannot be enforced, the remainder of the agreement shall remain in full force and effect, unless an injustice would thereby result.

84 Each party represents that he or she understands the meaning of the various provisions of this agreement, and that the text does set forth the agreement in the manner they had intended. The parties acknowledge that this agreement is the free and voluntary act of each and that they each believe it to be fair, just, and reasonable.

IN WITNESS, [name] and [name] have signed this agreement below and have placed their initials in the lower left margin of each page.

[Signed by wife-to-be]

Subscribed and sworn to before me on [date].

[Signed by notary public]
My commission expires:
[Signed by husband-to-be]

Subscribed and sworn to before me on [date].

[Signed by notary public]

My commission expires:

## Form 25  Separation agreement.

**NOTE:** Like the Complaint for Divorce, the Separation Agreement Form consists of a group of numbered paragraphs which may be selected as desired to fit the individual needs and desires of the client. Numbered paragraphs without brackets must be included in order to comply with Virginia law. Those with brackets are optional, although the subjects of the suggested paragraphs are usually included in separation agreements.

Numbering is according to subject matter, as follows:

01–09 *RECITALS*

   01   Marriage of the parties

   02   Children born to or adopted by the parties

   03   Separation of the parties

   04   Intent of agreement

   05   Competence of parties

   06   Disclosure of assets in attachments

   [07]   Intent that agreement be ratified and incorporated into any final decree

   [08]   Knowledge that if there is divorce, waiving right to equitable division of property and entitlement to or modification of spousal support

   09   Parties to lead separate lives

10–19 *CHILD CUSTODY*

   11   General welfare of children paramount; fostering of good relationship with both parents

   [12]   Joint legal and physical custody

*OR*

   [13]   Joint legal custody; primary physical custody in one parent; visitation

*OR*

   [14]   Shared physical custody

*OR*

[15] Sole custody in one parent; reasonable visitation

16 Modification of custody and visitation arrangements

[17] Restriction to residence in Virginia

[18] Restriction to overnight visits without adult member of opposite sex present

[19] Religious or moral training of child

20–29 *CHILD SUPPORT*

21 Child support payable by noncustodial parent; amount

22 Modification of child support; circumstances

[22.1] change with consumer price index

*or*

[22.2] change with age of child

*or*

[22.3] change with income of party or parties

*or*

[22.4] change with emancipation or change in custody

22.5 General provisions for modification

[23] Income tax exemptions

[24] Termination of child support; college education

[25] Camps, lessons, etc.

[26] Health insurance

[27] Extraordinary medical expenses not covered by insurance

[28] Death of obligor

[29] Life insurance

30–39 *SPOUSAL SUPPORT*

31 General

31.1 Amount of spousal support

*or*

31.2 Waiver of spousal support

32     Modification of spousal support; circumstances

    [32.1]   consumer price index

    [32.2]   change in income of party or parties

    [32.3]   expiration of specific time period

    [32.4]   completion of degree program

    [32.5]   general

[33]   Lump sum payment of support

[34]   Death of obligor spouse

[35]   Remarriage of dependent spouse

[36]   Cohabitation of dependent spouse

[37]   Tax consequences; treatment as alimony under § 71

[38]   Medical insurance until divorce

40–49 *PROPERTY DIVISION*

40     General release of rights in property

41     Separate property: Schedules A and B

42     Marital property: Schedule C; plan for distribution

[43]   Marital home to custodial parent; sale when last minor child reaches majority; upkeep of home; mortgage payments

*OR*

[44]   Purchase of marital home by one spouse; appraisal; method of payment

*OR*

[45]   Sale of marital home; appraisal; distribution of proceeds

[46]   Other real property; all deeds to transfer title

    46.1   transfer to one of spouses

    46.2   sale to outside party

47     Household furnishings

48     Automobiles

[49]   Payment of lump sum over time

**50–59 *TAX RETURNS***

51   Plan for current and future tax years

52   Refunds; penalties

[53]   Furnishing of tax returns for spousal or child support calculations

**60–69 *DEBTS AND OBLIGATIONS***

[61]   credit cards

[62]   individual debts and obligations

**70–79 *CONCLUDING PARAGRAPHS***

[71]   Modification: need for writing; circumstances; method

[72]   Incorporation into final decree of divorce

*OR*

[73]   Approval by court; no incorporation

*OR*

[74]   Agreement not to be filed with court

75   Agreement that separation not due to fault of either party

76   Whole understanding of parties, etc.

77   Fairness of agreement

78   Advice of independent counsel

79   Agreement to be governed by Virginia law

*SEPARATION AGREEMENT*

THIS AGREEMENT is made and entered into to take effect on this [date], by and between [name] (referred to as wife) and [name] (referred to as husband).

*RECITALS:*

01 Husband and wife were married in [locality] on [date].

02 [Number] children were born of their marriage (adopted by the parties). Their names are [names, dates of birth].

03 Due to certain unhappy differences, the parties mutually agreed to separate. They in fact commenced a marital separation on [date] and are presently living separate and apart.

04 The parties are entering into this agreement to settle the rights and

obligations of either or both of them (and especially to make provision for the care and support of their minor children).

It is expressly understood and agreed that this agreement is not executed for the purpose of the obtaining of a divorce from each other, nor is it an agreement or consent by either party for the other to obtain a divorce, yet it is here agreed and stipulated that the parties have separated by mutual consent and have agreed to live separate and apart because they feel that such is in their mutual best interests.

05 Each party is over the age of eighteen years, and is fully competent to make this agreement.

06 The parties have, to the best of their ability, fully and frankly disclosed all assets held by either or both of them to each other. These assets are listed in Schedules A to C.

[07] The parties intend that this agreement be presented to the court in the event either party brings an action for divorce, and that it be ratified, approved, and incorporated into any final decree of divorce.

[08] The parties acknowledge that by executing this agreement, they will waive any right to have a divorce court equitably distribute their property under Va. Code § 20-107.3. They further acknowledge that by executing this agreement and filing it with any divorce pleadings, the court will have no power to award spousal support or to modify spousal support except in accordance with the agreement.

09 The parties shall lead their separate lives and live separate and apart from each other as fully as though each were unmarried. Each may engage in any business or profession as each may choose, free from any influence from the other. Each may reside where he or she may choose, free from any restriction of the other. Each may choose his or her friends to associate with, whether they be of the same or the opposite sex, and the other shall not inquire as to the nature of the relationship, nor interfere with it in any way. The parties agree not to molest or harass each other at their respective places of employment, residence, on the streets or elsewhere.

WHEREFORE, for $1 and other good and valuable consideration, the parties agree and contract as follows:

11 Husband and wife share a concern for the welfare and best interests of their minor children, [names]. They each respect the other's parental role with the children and they agree that both of them are fit and proper parents. The parties agree to put no obstacle in the way of the maintenance of love and affection between each of them and the children. They will not belittle,

berate, scorn, ridicule, or condemn the other in the presence of the children and each will actively attempt to generate a feeling of good will between the other parent and the children. Although their personal lives may take them in separate directions, they intend to cooperate in their shared parenting arrangements. They realize that they cannot relieve the court of the ability to determine the best interests of the children regarding matters pertaining to them.

[12] The children shall be in the joint custody of husband and wife. This means that important parental decisions affecting the children's growth and development shall be made jointly whenever possible. The parents agree to consider the children's best interests in making these decisions. They agree regularly to advise one another on all important matters related to the children, with the goal of adopting a harmonious policy regarding the interests of the children. Each party agrees promptly to notify and to consult with the other with respect to any medical problems or illness of the children. Each party hereby agrees promptly to notify and to consult with the other with respect to any educational progress, education problems, and any change of schools or classes of the children. [Set forth arrangement of physical custody of children: weekday/weekend; school year/summer; alternating days; Monday through Wednesday/Thursday through Sunday are common arrangements.] The parents agree to confer from time to time in order to arrange a mutually convenient advance schedule, which shall be in writing if either parent so requests. Each parent also agrees to give thoughtful consideration to any request to the other for a change in the schedule to deal with unanticipated situations.

[13] The children shall be in the joint legal custody of [names]. This means that important parental decisions affecting the children's growth and development shall be made jointly whenever possible. The parents agree to consider the children's best interests in making these decisions. They agree regularly to advise one another on all important matters related to the children, with the goal of adopting a harmonious policy regarding the interests of the children. Each party agrees to promptly notify and to consult with the other with respect to any medical problems or illness of the children. Each party hereby agrees promptly to notify and to consult with the other with respect to any educational progress, education problems, and any change of schools or classes of the children.

[Names of children] shall have their principal residence with [name]. They shall spend reasonable amounts of time with [name]. This shall include a fair sharing of holidays and other special days. The children shall also be with [name] for certain additional times during the summer. In particular, they shall spend [set forth visitation schedule: every other weekend; one overnight and one evening per week are common]. [Name] shall assist with the care of the children on snow days, sick days and other times when the children are unexpectedly out of school.

The parties agree to confer from time to time in order to arrange a mutually convenient advance schedule, which shall be in writing if either parent so requests. Each parent also agrees to give thoughtful consideration to any request from the other for a change in the schedule to deal with unanticipated situations.

[14] [Names of children] shall have their principal residence with [name]. They shall spend reasonable amounts of time with [name]. This shall include a fair sharing of holidays and other special days. The children shall also be with [name] for certain additional times during the summer. In particular, they shall spend [set forth visitation schedule: every other weekend; one overnight and one evening per week are common.]

The parties agree to confer from time to time in order to arrange a mutually convenient advance schedule, which shall be in writing if either parent so requests. Each parent also agrees to give thoughtful consideration to any request from the other for a change in the schedule to deal with unanticipated situations.

15 [Name or names of child or children] shall have his (her)(their) principal residence with [name of first parent]. He (she)(they) shall spend reasonable amounts of time with [name of other parent]. This shall include a fair sharing of holidays and other special days. [Name or names of child or children] shall also be with [name of other parent] for certain additional times during the summer. In particular, he (she) (they) shall spend [set forth visitation schedule: every other weekend; one overnight and one evening per week are common].

[Name or names of child or children] shall have his (her) (their) principal residence with [name of other parent]. He (she) (they) shall spend reasonable amounts of time with [name of first parent]. This shall include a fair sharing of holidays and other special days. [Name or names] shall also be with [name of first parent] for certain additional times during the summer. In particular, he (she) (they) shall spend [set forth visitation schedule: every other weekend; one overnight and one evening per week are common.]

16 The parties agree to confer should circumstances change so that it appears to either or both of them that the best interests of a child or children may warrant a change in the custodial arrangement. Such circumstances might include a serious illness or accident on the part of one parent; an

increase or decrease in employment; an employment prospect outside the state or at a great distance from the other party within the state; or a desire by one or more of the children for a change in the custodial situation. If the parties cannot reach a mutually satisfactory resolution of the situation, they agree to seek mediation (arbitration) (counseling with clergy or other professional).

[17] The parties agree that it is in the best interests of the children that both have regular and extensive contact with both parents, and that this necessitates both parents living in the state of Virginia. They therefore agree that neither will relocate outside the state of Virginia without the advice and consent of the other party.

[18] The parties agree that it is in the best interests of the children that there be no overnight visitation while [name of husband or wife] has an overnight adult guest (of the opposite sex) to whom he (she) is not related.

[19] The parties agree that it is in the best interests of the children that they be raised according to the principles of the [religious organization. Set forth any provisions regarding attendance at religious services; religious instruction; dietary restrictions, and so forth].

21 The parties acknowledge that they cannot divest the court of the power to set or modify the amount of child support in the best interests of the children. Nevertheless, they agree that [name] should pay [name of other party] for the support and maintenance of the children the sum of [amount] per [period]. These sums shall be payable [set forth arrangement, such as on the first and fifteenth days of each month].

[22.1] The amount of child support established in the preceding paragraph may be modified as circumstances change. Specifically, the parties provide that the amount of support shall be adjusted yearly, according to changes in the consumer price index.

[22.2] The amount of child support established in the preceding paragraph may be modified as circumstances change. Specifically, the parties provide that the amount of support shall be increased by [sum] as each child reaches the age of [state age or ages], to begin with the next calendar month following the child's birthday.

[22.3] The amount of child support established in the preceding paragraph may be modified as circumstances change. Specifically, the parties provide that the amount shall be increased by the sum of [state amount per period] as [name of party]'s income increases by [state amount]. The amount shall be decreased by [state amount by which reduced per period].

[22.4] The amount of child support established in the preceding paragraph may be modified as circumstances change. Specifically, the parties provide that the amount of support shall be adjusted by reducing the amount owed by [sum] as each child reaches the age of 18 or is otherwise emancipated, or physical custody is placed with [name].

22.5 In some circumstances, the needs and best interests of the children may warrant a change in the amount of child support. The parties agree to confer in good faith regarding such a proposed change. If the parties cannot reach a mutually satisfactory resolution of the situation, they agree to seek mediation (arbitration) (counseling with clergy or other professional).

[23] The parties agree that [name] shall be entitled to claim [name of child or children] as a dependent (dependents) for income tax purposes pursuant to I.R.C. § 1215.

[24] The parties agree to discuss with each other and with the children the appropriate college and higher education needs and desires of each of them. The parties agree that such decisions shall be made giving due consideration to the needs, wishes, and abilities of the child. The parties agree to share in the financial obligations of all such agreed-upon higher education, in direct proportion to their total gross incomes from the prior calendar year (or state some alternative).

[25] The parties agree that they shall share expenses for summer camps, music or athletic lessons, special education or tutoring equally (in the proportion of [state amount]).

[26] The parties agree that [name] shall be responsible for maintaining health insurance coverage for the children.

[27] The parties agree that they shall share major medical expenses not covered by insurance in the following way [state proportion, or who is to pay for such expenses]. This includes orthodontic or dental care, eyeglasses, and psychiatric or other counseling not covered by insurance.

[28] The parties agree that the child support established by this agreement shall continue until all children are emancipated. Should [name of party] die before [names] reach the age of majority or complete college, the agreed upon amounts, as modified by paragraph 22, shall continue to be payable by the estate of [name].

[29] [Name] agrees to keep life insurance on his (her) life in the amount of [state amount] with [name of child or children] as beneficiaries until the children are emancipated (reach age 18) (complete a four year full-time college education).

31.1 [Name] shall pay to [name] the sum of [amount] per [period] for her (his) support and maintenance.

31.2 The parties expressly waive any claim either of them may have, now or in the future, to receive spousal support and maintenance (alimony) from the other. They release each other from any such claim after being advised of the provisions of Va. Code § 20-109. They are thus aware that any right which either of them might otherwise have to spousal support may never be revived, regardless of the circumstances.

32 The parties realize that under Va. Code § 20-109 the amount of spousal support and maintenance may only be modified as provided in this agreement. They therefore agree that spousal support may be modified as follows:

[32.1] After each full calendar year following the execution of this agreement, the parties shall obtain the consumer price index. The amount of spousal support established under paragraph 31 shall be adjusted according to the percentage increase or decrease of the consumer price index over that of the year of execution of this agreement.

[32.2] Before [date] of each year following the execution of this agreement, the parties agree to furnish each other with their federal income tax Form 1040 from the previous calendar year. The amount of spousal support established by paragraph 31 shall be increased or decreased based upon the proportionate change in the gross (taxable) income of [name or names].

[32.3] The parties agree that the amount of spousal support established by paragraph 31 shall be decreased by [amount] (terminated) after the expiration of [period] after execution of this agreement.

[32.4] The parties agree that the amount of spousal support established by paragraph 31 shall be decreased by [amount] (terminated) when [name] completes her (his) degree in [name of degree].

32.5 The parties agree that the amount of spousal support established by paragraph 31 may need to be adjusted due to changes in the circumstances of the parties. These include, but are not limited to, changes in the parties' employment, health, marital situation, custody arrangements for minor children, or modifications of the tax laws that affect the treatment of these payments. Should either party feel that an adjustment in the amount of spousal support is warranted, the parties agree to confer to attempt to resolve the situation amicably. Should they be unable to reach agreement, the parties agree to submit the matter to mediation (arbitration).

[33] [Name of payor] will pay [name] the sum of [amount] in lieu of spousal support and maintenance. Such payments will be made in installments of [amount] per month, payable over [number] months. This amount

shall be payable whether or not [name] remarries, and any unpaid balance shall constitute a lien against the estate of [name of payor], should he (she) die before all installments are paid.

[34] Payments made for spousal support and maintenance shall continue (terminate) upon the death of [name of payor spouse]. Future payments shall be made by [name of payor spouse]'s estate, and any arrearages shall constitute a debt owed by his (her) estate.

[35] Payments made for spousal support and maintenance shall continue (terminate) upon the remarriage of [name of recipient spouse].

[36] Payments made for spousal support shall terminate if [name of recipient spouse] cohabits with an adult member of the opposite sex to whom she (he) is not related by blood or marriage, or holds herself (himself) out as married to such person.

[37] The parties agree that payments for spousal support and maintenance under this agreement shall be treated as alimony for income tax purposes under I.R.C. § 71. That is, they will be deductible by [payor spouse] and taxable as income to [recipient spouse].

[38] The parties agree that [name] shall keep his (her) medical coverage for the benefit of [name of other spouse] unless or until the marriage ends in a final decree of divorce.

40 Except as otherwise here provided, each party hereby relinquishes and releases all statutory and common law rights which each may have or in the future may acquire to any property, real or personal, which the other now owns or may hereafter acquire, and each agrees that he or she will, upon the request of the other, execute and deliver such releases or assurances as may be desired by the other to indicate, demonstrate, or to carry out the release and relinquishment of such interests.

41 The parties agree that [name] is the sole and separate owner of certain property identified in Schedule A, and of the approximate value listed in that schedule. [Name] is the sole and separate owner of certain property identified in Schedule B and of the approximate value listed in that schedule.

42 The parties agree that the property identified and valued in Schedule C is marital property. The parties have agreed to divide the property as follows: [list which assets go to which spouse, with individual and total amounts].

[43] The parties jointly own as their marital residence the property located at [address]. They agree that [name], as primary custodian of the children, shall retain the exclusive use and possession of the marital home until such time as the last child becomes emancipated, by age or otherwise. At that

time, the home shall be sold and the proceeds divided equally (or specify some other proportion). Until that time, [name or names] shall be responsible for mortgage payments, taxes, insurance, and utility payments for the home. [Name] shall be responsible for routine maintenance and upkeep of the home. [Name or names] shall pay for a major repair or maintenance of the home, defined as one which costs over [sum]. These expenses shall be incurred only after advance consultation, except for emergency repairs, but neither party may unreasonably withhold consent for repairs.

[44] The parties jointly own the home located at [address]. They agree that [name] will purchase the share of [name] for the sum of [amount], (or for one-half the appraised value, as established by a written appraisal of [realtors]). Such payment may be made [period] in the amount of [sum], [Name] agrees to execute all necessary documents to enable [name] to obtain good title to these premises.

[45] The parties currently own the premises at [address] as their marital residence. They agree that it is to be sold after appraisal by [realtor or realtors]. The proceeds, net of the expenses of sale and the mortgage principal, are to be divided equally (or specify some other proportion).

(Until the property is sold, [name] shall be entitled to remain in the home. For this period, she (he) will be responsible for mortgage, insurance, utilities, routine maintenance and repairs) (making payments of [sum] per month to [name] in lieu of rent).

[46.1] The parties own real property located at [address]. They agree that this property is to be allocated to [name] and agree that all necessary documents related to such conveyance shall be executed by [name].

[46.2] The parties own real property located at [address]. They agree that this property is to be sold after valuation by [realtors] and that the proceeds, net of the expenses of sale and the mortgage principal, will be divided equally (or specify some other proportion).

47 The parties agree that the household furnishings listed in Schedule C shall be divided as follows: [specify method].

48 The parties agree that the [year, make and model of automobile] shall become [remain] the property of [name]. To the extent that the said automobile is not paid for, the remaining obligation shall be solely that of [name]. All documents necessary to effect these transactions shall be executed willingly and promptly by [name]. The parties agree that the [year, make and model of automobile] shall become (remain) the property of [name]. To the extent that the said automobile is not paid for, the remaining obligation shall be solely that of [name]. All documents necessary to effect

these transactions shall be executed willingly and promptly by [name].

[49] The parties agree that in addition to the foregoing division of property, the sum of [amount] will be paid by [name] to [name].

51 The parties will file a joint federal and state income tax return for each year in which filing such a joint return will result in less aggregate federal and/or state income tax obligations than would result from their filing separate returns. The federal and state income tax liability due with respect to any such joint return shall be allocated between the parties and paid by each of them out of his or her separate property in a manner such that the amount paid out by each shall bear the same ratio to the total tax payable with respect to such joint return as the federal gross income of each bears to the total federal gross income. Any additional assessments or costs of taxation by audit or other adjustment shall be similarly allocated between the parties.

52 Any refund resulting from joint federal and state declarations and returns shall be shared between the parties in the same proportion as their respective contributions to the tax payments. The parties agree to consult and cooperate in obtaining any refund to which they may be entitled, and agree to share the reasonable expenses of obtaining a refund in the same proportion as their respective contributions to the tax payments.

[53] The parties agree to furnish each other with copies of prior year's tax returns as soon as these become available, for use in establishing the amount of spousal or child support.

[61] The parties expressly agree to close any joint credit card or other accounts within 30 days of this agreement. This shall be accomplished by writing to each creditor requesting that the accounts either be closed or be converted into an account for the exclusive use and responsibility of one party.

[62] Except as otherwise set forth in this agreement, each party shall be solely responsible for his or her respective indebtedness incurred after the separation. Neither party may in the future incur any debts or liabilities, or make any contract, for which the other could legally be held responsible, except by mutual consent. If one party is required to make any payment for which the other is responsible under this agreement, the responsible party shall indemnify and hold harmless the party making that payment for all costs and damages incurred by that party, including attorney's fees and other costs.

[71] The parties realize that they may wish to modify this agreement at some time in the future, should some unforeseen contingency arise. Such a

modification must be in a writing signed by each of the parties. The parties agree that if they are unable to agree on a modification of this agreement, they shall seek resolution of their differences by submitting the matter to mediation (arbitration).

[72] The parties intend for this agreement to be submitted to the court in which any divorce action is filed and for it to be ratified, incorporated, and made a part of any final decree of divorce. The parties each agree not to oppose such incorporation and they agree that subsequently, this Agreement shall be enforceable as part of said decree or independently as a contract between the parties. In addition, the parties agree that any amendments or modification to this agreement entered into after such incorporation into a divorce decree shall be incorporated into an amended decree in order that the court record reflect the intent and meaning of the parties' agreements.

The parties understand that such filing and incorporation will mean that the amounts payable for spousal support and maintenance cannot be modified except in accordance with this agreement (that neither party will ever be entitled to spousal support and maintenance). Further, they understand that because of such incorporation, provisions relating to spousal support and maintenance, custody, child support and visitation may be enforced as with any other divorce decree, under Va. Code § 20-79 et seq., including use of the court's contempt powers.

[73] The parties agree that they shall submit this agreement to any divorce court for its review and approval, but that it shall not be made a part of any final decree nor incorporated by reference therein. The parties realize that under Va. Code § 20-109, the amounts payable for spousal support and maintenance cannot be modified except in accordance with this agreement (that neither party will ever be entitled to spousal support and maintenance), but provisions regarding child custody, child support and visitation will be enforced as with any other divorce decree under Va. Code § 20-79 et seq., including use of the court's contempt powers.

[74] The parties intend that this agreement not be filed with any pleadings or other papers pertaining to an absolute divorce, and therefore that this agreement will not be incorporated by reference in any final decree of divorce. Any remedies under this agreement will be contractual in nature.

75 The parties agree that the immediate circumstances leading to their separation may not be used by either of them as the basis for a charge of desertion or constructive desertion against each other.

76 The parties intend this agreement to set forth their present understanding in its entirety. There are no binding written or oral promises between

them which they presently wish to make, except as set forth in this agreement. If any of the provisions of this agreement shall for any reason become invalid or otherwise cannot be enforced, the remainder of the agreement shall remain in full force and effect, unless an injustice would thereby result.

77 The parties acknowledge that they each believe this agreement to be fair, just, and reasonable. The parties acknowledge that this agreement is the free and voluntary act of each.

78 The parties acknowledge that this agreement was reviewed by the separate and independent legal counsel of each prior to signing. Each party represents that he or she understands the meaning of the various provisions of this agreement, and that the text does set forth the agreement in the manner they had intended.

79 The parties intend that this agreement be interpreted and enforced under the laws of the Commonwealth of Virginia.

## Form 26   **Petition for adoption.**

VIRGINIA:
IN THE CIRCUIT COURT FOR THE COUNTY (CITY) OF [NAME]

In the matter of the adoption
of a child to be known as
[NAME] by
[Names of adoptive parents]

### *PETITION*

Your petitioners, [names of adoptive parents], respectively represent as follows:

1. They are husband and wife and reside in [name of locality]. They desire to adopt a child to be known as [adoptive name of child] (Birth Certificate Registration No. [number], registered in the State of [name of state]), an infant child under the age of fourteen years, not theirs by birth. Said child was born on [date of birth], and was surrendered to the [name of agency] by her (his) natural parents or welfare department for placement for adoption by said agency.

2. Said [agency] has given its consent to the adoption of this child by petitioners. The consent of said agency is attached hereto as Exhibit "A" and made a part hereof.

3. The child was placed in the home of petitioners by the [agency] and has lived in petitioner's home since [date].

WHEREFORE, your petitioners pray for leave to adopt said infant and that said child's name be changed to [name] and that to this end all necessary and proper orders be entered.

DATE: _____

_____
[Adoptive Parent]

_____
[Adoptive Parent]

By  _____
      Of Counsel
[Address of Counsel]

**Form 27    Consent to adoption.**

VIRGINIA:
IN THE CIRCUIT COURT FOR THE COUNTY (CITY) OF [NAME]

In the matter of the adoption
of a child to be known as
[NAME] by
[Names of adoptive parents]

### CONSENT TO ADOPTION

The [name of agency], a child placing agency, to whom a female (male) child to be named [name of child], born on [date of birth], at [locality], was surrendered for placement for adoption by her natural parents on [date of surrender], hereby gives consent to the adoption of said child by [names of adoptive parents], with whom said child was placed for adoption on [date of placement]. The required supervisory visits have been made, and the child has been placed in the adoptive home for the period required by law.

In witness whereof, the [name of agency] has caused this instrument to be signed by [its Director] this [date].

[NAME OF AGENCY]
By _____
[Director]

STATE OF VIRGINIA
COUNTY (CITY) OF

Subscribed and sworn to before me this [date].

[Signed by notary public]
My commission expires:

**Form 28**    **Order of reference for adoption.**

VIRGINIA:
IN THE CIRCUIT COURT FOR THE COUNTY (CITY) OF [NAME]

In the matter of the adoption
of a child to be known as
[NAME] by
[Names of adoptive parents]

### ORDER OF REFERENCE

On this day [names of adoptive parents], petitioners, jointly filed their petition to adopt a child, not theirs by birth, and to have the child's name changed to [name].

And it appearing to the court that the petitioners reside at [address, City or County, Virginia, Zip Code], that the child is now living in the home of the petitioners, having been placed by [agency], and that this court has jurisdiction over this proceeding pursuant to, it is therefore

§ 63.2-1201 of the Code of Virginia

ADJUDGED, ORDERED and DECREED that the clerk of this court forward a copy of the Petition and all exhibits with this order to the Commissioner of Social Services and to the Virginia State Welfare Department; and that said Virginia State Welfare Department shall make a thorough investigation of the matter in accordance with, and shall report thereon in writing to this Court within sixty (60) days after the copy of the petition herein is forwarded to it, and shall cause a copy of said report to be served upon the Commissioner of Public Welfare in accordance with the aforesaid statute. And it is further

§ 63.2-1228 of the Code of Virginia

ADJUDGED, ORDERED and DECREED that the Commissioner of Public Welfare shall notify this Court within thirty (30) days of his receipt of the report of the Virginia State Welfare Department of his approval or disapproval thereof, stating reasons for any further action on the report that he deems necessary. And it is further

ADJUDGED, ORDERED and DECREED that copies of the reports of the Virginia State Welfare Department and the Commissioner of Public Welfare shall be furnished by the reporting agency to petitioners' counsel of record at the same time said reports are furnished to the Court, subject to the requirement that such reports be returned to the Clerk of this Court, without duplication, to be disposed of in accordance with.

§ 63.2-1246 of the Code of Virginia

And this proceeding is continued, awaiting the filing of said report by the Virginia State Welfare Department.

Entered this _____ day of _____, 19_____.

_____

JUDGE

I ASK FOR THIS:

_____

**Form 29    Interlocutory order of adoption.**

VIRGINIA:
IN THE CIRCUIT COURT FOR THE COUNTY (CITY) OF [NAME]

In the matter of the adoption
of a child to be known as
[NAME] by
[Names of adoptive parents]

### *INTERLOCUTORY ORDER*

§ 63.2-1228 of the Code of Virginia

ON the ＿＿＿＿＿＿ st day of [month, year], petitioners [names of adoptive parents] appeared through counsel, and the Virginia State Welfare Department and the Commissioner of Public Welfare having filed their reports in this matter in accordance with, and the Order of Reference of this Court dated [date];

And it appearing to the Court that all requirements of the applicable statutes have been complied with; that petitioners [names] are proper persons adequately to maintain, care for, and train the infant child to be known as [name of child], whose adoption is the subject of this proceeding; that the child is suitable for adoption and that the best interests of the child will be promoted by her (his) adoption by petitioners and by changing her (his) name to [name] as requested in the petition; it is therefore

ADJUDGED, ORDERED and DECREED that the infant child to be known as [name] (Birth Certificate Registration Number [number], registered in the State of [state]) born of [natural parents] on [date of birth] in the State of [name of state], henceforth, subject to the probationary period provided for by, and subject further to the provisions of the Final Order of Adoption of this Court, will be, for all intents and purposes, the child of [names of adoptive parents], petitioners herein; and it is further

§ 63.2-1212 of the Code of Virginia

ADJUDGED, ORDERED and DECREED that upon entry of the Final Order of this Court herein, the name of said child shall be changed to [name]; and it is further

ADJUDGED, ORDERED and DECREED that the Clerk of this Court shall forward an attested copy of this Interlocutory Order to the Commissioner of Public Welfare and to the Virginia State Welfare Department.

Entered this ＿＿＿＿＿ day of ＿＿＿＿＿＿, 19＿＿＿＿＿.

_____

JUDGE

I ASK FOR THIS:

_____

## Form 30 Final order of adoption.

VIRGINIA:
IN THE CIRCUIT COURT OF THE COUNTY (CITY) OF [NAME]

In the matter of the adoption
of a child to be known as
[NAME] by
[Names of adoptive parents]

### FINAL ORDER

§ 63.2-1212 of the Code of Virginia

On the [date of hearing], petitioners [names of adoptive parents] appeared through counsel, and the Virginia State Welfare Department and the Commissioner of Public Welfare having filed their reports in this matter in accordance with, and more than six months having elapsed since the entry of the Interlocutory Order herein dated [date];

And it appearing to the Court that all requirements of the applicable statutes have been complied with; that petitioners [names] are proper persons to maintain, care for, and train said child, that said child is a suitable child for adoption by petitioners; that the Commissioner of Public Welfare recommends to the Court the entry of a final order of adoption of said child by petitioners [names]; and that the best interests of the child will be served by the entering of a Final Order of adoption herein, it is

ADJUDGED, ORDERED and DECREED that henceforth said child shall be, for all intents and purposes, the child of said petitioners, [names], and shall be entitled to all the rights and privileges, and subject to all the obligations, of a child of said petitioners born in lawful wedlock.

And it further appearing to the Court that the petition filed in this cause includes a prayer that the infant's name be changed to [name], it is further ADJUDGED, ORDERED and DECREED that henceforth said child's name shall be [name].

And it is further ORDERED that the Clerk of this Court shall forward an attested copy of this Order to the Commissioner of Public Welfare and to the Virginia State Welfare Department and shall make such reports of the adoption of this infant as are required by law.

Entered this _____ day of _____, 19_____.

_____
JUDGE

I ASK FOR THIS:

_____

# INDEX

[References are to sections.]

[References are to sections.]

[References are to sections.]

[References are to sections.]

[References are to sections.]

[References are to sections.]

[References are to sections.]

[References are to sections.]

[References are to sections.]

[References are to sections.]

[References are to sections.]

[References are to sections.]

[References are to sections.]

[References are to sections.]